The RAISE Development
Method

The RAISE Development Method

The RAISE Method Group

Chris George
Anne E. Haxthausen
Steven Hughes
Robert Milne
Søren Prehn
Jan Storbank Pedersen

PRENTICE HALL

London New York Toronto Sydney Tokyo Singapore
Madrid Mexico City Munich

First published 1995 by
Prentice Hall International (UK) Limited
Campus 400, Maylands Avenue
Hemel Hempstead
Hertfordshire, HP2 7EZ
A division of
Simon & Schuster International Group

Printed and bound in Great Britain at
the University Press, Cambridge

Library of Congress Cataloging-in-Publication Data

The RAISE development method / [the RAISE Method Group].
      p. cm.
   Includes bibliographical references and index.
   ISBN 0-13-752700-4
    1. Software engineering. 2. Computer software - Development.
   I. RAISE Method Group.
   QA76.758.R33   1995
   005.1'2 - dc20   95 - 1575
                                    CIP

British Library Cataloguing in Publication Data

A catalogue record for this book is available from
the British Library

ISBN 0-13-752700-4

1 2 3 4 5   99 98 97 96 95

For Bent Dandanell
1963–1993

Contents

Editorial preface

The aim of the BCS Practitioner Series is to produce books which are relevant for practising computer professionals across the whole spectrum of Information Technology activities. We want to encourage practitioners to share their practical experience of methods and applications with fellow professionals. We also seek to disseminate information in a form which is suitable for the practitioner who often has only limited time to read widely within a new subject area or to assimilate research findings.

The role of the BCS is to provide advice on the suitability of books for the Series, via the Editorial Panel, and to provide a pool of potential authors upon which we can draw. Our objective is that this Series will reinforce the drive within the BCS to increase professional standards in IT. The other partners in this venture, Prentice Hall, provide the publishing expertise and international marketing capabilities of a leading publisher in the computing field.

The response when we set up the Series was extremely encouraging. However, the success of the Series depends on there being practitioners who want to learn as well as those who feel they have something to offer! The Series is under continual development and we are always looking for ideas for new topics and feedback on how to further improve the usefulness of the Series. If you are interested in writing for the Series then please contact us.

The use of **formal methods** in the development of safety-critical systems is an increasingly important area of computing science. This book complements *The RAISE Specification Language* (RSL) book already published in the Practitioner Series. It describes a complete method for developing industrial-strength applications using RSL. In addition to a comprehensive description of the method, there is an extensive tutorial, with examples and supporting material such as standard specifications and guidelines for quality assurance. Together, the two RAISE books describe a valuable practical approach to using formal methods for software development.

Ray Welland
Computing Science Department, University of Glasgow

Editorial Panel Members
Frank Bott (UCW, Aberystwyth), Dermot Browne (KPMG Management Consulting), Nic Holt (ICL), Trevor King (Praxis Systems plc), Tom Lake (GLOSSA), Kathy Spurr (Analysis and Design Consultants), Mario Wolczko (University of Manchester)

Preface

RAISE is an acronym for "Rigorous Approach to Industrial Software Engineering". It was the name of a CEC funded ESPRIT project and now gives its name to a formal specification language, the RAISE Specification Language (RSL), an associated method and a set of tools. RSL was described in a previous volume in this series [23] and the tools have been commercially available for some time. In this volume the RAISE method is described.

RSL is a wide spectrum language: the same language can be used to formulate both initial, very abstract specifications and to express low level designs suitable for translation to programming languages. The method therefore encompasses:

- formulating abstract specifications
- developing these to successively more concrete specifications
- justifying the correctness of the development
- translating the final specification into a programming language

All these activities are described in this volume. In addition there is an appendix containing both useful general material (standard specifications of data types; quality assurance check lists) and formal material supporting the method (the formal properties of RSL specifications; proof rules for use in justifications).

RAISE takes seriously the word "industrial". The method is intended for use on real developments, not just toy examples. So this volume is aimed at professional software engineers, although it could also be used by students at graduate level. Familiarity with RSL, or at least an ability to read it, is assumed.

The RAISE technology has been developed as collective efforts in the ESPRIT RAISE (315) and LaCoS (5383) projects. Chapters 1–3 were written by Chris George, chapter 4 by Anne Haxthausen, chapter 5 by Jan Storbank Pedersen and the appendices by Chris George.

Acknowledgements

During the design of the RAISE method many people advised, influenced and reviewed the process.

M. Broy and *C.B. Jones*, as consultants to the RAISE project, reviewed early to mid-term RAISE and RSL research and development, and gave much appreciated insight and advice.

In addition to the RAISE Method Group, many people involved in the RAISE and LaCoS projects directly or indirectly contributed to the design of the method: *Claus Bendix Nielsen, Simon Brock, Peter Michael Bruun, Bent Dandanell, Tony Evans, Patrick Goldsack, David Grosvenor, Jesper Gørtz, Peter Haff, Klaus Havelund, Søren Heilmann, Hamid Lesan, Peter Olsen, Kim Ritter Wagner*.

In addition, *Dines Bjørner, Richard Granville, Bo Stig Hansen, Melanie Dymond Harper, Zoë Hellinger, Sue Lambert* and *Carolyn Salmon* gave much helpful advice during preparation of this book.

CHAPTER 1

Introduction

Computers are increasingly being used for tasks where failure threatens severe consequences, including loss of life. Computers play an essential role in controlling spacecraft, aircraft, trains, cars, nuclear reactors and hospital equipment — to name just a few of the more critical applications. Whether we are worried about our plane landing safely or our bank account being correct, we would agree that it is vital that the computer systems behind them are completely reliable.

Reliability, which we might broadly describe as doing the job the system is supposed to do, is a requirement of both the hardware and the software. This book is about the software component. Making software reliable is especially difficult: any program capable of doing anything interesting is so complex that it is impossible to test it completely.

An important technique to aid in increasing reliability of software is the use of *formal methods*. We will define this term in more detail later, but the basic idea is that it should be possible to *reason* about properties of software, or systems involving software. For example, if the requirements say that there must be at most one train in any section of track, one can produce a proof that the software will always reflect this.

Formal methods are not the complete answer. For a start, "proofs" can contain flaws. Non-trivial proofs tend to be large and difficult to do automatically, so typically some steps will be claimed as "obvious" and not proved formally. For any proofs that are done automatically we have to ask how we know the prover is correct. Then there are wider problems. How do we know that the model of the world contained in the software (in which there is only one train per section) is reflected in the real world? Development starts with a statement of requirements, written mostly in a natural language, such as English. Formal methods can offer assurance that the requirements are correct, by finding inconsistency and incompleteness, but assurance is not certainty. Also, using formal methods involves interpreting the requirements by creating a model of them (albeit mathematical and abstract) in another language. Such processes are liable to errors.

1

Formal methods do not replace testing, and must be applied with due regard to quality control and to cost effectiveness. But they are invaluable for improving reliability.

1.1   Structure of the book

The next two sections of this introductory chapter present the basic ideas behind development in RAISE and its role in software engineering. There are then two sections introducing formal systems and the formal aspects of RAISE. Finally we note the changes to RSL that have been made in this book to the description in the book on RSL [23].

Part I of the book consists of a single tutorial chapter. This expounds, mainly through examples, a particular but general method for specifying and developing software systems in RAISE.

Part II consists of chapters on techniques: chapter 3 on development, chapter 4 on justification and chapter 5 on translation. Each of these can be read sequentially but are mainly intended to be used for reference.

Part III consists of appendices containing purely reference material:

- Appendix A contains standard, reusable specifications.
- Appendix B presents the proof system used in the rest of the book.
- Appendix C provides quality assurance checklists for doing quality assurance of specifications and developments.
- Appendix D contains references.
- Appendix E contains two indexes. The first, of terms, shows where the technical terms particular to RAISE are introduced and discussed. The second, of proof rules, shows where these rules are defined and used.

1.2   Characteristics of RAISE

The RAISE method is based on a number of principles:

- separate development
- step-wise development
- invent and verify
- rigour

We will describe each of these principles.

1.2.1   Separate development

It is clear, if we want to develop systems of any size, that we must be able to decompose their description into components and compose the system from the (developed) components. This is just as true when the description is a specification as it is when it is a program.

It is also clear that for most systems it is necessary to have people (or teams of people) working on different components at the same time. There will then be entities — files, documents, etc. — that are being shared. This generates two difficulties. The first is that it must be clear who is responsible for updating such shared entities, and what the status of each version is at any particular time. This is a standard configuration control problem and not specific to formal methods. The second difficulty is that there must be no ambiguity about what such shared entities mean, and this causes rather more problems (or systems integration would be a simple task!). The typical problem is that one person writes a function that others want to use. It is easy enough to share the information about the name of the function, what parameters it has and what its result type is. But it is not so easy to be exact about the semantics of the function — particularly what it does under different boundary conditions and how it may affect other things. What can the users assume about these?

If we also consider the development of these shared components we discover an additional problem. What can the developer safely do that will not affect the users?

What we need is a clear, unambiguous statement that acts as an agreement or *contract* between the developer and the users. For the developer a contract says what he must provide; for the users it says what they may assume. If the users discover during development that they need more or different properties, they need to renegotiate the contract, but otherwise they can develop their components freely. If a developer discovers during development that he can only supply fewer or different properties, he needs to renegotiate the contract, but otherwise can develop freely as long as he preserves the properties he contracted to provide. This also means that it must be known who are the users and developers, so that it is clear who needs to be involved in renegotiation.

A specification of a module (or perhaps group of modules) can act as this contract. A specification says precisely what the essential properties of the thing being specified are. It is much better in this respect than something written in a programming language, because it can state the essentials and ignore the irrelevances. A specification allows controllable precision; it can be as precise or as imprecise as its specifier and users require. Imprecision is not the same thing as vagueness or lack of clarity. Our logic allows us to draw some conclusions from a specification and not others, so a specification (implicitly) states what is essential and what is irrelevant.

A program representing a contract avoids the problem of vagueness in an informal description, but its incapacity for ignoring the irrelevant creates another problem. A program is complete in the sense that it contains all the information to allow it to execute. It is therefore precise about what it does, and so a development of it will cause its existing properties to change. Hence it is of little use as a contract allowing for development.

So what is the role of the contract in development?

Figure 1.1 illustrates how separate development works in the simple case of the development of a module A that is used in a module B. The initial versions of B

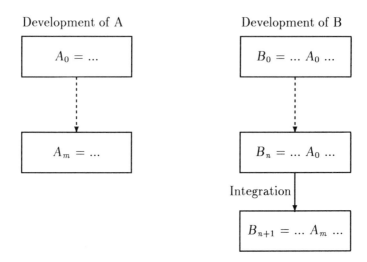

Figure 1.1: Separate development

and A are B_0 and A_0, and these are developed in n and m steps to B_n and A_m respectively. The module A_0 acts as the contract between the two developments; note that the reference in B to A is to A_0 at every stage but the last in B's development. When development is otherwise complete we integrate by using A_m instead of A_0 in B_n, to form B_{n+1}.

What we want is for the final system (A_m and B_{n+1}) to meet the original requirements. A set of sufficient conditions for this is:

- The initial modules (A_0 and B_0) together meet the requirements, i.e. have all the required properties.
- Each development step of A and B is an implementation step, i.e. each module implements the immediately preceding one. Implementation is introduced in section 1.6.

It is also useful to ensure that each B_i ($0 \le i \le n$) is a conservative extension of A_0. This simply means that only the developers of A are allowed to make decisions about the development of A. If the designers of B could also do so there would be a danger of contradictory decisions being taken. Conservative extension is introduced in section 1.6.2.

This picture of separate development can, of course, be scaled up to arbitrary numbers of separate components, and can be recursively applied so that components have sub-components, etc.

The picture we have presented of separate development is idealized. In practice it is rarely followed precisely. Important variations are:

- Not all requirements are met.
- Contracts may need to change.

- Some development steps may not be implementations.

We will consider each of these.

1.2.1.1 Requirements not met

The initial specifications may not meet all the requirements. This can happen for two reasons:

- Some requirements cannot be captured in RSL, because they are outside its scope. Typical requirements of this kind may be simple ones, like "the system will run on ... hardware under ... operating system and will be coded in ...", or more difficult ones like timing constraints. These are often termed *non-functional requirements*.
- Some requirements which can be captured in RSL are consciously deferred to later in development, because to include them at the beginning would make the initial specification too complex.

In either of these two cases we have to record the requirements not yet met and check that they are dealt with later. In both cases we will need to be reasonably sure that we can eventually deal with the requirements, or the development will have to be redone. In the second case of deferred requirements this means checking that the specification is more general than one reflecting the full requirements, but consistent with them.

1.2.1.2 Changing contracts

We may need to change a contract (like A_0) during development. This may be because the developers of B need properties additional to, or even different from, those they originally contracted for. It may be because the developers of A find it impossible, or costly either in terms of development time or in terms of the efficiency of the final implementation, to provide what they originally contracted to. In either case the contract can be renegotiated, i.e. at some point a development of A, A_i say, is created but is not an implementation of its predecessor. The developers of B must develop to B_j, say, using A_i and development continues from this point. This changing of contracts from A_0 to A_j is illustrated in figure 1.2.

This leaves the question of the relationship between the developments before and after the change in contract. It may be that we just consider the level at which the change took place a new start, re-validate against the requirements and continue. Usually, however, it is possible to express (formally) the relation between A_i and its predecessor and between B_j and its predecessor so that we know the relationship between the previous work and the new.

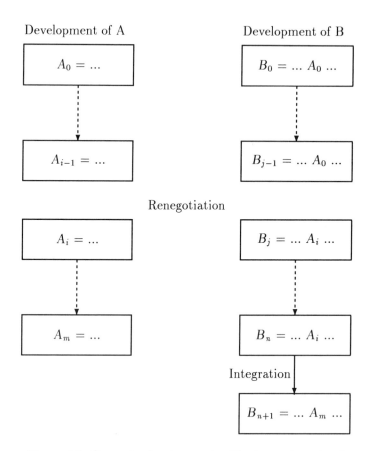

Figure 1.2: Separate development with changed contract

1.2.1.3   Non-implementation steps

We may need to make a non-implementation step during development. Typically the design we want to choose only works for a more restricted case than the one we are dealing with, and so we want to go back to the initial specification and change its properties. In theory what we should do is obvious — we should go back to the initial specification, make the changes and redo the development. The problem is that this may be a lot of work for a small change (particularly if we have been doing proofs). So are there any short cuts for situations where we are reasonably certain that the change is minor?

The first thing to say is that any such short cut is very dangerous, and should only be used with great care. That being said, we can examine some possibilities:

- If the change occurs in the development of A it may still be the case that the change we want to make is an implementation of our contract. If we can establish this there is no problem. For example, the usual way to establish that A_2 is an implementation of A_0 is that A_2 implements A_1 and A_1 implements A_0, with the result following from the transitivity of implementation. But it is quite valid to establish that A_2 implements A_0 directly. (The reason we don't do it as a matter of course is that the proof tends to be large and difficult; using the intermediate A_1 effectively decomposes the proof.) We can then choose to discard A_1 as a false step or retain it as a guide to the intuitions behind the development.

If, however, the change means that we are not implementing A_0, we should renegotiate the contract, as described above. It is very dangerous to weaken the formal relation between separate developments.

- If the change occurs in the development of B then, again, we may still be implementing B_0 (or B_j after a changed contract), and there is no real problem. But often this is not the case. At the system level, though, there are no other dependent developments and so we can decide to accept the change at this level without re-working the previous ones. What we should do is to formally document what the relation is and also informally document what the effective changes to the requirements are. If the original specification met the requirements and we are now changing its properties then, potentially at least, we are meeting changed requirements.

1.2.2 Step-wise development

The discussion about separate development assumed that there might be several steps in the development of A and B. It is indeed important that this is possible, that we can develop software in a sequence of steps. Then we can start with a suitable abstraction, decide what are the main design decisions we need to make, and what the dependencies are between them, and make a plan of the order in which we tackle them. Typical design decisions involve:

- providing explicit definitions for values previously given only signatures or implicit definitions or axioms
- providing explicit definitions for variables and channels previously referred to only by **any**
- giving concrete definitions for abstract types
- changing the definitions for types to allow more detailed or (potentially) more efficient functions over them (e.g. lists for sets)
- adding new definitions or axioms
- adding state variables, either locally to save values or globally to replace parameters
- changing the style of specification between applicative and imperative or between sequential and concurrent
- adding extra parameters or channels to express greater functionality

- making things more generally applicable (and hence more reusable) — such as adding parameters to schemes or widening the parameter types of functions
- removing constructs difficult to translate into the chosen target language

Dealing with one or more such decisions means we make a *development step*, we produce a new specification which we can verify conforms to the previous one. It is important to be able to make only one, or at least only a few, design decisions in each development step, to deal with one problem at a time.

Deciding what the major decisions are also gives us an overall plan of activities for the development. For example, for the lift system that we discuss in the tutorial (section 2.7) our top level plan is roughly:

- formulating an abstract specification by concentrating on producing suitable functions and axioms that can be validated against the requirements
- developing a concrete specification by designing a suitable global state type and definitions of the functions, so that the definitions can be checked to implement the axioms
- decomposing the global state into separate state components for the motor, doors and buttons
- introducing concurrency reflecting the different processes

Note that the problems being tackled here are, in order:

- meeting the main requirements
- designing a suitable global state type
- decomposing the state
- introducing concurrency

Of course there is some interplay between the design process and the problems to be tackled. Choosing different problems first would result in different problems arising. But deciding on this kind of top level plan is a critical step in starting a development.

The number of development steps from an initial specification will vary, but experience suggests that it is typically one or two. Main components will tend to have more steps than sub-components.

1.2.3   Invent and verify

There are techniques for development that rely on transformation, such as that developed by the CIP project in Munich [5]. With such a technique the developer starts with an expression and applies a transformation rule that creates a different but equivalent expression. Thus the developer is guaranteed a priori that the new expression is equivalent to the old one because the transformation rules are known to preserve equivalence.

In fact, doing RAISE justification is an example of a transformation technique, but applied to logical expressions rather than program expressions. Any formal application of correct proof rules produces a correct argument — there is no need to check it afterwards.

"Invent and verify", on the other hand, is a style that allows (in fact forces) the developer to invent a new design. Then, afterwards, the developer verifies its correctness.

The transformational route sounds easier, because there is only one step and correctness is guaranteed. What are the advantages of invent and verify?

- Transformational systems are very large for reasonably sized languages. The RSL justification editor currently has some 2000 rules. This is only a small system designed with the very particular purpose of doing justifications: most of the rules are equivalences. A design transformational system would be considerably larger because it would have a more general purpose and because it would not be restricted to equivalences. Equivalence may be useful for algorithms but not for data types where, for example, we often introduce redundancy. So the system would be extremely large with difficulties first in populating it and then in finding suitable rules.

  It can be argued, of course, that an extensible system would allow rules to be added as needed. But then one is back to invent and verify. One invents the rule one needs, verifies its correctness and then applies it. The rule is available to apply in future, but only if one has taken the trouble to suitably generalize it when inventing it.

- In practice transformational rules only apply in particular circumstances; showing that those circumstances hold generates "side conditions" that need to be proved. Hence the "and verify" part tends to be there anyway.

- It is easy given the invent and verify approach to invent several steps, perhaps changing one's mind several times, before deciding on the right approach and doing the verifications. With transformations the approach tends to be more formal from the start.

- In practice, as we noted when discussing separate development, some development steps will not be implementations and may, indeed, bear little formal relation to the previous level. But we may still wish to preserve the previous level as a guide to how we reached the new design. Hence we need to do "incorrect" steps, which runs counter to a "guaranteed correct" approach. There may still be opportunities for verification as well as invention in this case when we do postulate a formal relation.

It will be noticed that these are not objections to transformational approach in principle. Indeed, all these remarks could be made against doing justifications just by selecting rules and using them: a usable technique must allow lemmas to be defined and used (the "new rules"), side conditions to be generated, the justification of side conditions to be deferred and even goals to change in midstream via informal steps ("this amounts to showing ..."). Hence partly it is an engineering issue, and the real judgement the designers of the RAISE method made is that transformational systems are not yet sufficiently powerful to make all development transformational for a language like RSL.

1.2.4   Rigour

Development is difficult; proofs are much more so. It is impractical to prove every-thing, given the current state of theorem provers. And even if we could, with little effort, prove everything that is true, it is not clear that this ability would be suffi-cient. We often learn a lot from the failure of a proof, but we learn most from the precise details of the failure. So it is not enough merely to be able to do proof, we need to be able to *explore* properties of specifications.

Another problem is that, just as there are far too many possible test cases to execute in real time, so are there too many possible properties. As with testing, we have to look for the "interesting" cases, such as the boundary cases. And then we need to actually discharge the proofs for the suspect cases. There is another analogy with testing. If we had to repeat lots of "obvious" tests, our efficiency at spotting the problems would drop because the whole process would become so tedious. We should always be asking what is the most effective activity to help achieve our goals. In both proving and testing, suitable driving programs (programmed proof tactics, test harnesses and so on) reduce the human intervention and consequent tedium.

There is, of course, a danger that by selecting the cases to prove we miss the mistakes because it is "obvious" that they aren't there. Again, this is just like test case selection, where it is also dangerous but necessary to select a set of interesting cases. As with testing we use guidelines on test case selection and review by others to help avoid such pitfalls.

So it can be necessary to select the properties worthy of closer investigation, and to formally prove only those we suspect. But when we investigate some property in part informally we should also note down the argument, why we think it is true, as a normal part of documentation — as something to be reviewed now and referred to again later. We call an argument that may be wholly or partly informal a *justification*. Arguments that contain informal steps are termed *rigorous*. A justification that is completely formal is a *proof*.

Note that although we advocate rigorous rather than fully formal arguments, we still need the formal basis of the method. It is critical, if someone else challenges the correctness of an informal part of a justification, that we can formalize it and answer the challenge definitively.

1.3   Role of RAISE in software engineering

So far we have presented the characteristics of RAISE as a formal system. But this book is about *method*, and we need to examine what we mean by a method, and in particular what we mean by a formal method.

A method is a means of achieving something, and in the context of this book the something is the development of a *software system*. By "software system" we mean:

- a program, or collection of connected programs, written in some executable language. An executable language is one whose (well-formed) programs can be run on suitable hardware, usually after an automatic compilation process.
- associated documentation supporting the use and maintenance of the program(s).

Note that we include the documentation as well as the program. We will see that formal methods have most to do with production of the software, a lot to do with producing documentation supporting maintenance, and less to do with producing documentation supporting use.

A method consists essentially of procedures to be followed and techniques that facilitate the procedures.[1]

Procedures or activities are usually described in several layers. At the top are the major activities that collectively are said to form the software lifecycle, typically consisting of activities like requirements analysis and capture, architectural design, detailed design, coding, unit testing, integration, acceptance testing, maintenance. Within these major activities there are component activities like producing a particular kind of document (activity plan, architectural design, module design, coded module, test plan, test case, etc.), following a quality assurance procedure, changing an existing document, etc.

Together with these procedures identifying various kinds of activity there will be particular techniques that can be used. There are techniques for requirements analysis, for design, for doing reviews, for generating test cases, for analysing test coverage, etc.

Most of the RAISE method consists of techniques for four major procedures:

- specification
- development
- justification
- translation

Many detailed specification techniques are described in the book on RSL [23], and are not presented here, although there is some general advice in the tutorial part and good examples to follow throughout. Techniques for development, justification and translation are described in detail in part II.

Techniques must be related to the procedures that require them. Here we are in something of a difficulty. Particular suppliers and purchasers of software usually have their own notion of what method is to be used, generally embedded in their quality standards. Such standards will describe in detail what is meant by procedures like "test specification", say. They will prescribe the component procedures, their inputs and outputs, what techniques (and perhaps tools) are acceptable or mandated, what quality assurance procedures will be applied, etc. The use of for-

---

[1]Tools are commonly considered part of a method, because the method would be unusable without them. We believe tools to be essential for practical use of RAISE, but tools are not essential to understanding this book. Therefore the book does not make detailed reference to tools, though it does indicate which techniques can be supported by tools.

mal methods will affect some of these much more than others. It is unlikely, for example, to change substantially the order in which things are done, but it will change the proportion of time spent on some activities compared to others. Some techniques (like textual document preparation) will be affected little or not at all, some (like test case generation) may be changed because their inputs are different and perhaps available earlier, but will be essentially unchanged, while some (like design) will be radically different. So we do not want here to propose a method to replace everything in place already. Rather we want to explain how the RAISE method will affect typical methods in use already. We therefore need to describe at least some characteristics of a "typical" method, to explain how we use some of the basic terms.

We will use the following terms describing the top level procedures that are most affected when using RAISE:

specification starts with identified requirements, written mostly in a natural language such as English, and produces a description in RSL. For all but the most trivial systems this will be structured into a number of modules. The specification will define the behaviour of the system in sufficient detail to meet all the major functional requirements. This procedure covers what is often described as requirements analysis.

We shall often refer to the main output of this procedure as the *initial specification*. This is not because it is the first one written — there may be several versions attempted before one is selected, and we shall see later that producing a more concrete version to gain confidence in the more abstract is also a common technique. It is referred to as the initial specification because it is the basis for the more detailed specifications produced during development.

Ideally the initial specification will be free from "implementation bias", i.e. it should be possible to develop any possible correct final implementation from it. This is sometimes referred to by saying that the initial specification should define *what* the system is to do rather than *how* it is to do it. So, ideally, it should not reflect any architectural design decisions.

In practice there may be some variation from this. Large systems with many requirements will be hard to describe in a single module, and indeed may need to be modular because we use modularity as one means of dealing with complexity. While it is theoretically possible to use composition as well as decomposition to change the modular structure during development, it is unlikely in practice, and even less so with separate development. So initial specification often includes some architectural design.

development starts with the initial specification and produces a new, more detailed RSL specification (usually in a number of development steps) that conforms to the original and that is ready for translation — the *final specification*. This procedure is often called detailed design.

translation starts with the final specification in RSL and produces a program or collection of programs in some executable language(s). This procedure is often called coding.

Note that these procedures may apply to maintenance (when the inputs will also include the result of previous work) as well as to original development.

1.3.1   Validation and verification

There are two facets to showing correctness that are commonly distinguished, validation and verification:

validation is the check that we are creating what is required, i.e. that we are meeting the requirements. It can be expressed as the check that we are "solving the right problem". Since it is a check against requirements written in natural language it is necessarily informal.

verification is the check that the process of development is correct. Hence it includes in particular the formulation and justification of formal relations between development steps. It can be expressed as the check that we are "solving the problem right". Verification can be done with varying degrees of formality.

Validation requires that we are able to trace requirements, to relate them to where in the specification they are being met. We should be able to relate a functional requirement to either the initial specification or to a later development level. Once we know that a requirement has been captured we use verification to check that it remains captured.

It is also possible to relate non-functional requirements to development steps, since it is mainly these that drive the direction of development. Choice of a particular algorithm or data structure is often determined by a particular intended programming language or operating system, or by some capacity or efficiency requirement.

1.3.2   Analysing requirements

The great strength of formal methods is that in having to create a formal description of a system at an early stage in its development one is forced to make decisions about all kinds of things on which the requirements are silent or open to interpretation. This uncovers many problems with requirements documents — problems which are generally inherent in natural language documents no matter how carefully written.

The second important point to note is that it is particularly valuable to find errors and resolve ambiguities or contradictions at this early stage. It is a standard result that the later an error is discovered the more expensive it is to fix, both because of the work that needs to be re-done and because of the time elapsed.

Thirdly it is the experience of teams using formal methods that their common understanding of the problem improves through creating and discussing the specification. Just as requirements are couched in natural language, so is most communication between team members, and this too is open to misunderstandings and confusion. As a specification is developed and agreed it tends to give precise meanings to the components of the system, their functions, their interfaces, etc., and the communication between team members improves as a result. This effect has even been reported by teams who have previously worked together on similar systems, when they first attempt formal specifications.

Because of these effects it is sometimes worth re-writing the requirements from the specification, since this typically produces a document that has fewer omissions, contradictions and repetitions, is better structured and is more consistent in its terminology. This is particularly useful if the original document turns out to be very inadequate in these respects or if the customer is unable to understand the formal specifications. Playing back one's understanding of something is frequently a good way of checking that one has really understood it.

The value of doing a good job in producing the initial specification should be apparent. It follows that it is worth spending a considerable amount of time and effort on it, more than is usually spent on requirements analysis. A good initial specification will more than pay for itself in making development quick and reliable. Hence it is normal in the specification procedure to go through several iterations, to look for alternatives (particularly different architectures), to plan and sketch out the development route to see if there are any difficult steps that can be made easier, to create more concrete specifications that can be tested directly by symbolic execution or translated and run as prototypes. In fact a very iterative style of development in which, by the time the initial specification is agreed, most of the design work and even some translation has been done, seems well suited to formal specification among small teams. With larger teams working separately this is less practical as far as the interfaces are concerned, but can still be adopted for components.

"It is a long time before you start to code" is an accusation often made about formal development. Certainly it is expected, in using formal specification, and more so in using rigorous development, that coding will start late. But it should be quick and reliable (and may even be automatic for at least large parts). And any good development method encourages more work at the early stages, because rushing into code usually entails trying to debug one's way out of trouble later.

1.3.3   Maintaining correctness

Achieving a sound and correct starting point for detailed design is the first essential, and something that the clarity and logic of formal methods makes possible. Then we try to maintain the correctness; here the implementation relation in particular and the general ability to reason about specifications are important.

1.3.4   Concentration on discovery of errors as they are introduced

Software engineers spend much of their time finding and correcting errors. They also spend much of their time introducing them. Apart from those inherent in the requirements, all errors in software systems are introduced by their developers and maintainers. Hence our methods can usefully be directed at avoiding the introduction of errors or finding them immediately.

Errors fall into several categories:

- requirements that do not reflect the real desires or needs of the customer or user
- failure to meet requirements like performance or reliability that we try to design for but can rarely guarantee in advance
- misunderstandings of the requirements or previous development level
- slips by the developers or maintainers in not writing what they meant to write

The first category is often the most expensive to correct, the last probably the most common.

Using formal methods will help with the first category of error to the extent that the requirements are obviously unclear or incomplete, because in the analysis stage lots of questions will arise from the requirements and be resolved with their authors. But if the requirements say build X when they mean Y, and the request for X seems reasonable, there is little chance of any formal method detecting the problem. Building an early prototype to demonstrate is a good idea if this is likely to be a problem.

Formal methods have some difficulty with the second category of error — failure to meet requirements that cannot be easily expressed as a property of what particular components should do. Real-time requirements are a particular example, and how to deal with them is an active area of research. What we can do with such requirements is to use them as a guide to the direction in which we develop and the standards which we adopt. Thus to achieve performance or reliability requirements we will consider various potential architectures (including both software and hardware), use standard techniques to analyse their potential performance, failure rates, etc, and then guide our development towards the chosen architecture. To achieve particular quality levels in the product we will apply the appropriate standards in the development — and here formal methods have much to offer in achieving more reliability in the development process.

Formal methods also help with the third category of error, since formality sharply reduces the possibility of misunderstandings.

As for the fourth category of error, it is not clear if people are more or less likely to make errors in writing RSL than they would in other techniques. Tools can help in immediately pointing out some simple slips, and it is often the case that a type error in a specification indicates a deeper problem than just a slip.

But undoubtedly errors will be made in this way, and formal specifications are by no means easy to get right, just as programs are not easy to get right. But formal specifications do have two advantages over programs. First they can be verified against the previous level — against requirements by trying to prove requirements expressed formally, and against previous levels written in RSL by expressing implementation and then justifying it. Even if this process is only used to the extent of examining the proof obligations carefully, without actually making and recording any justification, it is very effective at discovering mistakes.

Secondly, formal specifications can be reviewed. Code reading is recognized as an effective way of discovering errors, and reading RSL is generally easier because it is more abstract and less detailed. So reviewing RSL, by people proficient in it and with check-lists of typical problems, is very effective.

1.3.5   Production of documentation enabling maintenance

Maintaining software is very expensive and very error-prone. Design documentation is typically missing or out-of-date.

Formal specifications, both initial and development specifications, can help considerably because they provide a means of understanding the code top-down. Comments in specifications can aid this process. Whether the change is an extension, an adaptation or a correction, it is possible to discover the module(s) affected and the first development level at which the change can be expressed, and for the development to be re-done from that point. The interfaces between RSL modules are all explicit, so it is easy to check what else is affected (usually using tools).

The process is also much easier (and likely to be followed) if all or most of the final specification is automatically translatable. This is also a crucial factor in the specifications being up-to-date. One of the problems with traditional design documentation is that once it has been created there is no real incentive to maintain it; changing the documentation as well as the code just seems like two jobs of which only one matters right now. The more we can make the code generated from designs the more likely it is that the designs will be consistent with the code.

1.4   Selective use

There are two important ways in which we can be selective in our use of RAISE: in how formal we choose to be and in what components of a system we choose to apply it to.

1.4.1   Degrees of formality

In section 1.2.4 we explained that it is not necessary (or sensible) to prove everything. In fact there is a more general principle: The degree of formality that you apply needs to be appropriate to the problem and an efficient way of tackling it. And there are many opportunities for being more or less formal in development. We may broadly classify three development styles:

formal specification only Formality is applied to the specification procedure. We write the specification with the aims of:

- achieving and recording a precise, unambiguous statement of what we understand the system is to do, as a basis for creating it now and maintaining it in the future
- using this as a guide to doing detailed design and writing the code, but using informal design techniques
- validating the specification against the requirements to discover any discrepancies and resolve them
- formulating test cases for use after coding

formal specification and rigorous development Formality is applied to the specification procedure as before, but also to the development procedure. This means that one writes both abstract and more concrete specifications and also records the development relations between them. These relations are then subject to examination and perhaps review, but are not justified.

formal specification and formal development We extend the previous step to doing the justifications as well. Our previous advice of always concentrating on the difficult or interesting parts and hence on doing justifications, including informal arguments, rather than full proofs, still stands, so perhaps this category should be called "formal specification and more rigorous development".

So what level should be adopted? Most experience with formal methods has been in using them at the first level, and certainly the formal specification procedure seems to be extremely effective because it finds so many ambiguities and omissions in the requirements. It is also effective in providing a basis for test cases and for determining expected results, and for providing documentation that can be used in maintenance. In terms of value (mainly increased confidence in the software) for effort it is extremely cost-effective.

But the first level alone still leaves the gap between the initial specification and the code. If we only intend to produce one level of specification, we may be tempted to make it very detailed, to capture all the requirements and be fairly close to the code. There is then a danger that we lose some of the advantages of formal specification in not being sufficiently abstract, and in creating specifications that are hard to reason about (whether mentally or on paper or with tools). Once we lose the ability to reason about what our specifications mean, we lose much of the point of producing them. Hence there are very good arguments for adopting the second level.

It is not necessary to adopt rigorous development uniformly. Our initial specification will provide a top-level decomposition into component systems, and some of these will require more development work than others. Some may be very simple and easily coded; some will be standard components for which we have already existing developments with translations.

Many of the benefits of the first level lie in error discovery — errors, omissions, contradictions or ambiguities in the requirements. Most of the benefits of the second level lie in error avoidance: having achieved a good initial specification we maintain conformity with it. It also produces a record of how the development was done that is very valuable in maintenance. The second level also produces RSL that may be automatically translated. In terms of cost-effectiveness — improved quality for effort — it may well be less effective than the first level, but it can still be a great improvement over the alternatives. (It is not unusual that increases in quality become more and more expensive to achieve.)

The third level, of actually doing justifications, continues the trend of increasing the effort substantially in return for a smaller return in quality improvement. Justification can be very time consuming and is almost certainly reserved for the more critical components. But it should be noted that it is here that there are possible gains that cannot be achieved (with any degree of reliability) in any other way. Even the simplest systems are far too complicated to test comprehensively, so that there are clear statistical limits that one can place on the reliability achievable through testing. The increasing use of parallel, distributed systems makes these problems even worse. There are already examples, such as the application by Bull in the ESPRIT LaCoS project [7], where previously undiscovered errors were discovered by justification.

Finally, it should be mentioned that it requires some experience to become a good specifier. It requires a little more to become a good rigorous designer, because it needs experience to judge what to develop first, how much detail to put in each development step, when to decompose, what previous developments can be re-used, which constructs will be easy or hard to translate into the chosen target language, how to take account of other constraints like timing problems, hardware, operating system, etc. It requires still more to be able to do justifications, because there are particular techniques to be learned. So teams new to formal methods should concentrate on formal specification before trying rigorous development, and justification skills should be developed later still.

1.4.2   Selective application of formality

In section 1.4.1 we saw that it is possible to be more or less formal in the way in which we apply formal methods. It is also the case that we may choose only to apply formal methods to parts of a system and not to others. There are two ways in which we can do this: selecting properties and selecting components. We will consider each of these.

1.4.2.1   Selecting properties

We can choose to specify only a few critical properties, like safety or security properties. We typically achieve two benefits from this:

- deeper understanding of the property itself through its capture in a formal language
- understanding (perhaps after some formal development) of how the system components need to interact in order to maintain the property

1.4.2.2 Selecting components

We can choose to specify only certain system components. Components for which formal methods are likely to be less useful include:

- standard components like databases or operating systems with which our system needs to interface. Specifying such an interface formally would involve specifying the relevant properties of the standard component, and this is rarely worthwhile.
- generic components which our system needs to instantiate. We would need to specify the generic component and also the code we need to write to make our particular instantiation. Such code is usually in some special language. For example, language processing systems (lexical analysers, parsers, compiler generators, syntax editors) will use specialized notations like "regular expressions" and BNF. Trying to use a general purpose specification language like RSL to specify input in these notations is likely to be clumsy, less clear and often no more abstract.

  User interfaces also come into this category. Modern systems typically use standard generic components to generate graphic user interfaces, and here the important features like appearance and response time are hard to specify effectively in a specification language.
- components whose behaviour is not regarded as very critical.
- existing components that were not formally specified and that we are adapting. This is a dangerous practice, of course, because it is precisely complex software with inadequate or outdated documentation that it is dangerous to adapt. But the cost of formally specifying an existing component first is usually hard to justify when the hope is to save development time by adaptation. In the long run it may be cheaper to start from scratch and develop properly, but this is unlikely to be apparent at the start. We note this category not to encourage it but to acknowledge it.

So the components we should specify formally are those whose correctness is critical and that we are creating from scratch or adapting.

Software that is developed formally is also easier to maintain and adapt, because the specification and development history provide effective documentation for these purposes. So other criteria for choosing formality are the expected lifetime of the system and the likelihood of re-use.

1.5   Formal systems

This section and the next on the RAISE implementation relation discuss aspects of RAISE as a formal system. This section discusses formal systems in general and may be skipped by readers with knowledge of the topic.

We have described RAISE as a *formal system*. What does this mean? A formal system has four essential components:

- a notation with a defined syntax
- a set of well-formedness rules
- a semantics
- a logic

If we take arithmetic expressions as an example, the syntax rules would say that terms like "1", "2", "+" and "1 + 2" are syntactically correct, but that terms like "1 +" and "+ +" are not.

Well-formedness rules cover the areas commonly known as "scope", "visibility" and "type" checking. If we extend our example to include booleans as well as arithmetic, and also to allow let expressions, then expressions like

> **let** x = 2 **in** 1 + y **end**

and

> **let** x = **true in** 1 + x **end**

may be violating scope/visibility and type rules respectively. (Though the first might be well-formed as a component of a larger let expression in which y is defined.)

The semantics of a system defines its meaning, usually in terms of some well-understood mathematical theory such as that for the natural numbers, or set theory. Semantics is usually only defined for well-formed terms.

For our simple example the relationship between our representation of arithmetic and booleans and mathematical natural numbers and truth values is obvious. But already we have the problem of explaining what a let expression means.

So far what we have considered includes programming languages, or at least programming languages that have been given a mathematical semantics. So is Ada, say, a formal system? For our purposes it still lacks the fourth element, a logic. This is what allows us to reason about terms in our system. For example, is it the case that the following equality is true?

$$1 + 2 = 2 + 1 \tag{1}$$

One way to answer this problem is to appeal to the semantics, to decide that the two expressions on either side of the equality symbol represent the mathematical natural number "3", that equality represents mathematical equality, and that therefore the answer is "yes". Another way, if our system is a programming language, is to test it and see. Essentially (assuming the execution of a program correctly follows its semantics) these are the same. We are "executing" the expression, symbolically or mechanically, to see what semantic value we get.

But if we have a logic we will have rules like

$$i + j = j + i \qquad\qquad\qquad (2)$$

together with rules for instantiating the names "i" and "j" with integers like "1" and "2". Now we can not only answer the problem of whether (1) is true without having to execute it, symbolically or otherwise, but we can also answer more general questions, like "Is 'i + 1' the same as '1 + i' for any integer 'i'?"

There is a cost in having a logic, a set of rules like (2), as well as a semantics: since we have two ways of answering questions we must ensure we get the same answers. In other words the logic must be consistent with the semantics. In RAISE we tackle this by starting with a small logic containing a minimal set of "basic" rules, which we can check against the semantics, and then checking other rules by showing how they are derived from the basic ones.

The formal system whose use we describe in this book is RAISE, based on its specification language, RSL. The book on RSL [23] describes its syntax, well-formedness rules and (informally) its semantics. (A deep knowledge of its semantics is not necessary for its use, but a definition is available [19].) An important aim of this book is to describe its logic. But it is worth considering first the question of why we need RSL. Why don't we provide a logic for Ada, or Pascal or any other programming language?

The reason is that these languages were designed for writing software. They have many "low-level" features like pointers that help us write efficient software. But such low-level features make reasoning very complicated, and so their logics would be very complicated. A specification language like RSL aims to make reasoning possible, and so it includes features (like abstract types and axioms) that make reasoning more tractable, and avoids features (like pointers) that make reasoning harder.

RSL is, however, a wide spectrum language because it is intended to be used not just for initial specification but also for development to languages like Ada or C++. Hence it includes some low-level features like variables with assignment and loops. We will see that, if we use only the sequential applicative features of RSL, reasoning is easier than when we include imperative and concurrent features. Hence the method encourages (but does not force) initial specifications to be sequential and applicative so that we can reason initially with some ease.

1.6 RAISE implementation relation

This section is more technical than the preceding sections of this chapter and assumes knowledge of RSL. It aims to provide some intuition for the notions of implementation and conservative extension.

Any formal system that aims to provide a means of development as well as a means of specification must provide a notion of implementation. That is, if module A_0 is developed to module A_1, we need to know if A_1 is a "correct" development. We say that A_1 is correct if it implements A_0, i.e. A_0 and A_1 are in the implementation relation. There are in fact several variations on the notion of implementation; the one in RAISE is chosen to meet two particular requirements that arise from the method requirements we have just been examining. If A_1 implements A_0, we want the following to hold:

property preservation: All properties that can be proved about A_0 can also be proved for A_1 (but not in general vice versa).

substitutivity: An instance of A_0 in a specification can be replaced by an instance of A_1, and the resulting new specification should implement the earlier specification.

Substitutivity means that we can develop parts of systems separately and then put them together safely.

Property preservation means that if we prove some properties of a module (and in particular if we prove it meets its requirements) and then we prove a development implements it, we know that the development also has the properties. In fact it ensures that implementation is transitive: if A_2 implements A_1 and A_1 implements A_0, A_2 implements A_0. So we can proceed from initial to final specification in a number of steps. We formally define the implementation relation in appendix B.8. A class expression *ce1* implements a class expression *ce0* if all the properties of *ce0* are true in the context of *ce1*. That is, the properties of *ce1* must imply the properties of *ce0*.

To understand implementation in practice we need to know what is meant by the (logical) properties of a class expression. The formal definition is in appendix B.8.2; intuitively it is just the collection of logical expressions that can be deduced from its definitions and axioms. We will call the collection of logical properties of a specification the *theory* of a specification.

So we see that the essential idea behind implementation is that the theory of the implementation needs to imply the theory of the class being implemented. This proof theoretic approach is one that RSL shares with Larch [13] and COLD-K [15, 9]. It contrasts with the "model theoretic" approach of Act One [8], OBJ [11], ASL [27] and Extended ML [26, 16], in which implementation is sub-classing of models. The advantage of the model theoretic approach is that it can allow observational equivalence. The disadvantage is that implementation is not so easy to prove because the proof theoretic notions are not so easily available [21]. (We will see in the section 2.8.4.1 that it is recommended and natural to write RSL in an abstract style that effectively specifies types by observational equivalence.)

We now look at some simple examples. Consider the class expression *S1* defined by

S1 =
    class
       value x, y : **Int**
    end

All this says is that there are names x and y of kind "value" and that they are integers. We call the collection of defined names with their kinds and types (or classes for schemes and objects) a *signature*. We have not constrained the values of x and y in any way. In fact because there are no constraints its theory reduces to **true**.

Now consider the class expression *S2*:

S2 =
   class
      value x, y : **Int**
      axiom x > y
   end

This has the same signature as *S1* but it also has an axiom. Since, apart from the axiom, x and y are unconstrained, the theory of *S2* can be presented as "x > y".

Does *S2* implement *S1*? It is a precondition for asking this question that the signature of *S2* should include the signature of *S1*. This relation we call *static implementation*. In fact the signatures of *S1* and *S2* are the same. So we have to prove

$$x > y \Rightarrow \textbf{true}$$

which is vacuously true.[2] Note that *S1* does not implement *S2*, since this would involve proving the reverse implication, which is not true for arbitrary integers x and y.

Now consider *S3*:

S3 =
   class
      value
         x : **Int** = 1,
         y : **Int** = 0
   end

The theory of *S3*, as you might expect, can be presented as

$$x = 1 \wedge y = 0$$

S3 has the same signature as *S1* and *S2*, and so we can ask what implementation relations hold. Does *S3* implement *S2*? We would need to prove

$$(x = 1 \wedge y = 0) \Rightarrow x > y$$

which is clearly true.

We can also see that *S3* implements *S1*, so we have a simple example of transitivity of implementation.

Now consider a fourth example *S4*:

S4 =
   class
      value x, y, z : **Int**
   end

This is like *S1* but it has an extra entity, the integer value z. Does it have any relation to *S1*? The signature of *S4* includes that of *S1*. The values are completely

---

[2]In such implications names like x and y are bound by their definitions in the implementing class, *S2* in this case.

unconstrained so its theory reduces to **true**. To check if *S4* implements *S1* we try to prove

true $\Rightarrow$ **true**

which is vacuously true: *S4* implements *S1*. Note that we cannot ask the question the other way round. *S1*'s signature does not include *S4*'s: *S1* does not define an integer *z*, so *S1* does not statically implement *S4*.

Consider a fifth scheme *S5*:

S5 =
  class
    value x, y, z : **Int**
    axiom x > z $\wedge$ z > y
  end

It should be clear that *S5* is an implementation of *S1*, *S2* and *S4*. The only interesting case is the second, where we need to prove

$(x > z \wedge z > y) \Rightarrow x > y$

which follows from the transitivity of ">".

So far we have had no hidden names. Now consider a sixth scheme *S6*:

S6 =
  hide z **in**
  class
    value x, y, z : **Int**
    axiom x > z $\wedge$ z > y
  end

(We could also have defined *S6* as "**hide** z **in** *S5*".) The signature of *S6* only includes the names that are not hidden, i.e. it only includes *x* and *y*.

S6 therefore cannot implement *S5* as *z* is in the signature of *S5* but not in the signature of *S6*: *S6* does not statically implement *S5*. The precondition for the implementation relation in the opposite direction is satisfied, however, as *S5* statically implements *S6*.

What is the theory of *S6*? We can in fact present its theory as

$$\exists z : \mathbf{Int} \bullet x > z \wedge z > y \qquad (1)$$

The only free names in (1) are *x* and *y*, the names in the signature of *S6*. It is not always possible to find such a finite presentation of the theory of a class involving hiding.

We can now see that *S5* does implement *S6*, since in *S5* the definition of a value *z* strictly between *x* and *y* implies (1), the existence of such a value. In fact the removal of a **hide** from a class expression always gives a trivial, but rarely very useful, example of implementation. *S6* also implements *S2* (which defined only *x* and *y* with the axiom that x > y), since (1) implies that *x* is greater than *y*.

Of rather more interest is whether we can get implementation by removing hidden entities. We can. For example, *S6* is implemented by, for example, *S7*:

S7 =
  class
    value
        x : **Int** = 2,
        y : **Int** = 0
  end

But *S6* is not implemented by *S2* since x being greater than y does not imply (1), that there necessarily exists a value between them. Similarly *S6* is not implemented by *S3* (in which x is 1 and y is 0).

So we see that implementation allows us to remove hidden entities, but that we need to take great care about the ways that properties involving the hidden entities affect the properties of the non-hidden entities.

1.6.1   Implementation meets its requirements

Having provided some intuition for the implementation relation we should check that it meets the requirements for property preservation and substitutivity that we identified earlier. We take the requirements in turn:

Property preservation   This is immediate from the definition of implementation.

Substitutivity   There are two questions here:

- Is the result of a replacement in some context always well-formed?
- Does the result of a replacement in some context always give implementation?

To answer the first question we note that since the new signature includes the old, replacing the old with the new cannot result in any names becoming undefined. The only possible problem is that of any extra names defined in the new.

First, we may get a result that is ill-formed. Consider the extending class expression

extend class value x : **Int end with class value** y : **Int end**

and then consider replacing either of the constituent class expressions with

class value x, y : **Int end**

This implements both of them, but replacing either with it would give multiple declarations of the same name in the extending class expression. Hence there is the possibility of ill-formedness of the result. (This only occurs with extending class expressions.)

There is also a possibility of "capture" of free names. Consider the following example:

class
   scheme S = **class value** x : **Int** = y **end**
   value y : **Int**
end

and then consider the class expression

class value x : **Int** = y **value** y : **Int end**

This class expression might be considered an implementation for the class expression of *S* — all we have done is add an extra declaration for *y*. But clearly the replacement of the old class expression with this one would change the theory of the context, the outer class expression. We would lose the equality between the x within *S* and the y outside it. Hence such a replacement cannot be allowed. But it is easy to avoid this problem. It is poor style to mention inside a class expression a name defined outside it, except for the names of modules defined either globally or as parameters. Then the only free names in a class expression will be parameter or global module names, and if we choose names different from either of these for modules declared inside class expressions, the problem is avoided.

So we can only allow replacement if the result is well-formed and if there is no capture of free names.

To answer the second question — does the result of a replacement in some context always give implementation? — we state in appendix B.8.6 the required "compositional" properties. Implementation can be shown to have these properties.

1.6.2   Conservative extension

We have so far distinguished between the signature of a class expression and its theory. Mathematicians often refer to these together as a "theory" (or, to be more precise in this case, a "typed theory"). Then they define a notion of *theory extension*. A theory *T2* extends a theory *T1* if *T2* adds to the entities and/or properties of *T1*. This is in fact the same as our notion of implementation.

We can then distinguish between *conservative extension* and *non-conservative extension*.

A theory *T2* conservatively extends a theory *T1* if every property of *T2* that can be expressed using entities defined in *T1* is a property of *T1*. In other words, *T2* adds no new properties to the entities from *T1*. An extension that is not conservative is non-conservative.

A formal definition of conservative extension can be found in appendix B.8.4. Here we try to give an intuition. Consider

scheme
   S1 = **class value** x : **Int axiom** x < 10 **end**,
   S2 = **extend** S1 **with class value** y : **Int** = x **end**

Call the properties that only involve the name x (the only name defined in *S1*) "*S1*-properties". The only *S1*-property available from the definition of *S1* is that x is less than 10. Since *S2* extends *S1* we may ask what are the *S1*-properties of *S2*.

The answer is, again, that x is less than 10. Since the *S1*-properties are unchanged by the extension we say that *S2* extends *S1* conservatively. But now consider

scheme

    S1 = **class value** x : **Int axiom** x < 10 **end**,
    S3 = **extend** S1 **with class value** y : **Nat** = x **end**

In *S3* it is possible to prove that x is at least zero as well as less than 10 (since it is equal to the natural number y). So the *S1*-properties of the extension are not the same as those of *S1*; *S3* extends *S1* non-conservatively.

Is conservative extension important? Often it is not, and indeed the extending class expression construct illustrated here is intended to provide a facility for extension in RSL that is typically non-conservative. When we consider single development steps, conservative extension is also rarely of use, since it amounts to taking no design decisions — only adding new entities is allowed.

However, conservative extension can be an important issue when we do separate development. Consider the following simple scenario. A contract between two teams says that there is a value x which is an integer. One team adds the property that it is positive. The other team adds the property that it is negative. What happens at integration? The result is that the specification as a whole is inconsistent; there is no possible program implementing it. This is obviously something to be avoided if possible.

The solution lies in noting that there is always only one team that is responsible for developing the module(s) representing the contract. It is their responsibility, and theirs alone, to strengthen its properties. When other teams use the module(s) in the contract they must be careful to ensure that the modules they are developing only extend the contract conservatively.

In practice this is not particularly difficult to ensure. There are essentially three ways that a separately developed component module can be used in other modules. If the component is a scheme it can be used in a formal parameter or to make an *embedded object* (an object defined inside a class expression). If the component is a *global object* (an object defined globally, i.e. not defined as a scheme parameter or within a class expression) its name can be mentioned in qualifications. As a result, all mentions of the entities defined in the component will be qualified — by the name of the formal parameter, by the name of the embedded object or by the name of the global object. We can then formulate the following rules. (The rules apply to any dependency, whether or not the thing being depended on is a contract with another development or not, because the rules are sensible ones anyway.)

1. Do not write axioms in which all the names are qualified.
2. In value, variable and channel definitions and axioms that involve qualified names, check that the defining types of the unqualified names do not make unwarranted assumptions about the types of the qualified names. In particular, if the unqualified name is defined to be in a subtype, this is "unwarranted" unless the definitions and axioms ensure that the value must be in the subtype because of the properties of the qualified names.

3. Beware of multiple axioms (or conjunctions) relating an unqualified name to different qualified ones.

For example

axiom A.x $\geq$ 0

breaks the first rule and should obviously be placed in the module defining x.

For the second rule consider

value
  y : **Nat** = A.x,
  f : **Int** $\rightarrow$ **Nat**
  f(x) $\equiv$ A.g(x)

Here the definition of y extends the object A conservatively only if x is constrained within the body of A to be a **Nat**. Otherwise the (sub)typing of y is unwarranted. Similarly the definition of f extends the object A conservatively only if g is constrained within the body of A to be a function that converges to a **Nat** for all **Int**s.

For the third rule consider

value y : **Int** $\bullet$ A.x $\leq$ y $\wedge$ y $\leq$ A.z

This implicit definition of y extends the object A conservatively only if it is true within the body of A that $x \leq z$.

The first rule seems very natural — the axiom is obviously in the wrong place. The second and third are more subtle and need care.

There is a fourth possibility that a type declared to be a sort in one module is extended non-conservatively by a declaration that makes the sort definitely non-empty. For example

value x : A.T

means that $A.T$ has at least one value in it. If there were no values, variables or channels of type T in A, this would be a non-conservative extension. Declarations of variables and channels of type $A.T$ can have the same non-conservative effect. However, since types are rarely implemented as empty this is unlikely to be a problem in practice.

So what should be done in the case

scheme
  SX = **class value** x : **Int end**,
  SY = **class value** y : **Int end**,
  S(X : SX, Y : SY) =
    class
      axiom X.x = Y.y
      ...
    end

This breaks the first rule, but where else can the axiom go? The way to deal with it is to note that there is a dependency between SX and SY; this is what the axiom says. Typically in practice it is clear which direction this dependency should take, but if it isn't we can make an arbitrary choice. Suppose we make *SY* dependent on *SX*. Then we reformulate as

scheme
   SX = **class value** x : **Int end**,
   SY(X : SX) = **class value** y : **Int axiom** y = X.x **end**,
   S(X : SX, Y : SY(X)) =
      class
         ...
      end

and this is consistent with the rules.

1.7   Changes to RSL

A few changes have been made to RSL as used in this volume since the original book describing RSL [23]:

- The expansion of explicit and implicit function definitions into signature and axiom has changed. The quantification in the axiom is over the given types of parameters rather than their maximal types. This approach is felt to be much more intuitive.
- The evaluation order of application expressions has been changed so that the function expression is evaluated before the parameters. This means that all evaluations in RSL are left-to-right.
- Axiom quantification (**forall**) is not used; axioms are quantified individually. This avoids counter-intuitive interpretations of axioms that did not mention all the names bound by the axiom quantification. This could be considered a stylistic restriction but is mentioned here as a reminder that **forall** should not be used. Similar remarks apply to $\forall$; care should be taken not to bind names not mentioned in the quantified expression.
- The rule that variables and channels from different objects are different has been extended to the actual parameters of schemes, so that the rule applies to formal parameters as well as objects defined within schemes or globally. This is a restriction on scheme instantiations and is necessary to ensure the compositionality of implementation.
- The map type constructor $\overrightarrow{m}$ has the new symbol $\overset{\sim}{\overrightarrow{m}}$. The original symbol has then been added to indicate the subtype of maps that have finite domains and are deterministic on application. That is, for any types *T1*, *T2*:

    T1 $\overrightarrow{m}$ T2 $\simeq$
      {| m : T1 $\overset{\sim}{\overrightarrow{m}}$ T2 •
        (**card dom** m **post true**) $\wedge$
        ($\forall$ x : T1 • x $\in$ **dom** m $\Rightarrow$ (m(x) **post true**)) |}

  Thus there are now finite maps as well as finite sets and lists. In addition, application of such maps to arguments in their domains is deterministic.

There are also two restrictions on the use of RSL that we follow in this book in order to ensure that the RSL implementation relation can be expanded.

- We do not use "embedded" scheme declarations, i.e. scheme declarations within class expressions or local expressions. There are also methodological reasons for this: we stated earlier that schemes should have as free names only the names of their parameters or of global modules. This restriction can also be overcome: since schemes may not be recursive it is possible to unfold all their instantiations and then remove their embedded definitions.
- We do not allow the classes of scheme formal parameters to hide any of the entities defined in them. This is a very minor restriction; it is very unlikely that one wants to include something in a parameter only to hide it. It might be convenient to define and hide a value to express a property, but it is then possible instead to assert in an axiom the existence of such a value.

Part I

Tutorial

CHAPTER 2

Tutorial

2.1   Introduction

This chapter is intended to illustrate how to specify and develop systems using RAISE. It concentrates on a particular style for consistency, and because this style has been shown to be useful and widely applicable in practice. But it is therefore not complete in showing all the possible ways to construct specifications and develop them. New users of RAISE should find it helpful to follow fairly closely in their own work; more experienced ones will be able to devise their own styles and techniques.

Before presenting the examples we discuss some alternatives in the styles of writing specifications. Section 2.2 considers the differences between applicative and imperative and between sequential and concurrent styles. Section 2.3 considers abstract and concrete styles. Section 2.4 distinguishes "system" and "subsidiary" modules and also introduces the notion of "hierarchical structuring". We then give an overview of the method in section 2.5.

Then three examples are presented in detail. Section 2.6 shows the specification and development of a simple information system (for controlling entry and exits of ships to a harbour). In section 2.7 we specify and develop a safety-critical concurrent control system (for a lift). These are followed in section 2.8 by the development of a data type (a bounded queue) from the specification of an initially abstract, applicative version into several alternative concrete versions, including applicative and imperative, sequential and concurrent, suitable for translation into a programming language. Finally a technical section 2.9 provides the theoretical underpinnings for the method used, in particular the development steps from applicative to imperative and from sequential to concurrent.

2.2   Choice of specification style

There are four main options:

applicative sequential: a "functional programming" style with no variables or concurrency

imperative sequential: with variables, assignment, sequencing, loops, etc. but
   with no concurrency

applicative concurrent: functional programming but with concurrency

imperative concurrent: with variables, assignment, sequencing, loops, etc. and
   concurrency

Applicative concurrent specifications are often inappropriate as the basis for programming language implementations; the main processes are recursive in structure
and their continued execution will keep increasing the size of the call stack. So unless we are implementing in an applicative language that can overcome this problem
we shall need to use an imperative style; the use of variables enables the recursion
to be replaced by a loop. Hence there are only three major kinds of module that
we are usually concerned with and that we shall concentrate on in this tutorial:
applicative sequential, imperative sequential and imperative concurrent. We will
generally abbreviate these to applicative, imperative and concurrent.

Our experience is that of the three, the applicative style is the easiest both to
formulate and to reason about in justifications. It also turns out that one can
easily start with applicative specifications and develop them into imperative or
concurrent ones. For this reason we will adopt this as the basis for the method in
the tutorial.

2.3   Abstractness

As well as distinguishing between applicative and imperative, sequential and concurrent styles of specification we can also distinguish between abstract and concrete
styles.

By abstractness we mean, in general, writing specifications to leave as many
alternative development routes open as possible. In other words, the fewer design
decisions we have taken in expressing a specification the more abstract it is. By
design decisions we mean things like

- deciding how to formulate a module using other modules
- deciding on a particular data structure
- deciding on a particular algorithm
- deciding what variables to use
- deciding what channels and patterns of communication to use

The opposite of "abstract" is "concrete". The distinction between the two is not a
black and white one, but we can characterize modules in each of the three categories
as tending to be abstract or concrete.

abstract applicative modules will use abstract types and will use signatures and
   axioms rather than explicit definitions for some or even all functions.

concrete applicative modules will use concrete types and will contain more explicit function definitions.

abstract imperative modules will not define variables but will use **any** in their accesses and will use axioms.

concrete imperative modules will define variables and will contain more explicit function definitions.

abstract concurrent modules will not define variables or channels but will use **any** in their accesses and will use axioms.

concrete concurrent modules will define variables and channels and will contain more explicit function definitions.

Again it must be stressed that these are relative rather than absolute distinctions. A module may be abstract in some ways and concrete in others. And certainly a system specification will contain modules in both varying styles and varying degrees of abstractness. We will also use the term *axiomatic* to describe a style of value definition in terms of signature and axiom.

We will adopt a naming convention in this tutorial that applicative modules will be prefixed "A_", imperative ones "I_" and concurrent ones "C_". We will also use the convention that the most abstract modules will be suffixed "0", more concrete ones "1", etc.

2.4   Kinds of module

Another distinction we can usefully draw is between *system modules* and *subsidiary modules*. System modules are those we are most concerned with developing; subsidiary ones are (as their name suggests) less important from the point of view of development.

2.4.1   System modules

System modules will form the majority of any specification. They are the modules we will develop from abstract to concrete and, typically, from applicative to imperative and possibly concurrent. They might be more precisely named "system or sub-system" modules since they correspond to what we see as the complete software system and its sub-systems. They will generally be expected to be finally implemented as software modules with dynamic state: in object oriented terms they will form the objects of the software system.

We will arrange for each system module to have a *type of interest*. For abstract applicative modules it corresponds to the standard use of the term by, for example, Guttag [12]. For a module specifying an abstract data type it is precisely that type: *Queue* or *Stack* or *Array* or whatever. For modules specifying software systems or sub-systems it is the type which is the "state" of the system or sub-system. For imperative (sequential or concurrent) modules the type of interest is the product of the types of any variables in the module and the types of interest of its component modules.

The first example in this tutorial is concerned with berthing ships in a harbour. The type of interest of the single system module of the initial applicative specification, *A_HARBOUR0*, is the abstract type *Harbour*. Later we decompose the specification into sub-systems for the set of ships waiting and the array of berths, so that the type of interest becomes defined by

type Harbour = P.Set × B.Array

where *P* and *B* are the objects instantiating the sub-systems. Their types of interest are, naturally, *Set* and *Array* respectively.

The third example is the development of a data type: the bounded queue. The type of interest in the single system module of the initial applicative specification, *A_QUEUE0*, is *Queue*, defined as an abstract type. When we develop this module this type becomes more concretely defined, but still remains the type of interest of any *QUEUE* module, whether applicative or imperative, sequential or concurrent. Some of the developments of *QUEUE* modules use *ARRAY* modules, which have a type of interest *Array*.

It is possible to write abstract imperative and concurrent modules in which the type of interest has no name: it is reflected purely in the occurrence of **read any** and **write any** in the signatures of some functions. And even in the development of such modules there may never be a type definition corresponding to it: it is implicit in the types of its variables and those of imperative modules instantiated as objects within it.

It is, of course, possible to write modules with no unique type of interest, for example by simply merging the applicative modules for two different data types. But we will not design system modules in this way, and so we will always be able to identify the type of interest. In applicative modules it will have a name and (in concrete versions) a defining type expression. In imperative modules it may or may not have a name, and may be a product of the types of variables and the types of interest of instantiated modules. (So the order of the types in such a product may be ambiguous; technically we can see its components rather than be able to form it uniquely.)

The method we propose for developing system modules starts, if possible, with a single applicative module whose type of interest therefore is intended to model the "state" of the entire system. We then develop this applicatively by making the state more concrete. This often involves introducing some sub-system modules with their own types of interest.

This process is complete when all the types involved are either

- RSL concrete types (like lists or maps) which we are happy to translate (either automatically or by hand) into the intended programming language, i.e. whose translations for these particular uses will be adequately efficient, or
- the types of interest of standard modules like those defined in appendix A for which we have sufficiently efficient translations already available or, again, can translate by hand

Then we can take the step of generating first imperative sequential modules and then, if we want a concurrent system, concurrent imperative modules from the applicative ones. This step will preserve the structure of the system modules: each applicative one will have an imperative counterpart, and the dependencies between the applicative modules will be mirrored by those between the imperative modules. The type of interest of an imperative module will be the same as the type of interest of its applicative counterpart (up to the ordering of product components).

Finally, we often wish to do more development, to improve the specification of some algorithms and to remove any under-specification still present. Then we are ready to translate.

2.4.2   Subsidiary modules

There are three kinds of subsidiary module: *type modules*, *auxiliary modules* and *parameter modules*.

Type modules are useful as a place to define all the types that we want to use across a specification, together with useful applicative functions on these types. In a large specification it may be useful to have several such modules, one for the development as a whole and one for each separate sub-development, so that if a team decide they want to put a new type into it they can do it in their local one. We recommend using global objects for this purpose as it avoids integration problems. Teams then only need to agree on a naming convention for such objects to avoid using the same names. Then there can be no name clashes between the types and functions defined, even if the types and functions themselves share names.

Type modules are usually only developed in very simple ways, such as by adding further types and functions.

Auxiliary modules are like type modules in that they are applicative. They are just convenient groupings of auxiliary functions on some concrete data type(s). An example would be a module collecting some useful functions on RSL lists, such as *reverse*, *is_ordered*, *is_permutation*. These should not be defined as part of the type module of a particular system because the module can be generic, parameterized by the type of element in the lists and perhaps the ordering relation.

Parameter modules are used to define parameters to other modules. They are usually applicative. We will only use parameters for two purposes:

- defining generic modules, i.e. modules we expect to instantiate more than once with different parameters, either in the current development or in the future
- allowing modules to share other imperative or concurrent ones. (Sharing in this sense is unusual; see section 3.8.3.1 for an example.)

For expressing the dependency of a module on others we will use either embedded objects or global objects instead of parameterization. Where possible we use embedded objects since they make the objects visible only in the class expression within which they are defined and, if not hidden, to other users of the scheme or object defined using that class expression. Where possible such embedded objects will be hidden.

This is not the only possible style, as all dependencies can be done using parameterization. But on systems of any size and complexity the parameter lists can become very lengthy.

We will follow object-oriented terminology and refer to a dependent module as a "client" and the modules it instantiates within it as "suppliers". We will say that class A is a *client* of class B if

- class B is instantiated as an object within class A, or
- class B is the body of a formal parameter of class A, or
- class B is instantiated as a global module and mentioned in class A, or
- A is a client of C and C is a client of B

If A is a client of B then B is a *supplier* of A.

This follows closely the common definition of the client–supplier relation (e.g. [17]) that a client has to use a supplier merely by referring to it, and extends to the transitive closure. The most important form of client–supplier relation is the first, where the supplier is instantiated within the client, since our method generally creates dependencies between imperative modules only in this particular form.

2.4.3   Hierarchical structuring

The aims of hierarchical structuring are:

- to make specifications more understandable by making it possible to understand a particular component by reference only to it and its suppliers
- to limit the effects of changes to a module to it and its clients
- to limit the properties of a module to it and its suppliers (rather than have them affected by its clients). In particular, to limit *interference* (changes to the state of a module by the functions of another) to changes in the states of suppliers by the functions of a client

There are several ways in which we achieve these aims:

- There should only be one type of interest in a module. If we need to define an array of queues of something, there will normally be three modules: a parameter module for "something", a module for "a queue of something" and a module for the "array of queues of something". We can see the notions of "something", queue and array all as distinct concepts and reflect this in the modularity.
- Clients should only extend their suppliers conservatively.
- A module A should only mention the entities of a module B if A is a client of B. In particular, if there are two embedded objects in a class expression, neither should call functions of the other. This is not possible if embedded objects are defined as instantiations of schemes because of the scope rules of RSL, but is possible if one of the objects is defined with a basic class expression. Not allowing calls between embedded objects is particularly important

in concurrent specifications, since the method we shall describe relies on non-interference between such objects.

- It is also usually a good idea to make clients refer only to the entities of their immediate suppliers. Names with multiple qualifications (*A.B.C...*) indicate a breach of this.
- Global objects should only be used with care. We suggested their use for type modules to save having too many parameters for system modules, but there is a concomitant risk that changes to such modules will affect many others.

The restriction on disallowing calls of functions between embedded objects needs to be broken when we want to model certain kinds of system. See the discussion on *sharing* in section 3.8.3.1.

2.5   Method overview

There are two aspects of a method:

- what is being produced, the particular artifacts
- the order in which they are produced

It is easy to confuse these, to assume that the dependencies between things produced means that one must produce them in a particular order (like "top-down" or "bottom-up"). Of course, there are some dependencies that force an order, like having a specification one can translate before running a translator, but in general there is room for flexibility and this is often very useful.

We will try to keep these aspects distinct, and describe first what is produced and then what ordering(s) of their production is appropriate.

2.5.1   What is produced

We concentrate here on the formal documents, mainly RSL specifications. The overall software engineering process will of course produce many other documents that are not particular to RAISE.

Our overall aim is a sequence of *specifications* of the system, where a specification is a collection of RSL modules, and a translation of it in some programming language. We will refer to each specification in the sequence as a *development level*, often abbreviated to *level*. Apart from type and parameter modules, the first specification (the initial specification) will usually be a single applicative system module. In subsequent levels there will usually be a module corresponding to each module in the previous level, but there may be additional modules. The notion of "correspondence" here is quite loose: we simply say that the module is developed from its corresponding predecessor, where development includes at least the techniques described in chapter 3. There are typically at most four levels in the sequence, and commonly only two. The final level (the final specification) contains only modules that are sufficiently close to the target programming language to be translatable, perhaps wholly or in part automatically.

There should also be a known and stated relation between the specifications in one level and the next, composed from relations between the modules in the specifications. We refer to the statement of such a relation between modules as a *development relation*. The relation stated needs to be compositional if possible (see appendix B.8.6) so that the relation between the level as a whole and the previous one can be determined from relations between the component modules. Such relations should be justified.

At some point there will usually be a switch in style, so that one level is applicative and the next and subsequent ones include imperative or concurrent modules. This will not be the case if the initial specification and the programming language of the final implementation share the same style.

There are some formal developments which only consist of part of a complete development. Sometimes we are only interested in specifying a problem and showing it has some properties. For example, we may have an existing, implemented system and wish to verify that it has some safety or security property. Then the task will be to construct a development in reverse, a process known as *reverse engineering*, back to a point at which the appropriate property can be stated as a theorem and justified. A similar process may be employed for maintaining an existing system, where in order to make some change we first reverse engineer it to an appropriate level of abstraction, make the change in the specification and redevelop. If the original development was formal the reverse engineering step will be unnecessary.

2.5.2 Order of production

There are three main stages involved:

- analysis
- design
- translation

The analysis stage produces the initial specification, the design stage the final specification and the translation stage the executable program. There is some notion of order here because each of these is needed as an input to its successor. But in practice the process is iterative.

Obviously we can try to work completely top down: we start with the first level, the initial specification, followed by the second, then the relation between the first and second and its justification, then the third, etc. If the requirements are clear and we know exactly how to design the system then this is fine. But in practice this is often not the case. Usually the requirements are far from clear or being understood, and often we are not sure what the best design will be. We need to explore, to spend time in the analysis stage. Experience with formal methods, and with RSL in particular, suggests that the process is extremely iterative; it takes a long time for the initial specification to settle down, and we need to try out designs before deciding on the initial specification. It is also the case that good initial specifications are hard to write, because the abstraction that is short and simple and at the same time adequate for expressing the important properties is hard to find and formulate.

Analysis also involves the issues that always arise in designing software. What are the objects we are concerned with? What are their attributes? What are the relations between them? Such questions are commonly the subject of other methods, whether termed "traditional", "structured" or "object oriented". We tend to use the terminology of object orientation because it seems to fit particularly well with RAISE. In fact it seems effective to start by answering these questions and developing the first specification to capture the answers to them. This first specification is unlikely to be the one we term "initial". In particular, it is likely to be too concrete and involve several modules. But in constructing it we should be aiming at analysing the requirements: coming to understand them, looking for inconsistencies, omissions, etc., looking for appropriate ways of modelling them. We will typically only sketch the parts that seem obvious and concentrate on what we see as possible difficulties. This technique of first constructing a more concrete and elaborated specification has been used with RSL on many projects and found very useful; see for example the experiences from the ESPRIT LaCoS project [6].

So we have a first specification, perhaps partly sketched. What now? There are two main options:

- We can complete the first specification and consider this the initial specification. It may even serve as the final specification as well, in which case we might be said to be doing formal specification rather than formal development. For some problems, generally in domains we know well, and for some components of larger problems, this is sufficiently effective.
- We can formulate an abstraction of the first specification to form the initial specification. We can then check that this first specification is an implementation of the abstraction, though in practice this does not seem very useful. Having formulated an abstraction for the initial specification, the first specification could be used as the second level. But what usually happens is that a new second level is formulated, often using some of the ideas in the first specification but in general differing from it in being more carefully constructed, more suitable for further development, etc. The aim of the first specification is requirements analysis; the aim of the initial specification and subsequent ones is requirements formalization and design (possibly for a generalization of the requirements). The difference in emphasis often means that the results are different.

  There is also the possibility, since the first specification is quite concrete, of translating it into a prototype. This may assist further in requirements analysis. We can test it to gain more confidence that its behaviour is correct; we can perhaps demonstrate it to the customer to gain confidence that its behaviour is appropriate.

This choice about how to start is the main way in which the order of activities must be flexible. Another important flexibility is in the idea of separate development discussed in chapter 1. Although we described what is produced as a sequence of levels, in fact each component may be developed largely separately.

The experience that development is typically iterative suggests that we need to try to reduce the inefficiency of this, the reworking. So we should

- concentrate on the parts that we expect to be more difficult, as reworking is usually caused by encounters with problems for which a solution requires a change in direction
- delay doing justifications until we are sure that the level we are justifying against the previous one is appropriate, which often means formulating later levels or trying to translate

2.6   First example: harbour

2.6.1   Aims of example

The example is a simple information system, with functions for changing the data, functions for interrogating the data, and invariant properties that the data must satisfy. There is no requirement for concurrent access.

2.6.2   Requirements

Ships arriving at a harbour have to be allocated berths in the harbour which are vacant and which they will fit, or wait in a "pool" until a suitable berth is available. Develop a system providing the following functions to allow the harbour master to control the movement of ships in and out of the harbour:

arrive: to register the arrival of a ship
dock: to register a ship docking in a berth
leave: to register a ship leaving a berth

The harbour is illustrated in figure 2.1.

We assume all ships will have to arrive and be waiting (perhaps only notionally) in the pool before they can dock. So we can picture the state transitions for ships in figure 2.2.

2.6.3   Initial formulation

We first ask what are the objects of the system. Mentioned in the requirements are ships, berths, pool and harbour. It also seems that the harbour is, for our purposes, a fixed collection of berths, while the number of ships in the pool will vary. We can show the entity relationships in figure 2.3.

Then we try to identify attributes of objects and see which ones may change dynamically. Ships have no attributes given in the requirements, except that they may or may not *fit* a berth. We could invent an attribute like *size* but we don't in

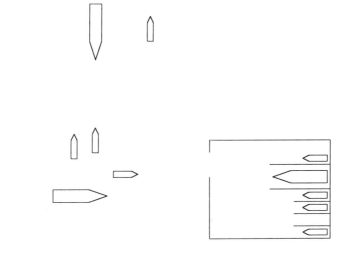

Figure 2.1: Harbour

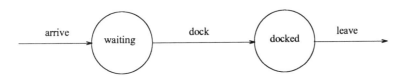

Figure 2.2: State transitions for ships

fact know if this is what determines fit. So we make a note that we will probably
need a function

fits : Ship × Berth → **Bool**

which we will leave underspecified, at least until we have discussed with the customers what they want here.

Berths change in that they may be vacant at one time and contain a ship at
another time. Hence what we might term *occupancy* is a dynamic attribute. This
suggests that a berth will be an RSL imperative object with possible state-changing
functions *enter* and *leave*, say.

The harbour seems to be a collection of berths. The members of this collection
are apparently fixed, and so we might well have in mind eventually modelling it as
an array.

The pool of waiting ships will change dynamically as ships arrive and dock.
So again there is the suggestion of an RSL imperative object with state-changing
functions *enter* and *leave*, say.

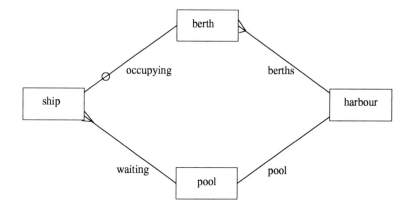

Figure 2.3: Entity relationships for harbour

There is often a choice of what we regard as attributes. We could have a dynamic attribute *location* for a ship, which might be *elsewhere, waiting* or *docked in berth k*. We could make ships into RSL imperative objects to model this. Then we would have duplicate information if we also had dynamic berths and pool of waiting ships. This would cause extra overhead in changing both objects consistently. Some systems are designed this way — usually when the amount of information is large, queries are common and need to be fast, and changes are less common. However, it is generally a dangerous practice and for this system it seems more appropriate to structure the system on the basis of the harbour and pool of waiting ships, and to calculate the location of a ship if we need to.

Now we can consider what are the invariants (properties that are always true) on the data. Possibilities are

- A ship can't be in two places at once.
- At most one ship can be in any one berth.
- A ship can only be in a berth it fits.

There are two ways to deal with such invariants. Where possible we build them into the model. If the occupancy of a berth is modelled as *vacant* or *occupied_by(s)* (where *s* is a ship), the model avoids any possibility of there being more than one ship in any one berth, and so guarantees the second invariant. (There is also the point that we shouldn't try to dock a ship into a berth that is occupied, but this is dealt with separately.) We have already decided to build into the model the fact that the collection of berths does not change, which could be considered an invariant.

The first invariant suggests the (imperative) predicate

$\forall$ s : Ship •
   $\sim$(waiting(s) $\land$ is_docked(s)) $\land$
   ($\forall$ b1,b2 : Berth •
      occupancy(b1) = occupied_by(s) $\land$ occupancy(b2) = occupied_by(s) $\Rightarrow$
        b1 = b2) $\land$
   ($\forall$ b : Berth • occupancy(b) = occupied_by(s) $\Rightarrow$ fits(s, b))

We expect in the initial specification to use an abstract type for the harbour. Having identified an invariant property captured by a predicate *consistent*, say, then we could use a subtype, as in

type
   Harbour_base,
   Harbour = {| h : Harbour_base • consistent(h) |}

This possibility can be adopted but it will require us to generate confidence conditions (see section 4.1.2) for the concrete applicative specification (when we find some concrete type for *Harbour_base*). Otherwise it is very easy to create a concrete applicative specification that passes the implementation check but does not maintain the invariant (and is thus inconsistent). It is a general rule that subtypes of abstract types should not be used unless confidence conditions of the concrete modules are generated and carefully checked.

Instead, we will express as a collection of axioms the property that the state-changing functions maintain the invariant, which makes the property more visible and will force us to justify it when we justify implementation. This may not seem too important in this example, but we shall see in the next example, the lift, that safety properties typically look like invariants.

For example, if *arrive* is a state-changing function and *consistent* a predicate expressing the invariant, we can write the axiom

axiom
   [arrive_consistent]
      $\forall$ s : Ship •
         arrive(s) **post** consistent() **pre** consistent() $\land$ can_arrive(s)

where *can_arrive* is a predicate expressing the precondition for *arrive*.

We now have some mental picture of the objects in the system. We can picture them as in figure 2.4, where only the state-changing functions are shown.

Although we could perhaps fairly easily specify this in RSL by first specifying schemes for *POOL*, *BERTH* and *BERTHS*, it is generally a good idea to try first for a single scheme without components that more closely matches the requirements, and keep the decomposed model in mind as a direction for development.

An alternative to this is to define the decomposed model first, to get more feel for how the system will go together, and possibly create an abstraction later. As we noted earlier, experience with using RAISE suggests that constructing a more concrete and decomposed system is a technique that is generally very successful.

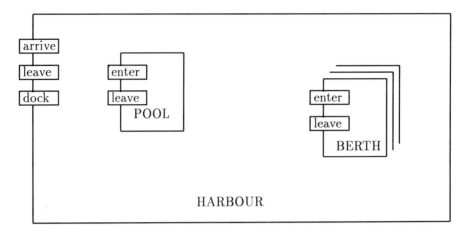

Figure 2.4: Harbour objects

2.6.4 Method overview

We want to proceed from applicative to imperative. So the particular method we
will use is as follows:

- Define a scheme *TYPES* containing types and attributes for the non-dynamic
  entities we have identified, and make a global object *T* for this.
- Define an abstract applicative module *A_HARBOUR0* containing the top level
  functions, the axioms relating these and the "invariants".
- Develop a sequence of concrete applicative modules, *A_HARBOUR1*, *A_HAR-
  BOUR2*, etc. which will introduce applicative component modules for the
  "pool" and "berths" components.
- Develop to a corresponding collection of imperative modules from the final
  applicative ones.
- Consider any efficiency improvements we can make to the imperative ones.
- Translate to the intended target language.

This outline of the method for a particular application we will call a *development
plan*. In practice such plans will include a number of other activities for documentation, testing, quality assurance, etc. together with schedules, effort to be used,
and so on.

2.6.5 Type module

From our initial thoughts we formulate the module *TYPES*:

scheme TYPES =
  class
    type
      Ship, Berth,
      Occupancy == vacant | occupied_by(occupant : Ship)
    value
      fits : Ship × Berth → **Bool**
  end

We then make a global object from *TYPES*:

object T : TYPES

2.6.6 Abstract applicative

To create an abstraction for the system we follow the method that will be described in more detail for the queue data type in section 2.8.4.1. But since this is a system specification rather than a data type like the queue we will try to formulate the system properties that we can specify at this point. We have already identified the notion of consistency, which we capture by a predicate.

The method is in summary:

- Define the type of interest as a sort (*Harbour*).
- Define the signatures of the functions we need.
- Categorize these functions as *generators* if the type of interest (or a type dependent on it) appears in their result types and as *observers* otherwise. (We shall see that the imperative counterparts to generators are functions that change (write to) the state. We have previously referred to these as "state-changing".) We find we have three generators: *arrives*, *docks* and *leaves*, and we identify two observers: *waiting* and *occupancy*.
- Formulate preconditions for any partial functions. All three generators are partial: there are situations where they cannot sensibly be applied. We therefore identify three functions (termed "guards") to express their preconditions: *can_arrive*, etc. All these guards are derived from (i.e. given explicit definitions in terms of) the observers.
- Define a function (*consistent*) to express the invariant, making it another derived observer.
- For each possible combination of non-derived observer and non-derived generator, define an axiom expressing the relation between them. We have three non-derived generators and two non-derived observers, so we have six such axioms.
- Add axioms expressing the notion that the non-derived generators maintain consistency. We have three such axioms.
- Hide the invariant function *consistent* and anything else not needed by clients of the module.

This gives the abstract applicative module *A_HARBOUR0*:

scheme A_HARBOUR0 =
  hide consistent **in**
  class
    type Harbour
    value
      /∗ generators ∗/
      arrives : T.Ship × Harbour $\xrightarrow{\sim}$ Harbour,
      docks : T.Ship × T.Berth × Harbour $\xrightarrow{\sim}$ Harbour,
      leaves : T.Ship × T.Berth × Harbour $\xrightarrow{\sim}$ Harbour,
      /∗ observers ∗/
      waiting : T.Ship × Harbour → **Bool**,
      occupancy : T.Berth × Harbour → T.Occupancy,
      /∗ derived ∗/
      consistent : Harbour → **Bool**
      consistent(h) ≡
        (∀ s : T.Ship •
          ∼ (waiting(s, h) ∧ is_docked(s, h)) ∧
          (∀ b1, b2 : T.Berth •
            occupancy(b1, h) = T.occupied_by(s) ∧
            occupancy(b2, h) = T.occupied_by(s) ⇒
              b1 = b2) ∧
          (∀ b : T.Berth •
            occupancy(b, h) = T.occupied_by(s) ⇒ T.fits(s, b))),
      is_docked : T.Ship × Harbour → **Bool**
      is_docked(s, h) ≡
        (∃ b : T.Berth • occupancy(b, h) = T.occupied_by(s)),
      /∗ guards ∗/
      can_arrive : T.Ship × Harbour → **Bool**
      can_arrive(s, h) ≡ ∼ waiting(s, h) ∧ ∼ is_docked(s, h),
      can_dock : T.Ship × T.Berth × Harbour → **Bool**
      can_dock(s, b, h) ≡
        waiting(s, h) ∧ ∼ is_docked(s, h) ∧
        occupancy(b, h) = T.vacant ∧ T.fits(s, b),
      can_leave : T.Ship × T.Berth × Harbour → **Bool**
      can_leave(s, b, h) ≡ occupancy(b, h) = T.occupied_by(s)
    axiom
      [waiting_arrives]
        ∀ h : Harbour, s1, s2 : T.Ship •
          waiting(s2, arrives(s1, h)) ≡ s1 = s2 ∨ waiting(s2, h)
            pre can_arrive(s1, h),

[waiting_docks]
    ∀ h : Harbour, s1, s2 : T.Ship, b : T.Berth •
      waiting(s2, docks(s1, b, h)) ≡ s1 ≠ s2 ∧ waiting(s2, h)
        pre can_dock(s1, b, h),
[waiting_leaves]
    ∀ h : Harbour, s1, s2 : T.Ship, b : T.Berth •
      waiting(s2, leaves(s1, b, h)) ≡ waiting(s2, h)
        pre can_leave(s1, b, h),
[occupancy_arrives]
    ∀ h : Harbour, s : T.Ship, b : T.Berth •
      occupancy(b, arrives(s, h)) ≡ occupancy(b, h)
        pre can_arrive(s, h),
[occupancy_docks]
    ∀ h : Harbour, s : T.Ship, b1, b2 : T.Berth •
      occupancy(b2, docks(s, b1, h)) ≡
        if b1 = b2 **then** T.occupied_by(s) **else** occupancy(b2, h) **end**
        pre can_dock(s, b1, h),
[occupancy_leaves]
    ∀ h : Harbour, s : T.Ship, b1, b2 : T.Berth •
      occupancy(b2, leaves(s, b1, h)) ≡
        if b1 = b2 **then** T.vacant **else** occupancy(b2, h) **end**
        pre can_leave(s, b1, h),
[arrives_consistent]
    ∀ h : Harbour, s : T.Ship •
      arrives(s, h) **as** h′ **post** consistent(h′)
        pre consistent(h) ∧ can_arrive(s, h),
[docks_consistent]
    ∀ h : Harbour, s : T.Ship, b : T.Berth •
      docks(s, b, h) **as** h′ **post** consistent(h′)
        pre consistent(h) ∧ can_dock(s, b, h),
[leaves_consistent]
    ∀ h : Harbour, s : T.Ship, b : T.Berth •
      leaves(s, b, h) **as** h′ **post** consistent(h′)
        pre consistent(h) ∧ can_leave(s, b, h)
end

In practice it will typically take several iterations before such a specification can be settled on. In particular, while the generators may be reasonably apparent from the requirements (ships can arrive and dock, etc.) it is often much less clear what good observers will be. Do we, for example, want one for the set of ships waiting? If one tries to use this as an observer it should soon become apparent that it can easily be defined as a derived observer from the simple observer *waiting* that we have used.

We have also omitted a constant of type *Harbour*, like *empty*. This is partly because the requirements were silent about initial conditions. In practice the ability to initialise (and perhaps reset) the system is a likely requirement and an *empty* constant would be required. Adding *empty* (and making the consequent changes in the remainder of the development) is left as an exercise for the reader.

2.6.6.1   Validation

Validating an initial specification means checking that it meets the requirements. In practice there are usually some requirements that are not expressed in the initial specification. These may be either

- requirements that cannot be expressed in RSL, the "non-functional" requirements, or
- requirements we have decided to defer because they are too detailed to include yet

Both these kinds of requirements will give direction to the development because we will need to deal with them at some point.

So validation means checking, for each requirement we can identify, that it is either correctly reflected in the initial specification or can be dealt with at some stage in the development plan. If we consider some of the requirements for the system, we can record:

1.	Ships can arrive and will be registered.	*A_HARBOUR0*
2.	Ships can be docked when a suitable berth is free.	*A_HARBOUR0*
3.	Docked ships can leave.	*A_HARBOUR0*
4.	Ships can only be allocated to berths they fit.	*A_HARBOUR0*
5.	Any ship will eventually get a berth.	outside system
6.	Any ship waiting more than 2 days will be flagged.	deferred to ...

We could of course give more precise references to requirements we believe to be met. Thus number 4 could have a reference to *can_dock*.

If we claim to meet a requirement but the claim is not immediate from the specification, we can formulate the requirement as a theorem and justify it.

This process will sometimes raise issues that we have not dealt with properly, causing us to rework the specification. We have assumed, for example, that the actual choice of a ship to fill a vacant berth is outside the system: we just provide the facilities for a user to make the choice. This may not be correct, or it may require a new function, to return, perhaps, a list of ships that can fit a berth, ordered by date of arrival.

Making such a list of requirements will also give us the opportunity to update the list as we do the development so that we can eventually show that all the deferred requirements are met. Showing where and how requirements are met is commonly called "requirements tracing".

2.6.7   Concrete applicative

A natural concrete type to use for *Harbour* is a set of waiting ships (which constitutes the pool) and an array of berths, for which we can use the standard modules *A_SET* and *A_ARRAY_INIT*, described in appendix A. We cannot be sure that the array will be applied to an index (for example to see if a berth is vacant) before it has been changed, and so we use the initialised version of the array (and we will initialise all occupancies to *vacant*).

We need *enter* and *leave* functions for both the set and the array. For the set these will be modelled by *add* and *remove* respectively. For the array both are modelled by a *change*, to an occupancy and a vacancy respectively.

Extending the type module
To instantiate *A_SET*, we need to provide a type *Elem*, and we can use the type *Ship* from the type module.

To instantiate *A_ARRAY_INIT*, we need to satisfy the requirements of the parameter *ARRAY_PARM_INIT* from section A.1. The type *Elem* will be *Occupancy* from the type module, and the value *init* will be *vacant*, also from the type module. We still need integers *min* and *max*, with *max* no less than *min*. We can add these to the type module, with an appropriate axiom. We could then model the type *Berth* as equal to the subtype of integers from *min* to *max*, but it is more general to leave *Berth* as a sort and say there is a function *indx* from *Berth* to this subtype: effectively the index of a berth is an attribute of it. We then leave open the possibility of there being other attributes of berths. Presumably there will need to be some others (and some attributes of ships) to enable us to eventually compute *fits*.

We therefore add the following definitions to the type module *TYPES*:

type
    Index = {| i : **Int** • i ≥ min ∧ max ≥ i |}
value
    min, max : **Int**,
    indx : Berth → Index
axiom
    [index_not_empty] max ≥ min,
    [berths_indexable]
        ∀ b1, b2 : Berth • indx(b1) = indx(b2) ⇒ b1 = b2

The axiom *berths_indexable* ensures that indexes identify berths uniquely.

We have chosen just to add these definitions to the type module directly rather than develop it to a new module *TYPES1*, say. This is the most convenient way to develop type modules. As here, the extensions to them are typically conservative and making formal developments of them would be more effort than is appropriate. We could if we wish proceed more formally by

- defining a new types module *TYPES1*

- justifying that *TYPES1* implements *TYPES*
- defining a new global object *T1* as an instantiation of *TYPES1*
- using *T1* in the developments of the system modules

Developing the system module

The method used to do this development step, in which we introduce component modules, will be described in more detail for the queue data type in section 2.8.4.7. In summary:

- Start by identifying a concrete type for the type of interest *Harbour*:

  type Harbour = P.Set × B.Array

  where *P* and *B* are the names of the objects that instantiate *A_SET* and *A_ARRAY_INIT* respectively. *P* represents the pool of waiting ships; *B* represents the array of berths.
- Create these objects *P* and *B*. We can use the global types module *T* to provide their actual parameters (with suitable fittings). For instance, the *Elem* type for the set module will be the type *Ship*, so that P models the pool of waiting ships.
- Define the non-derived functions *arrives*, *docks*, *leaves*, *waiting* and *occupancy* in terms of the functions provided by *A_SET* and *A_ARRAY_INIT*. The other functions are derived and so already have explicit definitions.
- Hide the objects *P* and *B* (along again with *consistent*). Only this module should have direct access to the objects' functions.

This gives us the concrete applicative module *A_HARBOUR1*:

scheme A_HARBOUR1 =
  hide P, B, consistent **in**
  class
    object
      /* pool of waiting ships */
      P : A_SET(T{Ship **for** Elem}),
      /* berths */
      B : A_ARRAY_INIT(T{Occupancy **for** Elem, vacant **for** init})
    type Harbour = P.Set × B.Array
    value
      /* generators */
      arrives : T.Ship × Harbour $\xrightarrow{\sim}$ Harbour
      arrives(s, (ws, bs)) ≡
        (P.add(s, ws), bs)
        pre can_arrive(s, (ws, bs)),
      docks : T.Ship × T.Berth × Harbour $\xrightarrow{\sim}$ Harbour
      docks(s, b, (ws, bs)) ≡
        (P.remove(s, ws), B.change(T.indx(b), T.occupied_by(s), bs))
        pre can_dock(s, b, (ws, bs)),

leaves : T.Ship × T.Berth × Harbour $\overset{\sim}{\to}$ Harbour
leaves(s, b, (ws, bs)) ≡
    (ws, B.change(T.indx(b), T.vacant, bs))
    pre can_leave(s, b, (ws, bs)),
/* observers */
waiting : T.Ship × Harbour → **Bool**
waiting(s, (ws, bs)) ≡ P.is_in(s, ws),
occupancy : T.Berth × Harbour → T.Occupancy
occupancy(b, (ws, bs)) ≡ B.apply(T.indx(b), bs),
/* invariant */
consistent : Harbour → **Bool**
consistent((ws, bs)) ≡
    (∀ s : T.Ship •
      ~ (P.is_in(s, ws) ∧ is_docked(s, (ws, bs)))) ∧
    (∀ b1, b2 : T.Berth •
      B.apply(T.indx(b1), bs) = T.occupied_by(s) ∧
      B.apply(T.indx(b2), bs) = T.occupied_by(s) ⇒ b1 = b2) ∧
    (∀ b : T.Berth •
      B.apply(T.indx(b), bs) = T.occupied_by(s) ⇒ T.fits(s, b))),
is_docked : T.Ship × Harbour → **Bool**
is_docked(s, (ws, bs)) ≡
    (∃ b : T.Berth • B.apply(T.indx(b), bs) = T.occupied_by(s)),
/* guards */
can_arrive : T.Ship × Harbour → **Bool**
can_arrive(s, (ws, bs)) ≡
    ~ P.is_in(s, ws) ∧ ~ is_docked(s, (ws, bs)),
can_dock : T.Ship × T.Berth × Harbour → **Bool**
can_dock(s, b, (ws, bs)) ≡
    P.is_in(s, ws) ∧ ~ is_docked(s, (ws, bs)) ∧
    B.apply(T.indx(b), bs) = T.vacant ∧ T.fits(s, b),
can_leave : T.Ship × T.Berth × Harbour → **Bool**
can_leave(s, b, (ws, bs)) ≡ B.apply(T.indx(b), bs) = T.occupied_by(s)
end

It would have been possible to define explicit *enter* and *leave* functions (plus observers) for the pool and berths. For example, we could have defined

object
    /* pool of waiting ships */
    P :
      use enter **for** add, leave **for** remove, waiting **for** is_in **in**
      A_SET(T{Ship **for** Elem}),
    /* berths */
    B :
      hide change, apply **in**

extend A_ARRAY_INIT(T{Occupancy **for** Elem, vacant **for** init}) **with**
class
    value
       enter : T.Ship × T.Berth × Array → Array
       enter(s, b, a) ≡ change(T.indx(b), T.occupied_by(s), a),
       leave : T.Berth × Array → Array
       leave(b, a) ≡ change(T.indx(b), T.vacant, a),
       occupancy : T.Berth × Array → T.Occupancy
       occupancy(b, a) ≡ apply(T.indx(b), a)
  end

Another possibility is to define a scheme for the pool that instantiates *A_SET* as an object, defines *enter*, *leave* and *waiting* functions, and hides the object. A similar scheme would be defined for the berths. This possibility, like the object definitions above, would give a better encapsulation of the supplier modules and would make the definitions of functions in *A_HARBOUR1* a little easier to read. For instance the body of *arrive* would be

    arrives(s, (ws, bs)) ≡ (P.enter(s, ws), bs)

In this small example we did not think the extra complication in the definitions of the objects for the pool and berths was worthwhile. In a larger example it would be.

2.6.7.1   Verification

We formulate the development relation *A_HARBOUR0_1*, which asserts that *A_HARBOUR1* implements *A_HARBOUR0*:

development_relation [A_HARBOUR0_1] A_HARBOUR1 $\preceq$ A_HARBOUR0

A development relation is a named statement of a relation between modules. This one takes the most simple form of the statement of an implementation relation ($\preceq$) between two versions of the harbour module.

Justification of this relation shows that the development step is correct. The justification amounts to showing that the axioms of *A_HARBOUR0* are true in *A_HARBOUR1*.

2.6.8   Concrete imperative

We describe *A_HARBOUR1* as "composite" because it instantiates other system modules (the set and array) within it. The method for developing from a composite applicative module to an imperative module is explained in detail in section 2.8.5.4. In summary:

- Define objects *P* and *B* as in the applicative version, but this time instantiating the imperative versions of the set and array modules respectively. There is no definition of the type of interest *Harbour*.

- Define imperative functions which correspond to the applicative ones. They have the same names. Generators have access **write any** and observers have access **read any**. Occurrences of the type of interest are removed from parameter and result types (and replaced by **Unit** if there are no other components in a parameter or result type).
- Define the bodies of the functions by adapting the applicative versions to use the imperative functions corresponding to the applicative ones. The general method for this adaptation is described in section 2.8.5.4 but is easy to follow intuitively for this example.

This gives the concrete imperative module *I_HARBOUR1*:

scheme I_HARBOUR1 =
   hide P, B, consistent **in**
   class
      object
         /* pool of waiting ships */
         P : I_SET(T{Ship **for** Elem}),
         /* berths */
         B : I_ARRAY_INIT(T{Occupancy **for** Elem, vacant **for** init})
      value
         /* generators */
         arrives : T.Ship $\xrightarrow{\sim}$ **write any Unit**
         arrives(s) ≡ P.add(s) **pre** can_arrive(s),
         docks : T.Ship × T.Berth $\xrightarrow{\sim}$ **write any Unit**
         docks(s, b) ≡
            P.remove(s) ; B.change(T.indx(b), T.occupied_by(s))
            pre can_dock(s, b),
         leaves : T.Ship × T.Berth $\xrightarrow{\sim}$ **write any Unit**
         leaves(s, b) ≡ B.change(T.indx(b), T.vacant) **pre** can_leave(s, b),
         /* observers */
         waiting : T.Ship → **read any Bool**
         waiting(s) ≡ P.is_in(s),
         occupancy : T.Berth → **read any** T.Occupancy
         occupancy(b) ≡ B.apply(T.indx(b)),
         /* invariant */
         consistent : **Unit** → **read any Bool**
         consistent() ≡
           (∀ s : T.Ship •
             ~ (P.is_in(s) ∧ is_docked(s)) ∧
            (∀ b1, b2 : T.Berth •
               B.apply(T.indx(b1)) = T.occupied_by(s) ∧
               B.apply(T.indx(b2)) = T.occupied_by(s) ⇒ b1 = b2) ∧
            (∀ b : T.Berth •
               B.apply(T.indx(b)) = T.occupied_by(s) ⇒ T.fits(s, b))),

is_docked : T.Ship → **read any Bool**
is_docked(s) ≡
   (∃ b : T.Berth • B.apply(T.indx(b)) = T.occupied_by(s)),
/* guards */
can_arrive : T.Ship → **read any Bool**
can_arrive(s) ≡ ∼ P.is_in(s) ∧ ∼ is_docked(s),
can_dock : T.Ship × T.Berth → **read any Bool**
can_dock(s, b) ≡
   P.is_in(s) ∧ ∼ is_docked(s) ∧
   B.apply(T.indx(b)) = T.vacant ∧ T.fits(s, b),
can_leave : T.Ship × T.Berth → **read any Bool**
can_leave(s, b) ≡ B.apply(T.indx(b)) = T.occupied_by(s)
end

2.6.8.1   Verification

Since this development step was from applicative to imperative, we need to decide what level of assurance we need for correctness. We can either

- check that the method for this transition has been followed correctly, or
- formulate the imperative axioms corresponding to the applicative axioms from *A_HARBOUR0* and justify them for *I_HARBOUR1*

Both of these are verifications since they check on the correctness of the development process. The first is informal and is almost certainly all that is necessary for this fairly straightforward development. The second is formal and can be done if we have any doubts or require the highest level of assurance of correctness. How to do it is described in section 2.9.

2.6.9   Further development

There are a few issues left to be resolved:

- The definition of *is_docked* still involves an existential quantifier and is probably not translatable yet. So we formulate a development of *I_HARBOUR1*, *I_HARBOUR2*, in which *is_docked* is defined by

value
   is_docked : T.Ship → **read any Bool**
   is_docked(s) ≡
      local variable found : **Bool** := **false**, indx : **Int** := T.min **in**
         while ∼ found ∧ indx ≤ T.max **do**
            found := B.apply(indx) = T.occupied_by(s) ; indx := indx + 1
         end ;
         found
      end

We can then formulate and justify the implementation relation between *I_HARBOUR2* and *I_HARBOUR1* to check this is correct.

- We have still left unspecified the types *Ship* and *Berth* and the values *min*, *max*, *fits* and *indx*; all defined in *TYPES*. In practice we should either have been able to define all of these by getting more detailed requirements, or we could regard them as system parameters to be instantiated for particular harbours.

  When we are in a position to make definite choices for these types and values we can define a new module, *TYPES1*, say. We then justify that *TYPES1* implements *TYPES* and create a new object *T1*, say. Now all we have to do at the translation stage is to use *T1* instead of *T*. The correctness of this follows from the compositionality of the implementation relation. If *TYPES1* implements *TYPES* then, if *T1 : TYPES1* and *T : TYPES*, for any specification *SPEC* in which the name *T1* does not occur, *SPEC[T1/T]* implements *SPEC*, where *SPEC[T1/T]* means *SPEC* with all free occurrences of *T* replaced by *T1*.

  It would be possible to create a new RSL specification by replacing all mentions of *T* by *T1* in all the modules, but, unless we actually need to use properties of *TYPES1* that were not in *TYPES* for further development of these modules, this is not necessary.

- Final implementation also assumes we have translations of the standard modules *I_ARRAY_INIT* and *I_SET* that are sufficiently efficient for our purposes. In the case of the latter, in particular, we might want a specialized translation if the set was to become large (though for this example it seems most unlikely).

2.6.10 Translation

Translation of this example is discussed in section 5.4.1.

Exercise Adapt *A_HARBOUR1* and *I_HARBOUR1* to meet the extra requirement that ships are docked in vacant berths in order of arrival, provided they fit. In other words, a ship *B* arriving after a ship *A* will only be docked before *A* if a berth is vacant that *B* will fit and *A* will not fit. As a consequence, *docks* will no longer have a parameter of type *T.Ship*.

A possible data type to use for the waiting ships is developed in the exercise at the end of section 2.8.

Also add to these modules a function to produce a report of the current status of the harbour, showing

- the names of ships waiting, in order, with the set of berths each will fit
- for each berth, the name of the ship in it or the fact that it is vacant

2.7   Second example: lift

2.7.1   Aims of example

The example is a simple safety-critical system involving concurrency.

We will want to be very careful to state the safety properties and justify them. Hence it is worth starting with an applicative specification and developing it into a concurrent one. So the example is designed to show

- how to specify axiomatically an applicative system satisfying safety properties
- how to develop such a system into one with explicit applicative functions over a global state
- how to decompose the applicative global specification into applicative components
- how to obtain a concurrent, decomposed system from the applicative one

The example also shows how to develop an asynchronous system, i.e. one in which there is no particular relation between the timing of different events (like buttons being pressed). Note also that some components (like buttons, doors and the lift motor) are hardware components; their specifications will describe the assumptions about them.

2.7.2   Requirements

A lift is required to serve a number of floors. Each floor has doors which must only be open when the lift is stationary at that floor. Each floor except the top one has a button to request the lift to stop there and then go up; each floor except the bottom one has a button to request the lift to stop there and then go down. The lift also has a button for each floor to request the lift to go to that floor.

2.7.2.1   Simplifying assumptions

- We do not distinguish between lift doors and floor doors. This reflects either that the lift cage has no door, or that the lift door and a floor door are constrained by hardware only to open and close together (when the lift is stationary at the floor).
- We only consider doors at each floor as being in one of two states: "open" (when the lift must be at the floor and stationary) and "shut" (when the lift may be elsewhere and/or moving).
- We do not consider the time taken for the lift to move or the doors to open or close. We will at the detailed level, however, have both "do" and "acknowledge" events for such actions and assume the hardware will tell us by the acknowledgements when the actions are completed.
- We do not consider lights on buttons or audible signals that the lift is stopping at a floor. We assume these will be done purely by hardware.

- We make some assumptions about the way the lift motor is controlled — these will be described later.
- We do not consider how to deal with hardware failures, or how to re-start the system after such a failure.
- We assume floors are numbered consecutively.

2.7.3 Initial formulation

A lift is an example of an asynchronous system, since buttons may be pressed at any time. In other words, there are external stimuli that may happen at any time, or may never happen. We have to be careful with such systems to make them "loosely coupled". We must not create the situation where a lift is waiting for one button to be pushed while a user is trying to push another.

We handle this problem quite naturally in our development style. There will be a button module with functions allowing a user to press it and allowing the lift to check if it has been pressed and to clear it. Each button is modelled as a separate process, so that there is no synchronization between users pressing buttons and the lift inspecting and clearing them.

2.7.3.1 System components

As usual we start by considering the objects of the system and whether they will have dynamic state:

- The lift itself will presumably change its position, direction and speed via commands to its motor.
- Doors will be open or closed.
- Buttons will be pressed (and lit) or cleared (and unlit).
- A floor could be dynamically "visited" by a lift or not but this would duplicate the lift position. So floors seem only to have static attributes, like their number, whether they are above or below other floors, whether they are the top or bottom floor.

Certainly it looks as if the lift motor, the doors and the buttons will have dynamic state and hence be modelled as RSL objects.

We can construct an entity relationship diagram (figure 2.5) illustrating the physical entities in the system.

We have not included a door for the lift cage because of our assumption that either the lift has no door or it is controlled by the floor door.

For our specification we will adopt a different structure between modules, since we do not feel constrained by the physical one: we remove the intermediate levels "Cage" and "Floor", merging the collections of buttons.

We can then picture the intended components in the specification as in figure 2.6 where only the generating functions are shown.

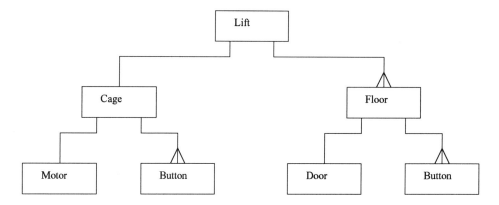

Figure 2.5: Physical entity relationships

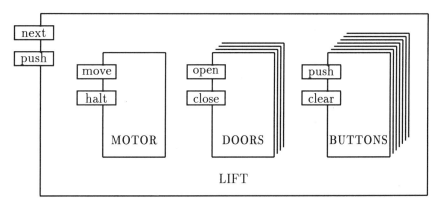

Figure 2.6: Specification components

It is not clear at present what the external functions of the component objects are. Certainly it must be possible to push any buttons. Does the lift then behave independently of external control (as long as there is no failure)? Or do we externally keep telling it to perform the next action? We have assumed the latter for now, but we will return to this question later.

Next comes the question of what attributes are necessary for these objects. In this case there is a question of how finely we need to model things. Are doors just open or closed, or do they also have intermediate opening and closing states? Do we need to go further and measure their current separation, their velocities and accelerations? Similar questions apply to the lift's movements.

The answers to such questions will lie in the detailed requirements (or should be clarified before we start if not stated there). Here we will just distinguish a door which is "closed" (by which we mean shut and locked) from a door which is "open", and demand that a door is open at a floor only when the lift is stationary at that floor. (Hence we shall ignore, for instance, the need to let a technician unlock a door manually when the motor fails.) The state transitions for each door are shown in figure 2.7.

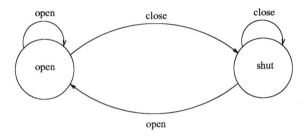

Figure 2.7: State transitions for a door

We will make similar assumptions about the lift. We will assume it can be sufficiently characterized by being halted at a floor (when the doors there may be open), or in some other state which we will call "moving". When halted it will be at a floor; it turns out to be convenient to always associate it with a floor even when moving, and this will be the (next) floor it is moving towards. When moving it must have a direction, up or down. Again it turns out to be convenient to associate a direction with the lift when it is halted, which is the direction in which it was last moving. A state transition diagram for the lift is shown in figure 2.8.

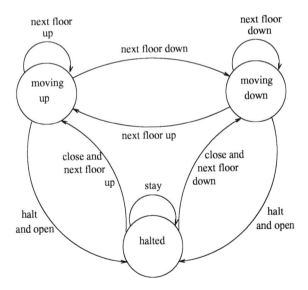

Figure 2.8: State transitions for lift

2.7.3.2   Types module

The preceding discussion gives us enough to formulate the type module for the system, which we will call *TYPES* and instantiate as the global object *T*:

scheme TYPES =
  class
    value
      min_floor, max_floor : **Int**,
      is_floor : **Int** → **Bool**
      is_floor(f) ≡ f ≥ min_floor ∧ f ≤ max_floor
    axiom [some_floors] max_floor > min_floor
    type
      Floor = {| n : **Int** • is_floor(n) |},
      Lower_floor = {| f : Floor • f < max_floor |},
      Upper_floor = {| f : Floor • f > min_floor |},
      Door_state == open | shut,
      Button_state == lit | clear,
      Direction == up | down,
      Movement == halted | moving,
      Requirement :: here : **Bool** after : **Bool** before : **Bool**
    value
      next_floor : Direction × Floor $\xrightarrow{\sim}$ Floor
      next_floor(d, f) ≡
        if d = up **then** f + 1 **else** f − 1 **end**
        pre is_next_floor(d, f),
      is_next_floor : Direction × Floor → **Bool**
      is_next_floor(d, f) ≡
        if d = up **then** f < max_floor **else** f > min_floor **end**,
      invert : Direction → Direction
      invert(d) ≡ **if** d = up **then** down **else** up **end**
  end

We have no indication that there will be any attributes of floors other than their numbers. Unlike the berths of the harbour system of section 2.6 we have chosen to model the type *Floor* directly as a subtype of **Int**. We assume that floors are numbered consecutively. This is merely for simplicity: we could have modelled floors as we did berths.

The type *Requirement* will be explained when we discuss below how buttons are checked.

2.7.3.3   Safety and liveness properties

For a control system like a lift there are usually two kinds of property that we are interested in. The first kind is that of *safety properties*. A safety property states that some situation must never arise, which we can formulate as "always the predicate describing the situation is false". Safety properties are generally not difficult to formulate in RSL.

The second kind of property is that of *liveness properties*. A liveness property says that something must eventually happen. Unfortunately such properties are generally difficult to express in RSL in their full generality. But we can provide an effective substitute, as we shall see.

2.7.3.4 Generators

As noted earlier we are dealing with an asynchronous system, with messages coming in at times and with frequencies beyond the influence of the lift controller, which is the part we want to specify. We need to ensure that the controller checks for new messages sufficiently frequently. For example, a detailed requirement for a lift might be that if it leaves a floor because there is a request to go to some floor above, and someone presses the up button at some intermediate floor before the lift passes it, the lift should stop there. A standard means of designing such a control system is as a small loop:

> **while true do**
>> read messages ;
>> take next appropriate action
> **end**

where "smallness" is measured by the amount of "action" that can be taken during each cycle. In our case the difference between the current floors before and after the next action will be limited to at most one, to meet the detailed requirement just mentioned. This means we assume that the lift motor is able to give a smooth trip across several floors although only given instructions to move one floor at a time.

This standard idea of a control loop also suggests what the generators should be: they should correspond to "read messages" and "take next action". The first will be a result-returning generator; it will tell us something about the state of the buttons and also change the state. It may not seem clear why such a function should generate a new state but it turns out this is the way to model it. It is as if there is the stream of all future button pushes encoded in the state, and this function reads the next set and changes the stream to the remaining stream. Leaving underspecified what the result of this function is and what the characteristics of the new state are means that it behaves just like a sensor seems to. This is the way that all such sensor functions should be modelled applicatively.

We do need to consider what the result type of this function should be. An array of boolean values for all buttons? The lift would need to do some processing on this: whether it should stop at the floor it is moving towards, for example, depends on whether the lift button for that floor is lit, or the button at the floor in the current direction is lit, or the button at the floor in the other direction is lit and there are no requests to go to further floors in the current direction. Clearly all this kind of processing can be done elsewhere, and we decide that the button sensor function, which we term *check_buttons*, will return a value of type *Requirement*, which is a record of three booleans, representing whether the lift is required *here*, *after* (i.e. at a later floor in the same direction) or *before* (i.e. at a floor in the opposite direction). We can make sure these predicates are false at the boundary cases (like *after* at the top floor). Calculation of these values from the buttons will clearly need the current floor and direction, but these can probably be obtained from the type of interest *Lift*, say. So we have a signature for *check_buttons*:

value

    check_buttons : Lift $\rightarrow$ T.Requirement $\times$ Lift

(Recall that T is the global instance of *TYPES*.)

Now we need a signature for *next*, the other generator suggested by the control loop. This presumably needs the results of *check_buttons*, so we have

value next : T.Requirement $\times$ Lift $\xrightarrow{\sim}$ Lift

check_buttons can be total so there is no need for a precondition. It is not clear yet what *next* should do if, say, *after* is true but it has reached the top. So we will leave it as partial for now. But we will defer defining its precondition.

2.7.3.5   Observers

We add the observers:

value

    movement : Lift $\rightarrow$ T.Movement,
    door_state : Lift $\rightarrow$ T.Floor $\rightarrow$ T.Door_state,
    floor : Lift $\rightarrow$ T.Floor,
    direction : Lift $\rightarrow$ T.Direction

2.7.3.6   Axioms

The normal method is next to try to define the observer–generator axioms, but in this case we will interpose an additional step. The initial purpose is to capture the critical properties of the lift. These we take to be:

- a safety property that the doors are always shut if the lift is not stationary at a floor (so people outside the lift cannot fall into the lift shaft), and open if the lift is stationary at a floor (so that people inside the lift can get out)
- a liveness property that the lift does something useful, that it will eventually get to and stop at a floor if requested there

The safety property can be expressed by an "invariant" function *safe*, with definition

safe(s) ≡
  (∀ f : T.Floor •
    (door_state(s)(f) = T.open) =
    (movement(s) = T.halted ∧ floor(s) = f))

As we noted earlier, liveness properties are harder to specify. What we can do, instead of trying to describe what "eventually" means, is describe some relation between a lift state and the next state. In fact this will be a relation over three states: the initial one, the one after *check_buttons* and the one after *next*.

Call these states *s*, *s'* and *s''*. We will express the properties that

- If *s* is safe, so are *s'* and *s''*.
- If the lift is halted in state *s''*, the lift was either wanted *here* or nowhere else, and the floor of *s''* is the same as the floor of *s*.
- If the lift is not halted in state *s''*, the lift was wanted either *after* or *before*, and the floor it is moving towards is next to the floor in state *s* and a valid floor.
- If the lift has changed direction between states *s* and *s''*, *after* must be false.

The first of these is the property that the invariant *safe* is maintained. We could specify it as a separate axiom but it is convenient in this case to include it as part of the liveness axiom. If we made it separate we would still use *safe(s)* as a precondition of the liveness axiom.

Another approach to stating liveness requirements is to form some measure of how close a state is to satisfying the property required and then show that the next state strictly reduces this measure. This can be quite tricky to do when, as here, each "read messages" part of the loop changes what is required. The argument that the lift will eventually reach a floor for which a button is lit is as follows:

- If the lift is currently halted somewhere else, *here* for that floor must be true. If *here* eventually becomes false, either *before* or *after* must be true and the lift must go into a non-halted state (which we hope means physically moving). But note that we make the assumption that *here* must become false. We are tempted to specify this (on the assumption that the lift clears the relevant buttons when it halts at a floor) but we cannot give any guarantee that someone does not immediately press one of them again. In fact we can never predict what the result of *check_buttons* will be (or we would restrict the ability of people to press buttons). We could specify at this level that the relevant buttons are cleared, of course, but

  - it would complicate the specification since it involves defining what those buttons are, and
  - it wouldn't help to specify safety or liveness, as we have seen

so we prefer to leave it as a requirement to be satisfied later.

Similarly, we assume that only the lift will be able to clear a button and so a button once pressed will stay lit. This in turn means that *before* and *after*, once true because a button is lit, will remain true until the lift either reaches the relevant floor or reverses direction, when *before* takes the value of *after* and vice versa.

It is never possible to guarantee absolutely that even a functioning lift will eventually do anything. Someone may hold the doors open somewhere indefinitely, for example. (We can, though, specify systems that detect such events and go into special states when they occur. Then liveness properties include assumptions about "normal" states as well as "safe" ones.)

- If we accept the assumption that the lift will not stay halted indefinitely anywhere, it will keep going to the "next" floor. There it may halt but, again, will eventually move. So we know that the lift always "makes progress".

    – If this movement is towards the floor in question, *after* is true and the lift is not allowed to change direction. So it must make progress until it reaches the floor.
    – If this movement is away from the floor in question, *before* is true. The lift must eventually change direction, since there are only finitely many floors in front of it, and *before* will stay true until it changes direction. When it changes direction, since *before* was true, *after* becomes true, and we have already established that it will eventually get to the floor in question.

Note that this analysis assumes the correct relation between the buttons and the values *here*, *before* and *after* for any floor. We will formalize these later and assume for now that they mean what we say they mean.

We now formulate the initial specification *A_LIFT0*:

scheme A_LIFT0 =
   hide movement, door_state, floor, direction, safe **in**
   class
      type Lift
      value
         /* generators */
         next : T.Requirement × Lift $\xrightarrow{\sim}$ Lift,
         check_buttons : Lift → T.Requirement × Lift,
         /* observers */
         movement : Lift → T.Movement,
         door_state : Lift → T.Floor → T.Door_state,
         floor : Lift → T.Floor,
         direction : Lift → T.Direction,
         /* derived */
         safe : Lift → **Bool**
         safe(s) ≡
            (∀ f : T.Floor •
               (door_state(s)(f) = T.open) =
               (movement(s) = T.halted ∧ floor(s) = f))

axiom
    [safe_and_useful]
      ∀ s : Lift •
        safe(s) ⇒
        let (r, s′) = check_buttons(s) **in**
          safe(s′) ∧
          let s″ = next(r, s′) **in**
            safe(s″) ∧
            (movement(s″) = T.halted ⇒
              (T.here(r) ∨ (∼ T.after(r) ∧ ∼ T.before(r))) ∧
              floor(s) = floor(s″)) ∧
            (movement(s″) = T.moving ⇒
              (T.after(r) ∨ T.before(r)) ∧
              T.is_next_floor(direction(s″), floor(s)) ∧
              floor(s″) = T.next_floor(direction(s″), floor(s))) ∧
            (direction(s) ≠ direction(s″) ⇒ ∼ T.after(r))
          end
        end
  end

2.7.3.7   Validation

As we did in section 2.6.6.1 we check that all the requirements are either reflected in the initial specification or catered for in the development plan. In this system the most important things to be checked are the safety and liveness properties; we will need to check that the definition of *is_safe* and the axiom *safe_and_useful* are adequate.

2.7.4   Development of main algorithm

The first aim is to define the function *next* and show that it satisfies *safe_and_-useful*. To do this we introduce two new generators *move* and *halt* and define *next* in terms of them. So *next* changes from being a generator to being a derived function.

   move changes the current floor to the next. To avoid having separate move-up and move-down functions it has a direction parameter, and changes the current direction to the value of this parameter. It also has a movement parameter, since if the lift is already moving *move* need not shut any doors, but otherwise the door of the current floor must be shut before the move. *halt* halts the lift at the current floor and opens (or unlocks) the doors. (We still need to specify later that it clears the buttons for that floor.)

   The preconditions for *move* and *halt* are *is_safe* and, for *move*, that there is a next floor. It is standard to make the safety or invariant predicate a precondition for generators, since the strategy is to show that it is preserved by *next*, which is defined in terms of *move* and *halt*. This allows us to effectively compute the precondition for *next* from its body, noting that it only calls *move* in the original direction when *after* is true, and in the opposite direction when *before* is true. This further allows us to compute a postcondition for *check_buttons*. The construction of *A_LIFT1* is otherwise according to the method for abstract applicative modules described in section 2.8.4.1.

scheme A_LIFT1 =
    hide movement, door_state, floor, direction, move, halt, safe **in**
    class
        type Lift
        value
          /* generators */
          move : T.Direction × T.Movement × Lift $\overset{\sim}{\to}$ Lift,
          halt : Lift → Lift,
          check_buttons : Lift → T.Requirement × Lift,
          /* observers */
          movement : Lift → T.Movement,
          door_state : Lift → T.Floor → T.Door_state,
          floor : Lift → T.Floor,
          direction : Lift → T.Direction,
          /* derived */
          next : T.Requirement × Lift $\overset{\sim}{\to}$ Lift
          next(r, s) ≡
            let d = direction(s) **in**
              case movement(s) **of**
                T.halted →
                  case r **of**
                    T.mk_Requirement(_, **true**, _) → move(d, T.halted, s),
                    T.mk_Requirement(_, _, **true**) →
                      move(T.invert(d), T.halted, s),
                    _ → s
                end,
                T.moving →
                  case r **of**
                    T.mk_Requirement(**true**, _, _) → halt(s),
                    T.mk_Requirement(_, **false**, **false**) → halt(s),
                    T.mk_Requirement(_, **true**, _) → move(d, T.moving, s),
                    T.mk_Requirement(_, _, **true**) →
                      move(T.invert(d), T.moving, s)
                end
            end
        end

pre
 (T.after(r) $\Rightarrow$ T.is_next_floor(direction(s), floor(s))) $\wedge$
 (T.before(r) $\Rightarrow$ T.is_next_floor(T.invert(direction(s)), floor(s))),
safe : Lift $\rightarrow$ **Bool**
safe(s) $\equiv$
 ($\forall$ f : T.Floor •
  (door_state(s)(f) = T.open) =
  (movement(s) = T.halted $\wedge$ floor(s) = f))

axiom
 [movement_move]
  $\forall$ s : Lift, d : T.Direction, m : T.Movement •
   movement(move(d, m, s)) $\equiv$ T.moving
    pre T.is_next_floor(d, floor(s)),
 [door_state_move]
  $\forall$ s : Lift, d : T.Direction, m : T.Movement, f : T.Floor •
   door_state(move(d, m, s))(f) $\equiv$
    if m = T.halted $\wedge$ floor(s) = f **then** T.shut
    else door_state(s)(f) **end**
    pre T.is_next_floor(d, floor(s)),
 [floor_move]
  $\forall$ s : Lift, d : T.Direction, m : T.Movement •
   floor(move(d, m, s)) $\equiv$ T.next_floor(d, floor(s))
    pre T.is_next_floor(d, floor(s)),
 [direction_move]
  $\forall$ s : Lift, d : T.Direction, m : T.Movement •
   direction(move(d, m, s)) $\equiv$ d **pre** T.is_next_floor(d, floor(s)),
 [move_defined]
  $\forall$ s : Lift, d : T.Direction, m : T.Movement •
   move(d, m, s) **post true pre** T.is_next_floor(d, floor(s)),
 [movement_halt] $\forall$ s : Lift • movement(halt(s)) $\equiv$ T.halted,
 [door_state_halt]
  $\forall$ s : Lift, f : T.Floor •
   door_state(halt(s))(f) $\equiv$
    if floor(s) = f **then** T.open **else** door_state(s)(f) **end**,
 [floor_halt] $\forall$ s : Lift • floor(halt(s)) $\equiv$ floor(s),
 [direction_halt]
  $\forall$ s : Lift • direction(halt(s)) $\equiv$ direction(s),
 [check_buttons_ax]
  $\forall$ s : Lift •
   check_buttons(s) **as** (r, s$'$)
  post
   movement(s$'$) = movement(s) $\wedge$
   door_state(s$'$) = door_state(s) $\wedge$
   floor(s$'$) = floor(s) $\wedge$

direction(s′) = direction(s) ∧
(T.after(r) ⇒ T.is_next_floor(direction(s′), floor(s′))) ∧
(T.before(r) ⇒ T.is_next_floor(T.invert(direction(s′)), floor(s′)))
end

2.7.4.1   Verification

We express the claim that *A_LIFT1* implements *A_LIFT0* by formulating this claim as a development relation and justifying it. This justification consists largely of justifying that the axiom *safe_and_useful* is true in *A_LIFT1*, i.e. that the algorithm will give a safe and useful lift.

2.7.5   Decomposition of the state

We decide to model the system in terms of three sub-systems: the doors, the buttons and the motor. Each of these has an abstract state and functions acting on this state with which we can decompose the actions of the generators of the *A_LIFT1* module.

scheme A_DOORS0 =
  class
    type Doors
    value
      /∗ generators ∗/
      open : T.Floor × Doors → Doors,
      close : T.Floor × Doors → Doors,
      /∗ observer ∗/
      door_state : Doors → T.Floor → T.Door_state
    axiom
      [door_state_open]
        ∀ f, f′ : T.Floor, s : Doors •
          door_state(open(f, s))(f′) ≡
            if f = f′ **then** T.open **else** door_state(s)(f′) **end**,
      [door_state_close]
        ∀ f, f′ : T.Floor, s : Doors •
          door_state(close(f, s))(f′) ≡
            if f = f′ **then** T.shut **else** door_state(s)(f′) **end**
  end

scheme A_BUTTONS0 =
  class
    type Buttons
    value
      /∗ generators ∗/
      clear : T.Floor × Buttons → Buttons,

check : T.Direction × T.Floor × Buttons → T.Requirement × Buttons
axiom
[check_result]
∀ s : Buttons, d : T.Direction, f : T.Floor •
check(d, f, s) **as** (r, s′)
post
(T.after(r) ⇒ T.is_next_floor(d, f)) ∧
(T.before(r) ⇒ T.is_next_floor(T.invert(d), f))
end

scheme A_MOTOR0 =
class
type Motor
value
/∗ generators ∗/
move : T.Direction × Motor $\xrightarrow{\sim}$ Motor,
halt : Motor → Motor,
/∗ observers ∗/
direction : Motor → T.Direction,
movement : Motor → T.Movement,
floor : Motor → T.Floor
axiom
[direction_move]
∀ s : Motor, d : T.Direction •
direction(move(d, s)) ≡ d **pre** T.is_next_floor(d, floor(s)),
[movement_move]
∀ s : Motor, d : T.Direction •
movement(move(d, s)) ≡ T.moving
pre T.is_next_floor(d, floor(s)),
[floor_move]
∀ s : Motor, d : T.Direction •
floor(move(d, s)) ≡ T.next_floor(d, floor(s))
pre T.is_next_floor(d, floor(s)),
[move_defined]
∀ s : Motor, d : T.Direction •
move(d, s) **post true pre** T.is_next_floor(d, floor(s)),
[direction_halt] ∀ s : Motor • direction(halt(s)) ≡ direction(s),
[movement_halt] ∀ s : Motor • movement(halt(s)) ≡ T.halted,
[floor_halt] ∀ s : Motor • floor(halt(s)) ≡ floor(s)
end

To formulate *A_LIFT2* we follow the method we used in section 2.6.7, using the following concrete type definition for *Lift*:

type Lift = M.Motor × DS.Doors × BS.Buttons

We also decide to remove the hidden functions *movement*, *door_state*, *floor* and *direction* as they are hidden and have simple definitions in terms of corresponding functions from the constituent objects (allowing us to easily unfold their occurrences). This in turn makes it sensible to define *A_LIFT2* in two stages, using a "BODY" module:

scheme A_LIFT2 = **hide** M, DS, BS, move, halt, safe **in** A_LIFT2_BODY

scheme A_LIFT2_BODY =
  class
    object
      /* motor */
      M : A_MOTOR0,
      /* doors */
      DS : A_DOORS0,
      /* buttons */
      BS : A_BUTTONS0
    type Lift = M.Motor × DS.Doors × BS.Buttons
    value
      /* generators */
      move : T.Direction × T.Movement × Lift $\xrightarrow{\sim}$ Lift
      move(d, m, (ms, ds, bs)) ≡
        (M.move(d, ms),
        if m = T.halted **then** DS.close(M.floor(ms), ds) **else** ds **end**,
        bs)
        pre T.is_next_floor(d, M.floor(ms)),
      halt : Lift → Lift
      halt((ms, ds, bs)) ≡
        (M.halt(ms), DS.open(M.floor(ms), ds), BS.clear(M.floor(ms), bs)),
      check_buttons : Lift → T.Requirement × Lift
      check_buttons((ms, ds, bs)) ≡
        let (r, bs') = BS.check(M.direction(ms), M.floor(ms), bs) **in**
          (r, (ms, ds, bs'))
        end,
      /* derived */
      next : T.Requirement × Lift $\xrightarrow{\sim}$ Lift
      next(r, (ms, ds, bs)) ≡
        let d = M.direction(ms) **in**
          case M.movement(ms) **of**
            T.halted →
              case r **of**
                T.mk_Requirement(_, **true**, _) →
                  move(d, T.halted, (ms, ds, bs)),
                T.mk_Requirement(_, _, **true**) →
                  move(T.invert(d), T.halted, (ms, ds, bs)),

$$\_ \rightarrow (\text{ms, ds, bs})$$
end,
T.moving →
case r **of**
T.mk_Requirement(**true**, _, _) → halt((ms, ds, bs)),
T.mk_Requirement(_, **false**, **false**) → halt((ms, ds, bs)),
T.mk_Requirement(_, **true**, _) →
move(d, T.moving, (ms, ds, bs)),
T.mk_Requirement(_, _, **true**) →
move(T.invert(d), T.moving, (ms, ds, bs))
end
end
end
pre
(T.after(r) ⇒ T.is_next_floor(M.direction(ms), M.floor(ms))) ∧
(T.before(r) ⇒
T.is_next_floor(T.invert(M.direction(ms)), M.floor(ms))),
safe : Lift → **Bool**
safe((ms, ds, bs)) ≡
(∀ f : T.Floor •
(DS.door_state(ds)(f) = T.open) =
(M.movement(ms) = T.halted ∧ M.floor(ms) = f))
end

2.7.5.1 Verification

We would like to state and justify a development relation between *A_LIFT1* and *A_LIFT2*. We could state this as

A_LIFT2 ⪯ A_LIFT1

but this relation cannot be justified since *A_LIFT1* defines and hides entities (*movement* and three other functions) that are not defined in *A_LIFT2*. We clearly do not need them as *A_LIFT2* defines all the non-hidden entities from *A_LIFT1*. What we do instead is to show that an extension of *A_LIFT2_BODY* (where the extension defines *movement* and the other three functions) implements *A_LIFT1*. We state the relation in the development relation *A_LIFT1_2*:

development_relation [A_LIFT1_2]
extend A_LIFT2_BODY **with**
class
value
movement : Lift → T.Movement
movement((ms, ds, bs)) ≡ M.movement(ms),

door_state : Lift → T.Floor → T.Door_state
door_state((ms, ds, bs)) ≡ DS.door_state(ds),

floor : Lift → T.Floor
floor((ms, ds, bs)) ≡ M.floor(ms),

direction : Lift → T.Direction
direction((ms, ds, bs)) ≡ M.direction(ms)

   end
 ⪯ A_LIFT1

If tools are available these will check that this relation is well-formed, i.e. that we
have included everything and not changed any signatures. We can then justify
this relation, which amounts to showing that the axioms from *A_LIFT1* hold in
A_LIFT2.

Note the following points:

- We needed to split *A_LIFT2* into a "BODY" and a hide to be able to construct
  this relation as the extension defining *movement*, etc. needs to be able to
  mention names like *M* hidden in *A_LIFT2*.
- The extension adding the hidden entities contains only explicit definitions,
  and hence is unlikely to be inconsistent. It also, for the same reason, is likely
  only to conservatively extend *A_LIFT2*.
- If we can be sure that the extension conservatively extends *A_LIFT2*, we can
  be sure that the properties of the entities defined in *A_LIFT2* are not affected
  by the extension. The extension used here is indeed conservative; how to
  demonstrate this is discussed in section 3.12.2.
- *A_LIFT1* involves hiding but this can be ignored in the justification since all
  the hidden names are now defined in the extension of *A_LIFT2_BODY*.

We can justify the development relation *A_LIFT1_2* to show that *A_LIFT2* implements *A_LIFT1*. Since implementation is transitive, this will show that *A_LIFT2*
implements *A_LIFT0*, and in particular that the decomposed design is still safe
and useful.

2.7.6   Development of components

Before making the shift to a concurrent system we will make the applicative components concrete by defining appropriate types for their types of interest. For each
component we follow the method described in detail later in section 2.8.4.6. In
summary:

- Choose a concrete RSL type for the type of interest. A possible type to use is
  the product of the result types of the non-derived observers, but other choices
  can be made. The important criterion is that all the observers can be defined
  in terms of the concrete type.

- Supply explicit bodies to functions using the RSL features available for the concrete type.

2.7.6.1 Motor

We need a concrete type for *Motor*. An obvious choice is

type Motor = T.Direction × T.Movement × T.Floor

since there are three observers in *A_MOTOR0* each giving one of the types in the product. The remainder of the formulation of *A_MOTOR1* is simple.

scheme A_MOTOR1 =
  class
    type Motor = T.Direction × T.Movement × T.Floor
    value
      /* generators */
      move : T.Direction × Motor $\xrightarrow{\sim}$ Motor
      move(d′, (d, m, f)) ≡
        (d′, T.moving, T.next_floor(d′, f))
          pre T.is_next_floor(d′, f),
      halt : Motor → Motor
      halt((d, m, f)) ≡ (d, T.halted, f),
      /* observers */
      direction : Motor → T.Direction
      direction((d, m, f)) ≡ d,
      movement : Motor → T.Movement
      movement((d, m, f)) ≡ m,
      floor : Motor → T.Floor
      floor((d, m, f)) ≡ f
  end

2.7.6.2 Doors

We only have one observer in *A_DOORS0*, with signature

    door_state : Doors → T.Floor → T.Door_state

This suggests the concrete type definition for the type of interest *Doors*

type Doors = T.Floor → T.Door_state

It may seem odd to regard a function type as sufficiently concrete (since function types are not generally available in programming languages), but when the parameter type of this function type is a finite type it can be developed to an array of objects. That is, we will have a single door module for each floor. This gives *A_DOORS1*:

scheme A_DOORS1 =
   class
      type Doors = T.Floor → T.Door_state
      value
         /* generators */
         open : T.Floor × Doors → T.Floor → T.Door_state
         open(f, s)(f') ≡ **if** f = f' **then** T.open **else** s(f') **end**,
         close : T.Floor × Doors → T.Floor → T.Door_state
         close(f, s)(f') ≡ **if** f = f' **then** T.shut **else** s(f') **end**,
         /* observer */
         door_state : Doors → T.Floor → T.Door_state
         door_state(s) ≡ s
   end

2.7.6.3 Buttons

We have no observers yet and so no clear guide as to what the concrete type should be. We also need to remember that we have not yet modelled the user function of pressing a button.

We have assumed that the lift has a button for each floor, and each floor has (at most) an "up" button and a "down" button. The bottom floor has only an "up" button; the top floor has only a "down" button; intermediate floors have both.

We remember that for the doors, where we expect to have an array, the concrete type was a function with parameter type *Floor* and result type *Door_state*. We can model the buttons with three such arrays: lift buttons, "up" floor buttons and "down" floor buttons. This suggests a product of function types for the concrete type, and we can formulate *A_BUTTONS1*:

scheme A_BUTTONS1 =
   hide required_here, required_beyond **in**
   class
      type
         Buttons =
            (T.Floor → T.Button_state) ×
            (T.Lower_floor → T.Button_state) ×
            (T.Upper_floor → T.Button_state)
      value
         /* generators */
         clear : T.Floor × Buttons → Buttons
         clear(f, (l, u, d)) ≡
            (λ f' : T.Floor • **if** f = f' **then** T.clear **else** l(f') **end**,
             λ f' : T.Lower_floor • **if** f = f' **then** T.clear **else** u(f') **end**,
             λ f' : T.Upper_floor • **if** f = f' **then** T.clear **else** d(f') **end**),
         check : T.Direction × T.Floor × Buttons → T.Requirement × Buttons,

```
/* observers */
required_here : T.Direction × T.Floor × Buttons → Bool
required_here(d, f, (lift, up, down)) ≡
    lift(f) = T.lit ∨
    d = T.up ∧
    (f < T.max_floor ∧ up(f) = T.lit ∨
     f > T.min_floor ∧
     down(f) = T.lit ∧ ~ required_beyond(d, f, (lift, up, down))) ∨
    d = T.down ∧
    (f > T.min_floor ∧ down(f) = T.lit ∨
     f < T.max_floor ∧
     up(f) = T.lit ∧ ~ required_beyond(d, f, (lift, up, down))),
required_beyond : T.Direction × T.Floor × Buttons → Bool
required_beyond(d, f, s) ≡
    T.is_next_floor(d, f) ∧
    let f' = T.next_floor(d, f) in
        required_here(d, f', s) ∨ required_beyond(d, f', s)
    end
```
axiom
```
[check_result]
    ∀ s : Buttons, d : T.Direction, f : T.Floor •
check(d, f, s) as (r, s')
    post
        r =
        T.mk_Requirement
            (required_here(d, f, s),
             required_beyond(d, f, s),
             required_beyond(T.invert(d), f, s))
```
end

Note that we have been able for the first time to define what *clear* does and how
here, *before* and *after* are computed.

2.7.6.4   Verification

For each of the applicative motor, doors, and buttons modules it is easy to formulate
and justify that the concrete version implements the abstract version.

2.7.6.5   Validation

Since we have elaborated *clear* and *here*, *before* and *after* for the buttons module for
the first time, we need to check that these are what is required. For example, *clear*
will clear the down button for a floor if the lift stops there on the way up (because of
some other request). We assume that in this situation it is most likely that anyone
waiting to go down will get into the lift and that therefore stopping again at this

floor on the way down will typically be a waste of time. This may be appropriate for a single lift system; it would not be for a multiple lift system. Conversely the lift will only stop when going up for a down button if there is no request for it to go higher. There are undoubtedly other, perhaps better, alternatives, but the primary purpose of this example is to show how such systems can be specified and developed rather than to discuss in detail control algorithms for lifts.

2.7.7   Introduction of concurrency

2.7.7.1   Lift

We have four concrete applicative modules to transform into concurrent ones. The easiest is the composition module *A_LIFT2*, which will become *C_LIFT2*. We follow the method described in detail later in section 2.8.6.4. In summary:

- Define objects *M*, *DS* and *BS* as in the applicative version, but this time instantiating concurrent imperative versions of the motor, doors and buttons modules.

  There is no definition of the type *Lift*.
- For each of the functions include in its type the access **in any out any** and remove the type of interest *Lift* from its parameter and result types (replacing by **Unit** if there are no other components in a parameter or result type).
- Define the bodies of the functions by adapting the applicative versions to use the imperative functions corresponding to the applicative ones. The general method for this adaptation is described in section 2.8.6.4 but is easy to follow intuitively for this example.
- Add an *init* function to call all the *init* functions of the constituent objects in parallel.

This gives *C_LIFT2*:

scheme C_LIFT2 =
    hide M, DS, BS, move, halt **in**
    class
        object
            /* motor */
            M : C_MOTOR1,
            /* doors */
            DS : C_DOORS1,
            /* buttons */
            BS : C_BUTTONS1

value
  /∗ generators ∗/
  move : T.Direction × T.Movement → **in any out any Unit**
  move(d, m) ≡
    if m = T.halted **then** DS.close(M.floor()) **end** ; M.move(d),
  halt : **Unit** → **in any out any Unit**
  halt() ≡
    let f = M.floor() **in** BS.clear(f) ; M.halt() ; DS.open(f) **end**,
  check_buttons : **Unit** → **in any out any** T.Requirement
  check_buttons() ≡ BS.check(M.direction(), M.floor()),
  /∗ derived ∗/
  next : T.Requirement → **in any out any Unit**
  next(r) ≡
    let d = M.direction() **in**
      case M.movement() **of**
        T.halted →
          case r **of**
            T.mk_Requirement(_, **true**, _) → move(d, T.halted),
            T.mk_Requirement(_, _, **true**) →
              move(T.invert(d), T.halted),
            _ → **skip**
          end,
        T.moving →
          case r **of**
            T.mk_Requirement(**true**, _, _) → halt(),
            T.mk_Requirement(_, **false**, **false**) → halt(),
            T.mk_Requirement(_, **true**, _) → move(d, T.moving),
            T.mk_Requirement(_, _, **true**) →
              move(T.invert(d), T.moving)
          end
      end
    end,
  /∗ initial ∗/
  init : **Unit** → **in any out any write any Unit**
  init() ≡ M.init() ∥ DS.init() ∥ BS.init(),
  /∗ control ∗/
  lift : **Unit** → **in any out any Unit**
  lift() ≡ **while true do** next(check_buttons()) **end**
end

(We have not yet formulated the component modules *C_MOTOR1*, etc., but the method is sufficiently regular for us to write down *C_LIFT2* even if we cannot type check it yet.)

We have now also included the control function *lift* that follows the pattern we indicated earlier: it repeatedly checks the buttons and does the next action. Why didn't we write the counterpart to this function in the applicative version *A_LIFT2* (or an earlier one)?

If we tried to write this function in the applicative version we would have written something like

value

    lift : Lift → Lift

    lift(s) ≡ lift(next(check_buttons(s)))

But this definition is likely to be contradictory. The function *lift* is claimed (by the total function arrow in its type) to be convergent when applied and (since it is applicative) must therefore terminate when applied. But such a function will in general not terminate. The concurrent counterpart is convergent because, although it involves an infinite loop this loop communicates. So we note again that the way to specify and analyse such systems starting from an applicative specification is in terms of a "next" function.

2.7.7.2   Motor

The motor is the easiest of the three components because it involves no component arrays. This module is sufficiently simple to follow the simplified method that will be described in detail later in section 2.8.6.3. In summary:

- Define a variable for each component of the applicative type of interest from *A_MOTOR1*.
- Give signatures to the functions corresponding to the applicative ones by adding the accesses **in any out any** and removing the type of interest *Motor* (as usual adding **Unit** where necessary).
- Define channels for (at least) the parameter and result types of the functions that are not **Unit**.
- Define the body of each function as an output of its parameter (unless of **Unit** type with no channel) followed by an input of its result (unless of **Unit** type with no channel).
- Add a "main" function (here called *motor*) which is a **while true do** loop containing an external choice between an expression for each of the other functions. Each of these expressions

  – inputs the parameter value from the function (if any), then
  – for generators, updates the variables as appropriate, then
  – outputs the result value to the function (if any).

  The updating of the variables and the result returned are the imperative counterparts to the bodies of the applicative functions.
- Define an *init* function that calls the main function after, possibly, initialising the variables.

scheme C_MOTOR1 =
  hide CH, V, motor **in**
  class
    object
      CH :
        class
          channel
            direction : T.Direction,
            floor : T.Floor,
            movement : T.Movement,
            move : T.Direction,
            halt, move_ack, halt_ack : **Unit**
        end,
      V :
        class
          variable
            direction : T.Direction,
            movement : T.Movement,
            floor : T.Floor
        end
    value
      /* main */
      motor : **Unit** → **in any out any write any Unit**
      motor() ≡
        while true do
          let d′ = CH.move? **in**
            CH.move_ack ! () ; V.direction := d′ ;
            V.movement := T.moving ; V.floor := T.next_floor(d′, V.floor)
          end []
          CH.halt? ; CH.halt_ack ! () ; V.movement := T.halted []
          CH.direction ! V.direction []
          CH.movement ! V.movement []
          CH.floor ! V.floor
        end,
      /* initial */
      init : **Unit** → **in any out any write any Unit**
      init() ≡ motor(),
      /* generators */
      /* assumes move only called when next floor in direction exists */
      move : T.Direction → **in any out any Unit**
      move(d) ≡ CH.move ! d ; CH.move_ack?,
      halt : **Unit** → **in any out any Unit**
      halt() ≡ CH.halt ! () ; CH.halt_ack?,

```
/* observers */
direction : Unit → in any out any T.Direction
direction() ≡ CH.direction?,
floor : Unit → in any out any T.Floor
floor() ≡ CH.floor?,
movement : Unit → in any out any T.Movement
movement() ≡ CH.movement?
```
end

Some design decisions are of interest here:

- Since the concrete state was a product of three components it was natural to use three variables.
- As with the channels, we have put the variables into an object *V* of their own to facilitate hiding them.
- We give no initial value to the variables. This reflects the intuition that it may be necessary to start or re-start the lift in any state. We might in this module want to assert that the lift is, say, stationary at the bottom floor and prepared to go up, but then it would not be applicable for a restart of the system in some other state. (Such a restart facility would need some additional functions to allow the system to be made safe before starting normal behaviour.)
- There are "acknowledgement" channels for the results of the *move* and *halt* functions, although these are of type **Unit**. This allows us to assume that the lift motor has actually carried out the corresponding action when the function terminates. Note that there is nothing in the specification about actually sending the commands to the physical motor. There are two ways of interpreting this specification (which will affect the way it is translated):
  - We regard the definition of *motor* as a specification of the *assumptions* about the hardware interface; it specifies that after doing a *move*, for example, the variables are set so that consequent functions like *floor* will obtain information that corresponds both to what the move was supposed to do (change the floor variable to the next floor) and also to what the physical lift has actually done. The functions *move*, *halt*, etc. are the interface to the hardware. In this case the translation of the module will ignore *motor* and translate the functions in terms of calls on the hardware.
  - We regard *motor* as implicitly calling the hardware functions in the appropriate places, such as telling the actual motor to move after receiving an input on the *CH.move* channel and then waiting for an acknowledgement from the motor before outputting on the *CH.move_ack* channel. In this case the *motor* function will be translated to include the appropriate hardware calls.

Which interpretation we take depends mostly on how close *motor* is to how the hardware actually operates. For the purposes of this tutorial we take the first interpretation.

Note that, if we take the second interpretation, the translation of *C_LIFT2* is also affected; we would need to make sure that its *init* function is invoked initially, since it will invoke the initial motor, door and button processes. With the first interpretation these are all "running" as hardware already.

- The applicative *move* function in *A_MOTOR1* had a precondition that involved a parameter, so we could not use the "if precondition then communicate else stop" style (see section 2.8.6.4). We can, however, check that in all calls of *move* the precondition (that there is a valid floor to move to) is true, so this is an instance where the check can be omitted. The check was in fact part of the proof of the *safe_and_useful* axiom earlier, since in that proof we could only unfold calls of *move* for which the precondition is true. Since this reduces the robustness of *C_MOTOR1* we have included a comment on this feature. A more robust implementation would include some code in the appropriate part of *motor*, which would require more knowledge about the hardware involved.

2.7.7.3 Doors

We need a method for decomposition into an object array. This is as follows:

- We have in the concrete type of interest a component which is a function type. The parameter type of this function type will be the type of the array index. (This can be done in RSL even if this type is infinite, but is typically only of use if the type is finite and fairly small. Otherwise we need to reconsider the concrete type.)
- We need a class expression for the array. We normally define this as a separate scheme.
- The type of interest of this scheme will be the result type of the function type, in this case *T.Door_state*.
- This method only makes sense if the current scheme is applicative and the development is to an imperative or concurrent one with an imperative or concurrent component.
- We need to define the functions of the component scheme. Usually this is very obvious, or soon becomes so, because they are the functions needed to model the (imperative or concurrent counterparts of the) functions in the current module. Any generator in the current module that changes or depends on an application of this component will need one or more corresponding functions; any observer that either produces a value of the type or in its body applies a value of the type will need one or more corresponding functions.
- We complete the definition of the functions of the component module and use them in the development of the current module.
- For a concurrent development, the *init* function in the current module will be defined as the parallel composition of the *init* functions of the components.

It is clear that the component module for a single door will need *open*, *close*, and *door_state* functions. We formulate it as the concurrent module *C_DOOR1*:

scheme C_DOOR1 =
    hide CH, door_var, door **in**
    class
        object
            CH :
                class
                    channel
                        open, close, open_ack, close_ack : **Unit**,
                        door_state : T.Door_state
                end
        variable door_var : T.Door_state
        value
            /* main */
            door : **Unit** → **in any out any write any Unit**
            door() ≡
                while true do
                    CH.open? ; CH.open_ack ! () ; door_var := T.open ⫿
                    CH.close? ; CH.close_ack ! () ; door_var := T.shut ⫿
                    CH.door_state ! door_var
                end,
            /* initial */
            init : **Unit** → **in any out any write any Unit**
            init() ≡ door(),
            /* generators */
            close : **Unit** → **in any out any Unit**
            close() ≡ CH.close ! () ; CH.close_ack?,
            open : **Unit** → **in any out any Unit**
            open() ≡ CH.open ! () ; CH.open_ack?,
            /* observer */
            door_state : **Unit** → **in any out any** T.Door_state
            door_state() ≡ CH.door_state?
    end

Note that as with the motor module:

- We have made no assumptions about the initial state.
- We have included acknowledgements so that we can assume that hardware interactions are completed when their functions terminate.

This allows us to formulate *C_DOORS1*:

scheme C_DOORS1 =
    hide DS **in**
    class
        object DS[f : T.Floor] : C_DOOR1

value
  /∗ initial ∗/
  init : **Unit** → **in any out any write any Unit**
  init() ≡ ∥ { DS[f].init() | f : T.Floor },
  /∗ generators ∗/
  open : T.Floor → **in any out any Unit**
  open(f) ≡ DS[f].open(),
  close : T.Floor → **in any out any Unit**
  close(f) ≡ DS[f].close(),
  /∗ observer ∗/
  door_state : T.Floor → **in any out any** T.Door_state
  door_state(f) ≡ DS[f].door_state()
end

2.7.7.4 Buttons

The method is just like that of section 2.7.7.3 except that we will need three arrays, each of the same component scheme *C_BUTTON1*. The state transitions for each button are shown in figure 2.9.

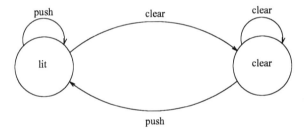

Figure 2.9: State transitions for a button

scheme C_BUTTON1 =
  hide CH, button, button_var **in**
  class
    object CH : **class channel** push, clear : **Unit**, check : T.Button_state **end**
    variable button_var : T.Button_state
    value
      /∗ main ∗/
      button : **Unit** → **in any out any write any Unit**
      button() ≡
        while true do
          CH.push? ; button_var := T.lit ⏐
          CH.clear? ; button_var := T.clear ⏐
          CH.check ! button_var

```
        end,
    /* initial */
    init : Unit → in any out any write any Unit
    init() ≡ button(),
    /* generators */
    push : Unit → in any out any Unit
    push() ≡ CH.push ! (),
    clear : Unit → in any out any Unit
    clear() ≡ CH.clear ! (),
    /* observer */
    check : Unit → in any out any T.Button_state
    check() ≡ CH.check?
end
```

As with the motor and doors, we have made no assumptions about the buttons initially.

The development step from *A_BUTTONS1* to *C_BUTTONS1* using arrays is now straightforward.

```
scheme C_BUTTONS1 =
    hide LB, UB, DB, required_here, required_beyond in
    class
        object
            /* lift buttons */
            LB[f : T.Floor] : C_BUTTON1,
            /* up buttons */
            UB[f : T.Lower_floor] : C_BUTTON1,
            /* down buttons */
            DB[f : T.Upper_floor] : C_BUTTON1
        value
            /* initial */
            init : Unit → in any out any write any Unit
            init() ≡
                || { LB[f].init() | f : T.Floor } ||
                || { UB[f].init() | f : T.Lower_floor } ||
                || { DB[f].init() | f : T.Upper_floor },
            /* generators */
            clear : T.Floor → in any out any Unit
            clear(f) ≡
                LB[f].clear() ;
                if f < T.max_floor then UB[f].clear() end ;
                if f > T.min_floor then DB[f].clear() end,
            /* observers */
            check : T.Direction × T.Floor → in any out any T.Requirement
            check(d, f) ≡
```

T.mk_Requirement
    (required_here(d, f),
      required_beyond(d, f),
      required_beyond(T.invert(d), f)),
required_here : T.Direction × T.Floor → **in any out any Bool**
required_here(d, f) ≡
    LB[f].check() = T.lit ∨
    d = T.up ∧
    (f < T.max_floor ∧ UB[f].check() = T.lit ∨
    f > T.min_floor ∧
    DB[f].check() = T.lit ∧ ∼ required_beyond(d, f)) ∨
    d = T.down ∧
    (f > T.min_floor ∧ DB[f].check() = T.lit ∨
    f < T.max_floor ∧
    UB[f].check() = T.lit ∧ ∼ required_beyond(d, f)),
required_beyond : T.Direction × T.Floor → **in any out any Bool**
required_beyond(d, f) ≡
    T.is_next_floor(d, f) ∧
    let f′ = T.next_floor(d, f) **in**
      required_here(d, f′) ∨ required_beyond(d, f′)
    end
end

2.7.7.5 Verification

Since this development step was from applicative to concurrent, we need to decide what level of assurance we need for correctness. We can either

- check that the method for this transition has been followed correctly, or
- formulate the concurrent axiom corresponding to the applicative *safe_and_useful* axiom from *A_LIFT0* and justify it for *C_LIFT2*.

Both of these are verifications since they check on the correctness of the development process. The first is informal and is generally all that is necessary. The second is formal and can be done if we have any doubts or require the highest level of assurance of correctness. How to do it is described in section 2.9.

2.7.8 Translation

Translation of this example is discussed in section 5.4.2.

Exercise Extend the example to allow for multiple lifts.
    The natural extension of the scheduling algorithm is probably too inefficient for multiple lifts as a request from a floor button would be passed to all lifts. This would ensure the one that can arrive first does so, but would mean all currently idle

lifts starting to move towards the floor. It is suggested, however, that a different algorithm is left as a separate, optional exercise.

2.8   Third example: queue

2.8.1   Aims of example

This example is of the development of a component, an abstract data type. The discussion is rather more detailed than in the previous examples, where the emphasis was on system specification and development and where the method summaries were written to reflect the particular example rather than offer full details. We will present in detail the method for specifying abstract applicative modules and for developing them to concrete and eventually imperative, sequential or concurrent modules.

The actual example is the simple (but not entirely trivial) example of a queue. To make it a little more realistic we will make the queue bounded, i.e. there will be a maximum number of elements it can hold.

2.8.2   Requirements

To start we need some requirements. The basic requirements for a bounded queue are that items may be extracted ("dequeued") only in the order in which they were inserted ("enqueued") and that at any time any number of items up to the maximum may have been enqueued and not yet dequeued. Note that in this case of a typical component rather than a complete system the requirements can usually be expressed in terms of the facilities (functions) to be provided. So we will have enqueue and dequeue functions, which we will abbreviate to *enq* and *deq* respectively. For formulating the boundedness we might also think of a "count" function, but since only two values of the count would probably be of interest (zero and the bound) we will choose instead to also have *is_empty* and *is_full* functions. The formulation of the queue largely consists of expressing the properties of these four functions.

2.8.3   Overview

There are a large number of specifications of the queue in this section. A particular development will only produce a few of these, and we first give an overview of the possible development routes and the sections relevant to them.

We always start with an abstract applicative specification, which is in this case *A_QUEUE0*. Its formulation is described in section 2.8.4.1.

We then decide how to develop this into a more concrete data structure. There are two choices:

- using the built-in RSL list type constructor. This gives the applicative concrete queue *A_QUEUE1*, described in section 2.8.4.6.
- using an array as a circular buffer. This gives the applicative concrete queue *A_QUEUE2*, described in section 2.8.4.7. Since *A_QUEUE2* instantiates another module (an array) we describe it as *composite*; its properties will be composed from the module(s) it instantiates. A module that does not instantiate others we describe as *single*.

  The technique of developing a module into a module that depends on others is *modular decomposition*. The ability to do so, and to compose the properties of a module from its particular properties and those of its components is critical to any method to be used for anything larger than the smallest problems.

Having developed to either *A_QUEUE1* or *A_QUEUE2*, if all we want is an applicative queue we are finished. But more typically we will need either an imperative or a concurrent queue. The first would be used in a purely sequential system, the latter in a concurrent one. In either case we will in general get greater efficiency because the queue value will not be passed as a parameter.

For an imperative queue, if we have developed to *A_QUEUE1* we develop *I_QUEUE1* from it in section 2.8.5.3 and we are finished. The overall development is illustrated in figure 2.10. Here the development steps are labelled "I" for implementation and "A_I" for applicative to imperative.

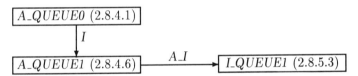

Figure 2.10: Development of *I_QUEUE1*

If we have developed to *A_QUEUE2* using an applicative array we develop to *I_QUEUE2* using an imperative array in section 2.8.5.4. The overall development is illustrated in figure 2.11. Here the development steps are labelled "I" for implementation, "A_I" for applicative to imperative and "C" for the clientship relation. For example, *A_QUEUE2* is a client of (instantiates) *A_ARRAY*.

For a single concurrent queue, we need to develop an imperative version first. So if we have developed to *I_QUEUE1* we develop *C_QUEUE1* as a client of it in section 2.8.6.3. The overall development is illustrated in figure 2.12.

The single concurrent queue *C_QUEUE1* has a sequential imperative supplier *I_QUEUE1*. The composite concurrent queue *C_QUEUE2* will have a concurrent supplier *C_ARRAY* that will in turn, we can presume, have its imperative supplier. So if we have developed to *A_QUEUE2* using the applicative array we can develop directly to *C_QUEUE2* as illustrated in figure 2.13.

There are also sections showing how to formulate abstract imperative modules (*I_QUEUE0* in section 2.8.5.1) and abstract concurrent modules (*C_QUEUE0* in

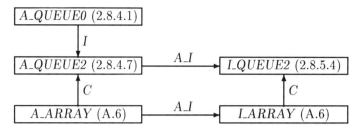

Figure 2.11: Development of *I_QUEUE2*

Figure 2.12: Development of *C_QUEUE1*

section 2.8.6.1). It is suggested that these sections are omitted in a first reading.

2.8.4   Applicative queue

In this section we develop first in section 2.8.4.1 an abstract applicative queue *A_QUEUE0* and then two alternative concrete versions: the "single" *A_QUEUE1* in section 2.8.4.6 and the "composite" *A_QUEUE2* in section 2.8.4.7.

2.8.4.1   Abstract applicative queue

The method in summary is

- define an abstract type of interest
- define a parameter module
- define the signatures of the constants and functions, taking care about whether functions are partial or total

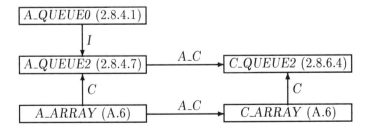

Figure 2.13: Development of *C_QUEUE2*

- formulate preconditions for partial function
- classify the functions as generators and observers
- define "observational" axioms relating the generators to the observers

Type of interest

We will need to identify the signatures of the functions required. It is immediately apparent that in the applicative case we need a type for the queue itself, the type of interest. In the abstract module this will be defined as an abstract type by a sort definition:

type Queue

Parameter module

The parameter type of *enq* will be *Elem* × *Queue* where *Elem* is the type of the things to be put on the queue. It seems appropriate to define a generic queue, so we need to define a parameter module. Is there anything else to put in it? We might immediately realize that it would be sensible to have the bound as a parameter as well. Should this go into the same parameter module or be a separate parameter? Our advice is that things that are unrelated can go into separate parameters, but it is not essential that they do. It turns out that, as long as parameters contain only applicative sequential entities (types, values and axioms), it is always possible to create the appropriate actual parameter(s) regardless of how many different objects the actual types or values are defined in. So it is largely a question of style, with the general advice to use fewer rather than more parameters for simplicity. In our case we will choose for simplicity to use just one parameter.

It looks reasonable to make the bound a natural number. Then we might ask if it is allowed to be zero. Such a question is often difficult to answer until we try to define the queue itself, when we may discover that allowing it to be zero will make some functions impossible to implement, so we might have to come back to the parameter module and change it. But certainly a permanently empty queue is useless, and so we will constrain the bound to be strictly positive. So we formulate the parameter module:

scheme ELEM = **class type** Elem **end**

scheme ELEM_BOUND =
    extend ELEM **with class value** bound : **Nat** • bound > 0 **end**

Considering the effect of the bound may have suggested that when the bound is 1 the queue should behave like a one place buffer. If we have such a buffer already defined we might make a note that a useful confidence check on the queue will be that it implements the one place buffer.

Total and partial functions

Now we consider the signatures of *enq* and *deq*. Are they to be total or partial? Certainly neither can be immediately defined as total, since *enq* may fail if the queue is full and *deq* if it is empty. There are two main approaches here:

1. We can make them partial and give them preconditions.
2. We can make them return a value indicating success or not. In the case of *deq* this can be achieved by a special "error" value of *Elem* (which should be defined in *ELEM_BOUND*) or by making it return a value of new variant type:

   type Deq_result == deq_fail | success(deq_res : P.Elem)

   This is preferable to defining *deq_fail* as a value of *Elem* in *ELEM_BOUND*. We don't have to check that *deq_fail* is never enqueued because it cannot be — it has a different type from *Elem*. In addition, modules using the queue module and forgetting to check the status value will usually be detected by type checking.

(There is another possibility: we can define subtypes like "non-empty-queue" and "non-full-queue" and make the functions total over such subtypes. For the purposes of this discussion this is effectively the same as the first alternative.)

Unfortunately it is difficult to decide between these two approaches without knowing how the queue will finally be implemented. These are the main possibilities:

- It may be possible to prove that the queue is never enqueued when full or dequeued when empty. In this case the first solution with preconditions is acceptable, though we might well think the queue not very suitable for reuse and not very robust against user errors.
- If the final implementation of the queue is to be concurrent, the natural development in the first case (as we shall see) will be to make the *enq* and *deq* functions unavailable when the queue is full and empty respectively. Then if the queue is running in parallel with one or more "writers" doing *enq* and one or more "readers" doing *deq* with the queue acting as a buffer, writers will be forced to wait while the queue is full and readers to wait while it is empty. In the second solution a writer will be able to make repeated unsuccessful communications with a full queue and readers with an empty one. This may be too inefficient.
- If the final implementation of the queue is to have one user (reader and writer), for the first alternative we would probably provide *is_empty* and *is_full* functions so that the user could check before using *deq* and *enq*. But this means that the user will make two calls on the queue each time, which will tend to be less efficient. (It is also less obvious if the formulator of a reader or writer module forgets to include the check.) The *is_full* and *is_empty* functions are of little use for a queue that may be used by multiple readers and writers: the result of such a function may not still hold at the next call of *enq* or *deq*.

The second approach, including a value indicating success or failure, should always be adopted when one expects to have multiple users and the precondition depends not just on the current value of the type of interest but also on the parameter(s). Consider for example a database relating keys to data values. The precondition for *lookup(k)* will be something like *is_in(k, db)*, which depends on the parameter to *lookup*, *k*, as well as *db*. For a concurrent database with multiple readers and writers we again cannot assume that the value returned by *is_in* will hold when we do the *lookup*, and we will see later that the method we are adopting will force the main database process to give some output after receiving the message to lookup a key; we cannot make the database unavailable to *lookup* in general, and can only calculate whether the lookup can succeed when the key has been received.

For this tutorial we will generally adopt the first approach (of partial functions with preconditions). There is then a simple technique to extend a module with partial functions to one with total ones. We will present such an extension for the queue in section 2.8.4.3 when we have completed the version with partial *enq* and *deq*.

So the signatures of *enq* and *deq* can finally be formulated, plus *is_full* and *is_empty*:

value
    enq : P.Elem $\times$ Queue $\xrightarrow{\sim}$ Queue,
    deq : Queue $\xrightarrow{\sim}$ P.Elem $\times$ Queue,
    is_full : Queue $\rightarrow$ **Bool**,
    is_empty : Queue $\rightarrow$ **Bool**

Preconditions
Next we formulate preconditions for each partial function (here *enq* and *deq*). It is generally best if preconditions are expressed as calls of functions, or possibly conjunctions of such calls. This may suggest additional functions. We have already identified *is_full* and *is_empty*, which we can use to formulate the preconditions of *enq* and *deq*.

Generators and observers
We classify the functions as either *generators*, which are those in which the type of interest (*Queue* in this case) occurs either directly in the result type or indirectly via type abbreviations, or *observers*, which are those in which it does not.

For instance, if we defined

type Elem_and_Queue = P.Elem $\times$ Queue
value deq : Queue $\xrightarrow{\sim}$ Elem_and_Queue

then *deq* would still be classified as a generator, as its result type depends on the type of interest *Queue*.

Constants

We consider the need for constants. Data types like queues commonly have a constant *empty*.

Whether to include *empty* depends on the requirements. If we are only developing an applicative queue then we may well intend to create instances of queues, and we cannot do that with our current generators. If we are developing an imperative or concurrent queue then there will be only one such queue for each object created from the queue module, and the question is whether we want either to be able to say that the queue is initially empty or be able at any point to make it empty. This is probably appropriate for queues, but may not be for other data types, like an array, for example.

We count constants which are either of the type of interest, or dependent on it, as generators. We have therefore identified the generators *empty*, *enq* and *deq*.

Axioms

For generators that are either constants or functions that only return a new value of the type of interest, we try to formulate "observer–generator" axioms. These are equational in form: each is an equivalence where the left-hand side applies an observer to a generator, such as

axiom
  [is_full_enq]
  ∀ e : P.Elem, q : Queue •
    is_full(enq(e,q)) ≡ ...
    pre ∼is_full(q)

For generators that return a result as well as a new value of the type of interest, we try to formulate axioms which are post expressions, such as

axiom
  [deq_ax]
  ∀ q : Queue •
    deq(q) **as** (e, q′) **post** e = ... ∧ is_full(q′) = ... ∧ is_empty(q′) = ...
    pre ∼ is_empty(q)

where the post expression includes one conjunct for the result and a conjunct for each observer applied to the new value of the type of interest.

We could also write axioms for non-result-returning generators in the post expression form, with a post expression like

  enq(e, q) **as** q′ **post** is_full(q′) = ... ∧ is_empty(q′) = ...

but we want to describe both styles.

We will describe axioms in one of these two forms, equational or post expression, as *observational axioms*.

It should be clear that, if there are g_1 non result-returning generators, g_2 result-returning generators and o observers, there will be $o * g_1$ axioms of the equational form and g_2 axioms of the post expression form, each of which will have a post expression with $(o + 1)$ conjuncts. Hence it is easy to check if everything is included. It is also apparent that the amount we have to write is proportional to the product of the number of generators and the number of observers. We need to minimize these numbers, a point we return to later, particularly in section 2.8.4.2.

Sometimes one or more axioms can be omitted because they would become vacuous. For example, suppose we had an observer *head* for the queue. The equational axiom for *head* and *empty* would be

axiom
    [head_empty]
        head(empty) ≡ ...
        pre ∼is_empty(empty)

and since the precondition would reduce to **false** the axiom would reduce to **true** even if we could find something to write on its right-hand side.

There are generally preconditions on the axioms. These preconditions are conjunctions of

- the precondition for the generator, if any, and
- the precondition for the observer(s), if any

If we formulate this set of observational axioms we are assured of the following:

consistency: For any value of the type of interest produced by a generator, and provided the appropriate preconditions hold, there is precisely one axiom for the result of applying an observer to the value, and precisely one axiom that gives the result if the generator is result-returning. Thus we are assured that we have very little danger of inconsistency through two axioms being applicable and giving different results. It is possible to write, for example,

    obs1(gen1(x)) ≡ obs2(gen2(x)),
    obs2(gen2(x)) ≡ ∼ obs1(gen1(x))

which gives a contradiction, but this is unlikely in practice. In our method of construction, where there is only an observer applied to a generator on the left-hand side, it is possible to avoid having generators on the right (or in the postconditions), and then such contradictions cannot arise.

completeness: If the terms on the right-hand sides of the equivalences, and the postconditions, do not involve the generators, and if the observers do not have preconditions, then (by repeated application of axioms) we can evaluate the result of an observer and the result of a result-returning generator applied to any term built up from the generators.

But we still have not done the hard part, which is formulating the right-hand sides and postconditions!

Exercise Find observational axioms that characterize an unbounded set, with constant *empty*, generators *add* and *remove*, and observer *is_in*. Can this be done with a bounded set? Can it be done with a stack or a queue, either bounded or unbounded?

Additional observers

You will find if you try the exercise above that it is impossible (with the constant and functions we have identified) to find a set of observational axioms that characterize a queue (bounded or unbounded). There are two alternatives to overcome this problem:

1. Add axioms relating generators.
2. Introduce one or more extra observers.

In the case of the queue it is possible to find a solution by adding axioms relating generators, but there are also known to be cases where this is impossible. There are, however, other reasons for choosing the second alternative:

- It is generally easier to formulate.
- It is possible to maintain the consistency and completeness results.
- It allows more implementations.

We hope to illustrate the first two points in what follows. But for the third we consider a possible generator-relating axiom:

axiom
> [deq_enq]
>> ∀ e : Elem, q : Queue •
>>> deq(enq(e,q)) ≡
>>>> **if** is_empty(q) **then** (e,q)
>>>> **else let** $(e',q') = $ deq(q) **in** $(e',$enq$(e,q'))$ **end**
>>> **end**

(This may also be an example of the first point; it is not particularly easy to formulate.)

The problem with such generator-relating axioms is that they involve equivalences between values of the type of interest (which our axioms never do). Consider a possible implementation of a queue as an array and a pair of pointers (intuitively a pointer to each end). An *enq* puts the new value in the array and increments one pointer; a *deq* reads a value and increments the other pointer. Now consider an *enq* followed by a *deq* to an initially empty queue. According to the axiom *deq_enq* above the new queue should be identical to the old, since we have as a consequence of it

> is_empty(q) ⇒ (deq(enq(e,q)) ≡ (e,q))

But we do not get the same (array, pointer, pointer) triple for the value q as before, because one array value has probably changed and both pointers have been incremented. So the axiom *deq_enq* will not hold for this implementation.

So we strongly advise only writing observational axioms. Then the properties of the type of interest will only be those that are observable.[1]

---

[1]This is not the only possible approach in RAISE. For example, it is possible to follow the Larch [13] approach, by introducing observational equivalence as part of the step from applicative to imperative.

What is the extra observer to be? An obvious choice might be *length*, since it should enable us to define *is_full* and *is_empty* and we know that *enq* and *deq* will (when their preconditions hold) increment it and decrement it respectively. But it turns out to be inadequate; there is still no way to complete *deq_ax*. An adequate alternative is to note that a queue can be seen as a list, and to define the extra observer by

type List_of_Queue = {| l : P.Elem* • **len** l ≤ P.bound |}
value list_of : Queue → List_of_Queue

We have used a subtype because it most accurately models the bounded queues.

Derived functions

Now we check if any of the observers or generators can be defined directly in terms of the others. We note that *is_full* and *is_empty* can be defined in terms of *list_of*. Such generators or observers are called *derived functions*. We can exclude them from the axioms (since the properties we would have expressed as axioms will follow from their definitions), so we now have one observer and three generators, for which the axioms will take the forms

axiom
  [list_of_empty] list_of(empty) ≡ ⟨⟩,

  [list_of_enq]
  ∀ e : P.Elem, q : Queue •
    list_of(enq(e, q)) ≡ list_of(q) ⌢ ⟨e⟩
    pre ∼ is_full(q),

  [deq_ax]
  ∀ q : Queue •
    deq(q) **as** (e, q′) **post** e = **hd** list_of(q) ∧ list_of(q′) = **tl** list_of(q)
    pre ∼ is_empty(q)

Note that these axioms take the form we wanted for completeness; the right-hand side expressions and postconditions do not involve the generators.

Making functions derived tends to make things clearer and also reduces the amount we have to write. If *is_full* and *is_empty* were not derived we would save their two definitions but have to write four more axioms (relating them to *empty* and *enq*) and add two more conjuncts to *deq_ax*.

Definedness axioms

If we are interested in doing proofs it is worth including extra axioms for the definedness of any partial (and non-derived) generators and observers. These take the form

axiom [f_defined] ∀ ... f(...) **post true pre** ...

where the precondition is as in the other axiom(s) for *f*. Such axioms for result-returning generators like *deq* can be derived from the other axioms, since these use post expressions (unless we made a mistake and the post expressions themselves are not total when the preconditions are true). For generators like *enq* the definedness axiom is not a consequence of the other axioms,[2] but presumably something we intend to ensure in any development. So we include the axiom *enq_defined*.

Definedness axioms will also be unnecessary when we have already included consistency axioms which use post expressions, like those in *A_HARBOUR0* in section 2.6.6.

The last thing to do is to remember to hide the new observer (and its result type). *list_of* was not required of us and there is no reason to make it visible. So we can finally formulate *A_QUEUE0*:

scheme A_QUEUE0(P : ELEM_BOUND) =
    hide List_of_Queue, list_of **in**
    class
        type Queue, List_of_Queue = {| l : P.Elem* • **len** l ≤ P.bound |}
        value
            /* generators */
            empty : Queue,
            enq : P.Elem × Queue $\overset{\sim}{\to}$ Queue,
            deq : Queue $\overset{\sim}{\to}$ P.Elem × Queue,
            /* hidden observer */
            list_of : Queue → List_of_Queue,
            /* derived */
            is_full : Queue → **Bool**
            is_full(q) ≡ **len** list_of(q) = P.bound,
            is_empty : Queue → **Bool**
            is_empty(q) ≡ list_of(q) = ⟨⟩
        axiom
            [list_of_empty] list_of(empty) ≡ ⟨⟩,
            [list_of_enq]
                ∀ e : P.Elem, q : Queue •
                    list_of(enq(e, q)) ≡ list_of(q) ⌢ ⟨e⟩ **pre** ∼ is_full(q),
            [deq_ax]
                ∀ q : Queue •
                    deq(q) **as** (e, q′)
                      post e = **hd** list_of(q) ∧ list_of(q′) = **tl** list_of(q)
                      pre ∼ is_empty(q),
            [enq_defined]
                ∀ e : P.Elem, q : Queue • enq(e, q) **post true pre** ∼ is_full(q)
    end

---

[2]Strictly speaking we can deduce from *list_of_enq* that *enq* terminates when its precondition is true, but not that it is deterministic. *deq_defined* implies both termination and determinacy.

We have added brief comments to distinguish the generators, observers and derived functions. These comments are useful to quality assurance reviewers (and ourselves in the future) to check that the construction of the module follows the method we have described.

Using variant types

It is natural to ask if a variant type definition would have been useful. Certainly it will give us a useful shorthand for some of the generators, and may provide us with an easy means of defining some observers if they correspond to destructors. To use a variant type we first decide on a sufficient set of generators for all values of the type. For the queue this will naturally be *empty* and *enq*. Then we can include any observers that correspond with destructors. But remember that such observers will then only apply to values that can be generated by their corresponding constructors. So for a stack, for example, we might be tempted to write

type Stack == empty | push(top : Elem, pop : Stack)

top and *pop* can probably not be applied to empty stacks, so their definition as destructors seems appropriate (and saves us writing axioms for them explicitly).

But now we have implicitly defined the axiom

axiom
  [pop_push]
  $\forall$ e : Elem, s : Stack • pop(push(e,s)) $\equiv$ s

and we know that such an axiom that relates generators causes problems with implementation. So we should not define destructors in variant types whose result types involve the type of interest (directly as here or indirectly through other types) unless we are sure that we want to implement the complete inverse of the corresponding constructor.[3]

There is also a choice illustrated here between defining *pop* as a result-returning generator (avoiding the need for *top*) just like our *deq*, and having separate *pop* and *top* functions. If in particular the intention is to develop to an imperative version where the discipline is intended to be that each element should only be popped once, having separate *pop* and *top* functions makes it harder to check that users of imperative stacks do so, and impossible to prove (unless we impose some extra machinery) that multiple readers of concurrent stacks can do so.

Using a variant type for queue, and noting that none of our observers correspond to possible destructors, we consider using the variant type definition

type Queue == empty | enq(P.Elem, Queue)

We need to consider the consequences of using such a variant type definition. To do so we first present the definitions which are together equivalent to it:

---

[3]These comments on whether to use variant types do not apply if applicative specifications are intended to express "abstract" properties, leaving imperative specifications to express "observational" properties, as in the Larch [13] approach.

type Queue
value
 empty : Queue,
 enq : P.Elem × Queue → Queue
axiom
 [empty_enq]
 ∀ e : P.Elem, q : Queue • empty ≠ enq(e,q),

 [Queue_induction]
 ∀ p : Queue → **Bool** •
  (p(empty) ∧ (∀ e : E.Elem, q : Queue • p(q) ⇒ p(enq(e,q)))) ⇒
   (∀ q : Queue • p(q))

If we compare this with *A_QUEUE0* we note several things:

totality of constructors: The constructor *enq* is here defined to be total, but *enq* in *A_QUEUE0* is not total because the queue is bounded. For this reason we cannot directly use a variant type. We could if we wished do the following instead:

type Queue == empty | enq1(P.Elem, Queue)
value
 enq : P.Elem × Queue $\xrightarrow{\sim}$ Queue
 enq(e,q) ≡ enq1(e,q) **pre** ∼is_full(q)

We would also hide *enq1*. This is sometimes a useful technique, especially when we want the rest of the variant type axioms without having to write them in full.

disjointness: A variant type also implicitly includes axioms saying that values constructed by different constructors are different. So you need to be sure that this is true. In our case there are two constructors and hence just one such axiom *empty_enq*. Such axioms are useful in that they make it possible to evaluate case expressions over values of the type of interest. They are generally harmless since they involve inequalities over this type rather than equalities, and they often hold anyway because of the presence of observers that can distinguish the two values (in this case *is_empty*). But if they might cause problems variant types should not be used.

induction: A variant type without a wildcard constructor also implicitly includes an induction axiom, in our case *Queue_induction*. This induction rule implies that all queues can be finitely generated by the two constructors in the variant type definition: *empty* and *enq*. This is very useful. However, the observer *list_of* allows us to calculate a finite RSL list from any term built from the generators (*empty*, *enq* and *deq*). Finite RSL lists form an inductive type, and theorems about queues that do not involve equality between queue values can be proved by induction on lists. For example, for our queue we cannot prove

  ∀ q : Queue • ∃ n : **Nat** • $deq^n(q)$ = empty

but we can prove

$$\forall\ q : \text{Queue} \bullet \exists\ n : \textbf{Nat} \bullet \text{is\_empty}(\text{deq}^n(q))$$

deq^n is meant to mean "apply *deq* *n* times" (discarding the element values returned and defaulting to the identity function when *n* is zero). In other words, we cannot prove that for any *Queue* value there is an *n* such that applying *deq* to it *n* times will make it precisely the same as the constant *empty*, but we can prove that we can create an empty queue that way. (Recall from the discussion about queues implemented as circular buffers that there may be more than one such buffer representing an empty queue.) In practice the slightly weaker, second property is sufficient. See also the discussion below on observational equivalence.

If the induction rule is not wanted it can be avoided by including an extra wildcard constructor:

type Queue == empty | enq(P.Elem, Queue) | _

If there is no wildcard constructor then there must be at least one constructor that is either a constant or has a parameter type that does not involve the type of interest (directly as with *enq* or indirectly through other types). Otherwise it can be shown that the type of interest is empty. The intuition behind this is that the induction rule implies that all values of the type of interest are finitely generated, but if all generators take arguments dependent on this type then the only possible values are infinitely generated.

We will not reformulate our example using variant types.

Observational equivalence

Before proceeding to develop the queue further we go back to the issue of avoiding axioms relating generators. We saw previously that this allowed us some implementations that would otherwise be unavailable. Another way of looking at this issue is that it gives us an "observational equivalence" over the type of interest. If we pose the question of whether two queue values are equal, there are several possibilities:

- They are identical expressions, so we know they are equal.
- One or more of our observers can distinguish them by giving different results when applied to them, so we know they cannot be equal.
- All the observers and result-returning generators give the same results but the expressions are not the same. We cannot tell if the values are equal, but we can regard them as *observationally equivalent*. Two expressions of the type of interest of a module are observationally equivalent if all observers and result-returning generators give the same results when applied to them (or cannot be applied to either because their preconditions do not hold).

Consider, for example, the expressions (for arbitrary *e*)

empty

and

let $(e',q') = \mathrm{deq}(\mathrm{enq}(e,\mathrm{empty}))$ **in** q' **end**

All the queue observers will agree about these two values: *list_of* gives the empty sequence for both (and hence the derived observers are bound to agree). The only result-returning generator, *deq*, cannot be applied to either as its precondition is false for both. So we conclude that they are observationally equivalent. However, we cannot prove from the axioms of *A_QUEUE0* that these two expressions have equal values. This is in fact a great advantage from the point of view of implementation, as we noted earlier. But although it looks like the theory is weak (since we can write down predicates that we cannot prove) it in fact causes no problems for the clients of the *A_QUEUE0*. Queue values that cannot be distinguished by the functions available to them can be regarded by clients as equivalent without any danger of inconsistency. If the theory is not strong enough this will become apparent in the lack of some function and can be rectified by its inclusion, without changing the principle. In particular we can add an *abstract equality* that models observational equivalence. See section 3.5.3 on how to define an abstract equality.

2.8.4.2   A more concrete approach

Formulating abstract modules usually involves several iterations. It is particularly important that abstract modules are well constructed because future development depends on them. Iterating until one is perfectly happy with the result, or until one is convinced one can't find a better one, is time well spent. Several attempts may be retained until one is settled on.

Also be aware of the option to decompose first. Where a natural specification would involve more than one data type with their own constructors, try to define them in separate modules. There is a good rule of thumb that if the type seems to involve more than two generators that are not constants or derived, one should consider a decomposition. For example, the module *A_HARBOUR0* in section 2.6.6 has three generator functions and is close to the point at which we would need to decompose in order to create an initial specification of reasonable size and complexity. If we did so, something like *A_HARBOUR1* would become the initial specification. We have to balance carefully the need to be abstract against the need to be simple and comprehensible.

Using abstract types is not always necessary and can lead to unnecessary length of specifications. Abstract types need only be used when the natural concrete types — particularly sets, lists and maps — would be too inefficient for the final implementation. Records (especially those not involving recursion) and products are frequently useful even in initial specifications. (Technically, records in RSL are considered abstract, but since they can typically be directly translated they can be considered concrete for the purposes of this discussion.)

Consider, for example, a specification of part of a (personal) banking system. We will need to record for each customer details like name, address, current balance, PIN number (for validating card transactions), card expiry date, overdraft limit, etc. We could model concretely something like

type

    Customer_id, Name, Address, Date, PIN_number,

    Customer_info = Customer_id $\overrightarrow{m}$ Customer_details,

    Customer_details ::

        name : Name

        address : Address

        balance : **Int**

        pin : PIN_number

        expiry : Date

        limit : **Int**

The first five types we expect to leave as abstract, and these would be immediate candidates for the type module.

    Suppose we tried to specify *Customer_info* abstractly. We would also have a number of functions to change details of a customer, like change_name, change_address, withdraw, deposit, issue_card, change_limit, etc., plus things like new_customer and remove_customer. We have identified at least 6 observers (corresponding to the components of *Customer_details*) plus probably *is_customer* and at least 8 generators, giving at least 56 axioms (or conjuncts in post expressions). These axioms will typically be stating things like changing an address doesn't change the overdraft limit. This is clearly unmanageable.

Decomposition

One thing to note is that the type *Customer_details* could be defined in one module and used in that defining *Customer_info*. This immediately partitions the generators and observers into two sets. And since

    o1 * g1 + o2 * g2 < (o1 + o2) * (g1 + g2)

for positive numbers of observers and generators, this decomposition will certainly give a reduction in the overall number of axioms (or conjuncts). But there are still likely to be at least 36 axioms or conjuncts in the module defining *Customer_details*.

    We can easily deal with this situation as well. There is no reason not to use the record type directly for this type, as a direct translation of it is almost certainly adequate. This defines the observers directly. We can even define many of the *change_* functions directly as reconstructors, by

type

    Customer_details ::

        name : Name ↔ change_name

        address : Address ↔ change_address

        balance : **Int** ↔ change_balance

        pin : PIN_number ↔ change_pin

        expiry : Date ↔ change_expiry

        limit : **Int** ↔ change_limit

and we are probably finished — all the axioms we want relating the observers and generators are implicitly given in this record type definition. We may need a few extra generators to change more than one component (if, for example, a new PIN number is given as well as a new expiry date when a new card is issued to replace a lost one) but these can easily be defined explicitly in terms of those we have.

The type we probably do want to make abstract is *Customer_info* in the other module, because a simple implementation of the RSL map type is unlikely to be sufficiently efficient. We could do this from scratch, starting with generators like *empty* and *add*, but there is a solution that is generally easier, and that we have in fact adopted for the queue example. We define *Customer_info* as a sort and define a hidden observer *map_of*, say, with signature

$$\text{map\_of} : \text{Customer\_info} \rightarrow (\text{Customer\_id} \xrightarrow{m} \text{Customer\_details})$$

As in the queue example, we will find that all the other observers become derived and we are only left with the axioms relating *map_of* to the generators. Thus by adding one observer we can typically reduce $o * g$ axioms to o definitions plus g axioms. What is more, we can use all the predefined operators for RSL maps in our definitions and axioms, which tends to make them shorter and more readable.

This technique of starting with concrete type definitions and then finding a suitable decomposition and abstracting where appropriate is one that is generally very successful. It is often worth going further and writing down some of the concrete value definitions based on the concrete type before doing the abstraction step. This gives us confidence that we have all the data we need in the types, that we can model the problem in this way, and often helps in formulating the abstract version.

Invariants

Before we leave this example it is worth considering another issue. What if a customer has more than one account? (The converse, joint accounts, is also possible but we will not deal with it here.) To deal with multiple accounts we could add a new type *Account_number*, say, and split *Customer_details* into, say, *Personal_details* (like name and address, that are constant across accounts) and *Account_details* (like balance, that are particular to accounts). When we come to consider the concrete types there are several alternative ways of defining them. One possibility is

type
    Personal_info = Customer_id $\xrightarrow{m}$ Personal_details,
    Account_info = Account_number $\xrightarrow{m}$ Account_details

where we would include the account numbers particular to a customer as part of his or her personal details.

Another alternative is

type
    Customer_info = Customer_id $\xrightarrow{m}$ Customer_details,
    Customer_details ::
        person : Personal_details
        accounts : Account_number $\xrightarrow{m}$ Account_details

These two alternatives are illustrated on the left and right of figure 2.14, where *C_id* is *Customer_id*, *P_d* is *Personal_details*, *A_n* is *Account_number*, *A_d* is *Account_-details* and *C_d* is *Customer_details*.

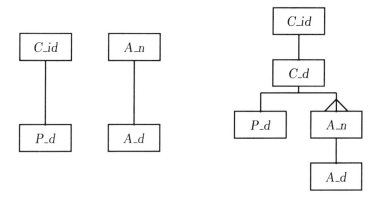

Figure 2.14: Entity relationship diagrams for bank accounts

Both these can hold the same information, but it turns out that the second of these is preferable even though at first sight it may look less natural (and may indeed be less like the final implementation where the two sets of data about customers are held separately). The entity relationship diagrams suggest that the second (on the right of figure 2.14) is better structured. There are two other reasons why the second is preferable:

- The first will need some axioms which are really invariants about the data: we will need to ensure that the set of account numbers in the domain of the second map is the union of all the account numbers found in the customer details, and that the sets of account numbers in different customer details are disjoint. No such axioms will be necessary in the second version. (It does not matter if account numbers are reused for different customers because the account details can only be found by knowing both the customer identifier and the account number.) It is this interdependence between the two maps in the first version that makes it difficult to use two modules corresponding to the two definitions, which is the first technique we considered to reduce complexity.
- When we create the abstract version, the first will need two observer functions, while the second needs only one. (It is possible to define a single observer in the first case but it would effectively be creating the second example in an obscure way.) This immediately tends to halve the number of axioms we need for the second compared to the first. We may need to define a few derived functions to unpack the more complicated data structure, but in general there is a definite gain.

There is a general rule that, where there are two maps with some invariant property relating them, a nested map structure is preferable. And one can draw the conclusion that a structure of type definitions that avoids (or reduces the complexity of) invariants is better than one that does not. We can see the solution with fewer invariants is a better fit to the problem. A similar example and discussion are in Jones' book on systematic software development [14].

2.8.4.3   Making functions total

We promised earlier to show how to make partial functions total. In our case *enq* and *deq* are the only partial functions provided by *A_QUEUE0*. We need first to define special values to indicate failure. For an observer or a result-returning generator (like *deq*) a convenient technique is to define a variant type, like

type Deq_result == deq_fail | deq_success(deq_res : P.Elem)

For a non-result-returning generator (like *enq*) we make it result-returning, the result being of a variant type like

type Enq_result == enq_fail | enq_success

We can now use these types to define an extension of *A_QUEUE0*:

scheme A_SAFE_QUEUE0(P : ELEM_BOUND) =
    hide enq, deq **in**
    extend A_QUEUE0(P) **with**
    class
      type
        Enq_result == enq_fail | enq_success,
        Deq_result == deq_fail | deq_success(deq_res : P.Elem)
      value
        safe_enq : P.Elem × Queue → Enq_result × Queue
        safe_enq(e,q) ≡
          if is_full(q) **then** (enq_fail,q) **else** (enq_success,enq(e,q)) **end**,
        safe_deq : Queue → Deq_result × Queue
        safe_deq(q) ≡
          if is_empty(q) **then** (deq_fail,q)
          else let (e,q') = deq(q) **in** (deq_success(e),q') **end end**
    end

For generators like *enq* and *deq*, as well as defining new results we need to decide what will be the new *Queue* value when they fail to have their normal effect. The most common thing to choose is (as here) to make the value unchanged.

It is also possible, of course, to define *A_SAFE_QUEUE0* from scratch rather than as an extension to *A_QUEUE0*, starting with the appropriate total types for *enq* and *deq* and otherwise following the method used for *A_QUEUE0*.

2.8.4.4 Method summary: abstract applicative formulation

1. Decide on the type of interest and whether it needs to be formulated as an abstract type. If it can be made concrete (including the use of a record), define it that way.
2. Consider whether the module should be decomposed into simpler ones. This sometimes occurs quite naturally because there seems to be more than one type of interest (often a main type and component types that could be defined separately). Decomposition can also be needed when there are more than two generators that are not constants or derived. If the module should be decomposed, do so, using the method for each module.
3. Consider whether the other types involved should come from a parameter (for a generic module) or from a global type module, and either define the parameter module or make sure the type module contains what is needed.
4. Formulate the signatures of the constants and functions needed. If the functions are not immediately total, decide between making them partial and making them total with result types that are variants including status values. For partial functions formulate their preconditions, which may suggest more observers. If the type of interest is concrete, add their definitions and go to step 11.
5. Classify the constants and functions into generators and observers according to whether or not the type of interest occurs (directly or indirectly) in their types (for constants) or result types (for functions).
6. Consider whether any generators or observers can be defined in terms of others, and if so give them explicit definitions and re-classify them as derived.
7. Consider whether a variant type or short record definition should be used for the type of interest, and if so formulate it. Remember to include any observers as destructors if appropriate. Remember to check that generators made into constructors are total; add new constructors and define the partial ones in terms of them otherwise.
8. For all the non-derived generators (including the constructors if a variant type definition is being used) and for observers that are not derived or defined as destructors, try to formulate the observational axioms. Remember to give axioms names.
9. If these axioms cannot be formulated, either invent one or more extra observers and return to step 6, or add generator–generator axioms, but be careful about the latter.
10. For the non-derived partial functions add definedness axioms.
11. Hide any functions and types that are not required to be available outside the module.
12. Include comments aimed at helping future readers to read and comprehend the module quickly.
13. Use tools if available to check the module is well-formed (no syntax, scope or type errors).

14. Use tools if available to generate and check confidence conditions for the module (see section 4.1.2).

15. If not entirely satisfied, keep iterating.

2.8.4.5   Concrete applicative queue

The main step in formulating a concrete applicative module from an abstract one is to decide on a suitable type to use for the abstract type *Queue*. The simplest choice is to take the product of the result types of the non-derived observers (or just the result type if there is only one). This will be an adequate basis for a concrete implementation since we know that all the non-derived observers can be defined in terms of it (they will just extract the corresponding component), the other observers are by construction derived, and all the properties of the generators are given in terms of the observers.

This assumes the non-derived observers have types of the form

$T \rightarrow U$

where T is the type of interest. If such an observer has a type of the form

$T \times U \rightarrow V$

then the contribution to the concrete type will be "$U \rightarrow V$", as if the observer's type had been written instead in a "curried" style

$T \rightarrow U \rightarrow V$

In *A_QUEUE0* we have just one non-derived observer, *list_of*, with type

Queue $\rightarrow$ List_of_Queue

and so the suggestion for the concrete type is its result type, *List_of_Queue*, i.e. bounded lists of elements. But before making this choice we need to consider the route to the final code in our programming language. There are several possibilities:

- We have an automatic translator that translates RSL lists. This translation is likely to use linked lists. Is this appropriate for our purposes? This is not immediately obvious for a queue, because we will be putting things on the back of the list when we do an enqueue. If the queue is long this will be quite inefficient. An implementation like one in which pointers to both ends of the queue are maintained, or (since we have a bounded list) a circular buffer, will be much more efficient. If we want such a special translation, it may be appropriate to go ahead with the development into RSL lists, translate using the translator and then modify the code to get an efficient translation. Effectively we use the translator to provide us with a template.

- If we decide we need a special implementation, such as a circular buffer, we may have one already available in a library of standard data types, in which case we should develop by defining a concrete queue in terms of it. There should already be a translation so we would then be finished.

- Otherwise we might decide that a circular buffer would be a useful addition to the library and we develop one first, and then use it as in the previous case.

In this tutorial we will present two applicative developments of the queue, one in terms of the RSL list constructor and one in terms of a circular buffer defined in terms of an array. The array module *A_ARRAY* is among the standard modules defined in appendix A and we assume there is already an implementation of it in our programming language.

2.8.4.6   Development to single applicative

The simplest style of development is to choose to develop the type of interest into a concrete RSL type that does not involve a type of interest from another system module, so that our module remains "single". For the concrete queue we can define

type Queue = {| l : P.Elem* • **len** l ≤ P.bound |}

Then we try to give definitions to all the constants and functions in terms of the operators available for lists in RSL. (Effectively we are making the observer *list_of* an identity.) We should get something like *A_QUEUE1*:

scheme A_QUEUE1(P : ELEM_BOUND) =
   class
      type Queue = {| l : P.Elem* • **len** l ≤ P.bound |}
      value
         /∗ generators ∗/
         empty : Queue = ⟨⟩,
         enq : P.Elem × Queue $\xrightarrow{\sim}$ Queue
         enq(e, q) ≡ q ⌃ ⟨e⟩ **pre** ∼ is_full(q),
         deq : Queue $\xrightarrow{\sim}$ P.Elem × Queue
         deq(q) ≡ (**hd** q, **tl** q) **pre** ∼ is_empty(q),
         /∗ observers ∗/
         is_full : Queue → **Bool**
         is_full(q) ≡ **len** q = P.bound,
         is_empty : Queue → **Bool**
         is_empty(q) ≡ q = ⟨⟩
end

Note we have made all the constant and function definitions explicit. This is often enough for the specification to be translatable.

We would like to state and justify a development relation between the abstract and concrete queues in a development relation. We need, as we did in section 2.7.5.1, to use an extension since *A_QUEUE1* does not define the entities *list_of* and *List_of_Queue* that were hidden in *A_QUEUE0*. This gives the development relation *A_QUEUE0_1*:

development_relation [A_QUEUE0_1]
   class object P : ELEM_BOUND **end** ⊢
      extend A_QUEUE1(P) **with**
         class
            type List_of_Queue = {| l : P.Elem* • **len** l ≤ P.bound |}

value
        list_of : Queue → List_of_Queue
        list_of(q) ≡ q
    end
    ⪯ A_QUEUE0(P)

The relation stated in this development relation is more complicated than those we have seen previously. We are formulating a relation between parameterized schemes *A_QUEUE0* and *A_QUEUE1*. To do so we need to create class expressions by applying the schemes to a suitable object. The schemes both have a formal parameter whose body is *ELEM_BOUND*, so we define an object with body *ELEM_BOUND* in the context of the implementation relation.

Confidence conditions

As well as checking that we have implementation we should be aware of possible inconsistencies in concrete modules. If there is an inconsistency it is possible to prove **true** = **false**, which means it is possible to prove anything, including the development relation we just asserted. We can look for some common forms of inconsistency by generating and justifying *confidence conditions* for a module. Confidence conditions are described in detail in section 4.1.2. Here we note that the most common conditions for applicative specifications are:

- For applications of functions or operators, any preconditions are true and the arguments are in the appropriate subtypes.
- For constant and function declarations, defining expressions are in the appropriate subtypes.

Confidence conditions can be generated by a tool. If we generate them for *A_QUEUE1*, in the first category we find that the applications of **hd** and **tl** in the body of *deq* both generate the condition that *q* is not empty, which is provable from the precondition of *deq*.

In the second category we find the conditions that the defining expression for *empty* and the bodies of *enq* and *deq* are in the subtype *Queue*, i.e. lists of length at most *P.bound*. These can also be justified. For *empty* we need the condition that *P.bound* is not negative, and for *enq* we need, as well as the subtype condition on the argument *q*, the precondition that the length of *q* is not already equal to *P.bound*.

Experience suggests that it is generally very useful to generate and inspect confidence conditions, as they often point to things that have been overlooked. It is usually sufficient to justify them only informally (as we did in the previous paragraph) rather than go through what can be quite tedious proofs. As their name suggests, confidence conditions are intended to help give more confidence in a specification, and in particular that particular kinds of common slips have been avoided. If the specification is inconsistent because a condition is not met, it is possible to prove anything about it — including its confidence conditions! So any proof of confidence conditions itself needs inspection to make sure it is not covering up an inconsistency.

2.8.4.7 Development to composite applicative

As in the previous version using the RSL list type, the aim is to make the abstract type *Queue* concrete. But instead of using the built-in type we will use a type provided (in part) by another module. The other module will become a supplier and the composite module its client. We start by considering the standard module *A_ARRAY* defined in appendix A.6.

This is constructed in the way described earlier for applicative modules. There is a generator *change* and an observer *apply*.

We can use the version of arrays without initialisation since the use of an array to model the queue will never apply an array to an index without previously setting the array for that index. *ARRAY_PARM* defines the type *Elem* as abstract, but makes the *Index* type the integers in a non-empty finite range. This is a restriction for the users of arrays but will make it possible for the developers of the array module to use finite arrays in an implementation. We allow *min* to be any integer rather than, say, zero, to allow flexibility.

To use the array as a circular buffer for the queue we need to define a concrete type for *Queue*. Since this concrete type will involve an array, we need to to instantiate *A_ARRAY*. This in turn means creating an object to meet the parameter requirement *ARRAY_PARM*.

A suitable concrete type for a queue is a product of an array, a value representing the current length of the queue, and an index representing the current position of the front of the queue, collectively forming a "circular buffer".

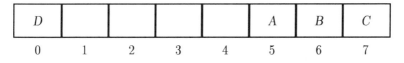

Figure 2.15: Circular buffer

Figure 2.15 illustrates a circular buffer of *bound* 8 holding the values *A*, *B*, *C*, *D* with *A* at the front. Hence the front position is 5 and the length is 4. To enqueue a value we calculate the appropriate position as the sum of the front and length modulo *bound*, i.e. $(5 + 4) \setminus 8$, which is 1. So an enqueue will be done by changing the array at position 1 and increasing the length to 5. To dequeue a value we return the value (*A*) at the front position, increment the front position modulo *bound* and decrement the length.

We then ask whether all such triples must represent queue values, or whether we should use subtypes. We note immediately that the length of a queue must lie between zero and *bound* inclusive. We also realize that we are using an uninitialised array for which *apply* is partial, while for a non-empty queue we must be able to obtain values within the queue. Hence we will need two subtypes, one for the length component and one for the triple:

type

Queue = {| (a, n, f) : A.Array × Length × A.Index • is_queue((a, n, f)) |},

Length = {| n : **Nat** • P.bound ≥ n |}

value

/∗ invariant ∗/

is_queue : A.Array × Length × A.Index → **Bool**

is_queue((a, n, f)) ≡

   (∀ i : **Nat** • i ∈ { 1 .. n } ⇒

      let k = (i + f − 1) \ P.bound **in** A.apply(k, a) **post true end**)

where *A* is an object which is an instance of *A_ARRAY*. We define this by

object

   X :

      class

         type Elem = P.Elem

         value min : **Nat** = 0, max : **Nat** = P.bound − 1

      end,

   A : A_ARRAY(X)

Note that where possible (as in the type *Length*) we use subtypes of components. The function *is_queue* could be unfolded and its definition removed, but it is generally clearer to define it separately and we shall see it plays a special role when we come to do the development to the imperative queue. This is why we use the comment that it represents an invariant. Note also that it is defined over the product *A.Array* × *Length* × *A.Index*, not over the type *Queue* it is used to define. (If any observers were used in its definition, these must also be defined over the product.)

We have chosen zero for *min* on the assumption that we know our intended programming language and this is how arrays are indexed in that language (and because it simplifies the definitions of our functions). We could if we wished defer this decision (and even allow the array to be larger than we need) by using an axiom in the object *X*:

object

   X :

      class

         type Elem = P.Elem

         value min, max : **Int**

         axiom [array_large_enough] max − min ≥ P.bound − 1

      end,

   A : A_ARRAY(X)

Note that in each case we can prove the axiom from *ARRAY_PARM*, that *max* ≥ *min*, from the condition in *ELEM_BOUND* that *P.bound* > 0. So the object *X* is in each case a suitable actual parameter for *A_ARRAY*.

Finally we hide anything either not defined or hidden in the abstract module, giving us *A_QUEUE2*:

scheme A_QUEUE2(P : ELEM_BOUND) =
   hide X, A, Length, is_queue **in**
   class
     object
       X :
         class
           type Elem = P.Elem
           value min : **Nat** = 0, max : **Nat** = P.bound $-$ 1
         end,
       A : A_ARRAY(X)
     type
       Queue = {| (a, n, f) : A.Array $\times$ Length $\times$ A.Index • is_queue((a, n, f)) |}
       Length = {| n : **Nat** • P.bound $\geq$ n |}
     value
       /∗ generators ∗/
       empty : Queue,
       enq : P.Elem $\times$ Queue $\xrightarrow{\sim}$ Queue
       enq(e, (a, n, f)) $\equiv$
         let back = (f + n) \ P.bound **in**
           (A.change(back, e, a), n + 1, f)
         end
         pre $\sim$ is_full((a, n, f)),
       deq : Queue $\xrightarrow{\sim}$ P.Elem $\times$ Queue
       deq((a, n, f)) $\equiv$
         let f′ = (f + 1) \ P.bound **in** (A.apply(f, a), (a, n $-$ 1, f′)) **end**
         pre $\sim$ is_empty((a, n, f)),
       /∗ observers ∗/
       is_full : Queue $\rightarrow$ **Bool**
       is_full((a, n, f)) $\equiv$ n = P.bound,
       is_empty : Queue $\rightarrow$ **Bool**
       is_empty((a, n, f)) $\equiv$ n = 0,
       /∗ invariant ∗/
       is_queue : A.Array $\times$ Length $\times$ A.Index $\rightarrow$ **Bool**
       is_queue((a, n, f)) $\equiv$
         ($\forall$ i : **Nat** • i $\in$ { 1 .. n } $\Rightarrow$
           let k = (i + f $-$ 1) \ P.bound **in** A.apply(k, a) **post true end**)
    axiom [empty_ax] is_empty(empty)
   end

Although the module is otherwise concrete, *empty* is still only characterized by an axiom, *empty_ax*. This is because any circular buffer with zero length can represent an empty queue; it does not matter what the contents of the array or the front position are.

We have used the same idea as we did in constructing *A_QUEUE1*; we have omitted the hidden *list_of* and *List_of_Queue* from *A_QUEUE2*. The development relation is *A_QUEUE0_2*:

development_relation [A_QUEUE0_2]
  class object P : ELEM_BOUND **end** ⊢
    extend A_QUEUE2(P) **with**
      class
        type List_of_Queue = {| l : P.Elem* • **len** l ≤ P.bound |}
        value
          list_of : Queue → List_of_Queue
          list_of(q) ≡
            if is_empty(q) **then** ⟨⟩
            else let (e, q′) = deq(q) **in** ⟨e⟩ ⌢ list_of(q′) **end**
            end
      end
    ⪯ A_QUEUE0(P)

As with the single concrete module *A_QUEUE1* we should also generate confidence conditions for *A_QUEUE2*. We obtain:

- a subtype condition from the definition of *X.max* that *P.bound* is at least 1
- subtype conditions that the defining expressions of *enq* and *deq* are in the subtype *Queue*
- conditions from the three places where the remainder by *P.bound* is calculated that *P.bound* is not zero
- conditions from the applications of *A.change* in *enq* and *A.apply* in *is_queue* that their first arguments, *back* and *k* respectively, are in the subtype *A.Index*

Most of these are immediate from the restriction that *P.bound* is strictly positive and the definitions of *X.max* and *X.min*. The conditions that *enq* and *deq* give queue values involves checking that the new lengths and front indices are in the right ranges and that *is_queue* is true, i.e. that the array can safely be applied to any index from the front of the queue to the back. For *deq* this is immediate since the queue is shortened. For *enq* the queue is lengthened by one and the last element set by *change*. We know that *apply* can be used for any changed index from the *apply_change* axiom in *A_ARRAY*. Checking these results carefully will give us confidence that we have not made any "off by one" errors that are common in using arrays.

2.8.5   Imperative queue

The main development method we adopt in this tutorial is as follows. For each module:

- Formulate an abstract applicative module first, then

- Formulate a concrete applicative module and show it implements the abstract applicative one, then
- Formulate a concrete imperative module from the concrete applicative one.
- If we want a concurrent module, formulate it from the imperative one.

The formulation of the concrete imperative module follows from the concrete applicative one in a very precise manner, and its properties are related to those of the concrete applicative one in a similarly precise manner. The same applies to developing the concrete concurrent module from the concrete imperative. This makes the formulation of abstract imperative or concurrent modules in general unnecessary. This style is proposed since the justifications to be done about correctness then come in the following places:

1. development from abstract applicative to concrete applicative
2. development from concrete imperative to concrete imperative
3. development from concrete concurrent to concrete concurrent

We do not in general do justifications about the step from applicative to imperative or imperative to concurrent because these steps are done according to precise rules (and could largely be automated).

The first kind of justification arises mainly from development of data structures. The justifications tend to cover the whole module. The second and third kinds come mainly from algorithm development, and the justifications tend to be local to particular functions. This approach also avoids the more difficult kinds of justifications relating abstract to concrete imperative and concurrent specifications.

However, this method does depend on doing standard steps from applicative to imperative and imperative to concurrent in a particular way. This allows us to infer rather than state the abstract properties of the imperative or concurrent versions. For many applications this should be sufficient, but for critical systems, or critical properties like safety properties, it may be necessary to state and prove the abstract imperative or concurrent properties. So in section 2.8.5.1 we describe how to formulate an abstract imperative queue. At a first reading readers may want to skip this section and go straight to the concrete version in section 2.8.5.2.

2.8.5.1   Abstract imperative queue

The method of this section can only be used if the generators are all either constants or have only one mention of the type of interest in their parameter types. It cannot be used, for example, for a *Tree* type with definition

type Tree == empty | node(Tree, Elem, Tree)

because *node* has two mentions of *Tree* in its parameter type. In such a case the method of section 2.8.5.3 may be used. An abstract applicative module may be used in that section instead of a concrete one, and, since types like *Tree* above can usually be translated directly using pointers, there may be no need to develop the abstract applicative module further. Alternatively, a development using object arrays is described in section 3.8.4.

We suggest formulating the applicative version of a module first. The abstract imperative version can then be constructed by the following method:

- Use the same module parameter (if any) as in the applicative module.
- Define imperative function signatures.
- Copy any auxiliary type or value definitions from the applicative module. (These are definitions not involving the type of interest.)
- Define imperative axioms.
- Define the bodies of derived imperative functions.
- Consider defining an initial axiom.
- Hide (the counterpart of) anything that was hidden in the applicative module.

We now consider in more detail the definitions of the imperative function signatures, axioms, function bodies and initial axioms.

Defining imperative function signatures

For each constant whose type is the type of interest we define a function with the same name of type **Unit** → **write any Unit**.

For each generator and each observer in the applicative module we define a function of the same name whose type is constructed from the corresponding applicative function's type by:

1. removing occurrences of the type of interest from the parameter and result types
2. inserting **Unit** in the parameter or result type if the type of interest was the only type in the parameter or result type respectively
3. retaining the total or partial function arrow
4. inserting **write any** in the case of a generator and **read any** in the case of an observer.

Defining imperative axioms

For each observer–constant and observer–generator axiom in the applicative module we define an axiom where:

1. the axiom name is the same as the applicative version
2. quantification is like the applicative version but without the quantification over the type of interest
3. the precondition (if any) is formulated using the function(s) that correspond to the functions used in the applicative precondition.
4. the body of the axiom takes one of the following forms:

   - If the applicative axiom is an equivalence

     $$obs(x,gen(y,q)) \equiv e$$

     where q is of the type of interest, the imperative axiom has the form

     $$gen(y) \; ; \; obs(x) \equiv gen(y) \; ; \; e'$$

where e' is the imperative counterpart of e.

If e mentions any observers (and remember our method precludes e from mentioning generators), let expressions are needed to ensure that these observers are evaluated on the right-hand side before the generator. For example, an applicative axiom often takes the form

$$\text{obs}(x,\text{gen}(y,q)) \equiv g(\text{obs}(f(x,y),q),z)$$

for some functions f, g and expression z. Here the imperative axiom would take the form

$$\text{gen}(y) ; \text{obs}(x) \equiv \textbf{let } r = \text{obs}(f(x,y)) \textbf{ in } \text{gen}(y) ; g(r,z) \textbf{ end}$$

- If the applicative axiom is a postcondition

  $$\text{gen}(x,q) \textbf{ as } (r,q') \textbf{ post } ... \text{obs}(y,q) ... \text{obs}(z,q') ... \textbf{ pre } ... \text{obs}(w,q) ...$$

  then the imperative one also involves a postcondition, and has the form

  $$\textbf{let } a = \text{obs}(y) \textbf{ in } \text{gen}(x) \textbf{ as } r \textbf{ post } ... a ... \text{obs}(z) ... \textbf{ pre } \text{obs}(w) ... \textbf{ end}$$

  Note that observers applied to q must be dealt with by introducing let expressions; observers applied to q' just become imperative observers.

There may also be other axioms in the applicative version. These may generally be dealt with using the techniques described in section 2.9.

Defining imperative derived functions

We also need to consider any functions that were derived in the applicative version, i.e. were given explicit definitions. In this case the bodies are rewritten using the corresponding imperative functions. Nested application must be replaced by let expressions or sequencing to ensure the evaluation order is correct. For example, if we start with the applicative expression

$$\text{obs1}(x,\text{obs2}(y,q),\text{gen}(z,q))$$

the evaluation order (being innermost first, and left to right if there are several parameters) is *obs2, gen, obs1*. Hence the imperative version of this expression is

$$\textbf{let } a = \text{obs2}(y) \textbf{ in } \text{gen}(z) ; \text{obs1}(x,a) \textbf{ end}$$

Defining an initial axiom

We also need to consider adding an *initial axiom*, to state what queue we want to have initially. We can leave this underspecified by not including such an axiom, but typically it is required. There are two ways to do this.

1. If there is a suitable generator like *empty* we can write

   axiom

   $[\text{initial}]$ **initialise** $\equiv$ **initialise** ; empty() $\hspace{2cm}$ (1)

   This says that *empty* does nothing new to the initial state, so one possible eventual implementation would be to initialise the queue by calling *empty*. It is possible to write, instead of the body of (1),

   initialise $\equiv$ empty() $\hspace{4cm}$ (2)

but for some developments (2) is too strong. If we have several variables and/or imperative supplier modules, the form (2) would force us to implement *empty* as initialising all of them, and this may be unnecessary. For example, in section 2.8.5.4 we develop the queue using a circular buffer and all *empty* needs to do is set the length of the buffer to zero.

2. If there is a suitable observer like *is_empty* we can write

axiom
    [initial] **initialise post** is_empty()

This is effectively the same as (1) and is perhaps clearer.

If we develop from an abstract imperative module to a concrete single imperative module (like *I_QUEUE1* in section 2.8.5.3), we will normally include suitable initial values for the variables we introduce and the initial axiom in the abstract module will be satisfied. If we develop to a composite imperative module (like *I_QUEUE2* in section 2.8.5.4), the initial axiom will normally be satisfied by the initial values of variables and the initial properties of the imperative supplier modules.

Following this method gives the following abstract imperative queue:

scheme I_QUEUE0(P : ELEM_BOUND) =
    hide List_of_Queue, list_of **in**
    class
        type List_of_Queue = {| l : P.Elem* • **len** l ≤ P.bound |}
        value
            /∗ generators ∗/
            empty : **Unit → write any Unit,**
            enq : P.Elem $\xrightarrow{\sim}$ **write any Unit,**
            deq : **Unit** $\xrightarrow{\sim}$ **write any** P.Elem,
            /∗ hidden observer ∗/
            list_of : **Unit → read any** List_of_Queue,
            /∗ derived ∗/
            is_full : **Unit → read any Bool**
            is_full() ≡ **len** list_of() = P.bound,
            is_empty : **Unit → read any Bool**
            is_empty() ≡ list_of() = ⟨⟩
        axiom
            [list_of_empty] empty() ; list_of() ≡ empty() ; ⟨⟩,
            [list_of_enq]
                ∀ e : P.Elem •
                    enq(e) ; list_of() ≡ **let** l = list_of() **in** enq(e) ; l ^ ⟨e⟩ **end**
                pre ∼ is_full(),
            [deq_ax]
                let l = list_of() **in**
                    deq() **as** e **post** e = **hd** l ∧ list_of() = **tl** l **pre** ∼ is_empty()
                end,
            [enq_defined] enq() **post true pre** ∼ is_full(),

[initial] **initialise post** is_empty()
   end

It should be clear that the imperative module will behave just like the applicative one, though it is perhaps not so clear just how to formalize "just like". We will come back to this issue in section 2.9.

2.8.5.2   Concrete imperative queue

As stated earlier in section 2.8.5 the main method being proposed here means that we have formulated the abstract applicative module (*A_QUEUE0* in our case) and developed this to either a single concrete applicative module (like *A_QUEUE1*) or a composite concrete applicative module (like *A_QUEUE2*). We show in the next two sections how to continue by developing a single concrete imperative module in the first case, and a composite concrete imperative module in the second.

2.8.5.3   Development to single imperative

The single concrete imperative module *I_QUEUE1* is developed from the applicative version *A_QUEUE1* by the following overall method:

- Use the same module parameter (if any) as in the applicative module.
- Define the state variable(s).
- Define an object as an instance of the applicative module:

  object A : A_QUEUE1(P)

- Define imperative functions.
- It is normally the case that the applicative module has no axioms, because we developed it applicatively first. But if it does, deal with them by creating corresponding imperative axioms, using the same technique as we used to develop the axioms in *I_QUEUE0* in section 2.8.5.1.
- Hide the variable(s) plus (the counterpart of) anything that was hidden in the applicative module plus A (unless it has been removed during the function definition stage).

We now consider in more detail the definitions of the state variables and of the imperative functions.

Defining state variables
We define a variable whose type is the concrete type of interest (*Queue* in this case):

variable queue : $\{| \ l : \text{P.Elem}^* \bullet \textbf{len } l \leq \text{P.bound} \ |\} := \langle \rangle$

It is quite likely that the concrete type of interest is a product (since this is how we suggested developing the applicative version when there is more than one non-derived observer). If so it is natural to define a variable for each component of the product.

We have also given the variable an initial value, making the queue initially empty. It is good practice always to give initial values for variables, even when a suitable value does not immediately suggest itself.

Defining imperative functions

For each constant whose type is the type of interest we define a function with the same name of type **Unit** → **write any Unit** that assigns to the variable(s) (*queue* in our case) the corresponding applicative value(s):

value

   empty : **Unit** → **write any Unit**
   empty() ≡ queue := A.empty

For each generator and each observer in the applicative module define a function of the same name whose type is constructed from the corresponding applicative function's type by:

1. removing occurrences of the type of interest from the parameter and result types
2. inserting **Unit** in the parameter or result type if the type of interest was the only type in the parameter or result type respectively
3. retaining the total or partial function arrow
4. inserting **write any** in the case of a generator and **read any** in the case of an observer.
5. adding bodies involving the variable(s) v, say, as follows:

   - An observer will have a body of the form
     obs(x) ≡ A.obs(x,v)
   - A non-result-returning generator will have a body of the form
     gen(x) ≡ v := A.gen(x,v)
   - A result-returning generator will have a body of the form
     gen(x) ≡ **let** (r,v′) = A.gen(x,v) **in** v := v′ ; r **end**

6. adding preconditions which are obtained from the applicative preconditions by using the corresponding imperative functions.

This gives a first (and adequate) set of function definitions. But we can often improve on these by "unfolding" the mentions of the applicative functions. For instance, the imperative definition of *deq* obtained by the above procedure is

   deq() ≡ **let** (r,q′) = A.deq(queue) **in** queue := q′ ; r **end**

"Unfolding" the applicative function gives

   deq() ≡ **let** (r,q′) = (**hd** queue, **tl** queue) **in** queue := q′ ; r **end**

and we have removed the call of the applicative function.

We can easily simplify this a little further, but it needs care and since we do not expect this step to be formally verified, but rather informally by quality control as "correct by construction" we would not advise taking it any further. If we wish we can even leave the original form mentioning *A.deq* and do the unfolding (and perhaps simplification) as a further development step. Since this further step will relate two concrete imperative specifications using the same types and variables, it is easily justified.

It should be apparent that by this unfolding we can often remove all occurrences of the applicative observers and generators. If this is so, it is tempting to remove the object *A*. However, doing so is only sensible if we are sure that the applicative module will never be modified and will never be used elsewhere, i.e. it was developed purely as a step in the construction of the imperative one. If these conditions are not met, removing it is likely to lead to duplicated code. For the purpose of our example we will assume these conditions are met and remove the applicative object.

Following this method gives the concrete imperative queue *I_QUEUE1*:

scheme I_QUEUE1(P : ELEM_BOUND) = **hide** queue **in** I_QUEUE1_BODY(P)

scheme I_QUEUE1_BODY(P : ELEM_BOUND) =
  class
    variable queue : {| l : P.Elem* • **len** l ≤ P.bound |} := ⟨⟩
    value
      /∗ generators ∗/
      empty : **Unit** → **write any Unit**
      empty() ≡ queue := ⟨⟩,
      enq : P.Elem $\xrightarrow{\sim}$ **write any Unit**
      enq(e) ≡ queue := queue ^ ⟨e⟩ **pre** ∼ is_full(),
      deq : **Unit** $\xrightarrow{\sim}$ **write any** P.Elem
      deq() ≡
        let (r, q′) = (**hd** queue, **tl** queue) **in** queue := q′ ; r **end**
        pre ∼ is_empty(),
      /∗ observers ∗/
      is_full : **Unit** → **read any Bool**
      is_full() ≡ **len** queue = P.bound,
      is_empty : **Unit** → **read any Bool**
      is_empty() ≡ queue = ⟨⟩
  end

We have chosen to separate out the "body" of *I_QUEUE1* as a separate module. The reason for this is that we want later on to express an implementation relation between *I_QUEUE1* and *I_QUEUE0* from the previous section. Using two modules where only one involves hiding makes this possible.

The method of formulation of *I_QUEUE1* from *A_QUEUE1* is quite precise and could be largely automated. Even if not automated it is so regular that it is very easy to check afterwards as part of quality assurance. It is possible, but somewhat complicated, to formalize the relationship between *A_QUEUE1* and *I_QUEUE1* (and we do this in section 2.9.3.1) but the idea behind our method is to make this step informal. It should be clear that the imperative module "behaves like" the applicative one and the idea is, generally, to leave this notion informal and check this step by quality assurance.

Before we finish this section we should comment on the relation between *LQUEUE1* and the abstract imperative module *LQUEUE0* developed in section 2.8.5.1. The relation is defined in the development relation *LQUEUE0_1*:

development_relation [LQUEUE0_1]
   class object P : ELEM_BOUND **end** ⊢

     extend LQUEUE1_BODY(P) **with**
       class
         type List_of_Queue = {| l : P.Elem* • **len** l ≤ P.bound |}
         value
           list_of : **Unit** → **read any** List_of_Queue
           list_of() ≡ queue
       end
     ⪯ LQUEUE0(P)

(It should now be apparent why we needed to define *LQUEUE1_BODY*; we need to be able to refer to the variable *queue* in the definition of *list_of*.) Justification of this relation is straightforward; part of it is done in section 4.4.6.

With the applicative version we also generated and checked confidence conditions. Do we need to do this for the imperative one? The answer is generally no. The conditions we obtain will mostly be the imperative counterparts of the applicative ones and will therefore hold by construction if we have followed the method carefully. In fact, if we generate the conditions for *LQUEUE1* we get conditions corresponding to those for *A_QUEUE1* plus a subtype one for the initialisation of the variable *queue*.

On the other hand, if we have made some other improvements as part of the applicative to imperative step, generating and inspecting the confidence conditions is a useful check that we have not made some kinds of mistake.

We also consider the relation of imperative confidence conditions to invariants in section 2.8.5.4.

2.8.5.4   Development to composite imperative

In the previous section 2.8.5.3 we developed a single concrete imperative module from a single concrete applicative module. In this section we will develop a composite concrete imperative module *LQUEUE2* from the composite concrete applicative *A_QUEUE2*. *LQUEUE2* will be a client of an imperative array module *LARRAY*, defined in section A.6. *LARRAY* is a standard module just like the applicative version *A_ARRAY* used by *A_QUEUE2*. It has been constructed from *A_ARRAY* in just the same way that *LQUEUE0* was constructed from *A_QUEUE0*. But the details of construction are not of much interest here: we expect to have a translation of imperative arrays already available. Hence we can just use the abstract module and develop it no further ourselves.

We can now develop the concrete imperative *I_QUEUE2* from the concrete applicative *A_QUEUE2* using a method very similar to that by which we developed the concrete imperative *I_QUEUE1* from the concrete applicative *A_QUEUE1*. The main difference is that the type of interest in *A_QUEUE2* is defined as (a subtype of) a product:

type
Queue = {| (a, n, f) : A.Array × Length × A.Index • is_queue((a, n, f)) |}

This suggests we might use three variables, one for each component. But in fact what we do is instantiate *I_ARRAY* as an object which will give us an imperative component object with a variable (or variables — we do not need to know how *I_ARRAY* is developed) for the first component. So we only need variables *length* and *front*, say, for the second and third components. The overall method is as follows:

- Instantiate imperative supplier modules.
- Add variables.
- Define imperative functions.
- Add axioms.
- Hide objects, variables and the counterparts to anything hidden in the applicative module.

We now consider in more detail the first four of these.

Instantiating imperative supplier modules
We replace the instantiations of the applicative module(s) (like *A_ARRAY*) with instantiations of the imperative module (like *I_ARRAY*) This may also involve copying other objects used to make actual parameters (like *X*). This gives

object
X : ...,
I : I_ARRAY(X)

Adding variables
We add variables for each component of the type of interest which is not the type of interest of a component module — if there are any such components. In our case there are two, and we have

variable
length : {| n : **Nat** • P.bound ≥ n |} := 0,
front : I.Index := X.min

Note that the type of *front* comes now from the object *I*.

Note also that we include initial values of the variables. We expect the queue to be initially empty, for which it is sufficient, as we shall see, to initialise only the *length* variable. *front* is initialised (arbitrarily) to the lowest value in its type.

Defining imperative functions
We define the functions with the same signatures as we did in *I_QUEUE1*.

We want to supply concrete definitions for each of the functions that correspond to concrete definitions in *A_QUEUE2* (which are all of them except *empty*). First, preconditions are written just like their applicative counterparts, using the corresponding imperative functions by dropping the type of interest parameters. In addition, if the applicative function has the type of interest *Queue* as a parameter (rather than the product type *A.Array* × *Length* × *A.Index*), it is normal to conjoin a call of the invariant function to the precondition. This is because the applicative version implicitly includes the subtype constraint on the type *Queue*. In the imperative version we are instead using the variables of this and component modules. These variables do not (separately) ensure that the subtype constraint on *Queue* is met. We can omit the condition if we are sure it is irrelevant. In our case *is_queue* provides a convergence condition for *apply* from the array module. This is obviously relevant to *deq*. If *apply* is not mentioned (directly or indirectly) in the body of a function, and we are convinced that no later development of such a function will cause it to be mentioned, there is no need to include *is_queue* in the function's precondition. We have only added a call of *is_queue* to the precondition of *deq*.

The bodies of the functions are constructed directly from those in *A_QUEUE2*. That is:

- An applicative observer will have a definition

  obs(x,(p,q,r,...)) ≡ expr

  and the imperative one will have the form

  obs(x) ≡ expr′

  We need to formulate *expr′*.

  The names *p,q,r,...* are bindings for the components of the applicative type of interest. These correspond either to the type of interest of a component imperative module or to one of the variables defined in this module.

  Suppose *p* corresponds to the type of interest of a component module. Then *p* will only occur in *expr* as an argument of an observer of a component applicative module and we just replace it with its imperative counterpart, dropping the type of interest parameter. So an expression in *expr* of the form

  A.obs(y,p)

  becomes in *expr′* an expression of the form

  I.obs(y)

  Suppose *q* corresponds to a variable *qv* defined in this module. Then occurrences of *q* in *expr* simply become occurrences of *qv* in *expr′*. This gives the following definitions for the observers:

value
　　is_full : **Unit** → **read any Bool**
　　is_full() ≡ length = P.bound,

is_empty : **Unit** → **read any Bool**
is_empty() ≡ length = 0

- Now we deal with the generators. These will take the applicative form

  gen(x,(p,q,r,...)) ≡ ... (e,(e1,e2,e3,...))

where *e* will be omitted if the generator is not result-returning.

The imperative counterpart we are trying to construct will take the form

gen(x) ≡ ... **let** z = e′ **in** e1′ ; e2′ ; e3′ ; ... z **end**

where, again, the let expression will be omitted if the generator is not result-returning.

Suppose again *p* is of the type of interest of a component module and *q* corresponds to a variable *qv* in the imperative module.

If *p* occurs as an argument of an applicative observer or generator we just replace by the imperative counterpart, dropping the *p* parameter. In addition, if *e1* is *p*, *e1′* is just **skip** (and can be omitted); the intuition here is that this part of the state is not being changed.

In the case of *q*, we replace *q* by *qv* except within *e2′*. If *e2* is *q*, *e2′* is again just **skip**. But otherwise *e2′* becomes an assignment to *qv* of the expression obtained from *e2* by the other rules. So if *e2* is, say,

q − 1

then *e2′* will be

qv := qv − 1

We need to be careful if a mention of *p*, say, occurs in *e2*. This will cause a problem since by the time we evaluate *e2′* the state of the variable or module corresponding to *p* will have been changed by *e1′*. Usually this problem can be solved by changing the order of *e1′*, *e2′*, etc. to make sure such references always come before the corresponding assignment or function invocation, but sometimes extra let expressions are needed.

Finally we need to obtain *e′*. This is obtained from *e* in the standard way, except that we have to be careful to evaluate it *before* the state changes from *e1′*, etc. Otherwise a mention of *qv*, say, would refer to the wrong value. This is why the form we suggest above puts *e′* in a let expression.

This gives the following definitions for the generators:

value
    enq : P.Elem $\xrightarrow{\sim}$ **write any Unit**
    enq(e) ≡
        let back = (front + length) \ P.bound **in**
            I.change(back, e) ; length := length + 1
        end
        pre ∼ is_full(),

deq : **Unit** $\overset{\sim}{\rightarrow}$ **write any** P.Elem
deq() $\equiv$
    let f′ = (front + 1) \ P.bound **in**
      let e = I.apply(front) **in**
        length := length − 1 ; front := f′ ; e
      end
    end
    pre ∼ is_empty() ∧ is_queue()

Adding axioms

We also need to consider any axioms. In our case we have one applicative axiom

axiom [empty_ax] is_empty(empty)

It is possible to deal with this axiom in the manner suggested in section 2.8.5.1. This would give the imperative axiom

axiom [empty_ax] empty() ; is_empty() $\equiv$ empty() ; **true**

But we can often improve on this. We know the definition of *is_empty* just checks for the length variable having the value zero. So *empty* will satisfy this axiom if it just sets this variable to zero. Moreover there are no other constraints on *empty*. This allows us to complete the definition of *empty*:

value
    empty : **Unit** → **write any Unit**
    empty() $\equiv$ length := 0

This gives us *I_QUEUE2*:

scheme I_QUEUE2(P : ELEM_BOUND) =
    hide X, I, length, front, is_queue **in**
    class
      object
        X :
          class
            type Elem = P.Elem
            value min : **Nat** = 0, max : **Nat** = P.bound − 1
          end,
        I : I_ARRAY(X)
      variable
        length : {| n : **Nat** • P.bound $\geq$ n |} := 0,
        front : I.Index := X.min
      value
        /* generators */
        empty : **Unit** → **write any Unit**
        empty() $\equiv$ length := 0,

enq : P.Elem $\overset{\sim}{\to}$ **write any Unit**
enq(e) ≡
    let back = (front + length) \ P.bound **in**
        I.change(back, e) ; length := length + 1
    end
    pre ∼ is_full(),
deq : **Unit** $\overset{\sim}{\to}$ **write any** P.Elem
deq() ≡
    let f′ = (front + 1) \ P.bound **in**
        let e = I.apply(front) **in**
            length := length − 1 ; front := f′ ; e
        end
    end
    pre ∼ is_empty() ∧ is_queue(),
/∗ observers ∗/
is_full : **Unit** → **read any Bool**
is_full() ≡ length = P.bound,
is_empty : **Unit** → **read any Bool**
is_empty() ≡ length = 0,
/∗ invariant ∗/
is_queue : **Unit** → **read any Bool**
is_queue() ≡
    (∀ i : **Nat** • i ∈ { 1 .. length } ⇒
        let k = (i + front − 1) \ P.bound **in** I.apply(k) **post true end**)
end

It may seem strange that we do not include an axiom of the form

axiom [invariant] □ is_queue()

This would preclude the need to include the invariant condition in any preconditions and make it clear that it must hold after any functions have been called. The problem with such an axiom is that it would mean that a composite module like *LQUEUE2* would most likely be a non-conservative extension of its components. For example, such an invariant would typically restrict the application of component functions in certain situations when the component module itself includes no such restriction. We have already warned about making such non-conservative extensions; they suggest poor structuring and they increase the likelihood of inconsistencies. In fact this possibility of inconsistency can be demonstrated for *LQUEUE2*. In the body of *enq* we have the sequence

    I.change(back, e) ; length := length + 1

The two expressions in sequence are "assignment disjoint", i.e. they cannot affect the same variables, and so they can be commuted, giving the equivalent expression

    length := length + 1 ; I.change(back, e)

Suppose this equivalent were used in the body of *enq*. After the first expression and before the second the length has been increased by one but we do not know that *apply* applied to *back* would be convergent until after the call of *change*. So *is_queue* does not necessarily *always* hold. This may seem a rather subtle case but the problem is a general one, which is why there are no imperative invariants in RSL. The notion of imperative invariance is not compositional.

In the applicative types of *empty*, *enq* and *deq* in *A_QUEUE2* the subtype *Queue* appears as a result. Where is the imperative counterpart of this condition? That is, after calling the imperative *empty*, *enq* or *deq*, do we know the invariant *is_queue* will hold (assuming for *deq* and *enq* that the invariant and any other precondition held before the call)?

Such conditions are precisely the imperative counterparts of some of the applicative confidence conditions. So we know that, if we generated and checked them for the applicative specification *A_QUEUE2* and followed the method correctly, they will hold for the imperative version.

If we require more confidence that invariance is maintained, it is insufficient to generate confidence conditions for a composite module like *I_QUEUE2* because there is no subtype covering the separate components. So instead we formulate the appropriate theorem:

theorem [I_QUEUE2_INVARIANCE]
  extend class object P : ELEM_BOUND **end with** I_QUEUE2(P) ⊢
    (empty() **post** is_queue()) ∧
    (∀ e : P.Elem • enq(e) **post** is_queue() **pre** is_queue() ∧ ∼is_full()) ∧
    (deq() **post** is_queue() **pre** is_queue() ∧ ∼is_empty())

This theorem can then be justified. Theorems record, and provide an opportunity to justify, properties of modules that are not stated as axioms but that we believe follow from the definitions of the module. They are used for two kinds of property:

1. properties that are relevant to showing that a specification meets its requirements
2. properties that are useful in justifications — perhaps of development relations or other theorems

I_QUEUE2_INVARIANCE is an example of the first kind. The second is like the use of a lemma in a justification but allows the property to be proved separately and to be used in more than one justification.

Development relations are similar to theorems but are statements of a relation between modules rather than about a single module.

We now consider any simplifications that will give performance improvements, but there are not likely to be many, or at least not significant ones. Such improvements are likely to come from component modules rather than a module like *I_QUEUE2* that uses components. So, provided *I_QUEUE2* can be translated, we are finished with the RSL development. In particular, if there are still any axioms we shall have to think how to remove them. This will typically involve taking some more design decisions. We did this in the case of defining *empty*, by deciding that only the *length* variable would be changed. We could also have defined *empty* by

value
   empty : **Unit** → **write any Unit**
   empty() ≡ length := 0 ; front := X.min

to take just one example.

2.8.6   Concurrent queue

As we remarked at the start of section 2.8.5, the main development method we are following means that before developing a concurrent module an applicative version will have been created in first abstract and then concrete versions, and an imperative sequential one from the concrete applicative. A concrete concurrent version may then be formulated based on the imperative one.

In this section, as in the imperative sequential case, we present first an abstract concurrent version of the queue in section 2.8.6.1. This is not part of the main method and at a first reading the reader may want to skip this section and go straight to the concrete version in section 2.8.6.2.

2.8.6.1   Abstract concurrent queue

We suggest formulating the imperative version of a module first (normally by developing this from an applicative version as described in section 2.8.5.2).

The overall method is as follows:

- Use the same parameter module (if any) as in the imperative module.
- Define an object as an instance of the imperative module:
  object I : I_QUEUE0(P)
- Define a function *main*:
  value main : **Unit** → **in any out any write any Unit**
- Define an initial function.
- Define the interface function signatures.
- Define concurrent axioms.
- Hide the name (*I* in our case) of the object which is an instance of the imperative module and *main*.

We now consider in more detail the definitions of the initial function, the interface function signatures and the axioms.

Defining an initial function

For each function corresponding to a constant in the applicative module whose type is the type of interest we have a choice. Commonly there is only one such function, like *empty*, and we want to start the queue in the empty state and never reset it. In that case we define *empty* as in:

value
    empty : **Unit** → **in any out any write any Unit**
    empty() ≡ I.empty() ; main()

In this case we refer to *empty* as an *initial function*, one that should be called once to start the concurrent process.

    Or we may want to be able to reset the queue to empty occasionally, i.e. to have *empty* available in the same way as functions like *enq*. In this case we define *empty* as in :

value empty : **Unit** → **in any out any Unit**

(note there is no **write any**) and instead of giving it an explicit definition we define an axiom like the following:

axiom
    [empty_ax]
    main() ∦ empty() ≡ I.empty() ; main()

If *empty* is not an initial function, we still have the problem that we have to start the queue initially, which means calling *I.empty* followed by *main*. But we do not want to export the object *I* containing the state variables; these must only be affected by starting the queue and then using the queue's functions. So we define an initial function *init*, say, and define it as a call of *I.empty* followed by a call of *main*:

value
    init : **Unit** → **in any out any write any Unit**
    init() ≡ I.empty() ; main()

If there is no function like *I.empty*, it is possible to invent one and add it to the imperative module, but it is also possible to define the body of the initial function as "*I*.**initialise** ; *main()*" instead.

Defining interface function signatures

For each of the other functions in the imperative module we define a function of the same name whose type is constructed from the corresponding imperative function's type by

- using a total function arrow
- removing the access descriptor **read any** or **write any**
- inserting the access descriptor **in any out any**.

We will refer to the functions (plus *empty* if we defined a separate initial function) as *interface functions* as they provide the interface to the module. We thus distinguish them from *main* and the initial function. Only *main* and the initial function include **write any** in their signatures; the interface functions have no access to the variables of the imperative module. It is essential for RSL concurrency that functions that may execute concurrently do not share access to variables.

    Note that all the functions have total arrows. This is because we expect to develop the interface functions as simple sequences of inputs and outputs and *main* as a loop containing an external choice of simple sequences of inputs, outputs and assignments. Such functions are in general total, and defining them as such eases any justifications we may want to do. The partiality in concurrent specifications typically comes from the parallel or interlocked composition of such functions, not in the functions themselves.

Defining concurrent axioms

For each such interface function we define an axiom like one of those in *C_QUEUE0* below:

scheme C_QUEUE0(P : ELEM_BOUND) =
    hide I, main **in**
    class
        object I : I_QUEUE0(P)
        value
          /* main */
          main : **Unit $\rightarrow$ in any out any write any Unit**,
          /* initial */
          empty : **Unit $\rightarrow$ in any out any write any Unit**
          empty() $\equiv$ I.empty() ; main(),
          /* generators */
          enq : P.Elem $\rightarrow$ **in any out any Unit**,
          deq : **Unit $\rightarrow$ in any out any** P.Elem,
          /* observers */
          is_full : **Unit $\rightarrow$ in any out any Bool**,
          is_empty : **Unit $\rightarrow$ in any out any Bool**
        axiom
          [enq_ax]
            $\forall$ e : P.Elem •
              main() $\|$ enq(e) $\equiv$ I.enq(e) ; main() **pre** $\sim$ I.is_full(),
          [deq_ax]
            $\forall$ test : P.Elem $\overset{\sim}{\rightarrow}$ **Unit** •
              main() $\|$ test(deq()) $\equiv$
                 let e = I.deq() **in** main() $\|$ test(e) **end**
                 pre $\sim$ I.is_empty(),
          [is_full_ax]
            $\forall$ test : **Bool** $\overset{\sim}{\rightarrow}$ **Unit** •
              main() $\|$ test(is_full()) $\equiv$
                 let b = I.is_full() **in** main() $\|$ test(b) **end**,
          [is_empty_ax]
            $\forall$ test : **Bool** $\overset{\sim}{\rightarrow}$ **Unit** •
              main() $\|$ test(is_empty()) $\equiv$
                 let b = I.is_empty() **in** main() $\|$ test(b) **end**
    end

The construction of the axioms is the same in each case:

- The left-hand side is a call of *main* interlocked with a call of the interface function, and this call is an argument to a *test* function if the interface function has a result type that is not **Unit**. *test* functions are needed in such axioms because the interlock operator may only be used with operands of type **Unit**. The right-hand side takes one of two forms:

    - If the interface function has a result type **Unit**, it is a sequence of a call of the imperative function (with the same argument as the concurrent one) and a call of *main*.
    - If the interface function has some other result type, it is a let expression binding the result of a call of the imperative function (with the same argument as the concurrent one) followed by a call of *main* interlocked with the test function applied to the let binding.

- Preconditions are the same as in the imperative module.

The intuition behind constructing the module in this way is that it is now possible to evaluate expressions like

empty() ∦ enq(a) ∦ enq(b) ∦ **let** x = deq() **in** ... **end**

since under appropriate conditions such an expression can be shown to be equivalent to

I.empty() ; I.enq(a) ; I.enq(b) ; **let** x = I.deq() **in** main() ∦ ... **end**

and then further evaluated using the axioms for the imperative functions.

The "appropriate conditions" referred to above are in particular that the *main* process will complete an interlocked composition with each interface function. That is, an interlock of *main()* with a call of an interface function will (possibly) change the state of variables and (possibly) produce a result but will always allow the interface function to terminate and leave the main process running. This is ensured by the four axioms in *C_QUEUE0*. Effectively each interface function acts like a transaction that locks the main process. This makes the use of interlock very useful in specifications of data types like the queue. Interlock is not suitable for main processes that allow portions of the execution of interface functions to be interleaved. For example, we did not try to specify the lift system in terms of a single process that could both move the lift and allow buttons to be pressed. We would, for example, expect the button transaction to take place within a movement of the lift. Instead, we decomposed the lift system into component processes executing concurrently that would each complete one transaction at a time.

It should be clear that the concurrent module will behave just like the imperative one, though it is perhaps not so clear just how to formalize "just like". We will come back to this issue in section 2.9.

2.8.6.2   Concrete concurrent queue

As stated earlier in section 2.8.5 the method we are following means that we have formulated the abstract applicative module (*A_QUEUE0* in our case) and developed this to either a single concrete imperative module (like *I_QUEUE1*) or a composite concrete imperative module (like *I_QUEUE2*). We show in the next two sections 2.8.6.3 and 2.8.6.4 how to develop further to a single concrete concurrent module in the first case, and a composite concrete concurrent module in the second.

The use of an imperative module means that the design of the variable(s) and the algorithms to manipulate them sequentially is already done. All we need to do is design the concurrent control structure.

2.8.6.3   Development to single concurrent

The single concrete concurrent module *C_QUEUE1* is developed from the imperative version *I_QUEUE1* by the following overall method:

- Use the same module parameter (if any) as in the imperative module.
- Define an object as an instance of the imperative module:

    object I : I_QUEUE1(P)
- Define a function *main*:

    value main : **Unit → in any out any write any Unit**
- Define an initial function.
- Define interface function signatures.
- Define channels.
- Define interface function bodies.
- Define the body of *main*.
- Hide the object *I*, the channels and the function *main*.

We now consider the definitions of the initial function, interface function signatures, channels, interface function bodies and body of *main* in more detail.

Defining an initial function

For each function corresponding to a constant in the applicative module whose type is the type of interest we have a choice. Commonly there is only one such function, like *empty*, and we want to start the queue in the empty state and never reset it. In that case we define *empty* as in:

value

   empty : **Unit → in any out any write any Unit**
   empty() ≡ I.empty() ; main()

In this case we refer to *empty* as an *initial function*, one that should be called once to start the concurrent process.

Or we may want to be able to reset the queue to empty occasionally, i.e. to have *empty* available in the same way as functions like *enq*. In this case the type of *empty* will be as above but without the **write any**, and it will be defined like the other interface functions described below.

If *empty* is not an initial function, we still have the problem that we have to start the queue initially, which means calling *I.empty* followed by *main*. But we do not want to export the object *I* containing the state variables; these must only be affected by starting the queue and then using the queue's functions. So we define an initial function *init*, say, and define it as a call of *I.empty* followed by a call of *main*:

value
    init : **Unit** → **in any out any write any Unit**
    init() ≡ I.empty() ; main()

If there is no function like *I.empty*, it is possible to invent one and add it to the imperative module, but it is also possible to define the body of the initial function as "*I*.**initialise** ; *main()*" instead.

For this example we will assume that *empty* will only be called initially and hence can provide the initial function.

Defining interface function signatures

For each of the other functions in the imperative module we define a function of the same name whose type is constructed from the corresponding imperative function's type by

- using a total function arrow
- removing the access descriptor **read any** or **write any**
- inserting the access descriptor **in any out any**

We will refer to the functions (plus *empty* if we defined a separate initial function) as *interface functions* as they provide the interface to the module. We thus distinguish them from *main* and the initial function. Only *main* and the initial function include **write any** in their signatures; the interface functions have no access to the variables of the imperative module. It is essential for RSL concurrency that functions that may execute concurrently do not share access to variables.

Defining channels

So far we have the signatures of all the functions. We also need to define channels, since each interface function will communicate with the *main* process. There will be at least one channel for each interface function, but there may be two. We decide as follows:

- If the interface function has parameter and result types that are both **Unit**, there will normally be just one channel, of type **Unit**.
- If the interface function has a parameter or result type that is **Unit** and a result or parameter type that is not **Unit**, there will normally be just one channel, of the non-unit type.

- If the interface function has non-unit parameter and result types, there will be two channels, one of each type.
- In the cases where there is "normally" just one channel it may still be appropriate to have two, by adding a second one of type **Unit**. We do this when timing (or relative timing) is important in the system and we want to make sure that whatever the *main* function does when it starts acting on a communication from an interface function is completed before anything else in the system is allowed to occur. This is typically the case when we are modelling some hardware function. There is an example of this earlier in this tutorial when we modelled a lift system. There is one component that opens and closes doors and another that moves the lift. These components are models of the hardware involved (door mechanisms and lift motor). Then it is important in sequences like

    close(f) ; move(f′)

or

    halt(f) ; open(f)

(where f, f' are floors) that we do not move towards another floor before the doors are closed or open the doors before a halt at a floor is completed.

This is only a problem when more than one *main* process from different modules is involved. We shall see that our method ensures that even with only one channel, interactions with the same *main* process cannot overlap.

It is also generally necessary, and certainly sensible, to make all the channel names distinct.

In the queue example we will assume that relative timing is not critical (since the queue will be software). It is also convenient to put all the channel definitions into an object so that we can hide them all together.

Defining interface function bodies

For each interface function we define a body which is simply an output of its argument on the channel corresponding to its parameter type (if any) followed by an input on the channel corresponding to its result type (if any).

Defining the body of the main function

We can now define the body of *main* as a **while true** loop containing an external choice between expressions, one expression for each interface function.

The most general form of the expression for an interface function *gen* with imperative precondition *I.can_gen* is

if I.can_gen() **then let** e = c1? **in** c2 ! I.gen(e) **end else stop end**

If there is no precondition, this reduces to the let expression. If the imperative *I.gen* has **Unit** parameter and a non-**Unit** result, the let expression reduces to the output expression. If the imperative *I.gen* has **Unit** result, the output expression is replaced by the call of *I.gen*. There is always at least one input or output and a call of *I.gen*.

So we have

value

    main : **Unit → in any out any write any Unit**

    main() ≡

        while true do

            if ∼ I.is_full() **then**

                let e = CH.enq? **in** I.enq(e) **end**

            else stop end []

            if ∼ I.is_empty() **then** CH.deq ! I.deq() **else stop end** []

            ...

        end

The use of **stop** may seem surprising. The point is that **stop** is a unit for external choice, i.e.

    expr [] **stop** ≡ expr

This means that if the queue is currently empty, say, the second choice from *main* is just **stop** and effectively disappears. So an empty queue cannot be dequeued.

Note that the guard of the if expression is evaluated before the input is received, so that no communication on the input channel can take place if it is false. If the guard depends on the value being input, this style cannot be used. Consider, for example, a database with a lookup interface function. Then the definition of *lookup* will be something like

    lookup(k) ≡ CH.lookup!(k) ; CH.lookup_res?

and the corresponding choice in the main process we might be tempted to write could be

    let k = CH.lookup? **in**

        if I.is_in(k) **then** CH.lookup_res!I.lookup(k) **else stop end**

    end

We can see that the first communication of the key will always succeed but then the main process will **stop** while the interface function *lookup* is still waiting for an input, and we will get deadlock. So we must instead make *lookup* a total function, by adopting one of the two possibilities:

- identifying a special value value of *Data* that cannot normally be stored in the database but can be returned as the result of looking up a key that is not present

- defining the result type of *lookup* not as *Data* but as, say

    type Lookup_res == not_found | res(data : Data)

The first of these is generally to be avoided since it relies on being able to identify a special value of *Data*, which is often a parameter. It also means that other specifications using the database can be written using *lookup* and forgetting to check whether the value returned is the special one; such a mistake will generate a type error in the other option.

This gives us *C_QUEUE1*:

scheme C_QUEUE1(P : ELEM_BOUND) =
  hide I, CH, main **in**
  class
    object I : I_QUEUE1(P)
    object CH : **class channel** enq, deq : P.Elem, is_full, is_empty : **Bool end**
    value
      /* main */
      main : **Unit** → **in any out any write any Unit**
      main() ≡
        while true do
          if ∼ I.is_full() **then let** e = CH.enq? **in** I.enq(e) **end**
          else stop end ⫿
          if ∼ I.is_empty() **then** CH.deq ! I.deq() **else stop end** ⫿
          CH.is_full ! I.is_full() ⫿
          CH.is_empty ! I.is_empty()
        end,
      /* initial */
      empty : **Unit** → **in any out any write any Unit**
      empty() ≡ I.empty() ; main(),
      /* generators */
      enq : P.Elem → **in any out any Unit**
      enq(e) ≡ CH.enq ! e,
      deq : **Unit** → **in any out any** P.Elem
      deq() ≡ CH.deq?,
      /* observers */
      is_full : **Unit** → **in any out any Bool**
      is_full() ≡ CH.is_full?,
      is_empty : **Unit** → **in any out any Bool**
      is_empty() ≡ CH.is_empty?
  end

If we wrote *C_QUEUE0* (described in the optional section 2.8.6.1) and want to express the relation between *C_QUEUE1* and *C_QUEUE0*, we need first of all to make a development of *C_QUEUE0* by substituting *I_QUEUE1* for the component *I_QUEUE0*. Call the result of this development *C_QUEUE0A*. *I_QUEUE1* implements *I_QUEUE0* (stated in the development relation *I_QUEUE0_1*) and so, since implementation is compositional, *C_QUEUE0A* implements *C_QUEUE0*. Then we can define the development relation *C_QUEUE0_1*:

development_relation [C_QUEUE0_1]
  class object P : ELEM_BOUND **end** ⊢ C_QUEUE1(P) ⪯ C_QUEUE0A(P)

If we did not create *C_QUEUE0A* first and tried to state that *C_QUEUE1* implements *C_QUEUE0* directly, we would get a static error in the relation since the object I instantiating L_QUEUE1 in C_QUEUE1 is not a static implementation of the corresponding object in C_QUEUE0; this is why the relation stated in L_QUEUE0_1 involved an extension.

Simplified method

The client–supplier relation between C_QUEUE1 and L_QUEUE1 gives a convenient separation between the imperative (state modifying and observing) part in the latter and the control part in the former. But for modules with very simple states it is possible to follow a combined method of development giving just one module. The result is that:

- The variables as well as the channels are defined in the same module.
- The component expressions in the *main* function will contain assignments to and reads of the variables.

An example of such a development was that of the lift motor in section 2.7.7.2.

2.8.6.4   Development to composite concurrent

We have two choices for development of a composite concurrent module, one that is internally sequential and one that is internally concurrent.

Recall that a composite module has one or more supplier modules. If there are more than one of these suppliers, functions of the composite module will typically involve calling functions of more than one supplier. So we could call these supplier functions either sequentially or in parallel. Since in our method the suppliers will have disjoint state variables and not be able to communicate, these are logically equivalent, but of course may have quite different efficiency characteristics when finally implemented.

Internally sequential

The method is precisely as in section 2.8.6.3 except that the object I is an instantiation of the composite sequential module L_QUEUE2 instead of the single sequential module L_QUEUE1.

Internally concurrent

This is obviously only worth doing when there is more than one component module, whereas for our example we have only an array module as component. But we show the development and indicate how several components would be dealt with.

We will use the concurrent array module C_ARRAY defined in section A.6. This is a standard module just like the abstract imperative version L_ARRAY. It has been constructed from L_ARRAY in just the same way that C_QUEUE0 was constructed from L_QUEUE0. But the details of construction are not of much interest here: we expect to have a translation of concurrent arrays already available. Hence we can use the abstract module and develop it no further ourselves.

We can now develop the concrete concurrent *C_QUEUE2* from the concrete applicative *A_QUEUE2* using a method very similar to that by which we developed the concrete imperative *I_QUEUE2* from the concrete applicative *A_QUEUE2*. The overall method is as follows:

- Use the same module parameter (if any) as in the applicative module.
- Instantiate the concurrent supplier modules.
- Define variables.
- Define channels for each function just as we did in section 2.8.6.3.
- Define the signature of the *main* process:

  value main : **Unit → in any out any write any Unit**
- Define an initial function.
- For each of the interface functions the definitions are precisely the same as in the single concurrent module *C_QUEUE1* in section 2.8.6.3.
- Define the body of *main*.
- Hide the objects, variables, channels and *main*.

We now consider in more detail instantiating the concurrent supplier modules, and defining the channels, the initial function and the body of *main*.

Instantiating the concurrent supplier modules
The type of interest in *A_QUEUE2* is a product:

type Queue = A.Array × Length × A.Index

As in the imperative case, the first component will be supplied by instantiating an array, for which we use the concurrent array *C_ARRAY*. So we create the appropriate object declarations for all such components

object
    X : ...
    C : C_ARRAY(X)

where the class of X is the same as in *I_QUEUE2*.

Defining variables
We define variables for the other components (if any) of the type of interest, just as we did in section 2.8.5.4 giving

variable
    length : {| n : **Nat** • P.bound ≥ n |} := 0,
    front : C.Index := X.min

The only change from *I_QUEUE2* is that the type of *front* comes now from the object *C*.

Defining an initial function
We need an initial function, either *empty* if this is not needed as an interface function or a special *init*, say. This will be the parallel composition of the initial process

of the component modules together with initial assignments to the variable(s) of this module followed by a call of *main*. In our case we will use *empty*, giving

value

    empty : **Unit → in any out any write any Unit**

    empty() ≡ C.init() ‖ (length := 0 ; main())

As we saw in the imperative case it is sufficient to change *length* to zero to make the queue empty; there is no need to change *front* as well.

    If there were several component modules in objects *C1*, *C2*, etc. with initial functions *empty*, *init*, etc., the definition of *empty* would take the form

value

    empty : **Unit → in any out any write any Unit**

    empty() ≡ C1.empty() ‖ C2.init() ‖ ... ‖ (length := 0 ; main())

Defining the body of the main function

We need to define the body of *main*. As in the single concurrent module *C_QUEUE1* in section 2.8.6.3 this consists of a **while true** loop containing an external choice between expressions dealing with each interface function. These expressions are obtained from the bodies of the corresponding function definitions in *L_QUEUE1* in section 2.8.5.3 in the obvious manner:

- Preconditions involving only parameters that can be expressed in terms of the variables of this module normally become expressions of the form

    if precondition **then** ... **else stop end**

    Other preconditions must be dealt with as described in the single concurrent case in section 2.8.6.3, basically by defining special effects and results for the cases when the preconditions are false.

- Results become outputs, so that a sequential expression

    ... ; e

    becomes

    ... ; CH.chan ! e

    To make such an expression more obviously guarded it is common to place such outputs earlier in the expression (taking care, of course, not to move the occurrence of *e* in front of any expressions whose execution will affect its value).

- Calls of functions from imperative modules become calls of functions from concurrent modules, and where possible (i.e. where they return **Unit** results) these are placed in parallel rather than sequence, so that for example

    I1.gen(x) ; I2.gen(y)

    becomes

    C1.gen(x) ‖ C2.gen(y)

    In RSL terms this is perfectly safe since, when (but not in general otherwise!) we construct things by the method described in this tutorial, there can be no "interference" between the functions of components: they do not share any variables or channels, i.e. they cannot communicate with each other in any way. In this case their component actions (communications and assignments) can be arbitrarily interleaved without affecting the result of their execution, and we achieve this interleaving by calling the functions in parallel. But we should only do this when it is not important that the first call terminates before the second. In some cases, particularly where the RSL components model hardware components, it may be important that one function is known to have terminated before the next one starts. There may be an "interference" in the real world (like doors opening and the lift moving affecting the same lift) that is not modelled in RSL. See the discussion earlier in section 2.8.6.3 on how to ensure a component's actions are completed when its interface function terminates.

This gives the module *C_QUEUE2*:

scheme C_QUEUE2(P : ELEM_BOUND) =
    hide X, C, CH, length, front, main **in**
    class
        object
            X :
                class
                    type Elem = P.Elem
                    value min : **Nat** = 0, max : **Nat** = P.bound − 1
                end,
            C : C_ARRAY(X),
            CH : **class channel** enq, deq : P.Elem, is_full, is_empty : **Bool end**
        variable
            length : {| n : **Nat** • P.bound ≥ n |} := 0,
            front : C.Index := X.min
        value
            /∗ main ∗/
            main : **Unit** → **in any out any write any Unit**
            main() ≡
                while true do
                    if length ≠ P.bound **then**
                        let e = CH.enq? **in**
                            let back = (front + length) \ P.bound **in**
                                C.change(back, e) ; length := length + 1
                          end
                      end
                  else stop end ⌷
                  if length ≠ 0 **then**
                      CH.deq ! C.apply(front) ;
                      let f′ = (front + 1) \ P.bound **in**

length := length − 1 ; front := f′
end
else stop end []
CH.is_full ! length = P.bound []
CH.is_empty ! length = 0
end,
/* initial */
empty : **Unit → in any out any write any Unit**
empty() ≡ C.init() ‖ (length := 0 ; main()),
/* generators */
enq : P.Elem → **in any out any Unit**
enq(e) ≡ CH.enq ! e,
deq : **Unit → in any out any** P.Elem
deq() ≡ CH.deq?,
/* observers */
is_full : **Unit → in any out any Bool**
is_full() ≡ CH.is_full?,
is_empty : **Unit → in any out any Bool**
is_empty() ≡ CH.is_empty?

end

Exercise Develop a bounded queue that has an additional selection mechanism
for *deq*; *deq* has an extra *test* parameter of type

P.Elem → **Bool**

so that *deq* removes (and returns) the first element *e* in the queue (if any) for which
test(e) is true.

Also include an observer *list_of* to give the elements in the queue, in order, and
an observer *next* that takes a *test* parameter like *deq* and returns the element (if
any) that would result from a call of *deq* with the same parameter.

deq and *next* should be total functions.

You may find the resulting specification useful for the exercise at the end of
section 2.6.

2.9   Formal relations between applicative, imperative and concurrent modules

This is a technical section that may be omitted at a first reading.

We have claimed that we can formalize the relation between applicative specifications and their imperative and concurrent counterparts, and that the development
steps involved could be largely automated. This claim needs supporting.

We shall provide some support here by

- identifying constraints on applicative specifications

- providing transformations which convert applicative specifications into imperative specifications
- outlining, through an example, how the imperative specifications obtained in this way can be extended conservatively to specifications that implement the applicative specifications

A treatment of more general applicative specifications will be indicated in section 3.8.4

2.9.1 Linear expressions

2.9.1.1 Informal assumptions

We have made some assumptions about applicative specifications:

- We assumed applicative generators and observers make at most one mention of the type of interest in their parameter and result types. If this is not the case there are a number of possibilities:

  - Two mentions of a type of interest in a parameter type (such as a concatenation function for lists) can often be dealt with by a simpler generator which deals with one element at a time (like a cons function for lists).
  - If there is a collection of values of the type of interest that is either fixed in number or bounded, the use of multiple component objects of the same scheme, either with a fixed collection of objects or with an object array, will often suffice.
  - Otherwise (as we noted previously in section 2.8.5.1 for trees, for example), we will have instantiated the applicative module in the imperative one. The imperative functions will be defined in terms of the applicative ones. Then applicative properties involving functions (like *node* for the type *Tree*) which have no imperative counterpart, will still hold applicatively. Other applicative properties will have imperative counterparts as described in the rest of this section.
    For an alternative approach see section 3.8.4.

- We assumed that applicative expressions do not involve more than one value of the type of interest at once. This is rarely a problem in practice, but may occur by chance (and often unintentionally). Consider, for example, the applicative expression

  let s' = gen1(x1,s) **in let** s'' = gen2(x2,s) **in** ... **end end**

  where s, s', etc. are of the type of interest. Where *gen2(x2,s)* occurs there are two state values in scope: s and s'. It should be clear that in the imperative version s will not normally be available, because we will use one variable and it will be overwritten by the imperative function *gen1*. Again, if we know how many such values are being "remembered" in the applicative version, we can deal with it by special techniques, such as extra variables in the imperative version or extra observers in the applicative one that "remember" enough about an earlier value. Usually, however, it was not intended anyway, i.e. we meant to write *gen2(x2,s')*.

2.9.1.2   Formal constraints

We need to make precise our ideas about what kinds of expression satisfy the assumptions we have just described. The intuition is that, if there is only one mention of a value of the type of interest being used at any one point in the order of execution of an applicative expression, we can find a corresponding imperative expression using a variable (or set of variables, or collection of imperative suppliers) to hold this value. We will call such applicative expressions *linear*. Then if the linear expression produces from a value *s* of the type of interest a new value *s'* and a result *r*, the corresponding imperative expression will change an existing imperative state *s* to an new imperative state *s'* and return the same value *r*.

More formally, a linear sequential applicative expression satisfies two conditions:

- There must be no name clashes if all names signifying members of the types of interest are replaced by identical names.
- There must be no function or operator taking as parameters more than one member of the type of interest. In particular there must be no equality or inequality test between members of the type of interest.

In this section we first define the class of applicative expressions we consider linear. Then in section 2.9.1.3 we show how to obtain the corresponding imperative expression from a linear one.

An applicative sequential expression is linear if it takes one of the following forms, where we take the phrase "type of interest" to mean "the type of interest or a type dependent on it"; the metavariables *s*, *s'* to range over values of the type of interest; the metavariables *x*, *y* to range over other types:

- an expression not mentioning any value of the type of interest
- an if expression of the form

    if expr **then** expr1 **else** expr2 **end**

    where *expr*, *expr1* and *expr2* are in linear form
- a local expression in which the constituent expressions are in linear form
- a case expression where the constituent expressions are in linear form, the type of expression being cased over is not of the type of interest, and the patterns do not involve generators or observers of that type
- an expression of the form

    let y = obs(x,s) **in** expr **end**

    where *obs* is an observer or derived observer with its definition in linear form and *expr* is linear

- an expression of the form

    let s$'$ = gen(x,s) **in** expr **end**

    where *gen* is a generator or derived generator with its definition in linear form and *expr* is linear and does not mention *s*
- an expression of the form

    let (y,s$'$) = gen(x,s) **in** expr **end**

    where *gen* is a generator or derived generator with its definition in linear form and *expr* is linear and does not mention *s*
- an infix expression of the form

    expr1 infix_op expr2

    where *expr1* and *expr2* are linear and either *expr1* or *expr2* is not of the type of interest.
- a prefix expression of the form

    prefix_op expr

    where *expr* is linear
- a boolean expression of one of the forms

    expr1 infix_connective expr2

    $\sim$ expr1

    where *expr1* and *expr2* are linear
- a post expression of the form

    expr1 **as** b **post** expr2 **pre** expr3

    where *expr1*, *expr2* and *expr3* are linear and if *expr1* is of the type of interest, *expr2* does not mention *s*.
- an equivalence expression of the form

    expr1 $\equiv$ expr2 **pre** expr3

    where *expr1*, *expr2* and *expr3* are linear, *expr1* is not of the type of interest, and either

    - neither *expr1* or *expr2* mention any generators, or
    - *expr2* does not mention *s*

2.9.1.3 Corresponding imperative expressions

The technique for obtaining the corresponding imperative expression *expr$'$* from a linear *expr* is as follows:

- if *expr* does not mention any value of the type of interest, *expr$'$* is identical to *expr*.
- an if expression of the form

    if expr **then** expr1 **else** expr2 **end**

    becomes

> **if** expr′ **then** expr1′ **else** expr2′ **end**

For, while, until and local expressions are handled in the same way.

- a case expression of the form

  > **case** expr **of**
  >   pattern1 → expr1,
  >   ...
  > **end**

  becomes

  > **case** expr′ **of**
  >   pattern1 → expr1′,
  >   ...
  > **end**

- an expression of the form

  > **let** y = obs(x,s) **in** expr **end**

  becomes

  > **let** y = obs(x) **in** expr′ **end**

- an expression of the form

  > **let** s′ = gen(x,s) **in** expr **end**

  becomes

  > gen(x) ; expr′

  In the following discussion we will assume that this is written as the equivalent let expression:

  > **let** dummy = gen(x) **in** expr′ **end**

  (where *expr′* does not mention *dummy*) so that we are always dealing with let expressions.

- an expression of the form

  > **let** (y,s′) = gen(x,s) **in** expr **end**

  becomes

  > **let** y = gen(x) **in** expr′ **end**

- an infix expression of the form

  > expr1 infix_op expr2

  becomes

  > expr1′ infix_op expr2′

- a prefix expression of the form

  > prefix_op expr

  becomes

  > prefix_op expr′

- a boolean expression of one of the forms

  > expr1 infix_connective expr2

$\sim$ expr1

becomes one of the forms

expr1$'$ infix_connective expr2$'$

$\sim$ expr1$'$

- for a post expression of the form

expr1 **as** b **post** expr2 **pre** expr3

we first consider the precondition *expr3*. If it mentions no generators then it just becomes *expr3$'$*. Otherwise it can be treated like "*expr3* $\equiv$ **true**"; see equivalence expressions below.

For the post expression, the transformation depends on whether the imperative expression we want is part of a sequential or concurrent specification. In the sequential case, the post expression becomes (ignoring the precondition)

expr1$'$ **as** b$'$ **post** expr2$'$

where b' is the result of removing from b any binding of the type of interest.

In the concurrent case we need to first rewrite the post expression as an equivalence expression using the proof rule *readonly_post_expansion* from appendix B and then transform the equivalence expression as shown below.

- for an equivalence expression of the form

expr1 $\equiv$ expr2 **pre** expr3

we first deal with the precondition as for post expressions.

For the equivalence, the transformation depends on whether the imperative expression we want is part of a sequential or concurrent specification. In the sequential case, if neither expression mentions any generators it becomes (ignoring the precondition)

$$\text{expr1}' \equiv \text{expr2}' \tag{1}$$

In the concurrent case, if neither expression mentions any generators it becomes (ignoring the precondition)

$$\forall \text{ test} : \text{T} \xrightarrow{\sim} \textbf{Unit} \bullet$$
$$\text{main}() \,\|\, \text{test}(\text{expr1}') \equiv \text{main}() \,\|\, \text{test}(\text{expr2}') \tag{2}$$

where T is the (common) maximal type of *expr1$'$* and *expr2$'$*, and *main()* is a call of the main process if the module is single, or the concurrent composition of the main processes from the component modules if the module is composite. If T is **Unit** (which will be the case if *expr1*'s type is the type of interest) (2) can be simplified to

$$\text{main}() \,\|\, \text{expr1}' \equiv \text{main}() \,\|\, \text{expr2}' \tag{3}$$

If *expr1* mentions any generators, *expr1$'$* will take the general form

let ... **in let** ... **in** e **end** ... **end** $\qquad(4)$

where e does not mention any generators. From our assumptions, *expr2* will not mention s. *expr2$'$* then takes the form

let ... **in let** ... **in** expr2 **end** ... **end**

where the let expressions are copied from (4). (We may need to rename some of the let bindings to avoid capturing any free names in *expr2*.) The resulting equivalence takes the form (1) in the sequential case, (2) (possibly simplified to (3)) in the concurrent case.

2.9.1.4   Examples

Post expressions
Consider the post expression from the axiom *deq_ax* from A_QUEUE0 in section 2.8.4.1:

> deq(q) **as** (e,q′) **post** e = **hd** list_of(q) ∧ list_of(q′) = **tl** list_of(q)
> **pre** ~is_empty(q)

This is not linear since deq(q) is of (by being dependent on) the type of interest *Queue*. We see that in the postcondition both q and q′ are in scope.

But we can rewrite the post expression in the form

> **let** l = list_of(q) **in**
> deq(q) **as** (e,q′) **post** e = **hd** l ∧ list_of(q′) = **tl** l **pre** ~ is_empty(q)
> **end**

and now it is linear. The corresponding imperative form is

> **let** l = list_of() **in**
> deq() **as** e **post** e = **hd** l ∧ list_of() = **tl** l **pre** ~ is_empty()
> **end**

which is the form of *deq_ax* in *I_QUEUE0* in section 2.8.5.1.

Case expressions
Note that we excluded the possibility of the expression being cased over being of the type of interest. This is because such a case expression would involve (effectively) comparing values of this type, and it should be apparent that an expression like

> s = s′

cannot be put into linear form. If we have such a case expression we need to rewrite it in some other way. For example, if we have

> **case** s **of**
> empty → ...
> add(x,s′) → ...
> **end**

then we can only partially put it in linear form by casing instead over one or more observers, something like

> **case** is_empty(s) **of**
> **true** → ...
> **false** → **let** x = first(s) **in let** s′ = second(s) **in** ... **end end**
> **end**

Now we have the problem that this expression in the imperative form will change the state through the call of *second*. So it depends on how s' is used. Often a more dramatic rewrite into separate axioms will suffice. Suppose, for example, the case expression occurs as part of a definition:

value
    length : S → **Nat**
    length(s) ≡
        case s **of**
            empty → 0,
            add(x,s') → 1 + length(s')
        end

Then we can rewrite this as

value length : S → **Nat**
axiom
    [length_empty]
    length(empty) = 0,
    [length_add]
    ∀ x : Elem, s : S • length(add(x,s)) = 1 + length(s)

and these axioms will rewrite into let expressions in linear form:

axiom
    [length_empty]
    let s = empty **in** length(s) = 0 **end**,
    [length_add]
    ∀ x : Elem, s : S •
    let n = length(s), s' = add(x,s) **in** length(s') = 1 + n **end**

(where in the second we have compressed the nested let expressions using a let definition list).

Quantified expressions

The definition of *safe*, a derived observer in *A_LIFT2*, is

value
    safe : Lift → **Bool**
    safe((ms, ds, bs)) ≡
        (∀ f : T.Floor •
            (DS.door_state(ds)(f) = T.open) =
            (M.movement(ms) = T.halted ∧ M.floor(ms) = f))

First we consider the intuitive problem. The idea of putting the defining expression of *safe* into linear form is that we can then easily transcribe it into a version to use in formulating theorems about the concurrent lift module *C_LIFT2*. Then each application of *door_state*, *movement* and *floor* will communicate with some other process to give the result. Clearly we will need to have much more information about the evaluation order than in the applicative case, and the quantification over *f* presents a problem.

More formally, if we consider the rules above for linear forms, we find that quantified expressions mentioning the type of interest are not amongst those classed as linear. We need to use let expressions to bring the applications of *door_state*, *movement* and *floor* outside the quantification. With the last two there is no problem, but *door_state* has *f* as an actual parameter and needs to be inside the scope of the quantification.

We need to replace the quantification with something else. Since we know there are only a finite number of floors, and *safe* corresponds to "every floor is safe", we can calculate a predicate for each floor and take their conjunction. One way to do this is with a loop. So we posit that an equivalent, linear form for the defining expression of *safe* is

local variable is_safe : **Bool** := **true in**
    let movement = M.movement(ms), floor = M.floor(ms) **in**
        for f **in** ⟨ T.min_floor .. T.max_floor ⟩ **do**
            let door_state = DS.door_state(ds)(f) **in**
                is_safe := is_safe ∧
                    (door_state = T.open) = (movement = T.halted ∧ floor = f)
            end
        end
    end ;
    is_safe
end

We can now produce the corresponding imperative definition for *safe*:

value
    safe : **Unit** → **in any out any Bool**
    safe() ≡
        local variable is_safe : **Bool** := **true in**
            let movement = M.movement(), floor = M.floor() **in**
                for f **in** ⟨ T.min_floor .. T.max_floor ⟩ **do**
                    let door_state = DS.door_state(f) **in**
                        is_safe := is_safe ∧
                            (door_state = T.open) = (movement = T.halted ∧ floor = f)
                    end
                end
            end ;
            is_safe
        end

2.9.2   Linear axioms

We saw in section 2.9.1 that we can form a corresponding imperative expression from a linear expression. This process is easily extendable to axioms.

For linear axioms that are post expressions or equivalences we have already seen how to create the corresponding imperative post expressions or equivalences.

For linear axioms that are not equivalences but boolean expressions we just add the implicit "$\equiv$ **true**" and proceed as for equivalences.

Example   If we just followed the rules above for the body of the axiom *safe_and_useful* in *A_LIFT0* is the boolean expression

safe(s) $\Rightarrow$
let (r, s$'$) = check_buttons(s) **in**
   safe(s$'$) $\wedge$
   let s$''$ = next(r, s$'$) **in**
      safe(s$''$) $\wedge$
      (movement(s$''$) = T.halted $\Rightarrow$
         (T.here(r) $\vee$ ($\sim$ T.after(r) $\wedge$ $\sim$ T.before(r))) $\wedge$
         floor(s) = floor(s$''$)) $\wedge$
      (movement(s$''$) = T.moving $\Rightarrow$
         (T.after(r) $\vee$ T.before(r)) $\wedge$
         T.is_next_floor(direction(s$''$), floor(s)) $\wedge$
         floor(s$''$) = T.next_floor(direction(s$''$), floor(s))) $\wedge$
      (direction(s) $\neq$ direction(s$''$) $\Rightarrow$ $\sim$ T.after(r))
   end
end

We can put this into linear form as

safe(s) $\Rightarrow$
let
   floor = floor(s), direction = direction(s), (r, s$'$) = check_buttons(s)
in
   safe(s$'$) $\wedge$
   let s$''$ = next(r, s$'$) **in**
      safe(s$''$) $\wedge$
      (movement(s$''$) = T.halted $\Rightarrow$
         (T.here(r) $\vee$ ($\sim$ T.after(r) $\wedge$ $\sim$ T.before(r))) $\wedge$
         floor = floor(s$''$)) $\wedge$
      (movement(s$''$) = T.moving $\Rightarrow$
         (T.after(r) $\vee$ T.before(r)) $\wedge$
         T.is_next_floor(direction(s$''$), floor) $\wedge$
         floor(s$''$) = T.next_floor(direction(s$''$), floor)) $\wedge$
      (direction $\neq$ direction(s$''$) $\Rightarrow$ $\sim$ T.after(r))
   end
end

The easiest way to check this re-formulation is correct is to prove it as a theorem of the module it came from. This is strictly not the same as proving it equivalent to the original: what is being proved is that it is a consequence of the original and the rest of the definitions and axioms. However, in practice it should be a sufficient check.

Having a linear expression we can form the corresponding imperative or concurrent axiom. In the lift case the development is concurrent and the first concurrent module is *C_LIFT2*. We can therefore formulate the following theorem:

C_LIFT2 ⊢
∀ test : **Bool** $\overset{\sim}{\rightarrow}$ **Unit** •
  let main =
    (λ() •
      M.motor() ‖
      ‖ { DS.DS[f].door() | f : T.Floor } ‖
      ‖ { BS.LB[f].button() | f : T.Floor } ‖
      ‖ { BS.UB[f].button() | f : BS.Lower_floor } ‖
      ‖ { BS.DB[f].button() | f : BS.Upper_floor }) **in**
    main() ‖ test(
      safe() ⇒
      let
        floor = floor(), direction = direction(), r = check_buttons()
      in
        safe() ∧
        let dummy = next(r) **in**
          safe() ∧
          (movement() = T.halted ⇒
            (T.here(r) ∨ (∼ T.after(r) ∧ ∼ T.before(r))) ∧
            floor = floor()) ∧
          (movement() = T.moving ⇒
            (T.after(r) ∨ T.before(r)) ∧
            T.is_next_floor(direction(), floor) ∧
            floor() = T.next_floor(direction(), floor)) ∧
          (direction ≠ direction() ⇒ ∼ T.after(r))
        end
      end)
      ≡
      main() ‖ test(
        let r = check_buttons(), dummy = next(r) **in true end**)
    end

In the right-hand side expression we have removed a number of the let expressions that correspond to observers like *safe* and *floor*. These can always be removed when the names bound by such let expressions have no occurrences. This can only be done for observers, not for generators like *next*, even though *dummy* has no occurrences, since only our observers have no effects on any variables.

This is the concurrent counterpart to the applicative *safe_and_useful* axiom, and if we want to gain additional confidence that the concurrent lift system is safe and useful, this is the theorem we should formulate and justify.

2.9.3 Justification

We have described how linear applicative expressions and axioms can be transformed into imperative sequential or concurrent expressions and axioms. We now demonstrate, through an example, how the imperative specifications obtained by these transformations can be extended conservatively to specifications which implement the applicative specifications. (More details can be found elsewhere [20].) We start with the sequential case, and then indicate the changes necessary to deal with the concurrent case.

The example we use is that of queues like those in section 2.8.

2.9.3.1 Sequential imperative

We need to construct an extension of the imperative specification. The overall construction using the queues as an example is illustrated in figure 2.16. The extension of *I_QUEUE0*, called *A_I_QUEUE0*, includes definitions of the applicative entities from *A_QUEUE0* in terms of the imperative ones from *I_QUEUE0*. The intention is to prove the implementation relation between *A_QUEUE0* and *A_I_QUEUE0*.

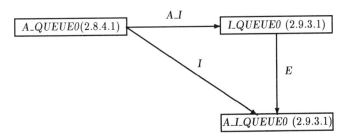

Figure 2.16: Development of *A_I_QUEUE0*

Result of the transformation
Applying the rules (given in sections 2.9.1 and 2.9.2) produces the following specification.

scheme I_QUEUE0(P : ELEM_BOUND) =
 class
  type List_of_Queue = {| l : P.Elem* • **len** l ≤ P.bound |}
  value
   /∗ generators ∗/
   empty : **Unit** → **write any Unit**,
   enq : P.Elem $\xrightarrow{\sim}$ **write any Unit**,

deq : **Unit** $\overset{\sim}{\to}$ **write any** P.Elem,
/* hidden observer */
list_of : **Unit** → **read any** List_of_Queue,
/* derived */
is_full : **Unit** → **read any Bool**
is_full() ≡ **len** list_of() = P.bound,
is_empty : **Unit** → **read any Bool**
is_empty() ≡ list_of() = ⟨⟩

  axiom
   [list_of_empty] empty() ; list_of() ≡ empty() ; ⟨⟩,
   [list_of_enq]
      ∀ e : P.Elem •
        let l = list_of() **in**
            enq(e) ; list_of() ≡ enq(e) ; l ⌢ ⟨e⟩ **pre** ∼ is_full() **end**,
   [deq_ax]
      let l = list_of() **in**
          deq() **as** e **post** e = **hd** l ∧ list_of() = **tl** l **pre** ∼ is_empty()
      end,
   [enq_defined] ∀ e : P.Elem • enq(e) **post true pre** ∼ is_full(),
   [initial] **initialise post** is_empty()
 end

We rewrote the body *list_of_enq* from *A_QUEUE0* as

  let l = list_of(q) **in**
      list_of(enq(e, q)) ≡ l ⌢ ⟨e⟩ **pre** ∼ is_full(q)
  end

to make it linear, and we introduced a similar let expression in the applicative *deq_ax*.

The resulting *I_QUEUE0* is almost identical to the *I_QUEUE0* defined in section 2.8.5.1. The only differences are that *List_of_Queue* and *list_of* have not been hidden (because we need them in the next step) and *list_of_enq* has a slightly different (but equivalent) form.

Exercise   Prove the equivalence of the axiom *list_of_enq* in the above version of *I_QUEUE0* and that in section 2.8.5.1. (You should defer this exercise until you have read chapter 4.)

Creation of the extension
If the imperative specification takes the form

  class decls **end**

then the extension (the step marked "E" in the figure) will take the form

  hide c′ **in extend use** c′ **for** c **in class** decls **end with class** decls′ **end**

where c is the name of any constant of the type of interest. (If there are several they are all renamed and hidden.)

If the original takes the form

hide names **in class** decls **end**

then the extension will take the form

hide names, c' **in**
use c' **for** c **in extend class** decls **end with class** decls$'$ **end**

This enables the declarations in *decls$'$* to mention names that were hidden in the original. *decls$'$* will consist of a number of declarations.

In our case we need the second version because *A_QUEUE0* hides *List_of_Queue* and *list_of* and we need to refer to the former and the imperative counterpart of the latter in the extension.

The declarations in *decls$'$* are:

- a definition of the type of interest, in our case

  type
      Queue =
          $\{| \ q : \textbf{Unit} \rightarrow \textbf{write any Unit} \cdot \ \Box \ q() \ ; \ \text{list\_of}() \equiv q() \ ; \ \text{list\_of}(q) \ |\}$

  Remember that in the initial applicative module the type of interest *Queue* is a sort, and hence open to any development. The normal applicative development is to develop the sort into a concrete type like a list. What we are showing here is that we can instead develop the sort into a function type. The particular type contains functions with **Unit** parameter that write to the state (still abstract) in such a way that calling the function and then evaluating the imperative observer *list_of* always gives the same result as applying the applicative observer *list_of* to the function. Different values of type *Queue* correspond to different queue states.

  If there were several non-derived observers there would be several equivalences in the subtype definition relating each imperative one to its applicative counterpart.

  Note that this construction depends on being able to pass a function (q of type *Queue*) as a parameter.

- a definition of each constant of the type of interest, in our case

  value empty : Queue = empty$'$

  Note that *empty* and *empty$'$* have the same maximal type, which is why we had to rename the *empty* exported from *I_QUEUE0*.

- for each applicative derived observer and non-constant generator, a value declaration with the same signature as in the applicative module and one of the following forms:

  - for a derived observer or generator, such as *is_empty*, the same definition as in the applicative specification:

value
    is_empty : Queue → **Bool**
    is_empty(q) ≡ list_of(q) = ⟨⟩
− for a non result-returning generator, such as *enq*:
value
    enq : P.Elem × Queue $\xrightarrow{\sim}$ Queue
    enq(e, q) ≡ (λ () • q() ; enq(e)) **pre** ∼ is_full(q)
− for a result-returning generator, such as *deq*:
value
    deq : Queue $\xrightarrow{\sim}$ P.Elem × Queue
    deq(q) **as** (e, q′) **post** (□ q() ; deq() ≡ q′() ; e)
    pre ∼ is_empty(q)

- for each applicative non-derived observer a value declaration with the same signature as in the applicative module but no definition
- for any other auxiliary definitions not already in the imperative module, copies of the applicative definitions.

This gives us the following scheme *A_I_QUEUE0*:

scheme A_I_QUEUE0(P : ELEM_BOUND) =
    hide List_of_Queue, list_of, empty′ **in**
    extend use empty′ **for** empty **in** I_QUEUE0(P) **with**
    class
        type
            Queue =
                {| q : **Unit** → **write any Unit** • □ q() ; list_of() ≡ q() ; list_of(q) |}
        value
            /∗ generators ∗/
            empty : Queue = empty′,
            enq : P.Elem × Queue $\xrightarrow{\sim}$ Queue
            enq(e, q) ≡ (λ () • q() ; enq(e)) **pre** ∼ is_full(q),
            deq : Queue $\xrightarrow{\sim}$ P.Elem × Queue
            deq(q) **as** (e, q′) **post** (□ q() ; deq() ≡ q′() ; e)
            pre ∼ is_empty(q),
            /∗ hidden observer ∗/
            list_of : Queue → List_of_Queue,
            /∗ derived ∗/
            is_full : Queue → **Bool**
            is_full(q) ≡ **len** list_of(q) = P.bound,
            is_empty : Queue → **Bool**
            is_empty(q) ≡ list_of(q) = ⟨⟩
    end

It can now be proved that this extension of the imperative module is an implementation of the initial applicative module. We have completed the construction depicted in figure 2.16, in particular that *A_I_QUEUE0* implements *A_QUEUE0*. So the extension to the imperative module *I_QUEUE0* will have as properties any axioms of the initial applicative module *A_QUEUE0*. But, of course, these properties look like properties of the extension, since they are applicative. In what sense are they properties of the extended imperative module *I_QUEUE0*? The non-derived applicative generators and observers are all defined in terms of their imperative counterparts, and hence so are the derived ones, so the properties of the applicative functions must in fact be properties of *I_QUEUE0* — provided the extension is conservative. We therefore need to check that the extension is indeed conservative.

Showing the extension is conservative

Sufficient conditions for such an extension to be conservative are described in section 3.9; broadly they are that there are no axioms and that any subtypes involved can be shown not to place any restrictions on the class being extended.

We have no axioms but we do have the subtype *Queue* and we claim that the applicative generators give values in this subtype. So, for example, we have to show that *empty*, and hence *empty'*, is in fact in the subtype *Queue* without just using the typing of *empty* as a justification. Note that the type *Queue* is quite restrictive. For example, $\lambda() \bullet \mathbf{skip}$ is not a value in *Queue* since that would require

$$\Box \; \mathbf{skip} \; ; \; \text{list\_of}() \equiv \mathbf{skip} \; ; \; \text{list\_of}(\lambda() \bullet \mathbf{skip})$$

i.e.

$$\Box \; \text{list\_of}() \equiv \text{list\_of}(\lambda() \bullet \mathbf{skip})$$

and since *list_of* can read the state but the right-hand side must be a constant value this cannot in general be true. We can see that any constant generator *c* in *Queue* must have the property that for some constant *l* of type *List_of_Queue*

$$\Box \; c() \; ; \; \text{list\_of}() \equiv c() \; ; \; l$$

We do indeed have such a property in *I_QUEUE0* for the constant generator *empty*; *l* is $\langle \rangle$.

For the generating functions of *I_QUEUE0*, we can see that they must have the property that the result of *list_of* after they are applied must be uniquely determined only by the result of *list_of* before they are called and any parameters. We can see from the axioms in *I_QUEUE0* that this is indeed true for *enq* and *deq*, and indeed will be true in general if we define observational applicative axioms as described in section 2.8.4.1 and transform them to imperative axioms according to the rules in sections 2.9.1 and 2.9.2.

2.9.3.2   Concurrent imperative

In this section we summarize the concurrent counterpart to section 2.9.3.1.

The concurrent imperative module uses the imperative sequential one as a supplier.

We then extend the concurrent imperative module with declarations similar to those for the sequential imperative case. We take the necessary extensions to *C_QUEUE0* from section 2.8.6.1 as our example:

- The type of interest definition takes the form

  type
    Queue =
      {| q : **Unit → in any out any write any Unit** •
        (∃ iq : **Unit → write any Unit** •
          q = (λ () • iq() ; main()) ∧
          (□ iq() ; list_of(q) ≡ iq() ; I.list_of()) ∧
          (∀ test : List_of_Queue $\xrightarrow{\sim}$ **Unit** •
            (□ q() ∥ test(list_of()) ≡ q() ∥ test(list_of(q))))) |}

- Non-derived observers are given the same signatures as in the applicative case, like

  value list_of : Queue → List_of_Queue

- Derived generators and observers have the same definitions as in the applicative specification, like

  value
    is_empty : Queue → **Bool**
    is_empty(q) ≡ list_of(q) = ⟨⟩

- Constants of the type of interest are defined in terms of the (renamed) constants from the specification being extended, as in

  value empty : Queue = empty′

- The other generators take forms like

  value
    enq : P.Elem × Queue $\xrightarrow{\sim}$ Queue
    enq(e, q) ≡ (λ () • q() ∥ enq()) **pre** ∼ is_full(q),

    deq : Queue $\xrightarrow{\sim}$ P.Elem × Queue
    deq(q) **as** (e, q′)
    post (∀ test : P.Elem $\xrightarrow{\sim}$ **Unit** • □ q() ∥ test(deq()) ≡ q() ∥ test(e))
    pre ∼ is_empty(q)

It should be clear that this is closely analogous to the sequential imperative extension. In the concurrent version we use "∥" instead of ";" and introduce test functions where necessary. Similar results to the sequential imperative version for implementation and conservative extension follow, justifying the overall argument that the concurrent imperative version is a correct version of the initial applicative one.

Part II

Techniques

CHAPTER 3

Development

3.1 Introduction

The main input to the development activity is the initial specification as a collection of related modules. The second input is the requirements that have yet to be met, as these have to be taken into account during the development process. Non-functional requirements will serve to push the development in particular directions, to make it suitable for a particular target language, or to tackle a foreseen problem, such as making a large or complex component space- or time-efficient. There will also be functional requirements not yet met because they are intended to be included at a particular level of development detail, or because the customer is not yet certain about them.

We start with some general discussion in this section about kinds of development step. Most of the rest of the chapter, sections 3.2 to 3.11, is concerned with techniques for making development steps. For each technique we describe the **purpose** of the development step, the **method** of its application, and what kind of **relation** it gives. There are also exercises for each technique.

Finally, in section 3.12 we look in more detail at how we can formulate and verify development relations, the statements of formal relations between modules.

We do not in this book describe design methods in general, or the attributes like cohesion and loose coupling that modules should have. Literature on object oriented design, such as [25], and its relation to formal methods, such as [17], is generally relevant.

To make a development step for a module we first formulate a new version of it. We are then interested in two things:

- the relation between the new version and the previous one
- the effect on clients of the module of replacing the previous version by the new one

These issues are obviously related. In particular, we will see that if the relation is *compositional* then the replacement will preserve the properties of clients of the module being developed. But we will discuss other kinds of development step, such as the development step from applicative to imperative, where the replacement would not even be well-formed.

3.1.1   Kinds of development step

We can categorize development steps by the kinds of relation we can establish between the new and old versions:

implementation: An *implementation* is a development step in which the relation between the old and new modules is the implementation relation, i.e. the original theory is only extended — all the properties that were true in the original remain true, but some possibilities resulting from under-specification may be removed. Implementation is formally defined in terms of the implementation relation in appendix B.8.3. Implementation is primarily important because, if an initial specification meets the requirements and its developments are all implementations of it, then they all meet the requirements. This is the ideal situation — the final implementation is guaranteed correct.

conservative extension: Conservative extension is a restriction of implementation in which the original theory is not extended (in the sense of having new properties) — all that is done is that new definitions are added. Conservative extension is important in structuring specifications: clients should only conservatively extend their suppliers. So the bodies of schemes should only conservatively extend their parameters, and class expressions containing embedded objects or referring to global modules should only conservatively extend the class expressions of the embedded objects or global modules. The reason for this is to allow separate development, with replacement of components' initial specifications with their developed ones, as described in section 1.6.2.

Conservative extension is also relevant to the establishment of implementation when entities hidden at one level are omitted in the next. In such a situation we in general show that a conservative extension of the new module (the extension defining the previously hidden, now missing, names) implements the old module. Conservative extension is defined in appendix B.8.4. Note that conservative extension is a special case of implementation; whenever we have conservative extension we have implementation.

static implementation: If a module B statically implements module A (and B does not define any names free in A), a replacement of A by B will be well-formed. Static implementation is described in the book on RSL [23]. Static implementation is also the relation that a class expression of an actual scheme parameter must hold to the class expression of the formal parameter. B statically implements A if the signature of B includes the signature of A.

In particular, if we retain or only add to the signature of a module, but change some of its properties, we will have a static implementation.

static change: If we do not have static implementation, any attempt to replace an old version of a module with a new one in general causes static errors (scope errors or type errors). So the relation is a change to the static properties and in this case to do replacement we have to change supplier and client modules simultaneously.

The main examples of static change we described in the tutorial were the development steps from applicative to imperative and from sequential to concurrent.

Implementation (and hence also conservative extension) is shown in appendix B.8.6 to be compositional. This means that, if all our development steps consist of implementations, the development of the whole system will give an implementation of the initial specification; all the properties of the original specification will be maintained. This is the ideal situation. Where we have only static implementation or static change we have to be careful to note how the properties are being changed.

3.1.2   Planning

The development stage may go through several development steps, and take up a substantial proportion of the overall time and effort. It therefore needs planning carefully.

For a system of any size there will be a number of sub-systems that can be developed separately, i.e. by different people working in parallel. These should be identified at the beginning of the development stage so that they can be planned and allocated. If the initial specification has been done well the interfaces between these sub-systems will be small and well understood. The smoothness of the development process will depend on these interfaces being stable, or having changes that are predicted in advance.

In planning the development of a system we therefore:

- identify sub-systems that can be developed separately
- plan in outline the development steps needed for each sub-system to meet its requirements not met by the initial specification — both functional and non-functional. Some such developments may result in further division into sub-sub-systems. Remember here to look for existing library modules that can be re-used or adapted.
- identify any development steps that will not be compositional, and try to mitigate or avoid these. Those that seem necessary should be planned as milestones marking a (one way) dependency between the separate developments.

Schedules and resources can then be allocated to the developments in the normal manner.

3.1.3   Example

Suppose the system has as a component a database. The module defining the database might well form a contract between the developers of the database itself and the developers of other component(s) which are the database's clients. An abstract specification of an applicative database might be

scheme DB_PARM = **class type** Key, Data **end**

scheme DB(P : DB_PARM) =
   class
      type Db
      value
         /* generators */
         empty : Db,
         put : P.Key × P.Data × Db → Db,
         /* observers */
         is_in : P.Key × Db → **Bool**,
         get : P.Key × Db $\overset{\sim}{\to}$ P.Data
      axiom
         [is_in_empty] ∀ k : P.Key • is_in(k, empty) ≡ **false**,
         [is_in_put]
            ∀ k, k′ : P.Key, i : P.Data, db : Db •
               is_in(k′, put(k, i, db)) ≡
                 k = k′ ∨ is_in(k′, db),
         [get_put]
            ∀ k, k′ : P.Key, i : P.Data, db : Db •
               get(k′, put(k, i, db)) ≡
                 if k = k′ **then** i **else** get(k′, db) **end**
                 pre k = k′ ∨ is_in(k′, db),
         [get_defined] ∀ k : P.Key, db : Db •
            get(k, db) **post true pre** is_in(k, db)
   end

If, for example, we used *DB* instead of *A_ARRAY_INIT* in *A_HARBOUR1* in the tutorial in section 2.6.7, we would have had in *A_HARBOUR1* an object formed from *DB* to give the collection of berths

object B : DB(T{Berth **for** Key, Occupancy **for** Data})

where *T* is an object formed from the types module *TYPES*. *A_HARBOUR* would then be a client of *DB*.

The specification of *DB* leaves a number of design decisions to be taken. In particular:

1. the addition of extra functions like *remove* for removing keys and their associated data from the database
2. the behaviour of *get* for a key that is not in the database

3. the organization of keys in the database (ordered, unordered, partly ordered by sub-divisions of the type *Key*, etc.)
4. a bound on the maximum size of the database (where by "size" we mean some measure of the quantity of information it can hold)
5. the possible development into an imperative form. If so:
   (a) the possible initial value, like *empty*
   (b) the (collection of) variable(s) and/or imperative supplier modules with variables, that will form the imperative state of the database
   (c) a possible further change to allow multiple concurrent access

If later versions may incorporate such design decisions, which decisions will have an effect on the clients of the database (the modules that use it)? We will only consider effects where clients are forced to change something, rather than purely beneficial ones where they can take advantage of a new feature, since what we are interested in are the additional costs of changes. We consider each in turn:

1. Additional functions like *remove* can generally be added without difficulty. Doing so is unlikely to change existing properties and so is a conservative extension (and therefore an implementation).
2. The definition of *get* on undefined keys may be handled in two main ways. One would be to make it return a variant type, one variant for success and one for failure. An alternative is to justify that modules using the database never look up undefined items. This is sometimes possible if it is a property of their algorithms. For example, a two-pass compiler might generate a symbol table on a first pass and read it on a second. The second pass can never try to look up a name not put in the symbol table by the first pass because it gets the identifiers from the same original input. Such a property is also possible to justify for a sequential database if all calls of *get* are guarded by calls of *is_in*.

   In the first case we would have a static change because of the change in the result type of *get*; in the second case (leaving *get* partial but checking that all its applications satisfy its precondition) there is no change to the database module.
3. Organizing the keys will require some development of the scheme *DB_PARM*, to define either an ordering relation or some division of the keys into kinds of key. This development will almost certainly be an implementation of *DB_PARM*. The development of *DB_PARM* can be used as the body of the formal parameter of a new version of *DB*. Such a development will provide implementation for an object like *B* above, the collection of berths, that is an instance of *DB* in a client. Hence from the client's point of view we will get implementation. The types module is typically the place where the necessary development would be made of the type (here *Berth*) used to supply the *Key* type so that the types module is a suitable implementation of the new *DB_PARM*.
4. There are two ways we could put a bound on the maximum "size" of the database. The first is to restrict the type *Key* to some finite type, so that

there is a known finite set of possible keys. This restriction is just like the other developments to *Key* discussed in point 3.

The alternative involves some changes to the module *DB*. Unfortunately such changes are not simple extensions to the properties of *DB*, because it is not possible to say "one can always add items to the database" (which is implied by the total arrow in the definition of *put*) and at the same time "there are circumstances when one cannot add items to the database" (e.g. when it is full) because the two statements are contradictory. So this change not only changes the detail of *DB* but will also involve changes to the clients of *DB*; they will have to check that they cannot cause the database to overflow or, more likely, include guards on all calls of *put* using an extra function *is_full* (to be defined in the bounded version of *DB*). This development will be a static implementation since the (maximal) type of *put* will not be changed; it will not be a compositional change since the properties of *DB* will change.[1]

5. The change from an applicative to an imperative style will be a static change since the signatures of the functions will change. Hence this step involves the clients changing simultaneously. As we saw in the tutorial, however, it is possible to make this change in a regular and predictable manner so that the changes are foreseeable in their form and their impact. In fact there is a precise sense in which the behaviour of the imperative version is "the same as" the behaviour of the applicative one. As for the related decisions:

   (a) The specification of an initial value for the database will not have any effects on its clients because there is no concept of an initial value in the applicative version. The decision can safely be made during the applicative to imperative design step.

   (b) The design of the state variables of the database, either within it or within supplier modules, should not have any effect on clients, because clients need not (and should not) have any sight of any such variables. They will refer to them in access clauses only in the form *B*.**any** (where *B* is the name of an object which is an instance of the database).

   (c) The decision on whether to allow concurrent access to the database is one that should be made at the same time as the development step from applicative to imperative. Although this is a static change, it is still possible to relate the properties of the applicative sequential and imperative concurrent versions.

So we can see that there is a range of possible kinds of development of *DB* that affect its clients in various ways. The important division is between those that are compositional (implementation and conservative extension) and those that are not. The ones that are not compositional will involve changes to clients and are best avoided if possible (by making the change to the initial specification). The exception to this is the change from applicative to imperative, either sequential or

---

[1] A more general version of *DB* could have made *put* partial, and included an underspecified *can_put* to use as a precondition. But we wanted an example of a non-compositional change.

concurrent. As we saw in the tutorial, the effects of this change can be predicted and hence allowed for.

Note that in all cases the clients' developers can choose when they use a new version of *DB* instead of the old one, since dependence between modules in RSL is always to a particular version of a module. There is no notion of dependence on an arbitrary version.

3.2   Removing under-specification

An early specification differs from a later one developed from it primarily in leaving out detail. We leave out detail so that we can concentrate on what is important at each stage in development, deferring what is less important. Under-specification is leaving out detail in such a way that it can be filled in later, and so removing under-specification is a natural part of development. (Since specifications, especially in the early stages, should be as general as possible and leave out everything except the absolutely necessary, under-specification is generally a virtue in spite of its name. It is its opposite, *over-specification*, that should be avoided.)

3.2.1   Replacing abstract types by more concrete ones

Purpose   Abstract types are not generally translatable directly into target languages. We need at some point to decide how we are going to represent them in terms of the types our chosen target language allows us. We may do this in one step, deciding perhaps a type is to be **Int** or **Char**, or we may take the decision in stages, deciding first perhaps that it is to be a record of several other types, some of which are as yet still abstract.

Method   An *abstract type* is one that has been given no type definition beyond its name; its definition takes the form

type id

It may be be developed into a concrete type by giving it a direct definition as some type expression, i.e.

type id = type_expr

It may also be developed as a variant type, union type or record type, so that it takes one of the following forms:

type id == variant−choice

type id = *type*_name−choice2

type id :: component_kind−string

Relation   All the developments in this section are implementations.

Exercise   According to this section

class type T **value** x : T **end**   (1)

is implemented by

class type T = {| n : **Nat** • n < 0 |} **value** x : T **end**   (2)

But (2) is contradictory; the type *T* is empty but a value x is declared to be in *T*.
Does (2) implement (1)?

3.2.2   Replacing variant types by concrete ones

Purpose   Variant types are a shorthand for abstract types plus various associated values (constructors, destructors, reconstructors), subtype names, and axioms relating these. They often do not need to be developed as they can be translated directly into a programming language. It may also be that we have created implementations of them previously in a library. But sometimes we will need to develop them to make them more concrete and amenable to translation into our chosen target language.

Method   A variant type may be developed into a concrete type if all the constructors, destructors, reconstructors and subtype names are also defined in terms of the concrete type, together with their definitions and axioms, and if the disjointness and induction axioms are either already true for the concrete type or are provided explicitly in the development. The method is to expand the variant type definition into its constituent type, value and axiom definitions (using the rules described in the RSL book [23]) and then to consider developments of each of these components in turn.

Relation   The development from variant to concrete type will be an implementation if the developments of the component type, value and axiom definitions are all implementations.

Example   Suppose we have a variant definition of the type *Queue*, where the type *El* is defined elsewhere:

type Queue == empty | enq(El, Queue)

then if we expand this definition we see it is equivalent to

type Queue
value
   empty : Queue,
   enq : El × Queue → Queue
axiom
   [empty_enq]
   ∀ el : El, q : Queue • empty ≠ enq(el, q),
   [Queue_induction]

∀ p : Queue → **Bool** •
   (p(empty) ∧ (∀ e : El, q : Queue • p(q) ⇒ p(enq(e, q)))) ⇒
     (∀ q : Queue • p(q))

and so we can develop it with, for example, the type *Queue* made concrete by being set equal to lists of elements, provided we also supply definitions for *empty* and *enq* plus either justification or statement of the disjointness axiom *empty_enq* and the induction axiom *Queue_induction*:

type Queue = El*
value
   empty : Queue = ⟨⟩,
   enq : El × Queue → Queue
   enq(e, q) ≡ q^⟨e⟩

Exercise

1. Define a *depth* function for the variant type *Queue* and for the concrete version. (The *depth* of an empty queue is zero; each *enq* increases it by one.)
2. Check that the concrete version of the queue implements the abstract one. For *Queue_induction* you will need to assume an induction rule for RSL lists that a predicate p holds for any list if:

   - p(⟨⟩) holds
   - p(el ⌢ ⟨e⟩) holds if p(el) does for any list *el* and element *e*.

   This is the "right" rule corresponding to *all_list_left_induction* defined in appendix B.6.

3.2.3 Replacing union and record definitions by concrete ones

Purpose Union and record type definitions are another way of writing variant definitions. So the purpose of developing them is the same as in section 3.2.2.

Method Union and record definitions may be rewritten as variant definitions using the rules in the RSL book [23]. They may then be developed as concrete type definitions using the rules in the previous section.

3.2.4 Extending variant types containing wildcards

Purpose Wildcards are included as a means of allowing for variant types to be extended later, either by the addition of more variants or by the addition of more components within a variant.

Method   There are two ways in which a variant type may contain a wildcard: as the whole variant or merely as its constructor name.

If the wildcard is a whole variant it may be developed in either of two ways:

1. It may be replaced by one or more variants.
2. It may be removed.

So if we have a variant type declaration

type id == variant−choice1 | _

this may be developed by either

type id == variant−choice1 | variant−choice2

(where variant−choice2 may include "_") or

type id == variant−choice1

If the wildcard appears as the constructor name, i.e. there are some components with it, it may be developed in three ways (or in any combination of the three):

1. Other variants may be added. So

    _(component_kind_list)

   may be developed into

    _(component_kind_list) | variant_choice

2. Further components may be added. So

    _(component_kind_list1)

   may be developed into

    _(component_kind_list1 , component_kind_list2)

3. The wildcard may be replaced by constructor name. So

    _(component_kind_list)

   may be developed into

    id_or_op(component_kind_list)

Remember that for the wildcard as a constructor the options may be used in combination. (Or simply note that after the first the second and third are still available, and after the second the first and third are.)

Relation   All these developments, for wildcards as whole variants or constructors, are implementations. They are conservative extensions only if the development retains a variant with a wildcard. (The presence of a wildcard prevents the inclusion of an induction axiom in the equivalent expansion in terms of types, value signatures and axioms.)

Exercise   Show that

type Colour == red | green | _   (1)

is implemented by

type Colour == red | green | blue   (2)

by expanding each into its equivalent sort, value and axiom definitions.

Would we have implementation if the wildcard were omitted from (1)?

3.2.5 Introducing destructors and reconstructors

Purpose   Destructors and reconstructors may be omitted at first if we are not sure whether or not we will need them. We can include them if we discover them to be useful, either for obtaining components (destructors) or replacing components (reconstructors).

Method   The destructors and reconstructors for component kinds in variants and short records are optional. Component kinds may be developed by their introduction. So if we have a component kind consisting only of a type expression, either a destructor or a reconstructor may be included. If it only has a destructor a reconstructor may be added; if it only has a reconstructor a destructor may be added.

It is not immediately apparent, and worth noting, that adding destructors can change the properties of the values of a type, and in particular can make case expressions deterministic when they were previously non-deterministic. Consider the variant type definitions

type Collection == empty | insert(Elem, Collection)   (1)

and

type Collection == empty | insert(first : Elem, rest : Collection)   (2)

The difference between these definitions is that for (2) the names *first* and *rest* are defined, together with the implicit axioms

axiom
  [first_insert]
  $\forall$ e : Elem, s : Collection • first(insert(e, s)) $\equiv$ e,
  [rest_insert]
  $\forall$ e : Elem, s : Collection • rest(insert(e, s)) $\equiv$ s

The extra axioms have two effects.

- First, these axioms would contradict an axiom
  axiom
    [insert_commutes]
    $\forall$ e1, e2 : Elem, s : Collection •
       insert(e1, insert(e2, s)) $\equiv$ insert(e2, insert(e1, s))
  since we could then use *first_insert* to prove that
    $\forall$ e1, e2 : Elem • e1 $\equiv$ e2
  (by applying *first* to each side) which is in general not true. So we can only consistently add an axiom like *insert_commutes* to the type definition (1) that

does not include the destructor *first*. This means that (2) defines a type that is more like "list" than "set", with *first* and *rest* corresponding to **hd** and **tl** respectively.

- Secondly, consider a case expression over an expression *exp* of type *Collection*:

  case exp **of**
  >   empty → ...,
  >   insert(e, s) → e
  end

  For the definition (2) the value returned in the second case branch must be the same as *first(exp)* and hence must be a unique value, as we can see from the implied axiom *first_insert*. But for the definition (1) the result returned in the second case branch may be non-deterministic. For example, if *exp* was *insert(e1, insert(e2, empty))* and we also had the axiom *insert_commutes*, the result of the case expression would be *e1* $\sqcap$ *e2*.

So we can see that adding destructors not only adds new functions with the appropriate properties: it also affects the properties of values of the type.

Relation   Introducing destructors and reconstructors always gives an implementation.

Exercise   Show that the development from (1) to (2) is not a conservative extension, by finding a property that does not mention *first* or *rest* and is true for (2) but may not be true for (1).

3.2.6   Extending signature definitions

Purpose   The least amount of information we can initially give about a value is its signature (its name and type). We do this so that we can later give more information about its value — either partial information in an implicit definition, or complete information in an explicit definition.

Method   If a value has only been given a signature, it may be developed by giving it an implicit or explicit definition. So

value single_typing

may be developed into

value single_typing • *pure_logical*_value_expr

or

value single_typing = value_expr

If the signature is not a *single_typing*, it must be split into separate definitions to be given definitions. For example

value x, y : **Int**

may be developed into

value
   x : **Int** = 0,
   y : **Int** • y > 0

A single_typing whose binding is an identifier and whose type expression involves a function arrow may be developed into an implicit or explicit function definition. So

value id : function_type_expr

may be developed into

value
   id : function_type_expr
   id formal_function_parameter−string ≡ value_expr opt−pre_condition
or
value
   id : function_type_expr
   id formal_function_parameter−string post_condition opt−pre_condition

Relation   All the developments in this section are implementations.

Exercise   Which of the following developments are implementations?

Original	Development
value x : **Nat**	**value** x : **Nat** • x < 2
value x : **Nat**	**value** x : **Int** • x < 2
value x : **Nat**	**value** x : **Int** = 1
value f : **Nat** → **Nat**	**value** f : **Nat** → **Nat** f(x) = x + 1
value f : **Nat** → **Nat**	**value** f : **Nat** → **Nat** f(x) **as** r **post** r > x

3.2.7 Replacing implicit value definitions by more explicit ones

Purpose   If we have given only an implicit definition for a value we must, at some point before we can hope to translate it into a target language, develop it into an explicit definition. We may choose to do this in one step, or we may choose to gradually restrict it towards a precise definition by strengthening its defining condition.

Method An implicit value or function definition may be replaced by either a less implicit definition or by an explicit one, provided the new definition has the same signature as the old and its definition is sufficient to imply the theory of the old one.

Less implicit definitions We see from appendix B.8.2 that the theory of an implicit value declaration is given by

properties(**value** id : T • p_eb) $\simeq$ ($\exists$ id' : T • id' = id) $\wedge$ (p_eb $\equiv$ **true**)

We have to show that these properties hold in the scope of the new definition. For example

value x : **Int** • x > 0

is implemented by

value x : **Int** • x > 0 $\wedge$ x < 10

since in the scope of the new definition

($\exists$ b : **Int** • b = x) $\wedge$ (x > 0 $\equiv$ **true**)

holds.

Note that the existential conjunct will always hold immediately if the new definition has a type which is equal to or a subtype of the old, since we will use the value as a "witness".

For implicit function definitions the theory is given by

properties(**value** id : T $\xrightarrow{\sim}$ a T1 id(b) **as** b' **post** ro_eb' **pre** ro_eb) $\simeq$
   ($\exists$ id' : T $\xrightarrow{\sim}$ a T1 • id' = id) $\wedge$
   ($\square$ $\forall$ b : T • id(**express**(b)) **as** b' **post** ro_eb' **pre** ro_eb)

(where the partial function arrows may be replaced by total function arrows).

Again the existential conjunct is generally satisfied by the same type being used in the new definition, so the condition reduces to proving the postcondition. If the new definition is implicit, i.e. involves a postcondition, this amounts to showing that

- The old precondition implies the new (with missing preconditions being taken to be **true**).
- The new postcondition always implies the old when the old precondition (if any) holds.

For example the implicit function definition

   f : **Nat** $\to$ **Nat**
   f(x) **as** r **post** r > x

is implemented by

   f : **Nat** $\to$ **Nat**
   f(x) **as** r **post** r > 2*x

since

   $\forall$ x : **Nat** • $\forall$ r : **Nat** • r > 2*x $\Rightarrow$ r > x

Explicit definitions For example

value x : **Int** • x > 0

is implemented by

value x : **Int** = 1

since in the context of the new definition

  $(\exists\, b : \textbf{Int} \bullet b = x) \wedge x > 0$

becomes

  $(\exists\, b : \textbf{Int} \bullet b = 1) \wedge 1 > 0$

which is clearly true. An explicit value or applicative function definition may be trivially rewritten as an implicit one and the rule above (that the new condition must imply the old) used to show implementation. For example,

  f : **Nat** → **Nat**
  f(x) **as** r **post** r>x

is implemented by

  f : **Nat** → **Nat**
  f(x) ≡ 2∗x + 1

since this is equivalent to

  f : **Nat** → **Nat**
  f(x) **as** r **post** r = (2∗x + 1)

and

  $\forall\, x : \textbf{Nat} \bullet \forall\, r : \textbf{Nat} \bullet r = (2*x + 1) \Rightarrow r > x$

For an imperative function this method may not work — the implicit form can have references to values of the variables before and after the execution of the function, while the explicit one will contain assignments. We proceed as in the following example.

Example Suppose we have a variable representing a stack as a list of elements

variable stack : Elem*

and implicitly specified *push* and *pop* functions

value
  push: Elem → **write** stack **Unit**
  push(e) **post** stack = ⟨e⟩^stack`,

  pop: **Unit** $\xrightarrow{\sim}$ **write** stack Elem
  pop() **as** r **post** stack` = ⟨r⟩^stack **pre** stack ≠ ⟨⟩

Now suppose we develop explicit definitions for *push* and *pop*:

value
  push: Elem → **write** stack **Unit**
  push(e) ≡ stack := ⟨e⟩^stack,

pop: **Unit** $\xrightarrow{\sim}$ **write** stack Elem

pop() $\equiv$ **let** r = **hd** stack **in** stack := **tl** stack ; r **end**

pre stack $\neq \langle\rangle$

We need to justify the properties of the old definitions in the context of these new ones. The theory of an implicit function definition (see appendix B.8.2) is given by

properties(**value** id : T $\xrightarrow{\sim}$ a T1 id(b) **as** b′ **post** ro_eb′ **pre** ro_eb) $\simeq$

    ($\exists$ id′ : T $\xrightarrow{\sim}$ a T1 • id′ = id) $\land$

    ($\Box \ \forall$ b : T • id(**express**(b)) **as** b′ **post** ro_eb′ **pre** ro_eb)

(where the partial function arrows may be replaced by total function arrows).

The first conjunct will be satisfied immediately if the new definition, as here, has the same type. So we need to justify the second conjunct. For *push* we have to justify

$$\Box \ \forall \ e : \text{Elem} \bullet \text{push}(e) \ \textbf{post} \ \text{stack} = \langle e\rangle\hat{\ }\text{stack}\grave{\ } \tag{1}$$

A post expression may be turned into an expression not involving **post** provided a convergence condition is satisfied. We use the proof rule

[post_expansion]

    e **as** b **post** ro_eb′ **pre** ro_eb $\simeq$

        (**let** v_hook$_1$ = v$_1$, ..., v_hook$_n$ = v$_n$,

             b = e **in** ro_eb′[v_hook$_i$/v$_i$`] **end**

        $\equiv$

        let b = e **in true end**) **pre** ro_eb

    when e **post true pre** ro_eb

where *ro_eb′[v_hook$_i$/v$_i$`]* means substitute *v_hook$_i$* for all free occurrences of $v_i\grave{\ }$ in *ro_eb′* $(1 \leq i \leq n)$. The names *v_hook$_i$* must be chosen so they do not occur in e or *ro_eb′*.

The "**when**" condition is the convergence condition.

The expression on the right-hand side of the proof rule effectively says that the postcondition is true after executing the expression e. e is executed on both sides of the equivalence so that its effects are allowed for. For a function like *push* which returns a **Unit** value, when the result naming is missing, the rule reduces to

    e **post** ro_eb′ **pre** ro_eb $\simeq$

        (**let** v_hook$_1$ = v$_1$, ..., v_hook$_n$ = v$_n$ **in**

             e ; ro_eb′[v_hook$_i$/v$_i$`] **end**

        $\equiv$

        e ; **true**) **pre** ro_eb

    when e **post true pre** ro_eb

We can apply *post_expansion* to (1). The applicability condition is immediately satisfied since *push* is defined to be a total function by its signature. We obtain (ignoring quantification, which commutes with $\Box$)

□ (**let** stack_hook = stack **in** push(e) ; stack = ⟨e⟩^stack_hook **end**

    ≡

    push(e) ; **true**)

To justify this we first use the rule *always_application1* to introduce an arbitrary initial assignment to the variable *stack*. This gives

∀ s : Elem* • □

    stack := s ; **let** stack_hook = stack **in** push(e) ; stack = ⟨e⟩^stack_hook **end**

    ≡

    stack := s ; push(e) ; **true**

We are in the scope of the new definition, so (since there is no precondition) we can unfold the applications of *push*, propagate the initial assignments using the rule *assignment_sequence_propagation* and absorb the let expression to obtain

∀ s : Elem* • □

    stack := s ; stack := ⟨e⟩^s ; stack = ⟨e⟩^s

    ≡

    stack := s ; stack := ⟨e⟩^s ; **true**

which is immediate after propagating the second assignment on the left-hand side of the equivalence.

For *pop* we need to justify

□ pop() **as** r **post** stack` = ⟨r⟩^stack **pre** stack ≠ ⟨⟩   (2)

When we apply the rule *post_expansion* to (2) we will obtain

□ **let** stack_hook = stack, r = pop() **in** stack_hook = ⟨r⟩^stack **end**

    ≡

    pop() ; **true pre** stack ≠ ⟨⟩   (3)

plus a side condition

pop() **post true pre** stack ≠ ⟨⟩   (4)

Informally, we can see that the side condition (4) is true as the precondition allows the call of *pop* to be unfolded. The only possibly non-convergent expressions in the definition of *pop* are "**hd** *stack*" and "**tl** *stack*" and these converge given the precondition. The main condition (3) can be tackled in the same way as we justified the condition (1) for *push*.

Note that the unfolds of *pop* will always go through if the old precondition implies the new. So we can summarize with the following checks to show that an explicit definition implements an originally implicit, now axiomatic, one:

- that the type of the new signature is a subtype of the type of the old signature
- that any precondition of the new is implied by a precondition of the old
- that the postcondition of the old is provable from the axiom or definition of the new

A slightly more complicated example of turning a post expression into an expression not involving **post** may be found in section 3.2.14.

Relation   Making value definitions more explicit gives implementation as long as the principles in this section are followed.

Exercise   Find explicit definitions implementing the following implicit ones:
value
    f : **Int** $\rightarrow$ **Int**
    f(x) **as** r **post** r $\geq$ 0 $\wedge$ (r = x $\vee$ r = 0 $-$ x),

    g : **Int*** $\xrightarrow{\sim}$ **Int**
    g(x) **as** r **post**
        r $\in$ **elems** x $\wedge$
        ($\forall$ i : **Int** • i $\in$ **inds** x $\Rightarrow$ x(i) $\leq$ r)
    pre x $\neq$ $\langle\rangle$

3.2.8   Replacing explicit value definitions with other explicit ones

Purpose   This may seem a waste of time but is commonly done to obtain a more efficient algorithm.

Method   An example which also involves introducing local definitions into a new explicit function may be found in section 3.2.9.

Relation   The theory of the old, explicit definition is given by
properties(**value** id : T = p_e) $\simeq$ ($\exists$ id$'$: T • id$'$ = id) $\wedge$ (id $\equiv$ p_e)
for a value and
properties(**value** id : T $\xrightarrow{\sim}$ a T1 id(b) $\equiv$ e **pre** ro_eb) $\simeq$
    ($\exists$ id$'$: T $\xrightarrow{\sim}$ a T1 • id$'$ = id) $\wedge$ ($\square$ $\forall$ b : T • id(**express**(b)) $\equiv$ e **pre** ro_eb)
for a function (where the partial function arrows may be replaced by total function arrows). If the new value or function has the same type as the old, the existential conjunct is part of the new theory. Hence we will then have implementation if the new explicit definition satisfies the second conjunct, i.e. if the new definition implies the old definition regarded as an axiom.

Exercise   Show that
value
    factorial : **Nat** $\rightarrow$ **Nat**
    factorial(x) $\equiv$ **if** x = 0 **then** 1 **else** x $*$ factorial(x$-$1) **end**
is implemented by
value
    factorial : **Nat** $\rightarrow$ **Nat**
    factorial(x) $\equiv$ **if** x $<$ 2 **then** 1 **else** x $*$ (x$-$1) $*$ factorial(x$-$2) **end**

3.2.9 Introducing local definitions

Purpose Local definitions are typically used to allow more efficient algorithms. The local definitions may introduce useful functions, variables, channels, or objects. They are made local for several reasons:

- They will not be exported from the module.
- They are textually close to the point at which they are used.
- Local variables and channels allow, respectively, imperative bodies for applicative functions, and concurrent bodies for sequential ones.

Method Local definitions are introduced into the body of a value definition and the value defined in terms of them.

Example A function for reversing a list of elements might be defined

value
    rev : Elem* → Elem*
    rev(l) ≡
        case l **of**
            ⟨⟩ → ⟨⟩,
            ⟨h⟩^t → rev(t)^⟨h⟩
        end

It is well known that this function is not as efficient as it might be as the basis for a programming language implementation because it is not tail recursive. We can introduce a local function *rev1* that is a more efficient form of *rev* and define *rev* in terms of it:

value
    rev : Elem* → Elem*
    rev(l) ≡
        local
            value
                rev1 : Elem* × Elem* → Elem*
                rev1(to_do, done) ≡
                    case to_do **of**
                        ⟨⟩ → done,
                        ⟨h⟩^t → rev1(t, ⟨h⟩^done)
                    end
        in rev1(l, ⟨⟩) **end**

Note that this is a case where *rev1* has a different interface from *rev* (it takes a pair of parameters) and so cannot be used directly to implement *rev*.

Another version of this example, where variables are used with the same purpose as the parameters of *rev1*, is

value
   rev : Elem* → Elem*
   rev(l) ≡
      local
         variable
            to_do : Elem* := l,
            done : Elem* := ⟨⟩
      in
         while to_do ≠ ⟨⟩ **do**
            done := ⟨**hd** to_do⟩^done ;
            to_do := **tl** to_do
         end ;
         done
      end

(The development of this version is described in section 3.3.3.) Note here that while the body of *rev* is imperative (using variables) the accesses to the variables do not appear in its signature as they are local to it. So this is an example of an imperative body for an applicative function.

For a third version of the same example, using an embedded object, suppose we have defined a scheme with a number of list processing functions, including a reverse function *rev*. We can provide a local instantiation of such a scheme to gain access to the reverse function. Such a scheme will presumably be parameterized, so we will need to provide it with a parameter of the appropriate kind. Suppose it is called *LIST_FUNS* and has a parameter *EL* : **class type** *El* **end**. Then our reverse function could be written

value
   rev : Elem* → Elem*
   rev(l) ≡
      local
         object
            E : **class type** El = Elem **end**,
            L : LIST_FUNS(E)
      in L.rev(l) **end**

Uniqueness of local declarations   It is important that the declarations in a local expression provide a unique meaning for each name they define to avoid non-determinacy. In particular:

- for value declarations, it must be possible to prove that there exists a unique value (within its type) for each name defined
- for variable declarations, there must be a unique initial value (within the variable's type).

There is a special function **removable** used in the proof rule *local_absorption* that is true only if the the local declarations define values and the initial values of variables uniquely and also if they only extend their surrounding class expression conservatively. The notion of conservative extension is added so that introducing or removing the local expression does not change the properties of the surrounding class expression.

removable will be satisfied if

1. local declarations only define type abbreviations, channel definitions, initialised variable definitions, explicit value definitions and object definitions with the same restrictions in their defining classes.
2. local declarations are consistent with subtypes as described in section 3.12.2.1.

Relation   Introducing local definitions will give an implementation if the new definition implements the old (plus any relevant axioms). The principles for showing implementation are in section 3.2.13, 3.2.14 or 3.2.15 if the old definition was in signature axiom form and was, respectively, applicative sequential, imperative sequential or concurrent; in section 3.2.7 if the old definition was implicit; in section 3.2.8 if the old definition was explicit.

Exercise   Define an implementation of the following function, using one or more local variables and a while loop:

value
  sum : **Int*** → **Int**
  sum(x) ≡ **if** x = ⟨⟩ **then** 0 **else** **hd** x + sum(**tl** x) **end**

3.2.10   Applicative decomposition of functions

Purpose   At a particular level of detail we will probably specify that a particular action is carried out by a single function, which we might specify by signature and possibly some axioms, or implicitly, or explicitly. As we introduce more detail we often want to break such actions down into component actions, perhaps introducing some new functions to perform particular parts, and then define the original action as some composition of the components. Such compositions may be functional, sequential or concurrent. The technique of defining component functions and then formulating the original action as some composition of these components is called *functional decomposition*.

Method   Sections 3.2.6, 3.2.7 and 3.2.8 describe how to create explicit functions to implement less explicit ones, so this section (and the two following ones) are purely about how to create and reason about the properties of compositions of functions.

Such compositions take one of three forms:

1. *functional composition* in which applying g to the result of applying f to x is written $g(f(x))$ or (equivalently) as $(g{\circ}f)(x)$
2. *sequential composition* in which applying g to the result of applying f to x is written $f(x)$; $g()$. In this case the result of f is recorded in some state change which is read (and perhaps further changed) by g
3. *concurrent composition* in which f and g are executed in parallel, typically with some communication between them, written using the parallel combinator as, for example, $f(x) \parallel g()$

In this section we discuss functional decomposition. Sequential decomposition is discussed in section 3.2.11 and concurrent decomposition in section 3.2.12.

Relation   Decompositions will be implementations if the composed functions together implement the original. So the implementation principles in sections 3.2.6, 3.2.7 and 3.2.8 are relevant here.

Example   Suppose we are concerned with a spelling checker. We might consider two phases — the first to separate out words and the second to check words against a dictionary, creating a list of mis-spelled words.

We might start with the following specification. We assume definition of a function *last* that returns the last element of a non-empty list. We also assume definitions of the predicates *is_word_char* and *is_in_dict*.

type
    Word = {| w : **Text** •
               w ≠ '''' ∧ (∀ c : **Char** • c ∈ **elems** w ⇒ is_word_char(c)) |}
value
    is_sub_word : Word × **Text** → **Bool**
    is_sub_word(w, t) ≡
        (∃ p, q : **Text** •
            t = p⌃w⌃q ∧
            (p = '''' ∨ ∼is_word_char(last(p))) ∧
            (q = '''' ∨ ∼is_word_char(**hd** q))),

    check : **Text** → Word*
    check(t) **as** l **post**
        (∀ w : Word • (w ∈ **elems** l) = (is_sub_word(w, t) ∧ ∼is_in_dict(w)))

A *Word* is a non-empty sequence of characters each of which satisfies *is_word_char*. A sub-word of a text is a word that is part of the text and that has on each side a text that is either empty or has a non-word character adjacent to the sub-word. A word is in the output sequence produced by *check* if and only if it is a sub-word of the text and is not in the dictionary.

This might be considered too loose a specification in that the mis-spelled words are allowed to appear in any order and might be duplicated, or it might be considered a good specification in that these unimportant matters are left for the implementor. Conversely, one could also argue that the use of a list for the result was poor setting of requirements — they ought to say "set".

We now consider the decomposition of this problem into two phases. The first will produce a sequence of words from the text. The second will check each word in the sequence against the dictionary. A functional decomposition might then produce for *check*

value

    check : **Text** → Word*

    check(t) ≡

      local

        value words : **Text** → Word*

        axiom

          words($''''$) ≡ $\langle\rangle$,

          ∀ t : **Text** •

            words(t) ≡ words(**tl** t) **pre** t ≠ $''''$ ∧ ~is_word_char(**hd** t),

          ∀ w : Word, r, t : **Text** •

            words(t) ≡ $\langle$w$\rangle$^words(r)

            pre t = w^r ∧ is_sub_word(w, t)

        value

          check_words : Word* → Word*

           check_words(l) ≡

             case l **of**

               $\langle\rangle$ → $\langle\rangle$,

               $\langle$h$\rangle$^t →

                 if is_in_dict(h)

                 then check_words(t)

                 else $\langle$h$\rangle$^check_words(t)

                 end

             end

      in check_words(words(t)) **end**

Exercise A stream of events is to be filtered, producing an output stream of events that satisfy three tests. Representing the streams as lists we have a specification

value

    test1, test2, test3 : Event → **Bool**,

    filter : Event* → Event*

    filter(el) ≡

      case el **of**

        $\langle\rangle$ → $\langle\rangle$,

$\langle h \rangle \widehat{\ } t \rightarrow$
    if test1(h) $\wedge$ test2(h) $\wedge$ test3(h) **then** $\langle h \rangle \widehat{\ }$filter(t)
    else filter(t) **end**
end

The implementation of the test functions means that *test1* is much faster in execution than *test2*, and *test2* much faster than *test3*, and processing speed is important. Define a functional decomposition of *filter*. If separate, specialized hardware is to be used for some of the tests, would a sequential or a concurrent decomposition be more appropriate?

3.2.11   Sequential decomposition of functions

Purpose   The same as the applicative case in section 3.2.10.

Method   We illustrate the method starting from the same example of the spelling checker from section 3.2.10.

For a sequential decomposition we create a variable to hold the output of *words* and the input of *check_words*, so our formulation of *check* is

value
  check : **Text** $\rightarrow$ Word*
  check(t) $\equiv$
    local
      variable wl : Word* := $\langle \rangle$
      value words : **Text** $\rightarrow$ **write** wl Unit
      axiom
        words('''') $\equiv$ **skip**,
        $\forall$ t : **Text** •
          words(t) $\equiv$ words(tl t) **pre** t $\neq$ '''' $\wedge$ ~is_word_char(**hd** t),
        $\forall$ w : Word, r, t : **Text** •
          words(t) $\equiv$ (wl := wl$\widehat{\ }\langle w \rangle$; words(r))
          pre t = w$\widehat{\ }$r $\wedge$ is_sub_word(w, t)
      value
        check_words : **Unit** $\rightarrow$ **write** wl Word*
          check_words() $\equiv$
            case wl **of**
              $\langle \rangle \rightarrow \langle \rangle$,
              $\langle h \rangle \widehat{\ } t \rightarrow$
                  if is_in_dict(h)
                  then wl := t ; check_words()
                  else wl := t ; $\langle h \rangle \widehat{\ }$check_words()
                  end
            end
    in words(t) ; check_words() **end**

Relation Decompositions will be implementations if the composed functions together implement the original. So the implementation principles in sections 3.2.6, 3.2.7 and 3.2.8 are relevant here.

Exercise The definition of the local imperative function *words* breaks the rules for uniqueness and conservativeness of local definitions from section 3.2.9; it uses axioms rather than an explicit definition. Develop it into an explicit form.

3.2.12 Concurrent decomposition of functions

Purpose The same as the applicative case in section 3.2.10.

Method The method is very similar to the applicative and sequential cases. We define processes and use channels to pass the values between them.

Since concurrent processes can only be of **Unit** type any results generated will need to be output on a channel or stored in a variable.

Relation Decompositions will be implementations if the composed functions together implement the original. So the implementation principles in sections 3.2.6, 3.2.7 and 3.2.8 are relevant here.

Exercise Define a concurrent decomposition of the *check* function from section 3.2.10. *words* should output each word as it finds it. This means that *words* will also need to signal the end of its output so that *check_words* can terminate.

3.2.13 Replacing applicative axioms by definitions

Purpose One way of describing the process of development is as a process of moving from a description of desired properties to a description of values with those properties. So the notion of replacing properties (typically expressed as axioms) by value definitions is a central one. In this section we deal with the applicative sequential case and in the following ones with the imperative sequential and concurrent versions. The uniform manner in which RSL treats these different aspects means that these three sections are very similar.

Method To replace an old description in which values have only signatures and are described by axioms by a new description based on definitions, we need to ensure that the old properties are preserved. The theory of the signature (see appendix B.8.2) is given by

properties(**value** id : T) $\simeq \exists$ id$'$: T • id$'$ = id which is just the existence of a value of the appropriate type, and will be preserved if the the signature of the new definition has a type which is a subtype of the type of the signature of the old definition.

The theory of an axiom is given by

properties(**axiom** [id] ro_eb) $\simeq$ $\Box$ ro_eb $\equiv$ **true**

So we also need to ensure that the old axioms are always true for the new values, i.e. we show that the axioms always follow as a consequence of our definitions. There is an immediate question of whether the definitions are explicit or implicit (i.e. involve postconditions). We will deal first with the explicit case.

Explicit definitions   If the definitions are explicit we can simply unfold instances of the value in the axioms and try to reduce them to **true**. For a typical axiom of the form *e1* $\equiv$ *e2* this presents no methodological problems.

Example   The stack axiom for *top* might be

axiom
$\quad$ $\forall$ s : Stack, e : Elem •
$\qquad$ top(push(e, s)) $\equiv$ e

If we have a definition for *top* in which we have implemented the type *Stack* as lists of elements we might have the following definitions for *push* and *top*:

value
$\quad$ push : Elem $\times$ Stack $\to$ Stack
$\quad$ push(e, s) $\equiv$ $\langle$e$\rangle$^s,
$\quad$ top : Stack $\overset{\sim}{\to}$ Elem
$\quad$ top(s) $\equiv$ **hd** s
$\quad$ **pre** s $\neq$ $\langle\rangle$

We ignore quantification, and note that ro_eb $\equiv$ **true** reduces to ro_eb when ro_eb is convergent, and that $\Box$ ro_eb reduces to ro_eb when ro_eb is pure. Thus the condition to be justified is

$\quad$ top(push(e, s)) $\equiv$ e

To justify this we simply unfold the instances of *push* and *top* (ensuring that the arguments are defined and that any preconditions are satisfied). This gives

$\quad$ **hd** $\langle$e$\rangle$^s $\equiv$ e

which is immediate.

But how do we interpret axioms that involve post expression? There are rules for rewriting post expressions as expressions not involving **post**. An expression

$\quad$ e **as** b **post** ro_eb′ **pre** ro_eb

in which e is read-only and in which ro_eb′ contains no pre-names is equivalent (using the rule *readonly_post_expansion*) to

$\quad$ **let** b = e **in** ro_eb′ **end** $\equiv$ **true pre** ro_eb

provided that

e **post true pre** ro_eb

i.e. that the precondition ensures that *e* converges. We will use such a rule to rewrite the condition obtained from the axiom and then try to justify it using our explicit definition.

Example Suppose we specify axiomatically a function to remove the smallest item from a list of integers:

value remove_min : **Int*** $\overset{\sim}{\to}$ **Int** × **Int***
axiom
    ∀ l : **Int*** •
       remove_min(l) **as** (i, l1)
         post (∀ j : **Int** • j ∈ **elems** l1 ⇒ i ≤ j) ∧
              (∃ l2, l3 : **Int*** • l2^⟨i⟩^l3 = l ∧ l2^l3 = l1)
         pre l ≠ ⟨⟩   (1)

An explicit definition to implement *remove_min* might be

value
    remove_min : **Int*** $\overset{\sim}{\to}$ **Int** × **Int***
    remove_min(l) ≡
       local
          value
          split : **Int*** × **Int*** × **Int*** → **Int** × **Int***
          split(left, right, to_do) ≡
             case to_do **of**
                ⟨⟩ → (**hd** right, left^(**tl** right)),
                ⟨h⟩^t →
                    if h ≤ **hd** right
                    then split(left^right, ⟨h⟩, t)
                    else split(left, right^⟨h⟩, t)
                    end
            end
            pre right ≠ ⟨⟩
        in split(⟨⟩, ⟨**hd** l⟩, **tl** l) **end**
       pre l ≠ ⟨⟩

The intuition behind *split* is that at any point *to_do* is the list of integers not yet examined, **hd** *right* is the smallest found so far, *left* is the list of those to the left of the smallest so far and **tl** *right* is the list of those to its right.

To justify that our definition implements the original specification of *remove_min*, we first note that the signature is unchanged. We then need to show original axiom (1) holds.

We use the rule *readonly_post_expansion* (which is applicable as all the expressions involved are pure, and so definitely read-only) to rewrite the condition from (1) as

∀ l : **Int*** •
   let (i, l1) = remove_min(l) **in**
      (∀ j : **Int** • j ∈ **elems** l1 ⇒ i ≤ j) ∧
      (∃ l2, l3 : **Int*** • l2^⟨i⟩^l3 = l ∧ l2^l3 = l1)
   end
   ≡
   true
   pre l ≠ ⟨⟩

which generates the side condition

remove_min(l) **post true pre** l ≠ ⟨⟩

The outline of the justification is now

- If *l* is empty the condition and side condition are vacuously true. If *l* is not empty we have a constructive algorithm for *remove_min* in terms of *split* (whose precondition we note is true) for which we can easily check that the recursion is well founded. (The third argument to *split* is initially finite, decreases in length by one on each recursive call, and *split* terminates when it is empty.) The only partial operators involved are occurrences of **hd** and **tl** protected by preconditions. So termination is guaranteed. In addition, all constructs are deterministic, so we have convergence, satisfying the side condition.

- For each recursive call of *split* the concatenation of its three arguments is constant, since

   left^right^(⟨h⟩^t) = (left^right)^⟨h⟩^t = left^(right^⟨h⟩)^t

On the first call they concatenate to *l*, and so on termination (since *to_do* is then empty) we must have

   left^right = l

We also note that *right* is always non-empty (on each call it has at least one element) and so we can construct *l2* and *l3* as *left* and **tl** *right* respectively.

- All that remains to be shown is that *i* is a minimal element of *l1*. We can see from the recursive calls of *split* that it is always true that

   1. **hd** *right* is no larger than any number in **tl** *right*
   2. **hd** *right* is no larger than any number in *left*

so **hd** *right* is no larger than any number in *left* or **tl** *right*, and hence in *left*^**tl** *right*. On termination *left*^**tl** *right* is equal to *l1*.

Implicit definitions If the new function definition is implicit we cannot adopt the approach of unfolding applications of the function. We have to justify the old axiom using the postcondition for the function. We can do this by noting that the theory of the new function (see appendix B.8.2) is given by

properties(value id : T $\xrightarrow{\sim}$ a T1 id(b) **as** b′ **post** ro_eb′ **pre** ro_eb) $\simeq$
    ($\exists$ id′ : T $\xrightarrow{\sim}$ a T1 • id′ = id) $\wedge$
    ($\Box$ $\forall$ b : T • id(**express**(b)) **as** b′ **post** ro_eb′ **pre** ro_eb)

(where the partial function arrows may be replaced by total function arrows).

The second conjunct gives us a theorem (in the form of a post expression) we can use in the justification of the old axiom. So we can use the *readonly_post_expansion* rule quoted earlier in this section to turn a post expression into an expression not involving **post**. The original axiom can then be justified to be a consequence of this new property (plus the properties of any other relevant new axioms and definitions.) However, it should be noted that having to show implementation of axioms by an implicit definition is not likely to be a common situation. There seems little point in replacing axioms by definitions until we are ready to write down explicit definitions.

Relation   If the principles given in this section are followed, the replacement of axioms by definitions will be an implementation.

Exercise   Provide an explicit definition for the applicative version of the function *words* from section 3.2.10.

3.2.14   Replacing sequential axioms by definitions

Purpose   This is the counterpart to section 3.2.13 when the functions involved are sequential imperative, i.e. they typically involve the sequential composition operator ";" and use variables.

Method   As in section 3.2.13 the first check is that the type of the signature of the new value definition is a subtype of the type of the signature of the old definition. We consider two cases, when the new definitions are explicit and implicit.

Explicit definitions   As with applicative functions, the theory of the old axiom is simply that the axiom is always true, and this gives the condition to be justified. The technique is basically to unfold applications of the functions in the condition.

Example   An axiom for an abstract imperative stack relating the generator *push* with the (hidden) observer *list_of* might be

axiom
    $\forall$ e : Elem •
        push(e) ; list_of() $\equiv$ **let** st = list_of() **in** push(e) ; $\langle e \rangle$^st **end**

If we implement the *Stack* type as a list of elements we might give the following explicit definitions for *push* and *list_of*:

variable stack : Stack
value
    push : Elem → **write** stack **Unit**
    push(e) ≡ stack := ⟨e⟩^stack,
    list_of : **Unit** → **read any** Stack
    list_of() ≡ stack

The condition to be justified is (ignoring quantification, which commutes with □, and noting that $ro\_eb \equiv$ **true** reduces to ro_eb when ro_eb is convergent)

    □ push(e) ; list_of() ≡ **let** st = list_of() **in** push(e) ; ⟨e⟩^st **end**

This can be justified by unfolding *push* and *list_of* and then using the techniques described in section 4.4.2.4.

But how do we interpret axioms that involve post expression? There is a rule *post_expansion* for turning a post expression into an expression not involving **post** that is presented in section 3.2.7. An expression

    e **as** b **post** ro_eb′ **pre** ro_eb

in which ro_eb' mentions pre-names $v_i\grave{}$ $(1 \leq i \leq n)$ may be rewritten by the proof rule

[post_expansion]
    e **as** b **post** ro_eb′ **pre** ro_eb ≃
        (**let** v_hook₁ = v₁, ..., v_hookₙ = vₙ,
            b = e **in** ro_eb′[v_hookᵢ/vᵢ\grave{}] **end**
        ≡
        let b = e **in true end**)
    pre ro_eb
  when e **post true pre** ro_eb

where $ro\_eb'[\,v\_hook_i/v_i\grave{}\,]$ means substitute v_hook_i for all free occurrences of $v_i\grave{}$ in ro_eb' $(1 \leq i \leq n)$. The names v_hook_i must be chosen so that they do not occur in e or ro_eb'.

Example We give a sequential imperative version of the specification used in section 3.2.13 for removing the smallest number from a list of numbers. We will hold the list of numbers in a variable and return the smallest as a result of the function *remove_min*. The axiomatic specification is

variable l : **Int***
value remove_min : **Unit** →̃ **write** l **Int**
axiom
    remove_min() **as** i
    post (∀ j : **Int** • j ∈ **elems** l ⇒ i ≤ j) ∧
          (∃ l2, l3 : **Int*** • l2^⟨i⟩^l3 = l\grave{} ∧ l2^l3 = l)
    pre l ≠ ⟨⟩

An explicit definition to implement *remove_min* might be

variable l : **Int**[*]
value
   remove_min : **Unit** $\xrightarrow{\sim}$ **write** l **Int**
   remove_min() $\equiv$
     local
       variable
         left : **Int**[*] := $\langle\rangle$,
         right : **Int**[*] := $\langle$**hd** l$\rangle$,
         to_do : **Int**[*] := **tl** l
       value
         split : **Unit** $\rightarrow$ **write any Int**
         split() $\equiv$
           while to_do $\neq \langle\rangle$ **do**
             let h = **hd** to_do **in**
               if h $\leq$ **hd** right
               then left := left^right ; right := $\langle$h$\rangle$
               else right := right^$\langle$h$\rangle$
               end
             end ;
             to_do := **tl** to_do
           end ;
            l := left^(**tl** right) ; **hd** right
         pre right $\neq \langle\rangle$
     in split() **end**
     pre l $\neq \langle\rangle$

To justify that our definition implements the original specification of *remove_min* we first note that the signature is unchanged. We then use the *post_expansion* rule quoted earlier to rewrite the condition obtained from the theory of the axiom involving **post**. The rewritten condition is

   $\square$ **let** l_hook = l, i = remove_min() **in**
     ($\forall$ j : **Int** • j $\in$ **elems** l $\Rightarrow$ i $\leq$ j) $\wedge$
     ($\exists$ l2, l3 : **Int**[*] • l2^$\langle$i$\rangle$^l3 = l_hook $\wedge$ l2^l3 = l)
   end
   $\equiv$
   let i = remove_min() **in true end**
   pre l $\neq \langle\rangle$

plus a side condition

   remove_min() **post true pre** l $\neq \langle\rangle$

Implicit definitions If the new function definition is implicit we cannot adopt the approach of unfolding applications of the function. We have to justify the old axiom using the postcondition for the function. We can do this by noting that the theory of the new function (see appendix B.8.2) is given by

properties(**value** id : T $\xrightarrow{\sim}$ a T1   id(b) **as** b′ **post** ro_eb′ **pre** ro_eb) $\simeq$
   ($\exists$ id′ : T $\xrightarrow{\sim}$ a T1 • id′ = id) $\wedge$
   ($\square$ $\forall$ b : T • id(**express**(b)) **as** b′ **post** ro_eb′ **pre** ro_eb)
(where the partial function arrows may be replaced by total function arrows).

The second component gives us a post expression as a theorem we can use in the justification of the old axiom. So we can use the *post_expansion* rule quoted earlier in this section to turn the a post expression into an expression not involving **post**. The original axiom can then be justified to be a consequence of this new theory (plus the theory of any other relevant new axioms and definitions.) However, it should be noted that having to show implementation of axioms by an implicit definition is not likely to be a common situation. There seems little point in replacing axioms by definitions until we are ready to write down explicit definitions.

Relation   If the principles given in this section are followed, the replacement of axioms by definitions will be an implementation.

Exercise   Show that the explicit definition of *remove_min* in this section implements its specification. (The argument is similar to that for the applicative version in section 3.2.13.)

3.2.15   Replacing concurrent axioms by definitions

Purpose   This is the counterpart to sections 3.2.13 and 3.2.14 when the functions involved are concurrent, i.e. they involve communication on channels.

Method   As in sections 3.2.13 and 3.2.14 the first check is that the new value definitions have the same signatures as the old.

This time there is no need to consider implicit definitions — there is no way to describe a non-terminating concurrent function by RSL postconditions. So we consider implementing axioms involving communication with explicit definitions.

The explicit form of an axiomatic description is easy to construct in outline from the axioms. The structure of the main process is a while loop containing an external choice over expressions that start with each possible initial input or output. These will usually comprise all the channels in the signature, but there may be some that only occur following a previous communication. So we have the form

   main() $\equiv$ **while true do** e_1 [] e_2 [] ... [] e_n **end**

Each expression e_i then generally takes the form

   communication ; ...

(where *communication* is an input or an output expression) but there are often cases when the communication is only possible under some conditions, in which case the usual form is

   if p() **then** communication ; ... **else stop end**

The technique for showing implementation is then basically as before — we unfold the function applications in the axioms and try to show them to be always true.

Example In the tutorial in chapter 2 we had an abstract concurrent queue *C_QUEUE0* defined in section 2.8.6.1 in part by

object I : I_QUEUE0(P)
value
   main : **Unit** → **in any out any write any Unit**,
   is_empty : **Unit** → **in any out any Bool**
axiom
   [is_empty_ax]
   ∀ test : **Bool** $\overset{\sim}{\to}$ **Unit** •
      main() ∥ test(is_empty()) ≡
         let b = I.is_empty() **in** main() ∥ test(b) **end**

We also had an implementation *C_QUEUE1* defined in section 2.8.6.3 in part by

object I : I_QUEUE1(P)
object CH : **class channel** is_empty : **Bool**, ... **end**
value
   main : **Unit** → **in any out any write any Unit**,
   main() ≡
      while true do
         ...
         ⫿
         CH.is_empty ! I.is_empty()
      end,
   is_empty : **Unit** → **in any out any Bool**
   is_empty() ≡ CH.is_empty?

To show this is an implementation, we show that each axiom of the abstract specification is true in the intended implementation, by unfolding the function applications and simplifying. In the case of *main* we will also need to "unroll" the while loop once. So we have

   main() ∥ test(is_empty())
≡
   main() ∥ **let** b = is_empty() **in** test(b) **end**
≡
   main() ∥ **let** b = is_empty_c? **in** test(b) **end**
≡
   ((... ⫿ is_empty_c! I.is_empty()) ; main()) ∥ **let** b = is_empty_c? **in** test(b) **end**
≡
   let b = I.is_empty() **in** main() ∥ test(b) **end**
as required.

Relation   If the principles given in this section are followed, the replacement of axioms by definitions will be an implementation.

Exercise   Check that the other axioms from *C_QUEUE0* hold in *C_QUEUE1*.

3.3   Changing between applicative and imperative

Purpose   There is a general choice of style between applicative, where all values passed between functions are passed as parameters, and imperative, where some values may be held in variables. The most common change is probably from applicative to imperative. This was discussed at some length in the tutorial in chapter 2. The main reasons for this change are that applicative specifications are easiest to reason about while imperative ones are often more efficient as the basis for programming language implementations. In this section we deal with the change to sequential imperative; that to concurrent imperative is dealt with in section 3.4.

Method   It is one of the aims of the design of RSL that applicative and imperative constructs are as similar as possible. This means that it is comparatively easy to change a specification from one style to the other. The method is described in the tutorial in chapter 2 and is only summarized here.

We need first to identify the type T of the variable(s), the "type of interest". (There may be more than one variable when this type is a product.) Suppose we have other types U and V not dependent on T and applicative functions f and g with signatures

value
   f : U × T → T,
   g : T → V

Then f is a generator of T and g is an observer of T. If in the imperative case we create the variable(s) of type T, the imperative version of f will write to them and g will read them. So the imperative counterpart is

variable ...
value
   f : U → **write any Unit**
   g : **Unit** → **read any** V

Note that any gaps in the types after we incorporate references to T in variable accesses are filled with **Unit**.

Each applicative generator and observer will have a corresponding imperative function. We can tabulate the types of the imperative functions corresponding to applicative constants of type T and applicative functions with types dependent on T:

Applicative	Imperative
T	**Unit → write any Unit**
$T \to T$	**Unit → write any Unit**
$(U \times T) \to T$	**U → write any Unit**
$T \to U$	**Unit → read any U**
$(U \times T) \to (V \times T)$	**U → write any V**

Now we consider what happens to applications of f and g in expressions. Describing this process abstractly, as we do in the remainder of this section, makes it sound more difficult than it is in practice. Readers may find it helpful to look first at the examples in sections 3.3.1, 3.3.2 and 3.3.3.

The applicative f will have calls of the form $f(e, s)$ which will become in the imperative form $f(e)$. Similarly the applications of g will be $g(s)$ in the applicative version and $g()$ in the imperative. But we have ignored the problem that in the applicative version f has result type T and in the imperative version f has result type **Unit**. For example, we might have applicative expressions of the form $g(f(e, s))$.

The problem is not difficult to solve. Any expression e' in which f occurs only in the form $f(e, s)$ can be written (assuming v is not free in e', that f is purely applicative and that $f(e, s)$ is convergent)

let $v = f(e, s)$ **in** $e'[v/f(e, s)]$ **end**

where the notation $e[x/y]$ means the expression formed by substituting x for every free occurrence of y in e. It is now clear that in the imperative version the v becomes a variable which is accessed directly, and so the imperative counterpart of e' will be

$f(e)$; e''

where e'' is a rewrite of $e'[v/f(e, s)]$ in which occurrences of v are typically replaced by "()" when they appear as arguments of functions with read access to the variable v. So in particular, $g(f(e, s))$ will become in the imperative formulation $f(e)$; $g()$ while, for example, $f(e, s) + f(e, s)$ would become $f(e)$; $v + v$.

3.3.1 Changing between function parameters and global variables

Purpose The overall purpose is that described in section 3.3. In this particular case we also wish to make the change apply to the interfaces of the functions involved.

Relation If the change between applicative and imperative increases the variable accesses in the types of one or more of the functions declared at the top level of the module, the change cannot be an implementation because it cannot be a static implementation. So the relation is then a static change.

Method   This is shown in the examples in the tutorial, such as the development of the imperative *I_QUEUE1* from the applicative *A_QUEUE1* in section 2.8.5.3.

Exercise   Suppose we define an applicative one place buffer:
scheme A_OPB(E : ELEM) =
    hide empty, opb, val **in**
    class
        type Opb == empty | opb(val : E.Elem)
        value
            /* generators */
            put : E.Elem × Opb $\xrightarrow{\sim}$ Opb
            put(e, b) ≡ opb(e) **pre** is_empty(b),
            get : Opb $\xrightarrow{\sim}$ E.Elem × Opb
            get(b) ≡ (val(b),empty) **pre** ∼is_empty(b),
            /* observer */
            is_empty : Opb → **Bool**
            is_empty(b) ≡ b = empty
    end
Develop the concrete sequential imperative version *I_OPB*.

3.3.2   Introducing or removing local variables

Purpose   The overall purpose is that described in section 3.3. In this particular case we do not wish to make the change apply to the types of the functions involved, and so any variables must be local.

Method   We introduce or remove variables, generally exchanging them for function parameters. In the extreme case we can have an imperative body for an applicative function, or vice versa. An example is given in section 3.3.3, where an applicative function for reversing a list is developed using two local variables and an imperative body.

Relation   If the variables introduced or removed are local to a function there is no change to the function type and so the change will be an implementation if the new function body implements the old. For the relevant principles see section 3.2.6 if variables are being introduced into a value previously only given a signature, section 3.2.7 if variables are being introduced into a value previously defined implicitly, and section 3.2.8 if the old and new versions are both explicit definitions.

Exercise   The function *can_be_true* is specified as follows:
value
    can_be_true : **Int** × **Int** × (**Int** → **Bool**) → **Bool**
    can_be_true(i, j, p) ≡ (∃ k : **Int** • i ≤ k ∧ k ≤ j ∧ p(k))

can_be_true(i, j, p) is true if there is at least one value in the range *i* to *j* for which the boolean function *p* returns true.

Develop an implementation of *can_be_true* using a local expression with a variable and a for loop.

Specify and develop a similar function *always_true*.

There is an example similar to *can_be_true* in the tutorial chapter in section 2.6.9. The development there uses two variables and a while loop. Is this preferable to one using one variable and a for loop?

3.3.3   Changing between recursion and iteration

Purpose   There are two possible purposes in changing between recursion and iteration — efficiency of execution and justification of properties.

Iteration in an implementation is generally more efficient than recursion, though the difference may be slight or non-existent if the recursion is tail recursion (which is the only kind that can always be conveniently changed to iteration) or if the recursion is not too deep, i.e. there are not likely to be many nested recursive calls. But if the recursion is deep, the difference can be very substantial. Iterative forms also often allow further efficiency improvements to be made.

Justifications in RSL are commonly based on equivalences between terms. In this they differ from some other logics for analysing sequential programs which decorate points in programs with assertions. For this reason it is generally easier in RSL to justify properties of recursive expressions than it is to justify properties of iterative expressions. Hence it is often worth formulating functions recursively at first, when we are more interested in showing they have various properties, and rewriting them later as iterative forms. This rewrite can be automatic for tail recursive functions. For others it is typically possible to justify inductively that an iterative form satisfies a recursive equation and so implements a recursive definition.

Method   The body of an applicative tail recursive definition typically takes the form

$$f(x) \equiv \textbf{if } p(x) \textbf{ then } g(x) \textbf{ else } f(h(x)) \textbf{ end} \qquad (1)$$

where p is the termination condition, g calculates the final result, and h modifies the parameter value on each recursive call. (If there are several parameters we can regard x as a product value.)

A natural imperative counterpart to this is

$$f() \equiv \textbf{if } p() \textbf{ then } g() \textbf{ else } h() \text{ ; } f() \textbf{ end} \qquad (2)$$

where we have variable(s) replacing the parameter(s), read by p, written by h and read and perhaps written by g.

The imperative definition (2) can clearly be replaced by

$$f() \equiv \textbf{while } {\sim}p() \textbf{ do } h() \textbf{ end } \text{ ; } g()$$

and this is the iterative version.

In order to keep the original applicative signature for f in the iterative version we can introduce a local expression within which the variable(s) are defined, initialised to the value(s) of the formal parameter(s). So the general form for the iterative counterpart to (1) is

> $f(x) \equiv$
> **local variable** $v : T := x$ **in**
>   **while** $\sim p()$ **do** $h()$ **end** ; $g()$
> **end**

Example   The body of the list reversing function using a local tail recursive function is

> $rev(l) \equiv$
> **local**
>   **value**
> $rev1 : Elem^* \times Elem^* \to Elem^*$
> $rev1(to\_do, done) \equiv$
>   **if** $to\_do = \langle\rangle$ **then** $done$
>   **else** $rev1(\textbf{tl}\ to\_do, \langle\textbf{hd}\ to\_do\rangle\char`^done)$ **end**
> **in** $rev1(l, \langle\rangle)$ **end**

The recursion is already within a local function *rev1*, so we can place our variables within the local expression. *rev1* has two parameters and so we need to introduce two variables. Our general scheme gives

> $rev(l) \equiv$
> **local**
>   **variable**
> $to\_do : Elem^* := l,$
> $done : Elem^* := \langle\rangle$
> **in**
>   **while** $to\_do \neq \langle\rangle$ **do**
> $done := \langle\textbf{hd}\ to\_do\rangle\char`^done$;
> $to\_do := \textbf{tl}\ to\_do$
>   **end** ;
> $done$
> **end**

The only point of difficulty here is that we must be careful about the order of updating of the variables in the body of the loop. A natural order might have followed the applicative evaluation order:

> $to\_do := \textbf{tl}\ to\_do$; $done := \langle\textbf{hd}\ to\_do\rangle\char`^done$

but we can see that the expression "**hd** *to_do*" would give the wrong result; the previous assignment has already discarded the head. There is a general technique for making sure such problems do not occur. Suppose we have actual parameters in the recursive call *e1*, *e2*, etc. and we introduce variables *v1*, *v2*, etc. Then the general form of the loop body is

let (x1, x2, ...) = (e1, e2, ...) **in**
    v1 := x1 ; v2 := x2 ; ...
end

But in general, judicious ordering of the assignments avoids the need for a let expression.

We can also see this problem in terms of the notion of linearity of expressions that we introduced in section 2.9.1. For lists, **tl** is a generator and **hd** is an observer. Hence the expression

$$(\textbf{tl}\ to\_do, \langle \textbf{hd}\ to\_do \rangle \char`^ done) \tag{1}$$

is not linear for *to_do*; evaluation of product expressions is left-to-right, so (1) is equivalent to

let to_do' = **tl** to_do **in** (to_do', ⟨**hd** to_do⟩^done) **end**

and *to_do* occurs in the scope of *to_do'*.

We can make (1) linear by introducing a let expression

let h = **hd** to_do **in** (**tl** to_do, ⟨h⟩^done) **end**

but we can also see that the reversal of (1)

(⟨**hd** to_do⟩^done, **tl** to_do)

would be linear, and the order of assignments we chose in the imperative version corresponds to this reversal.

We could instead have used a single variable for the pair of values, giving a single assignment, but this tends to be very unwieldy as we have to introduce several let expressions to separate the component values. In our case we would have something like

rev(l) ≡
    local
        variable z : Elem* × Elem* := (l, ⟨⟩)
    in
        while let (to_do, done) = z **in** to_do ≠ ⟨⟩ **end do**
            let (to_do, done) = z **in**
                z := (**tl** to_do, ⟨**hd** to_do⟩^done)
            end
        end;
        let (to_do, done) = z **in** done **end**
    end

Relation   Provided we follow the method presented in this section, or if we prove that the iterative form obeys the recursive equation, we will have an implementation going from the recursive to the iterative form.

Exercise   Use the techniques of this section to develop the recursive *split* function defined in section 3.2.13 into an iterative form.

3.4   Changing between sequential and concurrent

Purpose   There is a clear choice between systems composed of passive components and those composed of active components. While both may be given a function call interface and both may be imperative, the activities of passive systems are sequential. Active systems have main processes that are always executing or waiting for communications, and their execution may be concurrent.

The main methodological reason for being able to change from sequential to concurrent specifications is that (applicative) sequential specifications are generally much easier to reason about than concurrent ones. This was discussed at some length in the tutorial in chapter 2. It is also the case, conversely, that some systems are conveniently and naturally specified in terms of active components although the final implementation may be sequential.

Method   It is one of the aims of the design of RSL that sequential and concurrent constructs are as similar as possible. This means that it is comparatively easy to change a specification from one style to the other. The method is described in the tutorial in chapter 2 and is only summarized here.

We can distinguish two styles of concurrent formulation: the applicative and the imperative. As noted in the tutorial, the applicative concurrent style involves recursion which is generally inappropriate as an implementation technique for functions that are not intended to terminate, so we will present the imperative concurrent style (abbreviated to "concurrent"). We will assume that we are developing from imperative sequential to imperative concurrent; the reverse is also possible but not likely to be common, and would depend on the concurrent module having the kind of structure we shall develop here. We will also assume the sequential module is "single", i.e. that it has no imperative suppliers. (If it has, see section 2.8.6.4 in the tutorial.)

We first define an object I, say, that is an instance of the sequential module.

We define a single, non-terminating "main" function with type

> **Unit → in any out any write any Unit**

We also define an initial function, *init* say:

value
> init : **Unit → in any out any write any Unit**
> init() ≡ I.init() ; main()

where *I.init* is some suitable generator from the imperative sequential module.

Each sequential generator and observer will have a corresponding concurrent interface function that will be able to communicate with the main function. If the type of the sequential function is

> U → **write any** V

(where either or both of U and V may be **Unit**, the function arrow may be partial, and **write** may be **read**), then the corresponding concurrent interface function will have type

$U \rightarrow$ **in any out any** V

where the function arrow is always total.

So far we have examined the relationship between the signatures of the sequential and concurrent case. What about axioms or definitions for them?

The most general sequential function is a result returning generator, *gen* say, which has signature

gen : $U \xrightarrow{\sim}$ **write any** V

and an associated function *can_gen* used to express its precondition, with signature

can_gen : $U \rightarrow$ **read any Bool**

There will then be a corresponding concurrent interface function *gen*. The axiom for *gen* in the concurrent module is then

axiom
  [gen_ax]
  $\forall$ u : U, test : $V \xrightarrow{\sim}$ **Unit** •
    main() $\parallel$ test(gen(u)) $\equiv$ **let** v = I.gen(u) **in** main() $\parallel$ test(v) **end**
    pre I.can_gen(u)

If the type V is **Unit**, such axioms can be simplified by omitting the test function.

Example An example should make this clearer. We will take the simple but common instance of a database. It has as generators an *empty* to make the database empty, an *update* function to insert new values (or overwrite old ones). It has as observers an *is_in* function and a *look_up* function. The axioms simply record the properties:

- *is_in* returns true if a value with the right key has been inserted by *update* and false otherwise.
- If you *look_up* a value with a key that *is_in*, you obtain the correct value, namely the one inserted by the most recent *update* to that key.

The imperative sequential specification is

scheme LDB(X : **class type** Key, Data **end**) =
class
  value
    /* generators */
    empty : **Unit** $\rightarrow$ **write any Unit**,
    update : X.Key $\times$ X.Data $\rightarrow$ **write any Unit**,
    /* observers */
    is_in : X.Key $\rightarrow$ **read any Bool**,
    look_up : X.Key $\xrightarrow{\sim}$ **read any** X.Data

axiom
  [is_in_empty]
  ∀ k : X.Key • empty() ; is_in(k) ≡ empty() ; **false**,
  [is_in_update]
  ∀ k1, k2 : X.Key, v : X.Data •
    update(k2, v) ; is_in(k1) ≡
      if k1 = k2 **then** update(k2, v) ; **true**
      else let x = is_in(k1) **in** update(k2, v) ; x **end**
      end,
  [look_up_update]
  ∀ k1, k2 : X.Key, v : X.Data •
    update(k2, v) ; look_up(k1) ≡
      if k1 = k2 **then** update(k2, v) ; v
      else let x = look_up(k1) **in** update(k2, v) ; x **end**
      end
      pre k1 = k2 ∨ is_in(k1)
end

We can now define the concurrent imperative version using the sequential imperative version:

scheme C_DB(X : **class type** Key, Data **end**) =
hide I, main **in**
class
  object I : I_DB(X)
  value
    /∗ main ∗/
    main : **Unit** → **in any out any write any Unit**,
    /∗ initial ∗/
    init : **Unit** → **in any out any write any Unit**
    init() ≡ I.empty() ; main(),
    /∗ generators ∗/
    empty : **Unit** → **in any out any Unit**,
    update : X.Key × X.Data → **in any out any Unit**,
    /∗ observers ∗/
    is_in : X.Key → **in any out any Bool**,
    look_up : X.Key → **in any out any** X.Data
  axiom
    [empty_ax]
      main() ∥ empty() ≡ I.empty() ; main(),
    [update_ax]
    ∀ k : X.Key, v : X.Data •
      main() ∥ update(k, v) ≡ I.update(k,v) ; main(),

[is_in_ax]
$\forall$ k : X.Key, test : **Bool** $\overset{\sim}{\to}$ **Unit** •
   main() $\|$ test(is_in(k)) $\equiv$
      let b = I.is_in(k) **in** main() $\|$ test(b) **end**,
[look_up_ax]
$\forall$ k : X.Key, test : X.Data $\overset{\sim}{\to}$ **Unit** •
   main() $\|$ test(look_up(k)) $\equiv$
      let r = I.look_up(k) **in** main() $\|$ test(r) **end**
   pre I.is_in(k)
end

Relation   Changing from sequential to concurrent will change the interface at some level. It can only be an implementation if the interface changes are contained by **local** declarations, as we see in the following section. It will otherwise be a static change.

Exercise   Develop the sequential imperative one place buffer *I_OPB* from the exercise in section 3.3.1 to a concrete, concurrent version *C_OPB*.

3.4.1   Changing between sequential and concurrent decomposition

Purpose   It is sometimes convenient to change the body of a sequential function from a sequential to a concurrent style in order to employ an improved algorithm. We can keep the function itself sequential, and hence localize the effects of the change, if the channels involved are local.

Method   A sequential composition typically takes the form *g(f(x, s))* in the applicative case, and *f(x) ; g()* in the imperative case. In the first case *f* creates a value which *g* takes as a parameter. In the second *f* will write its result in a variable which may be read by *g*. In either case the execution of *f* is complete before *g* starts. The equivalent concurrent composition will take the form *(f(x) $\|$ g()) ; res* where a variable *res* is used to hold the result. (This is necessary as the expressions combined by "$\|$" must be of **Unit** type.) The parameter to *f* and the variable *res* can be replaced by an input and an output channel respectively if the context in which this parallel combination is placed is also concurrent.

   It is possible to exactly mimic the sequential case in the concurrent by making *f* complete its calculation, pass the result to *g* on some channel and then **skip**. *g* will only start its execution when it receives the input. But this is taking very little advantage of concurrency. If we want *f* and *g* to execute simultaneously (or pseudo-simultaneously on a single processor), we need to adapt the algorithm so that *f* sends its results to *g* piece by piece — a technique commonly known as "pipelining". It will then be found that *f* will terminate when it comes to the end of its input data (which we are assuming is passed in one piece). There is no way to make *g* recognize when *f* has terminated without a special communication. This can be on a separate channel or by means of a special piece of data on the main channel. (The former is probably preferable as it distinguishes data from control.)

An exercise producing such a decomposition may be found in section 3.2.12.

Relation   If the channels introduced or removed are local, there is no change to the external interface and so the change will be an implementation if the new function body implements the old. For the relevant principles see section 3.2.6 if channels are being introduced into a value previously only given a signature, section 3.2.7 if channels are being introduced into a value previously defined implicitly, and section 3.2.8 if the old and new versions are both explicit definitions.

Exercise   Define a concurrent decomposition of the *filter* function from the exercise in section 3.2.10.

3.5   Changing types

3.5.1   Making types finite

Purpose   Abstract types are commonly unbounded when we first define them, as they are then least constrained. However, we may need to bound them, to take account of memory sizes or word sizes during final implementation.

Method   We need to define:

1. a means of calculating a measure of the "size" of a value of a type. (This may be simple in the case of **Int** but require some extra value definition(s) for abstract or more complicated types.)
2. the effect on the functions generating values of the type, since they will typically need extra preconditions

There is another fundamental decision that needs to be taken. Finite types are usually types of values in which we store information (lists, stacks, queues, buffers, etc.) Hence the problem of size occurs in the functions that add to them. So there is a question of whether the precondition that will be used to check for the possibility to extend takes account of the current size of the value of the type only, or also takes account of the size of the item being added. The first of these options is the easiest to specify, and the latter should only be used when the items being added may vary considerably in size. Note in particular that if the precondition depends only on the current size of the value it can be neatly incorporated in a subtype definition of the form

type Extendable_T = {| t : T • size(t) < bound |}

It was stated above that we need both to define a measure for the type and also to consider adding preconditions to functions generating values of the type (or writing to variables of the type). Limiting the type without considering these functions may lead to contradictions, as demonstrated by the example below.

Example   If we have a queue definition and decide to add axioms to make the queue bounded in size, we might be tempted to simply add the following definition of a *depth* function and axiom restricting the depth of any queue:

value
 bound : **Nat**,
 depth : Queue → **Nat**
axiom
 depth(empty) = 0,
 ∀ q : Queue, el : Elem • depth(enq(el, q)) = depth(q)+1,
 ∀ q : Queue • depth(q) ≤ bound

Unfortunately, adding these extra definitions and axioms to a definition of an unbounded queue will create an inconsistent specification.[2]

The contradiction arises because we will have for the unbounded queue a function *enq* with signature

 enq : Elem × Queue → Queue

If we consider a queue *q*, say, of maximum depth and some element *e*, this signature says that *enq(e, q)* is a value of type *Queue*, and the definition of *depth* says that its depth will be *bound+1*. But the last axiom says that the depth of all queues is at most *bound*. So we can conclude that for some natural number *bound*

 bound+1 ≤ bound
i.e.
 1 ≤ 0

which is clearly a contradiction. So in this case we clearly not only have to introduce the axioms for boundedness but also change the signature of *enq*. A better definition of an applicative bounded queue is *A_QUEUE0*, defined in the tutorial in section 2.8.4.1.

Relation   Making types finite is not in general an implementation. We have already noted that simply trying to add the axioms stating that the type must be bounded leads to a contradiction. To avoid this contradiction we have to change other properties. In particular, unbounded types have a property of the form "it is always possible to add another item" — this is what we mean by "unbounded". Bounded types do not have this property. Hence we are not extending the theory of such a type and so do not have implementation. The relation will be a static implementation since maximally the types will be unchanged.

---

[2]Since the theory of an inconsistent specification entails **false**, any assertion is provable in it, including the assertion that it implements another specification. So an inconsistent specification is always an implementation. It is just not a very useful one!

Exercise   Create an abstract specification of sets of a bounded size by adapting the standard specification *A_SET* of unbounded sets in appendix A.2.

3.5.2   Changing concrete types

Purpose   The general advice on defining types is to make them abstract initially and to only make them concrete (i.e. give them a definition in terms of some combination of other types) when we are sure what representation is needed. But sometimes we will find we need to change from one concrete type to another — the development process is full of changed decisions! This section is concerned with what we do in this situation.

It is worth noting at the outset that in changing from one concrete type to another we do not in general obtain implementation. For example, if we have in one specification

type T = **Int-set**

and in another

type T = **Int**[*]

the second specification cannot be an implementation of the first (or vice versa) because the theory of lists is not an extension of that of sets — they are different. (Even more immediately, the second cannot implement the first because it is not a possible replacement for it. Attempting such a replacement would cause a type error in any expressions that assumed T to be the same as **Int-set**.)

Method   We first deal with the situation where the types appear to be different but are in fact the same. This can arise with the use of type abbreviations, so that

type
    T = U,
    U = V

and

type
    T = V,
    U = V

are clearly equivalent, and so no change is in fact involved.

Similarly, an apparent change in concrete types can arise with different expressions of subtypes. For example

type T = $\{|\ i : \textbf{Int} \cdot i{\geq}0 \wedge i{<}7\ |\}$

is clearly equivalent to

type T = $\{|\ n : \textbf{Nat} \cdot n{<}7\ |\}$

For subtypes of a common supertype we can use the rule that if we have for example

type
    T1 = $\{|\ x : T \cdot p1(x)\ |\}$,
                                             (1)

$$T2 = \{| \; x : T \cdot p2(x) \; |\} \tag{2}$$

the condition that *T1* and *T2* are equivalent reduces to

$$\forall \, x : T \cdot p1(x) \equiv p2(x)$$

We can also of course change the definitions of subtypes involving further subtypes to make them (ultimately) subtypes of maximal types. For instance, if we have in addition to the definitions (1) and (2) above

type T3 = $\{| \; x : T1 \cdot p3(x) \; |\}$

then this can be rewritten to the equivalent definition

type T3 = $\{| \; x : T \cdot p1(x) \wedge p3(x) \; |\}$

In this manner it can be checked whether subtypes of any common maximal type are equivalent.

In the rest of this section we are concerned with the problem of changing from one concrete type definition to another non-equivalent one. There are two possible situations:

1. We have just developed the concrete type from an abstract one.
2. We did not develop the concrete one from an abstract one, or we do have an abstraction but it was some development levels back and we have added a lot of detail since then.

In the first situation there is no problem — we re-develop from the abstract type as described in section 3.2.1. This will not overcome the problem noted above that the second concrete formulation will not implement the first, but they may both be implementations of the common abstraction, which is typically what we want.

In the second situation what we need is a simple way of obtaining an abstract type from a concrete one. We can then develop the abstract type into the new desired concrete one. This technique is important because it is a common and very useful development technique to start with a very concrete description of the problem using concrete types. This is generally easier to formulate than a more abstract version, and helps with the initial problems of understanding the requirements and looking for omissions and inconsistencies.

There is in fact a very easy and effective way of abstracting from a concrete type definition. The method is as follows. The techniques follow closely those presented in the tutorial section 2.8.4.1.

- First replace the type definition

  type T = type_expr

  with

  type T
  value obs : T → type_expr

  Now we have an abstract type *T* and an observer *obs*.
- Replace any other mentions of *type_expr* by *T*.
- Classify the other constants and functions with types dependent on *T* as observers and generators in the standard way.

- The observers will be definable directly in terms of *obs*, so they become derived functions with definitions.
- Some generators may be definable in terms of others, in which case they also become derived functions.
- For each of the other generators, define an *obs*_generator axiom if it does not return a result and an axiom using a post expression if it does.
- For any partial non-derived and non-result-returning generators add defined-ness axioms.
- Hide *obs*.

To complete the process of developing *T* to a different concrete type from the one we started with, we now have to implement our abstract version with the new concrete type, as described in section 3.2.1.

Example 1   Consider *A_QUEUE0* in section 2.8.4.1 as derived from the concrete version *A_QUEUE1* in section 2.8.4.6. In this case

- The observer *obs* is called *list_of*.
- The other observers *is_full* and *is_empty* are derived.
- The generators *empty* and *enq* are not result-returning and have axioms *list_of_empty* and *list_of_enq*.
- The generator *deq* is result-returning and has an axiom *deq_ax* involving a post expression.
- *enq* is the only partial generator that does not return a result, so the axiom *enq_defined* is added.

We can gain confidence in this abstraction in a very simple way: we check that the original concrete version implements the abstraction if we extend the concrete one with a definition of *obs* as the identity function on *T*.

As an example of the final step to a different concrete type we can take the development of *A_QUEUE2* from *A_QUEUE0* in section 2.8.4.7.

Example 2   Suppose we have a concrete specification of a set type:

CONC_SET(E : ELEM) =
   class
      type Set = E.Elem-**set**
      value
         empty : Set = {},
         add : E.Elem × Set → Set
         add(e, s) ≡ {e} ∪ s,
         remove : E.Elem × Set → Set
         remove(e, s) ≡ s \ {e},
         is_in : E.Elem × Set → **Bool**
         is_in(e, s) ≡ e ∈ s
   end

We want to create a new specification in which sets are modelled as lists, i.e. with a type definition

type Set = E.Elem*

We will call our observer *set_of*. Following the method for creating an abstraction we formulate *ABS_SET*:

ABS_SET(E : ELEM) =
   hide set_of **in**
   class
     type Set
     value
       /* generators */
       empty : Set,
       add : E.Elem × Set → Set,
       remove : E.Elem × Set → Set,
       /* observer */
       set_of : Set → E.Elem-**set**,
       /* derived */
       is_in : E.Elem × Set → **Bool**
       is_in(e, s) ≡ e ∈ set_of(s)
     axiom
       [set_of_empty] set_of(empty) ≡ {},
       [set_of_add]
       ∀ e : E.Elem, s : Set • set_of(add(e, s)) ≡ {e} ∪ set_of(s),
       [set_of_remove]
       ∀ e : E.Elem, s : Set • set_of(remove(e, s)) ≡ set_of(s) \ {e}
  end

We note that *is_in* is an observer and has been defined in terms of *set_of*.

None of the generators *empty*, *add* and *remove* return results, so their axioms take the form shown. None are partial so no definedness axioms are needed.

We can if we wish now show that *CONC_SET* extended by a definition of *set_of* as the identity function on *Set* implements *ABS_SET*. This is fairly obvious simply by inspection, since it amounts to replacing *set_of(e)* by *e* throughout *ABS_SET* and seeing if we get the definitions of *CONC_SET*.

We are now ready to define *LIST_SET* as a development of *ABS_SET*:

scheme LIST_SET(E : ELEM) =
  class
    type Set = E.Elem*
    value
      empty : Set = ⟨⟩,
      add : E.Elem × Set → Set
      add(e, s) ≡ ⟨e⟩^s,

remove : E.Elem × Set → Set
remove(e, s) ≡
    case s **of**
      ⟨⟩ → ⟨⟩,
      ⟨h⟩^t →
          if h = e **then** remove(e, t) **else** ⟨h⟩^remove(e, t) **end**
    end,
  is_in : E.Elem × Set → **Bool**
  is_in(e, s) ≡
    case s **of**
      ⟨⟩ → **false**,
      ⟨h⟩^t → e = h ∨ is_in(e, t)
    end
end

It is straightforward to show that *LIST_SET* implements *ABS_SET*, by showing that a conservative extension of *LIST_SET* defining *set_of* as **elems** implements *ABS_SET*.

Relation We have seen in this section that changing from one concrete type to another is not an implementation unless the concrete types happen to be equivalent. The relation will in general be a static change.

When the types are different we can obtain something like implementation by creating an abstraction of our old concrete type and then showing the new one to be an implementation of this abstraction.

We know that the abstraction will not be an implementation of the original concrete version. Can it be used instead of it? The answer is generally yes, provided two conditions are met:

- The new use type checks.
- Any equalities between values of the type of interest (expressed using "=" or "≡") are replaced by calls of an abstract equality defined as described in section 3.5.3.

The first check ensures that users are not applying operators or functions particular to the concrete type when they should be using the functions of the abstraction. Type checking will expose such applications, allowing them to be replaced by the appropriate functions (which might entail adding new functions).

The second condition cannot, unfortunately, be checked by type checking. It is not necessarily a problem, but such equalities will eventually be implemented as the built-in equalities on the implementing concrete type, and will generally be too strict. See section 3.5.3 for more details.

The relation to "retrieve" functions Readers familiar with VDM [14] will recognize that the implementation of the observer function *set_of* (by **elems** in this example) is the "retrieve" function used by VDM. They may then ask why there is no requirement in the method described here to show that this function is surjective ("onto"). The reason is that it is not necessary. All we ever have to show is that the properties of the abstract specification hold in the more concrete one. If the implementation is not "adequate" in the VDM sense, i.e. the concrete type does not have sufficient values, this will become apparent in the justification of the RSL implementation relation.

Exercise 1 The definitions in *LIST_SET* allow duplicates in the lists representing sets (which is why *remove* does not merely remove the first occurrence). Define a different version by

1. defining the type *Set* as equal to a subtype of lists not containing duplicates
2. defining *add* so that it only adds the item if it is not already present
3. defining *remove* to remove at most one item

Show that this new version also implements *ABS_SET*.

Exercise 2 Suppose we had modelled (unbounded) applicative bags concretely as

scheme LIST_BAG(E : ELEM) =
   class
      type Bag = E.Elem*
      value
         empty : Bag = $\langle \rangle$,
         add : E.Elem $\times$ Bag $\to$ Bag
         add(e, b) $\equiv \langle e \rangle \hat{\ } b$,
         remove : E.Elem $\times$ Bag $\xrightarrow{\sim}$ Bag
         remove(e, b) $\equiv$ **if** e = **hd** b **then** **tl** b **else** $\langle$**hd** b$\rangle \hat{\ }$remove(e, **tl** b) **end**
         pre count(e, b) > 0,
         count : E.Elem $\times$ Bag $\to$ **Nat**
         count(e, b) $\equiv$
            if b = $\langle \rangle$ **then** 0
            else if hd b = e **then** count(e, **tl** b) + 1 **else** count(e, **tl** b) **end**
            end
   end

and we wish instead to use the type definitions

type
   Nat1 = {| n : **Nat** $\bullet$ n > 0 |},
   Bag = E.Elem $\xrightarrow{m}$ Nat1

That is, we will model bags as finite maps from elements to their counts.

1. Formulate an abstract specification *ABS_BAG* of unbounded applicative bags. (A bounded version may be found in appendix A.3.)
2. Show that *LIST_BAG* is an implementation of *ABS_BAG*.

3. Complete the version based on maps and show that it implements *ABS_BAG*.

3.5.3   Adding abstract equalities

Purpose   Abstract types already have equalities (=) defined for them. If users use these equalities then, when the abstract type is implemented as a concrete type, the equality will be the equality on the concrete type. This equality is often inappropriate because it distinguishes values that abstractly should be considered the same. For example, considering the sets modelled as lists from section 3.5.2, the list values $\langle 1,2 \rangle$, $\langle 2,1 \rangle$ and $\langle 1,1,2 \rangle$ all abstractly represent the same set $\{1,2\}$ but are unequal as lists. So when users want to compare values of the type of interest, it is better to define an equality function to be used instead of the built-in equality symbol. We call such a function an *abstract equality*.

Note that, although presented here as a development technique, such an equality function would normally be included in the original formulation.

Method   The abstract equality is defined in terms of the non-derived observers. Values are abstractly equal if these observers cannot distinguish them. In other words, the abstract equality models the observational equivalence induced by the observers. The general abstract definition for a type of interest T is

value
    eql : T × T → **Bool**
    eql(t1, t2) ≡ obs1(t1) = obs1(t2) ∧ obs2(t1) = obs2(t2) ∧ ...

Note that, if *obs1*, say, returns a value which is the type of interest of another abstract module, the equality between its results should be replaced by a call of that type's abstract equality function.

Note that we only need to use the non-derived observers in this definition; the derived observers will also necessarily agree on abstractly equal values since they are defined in terms of the non-derived ones.

All this is quite straightforward. But there is another detail that we need to be concerned with. Users will expect the abstract equality to be a *congruence*. That is, it must be an equivalence (reflexive, symmetric and transitive) relation and it must also be the case that, for all functions, (abstractly) equal arguments give (abstractly) equal results. We need to check whether this is true for the non-derived generators in the specification.[3]

Example   Consider the specification *ABS_SET* from section 3.5.2. There is only one non-derived observer, *set_of*, so we would define the "equality"

value
    eql : Set × Set → **Bool**

---

[3]This is not quite the same as a congruence in the normal sense, for which we might need to add an induction axiom, and which would permit substitution of equals by equals.

eql(s1, s2) ≡ set_of(s1) = set_of(s2)

Now we need to check that (abstractly) equal arguments give (abstractly) equal results for all the functions in *ABS_SET*.

It should be clear that, for any *e* of type *E.Elem*,

eql(s1,s2) ⇒ is_in(e, s1) = is_in(e,s2)

i.e.

set_of(s1) = set_of(s2) ⇒ e ∈ set_of(s1) = e ∈ set_of(s2)

and similarly for derived observers in general. So in practice we only need to consider the non-constant generators. For *add* we have

eql(s1,s2) ⇒ eql(add(e,s1), add(e,s2))

i.e.

set_of(s1) = set_of(s2) ⇒ set_of(add(e,s1)) = set_of(add(e,s2))

i.e.

set_of(s1) = set_of(s2) ⇒ {e} ∪ set_of(s1) = {e} ∪ set_of(s2)

which is immediate. The check for *remove* is very similar. So in the case of *ABS_SET* we know that *eql* is an abstract congruence for the functions defined there. In fact, the manner of defining axioms for abstract applicative modules proposed in the tutorial in section 2.8.4.1 is sufficient to ensure this.

The danger comes if any generators or observers are defined more weakly. Suppose, for example, we had included in *ABS_SET* a function *choose*:

value

choose : Set $\overset{\sim}{\rightarrow}$ E.Elem

choose(s) **as** r **post** r ∈ set_of(s) **pre** ~is_empty(s)

choose looks at first like a derived observer, but is only defined implicitly. (We could only give an explicit definition by having some more information about the parameter type *Elem*.) The question is whether this definition is sufficient to ensure congruence, i.e. whether

eql(s1,s2) ∧ ~is_empty(s1) ∧ ~is_empty(s2) ⇒ choose(s1) = choose(s2)

This cannot be proved. So we add an axiom stating it:

axiom

[choose_congruent]

∀ s1,s2 : E.Elem • eql(s1,s2) ∧ ~is_empty(s1) ⇒ choose(s1) = choose(s2)

We have omitted the second, unnecessary call of *is_empty*.

When we come to implement *ABS_SET* as *LIST_SET*, there are two possible courses of action we can take over *choose*:

• We can try to give an explicit definition, such as

value

choose : Set $\overset{\sim}{\rightarrow}$ E.Elem

choose(s) ≡ **hd** s **pre** ~is_empty(s)

This will satisfy the postcondition for *choose* from *ABS_SET*, but it will not satisfy the axiom *choose_congruent*. We can demonstrate a counter-example:

$\langle 1,2 \rangle$ and $\langle 2,1 \rangle$ are abstractly equal but give different results for *choose* (1 and 2 respectively). Hence such an explicit definition is not an implementation. To put it another way, inclusion of the axiom *choose_congruent* prevented us implementing *choose* in a manner inconsistent with our expectation that abstractly equal sets behave like equal sets.

- We can retain the implicit specification of choose and the axiom *choose_congruent*. This will give us implementation, but means that we cannot make *choose* more explicit until we can make some assumptions about the type *E.Elem* and then define *choose* in terms of selecting the "most suitable" in terms of some total order. One could see this as a problem; conversely one could argue that *choose* is a difficult function to define for sets and we should have been very cautious about including it in the first place. It was only included here to demonstrate possible problems, not to suggest they are common.

Relation   Addition of an abstract equality to a module only adds definitions and is always an implementation. It is a conservative extension if no congruence axioms are added.

Exercise   Define an abstract equality function for bags as specified in *A_BAG* in appendix A.3.

   If this definition were added to *A_BAG* would any congruence axioms be needed?

3.5.4   Changing value signatures

Purpose   In all the principles for implementing values it has been stated that the type of the signature of new, implementing definition must be a subtype of the type of the signature of the old definition. But it is sometimes the case that the reverse can be true and still give implementation. This section shows how to deal with such a situation.

Method   To take an example, can we show that

value x : **Nat** • x<10

is implemented by

value x : **Int** = 1

The rule is that, if the types in the signature are different, either there is no possibility of implementation because the maximal types are different, or the maximal types are the same. If the maximal types are the same, we have to justify the theory of the old definition in the context of the new. For example, the theory of

value x : **Nat** • x<10

is (see appendix B.8.2)

$(\exists\, b : \mathbf{Nat} \cdot x = b) \wedge (x{<}10 \equiv \mathbf{true})$

and in the new context x is defined to be 1, which allows us easily to prove the theory.

For functions we need to be careful both about changes to parameter and result types but also about total and partial arrows. For example, suppose we ask if

value f : **Nat** → **Nat**

is implemented by

value
  f : **Int** $\xrightarrow{\sim}$ **Int**
  f(x) ≡ x + 1 **pre** x ≥ 0

The maximal type of both the old and new functions f is

  Int $\xrightarrow{\sim}$ **Int**

so we pass the static check.

The theory of the original typing is (see appendix B.8.2)

  ∃ b : **Nat** → **Nat** • b = f

so we have to justify this using the new f as a witness. Intuitively, we have to show for the new definition that, given a **Nat** as an argument, f will converge with a **Nat** result. This can indeed be proven from the new definition of f, where we can use the information in its definition, and so we have implementation.

Relation   Arbitrary changes of value signature will give static change. If the maximal types are the same, it will be static implementation. Changing signatures into supertypes can give implementation when there is sufficient other information in the new definition or in axioms to show that the original subtype restriction is true. However, it is rare in practice to change the types in value signatures when doing development.

Exercise   Is

value
  f : **Int** $\xrightarrow{\sim}$ **Nat**

implemented by

value
  f : **Int** → **Int**
  f(x) **as** r **post** r > **abs** x

If so, would it still be the case if the second definition was only a signature, i.e. did not have the postcondition?

Hint: intuitively, the way to interpret the first type of f is that, applied an integer argument, it may or may not terminate. If it does terminate the result must be a **Nat**.

3.6   Adding new definitions

Purpose   It is in general always possible to add definitions of new entities — objects, types, values, variables, channels or axioms — to any class expression and obtain an implementation of that class expression. Indeed, this is often a very natural means of developing specifications.

Method   There are two ways of adding new definitions:

- If the old class expression is a basic class expression (i.e. it consists of a string of declarations) we may formulate the new one by copying the old and inserting the new definitions.
- We may use the **extend** facility of RSL. This allows us to say more clearly what we are adding without having to copy all of the old.

The choice between these two depends on whether we wish to preserve the original for use elsewhere. If so, **extend** saves copying the original in the new, makes it much clearer what is being added (as well as giving a shorter formulation) and avoids maintenance problems in having two copies of something. Otherwise we just edit the original (rather than copying it) to include the extra definitions.

Relation   An extension of a class expression is always an implementation, i.e.

extend class_expr1 **with** class_expr2

implements *class_expr1*. If *class_expr2* contains either no axioms or axioms of a specific form, the result is often a conservative extension. For further information see the **relation** information in sections 3.6.1 and 3.6.2.

If the result is not a conservative extension, **extend** should be preferred to putting the new definitions into a class expression with the old either as a parameter to it or as an object definition inside it. Parameters and object definitions are intended to allow for "replacement" of the component and hence should only conservatively extend such a component (to reduce the chance of inconsistency). The **extend** construct is specifically intended to allow for non-conservative extension without replacement.

3.6.1   Adding non-axiom definitions

Purpose   As noted above, adding definitions is a convenient way of constructing specifications by formulating the basic entities first and adding extra ones later.

Method   The **extend** construct is usually the best way of achieving this as it makes it clear what is being added and what is being left unchanged. It should not be used, however, when there is a clear difference of hierarchical level between the old and new. If this notion of hierarchy is followed, the most common kinds of definition to be added with **extend** will be definitions of values and type abbreviations rather than of objects, abstract types, and variables (though all these are possible). The introduction of channels also suggests a change of level if there were no channels before, but adding an extra channel to a set already defined is not uncommon.

It is worth noting that, in practice, adding extra channels can only be done with **extend** if the signatures of processes use **any** rather than naming the channels individually and if the processes are defined axiomatically using "$\parallel$" rather than concretely in terms of "$\lceil \rceil$".

Extending with axioms is discussed in section 3.6.2.

Relation Adding new non-axiom definitions always gives an implementation. It is usually a conservative extension, as adding only non-axiom definitions can in general not add information to things already defined. There are some possible exceptions to the conservativeness of the extension, but these are mostly of more theoretical than practical interest.

One possible exception concerns the possible emptiness of types. Suppose we define an abstract type T:

type T

and then define a value v:

value v : T

The second definition now extends the first non-conservatively in that it asserts that there is at least one value v in the type T, i.e. that T is non-empty.

This may seem an unimportant problem since we are unlikely to define types without defining some values for them. It is a more realistic problem, however, when we consider subtypes. In the tutorial in chapter 2 there is an example of a bounded queue where the bound on the queue is in a parameter:

scheme ELEM_BOUND =
    extend ELEM **with class value** bound : **Nat** • bound > 0 **end**

while in, for example, the applicative module *A_QUEUE0* there is a type *List_of_-Queue* defined by the subtype expression

$\{| \ l : \ \text{P.Elem}^* \bullet \textbf{len} \ l \leq \text{P.bound} \ |\}$

where P is the formal parameter with class expression *ELEM_BOUND*.

Suppose we had omitted any restriction on *bound* and even allowed it to be negative by writing in *ELEM_BOUND*

value bound : **Int**

with no axiom. Then *List_of_queue* would be potentially an empty type. But the function *list_of*, defined by

value list_of : Queue → List_of_Queue

is total over the (abstract) type *Queue*. So if there were no values in *List_of_Queue* there could be none in *Queue*. But we have a constant *empty* of type *Queue*, so we know there is at least one value in *Queue*. Hence there would be a possible contradiction in the specification. This demonstrates that, without "*bound* > 0" in *ELEM_BOUND*, *A_QUEUE0* would extend it non-conservatively. With the *bound* being a **Nat** there is no possibility of contradiction (though all queues could be empty, in which case neither *enq* nor *deq* would ever have their preconditions satisfied). With our additional constraint that *bound* is strictly positive a queue must be able to hold at least one element.

Note that this example demonstrates a way of discovering non-conservative extension. If we can generate a contradiction in the extension (in this case the body of *A_QUEUE0*) by implementing the component being extended (the parameter *P*) in a particular way (taking *bound* to be negative), the extension is not conservative (except in the degenerate case where the class being extended is already contradictory). The solution may then be either to weaken the extension or, as we did in this case, to strengthen the theory of the class being extended.

Exercise   Add an *isin_range* function to *A_MAP* from appendix A.5, by completing

value
    isin_range : R.Elem $\times$ Map $\rightarrow$ **Bool**
    isin_range(r, m) $\equiv$ ...

3.6.2   Adding axioms

Purpose   There are two possible purposes in adding axioms:

- reducing under-specification by adding more constraints
- adding properties that can be deduced from existing properties and making them available for future use. This corresponds to the practice of proving and recording lemmas in theorem proving.[4]

Method   The method here is either to include the extra axiom(s), or to use the **extend** construct. Putting only axiom(s) in a new class expression, with the old as a parameter or as an internal object definition, is not generally appropriate. The axioms will be vacuous or else will extend the parameter or object non-conservatively.

It is important to check that the new axioms are not inconsistent with the old. For example, there is a description in section 3.5.1 of how adding axioms to make an unbounded type bounded can result in an inconsistent specification.

Relation   Adding axioms always gives implementation.

---

[4]It is preferable, however, to keep such derived properties separate as theorems since this is their purpose; it can be misleading to combine definitional axioms with derived properties. This also provides a reminder to justify that they are derivable, as any theorem should be justified.

Exercise   In the exercise in section 3.6.1 we added a concrete definition of *isin_-range* to *A_MAP*.

1. Show that *isin_range* could have been defined by means of a signature and three axioms (relating it to the generators *empty*, *add* and *remove*) by defining these axioms.

2. Which style of adding *isin_range* is preferable, the one now completed in this exercise (where it is an observer) or the one in the exercise in section 3.6.1 (where it is a derived observer)?

3. Show that the three axioms formulated in this exercise are consequences of the definition from the exercise in section 3.6.1.

4. The converse, i.e. that the body of the definition from the previous exercise (regarded as an axiom) follows from the three axioms, does not hold because there is no induction axiom in *A_MAP*. Add a suitable axiom so that the converse does hold.

3.7   Hiding

Purpose   In section 3.6 we were concerned with adding entities. The **hide** construct is more like a means of removing them. It does not actually remove them, but it makes them unavailable outside the hiding class expression. It has three main purposes:

- In making it impossible for clients to mention the names of the hidden entities, hiding controls the way in which such entities may be used. This is particularly important in the case of variables, when hiding the variables enforces a discipline that outside the hiding class expression the variable may only be accessed (read from or written to) via the functions that are provided for that purpose. This prevents unconstrained access and can be used, for example, to maintain certain invariant conditions. Thus we might wish to assert that the type of a variable is a particular subtype, or to assert that between calls of functions accessing some collection of variables that a certain relation holds between the values in the variables. If the variable(s) are hidden then, once we have justified that all the available functions maintain such conditions (and that initialisation establishes them), we can be sure that they will always hold between calls of the functions.

    Channels are usually hidden for the same reason — to ensure that the only access to the "main", server process is via the interface functions.

- Hiding names of entities also makes the names available for something else.

- Hidden entities need not be implemented as part of implementation (see section 3.9). It is sometimes the case that an entity found useful in a specification at one level is not needed at a later one and so should be hidden to save having to implement it. For example, we might initially specify a sorting algorithm implicitly using functions *is_permutation* and *is_sorted*. Once we have provided an explicit algorithm for the sort, such functions are unnecessary. Sometimes we can ensure that we do not need to implement them by enclosing them in a **local** construct, but sometimes we need to formulate them at the top level of a class expression and to then **hide** them.

Method   The method is no more than using the **hide** construct for the names we wish to be unavailable externally.

Relation   Hiding names in a class expression will not give an implementation of that class expression because names previously visible are no longer so. In fact the reverse is true. If we have

scheme
    A = **hide** defined_item_list **in** B

then *B* will be an implementation and a conservative extension of *A*.

Exercise   At the start of appendix A it is stated that some of the standard specifications could have been defined from others by extension, hiding and renaming. Demonstrate this by redefining *A_STACK* (from that appendix) in terms of *A_LIST* (also from that appendix).

    Does this give a better specification of *A_STACK* than the current one?

3.8   Using object arrays

Purpose   When we have a collection of entities of a type that is to be the type of interest of a module, we can use an object array. If there is a fixed but small number of such entities, we might alternatively introduce a fixed collection of object declarations:

object
    O1 : S,
    O2 : S,
    ...
    On : S

But this is more conveniently expressed as an object array:

type Index = {| i : **Int** • i ∈ {1..n} |}
object O[i : Index] : S

This is particularly so if n is large or if we ever want to calculate the index for a call of a function of *S*. In the latter case it is clumsy to have to write

    case e **of**
        1 → O1.f(...),
        ...
        n → On.f(...)
    end

when with the array we can write *O[e].f(...)*. We also need the array in the common cases where *n* is unknown or *Index* is an abstract type.

Method The collection of entities usually exhibits itself when our type of interest either is or includes a function or map type from the index type to the entity type. For example, in the lift example in the tutorial, in section 2.7.6.2, we have in the module *A_DOORS1* the type definition

type Doors = T.Floor → T.Door_state

where *T.Floor* is a type ranging over the integers representing the floor numbers. We are developing a system that is generic with respect to what the floor numbers are, so we don't know how many floors there are. The actual doors are pieces of hardware that, in the final system, we want to send messages to, so we want a decomposition with an object for each door and an object array is a natural choice. The method in this simple case was described in the tutorial in section 2.7.7.3. We will deal in the next four sections with more complicated cases.

3.8.1 Born-and-die objects

The first complication arises when the entities we want to model with the objects in the array are not always available. This may be because, for example, we need to model some hardware entities as "not always in service". Or it may be because we think of such entities as having existence which we dynamically start and finish, sometimes called "born-and-die" objects. This is normally exhibited by our function type being a map instead of a total function. Index values that are in the domain of the map in a particular state typically represent those objects that are "live". So in an applicative specification we will have something like

type Map = Index $\xrightarrow{m}$ T
value
   all_indices : Index-**set** = { i | i : Index},
   is_alive : Index × Map → **Bool**
   is_alive(i,m) ≡ i ∈ **dom** m,
   new : Map $\xrightarrow{\sim}$ Index × Map
   new(m) **as** (i,m′) **post** i ∉ **dom** m ∧ m′ = m ∪ [i ↦ T_init]
     pre dom m ⊂ all_indices,
   delete : Index × Map $\xrightarrow{\sim}$ Map
   delete(i,m) ≡ m\{i} **pre** is_alive(i,m),
   function : Index × Data × Map $\xrightarrow{\sim}$ Result × Map
   function(i,d,m) ≡
     let (r,t) = T_function(d,m(i)) **in** (r, m † [i ↦ t]) **end**
     pre is_alive(i,m)

all_indices and *is_alive* are just useful abbreviations. The generators are

- *new*, which adds an index to the map with some suitable initial T value, *T_init*, as its value, and returns this new "live" index
- *delete*, which removes an index from the map and so makes it cease to be "alive"
- a *function* (intended to be generic), which, provided the index is "live", calls the corresponding function for the type T, which in general will return a new T value and a result. The T value is used to update the map and the result is returned

Clients of this module are then able (provided all indices are not already live) to get a new index, call the functions of the corresponding map component and eventually, perhaps, delete the index again. We will refer to this module as the "manager" of the map (or object array when developed).

To develop such a module into one that includes an object array we note first that object arrays in RSL do not have dynamic parameter types. So we have to create an object array with parameter type *Index*. RSL objects can not start and stop existing, but they can instead start and stop being available or "live". We have a choice as to how we model the fact that in any particular state only a subset of them will be live:

- Have each object store its status as part of its state and return it on request. Then the set of live objects can be calculated by enquiring of each in turn.
- Store the set of "live" indices (or, equivalently, the "dead" ones) as part of the state of the manager.

The second is the more common implementation technique, and the one we shall follow here. We will store the free (i.e. dead, not in use) ones as a set using the standard *L_SET* module from appendix A.2.

So in our case we model as if our type, instead of being a map from *Index* to T, had been

Index-**set** $\times$ (Index $\rightarrow$ T)

which suggests the decomposition with a variable or module for the first component and a variable or module for the second. The first we could model concretely (in terms of RSL sets) as indicated, or more abstractly (using a standard *SET* module). The second is a function, and so an object array is indicated.

It is possible to do this development at the applicative level and then develop from applicative to imperative or concurrent, but, as with the lift example, it is quite straightforward to do both in one step.

We shall first need to extend *L_SET* with a function to *select* (and add) an arbitrary element not already present, and it is convenient also to add a *can_select* function:

scheme I_SET_SELECT(E : ELEM) =
   extend I_SET(E) **with**
   class
     value
       can_select : **Unit** → **read any Bool**
       can_select() ≡ ($\exists$ e : E.Elem • ~is_in(e)),
       select : **Unit** $\xrightarrow{\sim}$ **write any** E.Elem
     axiom
       [select_ax]
       $\forall$ e : E.Elem •
       let b = is_in(e) **in**
         select() **as** e′ **post** is_in(e′) ∧ (b ⇒ e ≠ e′) **pre** can_select()
       end
   end

This gives the following sequential imperative definitions in the manager module corresponding to the applicative ones above:

object
   E : **class type** Elem = Index **end**,
   I : I_SET_SELECT(E),
   O[i : Index] : I_T
value
   init : **Unit** → **write any Unit** = I.is_empty,
   is_alive : Index → **read any Bool** = I.is_in,
   new : **Unit** $\xrightarrow{\sim}$ **write any** Index
   new() ≡ **let** i = I.select() **in** O[i].T_init() ; i **end**
     pre I.can_select(),
   delete : Index $\xrightarrow{\sim}$ **write any Unit**
   delete(i) ≡ I.remove(i) **pre** is_alive(i),
   function : Index × Data $\xrightarrow{\sim}$ **write any** Result
   function(i,d) ≡ O[i].T_function(d)
     pre is_alive(i)

If the objects in the array are to run concurrently, we will need to use the concurrent rather than applicative version of *SET_SELECT* (making an object *C*, say). The concurrent version of *init* will need to initiate all the initial processes of the object array and the set process:

   init : **Unit** → **in any out any write any Unit**
   init() ≡ ‖{ O[i].init() | i : Index } ‖ C.init()

Note that *O[i].init()* is a call of the initial process for index *i*, while *O[i].T_init()* is a call of an interface function to set the state of the (running) process with index *i* to its initial value. We have to start all the processes initially and then (re-)initialise them when *new* is called.

3.8.2 Self conscious objects

It is sometimes necessary that the index of an object in the array is available in the object. In this case we need to instantiate each object in the array with its index.

We assume for simplicity that the *Index* type is available from a global types module and that the scheme, *A*, say, that is to form the objects of the array is not parameterized. (The extension to the parameterized case is simple.) There are two ways of instantiating each instance of *A* with a different value of *Index*:

- The first way is the apparently natural one of parameterization. We change A so that it is parameterized:

  scheme A (P : **class value** self : Index **end**) = ...

  and then we define the array by

  object O[i:Index] :
    hide X **in**
    extend
      class object X : **class value** self : Index = i **end end**
    with A(X)

  We have to include the definition of the actual parameter *X* in the class expression for the array, as each *X* must be different. Note that we use the fact that the value of the array index *i* is available in the class expression for the array.

- The parameterization method turns out to be very awkward. An alternative is to define *self* within the scheme *A*, but leave its value underspecified:

  scheme A = **class value** self : Index ... **end**

  Then we define the array by

  object O[i:Index] : **extend** A **with class axiom** self = i **end**

Another possibility would be to define a variable in *A* and set it to the index value as part of the initialisation of the object array. The two suggestions above seem preferable to using a variable in that they show clearly that for each instance of *A*, *self* is a constant value.

3.8.3 Communicating objects

It is a feature of the method described in the tutorial in chapter 2 that suppliers of a client cannot invoke each others' methods. This enforces a hierarchical design in which at each level the client controls any interactions between its suppliers. This in turn means that the system is comparatively easy to reason about in terms of the behaviour of its components. But it is a design restriction that can be too restrictive. In particular, we sometimes need to create arrays of objects that can communicate with each other.

A solution is to use collections of buffers as parameters to the schemes forming the array. There will be a buffer for each type of data the schemes need to input, and a buffer for each type of data the schemes need to output. Buffers may be simple one place buffers (just a channel) or may be more elaborate. For instance, suppose we need to create a "chain" of objects, so that each can communicate with those on either side of it. We can construct this as follows:

- Each object will need a collection of buffers on each side, one to connect with its predecessor and one with its successor. We define a scheme *BUFFS* to define this collection of buffers.
- The scheme *A*, say, to define the object array is then parameterized so it has a set of buffers on its "left" (*L*) and on its "right" (*R*):

  scheme A(L : BUFFS, R : BUFFS) = ...

- For finite chains we will need to consider the "end" element. Assume this has nothing to its "right". A natural way to deal with this is to define a special scheme *A_END* with only one *BUFFS* parameter:

  scheme A_END(L : BUFFS) = ...

- To form the chain, the type *Index* must be a total order, so it is either some subtype of the integers or can be bijectively mapped into them. For simplicity we take it to be a subtype of the integers:

  type Index = {| i : **Int** • i ∈ {min .. max} |}

- We will need an array of *BUFFS* that is one larger than the array of *A*, so we define

  type Index1 = {| i : **Int** • i ∈ {min .. max+1} |}

- We can now define the arrays we need:

  object
      B[i : Index1] : BUFFS,
      O[i : Index] : A(B[i], B[i+1]),
      E : A_END(B[max+1])

  Now the manager can communicate with *O*[*min*] on the buffers in *B*[*min*], and each *O*[*i*] communicates with its predecessor on the buffers in *B*[*i*] and with its successor on the buffers in *B*[*i+1*].

Other examples may be found in chapter 32 of the RSL book [23].

3.8.3.1   Sharing

In the immediately preceding discussion on communicating objects, the parameters *L* and *R* to the scheme *A* were not really to make *A* generic in the usual sense of allowing it to be instantiated with different types, different bounds, etc. In fact these are the first parameters we have used in this book that are not applicative; buffers will typically have some internal state. This use of imperative (sequential or concurrent) parameters we call *sharing*. We see that *O*[*i*] and *O*[*i+1*] will share buffer *B*[*i+1*] (for *i* of type *Index*). We allow this use of parameterization because there are some systems that are very difficult to specify without it. (It is possible to do without it for this example, but only if A is not defined as a scheme and instead its class expression is included in the definition of the array O.) However, such sharing needs to be done with great care. It means that objects defined within the same class (such as the elements of the arrays B and O) can communicate directly. This gives the possibility of interference, of the state of one object being changed by the functions of another, other than via the client–supplier relation. A function of the class in which the objects are defined will communicate only with $O[\,min\,]$ via the buffer $B[\,min\,]$, but such communications will have effects that ripple through the chain. Such systems need careful structuring so that the possible patterns of communication (and hence interference) are clear. We also need to be very careful about making concurrent communications with the chain, because this will often lead to non-deterministic behaviour.

Such problems are not peculiar to RAISE, of course. For example, a distributed database can be seen as a number of parallel processes that share common data. There are well-known problems in designing such a system, in particular maintaining consistency when changes are being made simultaneously.

We restrict this special use of the term "sharing" to imperative modules. There is obviously a sense in which, for example, the object T formed from the types module in the harbour example in the tutorial is shared between the waiting ships object and the berths object because it is a global object mentioned in both. Such applicative sharing is essential: types in particular need to be shared. It does not, however, produce the problems of interference and non-determinism that imperative sharing can.

3.8.4   Modelling heap storage

We stated in the tutorial chapter in section 2.8.5.1 that the main method presented there for developing imperative sequential modules would need to retain the applicative module if there were more than one mention of the type of interest in the domain of a generator, such as *node* for the Tree type:

type Tree == empty | node(left : Tree, val : E.Elem, right : Tree)   (1)

There is a technique for creating an imperative module in this situation that can handle the problem of allowing multiple values of the type of interest. The technique effectively models "heap storage" as an object array. We will illustrate it with two examples.

Example 1   The first example is an imperative version of trees:

scheme I_TREE(E : ELEM) =
   hide next, S, no_cycles **in**
   class
      type Tree = **Nat**
      variable next : **Nat** := 0

object
    S[x : {| i **Nat** • i ≥ 1 |}] :
        class variable left : Tree, val : E.Elem, right : Tree **end**
value
    empty : Tree = 0,
    node : Tree × E.Elem × Tree $\xrightarrow{\sim}$ **write any** Tree
    node(l, e, r) ≡
        next := next + 1 ;
        let t = next **in**
            S[t].left := l ; S[t].val := e ; S[t].right := r ; t
        end
        pre is_tree(l) ∧ is_tree(r),
    left : Tree $\xrightarrow{\sim}$ **read any** Tree
    left(t) ≡ S[t].left **pre** ∼ is_empty(t) ∧ is_tree(t),
    right : Tree $\xrightarrow{\sim}$ **read any** Tree
    right(t) ≡ S[t].right **pre** ∼ is_empty(t) ∧ is_tree(t),
    val : Tree $\xrightarrow{\sim}$ **read any** E.Elem
    val(t) ≡ S[t].val **pre** ∼ is_empty(t) ∧ is_tree(t),
    is_empty : Tree → **Bool**
    is_empty(t) ≡ t = 0,
    is_tree : Tree → **read any Bool**
    is_tree(t) ≡
        t = 0 ∨
        (t ≤ next ∧ no_cycles(t) ∧ is_tree(S[t].left) ∧ is_tree(S[t].right)),
    no_cycles : Tree → **read any Bool**
    no_cycles(t) ≡ ...
end

Trees are represented by natural numbers, which are either zero (for the empty tree) or indices into an array of tree elements consisting of three variables. The variable *next* is 1 less than the next unused object in the array. This provides a simple free storage method when storage is never freed. The definition of *no_cycles* is left as an exercise; it is the condition that it is not possible to follow the pointers in a tree in a circle.

It is possible with this approach for an arbitrary number of *Tree* values to exist. Hence it is also possible to extend *LTREE* with an abstract equality function *eql*, say, that compares trees without regard to the particular storage allocation.

We can relate this version closely to the applicative version (1). In (1) we will have axioms like

axiom
    [left_node]
        ∀ l,r : Tree, e : E.Elem • left(node(l,e,r)) ≡ l

The corresponding axiom for *L_TREE* can be written

axiom
   [left_node]
      ∀ l,r : Tree, e : E.Elem •
         let l' = node(l,e,r) **in** eql(left(l'),l) **end** ≡ node(l,e,r) ; **true**   (2)

Example 2   The tree example has an unbounded amount of storage and also never deallocates storage. Our second example puts a bound on the size of the object array being used and also allocates and deallocates storage in a similar manner to the example in section 3.8.1.

The example *L_QUEUE* below is another version of the bounded queue. It has components in the queue elements (the object array *S*) that point both forwards and backwards, and a complete queue is represented by a pair of indices for the front and back of the queue. This allows both *enq* and *deq* operations to take place in constant time. Figure 3.1 illustrates such a queue containing the elements A, B and C.

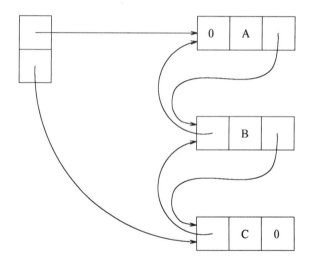

Figure 3.1: Queue

scheme L_QUEUE(E : ELEM_BOUND) =
   hide Index, X, F, S, connected, no_cycles **in**
   class
      type
         Queue :: front : Index back : Index,
         Index = {| i : **Nat** • i ≤ E.bound |}
      object
         X : **class type** Elem = Index **end**,

F : I_SET_SELECT(X),
S[x : {| i : Index • i ≥ 1 |}] :
    class variable front : Index, val : E.Elem, back : Index **end**
value
    empty : Queue = mk_Queue(0, 0),
    enq : E.Elem × Queue $\xrightarrow{\sim}$ **write any** Queue
    enq(e, q) ≡
        let f = front(q), b = back(q) **in**
            let b' = F.select(), f' = **if** f = 0 **then** b' **else** f **end in**
                S[b'].front := b ;
                S[b'].val := e ;
                S[b'].back := 0 ;
                if b ≠ 0 **then** S[b].back := b' **end** ; mk_Queue(f', b')
            end
        end
        pre F.can_select() ∧ is_queue(q),
    deq : Queue $\xrightarrow{\sim}$ **write any** E.Elem × Queue
    deq(q) ≡ ...,
    is_empty : Queue → **read any** Bool
    is_empty(q) ≡ q = mk_Queue(0, 0),
    is_queue : Queue → **read any** Bool
    is_queue(q) ≡
        let f = front(q), b = back(q) **in**
            is_empty(q) ∨ (no_cycles(f, b) ∧ connected(f, b)) **end**,
    no_cycles : Index × Index → **read any** Bool
    no_cycles(f, b) ≡ ...,
    connected : Index × Index → **read any** Bool
    connected(f, b) ...
end

Relation The introduction of object arrays is usually part of a development step from applicative to imperative, and so we will not expect to obtain implementation. We can often obtain the standard relation between applicative modules and imperative (sequential or concurrent) modules developed from them described in the tutorial in section 2.9.

Exercise 1 A system consists of an indexed collection of machines and a controller.

1. Specify (part of) such a system applicatively, including a function *reset_all* that can be used to reset all the machines to some value.
2. Develop the system into an imperative one using an object array. Assume each machine has a function *reset* that can be used to set its state to a particular value.

3. In the imperative version, does it matter whether the individual *resets* execute sequentially or in parallel? If not, what assumptions are you making?
4. Adapt your specifications so that *reset* returns a status value indicating "ok — done" or "busy — not done" and *reset_all* returns a list of indices for which the reset was not done. Is it necessary for the machines to be "self conscious" for this adaptation?

Exercise 2   In *L_TREE*:

1. Complete the definition of *no_cycles* from *L_TREE*. Hint: Note from the definition of *node* that the indices of the left and right branches must be strictly less than that of their parent.
2. Define the equality function *eql*.
3. Show that *node* always constructs a tree satisfying *is_tree* if its tree parameters satisfy it.
4. Justify the axiom (2).

Exercise 3   In *L_QUEUE*, complete the definitions of the functions *deq*, *no_cycles* and *connected*.

Exercise 4   In *L_QUEUE*, the use of a separate object F for the free storage is likely to be wasteful. Show how the free storage can be handled by the replacement of the objects X and F by a single variable pointing to a chain of free elements of the array S.

3.9   Removing hidden entities

Purpose   Sometimes we can remove all references to hidden entities (values, objects, etc.) So we would like, for example, to develop

   hide A **in class object** A : class_expr decls **end**

where decls does not mention A, to

   class decls **end**

In practice we will often do in one step the development from the first of these where decls *does* mention A to

   class decls′ **end**

where decls′ is the result of unfolding definitions from A, simplifying, etc. and does not mention A.

This often arises in the method, as illustrated in the tutorial in chapter 2, when we base imperative modules on applicative ones and then manage to unfold all the applicative entities. We would like to remove the applicative object before we translate.

Method   The method is simply to formulate as indicated above, removing the hidden entities and the **hide** clause.

Since we have removed hidden entities, to show implementation we show two things:

1. that extending the new class with the deleted definitions gives an implementation of the old class. For the example above we need to show

   extend class decls' **end with class object** A : class_expr **end** $\preceq$
   hide A **in class object** A : class_expr decls **end**

2. that the extension (the extending class expression to the left of the implementation relation above) is conservative

The first check is an implementation relation that we can justify. The second is, unfortunately, not in general provable since it amounts to showing that there are no assertions that can be proven about the extension that cannot be proven about decls'. There are, however, some rules that are sufficient to show that a particular kind of extension is conservative. See section 3.12.2.

Sometimes we have the problem that we cannot form the extension we wish because we want to hide something in the new class that needs to be visible in the declarations we want to remove. There was an example in section 2.8.5.3 when one of the hidden declarations to be removed mentioned the variable *queue* that needed to be retained, hidden, in *L_QUEUE1*. If we try to form an extension

extend L_QUEUE1 **with class value** f ... queue ... **end**

then it is ill formed because the occurrence of *queue* in the definition of f is not in the scope of the definition of *queue* hidden in *L_QUEUE1*. What we need to do is redefine *L_QUEUE1* (ignoring parameterization) as

scheme L_QUEUE1 = **hide** queue **in** L_QUEUE1_BODY

where *L_QUEUE1_BODY* is just the original intended definition of *L_QUEUE1* but without the **hide** clause. Now *queue* is visible outside *L_QUEUE1_BODY* (but not outside *L_QUEUE1*) and we can define the implementation relation we want, namely

extend L_QUEUE1_BODY **with class value** f ... queue ... **end** $\preceq$ L_QUEUE0

and justify this to show that *L_QUEUE1* implements *L_QUEUE0*.

It is also worth considering this example in terms of the rules for conservative extension described in section 3.12.2. The extending class expression in this case is

class
    type List_of_Queue = {| l : P.Elem* • **len** l $\leq$ P.bound |}
    value
        list_of : **Unit** $\rightarrow$ **read any** List_of_Queue
        list_of() $\equiv$ queue
end

We need to check that:

- there are only explicit definitions, and
- the extension is consistent with subtypes, i.e. any use of subtypes is consistent with the definitions.

We can see immediately that there are only explicit definitions. The type abbreviation is in itself harmless (even if the subtype were empty). But we have used subtypes in the type of *list_of*: its result is a subtype and it is total (the total functions being a subtype of the partial ones). We can see from the definition of *list_of* that its application just returns the value of the variable *queue*. An occurrence of a variable name is convergent, so *list_of* is total. The type of the variable (which is defined in *L_QUEUE2_BODY*) is in fact the same as the defining type expression for *List_of_Queue*, and we conclude that the definition of *list_of* is consistent with subtypes, and that the extension is conservative.

Why is no check on the non-emptiness of *List_of_Queue* needed, since it is the result type of *list_of*? In this case, although *list_of* would be an inconsistent definition, we know that *L_QUEUE2_BODY* would then also be inconsistent because the type of the variable *queue* would be empty. Any extension of an inconsistent specification is conservative. (This does not mean it might not be useful to check in the module defining the variable that its type is not empty.)

Relation   Removing hidden entities will give an implementation if it can be shown that a conservative extension of the new module implements the old module.

Exercise   Complete the following scheme definition:

scheme SORT0(E: LINEAR_ORDER) =
    hide is_permutation, is_ordered **in**
    class
        value
            sort : E.Elem* → E.Elem*
            sort(el) **as** el′ **post** is_permutation(el, el′) ∧ is_ordered(el′),
            ...
    end

Define *SORT1* with an explicit definition for the function *sort*. You may choose any sorting algorithm, or you might like to base it on *remove_min* from section 3.2.13. If you decide to introduce any new functions, remember to make them local or hide them. Omit *is_permutation* and *is_ordered*.

Define an implementation relation to show that *SORT1* implements *SORT0*. Check that the extension you use to define this relation is conservative. Check that the implementation relation holds.

Suppose *is_permutation* and *is_ordered* had been defined in an auxiliary module *LIST_FUNS*:

scheme LIST_FUNS(E : LINEAR_ORDER) = ...

Reformulate *SORT0* to use an embedded object instantiating *LIST_FUNS*. Such an object may not be needed in *SORT1*. Show that the implementation relation between *SORT1* and *SORT0* can still be expressed using a conservative extension.

3.10 Extending generality

Purpose When we first formulate a module, or a function inside a module, we tend to concentrate on the particular requirements we have been given. It is standard practice in programming to look for things that can be defined as separate functions and to separate them out into definitions, passing the values they need as parameters. Even if such a function is used only once and is not recursive (so that its call could be replaced with in-line code with advantage in program size as well as speed of execution) use of such functions may still be worthwhile because of the improvement in readability and maintainability of programs. There is then a possible generalization step in which an attempt is made to make such functions more generally useful so that they can be used in more than one context. To take a simple example, a function that is created to compare two values and return the largest might be generalized to one that takes a (non-empty) set or list of values and returns the largest. A further generalization, possible in a language that accepts functions as parameters, would be to formulate a function that returned the "largest" from a set or list of values when the measure of "larger" was defined by a function also passed as a parameter.

In specification we are concerned with similar generalizations for functions. But we are also concerned with generalizations at the module level. This is also a common concern in object oriented programming languages. So we would for example always parameterize a stack module so that we can easily instantiate it to any type we like (including stacks of stacks if we wish). The reason is partly the same as the programming one — we will get better structured specifications and we will only write things once rather than several times with minor differences. There is also a second reason: specifications should be re-usable — and in general more re-usable than programs because they are more abstract. For example, an implicit specification of what it means to sort a list may well refer only to the properties of the result — it is a permutation of the input and is sorted. It is usable as a specification of many implementations that use various sorting techniques (bubble sort, quicksort, etc.) and various ways of representing lists (chained with pointers, in arrays, etc.)

Method The overall method here is:

- Formulate (a module, function or axiom).
- Find a generalization, and formulate it.
- Replace the original as an instance of the generalization.

Various techniques for formulating generalizations are described in the following subsections.

Relation   Generalization typically involves changing the parameters to schemes or functions and so will typically be a static change.

3.10.1   Adding scheme parameters

Purpose   Adding parameters to schemes is a way of generalizing from particular modules that make assumptions about particular entities they use. Examples are:

types: We frequently create a type — a set, a list, a stack, a queue, a collection, etc. — of "something". "something" should always be made a parameter.

values: Systems tend to have many special constant values — the maximum depth of a stack, the set of indices of an array, etc. It is common advice in programming to give such a constant a name which is defined once and used everywhere else instead of repeating the value. This makes it easier to change, and avoids confusion with other constants. Making such a value a parameter is an improvement on this practice that is not usually available in programming languages (though the use of separate "header" files in some programming languages gives similar facilities).

Method   The method is the general one of re-formulation with a parameter and instantiation of the generalization to create the required instance. A number of examples of generalized schemes with parameters are presented in appendix A.

Relation   Adding parameters to schemes will generally give a static change since we are changing the scheme interface and so cannot expect replacement of a scheme with more parameters for one with less. We can, however, achieve implementation in terms of instantiations of such schemes. We simply have to provide extra object(s) to be used as the extra scheme arguments. For example, suppose we had a class expression with an instantiation of a scheme *INT_SET* providing sets of integers. The instantiation might look like

object S : INT_SET

If we then decided to generalize *INT_SET* to the parameterized one described in appendix A.2, we might instantiate it by

object
  I : **class type** Elem = **Int end**,
  S : A_SET(I)

If the remainder of the class expression that contained the original object definition is not changed, the new formulation will implement the old. (The identifier *I* must not already be the name of an entity in the class expression, but we can always choose some identifier that is not already in use as the name of an entity.)

Exercise   The concurrent schemes *C_DOOR1* and *C_BUTTON1* in the tutorial (sections 2.7.7.3 and 2.7.7.4) both describe similar classes. They have two states and functions to change and observe the states. Would it be possible to provide a single parameterized scheme that could be instantiated to provide both of these? If so, define a suitable scheme and define them both in terms of it.

3.10.2 Adding function parameters

Purpose The aim is very similar to section 3.10.1: to produce a function that is more generally useful. We avoid duplication of code and ease the maintenance problem. Justifications typically become shorter.

Method The method is again to formulate the generalization and then define the original function in terms of it.

Examples In the lift example in section 2.7 it would have been possible to define *move_up* and *move_down* functions. The addition of an extra "direction" parameter allowed these to be replaced by just one *move* function.

For a second example, suppose we have a function *min* to find the smallest item in a (non-empty) sequence. It is clear that the corresponding *max* function would look very similar. We can abstract from the particular comparison function used in *min*, "less than", to define a function that applies an arbitrary comparison, which might be instantiated by "less than" (to give *min*), "greater than" (to give *max*), "nearer to zero" (to give *smallest_absolute*), etc.

value
    best : (**Int** × **Int** → **Bool**) → **Int*** $\xrightarrow{\sim}$ **Int**
    best(comp)(seq) ≡
       if tl seq = ⟨⟩ **then hd** seq
       else
          let i = best(comp)(**tl** seq) **in**
            if comp(**hd** seq, i) **then hd** seq **else** i **end**
          end
       end
      pre seq ≠ ⟨⟩,

    min : **Int*** $\xrightarrow{\sim}$ **Int** =
      let lt = λ(x:**Int**, y:**Int**) • x < y **in** best(lt) **end**

Note that RSL does not support parametric polymorphism, so if we want a function that applies an arbitrary comparator to a sequence of arbitrary type, we need to use scheme parameters, as we saw in section 3.10.1.

Relation The new function will not have the same signature as the old and so cannot implement it directly. But, as when adding scheme parameters, we can still obtain implementation of the surrounding class expression. For example, we supplied a function equivalent to the original *min* in terms of *best* in the example above.

Exercise   Define a *filter* function for lists of an element type T by completing the following definition:

value

  filter : $(T \to \textbf{Bool}) \to T^* \to T^*$

  filter(p)(seq) $\equiv$ ...

filter(p)(seq) produces a new sequence containing only those elements of *seq* which give true when *p* is applied (and maintaining relative order of elements). You might like to reconsider the solution to the exercise in section 3.2.10 using *filter*.

  filter can also be used to specify other functions. For example

value

  is_in : $T \times T^* \to \textbf{Bool}$

  is_in(e, seq) $\equiv$ **let** eq $= (\lambda$ x : T $\bullet$ x $=$ e) **in** filter(eq)(seq) $\neq \langle \rangle$ **end**

Use *filter* to define

1. a function to remove all occurrences of an element from a sequence
2. a function to remove all duplicated elements from a sequence

3.10.3   Extending function parameter types

Purpose   A function with a parameter type that is not a maximal type is only partially useful because it cannot be applied to any value. If we can extend its parameter type it will be more useful.

Method   The method is first to change the type of the parameter.

  Sometimes the parameter type extension causes no difficulties. For example, a function defined on natural numbers may sometimes be changed to a function defined on all integers without any change to the body of its definition. Others are not so easy to generalize in this way. For instance, suppose we define the factorial function by

value

  factorial : $\textbf{Nat} \to \textbf{Nat}$

  factorial(n) $\equiv$ **if** n$=$0 **then** 1 **else** n$*$factorial(n$-$1) **end**

If we now change its type to $\textbf{Int} \to \textbf{Nat}$, we need to change the body of the definition as well, to handle negative arguments. Sometimes we can give a default result for the extra parameter values. For example, we might decide to let the factorial of a negative number be zero. To take another example, we could let the *pop* of an empty stack be the empty stack. But there is no such convenient default for *top*.

  Sometimes we will need to define some different "error handling" behaviour in order to extend function parameter types. This is discussed in section 3.10.5.

Note that weakening an explicit function's precondition is the same as extending its parameter type, and so the discussion here also applies to weakening preconditions.

Relation The new function will implement the old provided it agrees with the old on all the values in the original parameter type for which the precondition holds.

Exercise Define a factorial function that returns zero for negative arguments.

3.10.4 Weakening constraints

Purpose Another way of making things more general, and hence more generally useful, is to consider whether we have imposed constraints that are too strong. There are two typical ways in which this can occur:

- Postconditions of functions may be too strong.
- Axioms may be too strong or even unnecessary.

As an example of a postcondition of a function being too strong, consider two possible postconditions of a function to remove an element from a list:

value
    strong_remove : Elem × Elem* $\xrightarrow{\sim}$ Elem*
    strong_remove(e, seq) **as** res **post**
       ($\exists$ l, r : Elem* • l^r = res ∧ l^⟨e⟩^r = seq)
    pre e ∈ **elems** seq,
    weak_remove : Elem × Elem* $\xrightarrow{\sim}$ Elem*
    weak_remove(e, seq) **as** res **post elems** res = **elems** seq \ {e}
    pre e ∈ **elems** seq

weak_remove allows the order of the elements of the list to be changed, while *strong_remove* forces them to be unchanged. If the order is unimportant (i.e. we are using list as sets) this may be useful to the implementor. We have to be careful about altering other properties, of course — *weak_remove* will remove all copies of e and *strong_remove* just one. *weak_remove* may also change the number of occurrences of other elements.

The problem of axioms being too strong is just like that of functions. There is also the possibility of axioms being unnecessary. For example, we might define a type *Collection* abstractly by

type Collection == empty | add(Elem, Collection)

We now consider some possible additional axioms.

axiom
    [not_list]
       $\forall$ e1, e2 : Elem, s : Collection • add(e1, add(e2, s)) ≡ add(e2, add(e1, s))

The axiom *not_list* is certainly true of mathematical sets, but it may well not
be necessary here. Even if we want to use collections just for noting what is
in them and what is not, which is what mathematical sets essentially allow, the
ordering of the elements should be a design decision we can take later. A common
implementation technique for types like *Collection* is to use lists, and the axiom
not_list would make this difficult. So the axiom *not_list* should probably not be
included — it would be an example of over-specification.

This issue is also discussed in the tutorial chapter in section 2.8.4.1 where we
advise against generator-relating axioms.

Another possible additional axiom would disallow duplicates:

axiom
　　[not_bag]
　　　　$\forall$ e : Elem, s : Collection • is_in(e, s) $\Rightarrow$ add(e, s) = s

(Bags are sets with possibly duplicated elements.) It should come as no surprise
that *not_bag*, like *not_list*, is in general unnecessary and makes implementation
more difficult.

We can generalize our notion of avoiding generator relating axioms to avoiding
axioms which use equality or equivalence between terms of the type of interest.
The advice then covers axioms like *not_list* and *not_bag*. (We could formulate an
abstract equality as described in section 3.5.3 and use the equality in such axioms
instead of = or $\equiv$, but in general the axioms will turn out to be consequences of
the definition of the abstract equality and hence unnecessary.)

Finally we might add a signature for a function *choose* and add

axiom
　　[choose_ax]
　　　　$\forall$ e : Elem, s : Collection • choose(add(e, s)) = e

(*choose_ax*, together with the signature of *choose*, is equivalent to making *choose*
a destructor.)

choose_ax is another example of an axiom that is too strong. It would force us
to always *choose* the last element added. In fact, if both *not_list* and *choose_ax*
were added we would have a contradictory specification. Even without *not_list*, the
axiom *choose_ax* will be hard to implement. Suppose, for example, we implement
the collections as lists and decide to keep them ordered to facilitate searching. Then
to implement *choose* as constrained by this axiom we would have to keep track of
the last element added, not just, say, take the head of the list. So we should find
a weaker axiom for *choose*, say

axiom
　　[choose_ax]
　　　　$\forall$ s : Collection • s $\neq$ empty $\Rightarrow$ is_in(choose(s), s)

where we have also defined *is_in*.

Note that there is a connection between the ways in which the axioms *not_list*,
not_bag and *choose_ax* are too strong. If we are (abstractly) interested in sets as
opposed to lists, then certainly we want our functions (especially "query" functions

like *choose*) not to distinguish the order in which elements have been added. It turns out that such properties should be made properties of those functions, rather than enforced by axioms equating values of the abstract type, because this gives most freedom to implementors. They can retain extra information in the implementation of the type (like the ordering information in a list) while implementing the functions so that this extra information is immaterial. Thus the axiom for *choose* is wrong because it does not have this property — it depends on the order in which elements were added. Similarly, if we want sets rather than bags, a *remove* function should remove all instances, not just one, as otherwise *remove* depends on a *not_bag* property.

Method   The method here is to reformulate with the constraints changed or removed.

Relation   Weakening constraints will not give implementation precisely because some of the previously true properties will no longer hold. We may well obtain implementation in the reverse direction but this is unlikely to be of much interest here. We will obtain static implementation since signatures are not changed.

Exercise   Specify the *filter* function from the exercise in section 3.10.2 by means of a postcondition. Then weaken the condition to allow implementations where the relative order of elements may be changed.

3.10.5   Adding error handling

Purpose   Functions that are truly partial, that are undefined for some arguments, are always a problem. Whenever we have a call of such a function we have either to justify that the precondition holds or provide some suitable alternative behaviour (i.e. alternative to calling the function) for when the precondition does not hold. Such behaviour we will term "error handling". Sometimes we can safely extend the parameter type of the function to avoid the problem, and this is discussed in section 3.10.3. This section is concerned with the situation when no such extension is possible, or when we want to take definite distinctive action (like reporting the error, invoking special safety features, etc.)

Method   There are many ways of handling errors, and some programming languages provide special features like exception raising and handling that are not provided in RSL, so the advice in this section has to be of a fairly general nature.

We suggest that for most applications the question of how to handle errors can often be ignored in the initial specification. This may seem dangerous, but we have already stated that sometimes the initial specification should not attempt to cover all the requirements. It is more concerned with the main decomposition of the system into components and establishing as abstractly as possible the behaviour of those components. The system requirements may take one of two approaches to errors. They might require very definite action to be taken for error cases they foresee. On the other hand, they might offer only very general requirements like the logging of abnormal situations and a requirement that somehow the system should keep going if at all possible. Those errors for which the system requirements give some degree of latitude need not be considered in detail until enough development work has been done to help decide on the best course of action. Typically many other error possibilities are not foreseen in requirements and only arise during development — indeed their occurrence may be due to a particular design.

None of this should be interpreted as saying that we don't need to worry at all about errors until late in the development process. It is well known that some designs are much harder to make robust in their handling of errors than others. We are merely advocating the general advice that some concerns should be dealt with before others. A bad choice of where to start and a failure to keep the other concerns in the back of one's mind is always likely to cause problems.

One aim of doing formal development is to discover error cases not foreseen in the requirements. Hence the method needs to make such discovery likely.

When we define a function implicitly or axiomatically we should check that such a function exists. This is known as an *implementability* condition. Usually the only proof of such a condition is to perform the implementation, i.e. to find an explicit definition and check that it terminates (if it is supposed to) and satisfies the postcondition or axioms. Hence the initial check generally needs to be mental. Performing this mental check may suggest parameter or state values for which no satisfactory implementation exists, or which require special actions. Parameter values that require special actions may be handled within the function or elsewhere. We may want to clearly distinguish between "normal" and "abnormal" parameters and states. For instance we might define axioms in the style

axiom
    err_cond1 $\Rightarrow$ ...,
    err_cond2 $\Rightarrow$ ...,

    ...,
    $\sim$(err_cond1 $\vee$ err_cond2 ...) $\Rightarrow$ ...

A useful check on such axioms is that the conditions are mutually exclusive. We might later implement the function with a conditional expression to deal with the various cases:

value
    f : ...
    f(x) $\equiv$
        if err_cond1 **then** ...
        elsif err_cond2 **then** ...
        ...
        else ...
        end

From now on we will assume the error handling is to take place at or above the level of the call of our function, which will have a precondition or be defined on a parameter type involving subtypes. So we will at some stage be able to formulate the precise predicate establishing the conditions under which the function is known to be usable. So for each call of the function we must either establish that the predicate is already true, or else include some "guard" so that the function is not called when the predicate is not true. If we need such a guard, calls of the function will take the form

if p(x) **then** f(x) **else** handle error **end**   (1)

There are now two problems that we will deal with in turn. First there is the question of *discovery propagation*, which deals with trying to check the condition p during execution of f instead of, as in (1), before f is called. Secondly there is the question of *recovery propagation* which deals with the question of handling the error at the appropriate level.

Discovery propagation   There are good reasons for propagating the condition inwards. Consider, for example, the case where f is a look-up function on a database and p is the check that a key x is in the database. Then the expression (1) typically produces (in an implementation) two searches of the database — one to check the presence of the key and (if found) one to actually do the look-up. This is clearly very inefficient, and we would prefer to check the presence of the key during the look-up.[5] If the database has multiple concurrent readers the form (1) will also be inappropriate, since there is no guarantee that the result of p will still hold when f is executed. Including the check within f typically means changing the result type of f to indicate success or failure. This leads us to the issue of recovery propagation.

Recovery propagation   Handling an error usually means two things: calling a function that can handle it effectively — report to the user, try a different method, wait and try again, etc. — and also providing sufficient information for that function to take appropriate action. There are three main ways of doing this:

1. We can use some variable in which an appropriate error indication is deposited. Any expression calling a function which may set such a variable will need to check for the presence of a non-normal value in the variable following the function call and react accordingly. Such a variable may be fairly local, in which case there may be other such variables to further propagate the recovery outwards, or may be wider in scope to save actually passing the error indication on from one to another.

---

[5] Another possibility is to introduce a caching mechanism that stores separately the value corresponding to the key whose presence was last checked successfully. This still involves two interactions with the database but makes the second one very rapid.

2. We can define a new type for the result of functions within which errors may arise. Instead of a type T, say, it might be

   type Result $==$ fail $|$ ok(res $:$ T)

   Expressions containing calls of such functions will need to be modified to analyse the value returned.

3. We can provide an extra channel on which errors may be reported. Such channels may be fairly local, in which case there may be other such channels to further propagate the recovery outwards, or may be wider in scope to bypass inner processes.

Option 1 looks attractive at first because we seem to have to make only minor changes — we just include **write** access to such variables in the signatures of functions that may produce them. Calls of such functions will typically take the form

$$\text{v} := \text{f(x)} \; ; \; \textbf{if} \; \text{error\_var} = \text{ok} \; \textbf{then} \; ... \; \textbf{else} \; ... \; \textbf{end}$$

There are two dangers with this approach. First, there is the temptation to make such variables wide in scope to save the effort of mechanically passing the error on. This breaks the normal rules of good structuring, and makes it difficult to reason about system specifications. Secondly, there is the danger that, if the check after the call of f is ignored, i.e. no check for an error condition is made, the omission will not be noticed. This should be contrasted with adding the error condition to the value returned by f. Since its type is now different, expressions calling it will need to be changed or they will not type check.

In option 2 a call of f will typically take the form

```
case f(x) of
    fail → ...,
    ok(t) → ...
end
```

This has the advantage over option 1 of forcing the error to be handled at each level and of making it hard to ignore the error component of the returned value of f; taking $f(x)$ to be of type T instead of *Result* will generate a type error.

Option 2 does not work with processes because processes running in parallel may only return the **Unit** value. There is also the problem of restarting non-terminating processes, which will be necessary if we want the system to do anything other than terminate after the error is discovered. So for processes we have to either add the error value to an output that is to be produced or provide an extra channel. The first of these is analogous to option 2 in the sequential case and is generally to be preferred for the same reason — we might forget to do an input on an extra channel in writing other parts of the system. On the other hand, there may be no convenient output event which is about to occur when the error is detected, in which case the extra channel is needed. We may also think it better structuring to add a new channel for a new kind of information.

If the extra channel solution, option 3, is adopted, we should still note our normal structuring constraints and make it local in scope even if we have to have other channels for propagating the recovery further. Passing the message out in a structured manner is often also necessary for intermediate processes to be reset appropriately.

Relation   Discovery propagation tends to involve just enlarging parameter types and is therefore implementation, provided the behaviour on the original parameter type is unchanged. Recovery propagation tends to change interfaces and is therefore not implementation, but static change. If the error can be effectively handled at some level, levels outside it are not affected by recovery propagation and so may still be implementations, but there are usually at least some errors whose effects propagate to the outer interfaces of systems.

Exercise   Use the techniques described in the tutorial in section 2.8.4.3 to define a robust version of *A_MAP* from appendix A.5 (i.e. one in which all functions are total). Extend the ideas to produce robust versions of *I_MAP* and *C_MAP* from the same appendix.

3.11   Development in the large

Purpose   This section is about ways in which we can generate new specifications by replacing one component with another. This may seem to be much like other sections, where we have described replacing a value or type definition with another, but here we are speaking of components involving class expressions, so we are more involved with the structuring of our specifications.

The major issue is compositionality. That is, if we know the relation between two components (e.g. one implements the other), and we have a context in which one occurs, can we

- replace the occurring component with the other, and then
- deduce the relation between the new context and the old?

A method is in general regarded as compositional if it has general and reasonable rules for allowing the replacement and deducing the resulting relation. For RSL we are interested in the implementation relation between class expressions. In appendix B.8 we show the following for the implementation relation:

- Replacement is possible if the signature of the new includes the signature of the old, and if the replacement causes no capture of previously free names.
- The new context has the same relation to the original context as the replacing class expression to the class expression it replaces.

The second result about contexts is summarized as the implementation relation being compositional, defined in appendix B.8.6.

Method   The basic method is to replace a class expression by one that implements it. In the following sections we describe where class expressions may be replaced by others, and how we maintain implementation when we have implementations of the components.

Relation   As we noted above, replacing one class expression component with another that implements the original will give implementation of class expressions containing the component.

3.11.1   Building configurations

Purpose   We eventually need to assemble the developed components of a system so that we can translate them into the chosen target language. To do so we create a *configuration* by identifying the actual components to be used. A configuration will usually contain a number of RSL objects; it may also contain schemes if our target language allows schemes to be translated (as in Ada, for example, using generic packages).

Method   If we follow the development method proposed in the tutorial in chapter 2, our final specification will consist of

- one or more type modules instantiated as global objects
- a number of schemes used as parameters
- a "main" scheme containing a number of object declarations, each of which is an instantiation of a scheme defining a component. These schemes may in turn contain object declarations for sub-components also defined as schemes

Developing a global module causes no problems; it is discussed in section 3.11.3.

Schemes used as parameters are a special case because they rarely need to be developed. We discuss what happens when they are developed in section 3.11.2.

Apart from these we have a number of schemes, all but the main one instantiated as objects either globally or in others. (If our target language only allows objects to be translated, the main scheme will also be instantiated as an object.) Each of these instantiated schemes will have been subject to development, so in general there will be a version which is the finally developed one, and an earlier version which is instantiated (or perhaps versions if there is more than one instantiation). These earlier version(s) are the current "contracts" between the developments of the components.

The method is simply to replace all mentions of earlier versions with the final ones. This will be possible in the sense of giving a well-formed result if all the replacing versions statically implement the versions they replace. In general, when replacing class expressions by others, we need to be concerned about capture of free names, but all we are considering here is the replacement of one scheme name by another, and this problem cannot arise. If all the replacements are implementations, the new system will implement the old.

3.11.2   Changing the formal parameters of scheme definitions

Purpose   Sometimes we need to develop scheme parameters because we need to make more assumptions about what the parameter will provide.

Method   We saw in section 3.11.1 that, if we follow the proposed method, the parameterized schemes in our system are either the main one or are instantiated as objects in others. Changing the main scheme's parameter has no effects on the rest of the system. So the schemes for which changes in parameters have effects elsewhere always also have instantiations as well as definitions. It is sufficient to show that we obtain implementations of these instantiations. We illustrate by means of an example.

Example   Suppose we have a scheme defining a collection, parameterized with the standard scheme *ELEM*:

scheme COLLECTION(E : ELEM) = ...

and suppose we have an instantiation of this *COLLECTION* scheme as an object, where the type *Elem* is instantiated as a type *U*, say. For this we will need an actual parameter. This might take the case of a specially defined object, so that we have

object
    E : **class type** Elem = U **end**,
    T : COLLECTION(E)

Or we may have *U* defined as a type name in some object, like a global type module *G*, say, so that we did not need to define the object *E*, since we could write

object T : COLLECTION(G{U **for** Elem})

Now suppose we have a development of *COLLECTION* into *ORDERED_COL-LECTION*, which uses *LINEAR_ORDER* as its parameter (defined in appendix A.1). *LINEAR_ORDER* has the type *Elem* plus a total ordering *leq* and an equality *eql* on it. We want to instantiate *ORDERED_COLLECTION* instead of *COL-LECTION* to form the replacement object.

We will need first to define a total order on our type *U*. Suppose this is a function *lequ*. Then in the first case, where we have a special object *E*, we will now define

object
    E :
        class
            type Elem = U
            value
                leq : Elem × Elem → **Bool** = lequ,
                eql : Elem × Elem → **Bool**
                eql(x, y) ≡ leq(x ,y) ∧ leq(y, x)
        end,

T : ORDERED_COLLECTION(E)

In the second case, where we are using the global types module G as the actual parameter, it may be that *lequ* and *eqlu* are already defined in G, and we can simply write

object

T : ORDERED_COLLECTION(G{U **for** Elem, lequ **for** leq, eqlu **for** eql})

or it may be that we need to define *lequ* and/or *eqlu*. In this case we develop the global types module to $G2$, say, and use this instead of G.

In either of these cases, the development consists of

- developing E by adding definitions of the functions *leq* and *eql*, or developing G if necessary by adding definitions of the functions *lequ* and *eqlu*, and
- developing the definition of T from *COLLECTION(O)* to *ORDERED_COLLECTION(O')* where O and O' are respectively

  - the original object E and a development of it respectively, or
  - G and $G2$ (perhaps with a fitting), or
  - both the global object G (perhaps with a fitting)

The development of the definition of the object E by adding the definitions of *leq* and *eql*, or the development of G to $G2$ by a similar addition, always gives implementation. And any object implements itself. So in each case the object O is implemented by the object O'.

The development of the definition of the object T will give implementation provided

ORDERED_COLLECTION(O') $\preceq$ COLLECTION(O)

but we know O' implements O, and so by compositionality of implementation

COLLECTION(O') $\preceq$ COLLECTION(O)

Hence by transitivity of implementation it is sufficient to show

ORDERED_COLLECTION(O') $\preceq$ COLLECTION(O')

In summary: we will obtain implementation of the scheme instantiations if the class expression of the the new actual parameter (O') implements the class expression of the old actual parameter (O), and if the instantiation of the new scheme with O' implements an instantiation of the old scheme with O'.

3.11.3   Developing a global type module

Purpose   The method described in chapter 2 suggests defining a global type module with all the types we want to use generally but are not interested in developing, together with useful functions defined on these types. What happens when we need to add to this module a new type, or a new function? This can be dealt with easily.

Method   We have a global object:

object G : class_expr1

We simply add the things we need, either by extension of class_expr1:

object G2 : **extend** class_expr1 **with** ...   (1)

or by redefinition:

object G2 : class_expr2   (2)

We then change mentions of G in all other modules to mentions of $G2$. We can, if we do not wish to keep the original G as part of the history of the development, simply edit the definition of G itself. This will automatically change all references from the old G to the new one (though it will involve re-doing the type checking of all modules; tools will typically do this automatically).

Relation   We will obtain implementation if the class expression for $G2$ implements that for G. For (1) this is immediate; for (2) we need to justify

$\qquad$ class_expr2 $\preceq$ class_expr1

3.12   Verification of relations

In this section we see how the various kinds of relation that we identified at the start of this chapter can be verified, i.e. shown to be true.

implementation: If we are simply replacing in a client a mention of a module with a mention of another that implements it, there is nothing more to show since implementation is compositional.

Otherwise we are making more general changes to definitions and need to show implementation.

If the replacement module does not define some entities defined and hidden in the module being replaced, as we saw in section 3.9, we

- define an extension of the replacement module that defines the hidden items,
- show this extension is conservative, and
- show the extension implements the original module

Showing conservativeness of extension is described in section 3.12.2; showing implementation is described in section 3.12.1.

conservative extension: How to show an extension is conservative is described in section 3.12.2.

static implementation: Static implementation is decidable and therefore can be checked by tools.

If we have static implementation, it is commonly the case that the relation can be described as a partial implementation. Partial implementation is described in section 3.12.3.

static change In general it is difficult to relate modules with different signatures. However we saw in the tutorial chapter how it is possible to go from applicative to imperative (either sequential or concurrent) in a way that makes it possible to relate the properties of the applicative and imperative modules. The method for doing this suggests doing the development in a particular way so that in practice the relation can be assumed rather than stated, but it can be stated (and justified) if required. The relation, as we saw in section 2.9, involves showing that a conservative extension of the imperative module implements the applicative one.

Many other static changes are such that it is possible to describe them in terms of partial implementations; see section 3.12.3.

3.12.1   Showing implementation

The notion of implementation is basic to correct development in RSL because it is compositional, i.e. allows us to develop components separately.

In this section we consider in general how to decide if a development of a module is an implementation of that module.

Before proceeding, it is worth noting that we sometimes have a choice as to which implementation relation to establish. Suppose we start with a module $A0$. We then develop it into $A1$ and establish that $A1$ implements $A0$. We then perform a further development to $A2$. We could try to establish that $A2$ implements $A1$. Since implementation is a transitive relation this would also establish that $A2$ implements $A0$. This is likely to be the relation we are really interested in if $A0$ is the initial specification of this module. So would it be any better to show $A2$ implements $A0$ directly? In general this would be more difficult. $A2$ will be more similar to $A1$ than it is to $A0$ and this may outweigh any other considerations. Effectively the justifications that $A2$ implements $A1$ and that A1 implements $A0$ are a means of decomposing the justification that $A2$ implements $A0$. It may also be that $A1$ captures more requirements than $A0$, and we would not be checking that $A2$ also captured them if we only show that $A2$ implements $A0$.

Sometimes, however, $A2$ is not an implementation of A1 and yet is an implementation of $A0$. Working out the details of development often causes us to change direction slightly, so that, even if we see the ideas of $A2$ being a development of the ideas of $A1$, we may have changed the way we implement some of the original entities of $A0$. In this case we can obviously only justify the relation between $A2$ and $A0$.

In describing how to justify that one module implements another we will draw heavily on the definition of the **properties** of a declaration or class expression as defined in appendix B.8.2.

Technically we can only talk about one class expression implementing another. We then extend this to the idea of one object definition implementing another by saying that we will have an implementation relation between them if the class expressions defining the objects are in the implementation relation.

Similarly for scheme definitions: we will have an implementation relation between them if the class expressions defining the schemes are in the implementation relation and if there are the same formal parameters for each scheme. This is precisely what we normally need for separate development, but we can also develop and even add to scheme parameters and still obtain implementation of instantiations, as we saw in section 3.11.2.

So how do we show implementation between class expressions? A basic class expression consists of a string of declarations, each of which is a sequence of definitions. Each definition is of a particular *kind* — **object**, **type**, **value**, **variable**, **channel** or **axiom**. (Remember we are excluding scheme definitions from class expressions.) Apart from axioms, each kind of definition generally introduces a name for an entity of that kind, and one or more properties. There are some exceptions to this general rule — variant type definitions, union type definitions, short record definitions and multiple variable, channel and value declarations — but all these have expansions (described in the RSL book [23]) into strings of declarations containing definitions that do conform to the rule.

The general procedure in checking that a new class expression implements the old is as follows:

- For each non-axiom definition in the old class expression there must be a definition in the new class expression of the same kind and introducing the same name with the same maximal type or class.
- The **properties** of each definition in the old class expression must reduce to **true** in the new.

The first condition is static implementation and is defined in the RSL book [23]. We only deal here with the second, which is stated in appendix B.8.3 as a meta-rule allowing us to justify the implementation relation:

[implementation_introduction_inf]

$$\frac{ce1 \vdash \textbf{properties}(ce0)}{ce1 \preceq ce0}$$

when no_new_capture(ce1, ce0, **properties**(ce0)) ∧
    no_hiding(ce0) ∧ **no_scheme_defs**(ce0)   (1)

The first applicability condition is a check that the implementing class expression *ce1* does not capture any names that are free in *ce0*. This is necessary as such capture would in general change their properties.

The second applicability condition is a restriction reflecting the fact that the theory of a class expression can in general only be finitely presented by the **properties** function when there is no hiding involved. **no_hiding**(*ce0*) is true provided there are no names hidden in *ce0*. If the **no_hiding** restriction does not hold we can extend the implementing class expression conservatively with definitions of the missing names; see section 3.9 for details.

The third applicability condition is the restriction that we do not include scheme definitions (embedded schemes) in class expressions.

To use this meta-rule we need the definition of the **properties** function from appendix B.8.2. There are first a set of definitions explaining the **properties** of the various non-basic class expressions.

Apart from hiding class expressions, there are definitions for all the non-basic class expressions in terms of the **properties** of their components, so that the theory of any class expression satisfying the **no_hiding** and **no_scheme_defs** restrictions can ultimately be expanded into an expression involving the **properties** of a basic class expression, which is defined to be the conjunction of the **properties** of its definitions. There are then a series of definitions of the **properties** of each kind of definition. So, under some weak restrictions, the theory of an RSL class expression can be given in terms of a finite conjunction of assertions. For each class expression *ce0* the meta-rule (1) above is then really a shorthand for

$$\frac{ce1 \vdash assertion_1 \wedge ... \wedge assertion_n}{ce1 \preceq ce0}$$

when no_new_capture$(ce1, ce0, assertion_1 \wedge ... \wedge assertion_n) \wedge$
   no_hiding$(ce0) \wedge$ **no_scheme_defs**$(ce0)$

where each *assertion$_i$* is an assertion arising from a definition in *ce0*, and this can be rewritten

$ce1 \vdash assertion_1,$

...,

$$\frac{ce1 \vdash assertion_n}{ce1 \preceq ce0}$$

when no_new_capture$(ce1, ce0, assertion_1 \wedge ... \wedge assertion_n) \wedge$
   no_hiding$(ce0) \wedge$ **no_scheme_defs**$(ce0)$

With the exception of axioms, *ce1* will necessarily contain a definition corresponding to the one we are seeking to implement, because of the requirement of static implementation. But note that we are not restricted to the properties of the new definition alone in proving *assertion$_i$*: we have all of *ce1* in the context and can use all of its properties. This is particularly relevant for axioms, as it is typical that axioms in early specifications are implemented by means of definitions in later ones.

In the following discussion we consider each kind of definition in an "old" class expression and discuss what needs to be justified to show implementation of the definition by a "new" class expression. The typical sequent to be justified will be of the form

$C' \vdash assertion$

where C' is the new, implementing class expression.

3.12.1.1   Implementation of type definitions

A type definition establishes the name of the type. Type abbreviation definitions additionally establish equality between the type name and a type expression.

The theory of a sort definition is **true**, which gives nothing to justify.

The theory of an abbreviation definition is given by

properties(**type** Tid = T) $\simeq$ {id | id : Tid} = {id | id : T} so if in a new class expression C' we have an abbreviation definition

type Tid = T′

we can see that our condition to justify will be

$C' \vdash \{\text{id} \mid \text{id} : \text{Tid}\} = \{\text{id} \mid \text{id} : \text{T}\}$

i.e.

$C' \vdash \{\text{id} \mid \text{id} : \text{T}'\} = \{\text{id} \mid \text{id} : \text{T}\}$

So we have to show that the set of values in the new type is equal to the set of values in the old.

For union and short record definitions we can expand them into their equivalent variant definitions. For variant definitions, we can expand them into their equivalent sort, value and axiom definitions. These expansions are described in the RSL book [23].

It is not always necessary to expand the old and new definitions if they are both variant type definitions. Section 3.2.4 describes how variant types containing wildcards may be implemented by adding extra variants and constructors, and section 3.2.5 explains how variant type definitions may be implemented by definitions containing extra destructors and reconstructors.

3.12.1.2 Implementation of value definitions

A value definition establishes the name(s) of a constant or name of a function and its type. It may also give an implicit or explicit definition of its value.

Typings The theory of a typing is is given by

properties(**value** id : T) $\simeq \exists$ id′ : T • id′ = id

so in the new class expression we have to show that the value *id* is within the type T. Note that if T is maximal or a sort there will be nothing to show: the definition of the value *id* of the same type T or a subtype of it (necessary for static implementation) will be sufficient.

Explicit value definitions The theory is given by

properties(**value** id : T = p_e) $\simeq$ ($\exists$ id′ : T • id′ = id) $\wedge$ (id $\equiv$ p_e)

so we have to show, as with typings, that the value *id* is in the appropriate type and also that it is equivalent to the expression *p_e*.

Implicit value definitions The theory is given by

properties(**value** id : T • p_eb) $\simeq$ ($\exists$ id′ : T • id′ = id) $\wedge$ (p_eb $\equiv$ **true**)

so we have to show, as with typings, that the value *id* is in the appropriate type and also that the restriction *p_eb* holds.

Explicit function definitions   The theory is given by

properties(**value** id : T $\xrightarrow{\sim}$ a T1   id(b) $\equiv$ e **pre** ro_eb) $\simeq$

   ($\exists$ id′ : T $\xrightarrow{\sim}$ a T1 • id′ = id) $\wedge$ ($\Box$ $\forall$ b : T • id(**express**(b)) $\equiv$ e **pre** ro_eb)

(where the partial function arrows may be replaced by total function arrows).

   We have to show, as with typings, that the value *id* is in the appropriate type and also that application of the function is always equivalent to the expression *e* when the precondition holds.

   We need to take particular care with function types involving subtypes in their parameter and/or result types, or containing total function arrows, or containing access descriptors. Consider for example the explicit function definition

value
   f : **Nat** $\to$ **read** v **Nat**
   f(x) $\equiv$ ...

Part of its theory is

   $\exists$ b : **Nat** $\to$ **read** v **Nat** • b = f

To prove this for an implementing function *f* we would need to show for any **Nat** argument *x*, say, that *f(x)*

- does not access any channels,
- does not access any variables other than v,
- may read the variable v but cannot change it,
- converges, i.e. (since it does not communicate) terminates with a unique value, and
- returns a **Nat**.

Similar remarks apply to a function defined only as a typing or defined implicitly.

   Typically, of course, these properties are discharged by giving the implementing *f* the same type as the implemented one, but we also note that they will be discharged immediately provided parameter types only increase, result types only decrease, accesses only decrease, and partial arrows are replaced by total ones.

Implicit function definitions   The theory is given by

properties(**value** id : T $\xrightarrow{\sim}$ a T1   id(b) **as** b′ **post** ro_eb′ **pre** ro_eb) $\simeq$

   ($\exists$ id′ : T $\xrightarrow{\sim}$ a T1 • id′ = id) $\wedge$

   ($\Box$ $\forall$ b : T • id(**express**(b)) **as** b′ **post** ro_eb′ **pre** ro_eb)

(where the partial function arrows may be replaced by total function arrows).

   We have to show, as with typings, that the value *id* is in the appropriate type and also that the postcondition always holds when the precondition does.

3.12.1.3   Implementation of variable definitions

A single variable definition establishes the name of a variable, its type and (optionally) assigns an initial value to it.

If there is no initial assignment, the theory is given by

properties(**variable** v : T) $\simeq$
$\quad$ ($\square$ $\exists$ id : T • id = v) $\wedge$ ($\square$ $\forall$ id : T • v := id **post true**) $\wedge$
$\quad$ ($\exists$ id : T • $\square$ **initialise** ; v := id $\equiv$ **initialise**)

so we have to show that the new variable is always within the type T, that assignments to the new variable for any value in T will converge, and that the new variable has some unknown but fixed initial value of type T. The first and third conditions will be satisfied by a variable definition with the same variable name with type a (non-empty) subtype of T, and the second by a variable definition with the same variable name with type a supertype of T. So we can only implement by a variable with the same name and same type.

If there is an initialisation, the theory is given by

properties(**variable** v : T := p_e) $\simeq$
$\quad$ ($\square$ $\exists$ id : T • id = v) $\wedge$ ($\square$ $\forall$ id : T • v := id **post true**) $\wedge$
$\quad$ ($\square$ **initialise** ; v := p_e $\equiv$ **initialise**)

and in practice this means that the new variable as well as having the same name and type must be initialised to an equivalent value.

3.12.1.4   Implementation of channel definitions

A single channel definition establishes the name of a channel and its type.

The theory is given by

properties(**channel** c : T) $\simeq$
$\quad$ ($\exists$ id : T • **true**) $\wedge$ ($\square$ c? **post true**) $\wedge$ ($\square$ $\forall$ id : T • c ! id **post true**)

The first condition says that the channel has a non-empty type and the others that inputs and outputs of any value of the type must converge. This would allow implementation by a channel of the same name with a larger type, but in practice we need to use the same type to avoid possible contradictions in the types of functions involving input expressions.

3.12.1.5   Implementation of object definitions

An object definition establishes the name of the object and its class expression. An array object definition additionally establishes the type of the parameter.

We shall see that for a new object definition declaration to implement an old it must have the same name and its class expression must implement that of the old. Additionally, for arrays, the old array type must be a subtype of the new.

We could show this by examining the **properties** of object declarations, as we did for the other kinds of declaration, but the argument is fairly complicated if there is hiding involved. We appeal instead to the "compositionality" results for object declarations given in appendix B.8.6. The relevant meta-rules are

[object_implementation_inf1]

$$\frac{ce1 \preceq ce0}{\textbf{class object } O : ce1 \textbf{ end} \preceq \textbf{class object } O : ce0 \textbf{ end}}$$

[object_implementation_inf2]

$$\frac{\textbf{extend class value } b : T \textbf{ end with } ce1 \preceq}{\textbf{extend class value } b : T \textbf{ end with } ce0}$$
class object O[b : T] : ce1 **end** $\preceq$ **class object** O[b : T] : ce0 **end**

with the obvious extensions to several object parameters.

These express formally the results we claimed above, except for the possible enlargement of the type of the object parameter, which can be shown to hold as a consequence of these results.

3.12.1.6   Implementation of scheme definitions

A scheme definition establishes the name of the scheme, the names of its parameters (if any), their order, their class expressions, and the class expression of the scheme.

We shall see that for a new scheme definition declaration to implement an old one with the same parameters it must have the same name and its class expression must implement that of the old.

As with object declarations in the previous section, we appeal directly to the "compositionality" results from appendix B.8.6. For scheme declarations we have the meta-rules

[scheme_implementation_inf1]

$$\frac{ce1 \preceq ce0}{\textbf{class scheme } S = ce1 \textbf{ end} \preceq \textbf{class scheme } S = ce0 \textbf{ end}}$$

[scheme_implementation_inf2]

$$\frac{\textbf{extend class object } X : cex \textbf{ end with } ce1 \preceq}{\textbf{extend class object } X : cex \textbf{ end with } ce0}$$
class scheme S(X : cex) = ce1 **end** $\preceq$
  class scheme S(X : cex) = ce0 **end**

[scheme_implementation_inf3]

$$\frac{\textbf{extend class object } X[b : T] : cex \textbf{ end with } ce1 \preceq}{\textbf{extend class object } X[b : T] : cex \textbf{ end with } ce0}$$
class scheme S(X[b : T] : cex) = ce1 **end** $\preceq$
  class scheme S(X[b : T] : cex) = ce0 **end**

with the obvious extensions to several scheme and object parameters.

These express formally the results we claimed above.

It follows, of course, that instantiations of the new scheme will implement instantiations of the old scheme.

What if we want to develop the scheme parameters? We can in this case show that if we develop a scheme parameter to one that implements it then instantiations of the new scheme will implement instantiations of the old scheme. (We will also want to ensure, of course, that in such instantiations the actual parameters implement the new parameters as well as the old.) This is in fact a particular case of the more general discussion on developing scheme parameters in section 3.11.2. The more general discussion is relevant here since we are most unlikely to change a scheme parameter without at the same time developing the body of the scheme.

3.12.1.7 Implementation of axiom definitions

Axioms express logical properties. They may also be named but the names are ignored for the purposes of implementation.

The theory of an axiom is given by

properties(**axiom** [id] ro_eb) $\simeq$ $\square$ ro_eb $\equiv$ **true**

So the implementation check for an axiom is that it be shown to be always true in the new class expression. Any axiom name is ignored.

3.12.2 Showing conservative extension

An extension

extend ce1 **with** ce2 $\hfill$ (1)

is a conservative extension of *ce1* if all the properties of the extension that can be expressed in terms of the entities defined in *ce1* are true of *ce1*. Intuitively, the extension conserves the "*ce1*-properties". Conservative extension is formally defined in appendix B.8.4.

Unfortunately, conservativeness of an extension is not in general finitely expandable (unlike implementation) since the definition involves quantifying over all the "*ce1*-properties". However, it is possible to give a set of sufficient conditions for the extension (1) of *ce1* to be conservative. These are:

1. *ce2* contains no axioms.
2. *ce2* does not mention any subtypes, or if it does, any value, variable and channel definitions in *ce1* are consistent with those subtypes (see section 3.12.2.1).
3. Declarations in the body of any object declaration in *ce2* satisfy conditions 1, 2 and 3.

3.12.2.1 Consistency with subtypes

We need to explain what we mean by consistency with subtypes:

- For a variable or channel declaration or a value declaration that is a typing, it is sufficient for the subtype to be non-empty *without* using the variable,

channel or value declaration as evidence for the non-emptiness. In addition, if
the variable is initialised, the initialisation value must be within the subtype.
- For an explicit value or function definition the defining value must be within
  the subtype, *without* using the typing of the value name as evidence for this.
- For an implicit value or function definition there must exist a value within
  the subtype satisfying the restriction or (when any precondition is true) the
  postcondition, *without* using the typing of the value name as evidence for this.

Exercise   A scheme S is defined as follows:

scheme S =
  class
    type T = {| i : **Int** • p(i) |}
    value
      p : **Int** → **Bool**,
      a : T
  end

Decide which of the following declarations would extend S conservatively:

channel c : T
variable v : T
variable v : T := 0
variable v : T := a
value b : T
value b : T • b ≠ a
value f : **Int** → T
value f : **Int** → T   f(x) **as** r **post** r > a

3.12.3   Showing partial implementation

We saw in section 3.12.1 that an implementation relation

  ce1 ⪯ ce0

can generally be justified by justifying a (finite) collection of sequents of the form

  ce1 ⊢ assertion$_i$ (1)

where the *assertion$_i$* are the conjuncts of the **properties** of *ce0*. Note that these
are all in the context of, and hence properties of, *ce1*, the implementing class
expression.

    It is often the case that *ce1 partially implements ce0* in the sense that the
properties of the *ce1* are "close to" the properties (1) that would make it an implementation of *ce0*. We do not define "close to" formally, but intuitively we have
a partial implementation when some of the properties that would together give
implementation are true, some are true under restricted conditions, and some are
true when rewritten to take account of signature changes.

Example 1 A common instance of partial implementation is a development that makes a type bounded. Suppose we start with a specification of an abstract unbounded collection:

scheme COLLECTION(E : ELEM) =
  class
    type Collection
    value
      /* generators */
      empty : Collection,
      add : E.Elem × Collection → Collection,
      /* observers */
      is_in : E.Elem × Collection → **Bool**
    axiom
      [is_in_empty] $\forall$ e : E.Elem • is_in(e, empty) $\equiv$ **false**,
      [is_in_add]
        $\forall$ e, e' : E.Elems, s : Collection •
          is_in(e', add(e, s)) $\equiv$ e = e' $\lor$ is_in(e', s)
  end

and then we want to implement it with a scheme *BOUNDED_COLLECTION* with a maximum size to *Collection* and an observer *is_full*. First we will need to strengthen the parameter from *ELEM* to *ELEM_BOUND*, say, to include a bound. Now the conditions to show that a suitable instantiation of *BOUNDED_COLLECTION* implemented the corresponding instantiation of *COLLECTION* (as described in section 3.11.2) would expand to

  class object E : ELEM_BOUND **end**, BOUNDED_COLLECTION(E) $\vdash$
    $\forall$ e : E.Elem • is_in(e, empty) $\equiv$ **false**   (2)

and

  class object E : ELEM_BOUND **end**, BOUNDED_COLLECTION(E) $\vdash$
    $\forall$ e, e' : E.Elems, s : Collection •
    is_in(e', add(e, s)) $\equiv$ e = e' $\lor$ is_in(e', s)   (3)

But in fact, while (2) will hold in *BOUNDED_COLLECTION(E)*, (3) will not; add is no longer a total function and will have a precondition. But we can write instead the condition

  class object E : ELEM_BOUND **end**, BOUNDED_COLLECTION(E) $\vdash$
    $\forall$ e, e' : E.Elems, s : Collection • $\sim$is_full(s) $\Rightarrow$
    is_in(e', add(e, s)) $\equiv$ e = e' $\lor$ is_in(e', s)   (4)

So we can express the relation between *COLLECTION* and *BOUNDED_COL-LECTION* as the properties (2) and (4) and claim this as a partial implementation on the basis that these are close to the properties (2) and (3). We would also provide some textual commentary to explain the differences between the partial implementation conditions and the ones we would get from expanding the implementation relation; otherwise the partial implementation conditions are hard to interpret.

Expressing a relation as a variation on implementation also helps the developers of clients of the module understand what is changing; which properties of the old module are preserved, which are different and in what way.

This first example shows a relation that is a static implementation being described as a partial implementation. The next example shows the technique being applied to a static change.

Example 2   Suppose we generalize a function f from a scheme $S0$ by adding an extra, second parameter in a development $S1$. One way to deal with this is to give the more general function a new name and to define f in terms of it. Then we would expect to obtain implementation of $S0$ by $S1$. But suppose we do not do this; we just change the signature of f. Again we will see that we can form a partial implementation.

Suppose there is an axiom in $S0$ of the form

axiom

$\quad$ [g_f] $\forall$ x : T • g(f(x)) $\equiv$ e

where g is implemented in $S1$ and the expression e can be rewritten in terms of the entities defined in $S1$. Presumably the new f in $S1$ behaves the same as the old f when its new parameter has some particular constant value c, say. So we can write the corresponding property of $S1$ as

$\quad$ S1 ⊢ $\forall$ x : T • g(f(x, c)) $\equiv$ e

We can obviously generalize to several signature changes between $S0$ and $S1$.

This second example shows a relation that is a static change being described as a partial implementation.

3.12.3.1   Conclusion

In this section we have considered the various kinds of relations and shown that their verification involves verification of implementation, conservative extension and partial implementation.

Implementation involves the **properties** of all the different kinds of definition in RSL. We can, under some weak restrictions expressed in terms of **no_hiding** and **no_scheme_defs**, form the **properties** of any basic class expression simply by forming the conjunction of the **properties** of its constituent definitions. There are definitions (see appendix B.8) for the non-basic class expressions satisfying these restrictions in terms of the **properties** of their components, so that the **properties** of such a class expression can ultimately be expanded into a finite conjunction of assertions. We also have a technique of dealing with the case where **no_hiding** does not hold that involves extending the implementing class expression conservatively.

We have also seen that it is possible in practice to expand the implementation relation as a number of separate conditions, each consisting of one conjunct of the **properties** of the class being implemented in the context of the implementing class expression. This is convenient for justifications of implementation.

Conservative extension, unlike implementation, in general has no finite expansion into properties. In practice we show it by construction, by restricting the definitions we use and showing consistency with subtypes.

Partial implementation involves formulating the properties that are preserved (often close to those that would need to hold for implementation) and verifying them.

CHAPTER 4

Justification

One of the major reasons for expressing specifications in a formal language like RSL is to prove properties of the specifications. Which properties are we interested in? For a module, we may be interested in theorems about it. We may also be interested in checking that there is no unintended use of language constructs like division by zero. For a development step, we may be interested in a development relation stating how the new module should be related to the old module in order to be a correct development. In the tutorial, there were several examples of such development relations, e.g. *A_QUEUE0_1* in section 2.8.4.6. Formulating properties (also called conditions) about a module or development step and then trying to prove them is a way of ensuring correctness and detecting errors before further work is undertaken. This potentially reduces the effort devoted to testing software, not because testing should be reduced in scope, but because fewer errors in the code lead to fewer test failures and less re-work and re-testing.

In RAISE, a *justification* is an argument showing the truth of some condition. Such an argument can be totally formal, i.e. be a mathematical *proof* based on application of proof rules for RSL. Justification can, however, also be done more informally if this suits the practical or economic constraints associated with a particular industrial application. The idea of using informal arguments is to indicate how formal proofs could have been constructed. In other words, whenever informal arguments are used one should be convinced that it is possible to replace them with formal proofs. Such arguments, which depend on a formal underpinning but allow for informal steps, are called *rigorous*.

This chapter gives an introduction to the formulation of justifications and contains advice on techniques that can be used in constructing justifications.

Section 4.1 introduces the notion of justification conditions and section 4.2 the notion of justifications. The following sections 4.3, 4.4 and 4.5 give advice on techniques that can be used in constructing justifications. Section 4.3 gives general advice, while section 4.4 gives particular advice related to imperative constructs and section 4.5 particular advice related to concurrency.

The creation of justifications can be supported by computer-based tools. Which kind of support a tool can give is described in section 4.6. Some of the justification examples in this chapter have actually been produced using such a tool, but it is not the purpose of this book to explain how any specific tool operates.

4.1 Justification conditions

This section defines the notion of justification conditions and describes different kinds of justification conditions.

A *justification condition* (usually abbreviated to *condition*) is an assertion together with a context in which the assertion is to be interpreted. The context contains definitions (of objects, schemes, types, values, variables, channels and axioms) which define free names occurring in the assertion and state properties that can be assumed to be true in the assertion.

More precisely, a justification condition is a *sequent*,[1] i.e. it has one of the following forms:

- assertion
- context ⊢ assertion

An *assertion* is one of the following constructs:

- a logical value expression
- an implementation relation

and a *context* is a list of assumptions, where an *assumption* is one of the following constructs:

- a class expression
- a declaration
- an axiom assumption of the form *[id] ro_eb*, where *ro_eb* is a logical value expression

We say that a context *contains* all those definitions which its assumptions stand for. The RSL book [23] defines which definitions a class expression stands for. A declaration stands for its constituent definitions. An axiom assumption is short for the declaration **axiom** *[id] ro_eb*. The scope[2] of an assumption in a sequent extends to any assumption to its right and to the assertion.

A sequent of the form *assertion* is short for the sequent **class end** ⊢ *assertion*.

In practice, we do not display the full context of an assertion as the context may be quite large. For instance, we will typically not display definitions of global

---

[1]Formally, we should distinguish between *sequents* and *meta-sequents*, and between *assertions* and *meta-assertions*, as done in appendix B.8.3. This distinction serves to ensure that there are no circularities in the definition of the implementation relation. However, for the presentation in this chapter the distinction is not important and we ignore it and include meta-sequents in the term "sequent" and meta-assertions in the term "assertion".

[2]The *scope* of a declarative construct is a region of RSL text in which the identifiers and operators it introduces are potentially visible. However, there may be places where they are hidden, cf. the RSL book [23].

modules. Section 4.3.2 will describe the principles according to which the non-displayed (implicit) part of the context can be derived. We call the non-displayed part, *context*, of the context for the *context of the condition* and say that the condition *is interpreted in* or *has* the context *context*. So, if a condition, *ce* ⊢ *assertion*, is interpreted in *context*, then the *assertion* is interpreted in the context "*context, ce*". In other words, if we had displayed the whole context, the condition would have been *context, ce* ⊢ *assertion*.

A sequent of the form *context* ⊢ *assertion* (where the *context* is the full context) is true if *assertion* is true in all states in all models satisfying the definitions in the context *context*.

Section 4.3.2 will also explain how the definitions in the context of an assertion can be used to justify the assertion. For instance, if the assertion $x > 0$ has in its context an axiom $x = 1$, we can use this axiom to justify the assertion.

In RAISE there is a distinction between two kinds of conditions to be justified:

- formal conditions
- confidence conditions

These are described in the following two sections.

4.1.1   Formal conditions

Formal conditions are sequents whose truth is expected. Formal conditions appear as the sequents stipulated in theorems and development relations. The truth of a theorem can affect the formal correctness of a proof, since the theorem can be used in the proof. The truth of a development relation can affect the formal correctness of the way in which a configuration is built (e.g. when a specification is substituted for another specification, based on a stipulation that the implementation relation holds between them).

An example of a formal condition from a theorem
Assume the following definition of a global module, *I*:

    scheme I =
      class
        type El = **Int***
        value
          insert : **Int** × El → El
          insert(i, el) ≡ ⟨i⟩ ⁁ el,
          member : **Int** × El → **Bool**
          member(i, el) ≡ el ≠ ⟨⟩ ∧ (i = **hd** el ∨ member(i, **tl** el))
      end

and a theorem *T*, about it:

    theorem [T] I ⊢ ∀ i : **Int**, il : El • member(i, insert(i, il))

Then

I ⊢ ∀ i : **Int**, il : El • member(i, insert(i, il))

is a formal condition arising from the theorem *T*. This condition is to be interpreted in a context which contains the definition of the scheme *I*. In general, a formal condition is to be interpreted in a context containing those module definitions which were in the context[3] of the theorem or development relation from which it came.

An example of a formal condition from a development relation

Assume definitions of two global unparameterized schemes, *STACK0* and *STACK1* and the following development relation:

development_relation [STACK_DEV] STACK1 ⪯ STACK0

Then

STACK1 ⪯ STACK0

is a formal condition arising from the development relation *STACK_DEV*. This condition is to be interpreted in a context which contains the definitions of the modules *STACK0* and *STACK1*.

4.1.2   Confidence conditions

Confidence conditions are sequents whose truth increases the confidence that there is no unintended use of RSL constructs in a RAISE entity (module, theorem or development relation). The confidence conditions extend the normal static context conditions (such as maximal type correctness) in ensuring that constructs like division by zero do not occur. Such constructs are legal, so the construct is not formally incorrect and might be intended, but very probably the specifier has made a mistake.

For a given RAISE entity, one can systematically (or even automatically by a tool) generate confidence conditions sufficient to show that the RAISE entity does not contain such potentially unintended use of constructs. Each of the generated confidence conditions should be inspected, and it should be decided whether it is relevant, in which case it should be justified, or whether it is irrelevant (because a certain use of a construct was intended), in which case it should be ignored. Hence, confidence conditions differ from formal conditions in that they can be considered irrelevant.

We shall now give three examples of concerns that can give rise to the generation of confidence conditions:

- precondition satisfaction
- non-divergence
- subtype correctness

---

[3]Theorems and development relations are, like modules, to be interpreted in a context.

Precondition satisfaction
An explicitly defined partial function with a precondition can, according to the static context conditions, be applied to any actual parameter whose maximal type is the same as the maximal type of the formal parameter. In particular it is allowed to be applied to a parameter which does not satisfy the precondition, in which case the result of the application is under-specified. Since the specifier of the function has taken care to specify a precondition for the function, it is probably the intention that the precondition should hold for any actual parameter. Similar considerations hold for pre-defined operators. A natural choice is therefore to generate confidence conditions ensuring that pre-defined operators and user-defined functions are only applied to actual parameters which satisfy the preconditions. For instance, for the RSL expression ei_1 / ei_2, where ei_1 and ei_2 are read-only integer expressions, the confidence condition

$$ei_2 \neq 0$$

could be generated. The condition states that the precondition for the integer division operator should be satisfied.

Similarly, if *pop* is a function defined as follows

type
    Elem,
    Stack = Elem*
value
    pop : Stack $\overset{\sim}{\to}$ Stack
    pop(st) $\equiv$ **tl** st
    pre st $\neq \langle\rangle$

then for the RSL expression *pop(ast)*, where the actual parameter *ast* is a read-only expression possibly denoting an empty stack, the confidence condition

$$ast \neq \langle\rangle$$

could be generated. This condition states that the precondition for *pop* should be satisfied. It should be interpreted in a context which contains all those definitions which are in the context of the RSL expression *pop(ast)* from which it was generated. For example, if *pop(ast)* occurred in the expression

if ast $\neq \langle\rangle$ **then** pop(ast) **else** ... **end**

then the context of *pop(ast)* would be the context of the if expression plus the axiom *ast* $\neq \langle\rangle$.

Non-divergence
Some pre-defined operators are, according to the static context conditions, allowed to be applied to actual parameters for which the application is specified to diverge (to be equivalent to **chaos**). For instance, an application of the **card** operator to an infinite set will diverge. This property can in rare cases be exploited, for instance, one can test whether a set *s* is infinite by writing

card s $\equiv$ **chaos**

However, it is most likely that divergence is not wanted. A natural choice is therefore to generate confidence conditions ensuring that there are no such applications. For instance, for the RSL expression **card** s, where s is a possibly infinite set, the following confidence condition could be generated:

$$\sim(\textbf{card } s \equiv \textbf{chaos})$$

The condition states that s should be a finite set, since otherwise the **card** s would be **chaos**. However, **chaos** *may* be intended, as mentioned above, although that is not too likely. The condition can be approached in two ways: (1) ignore it as being irrelevant, because the effect was intended, or (2) try to argue that the condition holds, thereby ensuring that **chaos** will not arise. If the confidence condition is ignored, the specifier is advised to check carefully that the effect really was intended.

Subtype correctness

Confidence conditions can also be generated to ensure subtype correctness, i.e. that certain value expressions must denote values of certain subtypes.

An example of a subtype correctness condition is the requirement that functions whose formal parameter type is a subtype are only applied to actual parameters belonging to that subtype. As mentioned earlier, functions are allowed to be applied to any actual parameter belonging to the maximal type of the formal parameter type. In particular, they are allowed to be applied to actual parameters which do not belong to the formal parameter (sub-)type. However, if the specifier of the function has taken care to specify a subtype for the parameters, it is probably the intention that any actual parameter should belong to the subtype. A natural choice is therefore to generate confidence conditions reflecting this. For instance, if *pop* is a function defined over a subtype of non-empty finite stacks

> **type**
>   Elem,
>   Stack = Elem*,
>   NonEmptyStack = {| st : Stack • st $\neq$ $\langle\rangle$ |}
> **value**
>   pop : NonEmptyStack $\rightarrow$ Stack
>   pop(st) $\equiv$ **tl** st

then for the expression *pop(ast)*, where the actual parameter *ast* is a read-only expression possibly denoting an empty or infinite stack (maximal type checking only ensures that *ast* is of type *Elem$^\omega$*), the confidence condition

$$\text{ast} \neq \langle\rangle \wedge \sim(\textbf{len } \text{ast} \equiv \textbf{chaos})$$

could be generated. The condition states that the stack *ast* should belong to the subtype *NonEmptyStack*. An alternative formulation of the condition could be

$$\text{ast} \neq \langle\rangle \wedge (\exists \, t : \text{Elem}^* \bullet t = \text{ast})$$

4.2   General introduction to justification

The typical scenario for developing a justification is that the developer starts from a given condition whose truth should be justified. Such a condition is written within "half-brackets":

⌊condition⌋

and the whole construct is called a *goal*.[4]

An example of a goal is

⌊$I \vdash \forall i :$ **Int**, $il : El \bullet member(i, insert(i, il))$⌋

where I is the scheme defined in section 4.1.1. Note that this goal requires a context in which I is defined. In general, we assume that the context of a goal is given when we start the justification and we do not write it in the justification itself. This context should (at least) contain definitions of the free names occurring in the goal. In section 4.3.2.1 we elaborate further on this.

A common style of constructing a justification is to try to break the goal into simpler subgoals (whose truth ensures the truth of the original goal) by application of a proof rule or an informal argument. Then the simpler subgoals have to be justified. After a number of such simplifications, all subgoals may have been reduced to **true**, whereby the justification is completed. Such a strategy is conventionally known as *backwards reasoning* (because, as we shall see, it involves applying inference rules, as they are normally presented, upwards or backwards).[5] It is also possible to do forwards reasoning, where one starts from some known facts and then tries to establish a conclusion which coincides with the goal to be justified. Forwards reasoning is described in section 4.3.7.

To be more formal, a *justification* consists of a goal, and an *argument* that justifies the truth of the goal:

⌊condition⌋
argument

or more generally, it can consist of several subgoals and an argument for each of these:

- ⌊condition$_1$⌋
  argument$_1$

  $\vdots$

- ⌊condition$_n$⌋
  argument$_n$

An argument can for instance be a (backwards) application of a proof rule followed by an argument for each of the generated subgoals. In the following sections various kinds of arguments are described.

---

[4] For convenience, we sometimes use the term *goal* to mean the constituent condition of the goal.

[5] We could call this "bottom-up" reasoning, but this would conflict with the other common usage in which division of a task into sub-tasks is described as "top-down".

4.2.1 Proof rules and their application

Formal justification is based on the application of proof rules for RSL.

There are two kinds of proof rules:

- *equivalence rules* which are used to manipulate (sub-)terms of goals
- *inference rules* which are used to manipulate conditions of goals

These are explained in the following two sections.

In appendix B there is a collection of RSL proof rules which are always available (but not necessarily applicable) for any condition/subterm. For each condition/subterm there may be additional rules available. In section 4.3.2.2 we explain how these additional rules, which are called *context rules*, are derived from definitions in the context of the condition/subterm.

The rules are divided into basic and derived proof rules. A rule is *derived* if anything that can be proved using it can also be proved using only the basic rules. Hence, the derived rules are not necessary, but they have been introduced to shorten proofs.

The RSL proof rules are intended to be *sound*, but not necessarily *complete* with respect to the semantics of RSL [19]. That means that any condition that can be proved from them should evaluate to true according to the semantics, but not necessarily vice versa.

The proof rules were developed from the RSL proof theory [18] and a larger collection of derived rules can be found in the RAISE Justification Handbook [10].

4.2.1.1 Equivalence rules

An equivalence rule states that two RSL terms are equivalent. In a justification, equivalence rules can be used to manipulate goals by replacing subterms with equivalent subterms.

An equivalence rule has the form

$$t_1 \simeq t_2$$

where t_1 and t_2 are RSL terms of the same syntactic category. The rule states that t_1 and t_2 are equivalent, i.e. have the same semantics (meaning).

Rules for the syntactic category **value_expr** are termed *value rules*, rules for the syntactic category **type_expr** are termed *type rules*, etc.

Examples of value rules are

[not_false] $\sim$ **false** $\simeq$ **true**
[not_true] $\sim$ **true** $\simeq$ **false**
[dom_empty] **dom** [ ] $\simeq$ {}

and an example of a type rule is

[text_expansion] **Text** $\simeq$ **Char***

Each of the rules has a name written within square brackets. The first two rules state equivalences between logical value expressions, the third rule states an equivalence between set value expressions while the last one states an equivalence between type expressions. The rule, *not_false*, states that ∼ **false** is equivalent to **true**. The other rules are read in a similar way.

In a justification, equivalence rules can be used to manipulate goals: an equivalence rule can be *applied* to a subterm, t, of a goal, replacing the subterm with an equivalent term, t', obtaining a new goal. The context of the new goal is the same as that of the original goal. The term, t, is called the *matched term*, and the term, t', is called the *resulting term*. Equivalence rules can be applied left-to-right or right-to-left. If an equivalence rule is to be applied left-to-right, the left-hand side of the rule is called the *matching side*, and the right-hand side is called the *result side* (and vice versa for right-to-left application). An equivalence rule can only be applied to a (sub-)term, t, if t is of the same syntactic category as the rule, and if the matching side of the rule *matches* t. For simple rules, as those presented above, *matches* can be read as *is identical to*, and the resulting term is equal to the result side. As we shall see later, rules may contain term variables, and in this case matching is more complicated.

As mentioned earlier, justifications can be in backwards or forwards mode. This section only deals with application in backwards mode. Application in forwards mode is covered in section 4.3.7.

When an equivalence rule having a name, *name*, is applied to a subterm t of some goal in order to replace it with an equivalent term t', this is written

    ⌊...t...⌋
name:
    ⌊...t'...⌋

Note that one has to select a subterm t which the rule should be applied to. Which subterm was selected is, however, not written in the presentation of the justification — only the name of the rule used. As an example, *not_true* can be applied left-to-right to the subterm ∼ **true** in the goal

    ⌊∼ ∼ **true**⌋

in order to replace the subterm with the term **false**, obtaining the new goal

    ⌊∼**false**⌋

This is written

    ⌊∼ ∼ **true**⌋
not_true:
    ⌊∼ **false**⌋

We now have to argue for the truth of this new goal and can proceed by applying *not_false* to the term ∼ **false**:

    ⌊∼ ∼ **true**⌋
not_true:
    ⌊∼ **false**⌋
not_false:
    ⌊**true**⌋

As we have reached the goal $\llcorner$ **true** $\lrcorner$, which is fulfilled by definition, our justification is completed — we have proved the truth of our original goal $\llcorner \sim \, \sim$ **true** $\lrcorner$. (In this justification, the meaning of the original goal is the same as the meaning of the last goal, since the latter is obtained from the former by a sequence of replacements of terms with equivalent terms by which the meaning is not changed.)

The examples of equivalence rules shown so far have been very simple in the sense that each rule has defined exactly one equivalence between terms. However, there are more general equivalence rules which contain *term variables* which can be *instantiated* (i.e. replaced) with (actual) terms to give a particular equivalence. Hence, equivalence rules containing term variables are schemas for many equivalences.

An example of such a rule is

[empty_concatenation] $\langle \rangle \; \hat{} \; el \simeq el$

Here, *el* is a term variable which can be instantiated with any term which has the syntactic category **value_expr** and maximal type T^ω for some T. Hence, the rule states that for any list expression, *el*, the term, $\langle \rangle \; \hat{} \; el$, is equivalent to the term *el*.

Term variables can only be instantiated with certain terms — there are restrictions on

- the syntactic category
- certain static properties

of actual terms. These restrictions are, by convention, reflected by the name of the term variable, as explained in appendix B.3. For example, a term variable having the name *el* can only be instantiated with terms having the syntactic category **value_expr** and maximal type of the form T^ω.

In order to explain what it means to apply an equivalence rule containing term variables, we first explain what it means to instantiate the rule.

To *instantiate* a proof rule in a given context means to instantiate (i.e. replace) the term variables in the rule with actual terms and to expand applications of special functions. (Later we shall see that rules can also contain applications of special functions). An instantiation of an equivalence rule is *correct* if

- the syntactic and static restrictions for term variable instantiation (see appendix B.3) are satisfied in the given context
- both sides of the instantiated rule are well-formed in the given context. This constraint can be relaxed: "out-of-band names" may be accepted. See section 4.3.2.4 for an explanation of this issue.

An equivalence rule can only be *applied* to a term, t, in a particular context if

- t is of the same syntactic category as the rule
- the matching side of the rule *matches* t, i.e. it is possible to find a correct instantiation of the rule for which the matching side of the instantiated rule is identical to t

The resulting term is the instantiated result side.

An example of a left-to-right application of *empty_concatenation*, where *el* is instantiated with the term $\langle 5 + 2 \rangle$, is

$$\llcorner \langle \rangle \ \hat{} \ \langle 5 + 2 \rangle \equiv \langle 7 \rangle \lrcorner$$

empty_concatenation:

$$\llcorner \langle 5 + 2 \rangle \equiv \langle 7 \rangle \lrcorner$$

Another example of a rule with term variables is

[if_true] **if true then** e **else** e' **end** $\simeq$ e

An example of a left-to-right application of *if_true* is

$$\llcorner \textbf{if true then } 0 \textbf{ else } 1 \textbf{ end} \equiv 0 \lrcorner$$

if_true:

$$\llcorner 0 \equiv 0 \lrcorner$$

Here, e and e' are instantiated with 0 and 1, respectively. This instantiation satisfies the static restriction described in appendix B.3, that term variables whose names only differ in the number of primes (like e and e' in the rule *if_true*) must be instantiated with terms having the same maximal type.

The rule *if_true* can also be applied right-to-left to some term t. In this case, there are several possibilities for the term resulting from the application: it may be any term **if true then** t **else** t' **end** where t' is some value expression which has the same maximal type as t. Here one should make a choice such that the resulting goal looks promising with respect to completing the justification.

On the left- and right-hand sides of an equivalence rule, application of some *special functions* may occur. The names of these functions are always written in boldface, so they are easily recognizable. For instance, in the rule

[let_absorption3] **let** b = e **in express**(b) **end** $\simeq$ e

the special function **express** has been used. Special functions are functions which take RSL terms as arguments and return RSL terms as results. **express** is a special function which takes a binding and returns a value expression, which is obtained from the binding by bracketing any operators and otherwise leaving it unchanged.

When instantiating proof rules, applications of special functions must be expanded.

In appendix B.4 a description of the special functions and their evaluation is given.

Equivalence rules may also have *applicability conditions*, as explained in section 4.2.1.3.

4.2.1.2 Inference rules

An inference rule consists of a list of sequents called the *premises*, and a sequent called the *conclusion*, and states that the conclusion is true if the premises are true. Such a rule can be used to split a goal into n subgoals.

An inference rule has the form

$$\frac{p_1, \ ..., \ p_n}{p}$$

where $p_1, \ ..., \ p_n$ and p are sequents.[6] The rule states that the conclusion, p, is true if the premises, $p_1, \ ..., \ p_n$, are true, i.e. we can conclude (forwards) that p is true if we know that all p_i are true. Conversely, we can prove (backwards) p by proving all p_i.

Inference rules may contain term variables and special functions just like equivalence rules.

An example of an inference rule is

[and_split_inf]
$$\frac{ro\_eb, \ ro\_eb'}{ro\_eb \land ro\_eb'}$$

The rule has a name written within square brackets. The rule states that for any statically read-only logical value expressions, ro_eb and ro_eb', the conclusion, $ro\_eb \land ro\_eb'$, holds if each of the two premises, ro_eb and ro_eb', holds. This means that we can prove a condition $ro\_eb \land ro\_eb'$ by proving each of the conditions ro_eb and ro_eb' separately.

As mentioned earlier, justifications can be in backwards or forwards mode. In backwards mode, inference rules can only be *applied backwards* (upwards), while in forwards mode they can only be *applied forwards* (downwards). Backwards application is used to break a goal down into *subgoals*, which are then justified separately. Forwards application is used to make a conclusion from some known facts. This section only deals with backwards application. Forwards application is covered in section 4.3.7.

An inference rule can be applied backwards to the sequent, p, of a goal,[7] if the conclusion *matches* p, i.e. it is possible to find a correct instantiation of the inference rule for which the instantiated conclusion is identical to p. An instantiation of an inference rule is *correct* if

- the syntactic and static restrictions for term variable instantiation (see appendix B.3) are satisfied in the given context
- the instantiated premises and the instantiated conclusion are well-formed in the given context.

---

[6]In appendix B.8.3, which distinguishes between sequents and meta-sequents, there is also a distinction between inference rules and meta-inference rules. As we remarked earlier, we will generally ignore the distinction, but we will use the correct syntax; double horizontal lines will be used for meta-rules:

$$\frac{p_1, \ ..., \ p_n}{p}$$

[7]Unlike equivalence rules, however, it should be noted that inference rules can only be applied to the whole sequent constituting the goal — not to a subterm of a goal.

The result of the application is a list of goals whose sequents, p_1, ..., p_n, are the instantiated premises, and whose contexts are the same as that of the original goal, except for a few special cases explained later in this section. This is written

    ⌊P⌋
  name:

    ⌊P₁⌋

if there is only one premise ($n = 1$), or else

    ⌊P⌋
  name:

    • ⌊P₁⌋
    ⋮
    • ⌊Pₙ⌋

where the bullets indicate an itemized list of subgoals, and *name* is the name of the rule. We say commonly that an inference rule is applied to a goal meaning that it is applied to its sequent.

As an example, *and_split_inf* can be applied backwards to the goal

    ⌊x ≠ y ∧ x = z⌋

in order to break it into two subgoals, ⌊x ≠ y⌋ and ⌊x = z⌋. This is written

    ⌊x ≠ y ∧ x = z⌋
  and_split_inf:

    • ⌊x ≠ y⌋
    • ⌊x = z⌋

We now have to argue for the truth of each of these new goals. These arguments should be placed just after their respective goals, i.e. the form of the complete justification will be

    ⌊x ≠ y ∧ x = z⌋
  and_split_inf:

    • ⌊x ≠ y⌋
    argument₁
    • ⌊x = z⌋
    argument₂

where *argument₁* is an argument for the first subgoal, and *argument₂* is an argument for the second subgoal.

The sequents in the premises and conclusion of an inference rule will typically be logical value expressions as in the example above, but they may also be implementation relations and they may have explicit contexts (i.e. be of the form *context* ⊢ *assertion*.)

An example of an inference rule having a premise of the form *context* ⊢ *assertion* is

[all_subsumption_inf]
> **value** b : T ⊢ ro_eb
> ∀ b : T • ro_eb

and an example of an application of this rule is

⌊∀ n : **Nat** • n ≥ 0⌋
all_subsumption_inf :
⌊**value** n : **Nat** ⊢ n ≥ 0⌋

Note, how the context of the assertion $n ≥ 0$ in the new goal is the context of the assertion $∀ n : $ **Nat** $ • n ≥ 0$ in the original goal enriched with the value declaration **value** $n : $ **Nat**. However, the context of the goal (that is the implicit context of the assertion) is not changed.

There is another rule, *all_assumption_inf*, which is very similar to *all_subsumption_inf*, except that when applied backwards it moves the value declaration into the implicit context:

⌊∀ n : **Nat** • n ≥ 0⌋
all_assumption_inf :
⌊n ≥ 0⌋

all_assumption_inf is also more general in that it allows a typing list after '∀' instead of a single typing b : T. The rule is described in appendix B.9.

Another important example of a rule which changes the implicit context when applied is *class_assumption_inf*. It is described in appendix B.9.

As a special convention, if the application of an inference rule results in a goal of the form

⌊[id] ro_eb ⊢ ro_eb′⌋

we write

[id] ro_eb ⊢ ⌊ro_eb′⌋

instead, and we do not display [id] ro_eb ⊢ in the following steps of the justification. Here we have reduced the goal to ⌊ro_eb′⌋ by moving the axiom [id] ro_eb to the implicit context. An example of such an application is shown in section 4.2.1.3.

Hence, the application of inference rules may change the context of goals. The context of a goal is not explicitly written down at each point of the justification; instead it is indirectly represented as the context of the initial goal plus all definitions which have been added in previous steps.

Inference rules may also have *applicability conditions*, as explained in section 4.2.1.3.

4.2.1.3 Applicability conditions

We have already seen that the applicability of proof rules is restricted by syntactic and static constraints. Although such constraints can be fairly elaborate, for many rules application is only correct under further constraints which are not always statically decidable. Such constraints are called *applicability conditions*. These are expressed as logical value expressions in which term variables and application of special functions (for determining particular properties of terms) may occur.

Equivalence rules and inference rules with applicability conditions have the following forms, respectively:

$t_1 \simeq t_2$ **when** ro_eb

and

$$\frac{p_1, ..., p_n}{p}$$
when ro_eb

where *ro_eb* is an applicability condition. The equivalence rule states that when *ro_eb* is true t_1 and t_2 are equivalent. The inference rule states that, when *ro_eb* is true, p is true if p_1, ..., p_n, are true.

When a rule with an applicability condition is applied, the applicability condition gives rise to a *side condition* which should be justified separately. The side condition is the instantiated applicability condition and its context is the same as that of the term/goal to which the rule was applied.

In a justification, a side condition and the argument for its truth are enclosed by the keywords **since** and **end** and placed after the (last) goal resulting from the application. For instance, if there is one resulting goal in backwards mode, the form of the complete justification will be

    ⌊condition⌋
  name_of_rule:
    ⌊resulting_condition⌋
      since
          ⌊side_condition⌋
        argument_for_side_condition
      end
  argument_for_resulting_condition

If the side condition is a conjunction of m conditions we can instead write

    ⌊condition⌋
  name_of_rule:
    ⌊resulting_condition⌋
      since
        • ⌊side_condition$_1$⌋
          argument_for_side_condition$_1$
        ⋮
        • ⌊side_condition$_m$⌋
          argument_for_side_condition$_m$
      end
  argument_for_resulting_condition

Many side conditions will, in practice, be statically decidable or can be expanded to a conjunction of simpler conditions. So a tool need only generate side conditions which are not statically decidable, and it may expand a side condition to a conjunction of simpler side conditions, before presentation. Several justification examples in this book have been produced using such a tool.

An example of an equivalence rule with an applicability condition is

[equality_annihilation] e = e ≃ **true when convergent**(e) ∧ **readonly**(e)

In the applicability condition, two special functions, **convergent** and **readonly**, are used. These functions are described in appendix B.4. The rule states that $e = e$ is equivalent to **true** when convergent (i.e. is (a) deterministic and (b) either terminating or waiting for communication) and e is read-only (i.e. does not access any channels and does not write to any variables). The applicability condition is necessary. Otherwise we would for instance be able to prove that equalities like "(v := 1) = (v := 1)", "**chaos** = **chaos**" and "1 ⊓ 2 = 1 ⊓ 2" are equivalent to **true** which is wrong (the first equality is equivalent to "v := 1 ; **true**", the second to "**chaos**" and the third to "**true** ⊓ **false**").

There are two ways in which value equivalence rules with applicability conditions can be applied: the *standard application* shown above, where the instantiated applicability condition occurs as a side condition, and the *in-goal application* where the rule

$t_1 ≃ t_2$ **when** ro_eb

is applied left-to-right as if it had been written

$t_1 ≃$ **if** ro_eb ≡ **true then** t_2 **else** t_1 **end**

and right-to-left as if it had been written

if ro_eb ≡ **true then** t_1 **else** t_2 **end** ≃ t_2

i.e. the instantiated applicability condition does not occur as a side condition; instead it occurs as the guard in an **if** expression, where the **then** branch contains the resulting term obtained by standard application, and the **else** branch contains the matched term.

In-goal expansion should be used when the instantiated applicability condition accesses variables and must be simplified in the context of the remainder of the goal. See sections 4.4.3 and 4.4.6 for examples.

An example of an inference rule with an applicability condition is

[imply_deduction_inf]

$$\frac{[\text{id}] \; \text{ro\_eb} \vdash \text{ro\_eb}'}{\text{ro\_eb} \Rightarrow \text{ro\_eb}'}$$

when convergent(ro_eb) ∧ **pure**(ro_eb)

The inference rule states that, when *ro_eb* is convergent and pure, we can prove *ro_eb* ⇒ *ro_eb'* by proving *ro_eb'* in a context where *ro_eb* is assumed to be true.

An example of a backwards application of *imply_deduction_inf* is

$$\llcorner x = 0 \Rightarrow x \geq 0 \lrcorner$$
imply_deduction_inf:
$[\,x\_zero\,]\ x = 0 \vdash$
$$\llcorner x \geq 0 \lrcorner$$
...

The side conditions are trivially discharged since equality ($=$) is a total operator, and x is pure and convergent (any value name is pure and convergent) and so is 0.

Note that the term variable *id* is not matched by matching the goal against the conclusion and so can be instantiated to any identifier by the user.

4.2.2 Conclusion arguments

The justification of a goal is complete in backwards mode when the goal is reduced to one or more subgoals which are all trivially fulfilled: $\llcorner$**true**$\lrcorner$ or $\llcorner$context $\vdash$ **true**$\lrcorner$, and in forwards mode when a conclusion which coincides with the original goal is established.

In order to mark the completion of a justification, a *conclusion argument* consisting of the keyword **qed** is used, as in

$$\llcorner \sim\, \sim \textbf{true} \lrcorner$$
not_true:
$$\llcorner \sim \textbf{false} \lrcorner$$
not_false:
$$\llcorner \textbf{true} \lrcorner$$
qed

4.2.3 Irrelevance arguments

As explained in section 4.1.2, confidence conditions may be irrelevant if the situation they are intended to guard against is actually intended to occur. In such a case, it is not relevant to attempt a proof of the condition; in fact a proof may fail because the condition is not necessarily true. Instead, the confidence condition should explicitly be identified as irrelevant. This can be done by an *irrelevance argument*, which simply consists of the keyword **irrelevant**.

As an example, consider a fragment of a specification which allows for a certain set s to be finite or infinite:

if card s $\equiv$ **chaos then** 0 **else** 1 **end**

A systematic generation of confidence conditions for this fragment would investigate all sub-constructs for possible confidence conditions. In particular, the **card** s construct will generate the confidence condition that s should be finite in order to avoid **chaos**! But the possible evaluation of **card** s to **chaos** in this situation does no harm, since the expression as a whole still converges (to 0). The presented condition should then be considered irrelevant:

$\llcorner \sim (\textbf{card } s \equiv \textbf{chaos}) \lrcorner$
irrelevant

Note that irrelevance arguments are not informal. An informal argument asserts that some condition is **true** without formally proving it. An irrelevance argument does not assert anything about the truth or falsity of the condition.

Irrelevance arguments can only be applied to confidence conditions, not to formal conditions.

4.2.4 Comments

Any argument can be prefixed by comments, using the RSL syntax for comments as in

$\llcorner x \neq y \land x = z \lrcorner$
/* next we want to bring the left conjunct into an appropriate form */
inequality_expansion:
$\llcorner \sim (x = y) \land x = z \lrcorner$

4.2.5 Informal arguments

It may be tedious to do all steps in a justification in a totally formal way. Therefore, the RAISE method allows for *rigorous* arguments where some of the steps may be informal explanations. When one is convinced that a certain condition can be proved or that a certain condition can be replaced with another condition (by a number of formal steps), one can simply give an informal explanation instead of using formal arguments.

Hence, in addition to the application of proof rules, which constitutes formal proof steps, there are two kinds of informal arguments that can be used:

- *explanation arguments* which consist of a comment followed by the keyword **qed**. The comment should explain why the current goal is believed to be true.
- *replacement arguments* which consist of a comment followed by a new goal or list of new goals (as replacement for the otherwise current goal), and then an argument (formal or informal) for each new goal. The comment should explain why the new goal(s) can replace the old goal.

For example, an explanation argument is used in the following justification:

$\llcorner \langle \rangle \ ^\frown \ \langle 5 \rangle \ ^\frown \ \langle 7 \rangle \equiv \langle 5, 7 \rangle \lrcorner$
empty_concatenation:
$\llcorner \langle 5 \rangle \ ^\frown \ \langle 7 \rangle \equiv \langle 5, 7 \rangle \lrcorner$
/* which is obviously true */
qed

In the following justification a replacement argument is used:

⌊7 ∈ {(⟨5,7,3⟩ ⌢ ⟨⟩)(2)}⌋

/* as the application of the list to index 2 gives 7, this is equivalent to */

⌊7 ∈ {7}⌋

isin_singleton:

⌊7 = 7⌋

equality_annihilation:

⌊**true**⌋

qed

In both examples the informal step could have been replaced with a few formal steps.

4.2.6   Compact presentation of arguments

Justifications can grow rapidly. In order to make a justification more presentable, it is useful to hide some of the details by using a summary notation for applying a whole sequence of rules without showing the intermediate results (goals).

For example, a compact presentation of the justification of the theorem T from section 4.3.2.4 is

⌊I ⊢ ∀ i : **Int**, il : El • member(i, insert(i, il))⌋

class_assumption_inf, all_assumption_inf :

⌊member(i, insert(i, il))⌋

insert_def, member_def :

⌊⟨i⟩ ⌢ il ≠ ⟨⟩ ∧ (i = **hd** (⟨i⟩ ⌢ il) ∨ member(i, **tl** (⟨i⟩ ⌢ il)))⌋

empty_list_inequality, true_and :

⌊i = **hd** (⟨i⟩ ⌢ il) ∨ member(i, **tl** (⟨i⟩ ⌢ il))⌋

hd_concatenation, equality_annihilation :

⌊**true** ∨ member(i, **tl** (⟨i⟩ ⌢ il))⌋

true_or, **qed**

4.3   Doing justifications

The previous section gave a general introduction to justifications. This section contains advice on techniques that can be used in constructing justifications.

The scenario is that one starts from some goal

⌊condition⌋

whose truth should be justified. The challenge is then to construct an argument for this.

The goal can immediately be discharged by an irrelevance argument if the condition is an irrelevant confidence condition (the justifier has to decide whether it is), or by an explanation argument if the truth of the condition is obvious and there are no requirements for formality.

Otherwise the argument is made in several steps. In a typical step, we try to break a goal into simpler (sub-)goals using proof rules that are applicable to the goal or subterms of the goal.

In general, for the same goal there may be several different arguments, some of which are more elegant than others. It is not possible to give a general recipe on how to find an argument, and in particular not an elegant one. It can be difficult and is often an iterative process where various strategies are tried until a successful one is found. Here experience (as in any other creative process) and a computer-based assistant can be of great help.

In addition to finding an argument, there is also the challenge of presenting a justification in a readable way by structuring it and hiding less important details.

In this section we give some hints on possible strategies for constructing and presenting justifications. First, in subsection 4.3.1 we show some typical initial steps where the goal is reduced by enriching the implicit context, and in subsection 4.3.2 we show how contexts can be used. Then, in subsections 4.3.3, 4.3.4 and 4.3.7 we explain how justifications can be structured using substitutions, lemmas and forwards arguments, and in subsections 4.3.5, 4.3.6 and 4.3.8, we show how the well-known strategies of proof by case analysis, induction and contradiction can be applied.

4.3.1   Putting assumptions into the implicit context

Often the initial goal of a justification is a sequent of the form

⌞ce ⊢ assertion⌟

This is for instance usually the case for formal conditions coming from theorems about some given modules, as in

⌞I ⊢ ∀ i : **Int**, il : El • member(i, insert(i, il))⌟

from section 4.1.1.

A possible strategy for justifying such a goal is to try to simplify the assertion *assertion* to **true** obtaining the goal

⌞ce ⊢ **true**⌟

As in this case only the assertion *assertion* is manipulated, it would be better immediately to get the class expression out of the way, i.e. reducing the goal to

⌞assertion⌟

by not displaying the class expression *ce*, but moving it to the implicit context. This can be done using the rule *class_assumption_inf* which is described in appendix B.9. For our example we get

⌞I ⊢ ∀ i : **Int**, il : El • member(i, insert(i, il))⌟
class_assumption_inf:
⌞∀ i : **Int**, il : El • member(i, insert(i, il))⌟

Section 4.3.2.4 shows how the applications of *member* and *insert* can be unfolded using the definitions given in *I*.

Many goals are, as the goal we have reached above, a universally quantified expression of the form

⌞∀ typing-list • ro_eb⌟

A possible strategy for justifying this is to try to simplify *ro_eb* to **true** obtaining the goal

⌞∀ typing-list • **true**⌟

and then reducing this to **true** by applying the rule *all_annihilation*. As in this case only *ro_eb* is manipulated, it would be better immediately to get the quantification out of the way, i.e. reducing the goal to

⌞ro_eb⌟

by adding the value definitions of *typing-list* to the implicit context. This can be done using the tactic, *all_assumption_inf*, which is described in appendix B.9. For our example, this corresponds to saying that we can prove the universally quantified expression by proving *member(i, insert(i, il))* in a context containing the value definitions *i : Int* and *il : El*, i.e. under the assumption that *i* and *il* are an arbitrary integer and integer list, respectively:

⌞∀ i : **Int**, il : El • member(i, insert(i, il))⌟
all_assumption_inf:
⌞member(i, insert(i, il))⌟

4.3.2   Using context information

As stated in section 4.1, any condition is to be interpreted in a specific context. The same holds for any subterm of a condition.

The purpose of this section is to explain what the context is and how it can be exploited in a justification by using certain proof rules, which are called *context rules*.

First, in section 4.3.2.1, we recapitulate and elaborate on what the context of conditions and subterms is. Then, in section 4.3.2.2, we explain how the context rules are derived from the context, and finally, in sections 4.3.2.3–4.3.2.8, we give important examples of the usage of context rules.

4.3.2.1   Contexts

Any condition and any subterm of a condition is to be interpreted in a context containing definitions of schemes, objects, types, values, variables, channels and axioms.

It is important to know what the context is, as it can be exploited in the justification of the condition, as we shall see in the following sections. In this section we recapitulate and elaborate on what the context is.

The context of conditions

In justifications, we do not explicitly write the contexts of conditions appearing in it, but they can be derived according to the following rules:

1. For the initial goal:
   The context of the initial goal is to be provided outside the justification itself. This context should (at least) include:

   (a) if the goal is a formal condition, those module definitions which were in the context of the theorem or development relation from which it came

   (b) if the goal is a confidence condition arising from a subterm in a module, theorem or development relation, those module definitions which were in the context of the module, theorem or development relation plus local definitions from constructs (let definitions, typings, etc.) "enclosing" the subterm in the module, theorem or development relation

2. For subgoals:
   In the justification of a goal, subgoals may be generated. The context of these may be different from the context of the original goal, as in some steps definitions may be added to the context. The context of a subgoal is therefore the context of the initial goal plus all definitions which have been added in previous steps. Definitions may be added when inference rules are applied (see section 4.2.1.2). Important examples are the additions of axiom definitions from lemmas (see section 4.3.4) and case assumptions (see section 4.3.5). Informal steps (see section 4.2.5) and applications of equivalence rules (see section 4.2.1.1) do not change the context.

The context of subterms

The context of a subterm of a condition may differ from the context of the condition itself by having local definitions from declarative as well as non-declarative constructs "enclosing" the subterm in the condition.

For instance, in the condition

$$\llcorner\{\, 2 * n \mid n : \mathbf{Nat} \bullet n < 2 \,\} \equiv \{0, 2\}\lrcorner$$

the value definition, $n : \mathbf{Nat}$, belongs to the context of the expressions $n < 2$ and $2 * n$, and the axiom $n < 2$ belongs to the context of the expression $2 * n$.

The RAISE Specification Language book [23] defines the scope rules for declarative constructs and explains how declarative constructs give rise to definitions that are not axioms. Section 4.1 does the same for the syntactic extension of a **sequent** to RSL. Declarative constructs can also give rise to axioms:

- Axiom declarations give rise to their constituent axioms.
- Declarative constructs containing a restriction, • *ro_eb*, give rise to the axiom *ro_eb*, if *ro_eb* is pure.
- Patterns or bindings in which a value expression, *e*, is matched against a binding, *id_or_op*, give rise to the axiom *id_or_op* ≡ *e*, if *e* is pure and convergent.

The scope of a definition[8] from a declarative construct is the scope of the declarative construct from which the definition stems.

Non-declarative constructs can also give rise to axioms:

- Equivalence expressions, $e \equiv e'$ **pre** ro_eb, and post expressions, e **post** ro_eb' **pre** ro_eb, in which the precondition ro_eb is pure, give rise to the axiom ro_eb whose scope is the remaining part of the equivalence/post expression.
- If expressions, **if** eb **then** e **else** e' **end**, in which eb is pure and convergent, give rise to the axiom eb whose scope is e and the axiom $\sim eb$ whose scope is e'.
- Axiom prefix and infix expressions, and if expressions having elsif branches, give rise to axioms in a similar way (as they can be expanded to if expressions of the form **if** eb **then** e **else** e' **end**).

In general, a definition from a construct is in the context of a term if the term is within the scope of the definition.

Note that the axioms stated above do not have names, but a tool may automatically generate and keep track of names.

4.3.2.2   Context rules

The definitions in the context of a condition or subterm give rise to additional proof rules which are available for that condition or subterm. Such proof rules are called *context rules*. As with other proof rules, we distinguish between basic and derived context rules.

Context rules differ from other rules in that they may contain identifiers and operators which are not term variables, but are defined in the actual context. When applying such rules, matching requires identity for such identifiers and operators.

Basic context rules from axiom, type, value, variable, channel and object definitions
Each definition, *definition*, of an entity with a name, *id*, in the context of a condition/subterm gives rise to a number of equivalence rules which are available for that condition/subterm:

$$[\,name\,]\ ro\_eb_1 \simeq \textbf{true}$$
$$\vdots$$
$$[\,name\,]\ ro\_eb_n \simeq \textbf{true}$$

where

$$\textbf{properties}(\text{definition}) \simeq ro\_eb_1 \wedge ... \wedge ro\_eb_n$$

properties is defined in appendix B.8. If *definition* is an axiom, *name* is the name of the axiom, otherwise it is *id_def*, where *id* is the name being defined.

For example, if the context contains the definition

---

[8]Note that this also includes axioms.

value x : **Int** • x > 5

then, since

properties(**value** x : **Int** • x > 5) $\simeq$
    ($\exists$ id' : **Int** • id' = x) $\land$ (x > 5 $\equiv$ **true**)

the rules

[x_def] $\exists$ id' : **Int** • id' = x $\simeq$ **true**
[x_def] x > 5 $\equiv$ **true** $\simeq$ **true**

where x is not a term variable, are available.

Basic context rules from theorems and development relations
Each global theorem or development relation of the form

[id] context $\vdash$ ro_eb

gives rise to the equivalence rule

[id] ro_eb $\simeq$ **true**

which is available for any condition/subterm, whose context includes the context *context*.

Each global theorem or development relation of the form

[id] context $\vdash$ ce2 $\preceq$ ce1

gives rise to the (meta-)inference rule

[id]
$$\frac{\textbf{true}}{\text{ce2} \preceq \text{ce1}}$$

which is available for any condition, whose context includes the context *context*.

Care must, of course, be taken not to create circular arguments when we use theorems and development relations.

A justification of a theorem or development relation is *circular* (and hence not valid) if it depends on that theorem or development relation. A justification of a theorem or development relation, *id*, *depends on* a theorem or development relation, *id'*, if it uses *id'*, or if it uses a theorem or development relation which depends on *id'*. A justification *uses* a theorem or development relation if it applies a context rule which the theorem or development relation gives rise to.

Derived context rules
In practice, the basic context rules are not always in the most convenient form. In appendix B.10 we list some of the most useful context rules derivable from various forms of type, variable and value declarations and from axiom declarations respectively.

For example, if the context contains the definition

value
    f : **Nat** $\rightarrow$ **Nat**
    f(x) $\equiv$ x + 1

we obtain the derived context rule

[f_def] $f(e) \simeq e + 1$

when convergent$(e) \wedge$ **pure**$(e) \wedge$ **isin_subtype**$(e,$ **Nat**$)$

where e is a term variable, but f is not.

This rule can be used left-to-right to *unfold*, for example, *f(3)* to *3 + 1*, or right-to-left to *fold 3 + 1* to *f(3)*.

4.3.2.3   Using axioms

In this section we give three examples of how axioms in the context can be used. The first example illustrates how a value expression which is equal to the predicate of an axiom can be reduced to **true**. The second and third examples illustrate how axioms can be used if their predicates are universally quantified expressions and existentially quantified expressions, respectively.

Simple use of axioms

If the context contains an axiom

[id] ro_eb

then an occurrence of the term *ro_eb* can be reduced to **true**

       ⌊...ro_eb...⌋

  id:

       ⌊...**true**...⌋

using the derived context rule

[id] ro_eb $\simeq$ **true**

For example, if the context contains the following definitions

value

    x : **Int**,

    s : **Int-set**

axiom

    [ax1] $x \in s$,

the justification step

       ⌊...$x \in s$...⌋

  ax1:

       ⌊...**true**...⌋

can be done using the context rule

[ax1] $x \in s \simeq$ **true**

in which x and s are not term variables.

Using universal quantifications

If the context contains an axiom of the form

[id] $\forall$ b : T • ro_eb

then an occurrence of a term *ro_eb'* can be reduced to **true** using the derived context rule (cf. table B.3 in appendix B.10)

[id] **subst_expr**(e, b, ro_eb) $\simeq$ **true**
when **convergent**(e) $\wedge$ **pure**(e) $\wedge$ **isin_subtype**(e, T)

if there exists a pure and convergent value expression *e1* of the type *T* such that **subst_expr**(e1, b, ro_eb) is *ro_eb'*.

For example, if the context contains the definitions

value p : **Int** $\rightarrow$ **Bool**
axiom [p_nat] $\forall$ x : **Nat** $\bullet$ p(x)

the justification step

⌊p(2)⌋
p_nat :
⌊**true**⌋

can be done using the derived context rule

[p_nat] p(e) $\simeq$ **true**
when **convergent**(e) $\wedge$ **pure**(e) $\wedge$ **isin_subtype**(e, **Nat**)

in which *e* is a term variable, but *p* is not. (Note that **subst_expr**(e, x, p(x)) has been reduced to *p(e)* before presenting the rule.)

Using existential quantifications

If the context of a condition, *ro_eb'*, contains an axiom of the form

[id] $\exists$ b : T $\bullet$ ro_eb

then a general scheme for using this in the justification of the condition is

⌊ro_eb'⌋
imply_modus_ponens_inf :
  $\bullet$ ⌊$\exists$ b : T $\bullet$ ro_eb⌋
    id, **qed**
  $\bullet$ ⌊($\exists$ b : T $\bullet$ ro_eb) $\Rightarrow$ ro_eb'⌋
    exists_implies, all_assumption_inf :
      ⌊(ro_eb $\equiv$ **true**) $\Rightarrow$ ro_eb'⌋
  ...

For example, if the context contains the definitions

value s : **Int-set**
axiom [E] $\exists$ i : **Int** $\bullet$ i $\in$ s

the following justification can be done:

⌊s $\neq$ {}⌋
imply_modus_ponens_inf :
  $\bullet$ ⌊$\exists$ i : **Int** $\bullet$ i $\in$ s⌋
    E, **qed**
  $\bullet$ ⌊($\exists$ i : **Int** $\bullet$ i $\in$ s) $\Rightarrow$ s $\neq$ {}⌋

exists_implies, all_assumption_inf :

$\llcorner (i \in s \equiv \textbf{true}) \Rightarrow s \neq \{\} \lrcorner$

is_true :

$\llcorner i \in s \Rightarrow s \neq \{\} \lrcorner$

not_implies :

$\llcorner \sim (s \neq \{\}) \Rightarrow \sim (i \in s) \lrcorner$

inequality_expansion, not_not, not_isin_expansion :

$\llcorner s = \{\} \Rightarrow i \notin s \lrcorner$

imply_deduction_inf :

$[\,s\_empty\,]\ s = \{\} \vdash$

$\llcorner i \notin s \lrcorner$

s_empty:

$\llcorner i \notin \{\} \lrcorner$

not_isin_empty, **qed**

This example also illustrates the use of a context rule

$[\,s\_empty\,]\ s \simeq \{\}$

derived from the axiom assumption $[\,s\_empty\,]\ s = \{\}$.

Exercise   In a context containing the definitions

value s : **Int-infset**   **axiom** $[\,empty\,]\ \forall\, i : \textbf{Int} \cdot i \notin s$

prove the goal $\llcorner s = \{\} \lrcorner$.
Hint: use the rules *set_equality* and *isin_empty*.

4.3.2.4   Unfolding

Many goals contain names of entities defined in the context. There are a number
of equivalence rules for *unfolding* of type names, value names and function applications. Below we give some examples. Unfolding of variable names is discussed in
section 4.4.2.

Unfolding of type names
If the context contains a type abbreviation definition of the form

type Tid = T

then the derived context rule

$[\,Tid\_def\,]\ Tid \simeq T$

(where *Tid* and *T* are not term variables, but the identifier and type expression
from the type definition) can be applied to a type expression which is the name
Tid in order to replace it with the type expression *T*:

$\llcorner ...Tid... \lrcorner$

Tid_def:

$\llcorner ...T... \lrcorner$

Unfolding of value names

If the context contains an explicit value definition of the form

    value id : T = e

then the derived context rule

    [id_def] id $\simeq$ e

can be applied to a value expression which is the name *id* in order to replace it with the value expression *e*:

    ⌊...id...⌋
id_def:
    ⌊...e...⌋

Unfolding of function applications

If the context contains an explicit function definition of the form

    value
      f : T $\overset{\sim}{\rightarrow}$ a T1
      f(b) $\equiv$ e1

(where the partial function arrow $\overset{\sim}{\rightarrow}$ may be replaced by a total function arrow $\rightarrow$) then the derived context rule

    [f_def] f(e) $\simeq$ **subst_expr**(e, b, e1)
      when convergent(e) $\wedge$ **pure**(e) $\wedge$ **isin_subtype**(e, T)

(where *e* is a term variable, but *f* is not) is available. It can be applied to unfold an application *f(a)* of *f* to an actual parameter *a*, when *a* is pure, convergent and belongs to the type *T*:

    ⌊...f(a)...⌋
f_def:
    ⌊...e'...⌋

where *e'* is the result of **subst_expr***(a, b, e1)*. We saw an example earlier in section 4.3.2.2.

This is generalized in the obvious way to cases in which the function has several formal parameters.

Furthermore, it is generalized to the case where the function definition has a precondition, *ro_eb*. The derived context rule then has an extra conjunct in the applicability condition. This conjunct is the result of **subst_expr***(e, b, ro_eb)*.

To illustrate unfolding, we continue the justification started in section 4.3.1. First we unfold the application of *insert*:

    ⌊member(i, insert(i, il))⌋
insert_def :
    ⌊member(i, ⟨i⟩ ⌢ il)⌋

In the same way the application of *member* can now be unfolded. The complete justification is shown below:

⌊I ⊢ ∀ i : **Int**, il : El • member(i, insert(i, il))⌋
class_assumption_inf :
    ⌊∀ i : **Int**, il : El • member(i, insert(i, il))⌋
all_assumption_inf :
    ⌊member(i, insert(i, il))⌋
insert_def :
    ⌊member(i, ⟨i⟩ ⌢ il)⌋
member_def :
    ⌊⟨i⟩ ⌢ il ≠ ⟨⟩ ∧ (i = **hd** (⟨i⟩ ⌢ il) ∨ member(i, **tl** (⟨i⟩ ⌢ il)))⌋
empty_list_inequality :
    ⌊**true** ∧ (i = **hd** (⟨i⟩ ⌢ il) ∨ member(i, **tl** (⟨i⟩ ⌢ il)))⌋
true_and :
    ⌊i = **hd** (⟨i⟩ ⌢ il) ∨ member(i, **tl** (⟨i⟩ ⌢ il))⌋
hd_concatenation :
    ⌊i = i ∨ member(i, **tl** (⟨i⟩ ⌢ il))⌋
equality_annihilation :
    ⌊**true** ∨ member(i, **tl** (⟨i⟩ ⌢ il))⌋
true_or :
    ⌊**true**⌋
qed

It should be noted that unfolding may introduce *name confusion*, i.e. the resulting term may contain applied occurrences of names which are not visible because they were bound in a context different from the current. Such names are called *out-of-band names*.

As an illustration, assume that we want to justify the goal

⌊...g(n)...⌋

in a context containing the following definitions:

value
    i : **Int**,
    f : **Int** → **Int**
    f(j) ≡ i + j,
    g : **Int** → **Int**
    g(j) ≡ **let** i = j + 2 **in** i + f(j) **end**

First we unfold *g(n)* to get

⌊... **let** i = n + 2 **in** i + f(n) **end** ...⌋

And then we unfold *f(n)* to get

⌊... **let** i = n + 2 **in** i + (*i* + n) **end** ...⌋

Here, the *i* (shown in italics) is an out-of-band name — its corresponding definition (*i* : **Int**) is hidden by the let definition.

In a justification produced by hand, the out-of-band name must be avoided by applying *let_name_change* before unfolding *f(n)*:

⌊... **let** i = n + 2 **in** i + f(n) **end** ...⌋
let_name_change:
    ⌊... **let** i′ = n + 2 **in** i′ + f(n) **end** ...⌋
f_def :
    ⌊... **let** i′ = n + 2 **in** i′ + (i + n) **end** ...⌋

A justification tool may provide an alternative way of avoiding out-of-band names: it may be able to automatically apply renamings when necessary, or it may internally use unique, resolved names.

Exercise Prove the goal

    ⌊I ⊢ ∀ i : **Int** • ∼ member(i, ⟨⟩)⌋

where *I* is the scheme defined in section 4.1.1.

4.3.2.5 Folding

There may be situations where we want to fold application of names, e.g. to replace an expression $e′$ in a goal

    ⌊...$e′$...⌋

with a function application $f(a)$, where the context contains an explicit definition of the function f:

    value
        f : T $\overset{\sim}{\to}$ a T1
        f(b) ≡ e1

For this purpose we can use the derived context rule

    [f_def] f(e) ≃ **subst_expr**(e, b, e1)
        when convergent(e) ∧ **pure**(e) ∧ **isin_subtype**(e, T)

right-to-left. (Note that for any concrete function definition, **subst_expr**(e, b, e1) will be expanded before presenting the derived rule.)

For example, in a context containing the definition of *g* above, we can do the following folding:

    ⌊... **let** i = n + 2 **in** i + f(n) **end** ...⌋
g_def:
    ⌊... g(n) ...⌋

4.3.2.6 Using subtype information

Assume that in the context a value, *id1*, is declared to be of a certain type, *T1*, which is a subtype:

    id1 : T1

The question is now how we can use such subtype information in the proof of some condition involving *id1*.

For this purpose there are a number of proof rules.

First, there is the basic context rule

[id1_def] $\exists$ id′ : T1 • id′ = id1 $\simeq$ **true**

which the value definition gives rise to. This rule can be used in the justification of a condition, *ro_eb*, involving *id1* using the following scheme:

⌊ro_eb⌋
imply_modus_ponens_inf :
- ⌊$\exists$ id′ : T1 • id′ = id1⌋
  id_def, **qed**
- ⌊($\exists$ id′ : T1 • id′ = id1) $\Rightarrow$ ro_eb⌋
  ...

Alternatively, derived context rules such as those given in appendix B.10 can be used to give simpler justifications, as we see below.

In addition, there are several proof rules having applicability conditions of the form

isin_subtype(e, T)

If such a rule is instantiated such that *e* is replaced with *id1* and *T* with *T1*, we get the side condition

isin_subtype(id1, T1)

which is equivalent to **true**, as, from the definition of **isin_subtype** for read-only values in appendix B.4, it is equivalent to

$\exists$ id′ : T1 • id′ = id1

In the rest of this section we first discuss which rules to use when *T1* is

- a subtype expression
- the type **Nat**
- an abbreviation (a name) for a subtype expression

Then we explain how to use subtype information occurring in quantifications, and finally how to transform type expressions to equivalent subtype expressions.

Subtype expressions

Assume that in the context a value is declared to be of a certain subtype:

value id1 : {|b : T • p_eb|}

Then the derived context rule

[id1_def] **subst_expr**(id1, b, p_eb) $\simeq$ **true**

can be used to prove conditions involving *id1*.

For example, if the context contains the value definition

value count : {|i : **Int** • i > 0|}

we can use the derived context rule

[count_def] count > 0 $\simeq$ **true**

to prove conditions involving *count*.

The general scheme for proving a condition *ro_eb* involving a value name *id1* declared in the context to have the type $\{|b : T \cdot p\_eb|\}$ is

⌊ro_eb⌋
imply_modus_ponens_inf :
- ⌊ro_eb'⌋
  id1_def, **qed**
- ⌊ro_eb' $\Rightarrow$ ro_eb⌋
  ...

where *ro_eb'* is equivalent to **subst_expr***(id1, b, p_eb)*.

The type Nat

For the type **Nat** there is a derived proof rule *nat_value* (which is not a context rule):

[nat_value] ei $\geq$ 0 $\simeq$ **true**
    when convergent(ei) $\wedge$ **readonly**(ei) $\wedge$ **isin_subtype**(ei, **Nat**)

If the context contains the value definition

value n : **Nat**

this rule can for instance be used to directly reduce the expression $n \geq 0$ to **true**

⌊...n $\geq$ 0...⌋
nat_value:
    ⌊...**true**...⌋

since the subtype information given by the definition of *n* can be used to reduce each of the side conditions to **true**.

Abbreviations of subtype expressions

Any abbreviation definition of a subtype expression

type Tid = $\{|b : T \cdot p\_eb|\}$

in the context gives rise to a derived context rule

[Tid_def] **subst_expr**(e, b, p_eb) $\simeq$ **true**
    when
        convergent(e) $\wedge$ **pure**(e) $\wedge$ **isin_subtype**(e, Tid)

where *e* is a term variable.

Now, if we also have in the context the value definition

value id1 : Tid

Tid_def can be used to prove conditions involving *id1*.

For instance, if the context contains the definitions

type N1 = $\{|i : \textbf{Int} \cdot i > 0|\}$
value count : N1

we get from the first definition the context rule

[N1_def] e > 0 $\simeq$ **true**
   when convergent(e) $\wedge$ **pure**(e) $\wedge$ **isin_subtype**(e, N1)

where e is a term variable which can be instantiated with any integer value expression.

This rule can be used to directly reduce *count > 0* to **true**

   ⌊count > 0⌋
N1_def:

   ⌊**true**⌋

since the subtype information given by the definition of *count* can be used to reduce each of the side conditions **convergent**(count), **pure**(count) and **isin_subtype**-(*count, N1*) to **true**.

Subtype information in quantifications

For quantified expressions, the subtype information given in the quantification can be exploited using the equivalence rules *all_subtype* and *exists_subtype*, as illustrated by the following examples:

   ⌊$\forall$ n : {|i : **Int** • i > 0|} • n $\neq$ 0⌋
all_subtype:

   ⌊$\forall$ n : **Int** • (n > 0 $\equiv$ **true**) $\Rightarrow$ n $\neq$ 0⌋

   ⋮

   ⌊$\exists$ n : {|i : **Int** • i > 0|} • n $\neq$ 0⌋
exists_subtype:

   ⌊$\exists$ n : **Int** • n > 0 $\wedge$ n $\neq$ 0⌋

   ⋮

Transforming type expressions to equivalent subtype expressions

There are a number of equivalence rules for

- expanding types involving **Nat, -set**, *, $\xrightarrow[m]{}$ and $\rightarrow$ to subtypes of **Int, -infset**, $^\omega$, $\xrightarrow[m]{\sim}$ and $\xrightarrow{\sim}$, and **Text** to **Char***
- expanding a type expression T to a subtype expression {|b : T • **true**|}
- distributing subtype expressions through the type constructors $\times$, **-infset**, $^\omega$, $\xrightarrow[m]{\sim}$ and $\xrightarrow{\sim}$

In addition, there may be context rules derived from type abbreviations stating equivalences between type names and type expression.

These rules can be used to replace a type expression, *T1*, with an equivalent subtype expression, {|b : T • p_eb|}. This may be useful when we want to use the predicate, p_eb, from the equivalent subtype expression in the proof of a condition involving a value which is defined to have the type *T1*. This technique is illustrated in the following example:

⌊∀ (x,y) : **Nat** × **Nat** • x ≥ 0 ∧ y ≥ 0⌋

nat_expansion, nat_expansion:

⌊∀ (x,y) : {|x : **Int** • x ≥ 0|} × {|y : **Int** • y ≥ 0|} • x ≥ 0 ∧ y ≥ 0⌋

product_subtype:

⌊∀ (x,y) : {|(x,y) : **Int** × **Int** • x ≥ 0 ∧ y ≥ 0|} • x ≥ 0 ∧ y ≥ 0⌋

We can now proceed using *all_subtype*.

Exercise 1
Prove the goal

⌊∀ p : **Nat** × **Nat** • let (x,y) = p in x ≥ 0 ∧ y ≥ 0 end⌋

Hint: use *all_name_change*.

Exercise 2
Prove the goal

⌊~ (∃ x : {| i : **Int** • **false** |} • **true**)⌋

4.3.2.7 Using variant, union and short record type information

In the RAISE Specification Language book [23] are descriptions of how variant, union and short record type definitions can be expanded to sort definitions, value definitions, induction, disjointness, destructor and reconstructor axioms. In this book we use the convention that induction axioms are named *id_induction*, where *id* is the type name introduced by the definition; disjointness axioms relating two constructors, *con1* and *con2*, are named *con1_con2*; destructor axioms relating a destructor, *des*, to a constructor, *con*, are named *des_con*; and reconstructor axioms relating a reconstructor, *recon*, to a constructor, *con*, are named *recon_con*.

For instance,

type Tree == empty | node(left : Tree, elem : Elem ↔ newval, right : Tree)

can be expanded to a sort definition, some value definitions and the following axiom definitions:

axiom
    [Tree_induction]
        ∀ p : Tree → **Bool** •
            p(empty) ∧
            (∀ t1 : Tree, el : Elem, t2 : Tree •
                p(t1) ∧ p(t2) ⇒ p(node(t1,el,t2)))
            ⇒ (∀ t : Tree • p(t)),
    [empty_node]
        ∀ t1 : Tree, el : Elem, t2 : Tree • empty ≠ node(t1,el,t2),
    [left_node]
        ∀ t1 : Tree, el : Elem, t2 : Tree • left(node(t1,el,t2)) ≡ t1,

[elem_node]
  $\forall$ t1 : Tree, el : Elem, t2 : Tree • elem(node(t1,el,t2)) $\equiv$ el,
[right_node]
  $\forall$ t1 : Tree, el : Elem, t2 : Tree • right(node(t1,el,t2)) $\equiv$ t2
[newval_node]
  $\forall$ t1 : Tree, el, el1 : Elem, t2 : Tree •
    newval(el1,node(t1,el,t2)) $\equiv$ node(t1,el1,t2)

As stated in appendix B.8.2, we can obtain the properties of a variant definition by forming the conjunction of the properties of the definitions to which it can be expanded, and we get context rules from the properties in the usual way.

For instance, among the context rules that the variant type definition above give rise to is

[Tree_induction]
  $\forall$ t : Tree • e(t) $\simeq$ **true**
  when
    (**convergent**(e) $\wedge$ **pure**(e) $\wedge$ **isin_subtype**(e, Tree $\rightarrow$ **Bool**)) $\wedge$
    e(empty) $\wedge$
    ($\forall$ t1 : Tree, el : Elem, t2 : Tree • e(t1) $\wedge$ e(t2) $\Rightarrow$ e(node(t1,el,t2)))

where e is a term variable of syntactic category **value_expr** having the maximal type *Tree* $\overset{\sim}{\rightarrow}$ **Bool**.

Exercise   Use *Tree_induction* to prove, in a context containing the definition of *Tree* in this section, the goal

  $\llcorner \forall$ t : Tree • t = empty $\vee$ ($\exists$ l, r : Tree, el : Elem • t = node(l, el, r))$\lrcorner$

Hint: in section 4.3.6.3 another example of how to use *Tree_induction* is given.

4.3.2.8   Inconsistent contexts

When formulating theorems and development relations of the form

  [id] context $\vdash$ assertion

one has to be careful not to write an inconsistent context. A context is *inconsistent* if **false** is derivable from the properties of the declarations it contains. (See appendix B.8 for a definition of what the properties of declarations are.) If the context is inconsistent it is possible to prove that any assertion is true, no matter what the assertion is, in particular if it is **false**.

An example of inconsistent context is a declaration of a value *v* of an empty subtype:

  value v : {| i : **Int** • **false** |}

With this declaration in the context we can prove the condition **false**, since from the declaration we get the derived context rule (cf. table B.2 in appendix B.10)

  [v_def] **false** $\simeq$ **true**

A context that is not inconsistent is *consistent*.

4.3.3 Using substitutions

When a goal is large it is sometimes convenient to be able to simplify a sub-expression separately. There is a proof rule, *substitution1*

[substitution1] $e \simeq e'$ **when** $e \equiv e'$

which allows you to replace an expression e with what you believe is an equivalent expression e' and to do the justification that the two expressions are indeed equivalent "on the side".

The general pattern is

    ⌊ ... e ... ⌋
substitution1:
    ⌊ ... e' ... ⌋
       since
          ⌊$e \equiv e'$⌋
         argument
       end
    argument

So using substitutions is a way of structuring justifications. But it is more than that. It can be used as a technique for postponing the justification that e is equivalent to e' until you have investigated whether it is a reasonable strategy to replace e with e', i.e. whether you can find an argument for the goal ⌊ ... e' ... ⌋.

Substitutions can also be used when you find that it is easier to reduce e' to e than the opposite. An example of this is given in section 4.3.6.3.

A second substitution rule, *substitution2*

[substitution2]
    ro_eb $\simeq$ **true**
    when convergent(ro_eb) $\wedge$ ro_eb

is available for replacing a boolean subterm *ro_eb* with **true**:

    ⌊ ... ro_eb ... ⌋
substitution2:
    ⌊ ... **true** ... ⌋
       since
          ⌊ro_eb⌋
         argument
       end
    argument

substitution2 can for instance be useful in situations where we want to make a subterm of a goal into a goal itself so that inference rules can be applied to it.

An example of the use of *substitution2* is sketched below:

     ⌊ ... (∃ n : **Nat** • n = 0) ... ⌋

substitution2 :

     ⌊ ... (**true**) ... ⌋

    since

        ⌊∃ n : **Nat** • n = 0⌋

      exists_introduction_inf :

        ⌊0 = 0⌋

      argument

    end

  argument

4.3.4   Lemmas

It is often convenient to introduce lemmas during a justification (that is, to establish a result independently and name it), and then later use it one or more times by referring to its name.

The concept of lemmas is hence very similar to that of theorems. The difference lies in that a lemma belongs to the justification where it is introduced and can only be used there, while a theorem is introduced independently of any justification and can be used in several justifications. Lemmas should be used in preference to theorems when the result is not of general interest or when the result depends upon some context (including assumptions) that is only built up during a specific justification and therefore has to be local to that justification.

The way to introduce a lemma, *[L] ro_eb*, is to apply the following inference rule backwards:

  [lemma]

    [id] ro_eb ⊢ ro_eb′
    ———————————
    ro_eb′

    when convergent(ro_eb) ∧ **pure**(ro_eb) ∧ ro_eb

The layout of the justification then becomes

    ⌊ro_eb′⌋

  lemma :

  [L] ro_eb ⊢

    ⌊ro_eb′⌋

    since

        ⌊ro_eb⌋

      argument_for_lemma

    end

  argument

for pure and convergent *ro_eb*. The context rules from the lemma can then be used in the argument for *ro_eb′*. Note that the lemma itself is justified on the side as in

$\lfloor \forall$ i : {| i : **Int** • i > 0 |} • 0 / i + i / i = 1$\rfloor$
all_subtype, is_true :

$\lfloor \forall$ i : **Int** • i > 0 $\Rightarrow$ 0 / i + i / i = 1$\rfloor$
all_assumption_inf, imply_deduction_inf :
[assump] i > 0 $\vdash$

$\lfloor$0 / i + i / i = 1$\rfloor$
lemma :
[L] i $\neq$ 0 $\vdash$

$\lfloor$0 / i + i / i = 1$\rfloor$

since $\lfloor$i $\neq$ 0$\rfloor$ /* proof of [L] */ int_inequality, assump, true_or, **qed** **end**
zero_divide_int :

$\lfloor$0 + i / i = 1$\rfloor$

since $\lfloor$i $\neq$ 0$\rfloor$ L, **qed** **end**
divide_int_annihilation :

$\lfloor$0 + 1 = 1$\rfloor$

since $\lfloor$i $\neq$ 0$\rfloor$ L, **qed** **end**
simplify, **qed**

In the justification, the application of the rules *zero_divide_int* and *divide_int_-annihilation* both give the side condition $i \neq 0$. It was therefore convenient to introduce a lemma stating this predicate.

We produced this justification using a computer-based tool providing a tactic called *simplify*. *simplify* transforms a term to an equivalent one by applying a sequence of equivalence rules in one step.

4.3.5   Proof by case analysis

A possible strategy for justifying a condition, *ro_eb*, is to do a *case analysis*, i.e. to justify it for a number of different and exhaustive cases. This means that the condition should be justified under different assumptions, *ro_eb$_1$*, ..., *ro_eb$_n$*, and it should be justified that the disjunction of these assumptions is true.

The way to do case analysis is to apply the following inference rule backwards:

[case_analysis]

$\dfrac{[\text{id}_1]\ \text{ro\_eb}_1 \vdash \text{ro\_eb},\ ...,\ [\text{id}_n]\ \text{ro\_eb}_n \vdash \text{ro\_eb}}{\text{ro\_eb}}$

   when
      convergent(ro_eb$_1$) $\wedge$ ... $\wedge$ **convergent**(ro_eb$_n$) $\wedge$
      pure(ro_eb$_1$) $\wedge$ ... $\wedge$ **pure**(ro_eb$_n$) $\wedge$
      (ro_eb$_1$ $\vee$ ... $\vee$ ro_eb$_n$)

For pure and convergent assumptions the layout of the justification then becomes

⌊ro_eb⌋
case_analysis :
   • [assumpt$_1$] ro_eb$_1$ ⊢
         ⌊ro_eb⌋
      argument$_1$,

      ...
   • [assumpt$_n$] ro_eb$_n$ ⊢
         ⌊ro_eb⌋
      argument$_n$

   since
      ⌊ro_eb$_1$ ∨ ... ∨ ro_eb$_n$⌋
   argument
end

Case analysis is for instance a reasonable strategy in the justification of a property of a function which is defined by cases over the argument value. For example, if we wish to justify the condition

∀ x : **Int** • f(x) ≥ 0

in a context containing a definition of a function f for which $f(x)$ is defined for three different cases of x

value
   f : **Int** → **Int**
axiom
   [f_gt_0] ∀ x : **Int** • f(x) ≡ x + 2 **pre** x > 0,
   [f_is_0] f(0) ≡ 0,
   [f_lt_0] ∀ x : **Int** • f(x) ≡ 2 **pre** x < 0,

then a reasonable strategy is to use a case analysis over x, using the same three cases. However, before we can do that we first need to apply an *all_assumption_inf* in order to bring x into the context, since the identifiers in the case assumptions must be in the current context. The complete justification is

   ⌊∀ x : **Int** • f(x) ≥ 0⌋
all_assumption_inf :

   ⌊f(x) ≥ 0⌋
case_analysis :
   • [gt_0] x > 0 ⊢
         ⌊f(x) ≥ 0⌋
      f_gt_0 :
         ⌊x + 2 ≥ 0⌋
         since ⌊x > 0⌋ gt_0, **qed end**
      /* which can be proved using [gt_0] */ **qed**,

- $[$ is_0 $]$ x = 0 $\vdash$

    $\llcorner$ f(x) $\geq$ 0 $\lrcorner$

    is_0, f_is_0 :

    $\llcorner$ 0 $\geq$ 0 $\lrcorner$

    simplify, **qed**,
- $[$ lt_0 $]$ x < 0 $\vdash$

    $\llcorner$ f(x) $\geq$ 0 $\lrcorner$

    f_lt_0 :

    $\llcorner$ 2 $\geq$ 0 $\lrcorner$

        since $\llcorner$ x < 0 $\lrcorner$ lt_0, **qed end**

    simplify, **qed**

since

$\llcorner$ x > 0 $\vee$ x = 0 $\vee$ x < 0 $\lrcorner$ /* which is evident */ **qed**

end

Note that the preconditions from the axioms f_gt_0 and f_lt_0 appear as side conditions when context rules derived from the axioms are applied.

If there are only two cases, ro_eb' and ~ro_eb', then it is preferable to use the inference rule

$[$ two_cases_inf $]$

$\quad$ $[$ id $]$ ro_eb' $\vdash$ ro_eb,

$\quad$ $\underline{[$ id' $]} \sim$ ro_eb' $\vdash$ ro_eb

$\quad$ ro_eb

$\quad$ **when convergent**(ro_eb') $\wedge$ **pure**(ro_eb')

instead, as we then do not need to justify the disjunction of the cases. The layout then becomes

$\llcorner$ ro_eb $\lrcorner$

two_cases_inf :

- $[$ assumpt$_1$ $]$ ro_eb' $\vdash$

    $\llcorner$ ro_eb $\lrcorner$

    argument$_1$
- $[$ assumpt$_2$ $]$ ~ro_eb' $\vdash$

    $\llcorner$ ro_eb $\lrcorner$

    argument$_2$

for pure and convergent ro_eb'.

Exercise Use case analysis to prove the goal

$\llcorner$ $\forall$ x, y : **Int** $\cdot$ **abs** (x + y) $\leq$ **abs** x + **abs** y $\lrcorner$

4.3.6   Proof by induction

A possible strategy for justifying predicates of the form

$\forall$ b : T • ro_eb

where T is an inductive type (i.e. a type having an induction principle) is to prove (or rather justify) it by induction.

It is well-known that the *(stepwise) induction principle* for natural numbers can be used to prove that some property $p(n)$ holds for any natural numbers n: If it can be proved that the property holds for zero (i.e. $p(0)$ is true), and if, in addition, by assuming that the property holds for some arbitrary number n (i.e. $p(n)$ is true), it can be proved that it also holds for the next natural number $n+1$ (i.e. $p(n+1)$ is true), then one can conclude that the property $p(n)$ holds for any natural number n. In other words, according to the induction principle for natural numbers, predicates of the form

$\forall$ n : **Nat** • p(n)

(where $p(n)$ is not necessarily an application expression, but stands for any predicate in which n may occur) can be proved by proving

- a *base case*: p(0)
- an *induction step*: $\forall$ n : **Nat** • p(n) $\Rightarrow$ p(n+1)

Such a proof is called a (stepwise) *induction proof*. In the induction step $p(n)$ is called the *induction hypothesis*.

For the natural numbers, there is an alternative (more general) induction principle called the *complete induction principle* for natural numbers, according to which it can be proved that $p(n)$ is true for all natural numbers n by proving that for any natural number n, if $p(0)$, ..., and $p(n-1)$ hold then $p(n)$ also holds. In other words, by proving

$\forall$ n : **Nat** • ($\forall$ j : **Nat** • j < n $\Rightarrow$ p(j)) $\Rightarrow$ p(n)

Complete induction is most often used in proofs where $p(n)$ depends not just on the predecessor $(n-1)$ but on several previous numbers.

Similar induction and complete induction principles also exist for types other than the natural numbers.

In general, the induction principles state that predicates of the form

$\forall$ b : T • ro_eb   (1)

can be proved by proving a number of base cases and a number of induction steps.

Among the RSL equivalence rules there are a number of *induction rules* which can be used to do induction proofs for natural numbers, finite sets, finite lists, finite maps, and values of variant, short record and union types. The induction rules for natural numbers, finite sets, finite lists and finite maps are defined in appendix B, and the induction rules for variants, short records and unions are derived context rules, as described in section 4.3.2.7, in which ro_eb is of the form[9] e(b), where e

---

[9] There are differences between the formulations of the induction rules for built-in types and the formulation of those for variant, short record and union types. The reason for this is that the

is a term variable having the maximal type $T \overset{\sim}{\to}$ **Bool**.

The induction rules are all equivalences between **true** and predicates of the form (1) for different types T. Each rule has an applicability condition consisting of a conjunction of conditions, one for each base case and one for each induction step.

The typical layout of an induction proof having a base case and an induction step is therefore

    ⌊∀ b : T • ro_eb⌋
induction_rule_name:

    ⌊**true**⌋
    since

       •   ⌊base-case⌋
          argument_for_base-case
       •   ⌊induction-step⌋
          argument_for_induction-step

    end
  qed

Note that as the induction rules are equivalence rules, they can be applied to any (sub)term of a goal.

Some examples of use of induction rules are given below.

4.3.6.1   Example of stepwise induction

Consider the following specification of a function *sum* which for any natural number n gives the sum of the n first numbers:

   scheme SUM =
     class
       value
         sum : **Nat** → **Nat**
       axiom
         [sum_zero] $\text{sum}(0) \equiv 0$,
         [sum_n] $\forall$ n : **Nat** • $\text{sum}(n + 1) \equiv \text{sum}(n) + n + 1$
     end

sum is defined inductively:

- A basic clause defines *sum(0)*.
- An inductive clause defines *sum(n+1)* in terms of *sum(n)* for $n \geq 0$.

---

latter rules are (dynamically) created as context rules derived from induction axioms typically having the form $\forall\ p : T \to$ **Bool** • ... $\Rightarrow$ ($\forall\ b : T$ • $p(b)$)), while this is not necessary for the former rules — they have been formulated directly once and for all.

We now wish to prove the following condition:

$\forall$ n : **Nat** • sum(n) $\equiv$ n $*$ (n + 1)/2

As the condition involves *sum*, which is defined in an inductive way, a reasonable strategy for justifying it is to do a (stepwise) induction proof using the rule

[all_nat_induction]

$\quad$ $\forall$ b : **Nat** • ro_eb $\simeq$ **true**

$\quad$ **when** **subst_expr**(0, b, ro_eb) $\wedge$

$\quad\quad$ ($\forall$ b : **Nat** • ro_eb $\Rightarrow$ **subst_expr**(**express**(b) + 1, b, ro_eb))

This is done below:

$\quad$ $\llcorner$SUM $\vdash$ $\forall$ n : **Nat** • sum(n) $\equiv$ n $*$ (n + 1) / 2$\lrcorner$

class_assumption_inf :

$\quad$ $\llcorner\forall$ n : **Nat** • sum(n) $\equiv$ n $*$ (n + 1) / 2$\lrcorner$

all_nat_induction :

$\quad$ $\llcorner$**true**$\lrcorner$

$\quad$ **since**

$\quad\quad$ • $\quad$ $\llcorner$sum(0) $\equiv$ 0 $*$ (0 + 1) / 2$\lrcorner$

$\quad\quad$ sum_zero :

$\quad\quad\quad$ $\llcorner$0 $\equiv$ 0 $*$ (0 + 1) / 2$\lrcorner$

$\quad\quad$ /$*$ which is evident $*$/

$\quad\quad$ **qed**

$\quad\quad$ • $\quad$ $\llcorner\forall$ n : **Nat** • (sum(n) $\equiv$ n $*$ (n + 1) / 2) $\Rightarrow$

$\quad\quad\quad\quad$ (sum(n + 1) $\equiv$ (n + 1) $*$ (n + 1 + 1) / 2)$\lrcorner$

$\quad\quad$ all_assumption_inf, imply_deduction_inf :

$\quad\quad$ [ind_hyp] sum(n) $\equiv$ n $*$ (n + 1) / 2 $\vdash$

$\quad\quad\quad$ $\llcorner$sum(n + 1) $\equiv$ (n + 1) $*$ (n + 1 + 1) / 2$\lrcorner$

$\quad\quad$ sum_n :

$\quad\quad\quad$ $\llcorner$sum(n) + n + 1 $\equiv$ (n + 1) $*$ (n + 1 + 1) / 2$\lrcorner$

$\quad\quad$ ind_hyp :

$\quad\quad\quad$ $\llcorner$n $*$ (n + 1) / 2 + n + 1 $\equiv$ (n + 1) $*$ (n + 1 + 1) / 2$\lrcorner$

$\quad\quad$ /$*$ which can be shown using rules for arithmetic $*$/

$\quad\quad$ **qed**

$\quad$ **end**

qed

Exercise Use *all_list_left_induction* to justify the goal

$\quad$ $\llcorner\forall$ el : **Int*** • **len** el $\geq$ **card** (**elems** el)$\lrcorner$

4.3.6.2 Example of complete induction

Consider the specification of a function g:

> **scheme** A_FUN =
>> **class**
>>> **value**
>>>> $g : \textbf{Nat} \rightarrow \textbf{Nat}$
>>> **axiom**
>>>> $[\,g0\,]\ g(0) \equiv 8,$
>>>> $[\,g1\,]\ g(1) \equiv 11,$
>>>> $[\,gn\,]\ \forall\, n : \textbf{Nat} \cdot g(n) \equiv 3 * g(n-1) - 2 * g(n-2)\ \textbf{pre}\ n \geq 2$
>> **end**

g is defined inductively:

- A basic clause defines $g(0)$.
- A basic clause defines $g(1)$.
- An inductive clause defines $g(n)$ in terms of $g(n-1)$ and $g(n-2)$ for $n \geq 2$.

We wish to prove the condition

> $\forall\, n : \textbf{Nat} \cdot g(n) \equiv 3 * 2{\uparrow}n + 5$

As the condition involves g, which is defined in an inductive way in which $g(n)$ depends on g for several previous numbers $(g(n-1)$ and $g(n-2))$, a reasonable strategy for justifying it is to do a complete induction proof using the rule

> $[\,$all_nat_complete_induction$\,]$
>> $\forall\, b : \textbf{Nat} \cdot$ ro_eb $\simeq$ **true**
>> **when disjoint**$(b, b') \wedge$ **no_capture**$(b',$ ro_eb$) \wedge$
>>> $(\forall\, b : \textbf{Nat} \cdot$
>>>> $(\forall\, b' : \textbf{Nat} \cdot$ **express**$(b') <$ **express**$(b) \Rightarrow$
>>>>> **subst_binding**$(b', b,$ ro_eb$))$
>>> $\Rightarrow$ ro_eb$)$

This is done below:

> $\llcorner$A_FUN $\vdash \forall\, n : \textbf{Nat} \cdot g(n) \equiv 3 * 2 \uparrow n + 5\lrcorner$
>
> class_assumption_inf :
>> $\llcorner \forall\, n : \textbf{Nat} \cdot g(n) \equiv 3 * 2 \uparrow n + 5\lrcorner$
>
> all_nat_complete_induction :
>> $\llcorner$**true**$\lrcorner$
>> **since**
>>> $\llcorner \forall\, n : \textbf{Nat} \cdot$
>>>> $(\forall\, j : \textbf{Nat} \cdot j < n \Rightarrow (g(j) \equiv 3 * 2 \uparrow j + 5)) \Rightarrow$
>>>> $(g(n) \equiv 3 * 2 \uparrow n + 5)\lrcorner$
>>>
>>> all_assumption_inf :
>>>> $\llcorner (\forall\, j : \textbf{Nat} \cdot j < n \Rightarrow (g(j) \equiv 3 * 2 \uparrow j + 5)) \Rightarrow$
>>>> $(g(n) \equiv 3 * 2 \uparrow n + 5)\lrcorner$

case_analysis :
- [c0] n = 0 ⊢
    ⌊(∀ j : **Nat** • j < n ⇒ (g(j) ≡ 3 * 2 ↑ j + 5)) ⇒
      (g(n) ≡ 3 * 2 ↑ n + 5)⌋
  c0, c0, g0 :
    ⌊(∀ j : **Nat** • j < n ⇒ (g(j) ≡ 3 * 2 ↑ j + 5)) ⇒
      (8 ≡ 3 * 2 ↑ 0 + 5)⌋
  /* which simplifies to */
    ⌊(∀ j : **Nat** • j < n ⇒ (g(j) ≡ 3 * 2 ↑ j + 5)) ⇒ **true**⌋
  implies_true, **qed**,
- [c1] n = 1 ⊢
    ⌊(∀ j : **Nat** • j < n ⇒ (g(j) ≡ 3 * 2 ↑ j + 5)) ⇒
      (g(n) ≡ 3 * 2 ↑ n + 5)⌋
  ..., **qed**,
- [cn] n ≥ 2 ⊢
    ⌊(∀ j : **Nat** • j < n ⇒ (g(j) ≡ 3 * 2 ↑ j + 5)) ⇒
      (g(n) ≡ 3 * 2 ↑ n + 5)⌋
  imply_deduction_inf :
  [ind_hyp] ∀ j : **Nat** • j < n ⇒ (g(j) ≡ 3 * 2 ↑ j + 5) ⊢
    ⌊g(n) ≡ 3 * 2 ↑ n + 5⌋
  gn :
    ⌊3 * g(n − 1) − 2 * g(n − 2) ≡ 3 * 2 ↑ n + 5⌋
    since ⌊n ≥ 2⌋ cn, **qed end**
  ind_hyp :
    ⌊3 * (3 * 2 ↑ (n − 1) + 5) − 2 * g(n − 2) ≡ 3 * 2 ↑ n + 5⌋
    since
      - ⌊n − 1 < n⌋ /* which is evident */ **qed**
      - ⌊n − 1 ≥ 0⌋ /* which follows from [cn] */ **qed**
    end
  ind_hyp :
    ⌊3 * (3 * 2 ↑ (n − 1) + 5) − 2 * (3 * 2 ↑ (n − 2) + 5) ≡
      3 * 2 ↑ n + 5⌋
    since
      - ⌊n − 2 < n⌋ /* which is evident */ **qed**
      - ⌊n − 2 ≥ 0⌋ /* which follows from [cn] */ **qed**
    end
  /* which can be shown using rules for arithmetic */ **qed**
  since
    ⌊n = 0 ∨ n = 1 ∨ n ≥ 2⌋ /* which is evident */ **qed**
  end
end qed

4.3.6.3 Example of variant induction

Consider the following specification of a variant type *Tree* of trees and a function *count* which counts the number of node elements in a tree and a function *set* which gives the set of node elements in a tree:

    scheme TREE =
      class
        type
          Elem, Tree == empty | node(left : Tree, elem : Elem, right : Tree)
        value
          count : Tree $\rightarrow$ **Nat**,
          set : Tree $\rightarrow$ Elem-**set**
        axiom
          [count_empty] count(empty) $\equiv$ 0,
          [count_node]
            $\forall$ t1, t2 : Tree, el : Elem •
              count(node(t1, el, t2)) $\equiv$ count(t1) + 1 + count(t2),
          [set_empty] set(empty) $\equiv$ {},
          [set_node]
            $\forall$ t1, t2 : Tree, el : Elem •
              set(node(t1, el, t2)) $\equiv$ set(t1) $\cup$ {el} $\cup$ set(t2)
    end

We now wish to prove the condition

    $\forall$ t : Tree • **card** set(t) $\leq$ count(t)

A reasonable strategy for doing this is to do variant induction using the derived context rule, *Tree_induction* (see section 4.3.2.7), which the variant type definition of *Tree* gives rise to:

    $\llcorner$TREE $\vdash$ $\forall$ t : Tree • **card** set(t) $\leq$ count(t)$\lrcorner$
class_assumption_inf :
    $\llcorner$$\forall$ t : Tree • **card** set(t) $\leq$ count(t)$\lrcorner$
/* transform the goal to a form appropriate for Tree_induction */
substitution1 :
    $\llcorner$$\forall$ t : Tree • (λ t : Tree • **card** set(t) $\leq$ count(t))(t)$\lrcorner$
    since
       $\llcorner$**card** set(t) $\leq$ count(t) $\equiv$ (λ t : Tree • **card** set(t) $\leq$ count(t))(t)$\lrcorner$
       lambda_application, let_absorption4, is_annihilation, **qed**
    end
Tree_induction :
    $\llcorner$**true**$\lrcorner$

since

- ⌊(λ t : Tree • **card** set(t) $\leq$ count(t))(empty)⌋
  lambda_application, let_absorption4 :
  ⌊**card** set(empty) $\leq$ count(empty)⌋
  set_empty, count_empty :
  ⌊**card** {} $\leq$ 0⌋
  card_empty, leq_int_annihilation, **qed**

- ⌊$\forall$ t1 : Tree, el : Elem, t2 : Tree •
  (λ t : Tree • **card** set(t) $\leq$ count(t))(t1) $\wedge$
  (λ t : Tree • **card** set(t) $\leq$ count(t))(t2) $\Rightarrow$
  (λ t : Tree • **card** set(t) $\leq$ count(t))(node(t1,el,t2))⌋
  lambda_application, let_absorption4, lambda_application,
  let_absorption4, lambda_application, let_absorption4 :
  ⌊$\forall$ t1 : Tree, el : Elem, t2 : Tree •
  card set(t1) $\leq$ count(t1) $\wedge$ **card** set(t2) $\leq$ count(t2) $\Rightarrow$
  card set(node(t1,el,t2)) $\leq$ count(node(t1,el,t2))⌋
  all_assumption_inf, imply_deduction_inf :
  [ind_hyp]
  card set(t1) $\leq$ count(t1) $\wedge$ **card** set(t2) $\leq$ count(t2) $\vdash$
  ⌊**card** set(node(t1,el,t2)) $\leq$ count(node(t1,el,t2))⌋
  set_node, count_node :
  ⌊**card** (set(t1) $\cup$ {el} $\cup$ set(t2)) $\leq$
  count(t1) + 1 + count(t2)⌋
  card_union, card_union, card_singleton, minus_plus_int :
  ⌊**card** set(t1) + 1 + **card** set(t2) $-$ **card**(set(t1) $\cap$ {el}) $-$
  card ((set(t1) $\cup$ {el}) $\cap$ set(t2)) $\leq$
  count(t1) + 1 + count(t2)⌋
  /* which is true if we can prove */

  - ⌊**card** set(t1) $\leq$ count(t1)⌋
    ind_hyp, **qed**

  - ⌊**card** set(t2) $\leq$ count(t2)⌋
    ind_hyp, **qed**

end
qed

For an exercise using variant induction, see section 4.3.2.7.

4.3.7   Forwards reasoning

Until now we have only considered how to justify a condition using backwards reasoning, i.e. taking the given condition as the starting point, breaking it into simpler sub-conditions, and then justifying each of these.

Sometimes it is convenient to work the other way around: to make conclusions from known facts (sequents), after which the conclusion is then a known fact, etc., until the initial goal has been established as a conclusion. This is conventionally known as as *forwards reasoning* or *natural deduction*.

How to switch to forwards mode and how to do forwards reasoning is explained below.

4.3.7.1   Switching to forwards mode

It is possible to switch from backwards mode to forwards mode. This is done by using a *follows argument* which has the form

follows
    argument
end

where the embedded argument must be developed as a forwards argument.

4.3.7.2   Introducing facts

While the steps in a backwards argument manipulate goals, the steps in a forwards argument manipulate lists of facts, where a *fact* is a sequent which is known to be true in the current context and is written within half-brackets (just as a goal).

We start from the empty list of facts. Facts can be added to the current list of facts by *fact introductions* in a *from argument* which has the form

from fact_intro-list
    fact-list
    argument

Each of the embedded *fact_intros* introduces a fact. The result is a new list, *fact-list*, of facts, which is obtained by adding the introduced facts to the right of the current list of facts. *argument* is an argument in which this new list of facts can be manipulated.

A *fact_intro* can be either

- the name of an axiom (e.g. a lemma or case assumption) from the context optionally followed by the fact it represents (and introduces)
- a tautology, i.e. the fact ⌊**true**⌋

Note that before starting a forwards argument, we should define a number of lemmas that we expect to be useful as facts in the forwards argument.

4.3.7.3   Conclusion arguments

The following sections explain how the list of facts can be manipulated. When a fact is reached which is identical to the original goal of the follows argument the follows argument is complete. So the typical form of a forwards justification is

```
  ⌊condition⌋
    follows
      from ...
        ...
          ⌊condition⌋
        qed
      end
```

4.3.7.4   Application of inference rules

The main steps in a forwards justification are application of inference rules. An inference rule can be applied forwards to (a sublist of) the list of facts if the sequents, p_1, ..., p_n, in the facts *match* (in the right order) the premises of the inference rule, i.e. it is possible to find a correct instantiation of the inference rule for which the instantiated premises are identical to p_1, ..., p_n. The result of the application is a new list of facts which is obtained from the old list by replacing the (sub)list with a fact whose sequent, p, is the instantiated conclusion. This is written

$$\dots, \lfloor p_1 \rfloor, \dots, \lfloor p_n \rfloor, \dots$$
$$name \Rightarrow$$
$$\dots, \lfloor p \rfloor, \dots$$

where *name* is the name of the applied rule. Note that the name is followed by "$\Rightarrow$" rather than ":", in order to indicate that the argument is forwards. (Sub)lists of fact lists may be reordered to get them into the required order to match the premises of the inference rule to be applied.

Applicability conditions give rise to side conditions in the same way as in backwards application. The side conditions are goals which should be justified (initially at least) in backwards mode.

4.3.7.5   Application of equivalence rules

In forwards mode, equivalence rules can be used to manipulate lists of introduced facts by replacing subterms of the facts with equivalent subterms, in the same way as they can be used in backwards mode to manipulate goals by replacing subterms of the goals with equivalent subterms. The concept of *matching* and the notions of *matched term*, *resulting term*, etc. are the same. When an equivalence rule having a name, *name*, is applied forwards to a subterm, t, of a list of introduced facts in order to replace it with an equivalent term, t', this is written

$$\dots, \lfloor \dots t \dots \rfloor, \dots$$
$$name \Rightarrow$$
$$\dots, \lfloor \dots t' \dots \rfloor, \dots$$

Again, the name of an applied rule is followed by "⇒" rather than ":", and applicability conditions give rise to side conditions if standard application and not in-goal application is used.

4.3.7.6   Other forwards arguments

An *irrelevance argument* may *not* be applied.

A *commented argument* may be used as in backwards justifications.

A *replacement argument* may be used to replace the current list of facts with another list of facts.

An *explanation argument* may be used to terminate a forwards justification.

4.3.7.7   Example

For example, suppose that we have in the context the two axioms:

[a1] x ∈ s1 ∩ s2,
[a2] x ∈ s3

Then a justification of the condition $x \in s1 \land x \in s3$ could be

⌊x ∈ s1 ∧ x ∈ s3⌋
follows
   from
       [a1] ⌊x ∈ s1 ∩ s2⌋,
       [a2] ⌊x ∈ s3⌋
         ⌊x ∈ s1 ∩ s2⌋, ⌊x ∈ s3⌋
       isin_intersection ⇒
         ⌊x ∈ s1 ∧ x ∈ s2⌋, ⌊x ∈ s3⌋
       and_left_inf ⇒
         ⌊x ∈ s1⌋, ⌊x ∈ s3⌋
       and_split_inf ⇒
         ⌊x ∈ s1 ∧ x ∈ s3⌋
      qed
end

Exercise   In a context containing the definitions
   value k : **Int**
   axiom [k_greater_5] k > 5
use forwards reasoning to prove the goal
   ⌊k > 4⌋
using as facts the axiom *k_greater_5* and the lemma
   [greater_transitivity] ∀ x,y,z : **Int** • x > y ∧ y > z ⇒ x > z

Hint: use *all_instantiation_inf* to obtain the fact

⌊k > 5 ∧ 5 > 4 ⇒ k > 4⌋

from *greater_transitivity* and complete with *imply_modus_ponens_inf*.

4.3.8   Proof by contradiction

In some cases an efficient way to prove a condition is *by contradiction*. The strategy for such a proof is to assume that the condition, *ro_eb*, which is to be proved, is false, (i.e. assume ~ *ro_eb*), and then by a forwards proof show that this leads to a contradiction (i.e. the condition **false**).

A condition, *ro_eb*, is proved by contradiction by first applying the rule

[contradiction_inf1]
$$\frac{[\,\text{id}\,] \sim \text{ro\_eb} \vdash \textbf{false}}{\text{ro\_eb}}$$
when convergent(ro_eb) ∧ **pure**(ro_eb)

and then typically shifting to forwards mode. So the layout for a proof by contradiction is, for pure and convergent *ro_eb*

⌊ro_eb⌋
contradiction_inf1:
[assumpt] ~ ro_eb ⊢
    ⌊**false**⌋
follows
    from

        ...

            ⌊**false**⌋
        qed
end

If the condition to be proved is of the form ~ *ro_eb*, we could alternatively start by using the rule

[contradiction_inf2]
$$\frac{[\,\text{id}\,] \text{ro\_eb} \vdash \textbf{false}}{\sim \text{ro\_eb}}$$
when convergent(ro_eb) ∧ **pure**(ro_eb)

The layout then becomes

⌊~ ro_eb⌋
contradiction_inf2:
[assumpt] ro_eb ⊢
    ⌊**false**⌋

follows
>   **from**
>
>   ...
>
>   ⌊**false**⌋
>   **qed**
end

For example, in a context containing the following declarations

value
>   x, y : **Int**,
>   s: **Int-set**

axiom
>   [ax1] x ∈ s,
>   [ax2] ~ (y ∈ s)

a proof by contradiction can be used in the justification of ⌊~(x = y)⌋:

>   ⌊~(x = y)⌋
>   contradiction_inf2:
>   [assumpt] x = y ⊢
>
>   ⌊**false**⌋
>   **follows**
>   >   **from**
>   >
>   >   [ax1] ⌊x ∈ s⌋
>   >
>   >   ⌊x ∈ s⌋
>   >   assumpt ⇒
>   >
>   >   ⌊y ∈ s⌋
>   >   ax2 ⇒
>   >
>   >   ⌊**false**⌋
>   >   **qed**
end

Exercise   The example just presented suggests a general theorem where x and y are of some type T:

$$(\exists\, f : T \rightarrow \textbf{Bool} \cdot f(x) \wedge {\sim}f(y)) \Rightarrow x \neq y \tag{1}$$

1. Prove this by contradiction.
2. For convergent, read-only logical expressions *eb* and *eb'* we have the rule *not_implies*:

   $${\sim}eb \Rightarrow {\sim}eb' \simeq eb' \Rightarrow eb$$

   We could therefore do the proof of (1) by first rewriting the goal to

   $$\llcorner\; x = y \Rightarrow {\sim}(\exists\, f : T \rightarrow \textbf{Bool} \cdot f(x) \wedge {\sim}f(y))\; \lrcorner \tag{2}$$

   Do the proof from the goal (2).

Hint: the equality before the implication allows us to replace x by y in the expression after the implication. This makes this proof of (1) easier than the first and illustrates a useful strategy for proving implications where the expression on the right is an inequality.

4.4   Justification for imperative specifications

When justifying conditions involving imperative constructs, the techniques presented so far are still applicable. For instance, suppose we have a conventional implementation of an imperative stack using a state variable *st* containing a list, and we want to prove the standard axiom

$\forall$ x : Elem • push(x) ; top() $\equiv$ push(x) ; x

relating *push* and *top* (where *top* just reads the top of the stack, there being a separate *pop* operation). We will, as in an applicative setting, start by removing the quantification and unfolding the function applications. But then some additional advice on how to manipulate imperative constructs, e.g. how to unfold variable instances, is needed.

This section gives advice which is particularly related to the construction of justifications where imperative constructs are involved.

4.4.1   Fulfilling applicability conditions on variable access

Many proof rules have applicability conditions like

- **pure**(e)
- **readonly**(e)
- **assignment_disjoint**(e,e′)

on the variable access in value expressions (here e and e'). For a definition of the special functions used in these conditions, see appendix B.4.

In an applicative setting these conditions are always satisfied.

In an imperative setting, there may be situations where we wish to apply such a rule, but where the applicability condition is not fulfilled. In these situations, however, it is sometimes possible to rewrite the expression such that the inopportune accesses to variables are isolated in one sub-expression and the rule can be applied to another sub-expression for which the applicability condition becomes fulfilled.

A strategy for isolating inopportune variable accesses is to use evaluation,[10] associativity and commutativity rules in order to replace the term to which the rule

---

[10] An evaluation rule is a rule which for some construct gives the order in which sub-expressions are evaluated by stating an equivalence between the construct and a let expression. For example, the rule *application_evaluation* states that a function application is evaluated by first evaluating the function, then evaluating the argument, and finally evaluating the application.

should be applied with an expression having one of the two forms[11]

- **let** b = e_1 **in** e_2 **end**
- e_1 ; e_2

where only e_1 contains the inopportune variable accesses. Now the rule can be applied to e_2.

Examples of this are given in section 4.4.2.

If the inopportune variable access is a variable instance v (read access), an alternative strategy is to unfold this. In section 4.4.2, techniques for unfolding variable instances are given. Examples are given in sections 4.4.2 and 4.4.4.

4.4.2 Unfolding variable instances

There are situations where a reasonable strategy for the next step in a justification is to *unfold* a *variable instance* (a value expression which is a variable name), i.e. to replace it with an expression representing the value the variable contains at the point where the instance occurs.

Unfolding of variable instances can be a useful strategy for the same reasons as it can be useful to unfold value names and function applications: we can obtain an expression which makes it possible to further simplify the goal.

For example, unfolding of variable instances can be used as a strategy for removing read accesses from an expression, so that applicability conditions of the proof rule to be applied can be fulfilled, cf. section 4.4.1.

This section gives strategies for how instances of a variable v can be unfolded. First we will consider the situation where the instance occurs after an assignment to the variable itself, and then the situation where this is not the case.

4.4.2.1 After an assignment

In this section, we consider the situation where the instance occurs in an expression e' in a sequence starting with an assignment of the value of an expression e to the variable:

$$v := e ; e'$$

For the purpose of unfolding the variable instance, v, in e', the following rule can be used:

[assignment_unfold]
    $v := e ; v \simeq v := e ; e$
    when
        convergent($v := e$) $\wedge$ **readonly**(e) $\wedge$ **assignment_disjoint**($v := e, e$)

Note that when e is read-only, the last conjunct means that e must not read v.

---

[11] In fact sequences can be expanded to let expressions using the rule *sequence_expansion*. This indicates that a sequence is a derived form and that a let expression is the basic form.

If e' is v and the applicability condition is satisfied, the rule can be used directly, as shown in the following example, where we assume that v is declared to be a variable of type **Int**:

⌊v := 3 ; v ≡ v := 3 ; 3⌋
assignment_unfold:

⌊v := 3 ; 3 ≡ v := 3 ; 3⌋
is_annihilation, **qed**

But what if e' is not v or the applicability condition is not fulfilled? These issues are discussed in the next sections.

4.4.2.2 Placing the assignment in front of the instance

If e' is not v, but a more complicated expression like **abs** v, then it is necessary to perform some manipulations in order to bring the assignment directly in front of the v we wish to unfold, so that the rule *assignment_unfold* can be applied. This is shown in the following example, where e is assumed to be read-only and convergent, to be of the type of v and not reading v:

⌊v := e ; **abs** v ≡ v := e ; **abs** e⌋
prefix_op_evaluation

⌊v := e ; **let** x = v **in abs** x **end** ≡ v := e ; **abs** e⌋
sequence_let:

⌊**let** x = (v := e ; v) **in abs** x **end** ≡ v := e ; **abs** e⌋
assignment_unfold:

⌊**let** x = (v := e ; e) **in abs** x **end** ≡ v := e ; **abs** e⌋
sequence_let:

⌊v := e ; **let** x = e **in abs** x **end** ≡ v := e ; **abs** e⌋
let_absorption4:

⌊v := e ; **abs** e ≡ v := e ; **abs** e⌋
is_annihilation, **qed**

The general strategy is to use evaluation, associativity and commutativity rules in order to replace e' with a let expression of the form

let x = v **in** e″ **end**

and then to use *sequence_let* in order to place the v just after the assignment, whereupon *assignment_unfold* can be applied. After that, *sequence_let* can be used the other way in order to get the assignment out of the let expression.

Then, the let expression can be absorbed, replacing in $e″$ all occurrences of x with e. This can be done by using *let_absorption4* if e is pure and convergent, or by other manipulations for the less restrictive case where all occurrences of x in $e″$ are evaluated before any possible assignments in $e″$ to any variable that may be read by e:

⌊...v := e ; e'...⌋
/* after some manipulation with evaluation rules and the like, we get */
⌊...v := e ; **let** x = v **in** e″ **end**...⌋
sequence_let:
⌊...**let** x = (v := e ; v) **in** e″ **end**...⌋
assignment_unfold:
⌊...**let** x = (v := e ; e) **in** e″ **end**...⌋
sequence_let:
⌊...v := e ; **let** x = e **in** e″ **end**...⌋
/* after some manipulations, typically just let_absorption4, we may get */
⌊...v := e ; e‴...⌋

where $e‴$ is **subst_expr**(e, v, e') if $e″$ was **subst_expr**(x, v, e').

There is a derived equivalence rule, *assignment_sequence_propagation*, that does all these manipulations in one step. It applies to expressions of the form

v := e ; e'

when e is read-only and convergent, is of the type of v and does not read v. The result of the applications is

v := e ; e‴

where $e‴$ is obtained from e' by substituting the expression e for any instance of v that may be evaluated before any possible assignments to v or to any variables that may be read by e. Possible assignments to a variable are actual assignments and calls of functions with write access to the variable.

4.4.2.3 Fulfilling the instantiated applicability condition

If the applicability condition of *assignment_unfold* is not fulfilled (i.e. e is not read-only or it is not convergent or it reads the variable v) the strategies mentioned in section 4.4.1 can be used.

A strategy which can always be used is sketched here:

⌊...v := e ; v...⌋
assignment_evaluation:
⌊...**let** x = e **in** v := x **end** ; v...⌋
let_sequence:
⌊...**let** x = e **in** v := x ; v **end**...⌋
assignment_unfold:
⌊...**let** x = e **in** v := x ; x **end**...⌋

But there may be more elegant ways, as shown below.

Example of isolating inopportune write accesses

⌊v := (v2 := 5 ; 3) ; v ≡ v2 := 5 ; v := 3 ; 3⌋
assignment_sequence:
⌊v2 := 5 ; v := 3 ; v ≡ v2 := 5 ; v := 3 ; 3⌋
assignment_unfold:
⌊v2 := 5 ; v := 3 ; 3 ≡ v2 := 5 ; v := 3 ; 3⌋
is_annihilation, **qed**

Example of isolating and removing inopportune read accesses
Assume that we wish to unfold the instance of *v* succeeding the assignment in the goal

⌊...v := v + 1 ; v...⌋

However, we cannot apply *assignment_unfold*, as there is an inopportune read access in the right-hand side ($v + 1$) of the assignment. A strategy is to make the assignment pure by unfolding the instance of *v* in it. If there is a preceding assignment, we can use the techniques for unfolding described previously. An example of this is

⌊...v := 3 ; v := v + 1 ; v...⌋
assignment_sequence_propagation :
⌊...v := 3 ; v := 3 + 1 ; v...⌋
simplify :
⌊...v := 3 ; v := 4 ; v...⌋
assignment_unfold :
⌊...v := 3 ; v := 4 ; 4...⌋
...

If there is no preceding assignment, the technique explained in section 4.4.2.4 can be used.

4.4.2.4   Introducing arbitrary initial assignments

What can be done if we wish to unfold a variable instance *v* and there is no preceding assignment to it?

For instance, in

⌊v := v + 1 ; v := v − 1 ≡ **skip**⌋

we may wish to unfold the *v* on the right-hand of the first assignment so this right-hand side does not read *v* and therefore can be used when unfolding the *v* on the right-hand side of the second assignment.

If the condition is an equivalence expression, a post expression or an implication between equivalence expressions, a strategy is to introduce and make use of the □ ("for all possible states") that is implicit in any goal. Having introduced □ with the rule *always_elimination_inf*, we use one of the rules *always_application$m$*, $m =$ 1, 2 or 3, or *always_post_application$m$*, $m = 1$ or 2, to introduce arbitrary initial assignments to state variables.

For the example above we need *always_application1*:

[always_application1]

    $\Box\ e \equiv e' \simeq \forall$ id : Tv $\bullet\ \Box$ v := id ; e $\equiv$ v := id ; e'

  when

      no_capture(id, v) $\wedge$ **no_capture**(id, e) $\wedge$ **no_capture**(id, e') $\wedge$

      ($\Box$ **isin_subtype**(v, Tv)) $\wedge$ ($\Box\ \forall$ id : Tv $\bullet$ v := id **post true**)

The justification is as follows:

    $\llcorner$v := v + 1 ; v := v − 1 $\equiv$ **skip**$\lrcorner$

always_elimination_inf:

    $\llcorner\Box$ v := v + 1 ; v := v − 1 $\equiv$ **skip**$\lrcorner$

always_application1:

    $\llcorner\forall$ id : **Int** $\bullet\ \Box$

      v := id ; v := v + 1 ; v := v − 1 $\equiv$ v := id ; **skip**$\lrcorner$

  since

    • $\llcorner\Box\ \exists$ id : **Int** $\bullet$ id = v$\lrcorner$

       v_def, **qed**

    • $\llcorner(\Box\ \forall$ id : **Int** $\bullet$ v := id **post true**)$\lrcorner$

       v_def, **qed**

  end

where we have assumed that v is declared to have the type **Int**.

In this way we have obtained an assignment to v that precedes the instance we wish to unfold, and we can now proceed as usual. Continuing the example:

  all_assumption_inf:

    $\llcorner\Box$ v := id ; v := v + 1 ; v := v − 1 $\equiv$ v := id ; **skip**$\lrcorner$

  assignment_sequence_propagation:

    $\llcorner\Box$ v := id ; v := id + 1 ; v := v − 1 $\equiv$ v := id ; **skip**$\lrcorner$

  assignment_sequence_propagation:

    $\llcorner\Box$ v := id ; v := id + 1 ; v := (id + 1) − 1 $\equiv$ v := id ; **skip**$\lrcorner$

  ...

The general scheme for equivalence expressions without preconditions, and for a variable v of type T, is as follows:

    $\llcorner$e $\equiv$ e'$\lrcorner$

always_elimination_inf:

    $\llcorner\Box$ e $\equiv$ e'$\lrcorner$

always_application1:

    $\llcorner\forall$ id : **T** $\bullet\ \Box$ v := id ; e $\equiv$ v := id ; e'$\lrcorner$

> **since**
> > • $_\llcorner \square \; \exists \; id : T \bullet id = v \lrcorner$
> > > v_def, **qed**
> > • $_\llcorner \square \; \forall \; id : T \bullet v := id \; \textbf{post true} \lrcorner$
> > > v_def, **qed**
> **end**
> all_assumption_inf:
> > $_\llcorner \square \;\; v := id \; ; \; e \equiv v := id \; ; \; e' \lrcorner$
> /* now, variable instances of v in e and/or e$'$ can be unfolded
> using the introduced assignments */
> > ...

If the condition is either an equivalence expression with a precondition, or a post expression, or an implication between two equivalence expressions, similar techniques can be used.

Exercise   In a context containing
> **variable** x,y : **Int**

justify the goal
> $_\llcorner$x := x + y ; y := x − y ; x := x − y **post** x > y **pre** y > x$\lrcorner$

4.4.2.5   Using initialisations

If the context contains a variable declaration with an initialisation
> **variable**
> > v : T := e

then the context rule
> [v_def] **initialise** ; v := e $\simeq$ **initialise**

can be used.

For example, assume that in the abstract imperative specification *I_QUEUE0* in section 2.8.5.1 we had the axiom
> **initialise** ; is_empty() $\equiv$ **initialise** ; **true**

This states that initialising all variables to their initial values and then evaluating *is_empty()* is equivalent to initialising all variables to their initial values and then returning true. Suppose we wish to show that this axiom holds in *I_QUEUE2* from section 2.8.5.4. Then this can be justified using the derived context rule
> [queue_def] **initialise** $\simeq$ **initialise** ; queue := $\langle\rangle$

The justification is
> $_\llcorner$**initialise** ; is_empty() $\equiv$ **initialise** ; **true**$\lrcorner$
> is_empty_def :
> > $_\llcorner$**initialise** ; queue = $\langle\rangle$ $\equiv$ **initialise** ; **true**$\lrcorner$

queue_def, queue_def, sequence_associativity, sequence_associativity :

⌞**initialise** ; queue := $\langle\rangle$; queue = $\langle\rangle$ ≡ **initialise** ; queue := $\langle\rangle$; **true**⌟

assignment_sequence_propagation :

⌞**initialise** ; queue := $\langle\rangle$; $\langle\rangle$ = $\langle\rangle$ ≡ **initialise** ; queue := $\langle\rangle$; **true**⌟

simplify, **qed**

4.4.3 Avoiding imperative side conditions

When applying an equivalence rule, it may turn out that the instantiated applicability condition reads variables. Such a condition may be impossible to prove if it appears as a side condition (as in side conditions there is, as in any justification condition, an implicit quantification over all states). In this case in-goal application (as described in section 4.2.1.3) should be used.

For instance, in a context containing the following declarations

variable v : **Int**

value

   f : **Unit** → **write** v **Int**

   f() ≡ v : = v + 1 ; v **pre** v $\neq$ 0

any instance of the applicability condition for the derived context rule

[f_def]

   f() $\simeq$ v := v + 1 ; v

   when v $\neq$ 0

for unfolding applications of *f* will be

   v $\neq$ 0

which reads *v*. If we used the standard application of the rule in order to unfold *f()* in the following goal:

   ⌞v := 2 ; f() ≡ v := 3 ; 3⌟

we would get

   ⌞v := 2 ; v : = v + 1 ; v ≡ v := 3 ; 3⌟

      since

         ⌞v $\neq$ 0⌟

      end

Here, the side condition v $\neq$ 0 is implicitly quantified over all states, i.e. it is equivalent to

   □ v $\neq$ 0

and this condition is actually false, and therefore too strong a side condition.

If we use in-goal application instead, we get

   ⌞v := 2 ; **if** (v $\neq$ 0) ≡ **true then** v : = v + 1 ; v **else** f() **end** ≡ v := 3 ; 3⌟

which we can prove as sketched below:

⌊v := 2 ; if (v ≠ 0) ≡ **true then** v : = v + 1 ; v **else** f() **end** ≡ v := 3 ; 3⌋
is_true:

⌊v := 2 ; **if** v ≠ 0 **then** v : = v + 1 ; v **else** f() **end** ≡ v := 3 ; 3⌋
assignment_sequence_propagation:

⌊v := 2 ; **if** 2 ≠ 0 **then** v : = 2 + 1 ; v **else** f() **end** ≡ v := 3 ; 3⌋
/* which can be simplified to */

⌊v := 2 ; v : = 3 ; v ≡ v := 3 ; 3⌋
assignment_idempotence2:

⌊v : = 3 ; v ≡ v := 3 ; 3⌋
assignment_sequence_propagation, is_annihilation **qed**

4.4.4   Commuting sequences

There may be situations where we wish to commute two expressions in sequence.
For this purpose there are the following rules:

[sequence_commutativity1]
 eu ; eu′ ≃ eu′ ; eu
 when convergent(eu) ∧ **readwriteonly**(eu) ∧
  assignment_disjoint(eu, eu′)

[sequence_commutativity2]
 eu ; e ≃ **let** b = e **in** eu ; b **end**
 when convergent(eu) ∧ **readwriteonly**(eu) ∧
  assignment_disjoint(eu, e) ∧ **no_capture**(b, eu)

[sequence_commutativity3]
 eu ; eu′ ; e ≃ eu′ ; eu ; e
 when convergent(eu) ∧ **readwriteonly**(eu) ∧
  assignment_disjoint(eu, eu′)

The reason for the requirement that at most one of the expressions is able to
communicate (i.e. the other must be read-write-only) is that, if they could both
communicate, commuting them would have changed the meaning (the order of
communications being significant).

If the side conditions concerning assignment disjointness are not fulfilled, the
techniques described in section 4.4.1 can be used.

The rules can for instance be used to move inputs and outputs to the start of
sequences, in order to obtain expressions in standard form (see section 4.5.1.1) as
required by certain techniques explained in section 4.5 on justification involving
concurrency.

Example of moving output to the start of a sequence

For read-write-only and convergent *e* we want to commute the sequence v := e ; c!v

in some goal

⌊v := e ; c!v ; eu ≡ ...⌋

However, we cannot commute it using *sequence_commutativity3* because the second expression reads a variable (*v*) written to by the first, and hence the assignment disjointness condition is not fulfilled.

Here we can use the technique of removing the inopportune variable instance *v* by unfolding it. If *e* is read-only and does not read *v*, the unfolding can be obtained by *assignment_sequence_propagation*, and then *sequence_commutativity3* can be used:

⌊v := e ; c!v ; eu ≡ ...⌋

assignment_sequence_propagation:

⌊v := e ; c!e ; eu ≡ ...⌋

sequence_commutativity3:

⌊c!e ; v := e ; eu ≡ ...⌋

If *e* has write effects or reads *v*, *assignment_sequence_propagation* cannot be used immediately because its applicability condition is not fulfilled. In this case, one of the techniques mentioned in section 4.4.1 can be used.

Example of moving an input to the start of a sequence

We can move inputs to the start of sequences by similar techniques. We can, for example, justify

⌊v := e ; **let** b = c? **in** eu **end** ≡
    let x = c? **in** v := e ; **let** b = x **in** eu **end end**⌋

provided *e* is read-write-only and convergent and *x* is different from *b* and *v* and not free in *e* or *eu*. The justification is

⌊v := e ; **let** b = c? **in** eu **end** ≡
    let x = c? **in** v := e ; **let** b = x **in** eu **end end**⌋

sequence_let:

⌊**let** b = (v := e ; c?) **in** eu **end** ≡
    let x = c? **in** v := e ; **let** b = x **in** eu **end end**⌋

sequence_commutativity2:

⌊**let** b = **let** x = c? **in** v := e ; x **end in** eu **end** ≡
    let x = c? **in** v := e ; **let** b = x **in** eu **end end**⌋

let_associativity:

⌊**let** x = c? **in let** b = (v := e ; x) **in** eu **end end** ≡
    let x = c? **in** v := e ; **let** b = x **in** eu **end end**⌋

sequence_let:

⌊**let** x = c? **in** v := e ; **let** b = x **in** eu **end end** ≡
    let x = c? **in** v := e ; **let** b = x **in** eu **end end**⌋

is_annihilation, **qed**

4.4.5   Termination of loops

If there are until or while loops in a specification, it may be important to know that they terminate, and therefore relevant to formulate and justify conditions ensuring that they do.

Such conditions will be of one of the forms

> **do** eu **until** eb **end post true**

or

> **while** eb **do** eu **end post true**

4.4.5.1   Termination of until loops

A strategy for proving the termination of conditions of the first form is to transform the until loop into a sequence in which the second expression is a while loop, and then prove the termination of the sequence. The termination of a sequence can be proved by using the rule

> [sequence_convergence]
> eu ; e **post true** $\simeq$ **true**
> **when** (eu **post true**) $\land$ (eu ; (e **post true**) $\equiv$ eu ; **true**)

Hence, the general scheme for proving the termination of an until loop is

> $\llcorner$**do** eu **until** eb **end post true**$\lrcorner$

until_expansion :

> $\llcorner$eu ; **while** $\sim$(eb) **do** eu **end post true**$\lrcorner$

sequence_convergence :

> - $\llcorner$eu **post true**$\lrcorner$
>
>   ...
>
> - $\llcorner$eu ; (**while** $\sim$(eb) **do** eu **end post true**) $\equiv$ eu ; **true**$\lrcorner$
>
>   ...

4.4.5.2   Termination of while loops

A strategy for proving conditions of the second form is to apply the following rule left-to-right:

> [while_readonly_convergence]
> **while** ro_eb **do** eu **end post true** $\simeq$ **true**
> **when**
>   ($\Box$ **let** b = ro_ei **in** eu ; b > ro_ei **end** $\equiv$ eu ; **true pre** ro_eb) $\land$
>   ($\Box$ ro_ei < 0 $\Rightarrow$ $\sim$ ro_eb) $\land$
>   ($\Box$ (ro_eb **post true**) $\land$ (ro_ei **post true**))

It requires

- that the loop condition (*ro_eb*) is convergent

- that one can find a measure (integer expression), ro_ei, which is read-only and convergent, and which strictly decreases for any execution of the body of the loop and causes the loop condition (ro_eb) to be false when it becomes negative

Below is an example of a justification of the termination of a while loop:

⌞**class**
        variable v : **Nat** := 0
        value
          f : **Unit** → **write** v **Unit**
          f() ≡ **while** v ≤ 2 **do** v := v + 1 **end**
      end ⊢
      f() **post true**⌟
class_assumption_inf, f_def :
  ⌞**while** v ≤ 2 **do** v := v + 1 **end post true**⌟
/∗ use 2 − v as strictly decreasing measure ∗/
while_convergence :
  ⌞**true**⌟
  since
     - ⌞(□ **let** b = 2 − v **in** v := v + 1 ; b > 2 − v **end** ≡
              v := v + 1 ; **true**
              pre v ≤ 2)⌟
     /∗ introduce arbitrary initial assignment for v and propagate ∗/
     always_application2, all_assumption_inf :
       ⌞□ (v := v0 ; v ≤ 2 ≡ v := v0 ; **true**) ⇒
         (v := v0 ;
           let b = 2 − v **in**
             v := v + 1 ; b > 2 − v
           end ≡
             v := v0 ; v := v + 1 ; **true**)⌟
    assignment_sequence_propagation, assignment_sequence_propagation,
    assignment_sequence_propagation :
       ⌞□ (v := v0 ; v ≤ 2 ≡ v := v0 ; **true**) ⇒
         (v := v0 ;
           let b = 2 − v0 **in**
             v := v0 + 1 ; b > 2 − v
           end ≡
             v := v0 ; v := v0 + 1 ; **true**)⌟
    let_absorption4 :
       ⌞□ (v := v0 ; v ≤ 2 ≡ v := v0 ; **true**) ⇒
         (v := v0 ; v := v0 + 1 ; 2 − v0 > 2 − (v0 + 1) ≡
           v := v0 ; v := v0 + 1 ; **true**)⌟
    simplify, **qed**

- ⌊(□ 2 − v < 0 ⇒ ∼ (v ≤ 2))⌋
  simplify, **qed**
- ⌊(□ (v ≤ 2 **post true**) ∧ (2−v **post true**) ∧ **readonly**(2−v))⌋
  simplify, **qed**

    end
qed

Exercise In a context containing the definitions

    variable Q, R : **Int**
    value
        divide : **Int** × **Int** → **write** Q, R **Unit**
        divide(x, y) ≡
            R := x ; Q := 0 ; **while** y ≤ R **do** R := R − y ; Q := Q + 1 **end**
            pre y > 0

justify the goal

    ⌊∀ x, y : **Int** • divide(x, y) **post** x = R + y * Q ∧ y > R **pre** y > 0⌋

This is an example of showing that an explicit function (for doing integer division) implements its implicit specification in terms of a postcondition. Note that proving a postcondition for an expression implies proving termination of the expression.

    Hint: there are a number of rules that can be used to prove post expressions. For this exercise use *sequence_post*, *while_post* and *assignment_post_propagation*. The first of these rules can be used to establish that $x = R + y * Q$ before the while loop.

4.4.6 Example: justification of imperative queue development

This section shows how formal conditions arising from the development relation *I_QUEUE0_1* formulated in section 2.8.5.3 can be justified.

    As a first step, *class_assumption_inf* and *implementation_expansion_inf* are applied, by which we obtain the subgoals

- ⌊is_full() ≡ **len** list_of() = P.bound⌋
- ⌊is_empty() ≡ list_of() = ⟨⟩⌋
- ⌊empty() ; list_of() ≡ empty() ; ⟨⟩⌋
- ⌊∀ e : P.Elem •
      enq(e) ; list_of() ≡ **let** l = list_of() **in** enq(e) ; l ˆ ⟨e⟩ **end**
      pre ∼ is_full()⌋
- ⌊**let** l = list_of() **in**
      deq() **as** e **post** e = **hd** l ∧ list_of() = **tl** l **pre** ∼ is_empty()
          end⌋
- ⌊enq() **post true pre** ∼ is_full()⌋

The first three of these are simple to justify so we will not show the justifications. The last three subgoals are more complicated. As the principle for justifying these three are the same, we only show the justification of the first:

    ⌊∀ e : P.Elem •
        enq(e) ; list_of() ≡ **let** l = list_of() **in** enq(e) ; l^⟨e⟩ **end**
        pre ∼is_full()⌋

all_assumption_inf :

    ⌊enq(e) ; list_of() ≡ **let** l = list_of() **in** enq(e) ; l^⟨e⟩ **end** **pre** ∼is_full()⌋
/∗ in order to avoid imperative assumptions from the precondition,
    we introduce arbitrary initial assignments ∗/

always_elimination_inf, always_application2, all_assumption_inf :

    ⌊□ (queue := q ; ∼is_full() ≡ queue := q ; **true**) ⇒
        (queue := q ; enq(e) ; list_of() ≡
            queue := q ; **let** l = list_of() **in** enq(e) ; l^⟨e⟩ **end**)⌋
/∗ we can now make the left-hand side of the implication pure ∗/

is_full_def, assignment_sequence_propagation, sequence_is, simplify :

    ⌊□ ∼ (**len** q = P.bound) ⇒
        (queue := q ; enq(e) ; list_of() ≡
            queue := q ; **let** l = list_of() **in** enq(e) ; l^⟨e⟩ **end**)⌋
/∗ and then we can put it into the context as an assumption ∗/

always_implies2, imply_deduction_inf :

[not_full] ∼(**len** q = P.bound) ⊢

    ⌊□ queue := q ; enq(e) ; list_of() ≡
        queue := q ; **let** l = list_of() **in** enq(e) ; l^⟨e⟩ **end**⌋
/∗ We now expand and simplify the left-hand side of the equivalence. ∗/
/∗ In order to avoid imperative side conditions,
    we use in-goal application when unfolding enq. ∗/

enq_def :

    ⌊□ queue := q ;
        if ∼is_full() ≡ **true then** queue := queue^⟨e⟩ **else** enq(e) **end** ; list_of() ≡
        queue := q ; **let** l = list_of() **in** enq(e) ; l^⟨e⟩ **end**⌋

is_true, is_full_def, list_of_def :

    ⌊□ queue := q ;
        if ∼(**len** queue = P.bound) **then** queue := queue^⟨e⟩ **else** enq(e) **end**;
        queue ≡
        queue := q ; **let** l = list_of() **in** enq(e) ; l^⟨e⟩ **end**⌋

assignment_sequence_propagation, not_full, if_true,
assignment_sequence_propagation :

    ⌊□ queue := q ; queue := q^⟨e⟩ ; q^⟨e⟩ ≡
        queue := q ; **let** l = list_of() **in** enq(e) ; l^⟨e⟩ **end**⌋
/∗ the right-hand side is expanded and simplified in a similar way ∗/

list_of_def, enq_def, is_true, is_full_def,

assignment_sequence_propagation, let_absorption4, not_full, if_true :

$\llcorner\square$ queue := q ; queue := q^$\langle e \rangle$; q^$\langle e \rangle$ $\equiv$

queue := q ; queue := q^$\langle e \rangle$; q^$\langle e \rangle \lrcorner$

simplify, **qed**

Note that in-goal applications have been used for unfolding *enq* because otherwise we would get a side condition involving — after unfolding *is_full* — the value of the variable *queue*.

Note also that the technique of introducing arbitrary initial assignments explained in section 4.4.2.4 has been used.

4.5   Justification for concurrent specifications

When justifying conditions involving constructs for concurrency, the techniques presented so far are still applicable. This section gives advice which is particularly related to the construction of justifications where concurrency is involved.

It explains how let expressions and expressions in the combinators $\|$ and $\#$ can be expanded to more simple expressions.

4.5.1   Expansion to choice form

An expression of one of the forms

- $eu_1 \| eu_2$
- $eu_1 \# eu_2$
- **let** $b = e_1$ **in** e_2 **end**

can be expanded to an expression in *choice form*, i.e. an expression in which the outermost combinators are $[]$ and $\sqcap$, by

1. first ensuring that eu_1, e_1 and eu_2 are in a *standard form*, explained below, or are equivalent to **stop**, and, for $\|$ and $\#$, also ensuring that eu_1 and eu_2 are assignment disjoint
2. then using one of the expansion rules explained below

4.5.1.1   Standard form

An expression is in *basic standard form* if it is in one the following forms:

1. a *guarded convergent expression*, i.e. in one of the two forms

   (a) **let** $b = c?$ **in** e **end**
   (b) c ! e_1 ; e_2[12]

---

[12]Note that we have chosen $c ! e_1 ; e_2$ as a basic standard form and not the equivalent form **let** $b = c ! e_1$ **in** e_2 **end**, even though a sequence is a derived form and a let expression is the basic form. The reason for this choice is that sequences are more frequently used.

where e_1 is non-communicating, convergent and in the type of c,

i.e. **readwriteonly**$(e_1) \land$ **convergent**$(c!e_1)$

2. a non-communicating and convergent expression

e

i.e. **readwriteonly**$(e) \land$ **convergent**(e)

3. an external choice

$e_1 \,[]\, ... \,[]\, e_n$

between expressions, e_1, ..., e_n, $(n \geq 2)$ in basic standard forms 1 and 2.

Note that a basic standard form expression is convergent if one of the following holds:

- It is one of the first two forms.
- It is of the third form and all its constituents are guarded convergent expressions (of the first form) and no two of these start with an input on the same channel or an output on the same channel.

An expression is in *derived standard form* if it is in one the following forms:

1. a derived guarded convergent expression, i.e. in one of the three forms

   (a) $cu?\ ;\ e$
   (b) $cu?$
   (c) $c\ !\ e_1$

   where e_1 is non-communicating, convergent and in the type of c

2. an external choice

   $e_1 \,[]\, ... \,[]\, e_n$

   between expressions, e_1, ..., e_n, $(n \geq 2)$ in derived standard form 1 (at least one e_i should be in this form) and basic standard forms 1 and 2.

They are *derived* standard forms since they can be immediately rewritten into basic standard form expressions:

- $cu?\ ;\ e$ can be rewritten to **let** $b = cu?$ **in** e **end** using *sequence_expansion*
- $cu?$ can be rewritten to **let** $b = cu?$ **in skip end** using *let_absorption2*
- $c!e_1$ can be rewritten to $c!e_1\ ;$ **skip** using *let_absorption2* and *sequence_expansion*

An expression is in *standard form* if it is in basic standard form or in derived standard form.

Some expressions which are not in standard form can be transformed to an expression in standard form; see section 4.5.1.3.

4.5.1.2   The expansion rules

For eu_1, eu_2 and e_1 in standard form or equivalent to **stop**, and eu_1 and eu_2 assignment disjoint, the three expressions

$\text{eu}_1 \parallel \text{eu}_2$

$\text{eu}_1 \Vdash \text{eu}_2$

let b = e_1 **in** e_2 **end**

can be expanded to expressions in the choice form by using the rules *parallel_-expansion*, *interlock_expansion* and *let_expansion*.

Before explaining these rules, we give two examples where we explain intuitively how some expressions can be expanded.

Example 1

For the first example, consider the expression

let b = c? **in** v1 := b **end** $\parallel$ c ! e_1

It has the following possible behaviours:

- v1 := e_1
- **let** b = c? **in** v1 := b **end** ; c ! e_1
- c ! e_1 ; **let** b = c? **in** v1 := b **end**

The first behaviour is obtained if the left-hand side and the right-hand side of the expression communicate with each other. Such a behaviour is called an *internal behaviour*. The second and third behaviours are obtained if the left-hand or the right-hand side respectively communicates with the surroundings. Such behaviours are called *external behaviours*.

It is an internal choice whether

- it will be up to the surroundings to make an (external) choice between each of the external behaviours and the internal behaviour, or,
- the expression has the internal behaviour

Hence, the expression can be expanded to the choice form

$($

let b = c? **in** v1 := b **end** ; c ! e_1

$\Box$

c ! e_1 ; **let** b = c? **in** v1 := b **end**

$\Box$

v1 := e

$)$

$\sqcap$

v1 := e

The form of the expression is

(E $\Box$ I) $\sqcap$ I

where *I* is the possible internal behaviour and *E* is an external choice between the possible external behaviours.

Example 2

For the second example, the expression

   c ! e_1 || c ! e_2

can be expanded to

   c ! e_1 ; c ! e_2 []   c ! e_2 ; c ! e_1

In this case, the form of this expression is E. There are no possible internal behaviours that can contribute to the expansion.

General

In general, an expression of one of the forms

- eu_1 || eu_2
- eu_1 ⧺ eu_2
- **let** b = e_1 **in** e_2 **end**

where eu_1, eu_2 and e_1 are in standard form or equivalent to **stop**, and eu_1 and eu_2 are assignment disjoint, can be expanded to

- E, if there are no possible internal behaviours of the expression
- $(E \; [] \; I) \; [] \; I$, otherwise

Here, E is **stop** if there are no possible external behaviours of the expression, otherwise it is an external choice, $e_1 \; [] \; ... \; [] \; e_n$, between all the possible external behaviours e_1, ..., e_n ($n \geq 1$). Similarly, I is an internal choice, $i_1 \; [] \; ... \; [] \; i_m$, between all the possible internal behaviours i_1, ..., i_m ($m \geq 1$) of the expression.

In general, for expressions of the form

   $a_1 \; [] \; ... \; [] \; a_n \oplus b_1 \; [] \; ... \; [] \; b_m$ $(n \geq 1, m \geq 1)$

(where $\oplus$ is || or ⧺) the possible internal behaviours are all the possible internal behaviours which can be found by investigating each pair

   (a_i, b_j) $(1 \leq i \leq n, 1 \leq j \leq m)$

Such a pair gives rise to a possible internal behaviour if a_i or b_j is non-communicating (read-write-only), or if a_i and b_j start with a communication on the same channel, one with an input and the other with an output. The specific internal behaviour depends on the combinator $\oplus$. For the combinator ⧺, there are no external behaviours. For the combinator ||, each a_i ($1 \leq i \leq n$) and b_j ($1 \leq j \leq m$) which starts with an input or an output gives rise to a possible external behaviour.

For let expressions of the form

   let b = $a_1 \; [] \; ... \; [] \; a_n$ **in** e **end** $(n \geq 1)$

each a_i ($1 \leq i \leq n$) which starts with an input or an output gives rise to a possible external behaviour, and each a_i ($1 \leq i \leq n$) which is non-communicating (read-write-only) gives rise to a possible internal behaviour.

Absence of internal behaviour is modelled by **swap** and absence of external behaviour is modelled by **stop**.

All this is formalized in the expansion rules *parallel_expansion*, *interlock_expansion* and *let_expansion*, which can be found in appendix B.6.

In these expansion rules, some special functions **parallel_expand**, **interlock_expand** and **let_expand** are used. These functions are defined in appendix B.4 by rules that use the special (auxiliary) functions **parallel_ints**, **parallel_exts**, **interlock_ints**, **let_ints**, and **let_exts**, which are used to calculate *I* and *E*. The auxiliary functions are also defined by rules in appendix B.4, but only for arguments in basic standard form or **stop**. Corresponding rules for arguments in derived standard form are easily deduced.

4.5.1.3   Obtaining the right form

To apply the expansion rules for ‖, ⫿ and **let** we may need to convert their arguments to standard form expressions. This section gives, for three often encountered kinds of non-standard form expressions, ways of converting them to standard form expressions by applying proof rules.

If expressions
Sometimes we have an if expression whose branches are in standard form, where we need a standard form expression. In this case a suitable tactic is to do case analysis (using *two_cases_inf*) on the guard of the if expression and its negation. This will give two goals, each dealing with one of the branches of the if expression.

Test functions
It is also worth considering how we deal with interlocked expressions involving "test" functions. (A "test" function is a function that is used to convert an expression to an expression of type **Unit**, so that it can appear as an argument of the ⫿ combinator.) Suppose, for example, that we want to justify the following condition:

$\llcorner$C_STACK $\vdash$ $\forall$ st : Stack, test : **Bool** $\overset{\sim}{\to}$ **Unit** •

stack_p(st) ⫿ test(is_empty()) $\equiv$ stack_p(st) ⫿ test(**false**) **pre** st $\neq$ $\langle\rangle$ $\lrcorner$

where *C_STACK* is defined in section 4.5.1.4.

We start as follows:

class_assumption_inf, all_assumption_inf, pre_deduction_inf:

[st_not_empty] st $\neq$ $\langle\rangle$ $\vdash$

$\llcorner$stack_p(st) ⫿ test(is_empty()) $\equiv$ stack_p(st) ⫿ test(**false**)$\lrcorner$

Then we can unfold *stack_p(st)* to obtain an expression in standard form, but we cannot unfold *test(is_empty())*. Instead we can apply *application_evaluation* followed by unfolding *is_empty()*, so that *test(is_empty())* is replaced by something like

let b1 = test **in let** b2 = is_empty_c? **in** b1(b2) **end end**

Absorbing the outer let expression then gives

let b2 = is_empty_c? **in** test(b2) **end**

which is in standard form.

If input or output is not at the start

Examples of how to move an input or output to the start of a sequence, in order to obtain a standard form expression, are shown in section 4.4.4.

Hence

mp() ≡
  x := 1 ; c1!x ; mp()
  ⏷
  x := 2 ; c2!x ; mp()

can be rewritten as the better (and equivalent) form

mp() ≡
  c1!1 ; x := 1 ; mp()
  ⏷
  c2!2 ; x := 2 ; mp()

This is better both because the interlock/parallel expansion rule can now be applied to expressions where *mp()* is interlocked or put in parallel with another standard form expression, and also because its convergence is now much more apparent — it is clear that the variable x will be assigned 1 or 2 according to the communications offered by the environment, not according to an internal choice.

Exercise In a context containing the definitions

  channel c : **Int**   **variable** v : **Int**

justify the goal

  ⌞c!1 ∥ v:=c? ≡ (c!1 ; v:=c? ⏷ v:=c? ; c!1 ⏷ v:=1) ⏷ v:=1⌟

4.5.1.4 Example

Consider the specification of a stack process and its interface functions:

  scheme C_STACK =
    class
      type Elem, Stack = Elem*
      channel is_empty_c : **Bool**, push_c, top_c : Elem, pop_c : **Unit**
      value
        stack_p : Stack → **in any out any Unit**
        stack_p(st) ≡
          is_empty_c ! (st = ⟨⟩) ; stack_p(st)
          ⏷
          let b = push_c? **in** stack_p(⟨b⟩ ^ st) **end**
          ⏷

> **if** ~ (st = ⟨⟩) **then** pop_c? ; stack_p(**tl** st) **else stop end**
> []
> **if** ~ (st = ⟨⟩) **then** top_c ! **hd** st ; stack_p(st) **else stop end**,
> is_empty : **Unit** → **in any out any Bool**
> is_empty() ≡ is_empty_c?,
> push : **Elem** → **in any out any Unit**
> push(e) ≡ push_c ! e,
> pop : **Unit** → **in any out any Unit**
> pop() ≡ pop_c ! (),
> top : **Unit** → **in any out any Unit**
> top() ≡ top_c ?

   end

Suppose we want to justify the condition

   ∀ st : Stack, e : Elem •
   (stack_p(st) ‖ push(e)) ‖ pop() ≡ stack_p(st)   (1)

This can be done in two steps: First *stack_p(st) ‖ push(e)* can be reduced to the expression *stack_p(⟨e⟩ ^st)*, and then *stack_p(⟨e⟩ ^ st) ‖ pop()* can be reduced to *stack_p(st)*.

In both steps the arguments of ‖ are assignment disjoint and we can use the expansion rules after having converted the arguments to standard form expressions.

In the first step it turns out that *push(e)* can be unfolded to an expression in standard form, but *stack_p(st)* cannot. *stack_p(st)* unfolds to an external choice, where two of the choices are if expressions. It is therefore necessary to do a two case analysis on the guard of the if expressions and their negation, as explained in section 4.5.1.3.

The justification is

   ⌊C_STACK ⊢

      ∀ st : Stack, e : Elem • (stack_p(st) ‖ push(e)) ‖ pop() ≡ stack_p(st)⌋
   class_assumption_inf, all_assumption_inf :

   ⌊(stack_p(st) ‖ push(e)) ‖ pop() ≡ stack_p(st)⌋
   two_cases_inf:

   • [empty] st = ⟨⟩ ⊢

      ⌊(stack_p(st) ‖ push(e)) ‖ pop() ≡ stack_p(st)⌋
      /* first we unfold the stack and push processes */
      stack_p_def, push_def :

         ⌊ ((is_empty_c ! (st = ⟨⟩) ; stack_p(st) []
            let b = push_c? **in** stack_p(⟨b⟩ ^ st) **end** []
            if ~ (st = ⟨⟩) **then** pop_c? ; stack_p(**tl** st) **else stop end** []
            if ~ (st = ⟨⟩) **then** top_c ! **hd** st ; stack_p(st) **else stop end**)
            ‖ push_c ! e) ‖ pop() ≡
               stack_p(st)⌋

/∗ then using the case assumption we can reduce this to ∗/
simplify :

    ⌞ ((is_empty_c ! (st = ⟨⟩) ; stack_p(st) []
       let b = push_c? **in** stack_p((⟨b⟩ ⌢ st) **end**)
       ‖ push_c ! e) ‖ pop() ≡
         stack_p(st)⌟

interlock_expansion, simplify :

    ⌞stack_p(⟨e⟩ ⌢ st) ‖ pop() ≡ stack_p(st)⌟
/∗ the second step is proved in a similar way ∗/
  ...

- [not_empty] ∼(st = ⟨⟩) ⊢
    ⌞(stack_p(st) ‖ push(e)) ‖ pop() ≡ stack_p(st)⌟
/∗ this case is proved in a similar way ∗/
  ...

Exercise 1   Complete the justification above.

Exercise 2   The process *stack_p* is recursive and yet non-terminating, which may give problems in an implementation. An iterative version can be defined along the lines of

    stack_p : Stack → **in any out any Unit**
    stack_p(st) ≡
      local
        variable v : Stack := st
      in
        while true do ... **end**
      end

Complete the definition and then justify the same condition (1).

4.6 Tools support

When creating justifications there are two major tasks:

- Formulate justification conditions.
- Develop arguments for the truth of these conditions.

For both tasks it is a great help to have computer-based tools.

A tool that can generate confidence conditions for RSL modules, theorems and development relations can provide help in formulating conditions.

A justification editor can help develop arguments. In particular it can:

- do syntax and type checking
- keep track of the implicit context
- keep track of where informal arguments are used

- keep track of which proof rules are available. (In practice this means that it should have a rule base consisting of the proof rules which are always available and it should dynamically generate context rules which are available for the current goal and additional context rules which are available for subterms of the current goal.)
- generate and keep track of names for unnamed axioms
- handle out-of-band names
- for a given goal/term show the user the subset of rules that are applicable, i.e. are available and can match
- for a given goal/term apply an applicable rule (chosen by the user or a tool)
- evaluate applications of special functions
- simplify expressions automatically by applying several rules according to certain tactics
- allow tactics to be developed and applied
- allow replay of a proof when changes are made to the specification it is about

Tools meeting many of these requirements have been developed in the RAISE and LaCoS ESPRIT projects and are described in the RAISE tools manuals [3, 4].

CHAPTER 5

Translation

Once we have the final specification (low-level design) expressed in RSL, we are ready to produce code for the implementation in a programming language. We call the process of producing code from an RSL specification *translation*. The aim of this chapter is to provide guidelines on how to translate RSL specifications into code.

The implementation language for an RSL specification could be any programming language: a logic language like Prolog, a functional language like Lisp, or a more traditional procedural, imperative language, perhaps with some support for object oriented programming. The nature of the implementation language greatly affects the ease with which a given RSL specification can be translated into that language. Since we cannot here describe translation into all these different kinds of languages, we will restrict the guidelines to those relevant to procedural languages and will use Ada [1] as our programming language.

RSL is a general wide-spectrum specification and design language and *not* a special design language for any particular programming language. Hence, there are at least three issues to consider when looking at both RSL and an implementation language.

First of all, there are RSL constructs that are very far from those found in most programming languages. These constructs include sorts and axioms, postconditions, quantifications and other features that all have one thing in common: that they are typically used at the more abstract levels of RSL specification. Hence, all of these constructs should be eliminated on the way to the final specification that is to be subject to translation. Chapter 3 on development describes techniques for developing such constructs into more directly implementable ones.

Secondly, there are RSL constructs that can be translated into the programming language in a reasonably straightforward manner. This includes most of the algorithmic parts of RSL.

Thirdly, there might be concepts in the relevant programming language for which there are no immediately corresponding constructs in RSL but which we would still like to use; these include array types, physical layout of data structures and exceptions. Some of these, like the array types, we can model by a special RSL module and then provide an efficient manual translation that involves the desired programming language type. Others, like the physical data layout, are actually not supposed to be introduced before the coding. For the more difficult ones, like exceptions, the treatment depends on the intended use of the feature in the program. If we want to reason about exceptions at the RSL level, we need to construct a model of them, which may not be a trivial thing to do. Alternatively, we can say that the RSL specification defines all the "normal" cases only, and exceptions (and their handling) should be introduced during coding.

This chapter first addresses some general issues of translation. Then it presents more detailed translation guidelines for sequential specifications. After that a section specifically deals with translating concurrent specifications. Finally, the translation process is illustrated using the examples in chapter 2.

5.1   General issues of translation

This section discusses overall aspects related to translation.

5.1.1   Correctness of a translation

When performing a development step from one RSL module to a more detailed one, development relations are used to record the formal relation, for example implementation, between the modules. The concept of one module implementing another is well defined for RSL, but, when translating an RSL module into a programming language text, no such obvious relation exists. There are two problems in establishing such a relation.

First of all, the semantics of the programming language is typically not formalized, and even if it were, it would probably be impractical to relate it to the RSL semantics in such a way that a formal implementation relation between an RSL module and some programming language code could be established. One possibility would be to provide a complete formal semantics of the programming language expressed in RSL. But for any non-trivial language, like Ada, developing such a semantics would be an enormous task. Therefore, we have to rely on a language reference manual written in natural language, such as the one for Ada [1], and accept that an implementation is not formalizable and therefore not subject to formal justification.

The other problem is to decide, even without a formalization of the relation between an RSL module and code, what it means for a program to implement an RSL specification. Two issues then arise:

- In RSL, the "effects" of two expressions can be compared using "$\equiv$". Such a strong equivalence operator does not exist in programming languages and it cannot in general be implemented, since it can compare effects including side-effects, non-determinism and convergence. This has the implication that expressions involving ≡ cannot be directly translated (just as postconditions cannot be). The second is that there are semantically different RSL expressions whose difference cannot be observed at the code level. This is particularly the case for expressions containing an internal choice, since there is no fairness in RSL. For example, e1 ⌈⌉ e2 cannot be distinguished from e1 (or e2) without having a strong equivalence like ≡ or postconditions. Hence in certain cases it might be reasonable to consider code that is "more deterministic" than the RSL specification to be a correct translation.

- RSL contains composite types whose values can be arbitrarily large or even infinite. Even if we decide that infinite values are not to be translated, the arbitrarily large values are a problem. One approach is to use subtypes in the specification that is to be translated and handle the introduction of limits as a RAISE specification step as described in section 3.5.1. A similar but still different issue is translation of the built-in types **Int** and **Real**. For **Int** the subtype approach can be used. **Real** has the additional property that its values are arbitrarily precise. This property is not implementable in practice. There are two ways of dealing with this, depending on the role of reals in the specification. If the detailed behaviour related to the accuracy and range of the reals is not an issue, we can use an appropriate programming language type — in Ada, a floating point or a fixed point type. Alternatively, we can avoid using **Real** and even **Int** in the RSL specification and instead define and use RSL modules that specify the behaviour of the relevant programming language types. An example of such a model of the C++ integer types can be found in Reher [24].

5.1.2   Automatic and manual translation

For a subset of RSL, it is feasible to produce target language code automatically by a tool that is similar to a compiler. If such a tool (a translator) is available for the relevant target language, we would still need to decide which parts of a specification language should be automatically translated and which parts should be manually translated. In general we can adopt the following criteria:

- Manual translation should be used for:
  - user interfaces (e.g. communication with X windows)
  - composite structures that have particular requirements for their storage format or strict efficiency requirements
  - low-level RSL constructs that the translator does not support

- Automatic translation should be used for:
  - RSL modules other than the above
  - generating skeleton code for the otherwise manually translated modules in order to ensure a consistent set of interfaces

In general, hand-written code may have to be produced to interface automatically produced code with existing software.

In order to manage the combined use of hand translated and automatically translated constructs, we should modularize the RSL specification in such a way that the constructs that are to be translated by hand are localized in separate modules that can then be used by the parts to be automatically translated. For a module that is translated by hand the resulting code should be reviewed to ensure that it satisfies the properties expressed by the RSL specification.

5.1.3   Particular problems of translation

5.1.3.1   Translating a specification

A specification consists of a list of modules that are at the outermost level. RSL allows such modules to be defined in any order. Modules at this level correspond in a natural way to Ada library units (and their bodies), and translating them into library units leads to utilization of the Ada library with its separate compilation facilities.

Ada imposes a partial order on library units and, in contrast to RSL, entities *must* be defined before they are referred to. At the outermost level this means that non-cyclic **with** clauses must be established among the Ada units. Consider a specification consisting of the two modules

```
    object
      M1 :
        class
          value
            f : Int → Int
            f(x) ≡ if x > 0 then M2.g(x) else x end
      end
    object
      M2 :
        class
          value
            g : Int → Int
            g(x) ≡ if x > 10 then x else 2 * x end
      end
```

If we assume that a type `Int`, declared in a package `Int_Package`, is appropriate for **Int** (see section 5.2.4.1), this specification can be translated into

```
with Int_Package; use Int_Package;
package M1 is
  function f(x : in Int) return Int;
end M1;
```

```
with Int_Package; use Int_Package;
package M2 is
  function g(x : in Int) return Int;
end M2;

with M2;
package body M1 is
  function f(x : in Int) return Int is
  begin
    if x > 0 then
      return M2.g(x);
    else
      return x;
    end if;
  end f;
end M1;

package body M2 is
  function g(x : in Int) return Int is
  begin
    if x > 10 then
      return x;
    else
      return 2 * x;
    end if;
  end g;
end M2;
```

This example also shows the straightforward mapping from RSL objects to Ada packages. Similarly, schemes can in general be translated into generic packages, as described in section 5.2.1.1.

As not all Ada compiler systems are equally powerful when it comes to establishing a good elaboration order for library unit bodies, it is a good idea to add a **pragma ELABORATE** for all generic library packages (with bodies) that are mentioned in a **with** clause and also for library packages whose body elaboration is required before the elaboration of some other unit.

Note that in order to get an executable image for an Ada program, an Ada main program (usually a procedure) is needed for linking. Such a main program has to be hand-coded and will typically mention (some of) the translated library units in its context clause.

5.1.3.2   Name and structure equivalence of types

If we define in RSL (perhaps in two different modules)

type
    T1 = **Int** × **Bool**
type
    T2 = **Int** × **Bool**

then in RSL *T1* and *T2* are the same type. This is normally referred to as "structural equivalence" of types. In a number of programming languages, including Ada, two separate type definitions give rise to two different (incompatible) types, even when their structure is the same. This is often referred to as "name equivalence", because each type name denotes a different type. Therefore, in order to prevent a correct RSL specification being turned into an Ada program that will be rejected by a compiler due to type errors, it is important to define types only once in Ada and use subtypes to get the right names. Hence, in Ada the above RSL type definitions should be translated into

```
type T1 is
  record
    f_1 : Int;
    f_2 : Boolean;
  end record;

subtype T2 is T1;
```

(See section 5.2.4.2 for details on the translation of product type expressions.)

5.1.3.3   Evaluation order for expressions

In RSL, the order of evaluation of the sub-expressions of an expression is from left to right. Since the evaluation of expressions may have side-effects, it is important that the evaluation order is preserved by the translation. The programming language may have left the determination of the evaluation order of certain sub-expressions for the compiler implementer to decide. The most important examples of such sub-expressions are the actual parameters of subprogram calls and operands of infix operators. If the actual parameters or operands cannot be guaranteed to have no side-effects, auxiliary variables and assignments have to be introduced to enforce the RSL evaluation order in the translated code.

5.1.3.4   Names

In order to maintain as close a relation as possible between the RSL specification to be translated and the resulting code, the names used in the specification should be preserved in the code as far as possible. When trying to preserve the names, a number of issues have to be dealt with:

- The scope and visibility rules of RSL might not be the same as those of the programming language. The rules of RSL and Ada are fairly compatible, in that Ada is a block structured language with modules (packages and generic packages). The main source of difference is that RSL expressions, typically **let** and **local** expressions but also other composite expressions, may require the declaration of local entities. If the expression is the body of a function, the local declarative part of the corresponding Ada subprogram is the natural place for such additional declarations. If the expression is of type **Unit**, we can and should always introduce an Ada block statement to keep the names as local as possible. In all other cases, entities that need to be locally declared should be declared at the innermost enclosing declarative part, and if name conflicts arise from that, the names must be made unique.
- RSL is case sensitive, and a number of programming languages, including Ada, are not. This means that names that would otherwise become indistinguishable in a one-to-one translation sometimes have to be translated into different ones. Similarly, a convention should be adopted for the treatment of special symbols, particularly Greek letters and primes, that are not allowed in Ada identifiers.
- RSL has the possibility of overloading values. For languages that do not offer user-defined overloading, distinct names have to be used. For reasons of traceability between the final specification and the code, it is better to remove the overloading in the final RSL specification. Since Ada has overloading and the rules for resolving overloading in RSL and Ada are very similar, there is no reason for avoiding overloading in the final RSL specification when the target language is Ada. The few expressions that can be resolved in RSL but not in Ada can be handled by introducing a qualification in Ada.

Since we usually know which programming language will be used before writing the specification, the special rules of the language should be taken into account in the final specification in order to minimize the naming differences between the specification and the code.

5.2   Translating sequential specifications

This section follows the structure of the RSL syntax and describes how the individual non-concurrent language constructs can be translated. Issues related to translation of concurrent constructs are dealt with in section 5.3, while those related to the specification level have been dealt with in section 5.1.3.1.

5.2.1   Declarations

Translating a declaration will result in one or more declarations; in fact each definition in a declaration will become one or more declarations. Certain constructs, like modules and functions, give rise to both a declaration and a body.

One important difference between RSL and certain programming languages is that the order of declarations (and definitions) in RSL can be chosen freely, whereas the programming language requires that an entity is declared before it is referred to. This means that the declarations in the resulting declaration list may have to be topologically sorted in order to respect the "defined before use" requirement. In the case of Ada, this requirement also applies to generic formal parts.

5.2.1.1   Scheme declarations

The programming language may not have a construct that corresponds to schemes, which means that only objects can be translated.

The notion of being able to create instances based on a kind of template is handled by generic packages and instances in Ada. Hence, the general idea is to translate schemes into generic packages.

If the scheme is not parameterized, the Ada package should still be generic (and parameterless) to allow for several instantiations. This is particularly important if the scheme has a state, as each instance needs to have its own state. The class expression is translated into the generic package declaration and body; see section 5.2.2.

For a parameterized scheme, the differences between RSL schemes and Ada generics are important. The object definition list constituting the RSL formal scheme parameter has to be turned into a "flat" list of generic formal parameters to the generic package. This typically means that new unique names have to be found for the generic formal parameters in order to avoid name clashes. The new names can easily be constructed from the formal object name and the local name of the formal entity (see the example below).

A more interesting question is how the various formal parameters should be translated. In RSL, most parameterized schemes are parameterized with respect to types (often sorts) and values (constants and functions). Since a sort can be implemented by any type in the actual parameter object of a scheme instantiation, the generic package has to have enough information about the generic formal type to manipulate it correctly. Because an RSL type might be translated into an Ada type involving linked lists (see section 5.2.1.3), the Ada predefined equality and assign operations might not give the desired result. Therefore, in addition to the generic formal type corresponding to the sort, generic formal subprograms are needed for these characteristic operations.

Consider the following simple parameterized scheme, *DICTIONARY*:

scheme
    ELEM = **class type** Elem **end,**
    DICTIONARY(KEY : ELEM, DESCR : ELEM) =
      class
        ...
      end

The first scheme, *ELEM*, need not (and cannot meaningfully) be translated on its own, since it is only used for defining formal scheme parameters.

Formal scheme parameters are in RSL defined by one or more formal objects, here *KEY* and *DESCR*, that contain definitions of the formal entities, here the types *Elem*. In Ada, a generic formal parameter part consists of a "flat" list of generic formal parameters. Therefore the structure of the formal scheme parameters must be "flattened" as part of the translation. We have adopted the strategy of prefixing each of the non-overloadable entities, here the types *Elem* from *KEY* and *DESCR*, with the formal object names to make the identifiers introduced by the flattened declarations unique.

The generic package corresponding to *DICTIONARY* would be

```
generic
  type KEY_Elem is private;
  with function equal(x, y : in KEY_Elem) return Boolean is <>;
  with function copy(x : in KEY_Elem) return KEY_Elem is <>;
  with procedure assign(x : in out KEY_Elem;
                        y : in KEY_Elem) is <>;
  with procedure free(x : in out KEY_Elem) is <>;
  type DESCR_Elem is private;
  with function equal(x, y : in DESCR_Elem) return Boolean is <>;
  with function copy(x : in DESCR_Elem) return DESCR_Elem is <>;
  with procedure assign(x : in out DESCR_Elem;
                        y : in DESCR_Elem) is <>;
  with procedure free(x : in out DESCR_Elem) is <>;
package DICTIONARY is
  ...
end DICTIONARY;
```

```
(and a body)
```

The sorts are translated into formal private types, since they can be matched by any non-limited type at the point of instantiation. The formal **equal**, **copy** and **assign** routines are introduced to provide the right implementation of the RSL operations "=" and ":=". We have to take care that these names are not already used in the RSL specification. The formal parameter names, **x** and **y** are arbitrary, but they must obviously not be the same. The **free** procedures are needed in case more complex structures are built inside this module from one of the two sorts, as those structures may need **free** operations themselves to avoid running out of heap space. All of these characteristic operations are supplied with a default (**is <>**), which means that the matching actual subprograms need not be mentioned in the instantiation, but they have to exist at the point of instantiation for the defaulting to work. This means that types that are to be used as actual parameters have to have these four operations.

Values (constants and functions) occurring in formal scheme parameters should be translated into generic formal subprograms. The reason why constants are *not* translated into generic formal **in** parameters is that constants can be overloaded in RSL but not in Ada. Hence, in order to avoid conflicts with names introduced by the code of the class expression of the scheme, the constants are translated into parameterless generic formal subprograms. Moreover, since the use of defaults requires the actual parameters at the point of instantiation to be given in named notation, values defined in the same formal scheme parameter are not allowed to overload each other.

Variables occurring in formal scheme parameters are simply translated into generic formal **in out** parameters.

5.2.1.2 Object declarations

An object is typically translated into a module in the programming language if the language has modularity; if not, the specification will have to be "flattened" during the translation.

In a translation to Ada, each RSL object can be translated into a package. The form of the package depends on the class expression defining the object; see section 5.2.2 on class expressions.

Ada does not have anything like object arrays. Hence, each object in the array generally has to be declared as a separate package, which may be very cumbersome (or even infeasible for large or infinite object arrays). In special cases we might be able to arrive at better code than n Ada packages for an object array with n elements at the cost of having a less straightforward relation between the the RSL specification and the code. If each element in the object array contains a state component (one or more variables) and functions manipulating this state, and if the index type is sufficiently simple and not too large, we can do the following:

- Declare *one* package corresponding to the object array.
- Declare one or more arrays in Ada inside this package to hold the state.
- Define subprograms inside the package for state manipulation. The subprograms have one or more extra index parameters.
- Translate each call of the original manipulation functions into calls with the extra index parameters, e.g. in Ada *OBJ_ARR[i].f(e)* is translated into `OBJ_ARR.f(i,e)`.

The translation of the lift example in section 5.4.2 shows an example of translation of an object array that also contains concurrency.

5.2.1.3 Type declarations

An RSL type definition is translated into a type or perhaps a subtype declaration. In addition to the type declaration, it might be necessary to declare certain characteristic operations (as described in section 5.2.1.1) if the type is to be used as an actual parameter of a generic instantiation.

Translation of each of the different type definitions is done as follows:

Sort definitions In general, a sort should not be directly translated, but be subject to further development within RSL, in order to get closer to an existing programming language type.

There is one important exception to this: when the sort appears in a formal scheme parameter. Here, a sort definition means that there are no restrictions on the actual type except those coming from related values and axioms. The sort definition should then be translated into a generic formal private type with associated characteristic operations, as shown in section 5.2.1.1.

Variant definitions Variants are a convenient shorthand in RSL, but even though they stand for a sort, some operations and axioms, they are more readily translatable than the corresponding sort definition, operations and axioms.

One of the simplest forms of a variant type definition is one where all the alternatives are constant constructors and where there is no wildcard. Such a variant definition is translated into an enumeration type declaration in Ada. For example

   type Colour == red | green | blue

Ada type declaration:

```
type Colour is (red, green, blue);
```

This enumeration type satisfies both the disjointness and the induction axioms, since the three enumeration literals are all different and the type contains exactly three values. Moreover, the enumeration literals can be overloaded just like the RSL values.

If there are wildcards in a variant type definition, the module containing the definition should be developed further in RSL to remove the wildcard.

Variant type definitions containing record variants are often used to define recursive data structures, as in the following example of a tree structure. The example also illustrates translation of destructors and reconstructors.

   type Tree == empty | node(left : Tree, val : Elem ↔ repl_value, right : Tree)

Because of the varying size of a *Tree*, a linked list would be a natural translation. This results in the following declarations in the (potentially generic) package declaration corresponding to the enclosing class expression:

```
type Tree_kind is (empty, node);
type Tree_record(kind : Tree_kind := Tree_kind'First);
type Tree is access Tree_record;
type Tree_record(kind : Tree_kind := Tree_kind'First) is
  record
    case kind is
      when empty =>
        null;
```

```
      when node  =>
         left  :  Tree;
         val   :  Elem;
         right :  Tree;
      end case;
   end record;

   function empty return Tree;
   function node(t1 : in Tree; x : in Elem; t2 : in Tree)
            return Tree;

   function left(t : in Tree) return Tree;
   function val(t : in Tree) return Elem;
   function repl_val(x : in Elem; t : in Tree) return Tree;
   function right(t : in Tree) return Tree;

   function equal(t1, t2 : in Tree) return Boolean;
   function copy(t : in Tree) return Tree;
   procedure assign(t1 : in out Tree; t2 : in Tree);
   procedure free(t : in out Tree);
```

The type **Tree_kind** is used as the discriminant type for distinguishing the variant alternatives. Because of the possibility of overloading in Ada, the names **empty** and **node** are "re-used" as discriminant values. The discriminant itself (**kind**) is initialised to allow the structure to vary over time; the value is arbitrary, but using an attribute makes the code easier to maintain. The complete type declaration for **Tree_record** defines that an "empty" tree has no components (except the discriminant) and a "node" has the expected three components. If no destructor names are defined in the specification, we can use any locally unique identifier as the component name.

The subprogram declarations are fairly straightforward; see section 5.2.1.4 for more information on translating values.

Since the *Tree* is implemented using access types, we need to define the characteristic operations (**equal**, **copy**, **assign** and **free**) for the type **Tree** because the predefined operators "=" and ":=" do not give the desired result and there is no automatic garbage collection in Ada. The code for **assign** is shown in the following as an example.

The corresponding package body contains

```
function empty return Tree is
begin
   return new Tree_record'(kind  => empty);
end empty;
```

```
function node(t1 : in Tree; x : in Elem; t2 : in Tree)
          return Tree is
begin
  return new Tree_record'(kind  => node,
                          left  => copy(t1),
                          val   => copy(x),
                          right => copy(t2));
end node;

function left(t : in Tree) return Tree is
begin
  return t.left;
end left;

function val(t : in Tree) return Elem is
begin
  return t.val;
end val;

function repl_val(x : in Elem; t : in Tree) return Tree is
  l : Tree;
begin
  assign(l, t);
  assign(l.val, x);
  return l;
end repl_val;

function right(t : in Tree) return Tree is
begin
  return t.right;
end right;

function equal(t1, t2 : in Tree) return Boolean is
begin
  -- comparing two tree values
end equal;

function copy(t : in Tree) return Tree is
begin
  -- copying a tree value
end copy;
```

```
procedure assign(t1 : in out Tree; t2 : in Tree) is
  l : Tree := copy(t2);
begin
  free(t1);
  t1 := l;
end assign;

procedure free(t : in out Tree) is
begin
  -- deallocation of a complete tree
end free;
```

For variant types that are not recursively defined, the access type can and should be avoided, as shown in the following example:

type Result == fail | ok(res: T)

results in the following Ada code in the declaration (assuming T is a simple type without pointers):

```
type Result_kind is (fail, ok);
type Result(kind : Result_kind := Result_kind'First) is
  record
    case kind is
      when fail =>
        null;
      when ok =>
        res : T;
    end case;
  end record;

function fail return Result;
function ok(r : in T) return Result;
```

and in the body:

```
function fail return Result is
begin
  return Result'(kind => fail);
end fail;

function ok(r : in T) return Result is
begin
  return Result'(kind => ok, res => r);
end ok;
```

Union definitions   A union type definition should be translated in the same way as the equivalent variant type definition. However, any implicit coercions in the RSL specification have to be made explicit in Ada.

Short record definitions   A short record type definition should be translated into a record type and functions for construction and possibly destruction and/or reconstruction. The result should be similar to that of a variant type definition, except that no discriminant is needed since there is only one alternative, and no access type is needed if the structure is not recursive.

Abbreviation definitions   An abbreviation definition should be translated into a type or subtype declaration, depending on the type expression. A type declaration should be used if no corresponding programming language type has already been declared for the type expression; otherwise a subtype declaration must be used to avoid problems with the difference between name and structure equivalence of types, as described in section 5.1.3.2.

Translation of the various type expressions is described in section 5.2.4.

5.2.1.4   Value declarations

In order to keep the distance between the final RSL specification and the code from becoming too wide, only explicit value definitions and explicit function definitions should be considered readily translatable. Typings as well as implicit value and function definitions should be developed further in RSL before translation. An exception is if an abstract RSL module has been constructed with the purpose of capturing properties of existing concepts in the programming language or of programming language library routines; the module could for example be one that describes the relevant properties of arrays by typings and axioms. Typings may also be useful in scheme parameters.

Explicit value definitions   Since values in RSL can be overloaded, the general translation of an explicit value definition into Ada should result in a function declaration (and body). If the programming language does not have overloading, names have to be made unique either prior to translation or as part of the translation.

If the value is not a function in the RSL specification, it should become a parameterless function in Ada, and the defining expression translates to the body of that function. If required for reasons of efficiency, its definition can be translated into a constant declaration, provided a (sufficiently global) analysis of the specification has shown that the value is not overloaded and is not used in an actual parameter to a scheme instantiation.

If the value is a function, i.e. the type expression denotes a function type, then one of two cases apply. Either the expression is the name, perhaps qualified, of another function, in which case, the value definition can be translated into a subprogram renaming, or the value definition can be treated as an explicit function definition; see below.

Implicit value definitions   An implicit value definition should usually be developed further before translation.

Explicit function definition   An explicit function definition has a natural mapping onto a subprogram.

A function defined directly within a module is translated into a subprogram declaration that belongs to the declaration list translated from the module. A function defined in a local expression has both its declaration and its body in the declarative part of the block corresponding to the local expression. See section 5.2.5.23 for translation of local expressions.

The result type of the RSL function is used to determine whether it should become a function or a procedure. If the result type is **Unit**, the function should become a procedure, since RSL functions with result type **Unit** do not deliver any useful value and can occur before a semicolon.

In most programming languages, any type may be the result of a function. But since, as in Ada, there may not be function types in the programming language, an RSL function returning a function value may not be translatable. Similarly, for such languages a curried function cannot be translated, as it could deliver a function value when applied to only some of its parameters. Other programming languages, such as C++, do not have such restrictions.

The partiality or totality of a function does not influence the translation of an explicit function definition: the code for the function is that corresponding to the expression. For the translation of a total function to be correct, we must, however, be sure that the translated expression results in a subprogram that terminates. A precondition can be treated in either of two ways, depending on the pragmatics of the precondition. We can let the precondition have no influence on the code (except perhaps for a comment re-stating it in programming language terms), because the precondition is seen as something the developer has to ensure at every point of call, and the function is not responsible for its behaviour when the condition is violated. Alternatively, we can produce a more robust subprogram that, when called, checks its precondition before executing the code corresponding to the real RSL function expression, and raises an exception or similar if the check fails. This increased robustness has a price at execution time and is therefore primarily relevant when the subprogram is expected to be called from code that is not produced from an RSL specification.

The parameter type of a function is very often a product type. Few of these product types are used on their own in a specification, i.e. values of their type are not constructed, assigned to variables, etc. Their only role is to define parameter types. The best translation strategy for such product types is to adopt the following convention: If the parameter type of a function is a product type, the corresponding subprogram has one parameter for each element in the product. This number of parameters must then be present in the formal function application of the explicit function definition to allow the formal parameters of the subprogram to be established correctly. A function with parameter type **Unit** is most naturally translated into a parameterless function.

Some programming languages, including Ada, allow user-defined overloading of operators, as does RSL. Hence, both prefix and infix applications can be translated in formal function applications. However, each programming language only has a limited subset of the operators available in RSL; for the remaining ones suitable function names must be chosen, either as part of the translation or when developing the final RSL specification. The latter is recommended.

The value expression of an explicit function definition is translated into a function or procedure body based on the result type. Section 5.2.5 describes how a value expression is translated.

Implicit function definitions   An implicit function definition should usually be developed further before translation.

5.2.1.5   Variable declarations

A variable definition is translated into one or more variable declarations. If no type already exists for the type expression, a separate type declaration is needed.

One thing to be aware of with respect to initialisations is that turning them into Ada initialisation expressions will not always have the desired effect. For example, if a function that is defined in the same module is used in the initialisation expression, the exception **Program_Error** will be raised at run-time, since the function body cannot have been elaborated at the point of the variable declaration. For this reason, an alternative to directly initialising the Ada variables might be considered: to define an initialisation procedure for initialising *all* the variables that are defined at the same level. This procedure would then have to be called in the statement list of the body, at which point the elaboration is sufficiently progressed to guarantee the absence of **Program_Error**.

5.2.1.6   Channel declarations

See section 5.3 on translating concurrency.

5.2.1.7   Axiom declarations

An axiom should usually be considered not translatable except in very particular contexts, such as those described in section 5.2.1.4. Axioms appearing in formal scheme parameters should have no influence on the code (except perhaps for a comment re-stating them in programming language terms), because an axiom is seen as something the developer has to ensure at the points of instantiation.

5.2.2   Class expressions

5.2.2.1   Basic class expressions

A basic class expression can occur in a number of different contexts, each leading to its own rules for translation.

If a basic class expression occurs as the class expression of an object definition, the object definition translates into a module, which for Ada will be a package declaration and body (if needed). In the module, all the basic declarative items resulting from the translation of the class expression are placed in the visible part of the package declaration, and all the bodies, i.e. subprogram bodies and inner package and generic package bodies, if any, are placed in the package body. The translation of the various declarations in a basic class expression is described in their respective sections. The main concern at the class expression level is to put the resulting basic declarative items in a correct topological order that does not violate the "define before use" rule, if the language has such a rule.

A basic class expression that occurs as the class expression of a scheme definition translates into an Ada generic package declaration and body (if needed), unless the scheme is only used in formal scheme parameters; see section 5.2.1.1. The generic package is, apart from the generic formal part, constructed exactly as described above for a package corresponding to an object.

A basic class expression occurring in the formal parameter part of a parameterized scheme is used to determine the generic formal parameters, as described in section 5.2.1.1.

When a basic class expression is a constituent of another class expression, e.g. an extending class expression or a hiding class expression, it should be translated as described in the sections dealing with the enclosing class expression.

5.2.2.2   Extending class expressions

Like a basic class expression, an extending class expression can occur in a number of different contexts, each leading to its own rules for translation. In addition, the nature of the constituent class expressions influences the possible translations of the extending class expression.

An extending class expression occurring as the class expression of an object definition translates into the Ada package declaration and body (if needed) corresponding to the object. In practice, most extending class expressions that are to be translated have the form

extend MOD1(...) **with class ... end**

where *MOD1(...)* is a scheme instantiation. In Ada there are basically two ways of translating this. We can produce a package with an inner (nested) package instantiation corresponding to the instantiation of *MOD1*, re-export all the entities from the instantiation by Ada subtype declarations and subprogram renamings, and then add the declarations coming from the translation of the basic class expression. In this way the code produced for *MOD1* is re-used. Alternatively, the whole extending class expression could be turned into a corresponding "flat" basic class expression, and then the resulting basic class expression could be translated following the guidelines given in section 5.2.2.1. In this case, the first of those steps need not actually be physically done at the RSL level, but can be handled as part of the translation process. The first approach is preferable as it is more robust in maintenance terms.

If the class expression that is being extended is a basic class expression, we would naturally use the "flatten into a basic class expression" strategy. If the class expression that is being extended is a hiding or a renaming class expression, we would translate it according to the specific guidelines and then choose the nested or the "flattened" approach as before. Similar considerations apply in the rare cases where the second class expression is not a basic class expression.

An extending class expression that occurs as the class expression of a scheme definition is translated just as if it occurred as the class expression of an object definition, except that the result is a generic package; see section 5.2.1.1.

An extending class expression occurring in the formal parameter part of a parameterized scheme is used to determine the generic formal parameters, as described in section 5.2.1.1.

5.2.2.3 Hiding class expressions

There are basically two approaches for translating a hiding class expression. One is to move the hidden entities into the body of the Ada package or generic package that results from the translation of the constituent class expression. This is not always possible because of Ada's requirement for defining entities before they are used. The second approach is to produce a package or generic package with an inner package containing the usual code for the constituent class expression and then re-export (by Ada subtype declarations and subprogram renamings) only the non-hidden entities.

A hiding class expression occurring in the formal parameter part of a parameterized scheme is used to determine the generic formal parameters, as described in section 5.2.1.1.

5.2.2.4 Renaming class expressions

A renaming class expression can either be translated by translating the constituent class expression and applying the renaming as a substitution on the result, or by using an approach with an inner package like the one described for hiding class expressions. In the second approach, the Ada subtype declarations and subprogram renamings are used to provide the correct (new) names.

A renaming class expression occurring in the formal parameter part of a parameterized scheme is used to determine the generic formal parameters, as described in section 5.2.1.1.

5.2.2.5   Scheme instantiations

A scheme instantiation is generally translated into a package instantiation, unless it occurs in one of the particular contexts described above where better alternatives exist.

A scheme instantiation occurring in the formal parameter part of a parameterized scheme is used to determine the generic formal parameters, as described in section 5.2.1.1.

5.2.3   Object expressions

5.2.3.1   Element object expressions

The translation of an element object expression depends on how the object array is translated; see section 5.2.1.2.

5.2.3.2   Array object expressions

An array object expression can be translated like an object array; see section 5.2.1.2.

5.2.3.3   Fitting object expressions

A fitting object expression that occurs as an actual scheme parameter (which is normally the only place it occurs) is translated into a list of generic associations where the fitting is reflected in the names used in the associations.

5.2.4   Type expressions

For each type expression occurring in a specification, a corresponding programming language type must already exist or be defined, except for function types and product types used as function parameter types; see section 5.2.1.4. However, it is also important not to declare the same type twice, as discussed in section 5.1.3.2.

5.2.4.1   Type literals

Unit   Since the type literal **Unit** is intended to be used as the parameter or result type of functions in a specification, the type itself need not have a corresponding type in the programming language. The treatment of **Unit** in parameter types is described in section 5.2.1.4. If, however, we want to translate the type **Unit** on its own, it should be translated into a one-element enumeration type with an arbitrary enumeration literal.

Bool   All programming languages have a type that can be used as the implementation of **Bool**. The type **Bool** is translated into the predefined type `Boolean` in Ada.

Int   As discussed in section 5.1.1, the type **Int** causes a problem when we try to preserve the semantics of the specification, since **Int** has infinitely many values. If the type **Int** itself (as opposed to finite subtypes of it; see section 5.2.4.7) is actually used in a specification, the best strategy is to perform an analysis of the RSL specification to find the largest integer that is known to need a representation. Then (if possible) declare an integer type that is sufficiently large. For example, in Ada we could declare

```
type Int is range <:lower_bound:> .. <:upper_bound:>;
```

This type declaration has the advantage that the compiler will reject modules that require too large integers (instead of introducing exceptions to reject them at run-time). The type is called `Int` to indicate its relation to the RSL type **Int** and in order not to conflict with the predefined Ada type names such as `Integer`. Note that the RSL conversion operator **int** then needs to be translated into a function with a different name, since Ada is not case sensitive. This type should be declared in a library package, e.g. `Int_Package`, in order to provide adequate scope and visibility, and to ensure that different abbreviation type definitions result in compatible Ada subtype declarations.

Nat   The type **Nat** has the same translation problem as **Int**. But assuming that a type `Int` has been declared as described above, the declaration of an Ada subtype corresponding to **Nat** would be

```
subtype Nat is Int range 0 .. Int'Last;
```

This subtype should be declared in a library package to provide adequate scope and visibility.

Real   This type causes even more problems than **Int**, because of the additional aspect of accuracy discussed in section 5.1.1. If the type **Real** is used in a specification, the best strategy is to perform an analysis of the RSL specification to find the accuracy requirements and the largest real that is known to need a representation. Then (if possible) declare a floating point type that is sufficiently large and precise. For example, in Ada we could declare

```
type Real is digits <:decimal_precision:>
            range <:lower_bound:> .. <:upper_bound:>;
```

The type is called `Real` to indicate its relation to the RSL type **Real** and in order not to conflict with the predefined Ada type names such as `Float`. Note that the RSL conversion operator **real** then needs to be translated into a function with a different name, since Ada is not case sensitive. This type should be declared in a library package in order to provide adequate scope and visibility, and to ensure that different abbreviation type definitions result in compatible Ada subtype declarations.

Char   Since the type **Char** has as values the ASCII character set, it can be translated into the Ada type `Character`.

Text   Since **Text** is defined as **Char***, it can be arbitrarily long and we could consider translation strategies like those for general lists; see section 5.2.5.7. But character lists should be treated as a special case that warrants a more efficient implementation. The programming language may have a type that directly implements character strings of varying length. Ada has a predefined type `String`. However, once a variable of type `String` has been declared, its bounds (and therefore its length) are fixed. In order to allow for the dynamic behaviour of RSL texts, a record type with a discriminant, like the following, should be used as the translation of the type **Text**:

```
Text_Limit : constant := <:some_limit:>;
subtype Text_Index is Integer range 0 .. Text_Limit;
type Text(L : Text_Index := Text_Index'First) is
  record
    S : String(1..L);
  end record;
```

This type should be declared in a library package in order to provide adequate scope and visibility, and to ensure that different abbreviation type definitions result in compatible Ada subtype declarations.

5.2.4.2   Product type expressions

Product types play a special role as function parameter types, where they are used to determine the number of parameters of the resulting subprogram, as described in section 5.2.1.4. Product types that occur in other contexts should be translated into record types, as shown in the following example:

Char × **Bool**

should in Ada be translated into

```
record
  f_1 : Character;
  f_2 : Boolean;
end record;
```

The component names are arbitrary, and the only requirement is that they are locally unique within the record.

If the same product type occurs in several places within a specification, other than as parameter types, it is important to declare the record type only once and use subtype declarations for the other instances, as described in section 5.1.3.2.

5.2.4.3   Set type expressions

A set can be implemented in various ways depending on the element type, efficiency requirements, etc. Most books on data structures contain adequate structures for implementing sets that can be directly coded in the programming language. However, a few issues should be kept in mind:

- The predefined equality and assignment of the programming language type might not correspond to the RSL equality and assignment on sets.
- All set-related operations in RSL, which typically use special symbols, must be potentially available as functions in the program.
- For Ada, it is recommended that one (or perhaps more) generic package(s) is used to implement the set type constructor and that there is an instantiation for each specific, unique set type. The generic declaration could for example look like this:

```
generic
  type Elem_type is private;
  with function copy(e1 : Elem_type)
                return Elem_type is <>;
  with function equal(e1,e2 : Elem_type)
                return Boolean is <>;
  with procedure assign(e1 : in out Elem_type;
                  e2 : Elem_type) is <>;
  with procedure free(e1 : in out Elem_type) is <>;
package Set_Package is
  type Set is private;
  function empty_set return Set;
  function cons_set(e : Elem_type; s1 : Set) return Set;
  function card(s1 : Set) return integer;
  function member(e : Elem_type; s1 : Set) return Boolean;
  function union(s1: Set; s2 : Set) return Set;
  function inter(s1: Set; s2 : Set) return Set;
  function minus(s1: Set; s2 : Set) return Set;
  function supset(s1: Set; s2 : Set) return Boolean;
  function supseteq(s1: Set; s2 : Set) return Boolean;
  function subset(s1: Set; s2 : Set) return Boolean;
  function subseteq(s1: Set; s2 : Set) return Boolean;
  function equal(s1,s2 : Set) return Boolean;
```

```
      function copy(s1 : Set) return Set;
      procedure assign(s1: in out Set; s2 : Set);
      procedure free(s1 : in out Set);
    private
      -- full type declaration of type Set
    end Set_Package;
```

The body will then define subprogram bodies.

5.2.4.4   List type expressions

Precisely the same translation considerations apply to list type expressions as to
set type expressions described in section 5.2.4.3. There is one significant additional
aspect of lists that is relevant to translation: lists are implicitly related to sets
via the **inds** and **elems** operations. If one or both of these operations are needed
for a particular list type, then it is necessary to implement the corresponding set
types. This added complexity might lead to declaring several generic packages for
defining list type constructors, one providing both the **inds** and **elems** operations
and requiring the set types as additional generic parameters (to avoid type conflicts), and others that do not provide the **inds** and/or **elems** operations. An Ada
specification of the former is given here:

```
  with Int_Package; use Int_Package;
  generic
    type Elem_type is private;
    type Elem_set_type is private;
    type Integer_set_type is private;
    with function copy(e1 : Elem_type) return Elem_type is <>;
    with function equal(e1,e2 : Elem_type) return Boolean is <>;
    with procedure assign(e1 : in out Elem_type;
                          e2 : Elem_type) is <>;
    with procedure free(e1 : in out Elem_type) is <>;
    with function empty_set return Elem_set_type is <>;
    with function cons_set(e : Elem_type; s1 : Elem_set_type)
                  return Elem_set_type is <>;
    with function member(e : Elem_type; s1 : Elem_set_type)
                  return Boolean is <>;
    with function empty_set return Integer_set_type is <>;
    with function cons_set(e : Int; s1 : Integer_set_type)
                  return Integer_set_type is <>;
  package List_Package is
    type List is private;
    function empty_list return List;
    function cons_list(e : Elem_type; l1 : List) return List;
    function concat(l1 : List; l2 : List) return List;
```

```
      function hd(l1 : List) return Elem_type;
      function tl(l1 : List) return List;
      function apply(l1 : List; i : Int) return Elem_type;
      function len(l1 : List) return Int;
      function elems(l1 : List) return Elem_set_type;
      function inds(l1 : List) return Integer_set_type;
      function copy(l1 : List) return List;
      function equal(l1,l2 : List) return Boolean;
      procedure assign(l1: in out List; l2 : List);
      procedure free(l1 : in out List);
   private
      -- full type declaration of type List
   end List_Package;
```

The body will then define subprogram bodies.

5.2.4.5 Map type expressions

Maps are quite similar to lists from a translation point of view. Moreover, the
list considerations originating from the **inds** and **elems** operations are exactly the
same as those from the **dom** and **rng** operations of a map. This might, as with
lists, lead to declaring several generic packages for map type constructors. An Ada
specification of a generic package offering both operations is given here:

```
   generic
      type Domain_type is private;
      type Range_type is private;
      type Domain_set_type is private;
      type Range_set_type is private;
      with function copy(e1 : Domain_type) return Domain_type is <>;
      with function equal(e1,e2 : Domain_type) return Boolean is <>;
      with procedure assign(e1 : in out Domain_type;
                            e2 : Domain_type) is <>;
      with procedure free(e1 : in out Domain_type) is <>;
      with function copy(e1 : Range_type) return Range_type is <>;
      with function equal(e1,e2 : Range_type) return Boolean is <>;
      with procedure assign(e1 : in out Range_type;
                            e2 : Range_type) is <>;
      with procedure free(e1 : in out Range_type) is <>;
      with function empty_set return Domain_set_type is <>;
      with function cons_set(e : Domain_type; s1 : Domain_set_type)
                   return Domain_set_type is <>;
      with function member(e : Domain_type; s1 : Domain_set_type)
                   return Boolean is <>;
      with function inter(s1 : Domain_set_type; s2 : Domain_set_type)
```

```
                      return Domain_set_type is <>;
   with function equal(s1,s2 : Domain_set_type)
                      return Boolean is <>;
   with procedure free(s1 : in out Domain_set_type) is <>;
   with function empty_set return Range_set_type is <>;
   with function cons_set(e : Range_type; s1 : Range_set_type)
          return Range_set_type is <>;
   with function member(e : Range_type; s1 : Range_set_type)
          return Boolean is <>;
 package Map_Package is
   type Map is private;
   function empty_map return Map;
   function cons_map(d : Domain_type; r : Range_type; m1 : Map)
             return Map;
   function extend(m1,m2 : Map) return Map;
   function override(m1,m2 : Map) return Map;
   function dom(m1 : Map) return Domain_set_type;
   function rng(m1 : Map) return Range_set_type;
   function apply(m1 : Map; d : Domain_type) return Range_type;
   function restricted_by(m1 : Map; ds : Domain_set_type)
             return Map;
   function restricted_to(m1 : Map; ds : Domain_set_type)
             return Map;
   function copy(m1 : Map) return Map;
   function equal(m1,m2 : Map) return Boolean;
   procedure assign(m1: in out Map; m2 : Map);
   procedure free(m1 : in out Map);
 private
   -- full type declaration of type Map
 end Map_Package;
```

The body will then define subprogram bodies.

5.2.4.6   Function type expressions

Since the programming language might not have function types, a specification that
is to be translated should only contain function type expressions in explicit value
or function definitions. Translation of function types occurring in such contexts is
described in section 5.2.1.4.

5.2.4.7   Subtype expressions

An abbreviation type definition that introduces a name for a subtype expression
should be translated into a subtype declaration if the programming language has

subtypes, as Ada does. The restriction part of the subtype expression might not always be translatable; in such cases a subtype declaration should still be declared in order to introduce the RSL subtype name, but with no constraint. The only kinds of restrictions that can be translated into Ada are restrictions that limit a subtype to an interval, as they can be translated into range constraints, and restrictions that limit a variant type to a single value, as they can be translated into discriminant constraints.

If a subtype of **Int**, *Limited_Int* say, is defined with the purpose of reflecting the actual minimal and maximal values, e.g. *min_val* and *max_val*, needed by the specification, such a subtype should be translated in Ada into an integer type declaration of the form

```
type Limited_Int is range min_val .. max_val;
```

This type declaration would eliminate the need for a type that tries to implement the unlimited type **Int**, as described in section 5.2.4.1.

If a subtype expression appears in another context, e.g. in a function signature, we first declare a subtype and then use that subtype.

5.2.4.8   Bracketed type expressions

A bracketed type expression is translated as the enclosed type expression.

5.2.4.9   Access descriptions

Access descriptions are not translated into anything, as there is no corresponding concept in Ada and they do not affect the functionality of a function; they merely restrict what can occur in the expression that constitutes the body of the function.

5.2.5   Value expressions

RSL does not distinguish between "expressions" and "statements", which is something most programming languages, including Ada, do. This has two implications for the translation of expressions. First, some expressions should be translated into statements rather than expressions. They are easy to identify because their type is **Unit**, e.g. assignment expressions and function calls with result type **Unit**. Secondly, some structured RSL expressions, that might not be of type **Unit**, only have programming language counterparts that are statements, e.g. a case expression over a variant type. The translation of such an expression depends on the context, but it typically involves declaring an auxiliary variable that is assigned to in the structured statement and then used in the translation of the context. The declaration of auxiliary variables should take place as close to the expression as feasible and may therefore require the introduction of a block statement.

5.2.5.1   Value literals

Unit literal   The **Unit** value literal is intended to be used as the actual parameter of functions in a specification. Such functions are translated into parameterless functions, as described in section 5.2.1.4. Therefore the literal itself need not have a corresponding value in the program. If, however, the type **Unit** has been translated on its own, as described in section 5.2.4.1, the translation of the **Unit** literal is the corresponding enumeration literal.

Bool literals   A **Bool** literal is translated into the corresponding boolean literal; in Ada `true` and `false`.

Int literals   An **Int** literal is translated into the same programming language integer literal. The only possible problem is that it might be too large for the programming language type involved; see section 5.2.4.1.

Real literals   A **Real** literal is translated into the same real literal. There are two potential problems with this: the resulting real literal might be too large for the programming language type involved and, for Ada, the implicit conversion from universal real to the relevant Ada floating point type might result in a loss of precision; see section 5.2.4.1.

Char literals   A **Char** literal is translated into a corresponding programming language character literal.

Text literals   Assuming that the type **Text** for Ada has been translated as described in section 5.2.4.1, i.e. as the record type `Text`, a text literal is translated into a record aggregate:

```
Text'(L => <:the length:>, S => <:the string literal:>)
```

One should be aware that "escaped" characters in the RSL **Text** literal need to be dealt with as part of the translation.

5.2.5.2   Names

A name that appears as an expression is just translated as itself, as it is known to represent a value or a variable.

5.2.5.3   Pre-names

Pre-names only occur in postconditions, and they therefore need no translation.

5.2.5.4   Basic expressions

chaos   One would typically not find **chaos** in a specification that is to be translated. But if it occurs, it probably signals an error of some kind, and a reasonable translation would therefore be to raise an exception that should be declared in a library package.

skip   Since **skip** does nothing and is of type **Unit**, it is translated into a programming language statement that does nothing; for Ada this is the `null` statement.

stop   Apart from special uses of **stop** in combination with external choice, for which the translation is described in section 5.3, we would not expect **stop** to appear in a specification that is to be directly translated. But if it occurs, it probably signals an error of some kind, and a reasonable translation would therefore be to raise an exception that should be declared in a library package.

swap   One would typically not find **swap** in a specification that is to be translated. But if it occurs, it probably signals an error of some kind, and a reasonable translation would therefore be to raise an exception that should be declared in a library package.

5.2.5.5   Product expressions

A product expression that is the outermost actual parameter of an *n*-ary function is translated into *n* actual parameters. A product expression that occurs in other contexts should be translated into a qualified record aggregate corresponding to the guidelines for translating product type expressions; see section 5.2.4.2.

5.2.5.6   Set expressions

Assuming that the relevant set type expression has been translated using a generic package, as suggested in section 5.2.4.3, set expressions should be translated as follows, utilizing the overloading facility of Ada:

- Ranged set expression. This expression denotes an integer set. The corresponding programming language type is here called `Int_set`. An expression of the form {*expr1* .. *expr2*} is translated into

    - a declaration of an auxiliary variable:

        ```
        s :  Int_set := empty_set;
        ```

    - a statement:

        ```
        for i in T(expr1) ..  T(expr2) loop
          s := cons_set(i,s);
        end loop;
        ```

where $\mathcal{T}(e)$ is the translation of e. After this statement **s** is the value of the ranged set.

- Enumerated set expression. An expression of the form {*expr1*, *expr2*, ..., *exprn*} is translated into

  ```
  cons_set(T(expr1), cons_set(T(expr2), ...,
           cons_set(T(exprn), empty_set)...))
  ```

- Comprehended set expression. Such an expression is generally not directly translatable, but should be developed further.

5.2.5.7 List expressions

Assuming that the relevant list type expression has been translated using a generic package, as suggested in section 5.2.4.4, list expressions should be translated as follows, utilizing the overloading facility of Ada:

- Ranged list expression. This expression denotes an integer list. The corresponding programming language type is here called `Int_list`. An expression of the form ⟨*expr1* .. *expr2*⟩ is translated into

  - a declaration of an auxiliary variable:

    ```
    l : Int_list := empty_list;
    ```

  - a statement:

    ```
    for i in reverse T(expr1) ..  T(expr2) loop
      l := cons_list(i,l);
    end loop;
    ```

  where $\mathcal{T}(e)$ is the translation of e. After this statement l is the value of the ranged list.

- Enumerated list expression. An expression of the form ⟨*expr1*, *expr2*, ..., *exprn*⟩ is translated into

  ```
  cons_list(T(expr1), cons_list(T(expr2), ...,
            cons_list(T(exprn), empty_list)...))
  ```

- Comprehended list expression. Such an expression is generally not directly translatable, but should be developed further.

5.2.5.8 Map expressions

Assuming that the relevant map type expression has been translated using a generic package, as suggested in section 5.2.4.5, map expressions should be translated as follows, utilizing the overloading facility of Ada:

- Enumerated map expression. An expression of the form [*expr11* ↦*expr21*, *expr12* ↦*expr22*, ..., *expr1n* ↦*expr2n*] is translated into

```
cons_map(T(expr11),T(expr21),
     cons_map(T(expr12),T(expr22),
          cons_map(...,
               cons_map(T(expr1n),T(expr2n),
                    empty_map)...))
```

where $\mathcal{T}(e)$ is the translation of e.

- Comprehended map expression. Such an expression is generally not directly translatable, but should be developed further.

5.2.5.9 Function expressions

For languages that have function values, a function expression should be translated into a function definition, i.e. a name for the function typically has to be introduced, and this name can then be used in place of the function expression.

5.2.5.10 Application expressions

An application expression is a list application, a map application, or a function application. List and map applications have corresponding `apply` functions defined for the types; see sections 5.2.4.4 and 5.2.4.5. A function application expression is translated into a function or procedure call depending on the result type, as described in section 5.2.1.4. If the function is n-ary and it is being called with only one (composite) actual parameter, the translation must result in the subprogram getting n parameters. This can be done by component selection for the actual parameters. For example, for a function `g` with two formal parameters and an actual composite value `av`, the call will be `g(av.f_1, av.f_2)`, where `f_1` and `f_2` are the component names, as described in section 5.2.4.2. In the case of a complex actual parameter expression, e.g. one with side-effects, an auxiliary variable might have to be introduced.

5.2.5.11 Quantified expressions

A quantified expression is generally not directly translatable, but should be developed further.

5.2.5.12 Equivalence expressions

As discussed in section 5.1.1, equivalence expressions cannot be translated if there are side-effects, non-determinism or non-convergence involved. The only cases where it can be faithfully translated are those where the equality operator could be used, i.e. the arguments are read-only and convergent.

5.2.5.13   Post expressions

A value defined by a post expression should generally be developed further into an explicit function definition before translation. The only exception is post expressions used in formal scheme parameters, as they are ignored in the translation.

5.2.5.14   Disambiguation expressions

If the programming language does not have overloading, a disambiguation expression can be translated as the disambiguated expression. If overloading exists in the programming language, a disambiguation expression should be translated into a qualified expression to aid in overload resolution. The only requirement for the translation is that a type name must be defined for the type expression.

5.2.5.15   Bracketed expressions

A bracketed expression is translated into a bracketed expression.

5.2.5.16   Infix expressions

Value infix expressions   The translation of a value infix expression is determined by its infix operator; see section 5.2.7.

Axiom infix expressions   The translation of an axiom infix expression is determined by its infix connective; see section 5.2.8.

Statement infix expressions   The translation of a statement infix expression is determined by its infix combinator; see section 5.2.9.

5.2.5.17   Prefix expressions

Value prefix expressions   The translation of a value prefix expression is determined by its prefix operator; see section 5.2.7.

Axiom prefix expressions   The translation of an axiom prefix expression is determined by its prefix connective; see section 5.2.8.

Universal prefix expressions   A universal prefix expression is used to quantify over all states. This is not feasible to do in a program. It is therefore not considered suitable for translation.

5.2.5.18   Comprehended expressions

The only comprehended expressions that can be expected in a specification that is to be translated is one where the operator is ‖ or ⫿, which are often used in connection with object arrays. An example of translation of the former can be found in section 5.4.2. The latter may be translated into a `select` statement.

5.2.5.19   Initialise expressions

The expression **initialise** is intended to be used in axiomatic specifications for expressing properties of the initial state. Such properties should be achieved by means of explicit initialisations in specifications that are to be translated. There is one context where it might be relevant to translate **initialise**: when it is being used to re-initialise the state to an explicitly defined initial state. The translation of class expressions that are subject to such re-initialisations should declare a parameterless procedure, `initialise`, that contains assignments (see section 5.2.5.20) corresponding to the explicit initialisations of the local variables; **initialise** is then translated into a call of `initialise`.

5.2.5.20   Assignment expressions

For types translated into types involving access types, an assignment expression cannot be translated directly into a programming language assignment statement, since sub-structures have to be copied. Instead an `assign` procedure must be called; see section 5.2.1.3. For Ada, the overload resolution will then ensure that the appropriate `assign` procedure is called, provided that the correct visibility has been established.

For other types, the built-in Ada assignment can be used.

5.2.5.21   Input expressions

See section 5.3 for the translation of concurrent specifications.

5.2.5.22   Output expressions

See section 5.3 for the translation of concurrent specifications.

5.2.5.23   Structured expressions

Local expressions   If a local expression is the value expression of an explicit function definition, the locally declared entities can become local declarations within the subprogram body. A local expression of type **Unit** can be translated directly into a block statement. If the type of the local expression is not **Unit**, an auxiliary variable must be declared, followed by a block statement with a translation of the declaration of the entities of the local expression and a statement part that assigns the result to the auxiliary variable. That variable is then used at the place corresponding to the original local expression.

Let expressions Only the translation of let expressions containing explicit let definitions is feasible; a let expression containing a typing or an implicit let definition should be further developed prior to translation. An explicit let definition introduces one or more names in a local scope. Hence, in general, a block statement is needed. In that respect the translation of a let expression is similar to that of a local expression described above. The names introduced in a let definition may be overloaded, and therefore we may have to declare each of them as a parameterless function. If they are not locally overloaded, they should be declared as constants, since doing so makes the program both easier to read and more efficient.

If expressions If an if expression is the value expression of an explicit function definition, it can be translated into an `if` statement within the subprogram body, each branch having a `return` statement at the end. An if expression of type **Unit** can always be translated directly into an `if` statement — for languages without an `elsif` construct, nested `if` statements should be used. The translation of other if expressions will, for languages that do not have conditional expressions, require the introduction of an auxiliary variable, followed by an `if` statement that assigns a value to the variable in each branch. The variable is then used at the place corresponding to the original if expression.

Case expressions Whether a case expression can be translated into code that includes a case statement depends on the type of the value expression of the case expression and the nature of the patterns. As most programming languages only allow case statements over discrete types, and some even only over integer types, at least translations of case expressions over the types **Real** and **Text** have to result in `if` statements.

Variant types are often used in case expressions, and assuming that the variant type has been translated as described in section 5.2.1.3, case expressions can be translated into Ada for *Colour* and *Tree* as follows:

For *Colour*, assuming that *expr1*, *expr2* and *expr3* are of type **Unit**

```
case ce of
    red → expr1,
    green → expr2,
    _ → expr3
end
```

is directly translatable into

```
case T(ce) is
    when red => T(expr1)
    when green => T(expr2)
```

```
      when others => T(expr3)
    end case;
```

A wildcard pattern at the outermost level is translated into the Ada choice **others**. Inner wildcard patterns result in no local declarations for the corresponding components.

If the case patterns has not covered all possibilities, a final

when others => $T(\mathbf{swap})$

should be added. Following the guidelines of 5.2.5.4, $T(\mathbf{swap})$ will be **raise swap**, where **swap** is a user-defined exception.

For *Tree*, assuming that *expr1* and *expr2* are of type **Unit**

```
    case te of
        empty → expr1,
        node(l,v,r) → expr2
    end
```

is translated as follows. (Remember that a discrete type **Tree_kind** and a **kind** field were introduced to distinguish the two variants. This can now be used in translating the case expression.)

```
    aux_t :  constant Tree := T(te);

    . . .

    case aux_t.kind is
      when empty => T(expr1)
      when node =>
        declare
          l :  Tree := aux_t.left;
          v :  Elem := aux_t.val;
          r :  Tree := aux_t.right;
        begin
          T(expr2)
        end;
    end case;
```

The auxiliary constant **aux_t** is introduced to ensure that $T(te)$ is only evaluated once. We have assumed that *l*, *v* and *r* are not locally overloaded within *expr2*; if they had been overloaded they would have been translated into parameterless functions returning the appropriate fields. Note that if *Tree* had not had destructors, the RSL pattern matching would have been non-deterministic. We would typically ignore such kinds of non-determinism, as discussed in section 5.1.1, and produce code like the above.

If product or list patterns occur in a case expression, the case expression is translated into **if** statements with inner blocks for declaring entities resulting from the pattern matching.

If an inner pattern other than an identifier occurs in a case expression, the case expression is translated into (potentially nested) **if** statements with inner blocks for declaring entities resulting from the pattern matching.

If the type of a case expression is not **Unit**, an auxiliary variable must be declared, as explained for the translation of if expressions.

While expressions   A while expression can be directly translated into a **while** statement. If the translation of the logical value expression results in statements, its translation should be made into a parameterless function that is then called in the condition part of the **while** statement, or the statements should be placed prior to the loop as well as at the end of the loop.

An infinite RSL loop, i.e. one of the form **while true do ... end**, can be translated into an infinite loop of the target language instead of a **while** with a trivial condition.

Until expressions   If until statements do not exist in the target language, an until expression can be translated into a **while** statement by following the RSL context-independent expansion of until expressions. A better translation can be achieved by using an infinite loop with an exit statement. For example:

  do expr1 **until** expr2 **end**

in Ada becomes

```
loop
  T(expr1)
  exit when  T(expr2);
end loop;
```

For expressions   The list limitation of a for expression can be of any list type. Hence, in the resulting code, it may be necessary to build the list first and then loop from 1 to the length of the list. However, very often the list limitation is of the form

  id **in** ⟨expr1 .. expr2⟩

In such cases it would be unnecessary to build the list at all. Instead the resulting for loop can directly loop over the range. In Ada this would be

```
for id in  T(expr1)  ..   T(expr2) loop
  ...
end loop;
```

5.2.6   Names

Names should be preserved by the translation as much as possible; see section 5.1.3.4 for a discussion of this issue.

A qualified identifier with a non-empty qualification is translated into the same name when the target language allows, as Ada does. Qualification of operators might not be supported, in which case a different naming approach has to be adopted. In Ada, a qualified operator like *O.(+)* is translated into `O."+"`. This approach is applicable to all RSL operators which also exist in the target language. For the other RSL operators, identifiers will already have been introduced and the usual translation of qualified identifiers can be used; see 5.2.7.

5.2.7   Identifiers and operators

Not all RSL operators are necessarily operators in the target language. For these operators, identifiers have to be introduced by the translation.

5.2.7.1   Infix operators

The translation of an infix expression involving the equality or inequality operator depends on the type of the operands. If the translation of the operand type has introduced a special `equal` function, as described in section 5.2.1.3, then that function is called (negated in the case of inequality). Otherwise the built-in equality and inequality operators can be used directly.

Addition, subtraction, multiplication and division of integers and reals can be directly translated as long as no special implementation is required of those types; see section 5.2.1.3.

Exponentiation of integers can be translated directly into integer exponentiation. The target language might have limitations on real exponentiation, in which case a function needs to be introduced as part of the translation for the operation. This is the case for Ada, where the built-in exponentiation can only raise a floating point value to the power of an integer.

Function composition cannot be translated in all contexts. But if a function composition, with operands that are function names, occurs in a function value definition, it can be translated into nested function calls within the body of the function being defined.

Comparison operators for integers and reals can be directly translated as long as a special implementation of those types is not required; see section 5.2.1.3.

The set, list and map operators are translated into the function names as described in the translation of the type constructors in sections 5.2.4.3, 5.2.4.4 and 5.2.4.5.

5.2.7.2   Prefix operators

The integer and real **abs** can typically be translated directly into corresponding **abs** functions of the target language.

Application of the **real** conversion operator can typically be translated directly into a type conversion of the target language. Note that since Ada is not case sensitive, `real(e)` is the same as the predefined type conversion `Real(e)`.

The **int** conversion operator has the semantics of truncating the real value. In the target language the semantics of conversion to integer is often that of rounding to the nearest integer. Hence, we must define a function for doing the RSL conversion. Note that, if the guidelines of section 5.2.4.1 have been followed for translating the type **Int**, the function in Ada must have a name different from `int`.

The remaining prefix operators work on sets, lists and maps and they are translated into the function names, as described in the translation of the type constructors in sections 5.2.4.3, 5.2.4.4 and 5.2.4.5.

5.2.8   Connectives

5.2.8.1   Infix connectives

When translating infix connectives we must be aware of the short-circuit nature of their RSL semantics, e.g. that $a \wedge b$ is defined as **if** a **then** b **else false end**. This means that we have to be careful in deciding whether $\wedge$, for example, can be translated into a logical conjunction in the target language.

There are three infix connectives:

- Boolean and ($\wedge$). In Ada this would be translated into **and then**.
- Boolean or ($\vee$). In Ada this would be translated into **or else**.
- Boolean implication ($\Rightarrow$). This operator may not exist in the target language, but since $a \Rightarrow b$ is equivalent to $\sim a \vee b$, it can be translated as such.

5.2.8.2   Prefix connectives

There is only one prefix connective, the Boolean not ($\sim$) and it is translated into logical negation in the target language.

5.2.9   Infix combinators

There are five infix combinators:

- External choice ($\lceil\rceil$). This is only relevant to translation in the context of concurrent specifications; see section 5.3.
- Internal choice ($\lceil\rceil$). One would typically not use this in a specification that is to be translated. But if it occurs, we could adopt a pragmatic approach, inspired by the discussion of semantics preserving translation in section 5.1.1, and just translate the operand that is easiest to translate and ignore the other one — an internal choice made by "the translator".[1]

---

[1]This translation, however, does not fully reflect the original meaning

- Concurrent composition (∥). See section 5.3 on guidelines for translating concurrent specifications.
- Interlocked composition (∦). The interlock combinator in RSL is used to axiomatically specify the behaviour of one process (the one of interest) by interlocking it with other "test" processes. Hence, in a final RSL system specification the interlock operator is not expected to occur, and its translation is therefore not relevant.
- Sequential composition (;). This is translated into " ; ", but see also section 5.3 for the concurrency aspects.

5.3   Translating concurrent specifications

A programming language need not support concurrent programming at all, and even when it does, the concurrency concepts typically differ considerably between programming languages. Therefore it is not feasible to give general and still useful guidelines for translating RSL concurrency. Therefore this section only deals with the translation into a specific programming language that has a process concept, Ada.

The process concept of RSL and the tasking concept of Ada are both at a reasonably high level of abstraction. However, the two concepts are different, and there is no immediate general mapping from one to the other.

This section addresses a number of specific technical issues involved in translating RSL concurrency into Ada tasking.

5.3.1   Processes and tasks

When an RSL specification defines a process as a parallel composition of two (other) processes, concurrency is (logically) requested of the implementation. The natural and simple solution is therefore to introduce an Ada task for each of the two constituent RSL processes. At this level the mapping is almost trivial. However, in general all RSL expressions that access channels denote processes. For example, consider

    expr1 ; expr2

The result is a process obtained by first "executing" the process denoted by *expr1* and, when that terminates, "executing" the process denoted by *expr2*.

It would be unacceptable — both from a program structure and a run-time efficiency point of view — to produce Ada tasks for all such RSL process expressions that are sequential in nature. Hence, when considering the infix combinators of RSL, only the parallel combinator requires the generation of Ada tasks.

Additionally, there are certain requirements for maintaining locality in the translation. Consider

```
object
  S :
    class
      channel
        C1, C2, C3 : Int
      value
        P : Unit → in C1 out C2 Unit
        P() ≡ expr1,
        Q : Unit → in C3 Unit
        Q() ≡ expr2
    end
```

with the following potential use of P and Q:

$$S.P() \parallel S.Q() \tag{1}$$

Since both *expr1* and *expr2* are defined inside S, they may depend on its definition and the names visible where it is declared. Therefore one cannot generally macro-expand the expressions at the point of usage. Hence, one has to construct some sort of Ada unit for each of P and Q. In this particular case one can see — based on the value definitions of P and Q — that both P and Q have to be turned into task types because of their use of channels and access types and because of the dynamic activation of the tasks.

The Ada code for S will consist of the package specification

```
package S is
  task type P_type is
    entry C1;
    entry C2;
  end P_type;
  type acc_P_type is access P_type;

  task type Q_type is
    entry C3;
  end Q_type;
  type acc_Q_type is access Q_type;
end S;
```

and the body

```
package body S is
  task body P_type is
  begin
    T(expr1)
  end P_type;
```

```
   task body Q_type is
   begin
     T(expr2)
   end Q_type;
 end S;
```

and the expression (1) is translated as

```
   a_p_v : S.acc_P_type;
   a_q_v : S.acc_Q_type;
   ...
 begin
   ...
   a_p_v := new S.P_type;
   a_q_v := new S.Q_type;
```

where each of the two tasks runs independently after they have been allocated and activated.

5.3.2 Parameterized processes

An RSL process may be parameterized. Ada tasks cannot be parameterized as such. Instead, the argument can be transferred to the task using an entry call.

For example, the parameterized RSL process

value
    P : T → ... **Unit**
    P(x) ≡ expr(x)

can be translated into a task type with an additional entry (**Param**)

```
 task type P_type is
   entry Param(x :  in T);
 end P_type;

 task body P_type is
   x :  T;
 begin
   accept Param(x :  in T) do
     P_type.x := x;
   end Param;
   T(expr(x))
 end P_type;
```

5.3.3   Recursively defined processes

RSL processes that act as servers may be defined using a recursive structure, as in

value
P : **Unit** → ... **Unit**,
P() ≡ expr1 ; expr2 ; ... ; P()

though they would normally be defined using while expressions.

In Ada we do not want the task type corresponding to a recursive P to create a new task when it reaches the end. Instead, we should translate (as if a while expression had been used) into

```
task body P_type is
begin
  loop
    T(expr1); T(expr2); ...;
  end loop;
end P_type;
```

5.3.4   Communication

In both RSL and Ada, process interaction is based on synchronous communication with message passing. RSL processes communicate using unidirectional channels, where the receiving process need not be known by the sending process; only the channel name is used. Ada tasks communicate using entries. An entry is part of a task. Hence, a task that calls an entry needs to know the name of the task owning the entry. During task communication (a rendezvous) values can be passed both ways by using the general parameter passing mechanism known from procedures, using the modes **in**, **out** and **in out**.

Deciding which Ada task should *own* the entry and which tasks should *call* the entry is not always easy. A possible approach is to say that the tasks corresponding to the process(es) whose types define the channel as **in** should always own the entry, and the ones corresponding to processes defining it as **out** should just call the entry. However, this approach is not acceptable, since RSL allows the mixing of send and receive in external choices, and the only construct in Ada feasible for modelling external choice (combined with communication) is the "selective wait" statement, where entry calls cannot occur. This means that, depending on the actual process expressions, we would like sometimes to associate the entry with a task whose RSL process defines the channel as **in** and sometimes with one defining it as **out**. See the next section on how to determine the allocation of entries to tasks depending on the communication pattern in the RSL specification.

5.3.5   Translating special forms of concurrency

Often a concurrent RSL specification contains one or more "server" processes with interface functions to communicate with the servers. Each server is characterized by having an infinite loop (or recursion) and at each step offering various communications, both inputs and outputs, with external choice among them. Examples of such specifications are the modules *C_MOTOR1*, *C_DOOR1* and *C_BUTTON1* of the lift example in section 2.7. In this section, we present guidelines for translating such modules. As an example we use *C_DOOR1*, but ignore the fact that the lift example includes object arrays of *C_DOOR1*; see section 5.4.2 for the complete example. Moreover, we make the reasonable assumption that there is only going to be *one* server process, here *door*, per object. There should only be one such process. Otherwise, there would be several instances of it running in parallel and the interface functions would (non-deterministically) communicate with one of them.

The resulting generic package specification is simple and involves no concurrency; only the four subprograms corresponding to *init*, *close*, *open* and *door_state* need to be declared.

The subtype T_Door_state is needed because in Ada the subprogram name hides all other entities with the same name within its own declaration.

```
with T; use T;
generic
package C_DOOR1 is
  procedure init;
  procedure close;
  procedure open;
  subtype T_Door_state is T.Door_state;
  function door_state return T_Door_state;
end C_DOOR1;

package body C_DOOR1 is
  door_var : T.Door_state;

  task type door_type is
    entry CH_open;
    entry CH_close;
    entry CH_open_ack;
    entry CH_close_ack;
    entry CH_door_state(d : out T_Door_state);
  end door_type;

  type acc_door_type is access door_type;
  acc_door_var : acc_door_type;
```

```
task body door_type is
begin
  loop
    select
      accept CH_open; accept CH_open_ack; door_var := T.open;
    or
      accept CH_close; accept CH_close_ack; door_var := T.shut;
    or
      accept CH_door_state(d : out T_Door_state) do
        d := door_var;
      end CH_door_state;
    end select;
  end loop;
end door_type;

procedure door is
begin
  acc_door_var := new door_type;
end door;

procedure init is
begin
  door;
end init;

procedure close is
begin
  acc_door_var.CH_close; acc_door_var.CH_close_ack;
end close;

procedure open is
begin
  acc_door_var.CH_open; acc_door_var.CH_open_ack;
end open;

function door_state return T_Door_state is
  d_s : T_Door_state;
begin
  acc_door_var.CH_door_state(d_s);
  return d_s;
end door_state;
end C_DOOR1;
```

The main process *door* is translated into a task type and an access type. The reason for this is that ordinary tasks start automatically at package elaboration time, i.e. before `init` and therefore before `door` is called. Objects pointed to by an access value do not start until they are created by the `new` operation (here used in the body of `door`).

The channels are translated into entries of the `door_type` task type. The entries have been given a `CH_` prefix to ensure uniqueness and to indicate that they stem from the redundant object *CH*. All but `door_state` are parameterless because the channel type is **Unit**. The entry `door_state` gets an `out` parameter because the value is coming *from* the `door_state` process.

The variable `acc_door_var` is used to hold a pointer to the `door_state` process when it is started.

The body of `door_type` contains an infinite loop corresponding to the **while true do ... end**. The external choice is translated into a `select` statement. The only requirement in Ada is that each alternative must begin with an accept statement. This is easy to satisfy here, as for most processes, since all the alternatives in the specification are inputs or outputs.

The procedure `door` starts an instance of the `door_type` task and sets the variable to point to that instance. The procedure `init` simply calls `door`.

The procedures `close` and `open` call the entries using the variable as a prefix to communicate with the right task. Note that both `close_ack` and `open_ack` are entry calls, even though in RSL this communication goes "the other way". The reason for turning the direction around is to avoid `accept` statements in `close` and `open`, which means that they do not have to be tasks but can be procedures.

The function `door_state` declares a local variable for holding the result of calling the `door_state` entry.

Exercise Translate the RSL module *C_DOORS1* into UNIX[2] processes and sockets using C.

5.4 Translation examples

In this section the harbour and the lift examples developed in the tutorial chapter are translated into Ada. In addition some of the standard specifications that are used in the examples are translated.

5.4.1 The harbour example

The aim of this section is to illustrate translation of imperative, sequential specifications by translating the final imperative harbour developed in section 2.6 into Ada. The specification consists of the scheme *TYPES1*, which is a development of

---

[2]UNIX is a registered trademark of Bell Laboratories

TYPES, its global object instance *T1*, and *I_HARBOUR2*, which is like *I_HAR-BOUR1* except that every occurrence of the object name *T* is turned into *T1* and that *is_docked* has been refined, as described in section 2.6.

I_HARBOUR2 contains two local scheme instantiations that use the standard modules *I_ARRAY_INIT* and *I_SET*. We therefore also translate these two schemes in order to illustrate how Ada code for typical standard modules can be developed.

5.4.1.1   Translation of TYPES1 and T1

First we develop *TYPES* into *TYPES1* to make it translatable, as described in section 2.6.9. Then we translate *TYPES1* into Ada.

```
scheme
  TYPES1 =
    hide sizes, is_Berth in
      class
        type
          Ship :: name : Text  ship_size : Size,
          Berth_type :: number : Index  berth_size : Size,
          Berth = {| b : Berth_type • is_Berth(b) |},
          Size :: draught : Nat  length : Nat,
          Occupancy == vacant | occupied_by(occupant : Ship),
          Index = {| i : Int • i ≥ min ∧ max ≥ i |}
        value
          min : Int = 4,
          max : Int = 7,
          fits : Ship × Berth → Bool
          fits(s, b) ≡
            let mk_Size(ds, ls) = ship_size(s),
                mk_Size(db, lb) = berth_size(b) in
            ds ≤ db ∧ ls ≤ lb
            end,
          sizes : Size* =
            ⟨mk_Size(30, 100), mk_Size(20, 100),
              mk_Size(15, 50), mk_Size(20, 200)⟩,
          gen_Berth : Index → Berth
          gen_Berth(i) ≡
            mk_Berth_type(i, sizes(i − min + 1)),
          is_Berth : Berth_type → Bool
          is_Berth(b) ≡ let mk_Berth_type(i, s) = b in s = sizes(i) end,
          indx : Berth → Index = number
      end
```

The sort *Ship* from *TYPES* has been developed into a record type with some characteristics of a ship. The sort *Berth* in *TYPES* contains all the berths of a harbour.

Therefore in *TYPES1* it is defined as a subtype (of *Berth_type*) that contains the actual berths of a given harbour. *Berth_type* explicitly defines the characteristics of a berth. Both ships and berths are characterized by their size, which is used to determine whether a ship fits into a berth; the type *Size* is introduced to model the size of ships and berths.

The scheme is translated into a parameterless generic package. The class expression is a hiding class expression, and the general idea is to move the declaration of hidden entities into the body.

The types *Ship*, *Berth_type* and *Size* are short record types with no recursion involved. They can therefore be translated into Ada record types with functions for construction and destruction, as described in section 5.2.1.3.

The values *min* and *max* are not overloaded in this specification and can hence be translated into Ada constants. We assume the existence of an Int_Package, a Nat_Package and a Text_Package, as discussed in section 5.2.4.1.

The subtype *Index* is a subtype of *Int* and it constrains the values to a range. This means that it can be translated directly into an Ada integer subtype with the appropriate range constraint.

The restriction used in the subtype expression of *Berth* cannot be expressed as a constraint in Ada. Therefore the subtype declaration in Ada just defines Berth to be the same as Berth_type.

The type *Occupancy* is a variant type that does not involve recursion. It can hence be translated following the guidelines given in section 5.2.1.3, where the use of an access type is avoided.

The functions *gen_Berth* and *fits* are translated into function declarations that are placed in the generic package declaration and bodies that are placed in the generic package body.

The function *indx* is defined to be equal to *number*. This can be expressed directly in Ada by declaring indx using a renaming declaration.

```
with Int_Package; use Int_Package;
with Nat_Package; use Nat_Package;
with Text_Package; use Text_Package;
generic
package TYPES1 is
  type Size is
    record
      draught : Nat;
      length : Nat;
    end record;
  function mk_Size(d : in Nat; l : in Nat) return Size;
  function draught(s : in Size) return Nat;
  function length(s : in Size) return Nat;
```

```
type Ship is
  record
    name : Text;
    ship_size : Size;
  end record;
function mk_Ship(n : in Text; s_s : in Size) return Ship;
function name(s : in Ship) return Text;
function ship_size(s : in Ship) return Size;

min : constant Int := 4;
max : constant Int := 7;
subtype Index is Int range min .. max;

type Berth_type is
  record
    number : Index;
    berth_size : Size;
  end record;
function mk_Berth_type(n : in Index; b_s : in Size)
          return Berth_type;
function number(b_t : in Berth_type) return Index;
function berth_size(b_t : in Berth_type) return Size;

subtype Berth is Berth_type;

type Occupancy_kind is (vacant, occupied_by);
type Occupancy
       (kind : Occupancy_kind := Occupancy_kind'First) is
  record
    case kind is
      when vacant =>
        null;
      when occupied_by =>
        occupant : Ship;
    end case;
  end record;
function vacant return Occupancy;
function occupied_by(s : in Ship) return Occupancy;
function occupant(o : in Occupancy) return Ship;

function gen_Berth(i : in Index) return Berth;

function fits(s : in Ship; b : in Berth) return Boolean;
```

```
    function indx(b : Berth) return Index renames number;
end TYPES1;


with Set_Package;
with List_Package;
package body TYPES1 is

  function equal(x, y : in Size) return Boolean renames "=";

  function copy(x : in Size) return Size is
  begin
    return x;
  end copy;

  procedure assign(x : in out Size; y : in Size) is
  begin
    x := y;
  end assign;

  procedure free(x : in out Size) is
  begin
    null;
  end free;

  package Size_set_Package is
          new Set_Package(Elem_type => Size);
  use Size_set_Package;

  package Integer_set_Package is
          new Set_Package(Elem_type => Int);
  use Integer_set_Package;

  package Size_list_Package is
          new List_Package
                (Elem_type => Size,
                 Elem_set_type => Size_set_Package.Set,
                 Integer_set_type => Integer_set_Package.Set);
  use Size_list_Package;

  function sizes return Size_list_Package.List is
  begin
    return cons_list(mk_Size(30, 100),
              cons_list(mk_Size(20, 100),
                cons_list(mk_Size(15, 50),
```

```
                        cons_list(mk_Size(20, 200), empty_list))));
end sizes;

function mk_Size(d : in Nat; l : in Nat) return Size is
begin
  return Size'(draught => d, length => l);
end mk_Size;

function draught(s : in Size) return Nat is
begin
  return s.draught;
end draught;

function length(s : in Size) return Nat is
begin
  return s.length;
end length;

function mk_Ship(n : in Text; s_s : in Size) return Ship is
begin
  return Ship'(name => n, ship_size => s_s);
end mk_Ship;

function name(s : in Ship) return Text is
begin
  return s.name;
end name;

function ship_size(s : in Ship) return Size is
begin
  return s.ship_size;
end ship_size;

function mk_Berth_type(n : in Index; b_s : in Size)
          return Berth_type is
begin
  return Berth_type'(number => n, berth_size => b_s);
end mk_Berth_type;

function number(b_t : in Berth_type) return Index is
begin
  return b_t.number;
end number;
```

```
function berth_size(b_t : in Berth_type) return Size is
begin
  return b_t.berth_size;
end berth_size;

function vacant return Occupancy is
begin
  return Occupancy'(kind => vacant);
end vacant;

function occupied_by(s : in Ship) return Occupancy is
begin
  return Occupancy'(kind => occupied_by, occupant => s);
end occupied_by;

function occupant(o : in Occupancy) return Ship is
begin
  return o.occupant;
end occupant;

function gen_Berth(i : in Index) return Berth is
begin
  return mk_Berth_type(i, apply(sizes, i - min + 1));
end gen_Berth;

function is_Berth(b : Berth_type) return Boolean is
  i : Int := number(b);
  s : Size := berth_size(b);
begin
  return (s = apply(sizes,i));
end is_Berth;

function fits(s : in Ship; b : in Berth) return Boolean is
  s_size : Size := ship_size(s);
  b_size : Size := berth_size(b);
  ds : Nat := s_size.draught;
  ls : Nat := s_size.length;
  db : Nat := b_size.draught;
  lb : Nat := b_size.length;
begin
  return ds <= db and then ls <= lb;
end fits;
end TYPES1;
```

The global object *T1* is translated into a generic package instantiation, which is quite simple as TYPES1 is parameterless. The resulting Ada code is the following library unit:

```
with TYPES1;
package T1 is new TYPES1;
```

I_HARBOUR2 contains two local scheme instantiations that use the standard modules *I_ARRAY_INIT* and *I_SET*. We therefore translate these two schemes in order to illustrate how Ada code for typical standard modules can be developed.

5.4.1.2   Translation of I_ARRAY_INIT

I_ARRAY_INIT is an imperative module that is naturally translated into an implementation that uses an array variable. But before introducing the array, we will consider the structure of the module, including its parameter. The standard specification *I_ARRAY_INIT* is a scheme and is therefore translated into a generic package. The generic formal part is determined from the scheme *ARRAY_PARM_INIT* and the use of the formal entities within the class expression of *I_ARRAY_INIT*. *ARRAY_PARM_INIT* contains the sort *Elem* and a value *init* to be used as the initial elements of the array. The sort *Elem* is translated into a generic formal private type P_Elem, as described in section 5.2.1.1. However, not all of the formal subprograms are needed here. In order to implement the *change* operation, a formal assign procedure for the formal type *Elem* is needed. The value *init* is translated into a generic formal in parameter P_init, since it is not locally overloaded.

The formal values *min* and *max* are of type **Int**. We here assume that a translation of **Int** into an Ada integer type Int already exists and is placed in a library package Int_Package, which is therefore included in the context clause of the generic I_ARRAY_INIT package. *min* and *max* are not locally overloaded and can hence be translated into generic formal in parameters rather than formal functions. The formal axiom *[array_not_empty]* is ignored in the translation as it is a requirement on the instantiations and it cannot be captured in Ada, except in the form of a comment.

I_ARRAY_INIT is defined as an extension of *I_ARRAY* and we will translate it by "unfolding" the extend, as described in section 5.2.2.2. The translation of *I_ARRAY_INIT* results in a generic package declaration and a body, where the specification should contain only those declarations necessary to reflect the entities provided by *I_ARRAY_INIT*, i.e. one subtype and three operations. The remaining declarations, including the declaration of the array variable, should be placed in the body in order not to expose unnecessary information and to minimize the need for re-compilation if a different implementation of the local state is desired.

The condition of the subtype *Index* is of a kind that is immediately translatable into an Ada subtype with a range constraint. The signatures of the three operations directly lead to three subprogram declarations. *init* becomes a parameterless procedure because of the **Unit** parameter and result type; *change* becomes a two parameter procedure. Finally, *apply* becomes a function with the expected parameter and result types.

The RSL comments are turned directly into Ada comments, as Ada comments are allowed in all those places where they are allowed in RSL.

The resulting generic package declaration is

```
with Int_Package; use Int_Package;
generic
  type P_Elem is private;
  P_init : in P_Elem;
  with procedure assign(x : in out P_Elem; y : in P_Elem) is <>;
  P_min : in Int;
  P_max : in Int;
  -- requirement: [array_not_empty] P_max >= P_min
package I_ARRAY_INIT is
  subtype Index is Int range P_min .. P_max;
  -- generator
  procedure change(i : in Index; e : in P_Elem);
  -- observer
  function apply(i : in Index) return P_Elem;
  -- initial
  procedure init;
end I_ARRAY_INIT;
```

In the body of I_ARRAY_INIT, the array variable (state) holding the state is declared, taking its bounds from P_min and P_max. The init procedure initialises the whole array with the formal initial value of the element type in order to satisfy the axiom *[apply_init]*. The axiom *[initial]* is satisfied by calling the init procedure within the statement list of the package body. The axiom *[apply_total]* is satisfied because the apply function is defined for all values belonging to the subtype Index. The axiom *[apply_change]* effectively expresses that *change(i,e)* updates the *i*th array component and that *apply(i)* reads the *i*th component. The subprogram bodies hence only have to achieve this. Note that the formal subprogram assign is used instead of the predefined ":=", because nothing is known about the actual type corresponding to the formal sort *Elem* (and therefore the type P_Elem). If the change or apply operation is called, by mistake, with an index that is outside the subtype Index, the usual Ada dynamic check on indexing will fail and the exception Constraint_Error will be raised.

```
package body I_ARRAY_INIT is
  state : array (Index) of P_Elem;
```

```
-- generator
procedure change(i : in Index; e : in P_Elem) is
begin
  assign(state(i),e);
end change;

-- observer
function apply(i : in Index) return P_Elem is
begin
  return state(i);
end apply;

-- initial
procedure init is
begin
  for i in Index loop
     assign(state(i),P_init);
  end loop;
end init;

begin
  init;
end I_ARRAY_INIT;
```

5.4.1.3   Translation of I_SET

The standard specification *I_SET* can be translated using a number of different data structures as nothing is said directly in the specification about the state. Here we decide to translate it into a general linked structure. *I_SET* is translated into a generic package. The generic formal part is determined from the scheme *ELEM* and the actual need for operations within the package. The sort *Elem* is translated into a generic formal private type, as described in section 5.2.1.1, but only some of the characteristic operations are needed. We only need to include those that are actually used.

The translation of *I_SET* results in a generic package declaration and body, where the declaration contains only the subprogram declaration corresponding to the methods of *I_SET*.

```
generic
  type E_Elem is private;
  with function equal(x, y : in E_Elem) return Boolean is <>;
  with function copy(x : in E_Elem) return E_Elem is <>;
  with procedure assign(x : in out E_Elem; y : in E_Elem) is <>;
  with procedure free(x : in out E_Elem) is <>;
```

```
package I_SET is
  -- generators
  procedure empty;
  procedure add(e : in E_Elem);
  procedure remove(e : in E_Elem);
  -- observer
  function is_in(e : in E_Elem) return Boolean;
end I_SET;
```

Note that the declaration of I_SET contains nothing exposing the data structure holding the set; such information need not be given before the package body, which means that this generic package declaration can be used for several alternative implementations of a set.

The package body declares a variable (state) to hold the current value of the set. The set is implemented as an ordinary linked list. The generic subprogram Unchecked_Deallocation is needed to free storage when manipulating lists. It is locally instantiated as a U_D procedure used in defining the empty procedure that deallocates a complete list. The subprogram bodies must satisfy the axioms. This is straightforward to implement using traditional list operations. The axiom *[initial]* is satisfied because access variables are implicitly initialised to null in Ada. The procedure add ensures that an element does not occur more than once in the set implementation. Alternatively, we could have allowed duplicates (simpler insert) at the expense of the list getting longer (slower is_in) and remove having to reach the end of the list to remove all copies.

```
with Unchecked_Deallocation;
package body I_SET is
  type Node;
  type Set is access Node;
  type Node is
    record
      elem : E_Elem;
      next : Set;
    end record;
  state : Set;

  procedure U_D is new Unchecked_Deallocation(Node,Set);

  -- generators
  procedure empty is
    l_s : Set;
  begin
    while state /= null loop
      free(state.elem);
      l_s := state.next;
```

```
      U_D(state);
      state := l_s;
   end loop;
end empty;

procedure add(e : in E_Elem) is
begin
   if not is_in(e) then
      state := new Node'(elem => copy(e), next => state);
   end if;
end add;

procedure remove(e : in E_Elem) is
   current, prev : Set;
begin
   current := state;
   prev := null;
   while current /= null loop
      if equal(current.elem,e) then
         free(current.elem);
         if prev = null then
            state := current.next;
         else
            prev.next := current.next;
         end if;
         U_D(current);
         return;
      end if;
      prev := current;
      current := current.next;
   end loop;
end remove;

-- observer
function is_in(e : in E_Elem) return Boolean is
   l_s : Set := state;
begin
   while l_s /= null loop
      if equal(l_s.elem,e) then
         return true;
      end if;
      l_s := l_s.next;
   end loop;
```

```
        return false;
    end is_in;
end I_SET;
```

5.4.1.4   Translation of I_HARBOUR2

I_HARBOUR2 is translated into a generic package, where only the non-hidden entities are declared in the specification, i.e. the hidden objects are placed in the package body. The hidden function *consistent* is not used in the RSL specification and is therefore not translated.

The subtype T_Occupancy is needed because in Ada the subprogram name hides all other entities with the same name within its own declaration.

```
with Int_Package; use Int_Package;
with T1; use T1;
generic
package I_HARBOUR2 is
    -- generators
    procedure arrives(s : in T1.Ship);
    procedure docks(s : in T1.Ship; b1 : in T1.Berth);
    procedure leaves(s : in T1.Ship; b1 : in T1.Berth);

    -- observers
    function waiting(s : in T1.Ship) return Boolean;

    subtype T_Occupancy is T1.Occupancy;
    function occupancy(b1 : in T1.Berth) return T_Occupancy;


    function is_docked(s : in T1.Ship) return Boolean;

    -- guards
    function can_arrive(s : in T1.Ship) return Boolean;
    function can_dock(s: in T1.Ship; b1 : in T1.Berth)
             return Boolean;
    function can_leave(s : in T1.Ship; b1 : in T1.Berth)
             return Boolean;
end I_HARBOUR2;

with I_ARRAY_INIT;
with I_SET;
package body I_HARBOUR2 is
    function equal(x, y : in T1.Ship) return Boolean renames "=";
```

```
function copy(x : in T1.Ship) return T1.Ship is
begin
  return x;
end copy;

procedure assign(x : in out T1.Ship; y : in T1.Ship) is
begin
  x := y;
end assign;

procedure free(x : in out T1.Ship) is
begin
  null;
end free;


package P is new I_SET(E_Elem => T1.Ship);

procedure assign(x : in out T1.Occupancy;
                 y : in T1.Occupancy) is
begin
  x := y;
end assign;

package B is new I_ARRAY_INIT(P_Elem => T1.Occupancy,
                              P_init => T1.vacant,
                              P_min => T1.min,
                              P_max => T1.max);

-- generators
procedure arrives(s : in T1.Ship) is
begin
  P.add(s);
end arrives;

procedure docks(s : in T1.Ship; b : in T1.Berth) is
begin
  P.remove(s) ; B.change(T1.indx(b1), T1.occupied_by(s));
end docks;

procedure leaves(s : in T1.Ship; b1 : in T1.Berth) is
begin
  B.change(T1.indx(b1), T1.vacant);
end leaves;
```

```
-- observers
function waiting(s : in T1.Ship) return Boolean is
begin
  return P.is_in(s);
end waiting;

function occupancy(b1 : in T1.Berth) return T_Occupancy is
begin
  return B.apply(T1.indx(b1));
end occupancy;

function is_docked(s : in T1.Ship) return Boolean is
  found : Boolean := False;
  indx : T1.Index := T1.min;
begin
  while not found and then indx <= T1.max loop
    found := B.apply(indx) = T1.occupied_by(s);
    indx := indx + 1;
  end loop;
  return found;
end is_docked;

-- guards
function can_arrive(s : in T1.Ship) return Boolean is
begin
  return not P.is_in(s) and then not is_docked(s);
end can_arrive;

function can_dock(s: in T1.Ship; b1 : in T1.Berth)
          return Boolean is
begin
  return P.is_in(s) and then not is_docked(s) and then
         B.apply(T1.indx(b1)) = T1.vacant and then
         T1.fits(s, b1);
end can_dock;

function can_leave(s : in T1.Ship; b1 : in T1.Berth)
          return Boolean is
begin
  return B.apply(T1.indx(b1)) = T1.occupied_by(s);
end can_leave;
end I_HARBOUR2;
```

5.4.2 The lift example

The aim of this section is to illustrate translation of concurrent specifications by translating the final concurrent lift developed in section 2.7 into Ada.

5.4.2.1 Translation of **TYPES** and **T**

First the scheme *TYPES* and the global object *T* need to be translated.

The values *min_floor* and *max_floor* are not given specific values in *TYPES*. We could develop *TYPES* further in RSL into *TYPES1*, as with the scheme *TYPES* in the harbour example where limits were also decided upon. But in this case, since there is nothing else that needs further developing in *TYPES*, we decide to fix the two values as part of the translation process. The only thing to be aware of is that the values must satisfy the axiom *[some_floors]*; the values 1 and 10 will be used in this example.

The scheme itself is translated into a parameterless generic package.

The values *min_floor* and *max_floor* are not overloaded in this specification and can hence be translated into Ada constants. We assume the existence of an **Int_Package**, as discussed in section 5.2.4.1.

The function *is_floor* is translated into an Ada function declaration with the obvious signature and a body that is placed in the generic package body.

The types *Floor*, *Lower_floor* and *Upper_floor* are all subtypes of *Int* and they constrain the values to particular ranges. This means that they can be translated into Ada integer subtypes with the appropriate range constraints.

The types *Door_state*, *Button_state*, *Direction* and *Movement* are all variant types with only constructors. They can hence be translated into Ada enumeration types, as described in section 5.2.1.3.

The type *Requirement* is a short record type with no recursion involved. It can therefore be translated into an Ada record type and functions for construction and destruction, as described in section 5.2.1.3.

The functions *next_floor*, *is_next_floor* and *invert* are translated into Ada function declarations with the obvious signatures and bodies that are placed in the generic package body.

```
with Int_Package; use Int_Package;
generic
package TYPES is
  min_floor : constant Int := 1;
  max_floor : constant Int := 10;

  function is_floor(f : in Int) return Boolean;

  subtype Floor is Int range min_floor .. max_floor;
  subtype Lower_floor is Floor range Floor'First .. max_floor-1;
  subtype Upper_floor is Floor range min_floor+1 .. Floor'Last;
```

```
type Door_state is (open, shut);
type Button_state is (lit, clear);
type Direction is (up, down);
type Movement is (halted, moving);

type Requirement is
  record
    here : Boolean;
    after : Boolean;
    before : Boolean;
  end record;
function mk_Requirement(h : in Boolean;
                        a : in Boolean;
                        b : in Boolean) return Requirement;
function here(r : in Requirement) return Boolean;
function after(r : in Requirement) return Boolean;
function before(r : in Requirement) return Boolean;

function next_floor(d : in Direction; f : in Int) return Int;
function is_next_floor(d : in Direction; f : in Int)
          return Boolean;
function invert(d : in Direction) return Direction;
end TYPES;
```

The generic package body contains the bodies of the functions. *next_floor*, *is_next_floor* and *invert* contain **if** expressions that are not of type **Unit**. They are therefore translated into function bodies containing **if** statements with a **return** statement in each branch.

```
package body TYPES is
  function is_floor(f : in Int) return Boolean is
  begin
    return f >= min_floor and then f <= max_floor;
  end is_floor;

  function mk_Requirement(h : in Boolean;
                          a : in Boolean;
                          b : in Boolean) return Requirement is
  begin
    return Requirement'(here => h, after => a, before => b);
  end mk_Requirement;
```

```
function here(r : in Requirement) return Boolean is
begin
  return r.here;
end here;

function after(r : in Requirement) return Boolean is
begin
  return r.after;
end after;

function before(r : in Requirement) return Boolean is
begin
  return r.before;
end before;

function next_floor(d : in Direction; f : in Int) return Int is
begin
  if d = up then
    return f + 1;
  else
    return f - 1;
  end if;
end next_floor;

function is_next_floor(d : in Direction; f : in Int)
          return Boolean is
begin
  if d = up then
    return f < max_floor;
  else
    return f > min_floor;
  end if;
end is_next_floor;

function invert(d : in Direction) return Direction is
begin
  if d = up then
    return down;
  else
    return up;
  end if;
end invert;
end TYPES;
```

The global object T is translated into a generic package instantiation, which is quite simple as TYPES is parameterless. The resulting Ada code is the following library unit:

```
with TYPES;
package T is new TYPES;
```

5.4.2.2   Translation of C_LIFT2

In the specification of the concurrent lift presented in section 2.7.7.1, the top module is *C_LIFT2* and, even though the component modules like *C_MOTOR1* have not been translated yet, we can still translate *C_LIFT2* under the assumption that each of these used schemes are translated into generic packages.

C_LIFT2 is an unparameterized scheme which is translated into a parameterless generic package. The class expression is a hiding class expression, and the general idea is to move the declaration of hidden entities into the body.

The scheme depends on the global object T. Therefore, T is mentioned in the context clause of the the generic package declaration of C_LIFT2.

C_LIFT2 only provides values, which translate into subprogram declarations in the generic package declaration. As described in section 5.2.1.4, functions with **Unit** result are translated into procedures.

```
with T; use T;
generic
package C_LIFT2 is
   -- generators
   function check_buttons return T.Requirement;

   -- derived
   procedure next(r : in T.Requirement);

   -- initial
   procedure init;

   -- control
   procedure lift;
end C_LIFT2;
```

The generic package body contains declarative items corresponding to the hidden entities, which are three objects and two functions. In addition it contains the bodies of the subprograms declared in the generic package declaration.

The local (hidden) objects M, DS and BS are translated into generic package instantiations. Therefore the three generic packages, i.e. C_MOTOR1, C_DOORS1 and C_BUTTONS1, need to be mentioned in the context clause.

In the body of the **move** procedure the package name **M** is prefixed with **C_LIFT2** in order to avoid the conflict with the formal parameter name **m**. Alternatively, a new identifier could be chosen for the formal parameter.

The remaining subprogram bodies are very close to the corresponding RSL definitions. The only procedure that differs is **init**, where a parallel composition appears to have been sequentialized. However, as we shall see in the translation of *C_MOTOR1*, *C_DOORS1* and *C_BUTTONS1*, each of the local **init** procedures starts tasks that will run in parallel once started.

```
with C_MOTOR1;
with C_DOORS1;
with C_BUTTONS1;
with Int_Package; use Int_Package;
package body C_LIFT2 is
  package M is new C_MOTOR1;
  package DS is new C_DOORS1;
  package BS is new C_BUTTONS1;

  -- generators
  procedure move(d : in T.Direction; m : in T.Movement) is
  begin
    if m = T.halted then DS.close(C_LIFT2.M.floor); end if;
    C_LIFT2.M.move(d);
  end move;

  procedure halt is
    f : T.Floor := M.Floor;
  begin
    BS.clear(f);
    M.halt;
    DS.open(f);
  end halt;

  function check_buttons return T.Requirement is
  begin
    return BS.check(M.direction, M.floor);
  end check_buttons;

  -- derived
  procedure next(r : in T.Requirement) is
    d : T.Direction := M.direction;
  begin
    case M.movement is
      when T.halted =>
```

```
            if r.after then
              move(d, T.halted);
            elsif r.before then
              move(T.invert(d), T.halted);
            else
              null;
            end if;
          when T.moving =>
            if r.here then
              halt;
            elsif not r.after and then not r.before then
              halt;
            elsif r.after then
              move(d, T.moving);
            elsif r.before then
              move(T.invert(d), T.moving);
            end if;
        end case;
    end next;

    -- initial
    procedure init is
    begin
        M.init; DS.init; BS.init;
    end init;

    -- control
    procedure lift is
    begin
      loop
        next(check_buttons);
      end loop;
    end lift;
  end C_LIFT2;
```

5.4.2.3   Translation of C_MOTOR1

The scheme *C_MOTOR1* is translated into a generic package. Since the module involves concurrency and contains a server process with interface functions, the guidelines of section 5.3.5 are followed directly.

The package specification only needs to declare the six subprograms corresponding to the non-hidden functions.

The subtypes are needed because in Ada the subprogram name hides all other entities with the same name within its own declaration.

```
with T; use T;
generic
package C_MOTOR1 is
  -- initial
  procedure init;

  -- generators
  subtype T_Direction is T.Direction;
  procedure move(d : in T_Direction);
  procedure halt;

  -- observers
  function direction return T_Direction;
  subtype T_Floor is T.Floor;
  function floor return T_Floor;
  subtype T_Movement is T.Movement;
  function movement return T_Movement;
end C_MOTOR1;
```

The body of the C_MOTOR1 contains declarations corresponding to the hidden entities and the bodies of the subprograms. The object *V* is translated into a package
with three variables and it hence needs no body.

```
package body C_MOTOR1 is
  package V is
    direction : T.Direction;
    movement : T.Movement;
    floor : T. Floor;
  end V;

  --main
  task type motor_type is
    entry CH_direction(d : out T.Direction);
    entry CH_floor(f : out T.Floor);
    entry CH_movement(m : out T.Movement);
    entry CH_move(d : in T.Direction);
    entry CH_halt;
    entry CH_move_ack;
    entry CH_halt_ack;
  end motor_type;

  type acc_motor_type is access motor_type;
  acc_motor_var : acc_motor_type;
```

```
task body motor_type is
  d1 : T.Direction;
begin
  loop
    select
      accept CH_move(d : in T.Direction) do
        d1 := d;
      end CH_move;
      accept CH_move_ack;
      V.direction := d1;
      V.movement := T.moving;
      V.floor := T.next_floor(d1,V.floor);
    or
      accept CH_halt;
      accept CH_halt_ack;
      V.movement := T.halted;
    or
      accept CH_direction(d : out T.Direction) do
        d := V.direction;
      end CH_direction;
    or
      accept CH_movement(m : out T.Movement) do
        m := V.movement;
      end CH_movement;
    or
      accept CH_floor(f : out T.Floor) do
        f := V.floor;
      end CH_floor;
    end select;
  end loop;
end motor_type;

procedure motor is
begin
  acc_motor_var := new motor_type;
end motor;

-- initial
procedure init is
begin
  motor;
end init;
```

```
-- generators
procedure move(d : in T_Direction) is
begin
   acc_motor_var.CH_move(d); acc_motor_var.CH_move_ack;
end move;

procedure halt is
begin
   acc_motor_var.CH_halt; acc_motor_var.CH_halt_ack;
end halt;

-- observers
function direction return T_Direction is
   d : T_Direction;
begin
   acc_motor_var.CH_direction(d);
   return d;
end direction;

function floor return T_Floor is
   f : T_Floor;
begin
   acc_motor_var.CH_floor(f);
   return f;
end floor;

function movement return T_Movement is
   m : T_Movement;
begin
   acc_motor_var.CH_movement(m);
   return m;
end movement;
end C_MOTOR1;
```

5.4.2.4 Translation of C_DOORS1

The package specification only needs to declare the four subprograms corresponding to the functions.

```
with T; use T;
generic
package C_DOORS1 is
  -- initial
  procedure init;

  -- generators
  procedure open(f : in T.Floor);
  procedure close(f : in T.Floor);

  -- observer
  subtype T_Door_state is T.Door_state;
  function door_state(f : in T.Floor) return T_Door_state;
end C_DOORS1;
```

The scheme *C_DOORS1* contains an object array of *C_DOOR1*, with one door for each floor. Object arrays can be translated in two different ways, as described in section 5.2.1.2; we will follow the second approach described, namely to declare only one package for the array. This means that *C_DOOR1* is in a sense unfolded and the object array information placed within the resulting package. The translation of *C_DOOR1* is described in section 5.3.5. The main change in the package declaration of DS is that each function gets the floor number as an extra parameter.

The package body of DS contains declarations of array variables corresponding to the individual variables declared in the body of the translation of the original *C_DOOR1*; see section 5.3.5. Furthermore, we have to inform the **door_type** task which floor it is related to. This is done by introducing an **id** entry and calling it as part of starting the **door_state** task.

```
package body C_DOORS1 is
  package DS is
    procedure init(f : in T.Floor);
    procedure close(f : in T.Floor);
    procedure open(f : in T.Floor);
    function door_state(f : in T.Floor) return T_Door_state;
  end DS;

  package body DS is
    door_vars : array(T.Floor) of T.Door_state;

    task type door_type is
      entry CH_open;
      entry CH_close;
      entry CH_open_ack;
      entry CH_close_ack;
```

```
      entry CH_door_state(d : out T_Door_state);
      entry id(f : in T.Floor);
  end door_type;

  type acc_door_type is access door_type;
  acc_door_vars : array(T.Floor) of acc_door_type;

  task body door_type is
    fl : T.Floor;
  begin
    accept id(f : in T.Floor) do
      fl := f;
    end id;

    loop
      select
        accept CH_open; accept CH_open_ack;
        door_vars(fl) := T.open;
      or
        accept CH_close; accept CH_close_ack;
        door_vars(fl) := T.shut;
      or
        accept CH_door_state(d : out T_Door_state) do
          d := door_vars(fl);
        end CH_door_state;
      end select;
    end loop;
  end door_type;

  procedure door(f : in T.Floor) is
  begin
    acc_door_vars(f) := new door_type;
    acc_door_vars(f).id(f);
  end door;

  procedure init(f : in T.Floor) is
  begin
    door(f);
  end init;

  procedure close(f : in T.Floor) is
  begin
    acc_door_vars(f).CH_close; acc_door_vars(f).CH_close_ack;
  end close;
```

```
      procedure open(f : in T.Floor) is
      begin
        acc_door_vars(f).CH_open; acc_door_vars(f).CH_open_ack;
      end open;

      function door_state(f : in T.Floor) return T_Door_state is
        d_s : T_Door_state;
      begin
        acc_door_vars(f).CH_door_state(d_s);
        return d_s;
      end door_state;
    end DS;

    -- initial
    procedure init is
    begin
      for f in T.Floor loop
        DS.init(f);
      end loop;
    end init;

    -- generators
    procedure open(f : in T.Floor) is
    begin
      DS.open(f);
    end open;

    procedure close(f : in T.Floor) is
    begin
      DS.close(f);
    end close;

    -- observer
    function door_state(f : in T.Floor) return T_Door_state is
    begin
      return DS.door_state(f);
    end door_state;
  end C_DOORS1;
```

Exercise 1 Translate the module *C_BUTTONS1* into Ada. The structure should be similar to that of *C_DOORS1* and *C_MOTOR1*.

Exercise 2 Translate the examples of this chapter into another programming language that you are familiar with.

Part III

Appendices

Standard specifications

This section presents abstract specifications of some common data types. Each data type X has three abstract specifications: applicative sequential A_X, imperative sequential L_X and imperative concurrent C_X.

Some of these specifications could have been defined in terms of others (by extension, hiding and renaming). For example, bags could be defined in terms of maps; stacks and queues in terms of lists. This has not been done because it would make thing more obscure. Bags, for example, have their own particular characteristics; defining them in terms of maps tends to hide these.

A.1 Parameter schemes

We first define some standard schemes to be used as parameters:

scheme ELEM = **class type** Elem **end**

scheme ELEM_BOUND = **extend** ELEM **with class value** bound : **Nat** • bound $>$ 0 **end**

scheme ELEM_FINITE =
  extend ELEM **with**
  class axiom [elem_finite] **card** { e | e : Elem } **post true end**

scheme ELEM_NON_EMPTY =
  extend ELEM **with**
  class axiom [elem_non_empty] ∃ e : Elem • **true end**

scheme ARRAY_PARM =
  class
    type Elem
    value min, max : **Int**
    axiom [array_not_empty] max $\geq$ min
  end

scheme ARRAY_PARM_INIT = **extend** ARRAY_PARM **with class value** init : Elem **end**

PARTIAL_ORDER and hence *LINEAR_ORDER* (defined as an extension of *PARTIAL_ORDER*) include as well as an ordering relation *leq* an abstract equality *eql* defined in terms of *leq*. This means that ordered collections (defined later with *LINEAR_ORDER* as a parameter) can be used both to implement sets of elements with a linear order on the element type (with *leq* instantiated as the order and *eql* as the predefined equality) and to implement maps with a linear order on the domain type (with *Elem* instantiated as pairs of domain and range elements, *leq* as the order and *eql* as the predefined equality on the domain components of the pairs).

scheme PARTIAL_ORDER =
  extend ELEM **with**
    class
      value
        leq : Elem × Elem → **Bool**,
        eql : Elem × Elem → **Bool**
        eql(a, b) ≡ leq(a, b) ∧ leq(b, a)
      axiom
        [reflexive] ∀ a : Elem • leq(a, a),
        [transitive] ∀ a, b, c : Elem • leq(a, b) ∧ leq(b, c) ⇒ leq(a, c)
    end

scheme LINEAR_ORDER =
  extend PARTIAL_ORDER **with**
  class axiom [linear] ∀ a, b : Elem • leq(a, b) ∨ leq(b, a) **end**

A.2   Sets

All these sets are unbounded. Bounded versions could be constructed analogously to the queues in appendix A.8.

Applicative

scheme A_SET(E : ELEM) =
  class
    type Set
    value
      /* generators */
      empty : Set,
      add : E.Elem × Set → Set,
      remove : E.Elem × Set → Set,
      /* observer */
      is_in : E.Elem × Set → **Bool**
    axiom
      [is_in_empty] ∀ e : E.Elem • ∼ is_in(e, empty),
      [is_in_add] ∀ s : Set, e, e′ : E.Elem • is_in(e′, add(e, s)) ≡ e = e′ ∨ is_in(e′, s),
      [is_in_remove] ∀ s : Set, e, e′ : E.Elem • is_in(e′, remove(e, s)) ≡ e ≠ e′ ∧ is_in(e′, s)
  end

Imperative

scheme I_SET(E : ELEM) =
  class
    value
      /* generators */
      empty : **Unit** → **write any Unit**,
      add : E.Elem → **write any Unit**,
      remove : E.Elem → **write any Unit**,
      /* observer */
      is_in : E.Elem → **read any Bool**

axiom
 [is_in_empty] ∀ e : E.Elem • empty() ; is_in(e) ≡ empty() ; **false**,
 [is_in_add]
   ∀ e, e' : E.Elem • add(e) ; is_in(e') ≡ **let** b = is_in(e') **in** add(e) ; e = e' ∨ b **end**,
 [is_in_remove]
   ∀ e, e' : E.Elem • remove(e) ; is_in(e') ≡ **let** b = is_in(e') **in** remove(e) ; e ≠ e' ∧ b **end**,
 [initial] **initialise** ≡ **initialise** ; empty()
end

Concurrent

scheme C_SET(E : ELEM) =
 hide I, main **in**
 class
   object I : I_SET(E)
   value
     main : **Unit** → **in any out any write any Unit**,
     /∗ initial ∗/
     init : **Unit** → **in any out any write any Unit**
     init() ≡ I.empty() ; main(),
     /∗ generators ∗/
     empty : **Unit** → **in any out any Unit**,
     add : E.Elem → **in any out any Unit**,
     remove : E.Elem → **in any out any Unit**,
     /∗ observer ∗/
     is_in : E.Elem ⇀ **in any out any Bool**
   axiom
     [empty_ax] main() ∥ empty() ≡ I.empty() ; main(),
     [add_ax] ∀ e : E.Elem • main() ∥ add(e) ≡ I.add(e) ; main(),
     [remove_ax] ∀ e : E.Elem • main() ∥ remove(e) ≡ I.remove(e) ; main(),
     [is_in_ax]
       ∀ e : E.Elem, test : **Bool** $\xrightarrow{\sim}$ **Unit** •
         main() ∥ test(is_in(e)) ≡ **let** b = I.is_in(e) **in** main() ∥ test(b) **end**
 end

A.3 Bags

Bags, sometimes called multisets, allow multiple copies of elements. All these bags are bounded. Unbounded versions could be constructed analogously to the sets in appendix A.2.

Note that the bound is on the number of different elements in the bag, not on the total of their counts. This seems sensible in view of the likely implementations.

Applicative

scheme A_BAG(E : ELEM_BOUND) =
 class
   type Bag
   value
     /∗ generators ∗/
     empty : Bag,
     add : E.Elem × Bag $\xrightarrow{\sim}$ Bag,

remove : E.Elem × Bag $\overset{\sim}{\to}$ Bag,
/* observer */
count : E.Elem × Bag → **Nat**,
/* derived observer */
can_add : E.Elem × Bag → **Bool**
can_add(e, b) ≡
  card { e | e : E.Elem • count(e, b) > 0 } < E.bound ∨ count(e, b) > 0
axiom
  [count_empty] ∀ e : E.Elem • count(e, empty) ≡ 0,
  [count_add]
    ∀ b : Bag, e, e' : E.Elem •
      count(e', add(e, b)) ≡ **if** e = e' **then** count(e', b) + 1 **else** count(e', b) **end**
      pre can_add(e, b),
  [count_remove]
    ∀ b : Bag, e, e' : E.Elem •
      count(e', remove(e, b)) ≡ **if** e = e' **then** count(e', b) − 1 **else** count(e', b) **end**
      pre count(e, b) > 0,
  [add_defined] ∀ b : Bag, e : E.Elem • add(e, b) **post true pre** can_add(e, b),
  [remove_defined] ∀ b : Bag, e : E.Elem • remove(e, b) **post true pre** count(e, b) > 0
end

Imperative

scheme I_BAG(E : ELEM_BOUND) =
  class
    value
      /* generators */
      empty : **Unit** → **write any Unit**,
      add : E.Elem $\overset{\sim}{\to}$ **write any Unit**,
      remove : E.Elem $\overset{\sim}{\to}$ **write any Unit**,
      /* observer */
      count : E.Elem → **read any Nat**,
      /* derived observer */
      can_add : E.Elem → **read any Bool**
      can_add(e) ≡
        card { e | e : E.Elem • count(e) > 0 } < E.bound ∨ count(e) > 0
    axiom
      [count_empty] ∀ e : E.Elem • empty() ; count(e) ≡ empty() ; 0,
      [count_add]
        ∀ e, e' : E.Elem •
          add(e) ; count(e') ≡
            let n = count(e') **in if** e = e' **then** add(e) ; n + 1 **else** add(e) ; n **end end**
          pre can_add(e),
      [count_remove]
        ∀ e, e' : E.Elem •
          remove(e) ; count(e') ≡
            let n = count(e') **in**
              if e = e' **then** remove(e) ; n − 1 **else** remove(e) ; n **end**
            end
          pre count(e) > 0,
      [add_defined] ∀ e : E.Elem • add(e) **post true pre** can_add(e),

[remove_defined] ∀ e : E.Elem • remove(e) **post true pre** count(e) > 0,
[initial] **initialise** ≡ **initialise** ; empty()
end

Concurrent

scheme C_BAG(E : ELEM_BOUND) =
  hide I, main **in**
  class
    object I : I_BAG(E)
    value
      main : **Unit → in any out any write any Unit**,
      /* initial */
      init : **Unit → in any out any write any Unit**
      init() ≡ I.empty() ; main(),
      /* generators */
      empty : **Unit → in any out any Unit**,
      add : E.Elem **→ in any out any Unit**,
      remove : E.Elem **→ in any out any Unit**,
      /* observers */
      count : E.Elem **→ in any out any Nat**,
      can_add : E.Elem **→ in any out any Bool**
    axiom
      [empty_ax] main() ‖ empty() ≡ I.empty() ; main(),
      [add_ax] ∀ e : E.Elem • main() ‖ add(e) ≡ I.add(e) ; main() **pre** I.can_add(e),
      [remove_ax]
        ∀ e : E.Elem • main() ‖ remove(e) ≡ I.remove(e) ; main() **pre** I.count(e) > 0,
      [count_ax]
        ∀ e : E.Elem, test : **Nat** $\xrightarrow{\sim}$ **Unit** •
          main() ‖ test(count(e)) ≡ **let** n = I.count(e) **in** main() ‖ test(n) **end**,
      [can_add_ax]
        ∀ e : E.Elem, test : **Bool** $\xrightarrow{\sim}$ **Unit** •
          main() ‖ test(can_add(e)) ≡ **let** b = I.can_add(e) **in** main() ‖ test(b) **end**
  end

A.4 Lists

All these lists are unbounded. Bounded versions could be constructed analogously to the queues in appendix A.8.

Applicative

scheme A_LIST(E : ELEM) =
  hide list_of **in**
  class
    type List
    value
      /* generators */
      empty : List,
      cons : E.Elem × List → List,
      tail : List $\xrightarrow{\sim}$ List,

/* hidden observer */
list_of : List → E.Elem*,
/* derived observers */
is_empty : List → **Bool**
is_empty(l) ≡ list_of(l) = ⟨⟩,
head : List $\xrightarrow{\sim}$ E.Elem
head(l) ≡ **hd** list_of(l) **pre** ∼ is_empty(l)
axiom
[list_of_empty] list_of(empty) ≡ ⟨⟩,
[list_of_cons] ∀ e : E.Elem, l : List • list_of(cons(e, l)) ≡ ⟨e⟩ ⌢ list_of(l),
[list_of_tail] ∀ l : List • list_of(tail(l)) ≡ **tl** list_of(l) **pre** ∼ is_empty(l),
[tail_defined] ∀ l : List • tail(l) **post true pre** ∼ is_empty(l)
end

Imperative

scheme I_LIST(E : ELEM) =
hide list_of **in**
class
value
/* generators */
empty : **Unit** → **write any Unit**,
cons : E.Elem → **write any Unit**,
tail : **Unit** $\xrightarrow{\sim}$ **write any Unit**,
/* hidden observer */
list_of : **Unit** → **read any** E.Elem*,
/* derived observers */
is_empty : **Unit** → **read any Bool**
is_empty() ≡ list_of() = ⟨⟩,
head : **Unit** $\xrightarrow{\sim}$ **read any** E.Elem
head() ≡ **hd** list_of() **pre** ∼ is_empty()
axiom
[list_of_empty] empty() ; list_of() ≡ empty() ; ⟨⟩,
[list_of_cons]
∀ e : E.Elem • cons(e) ; list_of() ≡ **let** l = list_of() **in** cons(e) ; ⟨e⟩ ⌢ l **end**,
[list_of_tail] tail() ; list_of() ≡ **let** l = list_of() **in** tail() ; **tl** l **end pre** ∼ is_empty(),
[tail_defined] tail() **post true pre** ∼ is_empty(),
[initial] **initialise post** is_empty()
end

Concurrent

scheme C_LIST(E : ELEM) =
hide I, main **in**
class
object I : I_LIST(E)
value
main : **Unit** → **in any out any write any Unit**,
/* initial */
init : **Unit** → **in any out any write any Unit**
init() ≡ I.empty() ; main(),

```
      /* generators */
      empty : Unit → in any out any Unit,
      cons : E.Elem → in any out any Unit,
      tail : Unit → in any out any Unit,
      /* observers */
      is_empty : Unit → in any out any Bool,
      head : Unit → in any out any E.Elem
   axiom
      [empty_ax] main() ‖ empty() ≡ I.empty() ; main(),
      [cons_ax] ∀ e : E.Elem • main() ‖ cons(e) ≡ I.cons(e) ; main(),
      [tail_ax] main() ‖ tail() ≡ I.tail() ; main() pre ∼ I.is_empty(),
      [is_empty_ax]
         ∀ test : Bool ⥲ Unit •
            main() ‖ test(is_empty()) ≡ let b = I.is_empty() in main() ‖ test(b) end,
      [head_ax]
         ∀ test : E.Elem ⥲ Unit •
            main() ‖ test(head()) ≡ let e = I.head() in main() ‖ test(e) end
            pre ∼ I.is_empty()
end
```

A.5 Maps

All these maps are unbounded. Bounded versions could be constructed analogously to the queues in appendix A.8.

Applicative

```
scheme A_MAP(D : ELEM, R : ELEM) =
   class
      type Map
      value
         /* generators */
         empty : Map,
         add : D.Elem × R.Elem × Map → Map,
         remove : D.Elem × Map → Map,
         /* observers */
         is_in : D.Elem × Map → Bool,
         apply : D.Elem × Map ⥲ R.Elem
      axiom
         [is_in_empty] ∀ d : D.Elem • ∼ is_in(d, empty),
         [is_in_add]
            ∀ m : Map, d, d' : D.Elem, r : R.Elem •
               is_in(d', add(d, r, m)) ≡ d = d' ∨ is_in(d', m),
         [is_in_remove]
            ∀ m : Map, d, d' : D.Elem • is_in(d', remove(d, m)) ≡ d ≠ d' ∧ is_in(d', m),
         /* apply_empty not specified */
         [apply_add]
            ∀ m : Map, d, d' : D.Elem, r : R.Elem •
               apply(d', add(d, r, m)) ≡ if d = d' then r else apply(d', m) end
               pre d = d' ∨ is_in(d', m),
```

[apply_remove]
  ∀ m : Map, d, d′ : D.Elem •
    apply(d′, remove(d, m)) ≡ apply(d′, m) **pre** d ≠ d′ ∧ is_in(d′, m),
[apply_defined] ∀ m : Map, d : D.Elem • apply(d, m) **post true pre** is_in(d, m)
end

Imperative

scheme I_MAP(D : ELEM, R : ELEM) =
  class
    value
      /∗ generators ∗/
      empty : **Unit** → **write any Unit**,
      add : D.Elem × R.Elem → **write any Unit**,
      remove : D.Elem → **write any Unit**,
      /∗ observers ∗/
      is_in : D.Elem → **read any Bool**,
      apply : D.Elem $\xrightarrow{\sim}$ **read any** R.Elem
    axiom
      [is_in_empty] ∀ d : D.Elem • empty() ; is_in(d) ≡ empty() ; **false**,
      [is_in_add]
        ∀ d, d′ : D.Elem, r : R.Elem •
          add(d, r) ; is_in(d′) ≡ **let** b = is_in(d′) **in** add(d, r) ; d = d′ ∨ b **end**,
      [is_in_remove]
        ∀ d, d′ : D.Elem •
          remove(d) ; is_in(d′) ≡ **let** b = is_in(d′) **in** remove(d) ; d ≠ d′ ∧ b **end**,
      /∗ apply_empty not specified ∗/
      [apply_add]
        ∀ d, d′ : D.Elem, r : R.Elem •
          add(d, r) ; apply(d′) ≡
            if d = d′ **then** add(d, r) ; r **else let** r′ = apply(d′) **in** add(d, r) ; r′ **end end**
          pre d = d′ ∨ is_in(d′),
      [apply_remove]
        ∀ d, d′ : D.Elem •
          remove(d) ; apply(d′) ≡ **let** r = apply(d′) **in** remove(d) ; r **end**
          pre d ≠ d′ ∧ is_in(d′),
      [apply_defined] ∀ d : D.Elem • apply(d) **post true pre** is_in(d),
      [initial] **initialise** ≡ **initialise** ; empty()
  end

Concurrent

scheme C_MAP(D : ELEM, R : ELEM) =
  hide I, main **in**
  class
    object I : I_MAP(D, R)
    value
      main : **Unit** → **in any out any write any Unit**,
      /∗ initial ∗/
      init : **Unit** → **in any out any write any Unit**
      init() ≡ I.empty() ; main(),

/* generators */
empty : **Unit** → **in any out any Unit**,
add : D.Elem × R.Elem → **in any out any Unit**,
remove : D.Elem → **in any out any Unit**,
/* observers */
is_in : D.Elem → **in any out any Bool**,
apply : D.Elem → **in any out any** R.Elem
axiom
[empty_ax] main() ∦ empty() ≡ I.empty() ; main(),
[add_ax] ∀ d : D.Elem, r : R.Elem • main() ∦ add(d, r) ≡ I.add(d, r) ; main(),
[remove_ax] ∀ d : D.Elem • main() ∦ remove(d) ≡ I.remove(d) ; main(),
[is_in_ax]
  ∀ d : D.Elem, test : **Bool** $\xrightarrow{\sim}$ **Unit** •
    main() ∦ test(is_in(d)) ≡ **let** b = I.is_in(d) **in** main() ∦ test(b) **end**,
[apply_ax]
  ∀ d : D.Elem, test : R.Elem $\xrightarrow{\sim}$ **Unit** •
    main() ∦ test(apply(d)) ≡ **let** r = I.apply(d) **in** main() ∦ test(r) **end**
    pre I.is_in(d)
end

A.6 Arrays

Arrays are bounded, with indexes in a (non-empty) range from integers *min* to *max* inclusive.

Applicative: uninitialised

scheme A_ARRAY(P : ARRAY_PARM) =
  class
    type Array, Index = {| i : **Int** • i ≥ P.min ∧ i ≤ P.max |}
    value
      /* generator */
      change : Index × P.Elem × Array → Array,
      /* observer */
      apply : Index × Array $\xrightarrow{\sim}$ P.Elem
    axiom
      [apply_change]
        ∀ i, i′ : Index, e : P.Elem, a : Array •
          apply(i′, change(i, e, a)) ≡ **if** i = i′ **then** e **else** apply(i′, a) **end**
  end

Applicative: initialised

scheme A_ARRAY_INIT(P : ARRAY_PARM_INIT) =
  extend A_ARRAY(P) **with**
  class
    value
      /* generator */
      init : Array
    axiom
      [apply_init] ∀ i : Index • apply(i, init) ≡ P.init,
      [apply_total] ∀ i : Index, a : Array • apply(i, a) **post true**
  end

Imperative: uninitialised

scheme I_ARRAY(P : ARRAY_PARM) =
  class
    type Index = {| i : **Int** • i $\geq$ P.min $\wedge$ i $\leq$ P.max |}
    value
      /* generator */
      change : Index $\times$ P.Elem $\rightarrow$ **write any Unit**,
      /* observer */
      apply : Index $\xrightarrow{\sim}$ **read any** P.Elem
    axiom
      [apply_change]
        $\forall$ i, i$'$: Index, e : P.Elem •
          change(i, e) ; apply(i$'$) $\equiv$
          if i = i$'$ **then** change(i, e) ; e **else let** e$'$ = apply(i$'$) **in** change(i, e) ; e$'$ **end end**
  end

Imperative: initialised

scheme I_ARRAY_INIT(P : ARRAY_PARM_INIT) =
  extend I_ARRAY(P) **with**
  class
    value
      /* initial */
      init : **Unit** $\rightarrow$ **write any Unit**
    axiom
      [apply_init] $\forall$ i : Index • init() ; apply(i) $\equiv$ init() ; P.init,
      [apply_total] $\forall$ i : Index • apply(i) **post true**,
      [initial] **initialise** $\equiv$ **initialise** ; init()
  end

Concurrent: uninitialised

scheme C_ARRAY(P : ARRAY_PARM) =
  hide I, main **in**
  class
    object I : I_ARRAY(P)
    type Index = I.Index
    value
      main : **Unit** $\rightarrow$ **in any out any write any Unit**,
      /* initial */
      init : **Unit** $\rightarrow$ **in any out any write any Unit**
      init() $\equiv$ I.**initialise** ; main(),
      /* generator */
      change : Index $\times$ P.Elem $\rightarrow$ **in any out any Unit**,
      /* observer */
      apply : Index $\rightarrow$ **in any out any** P.Elem
    axiom
      [change_ax] $\forall$ i : Index, e : P.Elem • main() $\parallel$ change(i, e) $\equiv$ I.change(i, e) ; main(),

[apply_ax]
  ∀ i : Index, test : P.Elem $\xrightarrow{\sim}$ **Unit** •
    main() $\Vert$ test(apply(i)) ≡ **let** e = I.apply(i) **in** main() $\Vert$ test(e) **end**
end

Concurrent: initialised

C_ARRAY_INIT is obtained from *C_ARRAY* by replacing the parameter *ARRAY_PARM* with *ARRAY_PARM_INIT* and the instantiation of *I_ARRAY* with an instantiation of *I_ARRAY_INIT*.

A.7 Stacks

All these stacks are unbounded. Bounded versions could be constructed analogously to the queues in appendix A.8.

Applicative

scheme A_STACK (E : ELEM) =
  hide list_of **in**
  class
    type Stack
    value
      /* generators */
      empty : Stack,
      push : E.Elem × Stack → Stack,
      pop : Stack $\xrightarrow{\sim}$ E.Elem × Stack,
      /* hidden observer */
      list_of : Stack → E.Elem*,
      /* derived observer */
      is_empty : Stack → **Bool**
      is_empty(l) ≡ list_of(l) = ⟨⟩
    axiom
      [list_of_empty] list_of(empty) ≡ ⟨⟩,
      [list_of_push] ∀ e : E.Elem, l : Stack • list_of(push(e, l)) ≡ ⟨e⟩ ⌢ list_of(l),
      [pop_ax]
        ∀ l : Stack •
          pop(l) **as** (e, l′) **post** e = **hd** list_of(l) ∧ list_of(l′) = **tl** list_of(l)
          pre ∼ is_empty(l)
  end

Imperative

scheme I_STACK(E : ELEM) =
  hide list_of **in**
  class
    value
      /* generators */
      empty : **Unit** → **write any Unit**,
      push : E.Elem → **write any Unit**,
      pop : **Unit** $\xrightarrow{\sim}$ **write any** E.Elem,
      /* hidden observer */
      list_of : **Unit** → **read any** E.Elem*,

```
                /* derived observer */
                is_empty : Unit → read any Bool
                is_empty() ≡ list_of() = ⟨⟩
            axiom
                [list_of_empty] empty() ; list_of() ≡ empty() ; ⟨⟩,
                [list_of_push]
                    ∀ e : E.Elem • push(e) ; list_of() ≡ let l = list_of() in push(e) ; ⟨e⟩ ⌢ l end,
                [pop_ax]
                    let l = list_of() in pop() as e post e = hd l ∧ list_of() = tl l pre ∼ is_empty() end,
                [initial] initialise post is_empty()
            end
```

Concurrent

```
scheme C_STACK(E : ELEM) =
    hide I, main in
    class
        object I : I_STACK(E)
        value
            main : Unit → in any out any write any Unit,
            /* initial */
            init : Unit → in any out any write any Unit
            init() ≡ I.empty() ; main(),
            /* generators */
            empty : Unit → in any out any Unit,
            push : E.Elem → in any out any Unit,
            pop : Unit → in any out any E.Elem,
            /* observer */
            is_empty : Unit → in any out any Bool
        axiom
            [empty_ax] main() ∦ empty() ≡ I.empty() ; main(),
            [push_ax] ∀ e : E.Elem • main() ∦ push(e) ≡ I.push(e) ; main(),
            [pop_ax]
                ∀ test : E.Elem ⥲ Unit •
                    main() ∦ test(pop()) ≡ let e = I.pop() in main() ∦ test(e) end
                    pre ∼ I.is_empty(),
            [is_empty_ax]
                ∀ test : Bool ⥲ Unit •
                    main() ∦ test(is_empty()) ≡ let b = I.is_empty() in main() ∦ test(b) end
    end
```

A.8   Queues

See the tutorial in chapter 2. The applicative, imperative and concurrent abstract queues can be found in sections 2.8.4.1, 2.8.5.1 and 2.8.6.1 respectively. All these queues are bounded. Unbounded versions could be constructed analogously to the unbounded stacks in appendix A.7.

Proof rules

B.1 Introduction

This appendix is concerned with the formal machinery by which we can do justifications. In the next section we define the syntax and meanings of proof rules. Then section B.3 gives the rules for instantiating term variables in rules and section B.4 describes the special functions used in the rules.

Section B.5 describes the organization of the proof rules and how they are named. Section B.6 gives the basic rules for type and value expressions and typings, and section B.7 a number of rules derivable from the basic ones.

Section B.8 presents a number of proof rules about class expressions and in particular defines a function **properties** and the RSL implementation relation.

Section B.9 adds some additional rules that express justification tactics not expressed in the meta language for proof rules.

The **properties** of class expressions in the context of a justification allows us to derive context rules. The derivation of some useful context rules is presented in section B.10.

In total this appendix describes an axiomatic semantics of well-formed RSL specifications. (The formation rules, the static semantics, are described in the book on RSL [23].)

B.2 Syntax and meaning of the logical system

In this section we present first the syntax and meaning of proof rules. Then we add theorems and development relations.

B.2.1 Proof rules

Syntax

```
inference_rule ::=
  opt-sequent-list
  sequent
  opt-applicability_condition

sequent ::=
  context ⊢ assertion |
  assertion
```

context ::=
  assumption-list

assumption ::=
  class_expr |
  decl |
  axiom_assumption

axiom_assumption ::=
  [id] assertion

assertion ::=
  readonly_logical-value_expr

equivalence_rule ::=
  equivalence *opt*-applicability_condition

equivalence ::=
  value_equivalence |
  type_equivalence |
  typing_equivalence

value_equivalence ::=
  value_expr $\simeq$ value_expr

type_equivalence ::=
  type_expr $\simeq$ type_expr

typing_equivalence ::=
  typing $\simeq$ typing

applicability_condition ::=
  when assertion

The assertions in inference_rules and equivalence_rules may include applications of special functions. Special functions are described in section B.4. We do not extend the syntax for them since they can always be expanded into RSL terms; see section B.4 for details.

Identifiers in inference_rules and equivalence_rules that are free or declared in the rule are interpreted as term variables. Term variables are described in section B.3.

Context-independent Expansions

A sequent of the form assertion is short for **class end** $\vdash$ assertion.

A sequent of the form

assumption-list $\vdash$ ro_eb

is short for

assumption-list $\vdash$ $\square$ ro_eb

In other words, the logical value expressions in sequents hold in all states.

An assumption of the form decl is short for **class** decl **end**.

An assumption of the form

[id] ro_eb

is short for

class axiom [id] ro_eb **end**

An inference_rule of the form

$\dfrac{opt\text{-sequent-list}}{\text{sequent}}$
when ro_eb

is short for

$\dfrac{\text{ro\_eb,}\quad opt\text{-sequent-list}}{\text{sequent}}$

When an inference_rule has no sequents above the line, the line is omitted, giving a rule of the form

sequent *opt*-applicability_condition

In an inference_rule there may be a common context shared by all the sequents in it (after expanding any applicability_condition). For brevity and convenience this shared context is not mentioned explicitly in any of the sequents.

An equivalence_rule of the form

e $\simeq$ e$'$ **when** ro_eb

is short for the inference_rule (with no sequents above the line)

$\square$ ((ro_eb $\equiv$ **true**) $\Rightarrow$ (e $\equiv$ e$'$))

In other words, equivalence rules hold in all states in which their applicability conditions hold.

A equivalence_rule of the form

e $\simeq$ e$'$

is short for

e $\simeq$ e$'$ **when true**

A type_equivalence of the form

T $\simeq$ T$'$

is short for the value_equivalence

{id | id : T} $\simeq$ {id | id : T$'$}

Scope and Visibility Rules

The scope of each class_expr in a context of a sequent extends to any class expressions to its right and to the assertion.

In an inference_rule, assumptions common to all the sequents can be omitted from the rule. In an equivalence_rule, the expressions and the assertion in the applicability_condition are always evaluated in the same context, which is therefore omitted from the rule.

Context Conditions

An assertion must have the maximal type **Bool**.

Attributes

The maximal type of a sequent is Bool. A sequent statically accesses no variables or channels.

Meaning

An inference_rule of the form

context$_0$ ⊢ ro_eb$_0$

...

$$\frac{\text{context}_{n-1} \vdash \text{ro\_eb}_{n-1}}{\text{context}_n \vdash \text{ro\_eb}_n}$$

means "if

- for $0 \leq i \leq n$ any term variables in *context$_i$* ⊢ *ro_eb$_i$* are consistently instantiated and any special function applications expanded, and

- for $0 \leq i < j \leq n$ the instantiations of any term variables in *context$_j$* ⊢ *ro_eb$_j$* are consistent with the instantiations of any term variables in *context$_i$* ⊢ *ro_eb$_i$*, and

- for $0 \leq i \leq n-1$, the instantiated *ro_eb$_i$* is proved in instantiated *context$_i$* and for all states

then in instantiated *context$_n$* and for all states, instantiated *ro_eb$_n$* is proved."

The rules for instantiating term variables, and doing so consistently, are described in section B.3. The expansions of special functions are described in section B.4.

Congruence properties

An equivalence_rule allows one expression to be substituted for another whenever the assertion in the applicability_condition holds.

This does not in general hold for the arguments of special functions; see section B.4 for details.

B.2.2 Theorems and development relations

It is necessary in development to name and record *development relations* between modules. It is also useful to be able to name and record *theorems* about modules. Development relations and theorems are essentially named sequents; development relations typically mention implementation relations, and we also allow theorems to do so.

Syntax

development_relation_def ::=
  development_relation [id] meta_sequent

theorem_def ::=
  theorem [id] meta_sequent

meta_sequent, an extension of sequent to include implementation relations, is defined in section B.8.3.

Context Conditions

development_relation_defs and theorem_defs may not contain any term variables or applications of special functions.

Theorems and development relations provide named context rules, as described in section 4.3.2.2.

B.3   Rules for instantiation of term variables

A *term variable* is an identifier that is either free or declared within a proof rule. Term variables are *instantiated* (i.e. replaced) by actual terms when rules are instantiated. A term variable cannot be instantiated with an arbitrary term — there are restrictions on

- the syntactic category
- certain static properties (like maximal type)

of the actual term.

These restrictions are implicitly given by the names of the term variables, as explained below.

pure prefix	read-only prefix	name	syntactic category and static properties
		ce, ceo, ces, cex	class_expr
		decl	decl
		decls	opt-decl-string
		T, Td, Tr, Tv	type_expr
		a	opt-access_desc-string
p_	ro_	e	value_expr
p_	ro_	eu	*unit*-value_expr
p_	ro_	eb	*logical*-value_expr
p_	ro_	ei	*integer*-value_expr
p_	ro_	er	*real*-value_expr
p_	ro_	es	*set*-value_expr
p_	ro_	el	*list*-value_expr
p_	ro_	em	*map*-value_expr
p_	ro_	ef	*function*-value_expr
p_	ro_	efu	*function-with_unit_domain*-value_expr
p_		e_pair	value_expr_pair
		literal	value_literal
		infix_op	infix_op
		prefix_op	prefix_op
		b, bm, bp	binding
		ip	inner_pattern
		id	id
		q	*element*-object_expr
		Tid	*type*-id
		v	*variable*-id
		c	*channel*-id
		cu	*unit-channel*-id
		S	*scheme*-id
		O	*object*-id
		ch	char_character

Table B.1: Names of term variables and their syntactic category and some of their static properties

A name in its basic form consists of a name of a syntactic category (like *pattern*) or a string of letters (like *e* and *es*), possibly preceded by a prefix *p_* or *ro_*, and possibly followed by a suffix which is either numeric (as in *e1*) or consists of one or more primes (as in *es'*). A name can also be in one of the composite forms *opt_n*, *n_string*, *n_list*, *n_list2*, *n_choice*, *n_choice2*, *n_product*, *n_product2* and *opt_n_list*, where *n* is a basic name.

The syntactic restrictions are:

- If the name of a term variable is basic and (ignoring *p_* and *ro_*) starts with a name of a syntactic category, it can only be instantiated with terms of that syntactic category.

- If the name of a term variable is basic and (ignoring *p_* and *ro_*) starts with a string of characters, table B.1 shows what the required syntactic category is. For example, for *ce* the required syntactic category is class_expr.

- If the name of a term variable is composite, the required syntactic category is found by replacing the basic name occurring in it with its required syntactic category and replacing the underscores with hyphens, e.g. the required syntactic category of *opt_el_list* is *opt-*value_expr-*list*.

The static restrictions are:

- Some term variables have certain static properties, as indicated with italics in table B.1, and can only be instantiated with actual terms having these properties.

- Term variables prefixed *p_* or *ro_* may only be instantiated with actual terms that are pure or read-only respectively. Term variables with which these prefixes may be used are indicated in table B.1. (Note that expr_pairs are already read-only by definition.)

- Term variables of a rule must be instantiated consistently, i.e.:

  – Multiple occurrences of the same term variable must be instantiated with the same actual term.
  – Term variables (like *e* and *e'*) of syntactic category *value_expr* only differing in the number of primes in their names must be instantiated with value expressions having the same maximal type. (Note that there are no such requirements for term variables (like *e*, *e1* and *e2*) only differing in the numeric suffices.)
  – If *e* is instantiated with a value expression having a maximal type T, then any term variable *es* must be instantiated with a value expression having the maximal type T-**infset**, and any term variable *el* must be instantiated with a value expression having the maximal type T^ω.

B.4   Special functions used in proof rules

This section describes in alphabetic order a number of *special functions* used in the proof rules, mostly in applicability conditions.

For each special function, its type is given, and its evaluation is described either informally or by rules defining it.

In section B.2 we made the claim that the special functions do not add to the possible RSL expressions. This is ensured by defining all these special functions in terms of expansion rules, i.e. these functions are in effect macros. Then there will be no enlargement of RSL provided all such expansions can always be done when the term variables are instantiated, and produce expressions not involving special functions. The expansions may use

- case analysis of the structure of arguments

- equality between syntactic terms

- recursion over the structure of arguments (since the finiteness of terms makes such recursion well-founded)

- information from the static context, in particular

    - the maximal types of value, variable and channel names
    - the accesses of function names
    - the type expressions for which non-sort type names are abbreviations
    - the syntactic structures of formal parameters and defining classes for schemes[1]

Special functions must be evaluated without the application of any proof rules to their arguments. Proof rules such as those allowing renaming, or context rules such as those allowing folding and unfolding, could otherwise typically change their meaning. Hence the instantiation of proof rules must, after the instantiation of term variables, also include the complete expansion of all special function applications.

are_different

are_different : name × name → *logical*-value_expr

are_different(name1, name2) is equivalent to **true** only if name1 and name2 denote different entities.

are_different is defined by the rules

are_different(**express**(b1), **express**(b2)) ≃ **disjoint**(b1, b2)

are_different(q1.id1, q2.id2) ≃ **are_different**(q1, q2) ∨ **are_different**(id1, id2)

are_different(id1[p_e1], id2[p_e2]) ≃ **are_different**(id1, id2) ∨ p_e1 ≠ p_e2

An extension of **are_different** to deal with sets of accesses is used in the expansion of **assignment_disjoint**. Sets of accesses are different if the sets are disjoint, i.e. if each member of one set is different from each of those in the other set. Completed accesses are different if neither qualification is a prefix of the other. For example

are_different(O.**any**, O.O1.**any**) = **false**

are_different(O1.**any**, O2.O3.**any**) = **are_different**(O1, O2)

A name is different from a completed access if its qualification is not a prefix of the qualification of the completed access. For example

are_different(v, **any**) = **false**

are_different(O1.v, O2.**any**) = **are_different**(O1, O2)

Comprehended accesses are handled similarly. For example

are_different(O1[p_e].v, {O2.[i].**any** | i : T • p_eb}) =
are_different(O1, O2) ∨ p_e ∉ {i | i : T • p_eb}

Whether a qualified name or access is different from an unqualified completed access **any** depends on whether the first object name in the qualification is that of an object defined in the scope of the **any** (an embedded object), when it is not different, or that of an object defined elsewhere (a parameter or a global object), when it is different.

---

[1]The last two items might seem surprising as they seem to involve unfolding, but unfolding is statically calculable for non-sort type names and scheme names. It is not, for example, for functions. We include these two items purely for convenience in **is_maximal** (to make its expansion necessary as well as sufficient) and in **no_hiding** and **no_scheme_defs** (to avoid having to unfold all scheme instantiations before applying these functions).

assignment_disjoint

> **assignment_disjoint** : value_expr × value_expr → *logical*-value_expr

assignment_disjoint(e1, e2) is equivalent to **true** only if neither of the value expressions can write to variables that can be read (or written to) by the other. It is used when the evaluation order changes. For example

> v := 1 ; u := v ≡ u := v ; v := 1

is generally false, since u will receive the value 1 in the first expression but not necessarily in the second.

assignment_disjoint(e1, e2) is defined in terms of **are_different** applied to the possible read accesses of *e1* and the possible write accesses of *e2*, and vice versa. Possible accesses are actual accesses (mentions of a variable name) and access rights from the signatures of functions that are applied.

convergent

> **convergent** : value_expr → *logical*-value_expr

convergent is defined by the rule

> **convergent**(e) ≃ e **post true**

convergent is used in applicability conditions of some rules to ensure that term variables can only be instantiated with value expressions that are (a) deterministic and (b) either terminating or waiting for communication. This in particular means that the expressions are not equivalent to **stop**, **swap** or **chaos**.

For example, *e* in the rule

> [card_singleton]
>   **card** {e} ≃ 1 **when convergent**(e) ∧ **readonly**(e)

should only be instantiated with a convergent value expression. Otherwise it could, for example, be used to imply the equivalence

> **card** {**stop**} ≡ 1

which is false, since the left-hand side is equivalent to **stop** (function arguments are evaluated before the call is made).

As another example, *ei* in the rule

> [plus_int_same] ei + ei ≃ 2 * ei **when convergent**(ei) ∧ **readonly**(ei)

should only be instantiated with a deterministic value expression. Otherwise it could, for example, be used to imply the equivalence

> (1 ⌈⌉ 2) + (1 ⌈⌉ 2) ≡ 2 * (1 ⌈⌉ 2)

which is false, since the left-hand side is equivalent to 2 ⌈⌉ 3 ⌈⌉ 4 and the right-hand side to 2 ⌈⌉ 4.

disjoint

> **disjoint** : binding × binding → *logical*-value_expr

disjoint(b1, b2) is equivalent to **true** only if the two bindings introduce disjoint sets of identifiers and operators. It is used to ensure that when two new bindings appear in a rule they do not cause any name confusion. For example, "**disjoint**(a, (x, y))" is **true**, but "**disjoint**(x, (x, y))" is **false**.

express

> **express** : binding → value_expr

express converts binding to a value expression, simply by bracketing any operators and otherwise leaving it unchanged. It is used when a binding is introduced that also appears as an expression. For example, "**express**(x)" is "x", and "**express**((x, +))" is "(x, (+))".

interlock_expand, interlock_ints

> **interlock_expand** : *Unit*-value_expr × *Unit*-value_expr → *Unit*-value_expr
>
> **interlock_ints** : *Unit*-value_expr × *Unit*-value_expr → *Unit*-value_expr

interlock_expand is defined by the following rule:

> **interlock_expand**(eu, eu′) ≃
> **if isin_standard_form_or_stop**(eu) ∧
> **isin_standard_form_or_stop**(eu′) ∧
> (□ **assignment_disjoint**(eu, eu′))
> **then**
> **if** (**interlock_ints**(eu, eu′) ≡ **swap**) **then stop**
> **else interlock_ints**(eu, eu′)
> **end**
> **else** eu ⫴ eu′
> **end**

Rules defining **interlock_ints** when one of the arguments is **stop**:

> **interlock_ints**(**stop**, eu) ≃ **swap**

> **interlock_ints**(eu, **stop**) ≃ **swap**

Rules defining **interlock_ints** when one of the arguments is in basic standard form 3 and the other in standard form (see section 4.5.1.1):

> **interlock_ints**(eu [] eu′, eu″) ≃ **interlock_ints**(eu, eu″) ⌈⌉ **interlock_ints**(eu′, eu″)

> **interlock_ints**(eu″, eu [] eu′) ≃ **interlock_ints**(eu″, eu) ⌈⌉ **interlock_ints**(eu″, eu′)

Rules defining **interlock_ints** when both arguments are in basic standard forms 1 or 2 (see section 4.5.1.1):

> **interlock_ints**(eu, eu′) ≃ eu ; eu′
> **when readwriteonly**(eu) ∨ **readwriteonly**(eu′)

> **interlock_ints**(**let** b = c? **in** eu **end**, c!e ; eu′) ≃ **let** b = e **in** eu ⫴ eu′ **end**
> **when no_capture**(b, eu′)

> **interlock_ints**(c!e ; eu′, **let** b = c? **in** eu **end**) ≃ **let** b = e **in** eu′ ⫴ eu **end**
> **when no_capture**(b, eu′)

> **interlock_ints**(**let** b = c1? **in** eu **end**, c2!e ; eu′) ≃ **swap**
> **when are_different**(c1, c2)

> **interlock_ints**(c2!e ; eu′, **let** b = c1? **in** eu **end**) ≃ **swap**
> **when are_different**(c1, c2)

> **interlock_ints**(**let** b1 = c1? **in** eu **end**, **let** b2 = c2? **in** eu′ **end**) ≃ **swap**
> **interlock_ints**(c1!e1 ; eu, c2!e2 ; eu′) ≃ **swap**

is_maximal

> **is_maximal** : type_expr → *logical*-value_expr

is_maximal(T) is equivalent to **true** only if T is known to be maximal. It does not return **true** for a type involving a sort, since a sort can be developed into a subtype. Neither does it return **true** for a function type since potential accesses can be increased in a development. So **is_maximal**(T) is true if T is a built-in type other than **Nat** or **Text**, or formed from maximal types using ×, **-infset**, $^{\omega}$ or $\tilde{_{m}}$, or an abbreviation for a maximal type. Finally

> **is_maximal**({| b : T • p_eb |}) ≃ **is_maximal**(T) ∧ (∀ b : T • p_eb)

isin_standard_form_or_stop

> **isin_standard_form_or_stop** : value_expr → *logical*-value_expr

isin_standard_form_or_stop(e) is equivalent to **true** only if e is equivalent to **stop** or else is in standard form according to section 4.5.1.1. **isin_standard_form_or_stop** is used in the let and concurrency expansion rules.

isin_subtype

> **isin_subtype** : value_expr × type_expr → *logical*-value_expr

isin_subtype(e, T) is defined by the rule:

> **isin_subtype**(e, T) ≃
> ∃ id : T • (**let** id′ = e **in** id **end** ≡ e)
> **when** **no_capture**(id, e) ∧ **disjoint**(id, id′)

When e is read-only there is a derived rule:

> **isin_subtype**(e, T) ≃ ∃ id : T • id = e
> **when** **no_capture**(id, e) ∧ **readonly**(e)

let_expand, let_exts, let_ints

> **let_expand** : binding × value_expr × value_expr → value_expr
> **let_exts** : binding × value_expr × value_expr → value_expr
> **let_ints** : binding × value_expr × value_expr → value_expr

These functions are only defined if the structure of the binding matches the type of the second argument (a well-formedness condition on rules in which they are used). **let_expand** is defined by the following rule:

> **let_expand**(b, e, e1) ≃
> **if** **isin_standard_form_or_stop**(e)
> **then**
> **if** (**let_ints**(b, e, e1) ≡ **swap**)
> **then** **let_exts**(b, e, e1)
> **else** (**let_exts**(b, e, e1) [] **let_ints**(b, e, e1)) [] **let_ints**(b, e, e1)
> **end**
> **else let** b = e **in** e1 **end**
> **end**

Rule defining **let_exts** when the second argument is **stop**:

> **let_exts**(b, **stop**, e1) ≃ **stop**

Rule defining **let_exts** when the second argument is in basic standard form 3 (see section 4.5.1.1):

let_exts(b, e [] e′, e1) $\simeq$ let_exts(b, e, e1) [] let_exts(b, e′, e1)

Rules defining **let_exts** when the second argument is in basic standard form 1 or 2 (see section 4.5.1.1):

let_exts(b, e, e1) $\simeq$ **stop**
when readwriteonly(e)

let_exts(b2, **let** b1 = c? **in** e1 **end**, e2) $\simeq$ **let** b2 = **let** b1 = c? **in** e1 **end in** e2 **end**

let_exts(b, c!e1 ; e2, e3) $\simeq$ **let** b = c!e1 ; e2 **in** e1 **end**

Rule defining **let_ints** when the second argument is **stop**:

let_ints(b, **stop**, e1) $\simeq$ **swap**

Rule defining **let_ints** when the second argument is in basic standard form 3 (see section 4.5.1.1):

let_ints(b, e [] e′, e1) $\simeq$ **let_ints**(b, e, e1) [] **let_ints**(b, e′, e1)

Rules defining **let_ints** when the second argument is in basic standard form 1 or 2 (see section 4.5.1.1):

let_ints(b, e, e1) $\simeq$ **let** b = e **in** e1 **end**
when readwriteonly(e)

let_exts(b2, **let** b1 = c? **in** e1 **end**, e2) $\simeq$ **swap**

let_exts(b, c!e1 ; e2, e3) $\simeq$ **swap**

matches

> **matches** : value_expr $\times$ pattern $\rightarrow$ *logical*-value_expr

matches(e, pattern) is only defined if there exists a binding *b* such that **express**(b) is *e* (a well-formedness condition on rules in which it is used). **matches**(e, pattern) is equivalent to **true** only if *e* matches *pattern*. (*matches* is explained in the RSL book [23].) It is used to define case expressions.

no_capture

> **no_capture** : binding $\times$ value_expr $\rightarrow$ *logical*-value_expr

no_capture(b, e) is equivalent to **true** only if none of the free identifiers or operators in *e* are introduced in *b*. For example, we could apply *let_name_change* to

let x = 1 **in** y + x **end**

to obtain

let z = 1 **in** y + z **end**

but not to obtain

let y = 1 **in** y + y **end**

since the meaning of the original *y* would change — it would be "captured" by the let. So, "**no_capture**(z, y + x)" is **true**, but "**no_capture**(y, y + x)" is **false**.

Generalizations of **no_capture** in which the first argument may also be a list of names, or a declaration string, or a class expression, and the second argument may be a class expression, are used in the rules for local expressions and in the rules for class expressions in section B.8.

no_capture(names, term) is equivalent to **true** only if none of the free identifiers or operators in *term* is included in *names*.

no_capture(decls, term) is equivalent to **no_capture**(**class** decls **end**, term).

no_capture(ce, term) is equivalent to **true** only if none of the free identifiers or operators in *term* is defined in *ce*.

no_hiding

> **no_hiding** : class_expr → *logical*-value_expr

no_hiding(ce) is equivalent to **true** only if none of the identifiers or operators defined in *ce* are hidden, and if **no_hiding** also holds for the defining and formal parameter classes of any schemes instantiated within *ce*. **no_hiding** is used in describing the **properties** function in section B.8.

no_new_capture

> **no_new_capture** : binding × binding × value_expr → *logical*-value_expr

no_new_capture(b1, b2, e) is equivalent to **true** only if *b1* does not introduce any identifiers or operators that are free in *e* and not introduced by *b2*. That is, *b1* must not capture any identifiers that are not captured by *b2*. It is used in rules about changing names. The first binding is the new one, the second the old and the expression is in the scope of the old. For instance

> **let** (x, y) = (1, 2) **in** x + y + z **end**

can be (partly) renamed to

> **let** (x, w) = (1, 2) **in** x + w + z **end**

since **no_new_capture**((x, w), (x, y), x + y + z) is **true**. Note that **no_capture**((x, w), x + y + z) would be **false**, but capturing the identifier *x* is harmless since it was already captured by the binding we are changing. The name we must be careful not to capture is *z*.

Generalizations of **no_new_capture** in which the two first arguments may be class expressions and the third a class expression or a logical value expression are used in section B.8. **no_new_capture**(ce1, ce2, term) is equivalent to **true** only if *ce1* does not define any identifiers or operators that are free in *term* and not defined in *ce2*.

no_scheme_defs

> **no_scheme_defs** : class_expr → *logical*-value_expr

no_scheme_defs(ce) is equivalent to **true** only if *ce* contains no scheme definitions, and if **no_scheme_defs** also holds for the defining classes of any schemes instantiated within *ce*. **no_scheme_defs** is used in describing the **properties** function in section B.8.

no_scheme_insts

> **no_scheme_insts** : class_expr × *object*-name → *logical*-value_expr

no_scheme_insts(ce, O) is equivalent to **true** only if *ce* contains no scheme instantiations with O as an actual parameter. **no_scheme_insts** is used in the rules for object declarations in section B.8.1.2.

parallel_expand, parallel_exts, parallel_ints

> **parallel_expand** : *Unit*-value_expr × *Unit*-value_expr → *Unit*-value_expr
> **parallel_exts** : *Unit*-value_expr × *Unit*-value_expr → *Unit*-value_expr
> **parallel_ints** : *Unit*-value_expr × *Unit*-value_expr → *Unit*-value_expr

parallel_expand is defined by the following rule:

> **parallel_expand**(eu, eu') ≃
>   **if isin_standard_form_or_stop**(eu) ∧
>   **isin_standard_form_or_stop**(eu') ∧
>   (□ **assignment_disjoint**(eu, eu'))
>   **then**
>   **if parallel_ints**(eu, eu') ≡ **swap**
>   **then parallel_exts**(eu, eu') [] **parallel_exts**(eu', eu)
>   **else**
>   (**parallel_exts**(eu, eu') [] **parallel_exts**(eu', eu) [] **parallel_ints**(eu, eu')) ⌈⌉
>   **parallel_ints**(eu, eu')
>   **end**
>   **else** eu ∥ eu'
>   **end**

Rule defining **parallel_exts** when the first argument is **stop**:

> **parallel_exts**(**stop**, eu) ≡ **stop**

Rules defining **parallel_exts** when the first argument is in basic standard form 3 (see section 4.5.1.1):

> **parallel_exts**(eu [] eu', eu'') ≃ **parallel_exts**(eu, eu'') [] **parallel_exts**(eu', eu'')

Rules defining **parallel_exts** when the first argument is in basic standard form 1 or 2 (see section 4.5.1.1):

> **parallel_exts**(**let** b = c? **in** eu **end**, eu') ≃ **let** b = c? **in** eu ∥ eu' **end**
>   **when no_capture**(b, eu')

> **parallel_exts**(c!e ; eu, eu') ≃ c!e ; (eu ∥ eu')

> **parallel_exts**(eu, eu') ≃ **stop**

Rules defining **parallel_ints** when one of the arguments is **stop**:

> **parallel_ints**(**stop**, eu) ≡ **swap**

> **parallel_ints**(eu, **stop**) ≡ **swap**

Rules defining **parallel_ints** when one of the arguments is in basic standard form 3 and the other in standard form (see section 4.5.1.1):

> **parallel_ints**(eu [] eu', eu'') ≃ **parallel_ints**(eu, eu'') ⌈⌉ **parallel_ints**(eu', eu'')

> **parallel_ints**(eu'', eu [] eu') ≃ **parallel_ints**(eu'', eu) ⌈⌉ **parallel_ints**(eu'', eu')

Rules defining **parallel_ints** when both arguments are in basic standard form 1 or 2 (see section 4.5.1.1):

parallel_ints(eu, eu′) ≃ eu ; eu′
when readwriteonly(eu) ∨ **readwriteonly**(eu′)

parallel_ints(**let** b = c? **in** eu **end**, c!e ; eu′) ≃ **let** b = e **in** eu ∥ eu′ **end**
when no_capture(b, eu′)

parallel_ints(c!e ; eu′, **let** b = c? **in** eu **end**) ≃ **let** b = e **in** eu′ ∥ eu **end**
when no_capture(b, eu′)

parallel_ints(**let** b = c1? **in** eu **end**, c2!e ; eu′) ≃ **swap**
when are_different(c1, c2)

parallel_ints(c2!e ; eu′, **let** b = c1? **in** eu **end**) ≃ **swap**
when are_different(c1, c2)

parallel_ints(**let** b1 = c1? **in** eu **end**, **let** b2 = c2? **in** eu′ **end**) ≃ **swap**

parallel_ints(c1!e1 ; eu, c2!e2 ; eu′) ≃ **swap**

properties

properties : class_expr → *logical*-value_expr

Provided **no_hiding**(ce) and **no_scheme_defs**(ce) hold, **properties**(ce) is a logical value expression which, together with the signature of *ce*, is a theory presentation of *ce*. It is defined in section B.8. (To ensure completeness of the definition it is arbitrarily defined to be **false** if **no_hiding**(ce) or **no_scheme_defs**(ce) does not hold.)

pure

pure : value_expr → *logical*-value_expr

pure(e) is equivalent to **true** only if *e* does not dynamically access any variables or channels. It is defined by the rule

pure(e) ≃ ∃ id : **Unit** $\overset{\sim}{\to}$ T • (id() ≡ e)

where T is the maximal type of *e*. It is used when it is necessary that an expression has the same value in all states. For instance, it is used in the applicability condition of the rule *always_absorption*.

pure is often checked statically from static accesses but this is not always sufficient. For example, it is not statically decidable whether

if eb **then** e1 **else** e2 **end**

is pure if *eb* and *e1* are but *e2* is not.

qualify

qualify : object_expr × class_expr × *logical*-value_expr → *logical*-value_expr
qualify : object_expr × class_expr × class_expr → class_expr

qualify returns a logical value expression or class expression generated from its third argument by qualifying with its first argument each free occurrence of any identifier or operator defined in its second argument. For example

qualify(O, **class value** x : **Int end**, x > y) ≃ O.x > y

qualify is used in the proof rules for object declarations in sections B.8.1.2 and B.8.2.

readonly

> **readonly** : value_expr → *logical*-value_expr

readonly(e) is equivalent to **true** only if *e* does not dynamically write to any variables or access any channels. It is used in particular when the application of a rule would change the number of occurrences of an expression. For instance, it is used in the applicability condition of the rule:

> [card_singleton]
> **card** {e} ≃ 1 **when convergent**(e) ∧ **readonly**(e)

Otherwise the rule could be used to imply the equivalence

> **card** {x := 1 ; x} ≡ 1

which is false, since the left-hand side is equivalent to

> x := 1 ; **card** {x}

which returns the value 1 but also has the effect of assigning to *x*.

readonly is defined by the rule

> **readonly**(e) ≃ ∃ id : **Unit** $\overset{\sim}{\to}$ **read** a T • (id() ≡ e)

where *T* is the maximal type of *e* and the access *a* is the possible read accesses of *e*. Possible read accesses are actual reads of variables and the read accesses in the signatures of functions that are applied.

readonly is often checked statically from static accesses but this is not always sufficient. For example, it is not statically decidable whether

> **if** eb **then** e1 **else** e2 **end**

is read-only if *eb* and *e1* are but *e2* is not.

readwriteonly

> **readwriteonly** : value_expr → *logical*-value_expr

readwriteonly(e) is equivalent to **true** only if *e* does not dynamically access any channels. It is used when we need to know that an expression cannot be waiting to do an input or an output. For example, when considering an output expression *c!e*, we can be sure that the first communication it might make will be an output on channel *c* only if we know that e cannot input or output.

readwriteonly is defined by the rule

> **readwriteonly**(e) ≃ ∃ id : **Unit** $\overset{\sim}{\to}$ **write** a T • (id() ≡ e)

where *T* is the maximal type of *e* and the access *a* is the possible variable accesses of *e*. Possible accesses are actual mentions of variables and the read and write accesses in the signatures of functions that are applied.

readwriteonly is often checked statically from static accesses but this is not always sufficient. For example, it is not statically decidable whether

> **if** eb **then** e1 **else** e2 **end**

is read-write-only if *eb* and *e1* are but *e2* is not.

removable

> **removable** : decl-string → *logical*-value_expr

removable is used in the rule *local_absorption*. **removable**(decls) is equivalent to **true** only if *decls* define values and the initial values of variables uniquely and also if the definitions in *decls* are consistent with subtypes, so that they only extend their context conservatively. See section 3.2.9 for more details.

subst_binding

subst_binding : binding $\times$ binding $\times$ value_expr $\rightarrow$ value_expr

subst_binding(b1, b2, e) is only defined if the structure of *b1* matches the maximal type of *b2* (a well-formedness condition on rules in which it is used). For example, "**subst_binding**((a, b), z, e)" is only defined if the maximal type of *z* is a product of length 2. **subst_binding**(b1, b2, e) is the value expression formed from *e* by replacing all free occurrences of identifiers or operators introduced in *b2* by occurrences of the corresponding identifiers or operators introduced in *b1*. For example

subst_binding((x, y), (a, b), a + b) $\simeq$ x + y

The maximal type of the new value expression is the same as the maximal type of *e*. The result is typically, as in the example above, obtained by standard textual substitution. But changing the structure of the bindings is also allowed; this will involve introducing let expressions. For example

subst_binding(z, (a, b), a + b) $\simeq$
let (a, b) = **express**(z) **in** a **end** + let (a, b) = **express**(z) **in** b **end**

subst_binding is used in rules for name changing.

A generalization of **subst_binding** in which the second argument is extended to allow a pattern is used in the rules defining case expressions:

subst_binding : binding $\times$ pattern $\times$ value_expr $\rightarrow$ value_expr

This generalization is defined by the following rules:

subst_binding(b, value_literal, e) $\simeq$ e

subst_binding(b, name, e) $\simeq$ e

subst_binding(b, _, e) $\simeq$ e

subst_binding(b, $(ip_1,...,ip_n)$, e) $\simeq$
let $(b_1,...,b_n)$ = **express**(b) **in**
  subst_binding(b_1, ip_1,
    subst_binding(...
      subst_binding(b_n, ip_n, e)...)) **end**
when
  no_new_capture($(b_1,...,b_n)$, $(ip_1,...,ip_n)$, e) $\wedge$
  disjoint($(b_1,...,b_n)$, b) $(n \geq 2)$

subst_binding(b, name(ip_list), e) $\simeq$
let b2 : T2 • name(**express**(b2)) = **express**(b)
in subst_binding(b2, (ip_list), e) **end**
  when no_new_capture(b2, (ip_list), e) $\wedge$
    disjoint(b2, b)

subst_binding(b, $\langle\rangle$, e) $\simeq$ e

$\textbf{subst\_binding}(b, \langle ip_1,...,ip_n \rangle, e) \simeq$
$\quad \textbf{let } b_1 = \textbf{hd express}(b),$
$\qquad ...$
$\qquad b_n = \textbf{hd (tl }...(\textbf{tl express}(b)) \ ... \ )$
$\quad \textbf{in}$
$\quad \ \textbf{subst\_binding}(b_1, ip_1,$
$\qquad \textbf{subst\_binding}(...$
$\qquad \ \ \textbf{subst\_binding}(b_n, ip_n, e)...))$
$\quad \textbf{end}$ $\hfill (n \geq 1)$

$\textbf{subst\_binding}(b, \langle \rangle \hat{} ip, e) \simeq$
$\quad \textbf{subst\_binding}(b, ip, e)$

$\textbf{subst\_binding}(b, \langle ip_1,...,ip_n \rangle \hat{} ip, e) \simeq$
$\quad \textbf{let } b_1 = \textbf{hd express}(b),$
$\qquad ...$
$\qquad b_n = \textbf{hd (tl }...(\textbf{tl express}(b)) \ ... \ ),$
$\qquad b' = \textbf{tl (tl }...(\textbf{tl express}(b)) \ ... \ )$
$\quad \textbf{in}$
$\quad \ \textbf{subst\_binding}(b_1, ip_1,$
$\qquad \textbf{subst\_binding}(...$
$\qquad \ \ \textbf{subst\_binding}(b_n, ip_n,$
$\qquad \quad \textbf{subst\_binding}(b', ip, e))...))$
$\quad \textbf{end}$ $\hfill (n \geq 1)$

$\textbf{subst\_binding}(b, id\_or\_op, e) \simeq e[\,b/id\_or\_op\,]$

$\textbf{subst\_binding}(b, =name, e) \simeq e$

The expression *e[b/id_or_op]* means *e* with **express**(b) substituted for every free occurrence of *id_or_op*.

subst_expr

$\textbf{subst\_expr}$: value_expr $\times$ binding $\times$ value_expr $\rightarrow$ value_expr

subst_expr(e1, b, e) is only defined if *e1* has a maximal type the same as the maximal type of *b* (a well-formedness condition on rules in which it is used). **subst_expr** is very similar to **subst_binding**, but the first argument is an expression rather than a binding. For example

$\textbf{subst\_expr}(e, x, x + x) \simeq e + e$

The maximal type of the resulting value expression is the same as the maximal type of the third parameter.

As with **subst_binding**, a let expression is needed if the structure of the expression does not match the structure of the binding. For example

$\textbf{subst\_expr}(f(), (x, y), x + y) \simeq$
$\quad \textbf{let } (x, y) = f() \textbf{ in } x \textbf{ end} + \textbf{let } (x, y) = f() \textbf{ in } y \textbf{ end}$

subst_id

$\textbf{subst\_id}$: id $\times$ id $\times$ value_expr $\rightarrow$ value_expr
$\textbf{subst\_id}$: id $\times$ id $\times$ class_expr $\rightarrow$ class_expr

subst_id(id1, id2, e) is the value expression formed from e by replacing all free occurrences of *id2* by *id1*. **subst_id**(id1, id2, ce) is the class expression formed from *ce* by replacing all free occurrences of *id2* by *id1*. **subst_id** is effectively **subst_binding** restricted to identifiers and then generalized to include class expressions.

B.5   Organization and naming of proof rules

The rules are listed in the following two sections as *basic* rules and *derived* rules. The collection of basic rules is known not to be complete; there are some difficulties, particularly in the areas of union types, local declarations and overloading. See the original proof theory for RSL [18] for further discussion. In addition, there are no rules for the literals and operators of the integers and reals (apart from induction for the natural numbers): we assume the normal laws of arithmetic.

The basic rules are designed to be as complete as possible and to be consistent. Having only the basic rules available for justifications makes justifications very long; they can be considerably shortened by the use of derived rules. A rule is derived if anything that can be proved using it can also be proved using the basic rules. The current RAISE justification editor has something like 2000 rules. The derived rules collected in this appendix are merely those that are used in the justifications elsewhere in the book.

There are a number of principles that guide the selection of basic rules and their naming. (Derived rules follow the same naming convention.)

Before considering these in detail, note that the name of an equivalence rule describes the rule read left-to-right. For inference rules, the name always ends "_inf" and generally describes the rule upwards.

B.5.1   Value expressions

Many constructs have expansions into others for which they are abbreviations; such rules are called X_expansion where X indicates the name of the construct. For example, *sequence_expansion* changes a sequence to a let expression:

[sequence_expansion]
  eu ; e $\simeq$ **let** b = eu **in** e **end**
    when no_capture(b, e)

There are defaults for all optional components in RSL; rules for adding these are called opt_X. For example, *opt_as* allows a result_naming to be included:

[opt_as]
  e **post** ro_eb $\simeq$ e **as** b **post** ro_eb
    when no_capture(b, ro_eb)

Application of rules in the two categories above removes a number of constructs from further consideration. Evaluation rules may then be used to make explicit the order of evaluation of a construct. These are particularly important when expressions communicate or write to variables. For example

[infix_op_evaluation]
  e infix_op e1 $\simeq$
    let b = e **in let** b1 = e1 **in express**(b) infix_op **express**(b1) **end end**
    when disjoint(b, b1) $\wedge$ **no_capture**(b, e1)

shows that order of evaluation is left to right for applications of infix operators. Evaluation rules also make it possible to reduce most expressions to let expressions in which the constituent value expressions are read-only.

There are rules we can apply when the constituents of let expressions are not convergent, such as

[let_annihilation1]
let b = **chaos** : T **in** e1 : T1 **end** $\simeq$ **chaos** : T1

and

[let_int_choice1]
let b = e $\lceil\rceil$ e$'$ **in** e1 **end** $\simeq$
let b = e **in** e1 **end** $\lceil\rceil$ **let** b = e$'$ **in** e1 **end**

So it is possible to restrict other basic rules to ones with read-only and convergent component expressions. We have not done this here, but have instead tried to keep the applicability conditions minimal.

The examples above illustrate two other naming conventions. X_annihilation is the name of a rule that reduces an X to one of the RSL basic expressions (**chaos**, **skip**, **stop** or **swap**) or to **true** or **false**.

X_Y is a distributivity rule; it shows how the construct X distributes through the construct Y. So a *let_int_choice* rule distributes a let through an internal choice.

A number is used at the end of a rule name when there are several rules with otherwise identical names.

There are a number of other categories of rule. X_convergence is a rule for showing the convergence of an X, i.e. "**X post true**". For example

[is_convergence]
(e $\equiv$ e$'$) **post true** $\simeq$ **true**

shows that equivalence expressions are always convergent.

An X_reduction rule can be used to reduce an X to a simpler expression. For example

[is_reduction]
e $\equiv$ e$'$ $\simeq$ e = e$'$
when convergent(e) $\wedge$ **readonly**(e) $\wedge$ **convergent**(e$'$) $\wedge$ **readonly**(e$'$)

allows, under particular conditions, the reduction of equivalence to equality.

X_absorption removes the construct X. For example

[if_absorption]
if eb **then true else false end** $\simeq$ eb

removes the if expression.

X_name_change is a rule for changing the identifiers and operators defined by an X construct.

X_replacement is a rule that allows the equivalence between two X constructs to be expressed in terms of equivalences between component expressions.

There are X_commutativity, X_transitivity, X_associativity and X_idempotence rules for constructs with these properties.

Finally, there are X_unwinding rules for iterative and comprehended expressions.

There are also some other principles to note about the organization of the basic rules. For each (maximal) type constructor in RSL (**-infset**, $^{\omega}$, $\widetilde{m}$, $\times$, $\xrightarrow{\sim}$) we decide

- what are the generators

- what are the observers

- what is derived

The rules should then

- define the observers for each of the generators

- define equality and the derived constructs either in terms of the observers or in terms of expansion rules

- where appropriate, define induction rule(s) for finite values

The generators for sets are the empty set "{}", the singleton set constructor "{_}", the union operator "∪" and set comprehension. The only observer is "∈". The enumerated and ranged sets are derived (and defined by expansion rules). Other operators like "∩" are also derived (and defined in terms of "∈"). Finally, we note that finite sets can be generated by the empty, singleton and union constructs and this gives us the basis for the induction rule.

Lists and maps have similar constructors to sets (empty, singleton, concatenation (lists) or union (maps), and comprehension). They are observed by **inds** and **dom** respectively, together with application. List comprehensions are defined by an unwinding rule rather than considering comprehension as basic. List induction is based on the empty, singleton and concatenation generators. For finite maps for which application is deterministic (the subtype "$_{\overrightarrow{m}}$"), override is a more convenient generator than union, so override with empty and singleton is used to define map induction.

Products are generated by product expressions and observed by let expressions.

Function expressions are generated using "λ" and observed by application.

B.5.2   Type expressions

There is a "normal form" for type expressions, which is the subtype expression

{| b : T • p_eb |}

where T is maximal. So most of the rules for type expressions show how to rewrite a type to this form. There are no observers for type expressions in RSL, but the **isin_subtype** special function is effectively an observer and is important in the proof theory.

There are also rules for distributing the predicates in subtypes through value expressions that include typings, like quantified expressions and comprehensions.

B.6   Basic rules

Type expressions

[type_equivalence]
T $\simeq$ T$'$
  when { b | b : T } = { b | b : T$'$ }

[nat_expansion]
  Nat $\simeq$ {| b : **Int** • **express**(b) $\geq$ 0 |}

[text_expansion]
  Text $\simeq$ **Char***

[subtype_evaluation]
  {| b : T • p_eb |} $\simeq$
    {| b : T • p_eb $\equiv$ **true** |}

[product_subtype]
  {| b1 : T1 • p_eb |} $\times$ {| b2 : T2 • p_eb$'$ |} $\simeq$
    {| (b1, b2) : T1 $\times$ T2 • p_eb $\wedge$ p_eb$'$ |}
  when disjoint(b1, b2) $\wedge$
    no_capture(b1, p_eb$'$) $\wedge$
    no_capture(b2, p_eb)

[finite_set_expansion]
  T-**set** $\simeq$
    {| b : T-**infset** •
      card express(b) **post true** |}

[infinite_set_subtype]
  {| b : T • p_eb |}-**infset** $\simeq$
    {| b1 : T-**infset** •
      $\forall$ b : T •
        express(b) $\in$ **express**(b1) $\Rightarrow$ p_eb |}
  when disjoint(b1, b) $\wedge$
    no_capture(b1, p_eb)

[finite_list_expansion]
  T* $\simeq$
    {| b : T$^\omega$ •
      len express(b) **post true** |}

[infinite_list_subtype]
  {| b : T • p_eb |}$^\omega$ $\simeq$
    {| b1 : T$^\omega$ •
      $\forall$ b : T •
        express(b) $\in$ **elems express**(b1) $\Rightarrow$
        p_eb |}
  when disjoint(b1, b) $\wedge$
    no_capture(b1, p_eb)

[finite_map_expansion]
  T1 $\overrightarrow{m}$ T2 $\simeq$
    {| bm : T1 $\overrightarrow{\widetilde{m}}$ T2 •
      (**card dom express**(bm) **post true**) $\wedge$
      ($\forall$ b1 : T1 •
        express(b1) $\in$ **dom express**(bm) $\Rightarrow$
          ((**express**(bm))(**express**(b1))
          post true)) |}
  when disjoint(bm, b1)

[infinite_map_subtype]
  {|b1 : T1 • p_eb|} $\overrightarrow{\widetilde{m}}$ {|b2 : T2 • p_eb$'$|} $\simeq$
    {| b : T1 $\overrightarrow{\widetilde{m}}$ T2 •
      dom express(b) $\subseteq$
        {b1 | b1 : T1 • p_eb} $\wedge$
      rng express(b) $\subseteq$
        {b2 | b2 : T2 • p_eb$'$} |}
  when no_capture(b, p_eb) $\wedge$
    no_capture(b, p_eb$'$)

[total_function_expansion]
  T $\rightarrow$ a T1 $\simeq$
    {| b1 : T $\xrightarrow{\sim}$ a T1 •
      $\forall$ b2 : T • $\square$
        (**express**(b1))(**express**(b2))
        post true |}
  when disjoint(b1, b2)

[function_subtype_argument]
  {| b1 : T1 • p_eb |} $\xrightarrow{\sim}$ a T2 $\simeq$ T1 $\xrightarrow{\sim}$ a T2
  when is_maximal(T2)

[function_subtype_result]
  T1 $\xrightarrow{\sim}$ a {| b2 : T2 • p_eb |} $\simeq$
    {| b : T1 $\xrightarrow{\sim}$ a T2 •
      $\forall$ b1 : T1 •
        $\square$
          (**express**(b))(**express**(b1)) $\equiv$
          let b2$'$ =
            (**express**(b))(**express**(b1)) **in**
          if $\exists$ b2 : T2 • p_eb $\wedge$
            express(b2) = **express**(b2$'$)
          then express(b2$'$)
          else chaos end
          end |}
  when disjoint(b, b1) $\wedge$
    disjoint(b2, b2$'$) $\wedge$
    no_capture(b2$'$, p_eb)

[subtype_name_change]
$\{| \ b1 : T \bullet p\_eb \ |\} \simeq$
$\quad \{| \ b2 : T \bullet$
$\quad \text{subst\_binding}(b2, b1, p\_eb) \ |\}$
$\text{when } \textbf{no\_new\_capture}(b2, b1, p\_eb)$

[subtype_reduction]
$\{| \ b : T \bullet \textbf{true} \ |\} \simeq T$

[subtype_subtype]
$\{| \ b : \{| \ b : T \bullet p\_eb' \ |\} \bullet p\_eb \ |\} \simeq$
$\quad \{| \ b : T \bullet p\_eb' \wedge p\_eb \ |\}$

[type_bracket_reduction]
$(T) \simeq T$

Value expressions

[imply_modus_ponens_inf]
$\text{ro\_eb},$
$\dfrac{\text{ro\_eb} \Rightarrow \text{ro\_eb}'}{\text{ro\_eb}'}$

[and_split_inf]
$\text{ro\_eb},$
$\dfrac{\text{ro\_eb}'}{\text{ro\_eb} \wedge \text{ro\_eb}'}$

[and_left_inf]
$\dfrac{\text{ro\_eb} \wedge \text{ro\_eb}'}{\text{ro\_eb}}$

[and_right_inf]
$\dfrac{\text{ro\_eb} \wedge \text{ro\_eb}'}{\text{ro\_eb}'}$

[contradiction_inf1]
$\dfrac{[\,\text{id}\,] \sim \text{ro\_eb} \vdash \textbf{false}}{\text{ro\_eb}}$
$\text{when } \textbf{convergent}(\text{ro\_eb}) \wedge \textbf{pure}(\text{ro\_eb})$

[imply_deduction_inf]
$\dfrac{[\,\text{id}\,] \ \text{ro\_eb} \vdash \text{ro\_eb}'}{\text{ro\_eb} \Rightarrow \text{ro\_eb}'}$
$\text{when } \textbf{convergent}(\text{ro\_eb}) \wedge \textbf{pure}(\text{ro\_eb})$

[case_analysis]
$[\,\text{id}_1\,] \ \text{ro\_eb}_1 \vdash \text{ro\_eb},$
$...,$
$\dfrac{[\,\text{id}_n\,] \ \text{ro\_eb}_n \vdash \text{ro\_eb}}{\text{ro\_eb}}$
$\text{when } \textbf{convergent}(\text{ro\_eb}_1) \wedge ... \wedge$
$\quad \textbf{convergent}(\text{ro\_eb}_n) \wedge$
$\quad \textbf{pure}(\text{ro\_eb}_1) \wedge ... \wedge \textbf{pure}(\text{ro\_eb}_n) \wedge$
$\quad (\text{ro\_eb}_1 \vee ... \vee \text{ro\_eb}_n)$

Value literals

[literal_convergence]
literal $\textbf{post true} \simeq \textbf{true}$

[empty_text]
$'''' \simeq \langle \rangle : \textbf{Text}$

[singleton_text]
$''\text{ch}'' \simeq \langle '\text{ch}' \rangle$

[text_string_expansion]
$''\text{ch ch\_string}'' \simeq \langle '\text{ch}' \rangle \ \hat{} \ ''\text{ch\_string}''$

Basic value expressions

[bool_disjoint]
$\sim (\textbf{true} \equiv \textbf{false}) \simeq \textbf{true}$

[skip_expansion]
$\textbf{skip} \simeq ()$

Set value expressions

[ranged_set_expansion]
$\{ \ \text{ro\_ei} \ .. \ \text{ro\_ei}' \ \} \simeq$
$\quad \textbf{if } \text{ro\_ei} \leq \text{ro\_ei}'$
$\quad \textbf{then } \{\text{ro\_ei}\} \cup \{ \ \text{ro\_ei} + 1 \ .. \ \text{ro\_ei}' \ \}$
$\quad \textbf{else } \{\} : \textbf{Int-set end}$
$\text{when } \textbf{convergent}(\text{ro\_ei}) \wedge$
$\quad \textbf{convergent}(\text{ro\_ei}')$

[set_enumeration_expansion]
$\{\text{ro\_e}, \text{ro\_e\_list}\} \simeq \{\text{ro\_e}\} \cup \{\text{ro\_e\_list}\}$

[singleton_set_evaluation]
$\{\text{ro\_e}\} \simeq \textbf{let } b = \text{ro\_e } \textbf{in } \{\textbf{express}(b)\} \textbf{ end}$

[isin_empty]
 e ∈ {} ≃ **false**
 when convergent(e) ∧ **readonly**(e)

[isin_singleton]
 e ∈ {ro_e′} ≃ e = ro_e′

[set_name_change]
 { ro_e | b1 : T1 • ro_eb } ≃
 { **subst_binding**(b2, b1, ro_e) |
 b2 : T1 •
 subst_binding(b2, b1, ro_eb) }
 when no_new_capture(b2, b1, ro_e) ∧
 no_new_capture(b2, b1, ro_eb)

[isin_comprehension]
 ro_e ∈ { ro_e′ | b : T1 • ro_eb } ≃
 ∃ b : T1 • ro_eb ∧ ro_e = ro_e′
 when convergent(ro_e) ∧
 no_capture(b, ro_e)

[opt_restriction_set_comprehension]
 { ro_e | b : T1 } ≃ { ro_e | b : T1 • **true** }

List value expressions

[ranged_list_expansion]
 ⟨ ei .. ei′ ⟩ ≃
 let b = ei **in**
 let b′ = ei′ **in**
 if express(b) ≤ **express**(b′) **then**
 ⟨**express**(b)⟩ ⌢
 ⟨**express**(b)+1 .. **express**(b′)⟩
 else
 ⟨⟩ : Int*
 end end end
 when disjoint(b, b′) ∧ **no_capture**(b, ei′)

[list_enumeration_expansion]
 ⟨e, e_list⟩ ≃ ⟨e⟩ ⌢ ⟨e_list⟩

[singleton_list_evaluation]
 ⟨e⟩ ≃ **let** b = e **in** ⟨**express**(b)⟩ **end**

[inds_empty]
 inds ⟨⟩ ≃ {}

[inds_singleton]
 inds ⟨e⟩ ≃ {1}
 when convergent(e) ∧ **readonly**(e)

[singleton_list_application]
 ⟨e⟩(1) ≃ e

[list_name_change]
 ⟨ e | b1 **in** ro_el • ro_eb ⟩ ≃
 ⟨ **subst_binding**(b2, b1, e) |
 b2 **in** ro_el •
 subst_binding(b2, b1, ro_eb) ⟩
 when no_new_capture(b2, b1, e) ∧
 no_new_capture(b2, b1, ro_eb)

[list_comprehension_evaluation]
 ⟨ e | b **in** ro_el • ro_eb ⟩ ≃
 let b1 = ro_el **in**
 ⟨ e | b **in express**(b1) • ro_eb ⟩ **end**
 when no_new_capture(b1, b, e) ∧
 no_new_capture(b1, b, ro_eb)

[list_comprehension_replacement]
 ⟨ e1 | b **in** ro_el : T^ω • ro_eb ⟩ ≃
 ⟨ e1′ | b **in** ro_el • ro_eb′ ⟩
 when convergent(ro_el) ∧
 no_capture(b, ro_el) ∧
 (□ ∀ b : T •
 express(b) ∈ **elems** ro_el ⇒
 (**if** ro_eb ≡ **true then** ⟨e1⟩ **else** ⟨⟩ **end** ≡
 if ro_eb′ ≡ **true then** ⟨e1′⟩ **else** ⟨⟩ **end**)) ∧
 isin_subtype(ro_el, T^ω)

[list_comprehension_unwinding]
 ⟨ e | b **in** ro_el : T^ω • ro_eb ⟩ ≃
 if ro_el = ⟨⟩ **then** ⟨⟩
 else
 let b = **hd** ro_el **in**
 if ro_eb ≡ **true then** ⟨e⟩ **else** ⟨⟩ **end**
 end ⌢ ⟨ e | b **in tl** ro_el • ro_eb ⟩
 end
 when convergent(ro_el) ∧
 no_capture(b, ro_el) ∧
 (∀ b : T •
 express(b) ∈ **elems** ro_el ∧
 (ro_eb ≡ **true**) ⇒
 assignment_disjoint(e, ro_eb)) ∧
 isin_subtype(ro_el, T^ω)

[opt_restriction_list_comprehension]
 ⟨ e | b **in** ro_el ⟩ ≃
 ⟨ e | b **in** ro_el • **true** ⟩

Map value expressions

[map_enumeration_expansion]
[e_pair, e_pair_list] $\simeq$ [e_pair] $\cup$ [e_pair_list]

[singleton_map_evaluation]
[ro_e $\mapsto$ ro_e1] $\simeq$
  let b = ro_e **in let** b1 = ro_e1 **in**
  [**express**(b) $\mapsto$ **express**(b1)] **end end**
when disjoint(b, b1) $\wedge$
  no_capture(b, ro_e1)

[dom_empty]
  dom [] $\simeq$ {}

[dom_singleton]
  dom [ro_e $\mapsto$ ro_e1] $\simeq$ {ro_e}
when convergent(ro_e1)

[singleton_map_application]
[ro_e $\mapsto$ ro_e1](ro_e) $\simeq$ ro_e1
when convergent(ro_e)

[dom_comprehension]
  dom [ro_e $\mapsto$ ro_e1 | b : T2 • ro_eb] $\simeq$
  { ro_e | b : T2 • ro_eb }

[map_comprehension_application]
[ro_e $\mapsto$ ro_e1 | b : T2 • ro_eb](ro_e$'$) $\simeq$
  $\bigcap$ { ro_e1 | b : T2 •
    ro_eb $\wedge$ (ro_e = ro_e$'$) }
when convergent(ro_e) $\wedge$
  convergent(ro_e$'$) $\wedge$
  no_capture(b, ro_e$'$) $\wedge$
  ro_e$'$ $\in$ { ro_e | b : T2 • ro_eb }

[map_name_change]
[ro_e $\mapsto$ ro_e1 | b1 : T2 • ro_eb] $\simeq$
[**subst_binding**(b2, b1, ro_e) $\mapsto$
  subst_binding(b2, b1, ro_e1) |
    b2 : T2 •
    subst_binding(b2, b1, ro_eb)]
when no_new_capture(b2, b1, ro_e) $\wedge$
  no_new_capture(b2, b1, ro_e1) $\wedge$
  no_new_capture(b2, b1, ro_eb)

[opt_restriction_map_comprehension]
[ro_e $\mapsto$ ro_e1 | b : T2] $\simeq$
[ro_e $\mapsto$ ro_e1 | b : T2 • **true**]

Function value expressions

[lambda_expansion1]
λ () • e $\simeq$ λ b : **Unit** • e
when no_capture(b, e)

[lambda_expansion2]
λ (b : T1) • e $\simeq$ λ b : T1 • e

[lambda_name_change]
λ b1 : T1 • e $\simeq$
  λ b2 : T1 • **subst_binding**(b2, b1, e)
when no_new_capture(b2, b1, e)

[lambda_convergence]
(λ b : T1 • e) **post true** $\simeq$ **true**

[lambda_application]
(λ b : T • e1)(e) $\simeq$
  let b = e **in** e1 **end**
when convergent(e) $\wedge$
  isin_subtype(e, T)

Application expressions

[application_expansion1]
e(opt_e1_list)(opt_e2_list) $\simeq$
  (e(opt_e1_list))(opt_e2_list)

[application_expansion2]
e(opt_e_list) $\simeq$ e((opt_e_list))

[application_evaluation]
e(e1) $\simeq$
  let b = e **in**
    let b1 = e1 **in**
    (**express**(b))(**express**(b1)) **end end**
when disjoint(b, b1) $\wedge$ **no_capture**(b, e1)

Quantified expressions

[all_nat_induction]
$\forall$ b : **Nat** • ro_eb $\simeq$ **true**
  when
  subst_expr(0, b, ro_eb) $\wedge$
  ($\forall$ b : **Nat** • ro_eb $\Rightarrow$
    subst_expr(**express**(b) + 1, b, ro_eb))

[all_set_induction]
 ∀ b : T-**set** • ro_eb ≃ **true**
 when
 subst_expr({}, b, ro_eb) ∧
 disjoint(b,b1) ∧ **no_capture**(b1,ro_eb) ∧
 (∀ b : T-**set** • ∀ b1 : T •
 ro_eb ∧ **express**(b1) ∉ **express**(b) ⇒
 subst_expr(
  express(b) ∪ {**express**(b1)}, b, ro_eb))

[all_list_left_induction]
 ∀ b : T* • ro_eb ≃ **true**
 when
 subst_expr(⟨⟩, b, ro_eb) ∧
 disjoint(b,b1) ∧ **no_capture**(b1,ro_eb) ∧
 (∀ b : T* • ∀ b1 : T •
 ro_eb ⇒
  subst_expr(
  ⟨**express**(b1)⟩ ⁀ **express**(b), b, ro_eb))

[all_map_overide_induction]
 ∀ b : T1 →ₘ T2 • ro_eb ≃ **true**
 when
 subst_expr([ ], b, eb) ∧ **disjoint**(b1,b2) ∧
 disjoint(b,b1) ∧ **no_capture**(b1,ro_eb) ∧
 disjoint(b,b2) ∧ **no_capture**(b2,ro_eb) ∧
 (∀ b : T1 →ₘ T2 • ∀ b1 : T1, b2 : T2 •
 ro_eb ⇒
  subst_expr(
  express(b) †
  [**express**(b1) ↦ **express**(b2)],
  b, ro_eb))

[exists_expansion]
 ∃ b : T • ro_eb ≃
 ~ (∀ b : T • ~ (ro_eb ≡ **true**))

[exists_unique_expansion]
 ∃! b : T • ro_eb ≃
 ∃ b : T •
 ro_eb ∧
 (∀ b′ : T •
 subst_binding(b′, b, ro_eb) ⇒
  express(b) = **express**(b′))
 when no_new_capture(b′, b, ro_eb)

[all_name_change]
 ∀ b : T • ro_eb ≃
 ∀ b′ : T • **subst_binding**(b′, b, ro_eb)
 when no_new_capture(b′, b, ro_eb)

[all_evaluation]
 ∀ b : T • ro_eb ≃
 ∀ b : T • (ro_eb ≡ **true**)

[all_convergence]
 (∀ b : T1 • ro_eb) **post true** ≃ **true**

[all_commutativity]
 ∀ b1 : T1 • ∀ b2 : T2 • ro_eb ≃
 ∀ b2 : T2 • ∀ b1 : T1 • ro_eb
 when disjoint(b1, b2)

[all_product1]
 ∀ (b1, b2) : T1 × T2 • ro_eb ≃
 ∀ b1 : T1 • ∀ b2 : T2 • ro_eb
 when disjoint(b1, b2)

[all_product2]
 ∀ (b, b_list2) : T × T_product2 •
 ro_eb ≃
 ∀ b : T •
 ∀ (b_list2) : T_product2 • ro_eb
 when disjoint(b, b_list2)

[all_implies]
 (∀ b : T • ro_eb) ⇒ (∀ b : T • ro_eb′) ≃
 true
 when ∀ b : T • (ro_eb ≡ **true**) ⇒ ro_eb′

[all_subtype]
 ∀ b : {| b : T • p_eb′ |} • ro_eb ≃
 ∀ b : T • (p_eb′ ≡ **true**) ⇒ ro_eb

[all_always]
 ∀ b : T • □ ro_eb ≃
 □ ∀ b : T • ro_eb

[all_application]
 ∀ b : T • **express**(b) = ro_e ⇒ ro_eb ≃
 let b = ro_e **in** ro_eb ≡ **true end**
 when convergent(ro_e) ∧
 no_capture(b, ro_e) ∧
 isin_subtype(ro_e, T)

[all_subsumption_inf]
 $\dfrac{\textbf{value } b : T \vdash \text{ro\_eb}}{\forall\, b : T \bullet \text{ro\_eb}}$

[all_deduction_inf]
 $\dfrac{\forall\, b : T \bullet \text{ro\_eb}}{\textbf{value } b : T \vdash \text{ro\_eb}}$

[all_elimination_inf]
$\exists$ b : T • **true**,
$\underline{\forall\ b\ :\ T\ \bullet\ ro\_eb}$
ro_eb
when no_capture(b, ro_eb)

[exists_unique]
$\exists$! b1 : T •
(e $\equiv$ **let** b2 = e **in express**(b1) **end**) $\simeq$
true
when
convergent(e) $\wedge$ **readwriteonly**(e) $\wedge$
no_capture(b1, e) $\wedge$ **isin_subtype**(e, T)

Equivalence expressions

[is_pre]
e $\equiv$ e$'$ **pre** ro_eb $\simeq$
(ro_eb $\equiv$ **true**) $\Rightarrow$ (e $\equiv$ e$'$)

[is_convergence]
(e $\equiv$ e$'$) **post true** $\simeq$ **true**

[is_reduction]
e $\equiv$ e$'$ $\simeq$ e = e$'$
when convergent(e) $\wedge$ **readonly**(e) $\wedge$
convergent(e$'$) $\wedge$ **readonly**(e$'$)

[is_true]
eb $\equiv$ **true** $\simeq$ eb
when convergent(eb) $\wedge$ **readonly**(eb)

[is_annihilation]
e $\equiv$ e $\simeq$ **true**

[is_commutativity]
e $\equiv$ e$'$ $\simeq$ e$'$ $\equiv$ e

[is_transitivity]
e $\equiv$ e$''$ $\simeq$ **true**
when (e $\equiv$ e$'$) $\wedge$ (e$'$ $\equiv$ e$''$)

Post expressions

[post_as_pre]
e **as** b **post** ro_eb **pre** ro_eb$'$ $\simeq$
(ro_eb$'$ $\equiv$ **true**) $\Rightarrow$ (e **as** b **post** ro_eb)

[post_pre]
e **post** ro_eb **pre** ro_eb$'$ $\simeq$
(ro_eb$'$ $\equiv$ **true**) $\Rightarrow$ e **post** ro_eb

[post_expansion]
e **as** b **post** ro_eb $\simeq$
(**let** b = e **in** ro_eb **end** $\equiv$
let b = e **in true end**)
when convergent(e)

[post_convergence]
(e **as** b **post** ro_eb) **post true** $\simeq$ **true**

[opt_as]
e **post** ro_eb $\simeq$ e **as** b **post** ro_eb
when no_capture(b, ro_eb)

[post_name_change]
e **as** b1 **post** ro_eb $\simeq$
e **as** b2
post subst_binding(b2, b1, ro_eb)
when no_new_capture(b2, b1, ro_eb)

[pre_name_absorption]
e **as** b **post let** b1 = v` **in** ro_eb **end** $\simeq$
let b1 = v **in** e **as** b **post** ro_eb **end**
when disjoint(b, b1) $\wedge$
no_capture(b1, e)

Disambiguation expressions

[disambiguation_evaluation]
e : T $\simeq$ **let** b = e **in express**(b) : T **end**

[disambiguation_absorption]
e : T $\simeq$ e
when convergent(e) $\wedge$ **isin_subtype**(e, T)

Bracketed value expressions

[bracket_expansion]
(e) $\simeq$ e

Prefix expressions

[always_evaluation]
$\square$ ro_eb $\simeq$ $\square$ (ro_eb $\equiv$ **true**)

[always_convergence]
($\square$ ro_eb) **post true** $\simeq$ **true**

[always_absorption]
$\square$ ro_eb $\simeq$ ro_eb
when convergent(ro_eb) $\wedge$ **pure**(ro_eb)

[always_idempotence]
□ □ ro_eb ≃ □ ro_eb

[always_application1]
□ e ≡ e′ ≃
∀ id : Tv • □ v := id ; e ≡ v := id ; e′
when
no_capture(id, v) ∧ **no_capture**(id, e) ∧
no_capture(id, e′) ∧
(□ **isin_subtype**(v, Tv)) ∧
(□ ∀ id : Tv • v := id **post true**)

[always_post_application1]
□ e **as** b **post** ro_eb ≃
∀ id : Tv • □
v := id ; (e **as** b **post** ro_eb) ≡
v := id ; **true**
when
no_capture(id, v) ∧ **no_capture**(id, e) ∧
no_new_capture(id, b, ro_eb) ∧
(□ **isin_subtype**(v, Tv)) ∧
(□ ∀ id : Tv • v := id **post true**)

[always_implies1]
(□ ro_eb) ⇒ (□ ro_eb′) ≃ **true**
when □ (ro_eb ≡ **true**) ⇒ ro_eb′

[always_elimination_inf]
□ ro_eb
―――――
ro_eb

Comprehension expressions

[ext_choice_comp_name_change]
[] { e | b1 : T1 • ro_eb } ≃
[] { **subst_binding**(b2, b1, e) |
b2 : T1 •
subst_binding(b2, b1, ro_eb) }
when no_new_capture(b2, b1, e) ∧
no_new_capture(b2, b1, ro_eb)

[int_choice_comp_name_change]
⊓ { e | b1 : T1 • ro_eb } ≃
⊓ { **subst_binding**(b2, b1, e) |
b2 : T1 •
subst_binding(b2, b1, ro_eb) }
when no_new_capture(b2, b1, e) ∧
no_new_capture(b2, b1, ro_eb)

[parallel_comp_name_change]
|| { eu | b1 : T1 • ro_eb } ≃
|| { **subst_binding**(b2, b1, eu) |
b2 : T1 •
subst_binding(b2, b1, ro_eb) }
when no_new_capture(b2, b1, eu) ∧
no_new_capture(b2, b1, ro_eb)

[opt_restriction_ext_choice_comp]
[] { e | b : T1 } ≃ [] { e | b : T1 • **true** }

[opt_restriction_int_choice_comp]
⊓ { e | b : T1 } ≃ ⊓ { e | b : T1 • **true** }

[opt_restriction_parallel_comp]
|| { eu | b : T1 } ≃ || { eu | b : T1 • **true** }

[ext_choice_empty]
[] { e : T | b : T1 • ro_eb } ≃ **stop** : T
when ~ (∃ b : T1 • ro_eb)

[ext_choice_comp_unwinding]
[] { e | b : T1 • ro_eb } ≃
let b = ro_e1 **in** e **end**
[]
[] { e | b : T1 •
ro_eb ∧ ~ (**express**(b) = ro_e1) }
when no_capture(b, ro_e1) ∧
convergent(ro_e1) ∧ **pure**(ro_e1) ∧
isin_subtype(ro_e1, {| b : T1 • □ ro_eb |})

[int_choice_empty]
⊓ { e : T | b : T1 • ro_eb } ≃ **swap** : T
when ~ (∃ b : T1 • ro_eb)

[int_choice_comp_unwinding]
⊓ { e | b : T1 • ro_eb } ≃
let b = ro_e1 **in** e **end**
⊓
⊓ { e | b : T1 •
ro_eb ∧ ~ (**express**(b) = ro_e1) }
when no_capture(b, ro_e1) ∧
convergent(ro_e1) ∧ **pure**(ro_e1) ∧
isin_subtype(ro_e1, {| b : T1 • □ ro_eb |})

[parallel_empty]
|| { eu | b : T1 • ro_eb } ≃ **skip**
when ~ (∃ b : T1 • ro_eb)

[parallel_comp_unwinding]
$\| \{$ eu $\mid$ b : T1 • ro_eb $\} \simeq$
let b = ro_e1 in eu end
$\|$
$\| \{$ eu $\mid$ b : T1 •
   ro_eb $\wedge \sim$ (**express**(b) = ro_e1) $\}$
when no_capture(b, ro_e1) $\wedge$
  convergent(ro_e1) $\wedge$ **pure**(ro_e1) $\wedge$
  isin_subtype(ro_e1, $\{|$b : T1 • $\Box$ ro_eb$|\}$) $\wedge$
  ($\Box \forall$ b : T1 •
   ro_eb $\wedge \sim$ (**express**(b) = ro_e1) $\Rightarrow$
   ($\Box$ **assignment_disjoint**(eu,
    let b = ro_e1 in eu end)))

Initialise expressions

[initialise_convergence]
initialise post true $\simeq$ **true**

[initialise_idempotence]
initialise ; **initialise** $\simeq$ **initialise**

Assignment expressions

[assignment_evaluation]
v := e $\simeq$
 let b = e in v := **express**(b) **end**
when no_capture(b, v)

[assignment_unfold]
v := e ; v $\simeq$ v := e ; e
when convergent(v := e) $\wedge$ **readonly**(e) $\wedge$
 assignment_disjoint(v := e, e)

[assignment_idempotence1]
v := e ; v := e$'$ $\simeq$ v := e$'$
when convergent(v := e) $\wedge$ **readonly**(e) $\wedge$
 assignment_disjoint(v := e, e$'$)

[assignment_reduction]
v := v $\simeq$ **skip**,

Input expressions

[input_reduction]
 let b1 = c? in e1 end $\|$
 let b2 = c? in e1$'$ end $\simeq$
 let b1 = c? in e1 end $\|$
 let b2 = c? in e1$'$ end

Output expressions

[output_evaluation]
c ! e $\simeq$ let b = e in c ! **express**(b) **end**
when no_capture(b, c?)

[output_reduction]
(c ! e ; eu) $\|$ (c ! e$'$; eu$'$) $\simeq$
 (c ! e ; eu) $\|$ (c ! e$'$; eu$'$)
when
 convergent(e) $\wedge$ **readwriteonly**(e) $\wedge$
 convergent(e$'$) $\wedge$ **readwriteonly**(e$'$)

Local expressions

[local_absorption]
local decls **in** e **end** $\simeq$ e
when no_capture(decls, e) $\wedge$
 removable(decls)

[local_let]
local decls **in let** b = e **in** e1 **end end** $\simeq$
let b = **local** decls **in** e **end in** e1 **end**
when no_capture(decls, e1)

[local_variable]
local
 variable v : T := p_e decls
in e1 **end** $\simeq$
 local
  variable v : T := p_e decls
 in v := p_e ; e1 **end**
when no_capture(**variable** v : T, p_e)

[local_int_choice]
local decls **in** e $\|$ e$'$ **end** $\simeq$
 local decls **in** e **end** $\|$
 local decls **in** e$'$ **end**

[local_ext_choice]
local decls **in** e $\|$ e$'$ **end** $\simeq$
 local decls **in** e **end** $\|$
 local decls **in** e$'$ **end**

[local_parallel]
local decls **in** eu $\|$ eu$'$ **end** $\simeq$
 local decls **in** eu **end** $\|$ eu$'$
when no_capture(decls, eu$'$) $\wedge$
 convergent(**local** decls **in** eu **end**) $\wedge$
 ($\Box$ **assignment_disjoint**(
  local decls **in** eu **end**, eu$'$))

[local_interlock]
 local decls in eu ‖ eu′ end ≃
  local decls in eu end ‖ eu′
 when no_capture(decls, eu′) ∧
  convergent(local decls in eu end) ∧
  (□ assignment_disjoint(
    local decls in eu end, eu′))

[local_convergence]
 local decls in e end post true ≃ true
 when local decls in e post true end

Let expressions

[let_def_list_expansion]
 let let_def, let_def_list in e end ≃
  let let_def in
   let let_def_list in e end end

[let_record_expansion]
 let record_pattern = e in e1 end ≃
  case e of record_pattern → e1 end

[let_list_expansion]
 let list_pattern = e in e1 end ≃
  case e of list_pattern → e1 end

[opt_restriction_implicit_let]
 let b : T1 in e end ≃
  let b : T1 • true in e end

[implicit_let_expansion]
 let b : T1 • ro_eb in e end ≃
  ⌈⌉ { e | b : T1 • ro_eb }

[let_replacement]
 let b = e in e1 end ≃
  let b′ = e′ in e1′ end
 when
  convergent(e) ∧ (e ≡ e′) ∧
  no_new_capture(b, b′, e1′) ∧
  (∀ b : T •
   □ e1 ≡ subst_binding(b, b′, e1′)) ∧
  isin_subtype(e, T) ∧ isin_subtype(e′, T)

[let_name_change]
 let b = e in e1 end ≃
  let b′ = e in
   subst_binding(b′, b, e1) end
 when no_new_capture(b′, b, e1)

[let_evaluation]
 let b = e in e1 end ≃
  let b1 = e in
   let b = express(b1) in e1 end end
 when no_new_capture(b1, b, e1)

[let_convergence]
 let b = e1 in e end post true ≃
  let b = e1 in e post true end ≡
   let b = e1 in true end
 when
  convergent(e1) ∧ readwriteonly(e1)

[let_input_convergence]
 let b = c? in e end post true ≃ true
 when convergent(c?)

[let_output_convergence]
 let b = c!e in e1 end post true ≃ true
 when convergent(c!e)

[let_annihilation1]
 let b = chaos : T in e1 : T1 end ≃
  chaos : T1

[let_annihilation2]
 let b = stop : T in e1 : T1 end ≃
  stop : T1

[let_annihilation3]
 let b = swap : T in e1 : T1 end ≃
  swap : T1

[let_annihilation4]
 let b = e in chaos end ≃ chaos
 when
  convergent(e) ∧ readwriteonly(e)

[let_annihilation5]
 let b = e in stop end ≃ stop
 when
  convergent(e) ∧ readwriteonly(e)

[let_annihilation6]
 let b = e in swap end ≃ swap
 when
  convergent(e) ∧ readwriteonly(e)

[let_absorption1]
let b = e in e1 end $\simeq$ e1
when no_capture(b, e1) $\wedge$
convergent(e) $\wedge$ readonly(e)

[let_absorption2]
let b = eu in skip end $\simeq$ eu

[let_absorption3]
let b = e in express(b) end $\simeq$ e

[let_absorption4]
let b = e in e1 end $\simeq$
subst_expr(e, b, e1)
when convergent(e) $\wedge$ pure(e)

[let_idempotence]
let b1 = e in
let b2 = e in e1 end end $\simeq$
let b1 = e in
subst_binding(b1, b2, e1) end
when convergent(e) $\wedge$ readonly(e) $\wedge$
no_capture(b1, e)

[let_commutativity]
let b1 = e1 in let b2 = e2 in e end end $\simeq$
let b2 = e2 in let b1 = e1 in e end end
when
convergent(e1) $\wedge$ readwriteonly(e1) $\wedge$
assignment_disjoint(e1, e2) $\wedge$
no_capture(b1, e2) $\wedge$
no_capture(b2, e1) $\wedge$
disjoint(b1, b2)

[let_associativity]
let b1 = let b2 = e1 in e end in e2 end $\simeq$
let b2 = e1 in let b1 = e in e2 end end
when
disjoint(b1, b2) $\wedge$ no_capture(b2, e2)

[let_product1]
let (b, b1) = (e, e1) in e2 end $\simeq$
let b = e in let b1 = e1 in e2 end end
when disjoint(b, b1) $\wedge$ no_capture(b, e1)

[let_product2]
let (b, b_list2) = (e, e_list2) in e1 end $\simeq$
let b = e in
let (b_list2) = (e_list2) in e1 end end
when disjoint(b, (b_list2)) $\wedge$
no_capture(b, (e_list2))

[let_if1]
let b = if eb then e else e$'$ end in
e1 end $\simeq$
if eb then
let b = e in e1 end
else
let b = e$'$ in e1 end
end

[let_if2]
let b = e1 in
if eb then e else e$'$ end end $\simeq$
if let b = e1 in eb end then
let b = e1 in e end
else
let b = e1 in e$'$ end
end
when convergent(e1) $\wedge$ readonly(e1) $\wedge$
assignment_disjoint(e1, eb)

[let_application]
let b = e1 in e2(e) end $\simeq$
let b = e1 in e2 end(
let b = e1 in e end)
when convergent(e1) $\wedge$ readonly(e1) $\wedge$
assignment_disjoint(e1, e2)

[let_all]
let b1 = e in $\forall$ b2 : T1 $\bullet$ ro_eb end $\equiv$
let b1$'$ = e in true end
$\simeq$
$\forall$ b2 : T1 $\bullet$
let b1 = e in ro_eb end $\equiv$
let b1 = e in true end
when
disjoint(b1, b2) $\wedge$ no_capture(b2, e)

[let_exists]
$\exists$ b2 : T1 $\bullet$
let b1 = e in ro_eb end $\equiv$
let b1 = e in true end $\simeq$
true
when disjoint(b1, b2) $\wedge$
no_capture(b2, e) $\wedge$
convergent(e) $\wedge$ readwriteonly(e) $\wedge$
(let b1 = e in $\exists$ b2 : T1 $\bullet$ ro_eb end $\equiv$
let b1 = e in true end)

[let_always]
☐ ro_eb ≃ **true**
when
  convergent(e) ∧ readwriteonly(e) ∧
  no_capture(b, ro_eb) ∧
  (**let** b = e **in** ☐ ro_eb **end** ≡
  let b = e **in true end**)

[let_is]
let b = e1 **in** e ≡ e′ **end** ≃
  let b = e1 **in** e **end** ≡
  let b = e1 **in** e′ **end**
when convergent(e1) ∧ **readonly**(e1)

[let_ext_choice]
let b = e1 **in** e [] e′ **end** ≃
  let b = e1 **in** e **end** []
  let b = e1 **in** e′ **end**
when
  convergent(e1) ∧ **readwriteonly**(e1)

[let_int_choice1]
let b = e [] e′ **in** e1 **end** ≃
  let b = e **in** e1 **end** []
  let b = e′ **in** e1 **end**

[let_int_choice2]
let b = e1 **in** e [] e′ **end** ≃
  let b = e1 **in** e **end** []
  let b = e1 **in** e′ **end**
when
  convergent(e1) ∧ **readwriteonly**(e1)

[let_parallel]
let b = e1 **in** eu ∥ eu′ **end** ≃
  let b = e1 **in** eu **end** ∥ eu′
when no_capture(b, eu′) ∧
  convergent(e1) ∧ **readwriteonly**(e1) ∧
  (☐ **assignment_disjoint**(
    let b = e1 **in** eu **end**, eu′))

[let_interlock]
let b = e1 **in** eu ∦ eu′ **end** ≃
  let b = e1 **in** eu **end** ∦ eu′
when no_capture(b, eu′) ∧
  convergent(e1) ∧ **readwriteonly**(e1) ∧
  (☐ **assignment_disjoint**(
    let b = e1 **in** eu **end**, eu′))

[let_expansion]
let b = e **in** e1 **end** ≃ **let_expand**(b, e, e1)
when
  isin_standard_form_or_stop(e)

If expressions

[if_expansion1]
if eb **then** eu **end** ≃
  if eb **then** eu **else skip end**

[if_expansion2]
if eb **then** eu **else_if_branch_string end** ≃
  if eb **then** eu **else_if_branch_string**
  else skip end

[if_expansion3]
if eb **then** e
elsif eb′ **then** e′ **else_if_branch_string**
else e″ **end** ≃
  if eb **then** e
  else
    if eb′ **then** e′
    else_if_branch_string else e″ **end**
  end

[if_evaluation]
if eb **then** e **else** e′ **end** ≃
  let id = eb **in**
  if id **then** e **else** e′ **end end**
when no_capture(id, e) ∧
no_capture(id, e′)

[if_reduction1]
if eb **then** eb **else** eb′ **end** ≃
  if eb **then true else** eb′ **end**
when convergent(eb) ∧ **readonly**(eb)

[if_reduction2]
if eb **then** eb′ **else** eb **end** ≃
  if eb **then** eb′ **else false end**
when convergent(eb) ∧ **readonly**(eb)

[if_annihilation1]
if eb **then** eb **else true end** ≃ **true**
when convergent(eb) ∧ **readonly**(eb)

[if_annihilation2]
if eb **then false else** eb **end** ≃ **false**
when convergent(eb) ∧ **readonly**(eb)

[if_true]
  if true then e **else** e′ **end** ≃ e

[if_false]
  if false then e **else** e′ **end** ≃ e′

[if_absorption]
  if eb **then true else false end** ≃ eb

[if_idempotence1]
  if eb **then**
    if eb **then** e **else** e′ **end**
  else
    if eb **then** e″ **else** e‴ **end**
  end ≃
    if eb **then** e **else** e‴ **end**
  when convergent(eb) ∧ **readonly**(eb)

[if_idempotence2]
  if eb **then** e **else** e **end** ≃
    let b = eb **in** e **end**
  when no_capture(b, e)

[if_commutativity]
  if eb
  then if eb′ **then** e **else** e′ **end**
  else if eb′ **then** e″ **else** e‴ **end**
  end ≃
    if eb′
    then if eb **then** e **else** e″ **end**
    else if eb **then** e′ **else** e‴ **end**
    end
  when convergent(eb) ∧ **readonly**(eb) ∧
    assignment_disjoint(eb, eb′)

[if_associativity]
  if if eb **then** eb′ **else** eb″ **end**
  then e **else** e′ **end** ≃
    if eb
    then if eb′ **then** e **else** e′ **end**
    else if eb″ **then** e **else** e′ **end**
    end

[if_application]
  if eb **then** e1(e) **else** e1′(e′) **end** ≃
    if eb **then** e1 **else** e1′ **end**
    (**if** eb **then** e **else** e′ **end**)
  when convergent(eb) ∧ **readonly**(eb) ∧
    assignment_disjoint(eb, e1) ∧
    assignment_disjoint(eb, e1′)

[if_all]
  if ro_eb
  then ∀ b : T • ro_eb′
  else ∀ b : T • ro_eb″
  end ≃
    ∀ b : T •
    if ro_eb **then** ro_eb′ **else** ro_eb″ **end**
  when no_capture(b, ro_eb) ∧
    convergent(ro_eb)

[if_always]
  if ro_eb **then** □ ro_eb′ **else** □ ro_eb″ **end** ≃
    □ **if** ro_eb **then** ro_eb′ **else** ro_eb″ **end**
  when convergent(ro_eb) ∧ **pure**(ro_eb)

[if_is]
  if eb **then** e **else** e″ **end** ≡
    if eb **then** e′ **else** e‴ **end** ≃
      if eb **then** e ≡ e′ **else** e″ ≡ e‴ **end**
  when
    convergent(eb) ∧ **readonly**(eb)

[if_ext_choice]
  if eb **then** e **else** e″ **end** []
    if eb **then** e′ **else** e‴ **end** ≃
      if eb **then** e [] e′ **else** e″ [] e‴ **end**
  when
    convergent(eb) ∧ **readwriteonly**(eb)

[if_int_choice]
  if eb **then** e **else** e″ **end** ⊓
    if eb **then** e′ **else** e‴ **end** ≃
      if eb **then** e ⊓ e′ **else** e″ ⊓ e‴ **end**
  when
    convergent(eb) ∧ **readwriteonly**(eb)

[if_parallel]
  if eb **then** eu ‖ eu′ **else** eu″ ‖ eu′ **end** ≃
    if eb **then** eu **else** eu″ **end** ‖ eu′
  when
    convergent(eb) ∧ **readwriteonly**(eb) ∧
    (□ **assignment_disjoint**(eb, eu′))

[if_interlock]
  if eb **then** eu ‖| eu′ **else** eu″ ‖| eu′ **end** ≃
    if eb **then** eu **else** eu″ **end** ‖| eu′
  when
    convergent(eb) ∧ **readwriteonly**(eb) ∧
    (□ **assignment_disjoint**(eb, eu′))

Case expressions

[case_expansion1]
case e **of** _ → e1 **end** ≃
let b = e **in** e1 **end**
when no_capture(b,e1)

[case_expansion2]
case e **of** case_branch **end** ≃
case e **of** case_branch, _ → **swap end**

[case_expansion3]
case e **of**
pattern → e1,
case_branch_list
end ≃
let b = e **in**
if matches(**express**(b), pattern)
then subst_binding(b, pattern, e1)
else
case express(b) **of** case_branch_list **end**
end end
when no_capture(b, e1) ∧
no_capture(b, case_branch_list),

While expressions

[while_unwinding]
while eb **do** eu **end** ≃
if eb
then eu ; **while** eb **do** eu **end**
else skip end

[while_replacement]
while eb **do** eu **end** ≃
while eb′ **do** eu′ **end**
when
□ **if** eb **then** eu **end** ≡ **if** eb′ **then** eu′ **end**

[while_convergence]
while eb **do** eu **end post true** ≃ **true**
when
(□
let b = ro_ei **in** eu ; b > ro_ei **end** ≡
eu ; **true**
pre (eb ≡ **let** b = eb **in true end**)) ∧
(□ ro_ei < 0 ⇒
(eb ≡ **let** b = eb **in false end**)) ∧
(□ (eb **post true**) ∧ (ro_ei **post true**))

Until expressions

[until_expansion]
do eu **until** eb **end** ≃
eu ; **while** ∼ eb **do** eu **end**

For expressions

[for_expansion]
for b **in** ro_el • ro_eb **do** eu **end** ≃
let id = ⟨ eu | b **in** ro_el • ro_eb ⟩ **in**
skip end

Infix operators

[infix_op_evaluation]
e infix_op e1 ≃
let b = e **in**
let b1 = e1 **in**
express(b) infix_op **express**(b1)
end end
when disjoint(b, b1) ∧
no_capture(b, e1)

[unit_equality]
eu = () ≃ **true**
when convergent(eu) ∧ **readonly**(eu)

[true_or_false]
eb = **true** ∨ eb = **false** ≃ **true**
when convergent(eb) ∧ **readonly**(eb)

[product_equality1]
(e, e1) = (e′, e1′) ≃
e = e′ ∧ e1 = e1′
when convergent(e) ∧ **readonly**(e) ∧
convergent(e′) ∧ **readonly**(e′) ∧
convergent(e1) ∧ **readonly**(e1) ∧
convergent(e1′) ∧ **readonly**(e1′)

[product_equality2]
(e, e_list2) = (e′, e′_list2) ≃
e = e′ ∧ (e_list2) = (e′_list2)
when convergent(e) ∧ **readonly**(e) ∧
convergent(e′) ∧ **readonly**(e′) ∧
convergent(e_list2) ∧ **readonly**(e_list2) ∧
convergent(e′_list2) ∧ **readonly**(e′_list2)

[set_equality]
ro_es = ro_es′ ≃
  ∀ b : T •
   (**express**(b) ∈ ro_es) =
   (**express**(b) ∈ ro_es′)
  when no_capture(b, ro_es) ∧
  no_capture(b, ro_es′) ∧
  convergent(ro_es) ∧ **convergent**(ro_es′) ∧
  isin_subtype(ro_es,T-infset) ∧
  isin_subtype(ro_es′,T-infset)

[list_equality]
ro_el = ro_el′ ≃
  inds ro_el = **inds** ro_el′ ∧
  (∀ b : **Int** •
   express(b) ∈ **inds** ro_el ⇒
   (ro_el(**express**(b)) ≡
   ro_el′(**express**(b))))
  when no_capture(b, ro_el) ∧
  no_capture(b, ro_el′) ∧
  convergent(ro_el) ∧ **convergent**(ro_el′)

[map_equality]
ro_em = ro_em′ ≃
  dom ro_em = **dom** ro_em′ ∧
  (∀ b : T •
   express(b) ∈ **dom** ro_em ⇒
   (ro_em(**express**(b)) ≡
   ro_em′(**express**(b))))
  when no_capture(b, ro_em) ∧
  no_capture(b, ro_em′) ∧
  convergent(ro_em) ∧
  convergent(ro_em′) ∧
  isin_subtype(ro_em, T $\underset{\widetilde{m}}{\sim}$ T1) ∧
  isin_subtype(ro_em′, T $\underset{\widetilde{m}}{\sim}$ T1)

[inequality_expansion]
e ≠ e′ ≃ ∼ (e = e′)

[greater_int_expansion]
ei > ei′ ≃ ∼ (ei ≤ ei′)

[greater_real_expansion]
er > er′ ≃ ∼ (er ≤ er′)

[less_int_expansion]
ei < ei′ ≃ ∼ (ei ≥ ei′)

[less_real_expansion]
er < er′ ≃ ∼ (er ≥ er′)

[geq_int_expansion]
ei ≥ ei′ ≃ ei′ ≤ ei
  when
   convergent(ei) ∧ **readwriteonly**(ei) ∧
   assignment_disjoint(ei, ei′)

[geq_real_expansion]
er ≥ er′ ≃ er′ ≤ er
  when
   convergent(er) ∧ **readwriteonly**(er) ∧
   assignment_disjoint(er, er′)

[proper_superset_expansion]
es ⊃ es′ ≃ ∼ (es ⊆ es′)

[proper_subset_expansion]
es ⊂ es′ ≃ ∼ (es ⊇ es′)

[superset_expansion]
es ⊇ es′ ≃ es′ ⊆ es
  when
   convergent(es) ∧ **readwriteonly**(es) ∧
   assignment_disjoint(es, es′)

[subset_expansion]
es ⊆ es′ ≃ es ∪ es′ = es′
  when convergent(es′) ∧ **readonly**(es′)

[isin_convergence]
e ∈ es **post true** ≃ **true**
  when convergent(e) ∧
   readwriteonly(e) ∧ **convergent**(es)

[not_isin_expansion]
e ∉ es ≃ ∼ (e ∈ es)

[isin_difference]
e ∈ (es \ es′) ≃ e ∈ es ∧ e ∉ es′
  when convergent(e) ∧ **readonly**(e) ∧
   convergent(es′) ∧ **readonly**(es′) ∧
   assignment_disjoint(e, es)

[dom_restriction_by]
dom (em \ es) ≃ **dom** em \ es

[restriction_by_application]
(ro_em \ ro_es)(ro_e) ≃ ro_em(ro_e)
  when convergent(ro_em) ∧
   convergent(ro_es) ∧ **convergent**(ro_e) ∧
   ro_e ∈ **dom** (ro_em \ ro_es)

[inds_concatenation1]
  inds (el $\frown$ el$'$) $\simeq$
  inds el $\cup$
  {**express**(b) + **len** el | ·
    b : **Int** • **express**(b) $\in$ **inds** el$'$ $\equiv$ **true**}
  when no_capture(b, el) $\wedge$
  no_capture(b, el$'$) $\wedge$
  convergent(**len** el)

[inds_concatenation2]
  inds (el $\frown$ el$'$) $\simeq$ **inds** el
  when (**len** el $\equiv$ **chaos**) $\wedge$ **readonly**(el$'$)

[concatenation_application1]
  (ro_el $\frown$ ro_el$'$)(ro_ei) $\simeq$
  if ro_ei $\in$ **inds** ro_el **then** ro_el(ro_ei)
  else ro_el$'$(ro_ei $-$ **len** ro_el) **end**
  when convergent(ro_el) $\wedge$
    convergent(ro_el$'$) $\wedge$ **convergent**(ro_ei) $\wedge$
    convergent(**len** ro_el) $\wedge$
    ro_ei $\in$ **inds** (ro_el $\frown$ ro_el$'$)

[concatenation_application2]
  (ro_el $\frown$ el$'$)(ro_ei) $\simeq$ ro_el(ro_ei)
  when convergent(ro_el) $\wedge$
    convergent(el$'$) $\wedge$ **readonly**(el$'$) $\wedge$
    convergent(ro_ei) $\wedge$
    (**len** ro_el $\equiv$ **chaos**) $\wedge$ ro_ei $\in$ **inds** ro_el

[isin_union]
  e $\in$ (es $\cup$ es$'$) $\simeq$ e $\in$ es $\vee$ e $\in$ es$'$
  when convergent(e) $\wedge$ **readonly**(e) $\wedge$
    convergent(es$'$) $\wedge$ **readonly**(es$'$) $\wedge$
    assignment_disjoint(e, es)

[dom_union]
  dom (em $\cup$ em$'$) $\simeq$ **dom** em $\cup$ **dom** em$'$

[union_application]
  (ro_em $\cup$ ro_em$'$)(ro_e) $\simeq$
  if ro_e $\in$ **dom** ro_em $\setminus$ **dom** ro_em$'$
  then ro_em(ro_e)
  else
    if ro_e $\in$ **dom** ro_em$'$ $\setminus$ **dom** ro_em
    then ro_em$'$(ro_e)
    else ro_em(ro_e) $\sqcap$ ro_em$'$(ro_e) **end**
  end
  when convergent(ro_em) $\wedge$
    convergent(ro_em$'$) $\wedge$ **convergent**(ro_e) $\wedge$
    ro_e $\in$ **dom** (ro_em $\cup$ ro_em$'$)

[dom_override]
  dom (em $\dagger$ em$'$) $\simeq$ **dom** em $\cup$ **dom** em$'$

[override_application]
  (ro_em $\dagger$ ro_em$'$)(ro_e) $\simeq$
  if ro_e $\in$ **dom** ro_em$'$
  then ro_em$'$(ro_e)
  else ro_em(ro_e) **end**
  when convergent(ro_em) $\wedge$
    convergent(ro_em$'$) $\wedge$ **convergent**(ro_e) $\wedge$
    ro_e $\in$ **dom** (ro_em $\dagger$ ro_em$'$)

[dom_restriction_to]
  dom (em / es) $\simeq$ **dom** em $\cap$ es

[restriction_to_application]
  (ro_em / ro_es)(ro_e) $\simeq$ ro_em(ro_e)
  when convergent(ro_em) $\wedge$
    convergent(ro_es) $\wedge$ **convergent**(ro_e) $\wedge$
    ro_e $\in$ **dom** (ro_em / ro_es)

[dom_composition]
  dom (ro_em1 $^{\circ}$ ro_em) $\simeq$
  { **express**(b) |
    b : T •
      express(b) $\in$ **dom** ro_em $\wedge$
      ro_em(**express**(b)) $\in$ **dom** ro_em1 }
  when
    convergent(ro_em) $\wedge$
    convergent(ro_em1) $\wedge$
    no_capture(b, ro_em) $\wedge$
    no_capture(b, ro_em1) $\wedge$
    isin_subtype(ro_em, T $\xrightarrow{\sim}_{\widetilde{m}}$ T1)

[composition_map_application]
  (ro_em1 $^{\circ}$ ro_em)(ro_e) $\simeq$
  ro_em1(ro_em(ro_e))
  when convergent(ro_em) $\wedge$
    convergent(ro_em1) $\wedge$ **convergent**(ro_e) $\wedge$
    ro_e $\in$ **dom** (ro_em1 $^{\circ}$ ro_em)

[composition_function_application]
  (ef1 $^{\circ}$ ef)(e) $\simeq$ ef1(ef(e))
  when convergent(e) $\wedge$ **readonly**(e) $\wedge$
    convergent(ef) $\wedge$ **readonly**(ef) $\wedge$
    convergent(ef1) $\wedge$ **readonly**(ef1)

[isin_intersection]
e ∈ (es ∩ es′) ≃ e ∈ es ∧ e ∈ es′
when convergent(e) ∧ **readonly**(e) ∧
convergent(es′) ∧ **readonly**(es′) ∧
assignment_disjoint(e, es)

Prefix operators

[prefix_op_evaluation]
prefix_op e ≃
  let b = e **in** prefix_op **express**(b) **end**

[abs_int_expansion]
abs ei ≃
if ei ≥ 0 **then** ei **else** 0 − ei **end**
when convergent(ei) ∧ **readonly**(ei)

[abs_real_expansion]
abs er ≃
if er ≥ 0.0 **then** er **else** 0.0 − er **end**
when convergent(er) ∧ **readonly**(er)

[card_expansion]
card ro_es ≃ 1 + **card** (ro_es \ {ro_e})
when convergent(ro_e) ∧
  convergent(ro_es) ∧ ro_e ∈ ro_es

[empty_set_equality]
es = {} ≃ **card** es ≡ 0
when convergent(es) ∧ **readonly**(es)

[len_expansion]
len el ≃ **card** (**inds** el)

[inds_convergence]
inds el **post true** ≃ **true**
when convergent(el)

[inds_expansion]
∀ b : **Int** •
 express(b) ∈ **inds** ro_el ⇒
  1 ≤ **express**(b) ∧
  (∀ b′ : **Int** •
   1 ≤ **express**(b′) ∧
   express(b′) ≤ **express**(b) ⇒
    express(b′) ∈ **inds** ro_el) ≃ **true**
when
 convergent(ro_el) ∧ **disjoint**(b, b′) ∧
 no_capture(b, ro_el) ∧
 no_capture(b′, ro_el)

[elems_expansion]
elems ro_el ≃
  { ro_el(**express**(b)) |
   b : **Int** • **express**(b) ∈ **inds** ro_el }
when
 convergent(ro_el) ∧ **no_capture**(b, ro_el)

[hd_expansion]
hd ro_el ≃ ro_el(1)
when convergent(ro_el) ∧ 1 ∈ **inds** ro_el

[inds_tail]
inds (**tl** ro_el) ≃
  { **express**(b) − 1 | b : **Int** •
   express(b) ∈ **inds** ro_el ∧
   express(b) > 1 }
when convergent(ro_el) ∧ 1 ∈ **inds** ro_el

[tl_application]
(**tl** ro_el)(ro_ei) ≃ ro_el(ro_ei + 1)
when convergent(ro_ei) ∧
 convergent(ro_el) ∧ ro_ei ∈ **inds** (**tl** ro_el)

[dom_convergence]
dom em **post true** ≃ **true**
when convergent(em)

[rng_expansion]
rng ro_em ≃
  { **express**(b1) |
   b1 : T1 •
   ∃ b : T •
    express(b) ∈ **dom** ro_em ∧
    (ro_em(**express**(b)) ≡
     (ro_em(**express**(b)) ⫿
     express(b1))) }
when
 convergent(ro_em) ∧ **disjoint**(b, b1) ∧
 no_capture(b, ro_em) ∧
 no_capture(b1, ro_em) ∧
 isin_subtype(ro_em, T $\underset{\widetilde{m}}{\rightarrow}$ T1)

Combinators

[ext_choice_replacement]
e ⫿ e′ ≃ e″ ⫿ e‴
when (e ≡ e″) ∧ (e′ ≡ e‴)

[ext_choice_annihilation]
chaos ⫿ e : T ≃ **chaos** : T

[ext_choice_absorption]
stop □ e ≃ e

[ext_choice_idempotence]
e □ e ≃ e

[ext_choice_commutativity]
e □ e′ ≃ e′ □ e

[ext_choice_associativity]
e □ (e′ □ e″) ≃ e □ e′ □ e″

[ext_choice_int_choice]
e □ (e′ ⊓ e″) ≃ (e □ e′) ⊓ (e □ e″)

[int_choice_replacement]
e ⊓ e′ ≃ e″ ⊓ e‴
when (e ≡ e″) ∧ (e′ ≡ e‴)

[int_choice_annihilation]
chaos ⊓ e : T ≃ **chaos** : T

[int_choice_absorption]
swap ⊓ e ≃ e

[int_choice_idempotence]
e ⊓ e ≃ e

[int_choice_commutativity]
e ⊓ e′ ≃ e′ ⊓ e

[int_choice_associativity]
e ⊓ (e′ ⊓ e″) ≃ e ⊓ e′ ⊓ e″

[int_choice_ext_choice]
e ⊓ (e′ □ e″) ≃ (e ⊓ e′) □ (e ⊓ e″)

[parallel_replacement]
eu ∥ eu′ ≃ eu″ ∥ eu‴
when (eu ≡ eu″) ∧ (eu′ ≡ eu‴) ∧
(□ **assignment_disjoint**(eu, eu′)) ∧
(□ **assignment_disjoint**(eu″, eu‴))

[parallel_annihilation]
chaos ∥ eu ≃ **chaos** : **Unit**

[parallel_absorption]
skip ∥ eu ≃ eu

[parallel_commutativity]
eu ∥ eu′ ≃ eu′ ∥ eu
when □ **assignment_disjoint**(eu, eu′)

[parallel_associativity]
eu ∥ (eu′ ∥ eu″) ≃ eu ∥ eu′ ∥ eu″
when (□ **assignment_disjoint**(eu, eu′)) ∧
(□ **assignment_disjoint**(eu′, eu″)) ∧
(□ **assignment_disjoint**(eu, eu″))

[parallel_expansion]
eu ∥ eu′ ≃ **parallel_expand**(eu, eu′)
when
isin_standard_form_or_stop(eu) ∧
isin_standard_form_or_stop(eu′) ∧
(□ **assignment_disjoint**(eu, eu′))

[parallel_int_choice]
eu ∥ (eu′ ⊓ eu″) ≃ (eu ∥ eu′) ⊓ (eu ∥ eu″)

[interlock_replacement]
eu ⫴ eu′ ≃ eu″ ⫴ eu‴
when (eu ≡ eu″) ∧ (eu′ ≡ eu‴) ∧
(□ **assignment_disjoint**(eu, eu′)) ∧
(□ **assignment_disjoint**(eu″, eu‴))

[interlock_annihilation]
chaos ⫴ eu ≃ **chaos** : **Unit**

[interlock_absorption]
skip ⫴ eu ≃ eu

[interlock_commutativity]
eu ⫴ eu′ ≃ eu′ ⫴ eu
when □ **assignment_disjoint**(eu, eu′)

[interlock_expansion]
eu ⫴ eu′ ≃ **interlock_expand**(eu, eu′)
when
isin_standard_form_or_stop(eu) ∧
isin_standard_form_or_stop(eu′) ∧
(□ **assignment_disjoint**(eu, eu′))

[interlock_int_choice]
eu ⫴ (eu′ ⊓ eu″) ≃ (eu ⫴ eu′) ⊓ (eu ⫴ eu″)

[sequence_expansion]
eu ; e ≃ **let** b = eu **in** e **end**
when **no_capture**(b, e)

Connectives

[implies_expansion]
  eb $\Rightarrow$ eb$'$ $\simeq$ **if** eb **then** eb$'$ **else true end**

[or_expansion]
  eb $\vee$ eb$'$ $\simeq$ **if** eb **then true else** eb$'$ **end**

[and_expansion]
  eb $\wedge$ eb$'$ $\simeq$ **if** eb **then** eb$'$ **else false end**

[not_expansion]
  $\sim$ eb $\simeq$ **if** eb **then false else true end**

Typings

[typing_list_expansion]
  $b_1 : T_1, ..., b_n : T_n \simeq$
    $(b_1, ..., b_n) : T_1 \times ... \times T_n$

[multiple_typing_expansion]
  $b_1, ..., b_n : T \simeq$
    $(b_1, ..., b_n) : T \times ... \times T$

B.7 Derived rules

Value expressions

[multiple_and_split_inf]
$$\frac{ro\_eb_1, \\ ..., \\ ro\_eb_n}{ro\_eb_1 \land ... \land ro\_eb_n}$$

[contradiction_inf2]
$$\frac{[\,id\,]\ ro\_eb \vdash \textbf{false}}{\sim ro\_eb}$$
when convergent(ro_eb) $\land$ **pure**(ro_eb)

[two_cases_inf]
$$\frac{[\,id\,]\ ro\_eb' \vdash ro\_eb, \\ [\,id'\,] \sim ro\_eb' \vdash ro\_eb}{ro\_eb}$$
when convergent(ro_eb') $\land$ **pure**(ro_eb')

[lemma]
$$\frac{[\,id\,]\ ro\_eb \vdash ro\_eb'}{ro\_eb'}$$
when convergent(ro_eb) $\land$ **pure**(ro_eb) $\land$
ro_eb

Quantified expressions

[all_nat_complete_induction]
$\forall$ b : **Nat** • ro_eb $\simeq$ **true**
when disjoint(b, b') $\land$
no_capture(b', ro_eb) $\land$
($\forall$ b : **Nat** •
($\forall$ b' : **Nat** •
express(b') < **express**(b) $\Rightarrow$
subst_binding(b', b, ro_eb))
$\Rightarrow$ ro_eb)

[all_instantiation_inf]
$$\frac{\forall\ b\ :\ T\ \bullet\ ro\_eb}{\textbf{subst\_expr}(e,\ b,\ ro\_eb)}$$
when convergent(e) $\land$ **pure**(e) $\land$
isin_subtype(e, T)

[all_annihilation]
$\forall$ typing_list • **true** $\simeq$ **true**

[exists_introduction_inf]
$$\frac{\textbf{subst\_expr}(e,\ b,\ ro\_eb)}{\exists\ b\ :\ T\ \bullet\ ro\_eb}$$
when convergent(e) $\land$ **pure**(e) $\land$
isin_subtype(e, T)

[exists_subtype]
$\exists$ b : {| b : T • p_eb' |} • ro_eb $\simeq$
$\exists$ b : T • p_eb' $\land$ ro_eb

[exists_unique_readonly]
$\exists$! b : T • (e $\equiv$ **express**(b)) $\simeq$
true
when convergent(e) $\land$ **readonly**(e) $\land$
no_capture(b, e) $\land$ **isin_subtype**(e, T)

[exists_implies]
($\exists$ b : T • ro_eb) $\Rightarrow$ ro_eb' $\simeq$
$\forall$ b : T • (ro_eb $\equiv$ **true**) $\Rightarrow$ ro_eb'
when convergent(ro_eb') $\land$
no_capture(b, ro_eb')

Equivalence expressions

[substitution1]
e $\simeq$ e'   **when** e $\equiv$ e'

[substitution2]
ro_eb $\simeq$ **true**
when convergent(ro_eb) $\land$ ro_eb

[pre_deduction_inf]
$$\frac{[\,id\,]\ ro\_eb \vdash e \equiv e'}{e \equiv e'\ \textbf{pre}\ ro\_eb}$$
when convergent(ro_eb) $\land$ **pure**(ro_eb)

Post expressions

[opt_pre1]
e **post** ro_eb $\simeq$ e **post** ro_eb **pre true**

[opt_pre2]
e **as** b **post** ro_eb $\simeq$
e **as** b **post** ro_eb **pre true**

[readonly_post_expansion]
e **as** b **post** ro_eb' **pre** ro_eb $\simeq$
let b = e **in** ro_eb' **end** $\equiv$ **true pre** ro_eb
when
readonly(e) $\land$ (e **post true pre** ro_eb)

[sequence_post]
  eu ; e **post** ro_eb″ **pre** ro_eb $\simeq$ **true**
  when (eu **post** ro_eb′ **pre** ro_eb) $\wedge$
  (eu ; (e **post** ro_eb″ **pre** ro_eb′) $\equiv$
  eu ; **true**) **pre** ro_eb

[while_post]
  while ro_eb **do** eu **end**
  post ro_eb′ $\wedge \sim$ ro_eb **pre** ro_eb′ $\simeq$
  true
  when
  ($\square$ eu **post** ro_eb′ **pre** ro_eb′ $\wedge$ ro_eb) $\wedge$
  (**while** (ro_eb′ $\equiv$ **true**) $\wedge$ ro_eb **do** eu **end**
  post true)

[pre_post_deduction_inf]
  $\dfrac{[\,id\,]\ ro\_eb' \vdash e\ \textbf{as}\ b\ \textbf{post}\ ro\_eb}{e\ \textbf{as}\ b\ \textbf{post}\ ro\_eb\ \textbf{pre}\ ro\_eb'}$
  when convergent(ro_eb′) $\wedge$ **pure**(ro_eb′)

Prefix expressions

[always_implies2]
  $\square$ ro_eb $\Rightarrow$ ro_eb′ $\simeq$ ro_eb $\Rightarrow$ ($\square$ ro_eb′)
  when pure(ro_eb)

[always_application2]
  $\square$ e $\equiv$ e′ **pre** ro_eb $\simeq$
  $\forall$ id : Tv • $\square$
  (v := id ; ro_eb $\equiv$ v := id ; **true**) $\Rightarrow$
  (v := id ; e $\equiv$ v := id ; e′)
  when
  no_capture(id, v) $\wedge$ **no_capture**(id, e) $\wedge$
  no_capture(id, e′) $\wedge$
  no_capture(id, ro_eb) $\wedge$
  ($\square$ **isin_subtype**(v, Tv)) $\wedge$
  ($\square \forall$ id : Tv • v := id **post true**)

[always_application3]
  $\square$ ((eb $\equiv$ eb′) $\Rightarrow$ (e $\equiv$ e′)) $\simeq$
  $\forall$ id : Tv • $\square$
  (v := id ; eb $\equiv$ v := id ; eb′) $\Rightarrow$
  (v := id ; e $\equiv$ v := id ; e′)
  when
  no_capture(id, v) $\wedge$ **no_capture**(id, e) $\wedge$
  no_capture(id, e′) $\wedge$ **no_capture**(id, eb) $\wedge$
  no_capture(id, eb′) $\wedge$
  ($\square$ **isin_subtype**(v, Tv)) $\wedge$
  ($\square \forall$ id : Tv • v := id **post true**)

[always_post_application2]
  $\square$ e **as** b **post** ro_eb′ **pre** ro_eb $\simeq$
  $\forall$ id : Tv • $\square$
  v := id ; (e **as** b **post** ro_eb′ **pre** ro_eb) $\equiv$
  v := id ; **true**
  when
  no_capture(id, v) $\wedge$ **no_capture**(id, e) $\wedge$
  no_capture(id, ro_eb) $\wedge$
  no_new_capture(id, b, ro_eb′) $\wedge$
  ($\square$ **isin_subtype**(v, Tv)) $\wedge$
  ($\square \forall$ id : Tv • v := id **post true**)

Assignment expressions

[assignment_idempotence2]
  v := e ; v := e′ ; e1 $\simeq$ v := e′ ; e1
  when convergent(v := e) $\wedge$ **readonly**(e) $\wedge$
  assignment_disjoint(v := e, e′)

Local expressions

[local_sequence1]
  local decls **in** eu ; e **end** $\simeq$
  local decls **in** eu **end** ; e
  when no_capture(decls, e)

[local_sequence2]
  local decls **in** eu ; e **end** $\simeq$
  eu ; **local** decls **in** e **end**
  when no_capture(decls, eu) $\wedge$
  convergent(eu)

Let expressions

[let_sequence]
  let b = e1 **in** eu ; e **end** $\simeq$
  let b = e1 **in** eu **end** ; e
  when no_capture(b, e)

If expressions

[if_infix_op]
  if eb **then** e **else** e′ **end** infix_op e1 $\simeq$
  if eb **then** e infix_op e1
  else e′ infix_op e1 **end**

While expressions

[while_readonly_convergence]
  while ro_eb **do** eu **end post true** $\simeq$ **true**
  when
    ($\Box$
    let b = ro_ei **in** eu ; b > ro_ei **end** $\equiv$
    eu ; **true pre** ro_eb) $\wedge$
    ($\Box$ ro_ei < 0 $\Rightarrow$ $\sim$ ro_eb) $\wedge$
    ($\Box$ (ro_eb **post true**) $\wedge$ (ro_ei **post true**))

Infix operators

[equality_annihilation]
  e = e $\simeq$ **true**
  when convergent(e) $\wedge$ **readonly**(e)

[int_inequality]
  ei $\neq$ ei$'$ $\simeq$
  ei < ei$'$ $\vee$ ei$'$ < ei
  when convergent(ei) $\wedge$ **readonly**(ei) $\wedge$
    convergent(ei$'$) $\wedge$ **readonly**(ei$'$)

[geq_int_transitivity]
  ro_ei $\geq$ ro_ei$''$ $\simeq$ **true**
  when convergent(ro_ei) $\wedge$
    convergent(ro_ei$'$) $\wedge$ **convergent**(ro_ei$''$) $\wedge$
    (ro_ei $\geq$ ro_ei$'$ $\wedge$ ro_ei$'$ $\geq$ ro_ei$''$)

[leq_int_annihilation]
  ei $\leq$ ei $\simeq$ **true**
  when convergent(ei) $\wedge$ **readonly**(ei)

[nat_value]
  ei $\geq$ 0 $\simeq$ **true**
  when convergent(ei) $\wedge$ **readonly**(ei) $\wedge$
    isin_subtype(ei, **Nat**)

[zero_divide_int]
  0 / ro_ei $\simeq$ 0
  when convergent(ro_ei) $\wedge$ ro_ei $\neq$ 0

[divide_int_annihilation]
  ro_ei / ro_ei $\simeq$ 1
  when convergent(ro_ei) $\wedge$ ro_ei $\neq$ 0

[plus_int_same]
  ei + ei $\simeq$ 2 $*$ ei
  when convergent(ei) $\wedge$ **readonly**(ei)

[minus_plus_int]
  ei $-$ ei$'$ + ei$''$ $\simeq$ ei + ei$''$ $-$ ei$'$
  when
    convergent(ei$'$) $\wedge$ **readwriteonly**(ei$'$) $\wedge$
    assignment_disjoint(ei$'$, ei$''$)

[not_isin_empty]
  e $\notin$ {} $\simeq$ **true**
  when convergent(e) $\wedge$ **readonly**(e)

[empty_list_inequality]
  $\langle$e$\rangle$ $^\frown$ el $\neq$ $\langle\rangle$ $\simeq$ **true**
  when convergent(e) $\wedge$ **readonly**(e) $\wedge$
    convergent(el) $\wedge$ **readonly**(el)

[empty_concatenation]
  $\langle\rangle$ $^\frown$ el $\simeq$ el

Prefix operators

[card_empty]
  card {} $\simeq$ 0

[card_singleton]
  card {e} $\simeq$ 1
  when convergent(e) $\wedge$ **readonly**(e)

[card_union]
  card (es $\cup$ es$'$) $\simeq$
    card es + **card** es$'$ $-$ **card** (es $\cap$ es$'$)
  when
    convergent(**card** es) $\wedge$ **readonly**(es) $\wedge$
    convergent(**card** es$'$) $\wedge$ **readonly**(es$'$)

[hd_concatenation]
  hd ($\langle$e$\rangle$ $^\frown$ el) $\simeq$ e
  when convergent(el) $\wedge$ **readonly**(el)

Connectives

[true_and]
  true $\wedge$ eb $\simeq$ eb

[true_or]
  true $\vee$ eb $\simeq$ **true**

[and_true]
  eb $\wedge$ **true** $\simeq$ eb

[implies_true]
  eb $\Rightarrow$ **true** $\simeq$ **true**
  when convergent(eb) $\wedge$ **readonly**(eb)

[not_true]
$\sim$ **true** $\simeq$ **false**

[not_false]
$\sim$ **false** $\simeq$ **true**

[not_not]
$\sim \sim$ eb $\simeq$ eb

[and_annihilation]
eb $\wedge \sim$ eb $\simeq$ **false**
when convergent(eb) $\wedge$ **readonly**(eb)

[not_and]
$\sim$ (eb $\wedge$ eb$'$) $\simeq \sim$ eb $\vee \sim$ eb$'$,

[not_implies]
$\sim$ eb $\Rightarrow \sim$ eb$' \simeq$ eb$' \Rightarrow$ eb
when convergent(eb) $\wedge$ **readonly**(eb) $\wedge$
convergent(eb$'$) $\wedge$ **readonly**(eb$'$)

Combinators

[assignment_sequence]
v := (eu ; e) $\simeq$ eu ; v := e

[sequence_commutativity1]
eu ; eu$' \simeq$ eu$'$; eu
when convergent(eu) $\wedge$
readwriteonly(eu) $\wedge$
assignment_disjoint(eu, eu$'$)

[sequence_commutativity2]
eu ; e $\simeq$ **let** b = e **in** eu ; b **end**
when convergent(eu) $\wedge$
readwriteonly(eu) $\wedge$
assignment_disjoint(eu, e) $\wedge$
no_capture(b, eu)

[sequence_commutativity3]
eu ; eu$'$; e $\simeq$ eu$'$; eu ; e
when convergent(eu) $\wedge$
readwriteonly(eu) $\wedge$
assignment_disjoint(eu, eu$'$)

[sequence_associativity]
(eu ; eu$'$) ; e $\simeq$ eu ; eu$'$; e

[sequence_is]
eu ; e $\equiv$ eu ; e$' \simeq$ e $\equiv$ e$'$
when convergent(eu) $\wedge$
readwriteonly(eu) $\wedge$
assignment_disjoint(eu, e) $\wedge$
assignment_disjoint(eu, e$'$)

[sequence_let]
eu ; **let** b = e1 **in** e$'$ **end** $\simeq$
let b = eu ; e1 **in** e$'$ **end**

[sequence_convergence]
eu ; e **post true** $\simeq$ **true**
when (eu **post true**) $\wedge$
(eu ; (e **post true**) $\equiv$ eu ; **true**)

B.8 Properties of specifications

The primary purpose of a specification is to describe the properties of the system being specified. In this section, we define the properties of a specification in terms of a special function **properties**. The result of applying **properties** to a class expression is a conjunction of logical value expressions.

Conventionally, a theory presentation comprises the (recursively enumerable) set of assertions that are provable from the theory presentation, together with the signature of the theory presentation. We will see that **properties** together with the signature provide a theory presentation of a class expression (except when hiding or scheme definitions occur in the class expression). The original class expression is also a theory presentation, of course. The purpose of the **properties** function is to provide a definition of the properties in a form suitable for extracting context rules, and also to provide a convenient way of justifying implementation.

The **properties** of a specification is the conjunction of the **properties** of its components.

We also use the **properties** function to define inconsistency. A class expression is *inconsistent* if **false** is provable from its **properties**. A class expression that is not inconsistent is *consistent*. A specification is consistent if all its class expressions are.

B.8.1 Proof rules for classes and objects

We present here a number of proof rules mainly applying to the contexts of justifications. Readers more interested in the consequences of these rules for defining the implementation relation and its properties may prefer to omit this section.

B.8.1.1 Proof rules for class expressions

[extend_introduction_inf]
$$\frac{ce1,\ ce2,\ ce3 \vdash ro\_eb}{\textbf{extend}\ ce1\ \textbf{with}\ ce2,\ ce3 \vdash ro\_eb}$$

[extend_elimination_inf]
$$\frac{\textbf{extend}\ ce1\ \textbf{with}\ ce2,\ ce3 \vdash ro\_eb}{ce1,\ ce2,\ ce3 \vdash ro\_eb}$$

[assumption_commutativity_inf]
$$\frac{ce2,\ ce1,\ ce3 \vdash ro\_eb}{ce1,\ ce2,\ ce3 \vdash ro\_eb}$$
when no_capture(ce1, ce2) $\wedge$ **no_capture**(ce2, ce1)

[hide_introduction_inf]
$$\frac{ce1,\ ce2 \vdash ro\_eb}{\textbf{hide}\ names\ \textbf{in}\ ce1,\ ce2 \vdash ro\_eb}$$
when no_capture(names, ce2) $\wedge$ **no_capture**(names, ro_eb)

[hide_elimination_inf]
$$\frac{\textbf{hide}\ names\ \textbf{in}\ ce1,\ ce2 \vdash ro\_eb}{ce1,\ ce2 \vdash ro\_eb}$$

[hide_rename_introduction_inf]
$$\frac{\textbf{hide}\ id\ \textbf{in}\ ce1,\ ce2 \vdash ro\_eb}{\textbf{hide}\ id'\ \textbf{in}\ \textbf{use}\ id'\ \textbf{for}\ id\ \textbf{in}\ ce1,\ ce2 \vdash ro\_eb}$$

[hide_rename_elimination_inf]

$$\frac{\textbf{hide } \text{id}' \textbf{ in use } \text{id}' \textbf{ for } \text{id } \textbf{in } \text{ce1, ce2} \vdash \text{ro\_eb}}{\textbf{hide } \text{id } \textbf{in } \text{ce1, ce2} \vdash \text{ro\_eb}}$$

[rename_introduction_inf]

$$\frac{\text{ce1, ce2} \vdash \text{ro\_eb}}{\textbf{use } \text{id}' \textbf{ for } \text{id } \textbf{in } \text{ce1, } \textbf{subst\_id}(\text{id}', \text{id, ce2}) \vdash \textbf{subst\_id}(\text{id}', \text{id, ro\_eb})}$$
$$\textbf{when no\_capture}(\text{id}', \text{ce2}) \wedge \textbf{no\_capture}(\text{id}', \text{ro\_eb})$$

[rename_elimination_inf]

$$\frac{\textbf{use } \text{id}' \textbf{ for } \text{id } \textbf{in } \text{ce1, } \textbf{subst\_id}(\text{id}', \text{id, ce2}) \vdash \textbf{subst\_id}(\text{id}', \text{id, ro\_eb})}{\text{ce1, ce2} \vdash \text{ro\_eb}}$$
$$\textbf{when no\_capture}(\text{id, ce2}) \wedge \textbf{no\_capture}(\text{id, ro\_eb})$$

[parameter_rename_inf1]

$$\frac{\textbf{scheme } S(O : \text{ce1}) = \text{ce2, ce3} \vdash \text{ro\_eb}}{\textbf{scheme } S(O' : \text{ce1}) = \textbf{subst\_id}(O', O, \text{ce2}), \text{ce3} \vdash \text{ro\_eb}}$$
$$\textbf{when no\_capture}(O', \text{ce2})$$

[parameter_rename_inf2]

$$\frac{\textbf{scheme } S(O[\,b : T\,] : \text{ce1}) = \text{ce2, ce3} \vdash \text{ro\_eb}}{\textbf{scheme } S(O'[\,b' : T\,] : \textbf{subst\_binding}(b', b, \text{ce1})) = \textbf{subst\_id}(O', O, \text{ce2}), \text{ce3} \vdash \text{ro\_eb}}$$
$$\textbf{when no\_capture}(O', \text{ce2}) \wedge \textbf{no\_new\_capture}(b', b, \text{ce1})$$

[scheme_fold_inf1]

$$\frac{\textbf{scheme } S = \text{ce1, ce1, ce2} \vdash \text{ro\_eb}}{\textbf{scheme } S = \text{ce1, } S, \text{ce2} \vdash \text{ro\_eb}}$$

[scheme_fold_inf2]

$$\frac{\textbf{object } O : \text{ce1, } \textbf{scheme } S(O : \text{ce2}) = \text{ce3, } \textbf{properties}(\textbf{object } O : \text{ce2}), \text{ce3, ce4} \vdash \text{ro\_eb}}{\textbf{object } O : \text{ce1, } \textbf{scheme } S(O : \text{ce2}) = \text{ce3, } S(O), \text{ce4} \vdash \text{ro\_eb}}$$
$$\textbf{when no\_hiding}(\text{ce2}) \wedge \textbf{no\_scheme\_defs}(\text{ce2})$$

[scheme_fold_inf3]

$$\frac{\begin{array}{c}\textbf{object } O[\,b : T\,] : \text{ce1, } \textbf{scheme } S(O[\,b : T\,] : \text{ce2}) = \text{ce3,} \\ \textbf{properties}(\textbf{object } O[\,b : T\,] : \text{ce2}), \text{ce3, ce4} \vdash \text{ro\_eb}\end{array}}{\textbf{object } O[\,b : T\,] : \text{ce1, } \textbf{scheme } S(O[\,b : T\,] : \text{ce2}) = \text{ce3, } S(O), \text{ce4} \vdash \text{ro\_eb}}$$
$$\textbf{when no\_hiding}(\text{ce2}) \wedge \textbf{no\_scheme\_defs}(\text{ce2})$$

[scheme_unfold_inf1]

$$\frac{\textbf{scheme } S = \text{ce1, } S, \text{ce2} \vdash \text{ro\_eb}}{\textbf{scheme } S = \text{ce1, ce1, ce2} \vdash \text{ro\_eb}}$$

[scheme_unfold_inf2]

$$\frac{\textbf{object } O : \text{ce1, } \textbf{scheme } S(O : \text{ce2}) = \text{ce3, } S(O), \text{ce4} \vdash \text{ro\_eb}}{\textbf{object } O : \text{ce1, } \textbf{scheme } S(O : \text{ce2}) = \text{ce3, } \textbf{properties}(\textbf{object } O : \text{ce2}), \text{ce3, ce4} \vdash \text{ro\_eb}}$$
$$\textbf{when no\_hiding}(\text{ce2}) \wedge \textbf{no\_scheme\_defs}(\text{ce2})$$

[scheme_unfold_inf3]

$$\frac{\textbf{object } O[\,b : T\,] : ce1, \textbf{ scheme } S(O[\,b : T\,] : ce2) = ce3, S(O), ce4 \vdash \text{ro\_eb}}{\begin{array}{l} \textbf{object } O[\,b : T\,] : ce1, \textbf{ scheme } S(O[\,b : T\,] : ce2) = ce3, \\ \textbf{properties}(\textbf{object } O[\,b : T\,] : ce2), ce3, ce4 \vdash \text{ro\_eb} \end{array}}$$

when no_hiding(ce2) ∧ no_scheme_defs(ce2)

The rules for folding and unfolding schemes depend on the classes of formal parameters not hiding any names (expressed by **no_hiding**) and not containing any scheme definitions (expressed by **no_scheme_defs**).

These rules can obviously be generalized for arbitrary numbers of parameters.

From these rules we can derive many other rules relating the different forms of class expression. The derived rules describe such properties as idempotence, commutativity, associativity, and, above all, distributivity of one class expression constructor (such as hide) through another (such as extend).

B.8.1.2 Proof rules for object declarations

[object_introduction_inf1]

$$\frac{ce1, ce2 \vdash \text{ro\_eb}}{\textbf{object } O : ce1, \textbf{qualify}(O, ce1, ce2) \vdash \textbf{qualify}(O, ce1, \text{ro\_eb})}$$

when no_capture(object O : ce1, ce2) ∧ no_capture(object O : ce1, ro_eb)

[object_introduction_inf2]

$$\frac{\textbf{value } b : T, ce1, ce2 \vdash \text{ro\_eb}}{\begin{array}{l} \textbf{value } b : T, \textbf{object } O[\,b : T\,] : ce1, \\ \textbf{qualify}(O[\,\textbf{express}(b)\,], ce1, ce2) \vdash \textbf{qualify}(O[\,\textbf{express}(b)\,], ce1, \text{ro\_eb}) \end{array}}$$

when no_capture(object O[b : T] : ce1, ce2) ∧ no_capture(object O[b : T] : ce1, ro_eb)

[object_elimination_inf1]

$$\frac{\textbf{object } O : ce1, \textbf{qualify}(O, ce1, ce2) \vdash \textbf{qualify}(O, ce1, \text{ro\_eb})}{ce1, ce2 \vdash \text{ro\_eb}}$$

when no_capture(ce1, qualify(O, ce1, ce2)) ∧ no_scheme_insts(ce2, O)

[object_elimination_inf2]

$$\frac{\begin{array}{l} \textbf{value } b : T, \textbf{object } O[\,b : T\,] : ce1, \\ \textbf{qualify}(O[\,\textbf{express}(b)\,], ce1, ce2) \vdash \textbf{qualify}(O[\,\textbf{express}(b)\,], ce1, \text{ro\_eb}) \end{array}}{\textbf{value } b : T, ce1, ce2 \vdash \text{ro\_eb}}$$

when (∀ b : T • no_capture(ce1, qualify(O[express(b)], ce1, ce2))) ∧ no_scheme_insts(ce2, O)

qualify is a special function that returns a class expression or logical value expression generated from the third argument by qualifying with the first argument each free occurrence of an identifier or operator defined in the second argument.

no_scheme_insts(ce, O) expresses the condition that ce does not contain any scheme applications with O as an actual parameter.

The rules for object arrays can obviously be generalized for arbitrary numbers of parameters.

B.8.2 Definition of the "properties" function

We can now present the rules for the properties of all the class expressions not involving hiding or scheme definitions:

properties(**class** decl decls **end**) ≃ **properties**(decl) ∧ **properties**(**class** decls **end**)

properties(**class end**) $\simeq$ **true**

properties(**extend** ce1 **with** ce2) $\simeq$ **properties**(ce1) $\wedge$ **properties**(ce2)
  when no_capture(ce2, ce1)

properties(**use** id$'$ **for** id **in** ce) $\simeq$ **subst_id**(id$'$, id, **properties**(ce))
  when no_capture(id$'$, ce)

scheme S = ce1 $\vdash$ **properties**(S) = **properties**(ce1)

object O : ce1, **scheme** S(O : ce2) = ce3 $\vdash$
  properties(S(O)) = (**properties**(**object** O : ce2) $\wedge$ **properties**(ce3))
  when no_hiding(ce2) $\wedge$ **no_scheme_defs**(ce2)

object O[b : T] : ce1, **scheme** S(O[b : T] : ce2) = ce3 $\vdash$
  properties(S(O)) = (**properties**(**object** O[b : T] : ce2) $\wedge$ **properties**(ce3))
  when no_hiding(ce2) $\wedge$ **no_scheme_defs**(ce2)

We have allowed properties of declarations by natural extension: we define
properties(**class** decl **end**) to mean **properties**(decl). Here are the rules for **properties** of
declarations:

properties(**type** Tid) $\simeq$ **true**

properties(**type** Tid = T) $\simeq$ {id | id : Tid} = {id | id : T}

properties(**value** id : T) $\simeq$ $\exists$ id$'$: T $\bullet$ id$'$ = id

properties(**value** id : T $\bullet$ p_eb) $\simeq$ ($\exists$ id$'$: T $\bullet$ id$'$ = id) $\wedge$ (p_eb $\equiv$ **true**)

properties(**value** id : T = p_e) $\simeq$ ($\exists$ id$'$: T $\bullet$ id$'$ = id) $\wedge$ (id $\equiv$ p_e)

properties(**value** id : T $\xrightarrow{\sim}$ a T1 id(b) **as** b$'$ **post** ro_eb$'$ **pre** ro_eb) $\simeq$
  ($\exists$ id$'$: T $\xrightarrow{\sim}$ a T1 $\bullet$ id$'$ = id) $\wedge$ ($\square$ $\forall$ b : T $\bullet$ id(**express**(b)) **as** b$'$ **post** ro_eb$'$ **pre** ro_eb)

properties(**value** id : T $\xrightarrow{\sim}$ a T1 id(b) $\equiv$ e **pre** ro_eb) $\simeq$
  ($\exists$ id$'$: T $\xrightarrow{\sim}$ a T1 $\bullet$ id$'$ = id) $\wedge$ ($\square$ $\forall$ b : T $\bullet$ id(**express**(b)) $\equiv$ e **pre** ro_eb)

properties(**variable** v : T) $\simeq$
  ($\square$ $\exists$ id : T $\bullet$ id = v) $\wedge$ ($\square$ $\forall$ id : T $\bullet$ v := id **post true**) $\wedge$
  ($\exists$ id : T $\bullet$ $\square$ **initialise** ; v := id $\equiv$ **initialise**)

properties(**variable** v : T := p_e) $\simeq$
  ($\square$ $\exists$ id : T $\bullet$ id = v) $\wedge$ ($\square$ $\forall$ id : T $\bullet$ v := id **post true**) $\wedge$
  ($\square$ **initialise** ; v := p_e $\equiv$ **initialise**)

properties(**channel** c : T) $\simeq$
  ($\exists$ id : T $\bullet$ **true**) $\wedge$ ($\square$ c? **post true**) $\wedge$ ($\square$ $\forall$ id : T $\bullet$ c ! id **post true**)

properties(object O : ce) $\simeq$
qualify(O, ce, **properties**(ce)) $\wedge$ ($\square$ **initialise** ; O.**initialise** $\equiv$ **initialise**)
when no_hiding(ce) $\wedge$ **no_scheme_defs**(ce)

properties(object O[b : T] : ce) $\simeq$
($\forall$ b : T •
  qualify(O[**express**(b)], ce, **properties**(ce)) $\wedge$
  ($\square$ **initialise** ; O[**express**(b)].**initialise** $\equiv$ **initialise**))
when no_hiding(ce) $\wedge$ **no_scheme_defs**(ce)

properties(axiom [id] ro_eb) $\simeq$ $\square$ ro_eb $\equiv$ **true**

The rules for variant type declarations are obtained by first expanding the variant type definitions into their component type, value and axiom declarations and then obtaining the properties of each. Union and short record type declarations are handled by expanding them into variant type declarations and then expanding those. The relevant expansions are given in the RSL book [23]. Other expansions, such as those for multiple typings, variable and channel definitions, are also needed for a complete definition.

The rules for partial functions (with "$\xrightarrow{\sim}$") have counterparts for total functions (with "$\rightarrow$").

initialise is a built-in RSL expression that informally means "give all variables their initial values". So the **properties** of an uninitialised variable definition includes a property that the variable has some (fixed but unknown) initial value, while the **properties** of an initialised variable definition includes a property that **initialise** will give it the initial value. The **properties** of an object declaration includes the property that **initialise** will include initialising the object.

For any declaration other than a scheme or an object declaration the effect of the declaration is succinctly expressed by the rule

decl $\vdash$ **properties**(decl)

For an object declaration in which the class expression satisfies the **no_hiding** and **no_scheme_defs** restriction, it is also the case that

object_decl $\vdash$ **properties**(object_decl)

However, the rules given earlier for introducing and eliminating object declarations are more general, and can be taken as defining the meanings of object declarations.

B.8.3 Implementation relation

A class *ce1* implements a class *ce0* (in a given context) when the following conditions hold:

- the signature of *ce1* includes that of *ce0*
- for any *ce2* and *ro_eb* such that **no_new_capture**(ce1, ce0, ce2) and **no_new_capture**(ce1, ce0, ro_eb), if

  ce0, ce2 $\vdash$ ro_eb

  is provable by using inference rules and equivalence rules, then

  ce1, ce2 $\vdash$ ro_eb

  is provable by using inference rules and equivalence rules.

We write "*ce1* implements *ce0*" as "*ce1* $\preceq$ *ce0*".

We did not allow implementation relations in our syntax for assertions in section B.2 because we need to avoid circularities between the implementation relation and assertions; the implementation relation is defined in terms of what is provable from assertions. We therefore now extend the syntax to allow *meta-rules*; the meta-rules are consequences of the definition of implementation. We can only manipulate terms which are or include "$\preceq$" using meta-rules.

Syntax

meta_inference_rule ::=
opt-meta_sequent-list
——————————
meta_sequent
opt-applicability_condition

meta_sequent ::=
context ⊢ meta_assertion |
meta_assertion

meta_assertion ::=
implementation_relation |
assertion

implementation_relation ::=
class_expr ⪯ class_expr

goal ::=
⌊ meta_sequent ⌋

implementation_relations may contain applications of special functions.

    Identifiers in meta_inference_rules that are free or declared in the rule are interpreted as term variables.

Context-independent Expansions

A meta_sequent of the form meta_assertion is short for **class end** ⊢ meta_assertion.

    A meta_inference_rule of the form

opt-meta_sequent-list
——————————
meta_sequent
when ro_eb

is short for

ro_eb,
opt-meta_sequent-list
——————————
meta_sequent

When an meta_inference_rule has no sequents above the line, the line is omitted, giving a rule of the form

meta_sequent *opt*-applicability_condition

In a meta_inference_rule there may be a common context shared by all the sequents in it (after expanding any applicability_condition). For brevity and convenience this shared context is not mentioned explicitly in any of the sequents.

Scope and Visibility Rules

The scope of each class_expr in a context of a meta_sequent extends to any class expressions to its right and to the meta_assertion.

    In a meta_inference_rule, assumptions common to all the meta-sequents can be omitted from the rule.

Context Conditions

A meta_inference_rule must contain at least one implementation_relation (to avoid confusion with inference_rules).

A goal may not contain any term variables or applications of special functions.

Attributes

An implementation_relation is read-only with maximal type Bool. The maximal type of a meta_-sequent is Bool. A meta_sequent statically accesses no variables or channels.

Meaning

The meaning of an implementation_relation was presented at the start of this section. The definition of the meaning of a meta_inference_rule is just like that for an inference_rule as described in section B.2. Briefly, the conclusion holds when all the premises do.

We then have a number of results:

1. By induction over the structure of class expressions, given a **no_hiding** and **no_scheme_-defs** restriction for the formal parameters of any scheme instantiations, we can prove that for every class expression *ce1* there is a class expression *ce2* such that

   ce1 $\preceq$ ce2 and ce2 $\preceq$ ce1

   and *ce2* contains no scheme instantiations.

2. By induction over the structure of *ce0*, given **no_hiding**(ce0), **no_scheme_defs**(ce0) and **no_new_capture**(ce1, ce0, **properties**(ce0)), we can prove that

   extend ce1 **with class axiom properties**(ce0) **end** $\preceq$ ce0

3. It follows that if the signature of *ce1* includes the signature of *ce0*, **no_hiding**(ce0), **no_-scheme_defs**(ce0), and **no_new_capture**(ce1, ce0, **properties**(ce0)), then

   ce1 $\preceq$ ce0

   if

   ce1 $\preceq$ **extend** ce1 **with class axiom properties**(ce0) **end**

The third result gives the meta-rule:

[implementation_introduction_inf]

$$\frac{\text{ce1} \vdash \textbf{properties}(\text{ce0})}{\text{ce1} \preceq \text{ce0}}$$

when no_new_capture(ce1, ce0, **properties**(ce0)) $\wedge$
   no_hiding(ce0) $\wedge$ **no_scheme_defs**(ce0)

Note that in this book we adopt the convention that proof rules are only defined when the terms in them are well formed. Hence, implicit in this definition is the condition that *ce1* statically implements *ce0*. Static implementation is defined in the RSL book [23]. Broadly, it is the condition that *ce1* defines all the types, values, variables, channels, schemes and objects that *ce0* does, with the same names and maximal types or classes, i.e. that the signature of *ce1* includes the signature of *ce0*.

In addition, the first applicability condition checks that none of the names occurring free in the properties of *ce0* and not defined in *ce0* are defined (and so "captured") in *ce1*.

The second applicability condition checks that there are no names hidden in *ce0*. We discuss hiding further in section B.8.5.

The third applicability condition checks that there are no scheme definitions in *ce0*.

Intuitively, we can say that $ce1 \preceq ce0$ if $ce1$ statically implements $ce0$ and preserves its properties.

When *implementation_introduction_inf* is applied to a goal that is an implementation relation, the application of **properties** is expanded into a conjunction of assertions, each of which is a read-only logical value expression. Hence we obtain a goal of the form

$\llcorner\ ce1 \vdash ro\_eb_1 \wedge ... \wedge ro\_eb_n\ \lrcorner$

This can be further split into separate goals, each of the form

$\llcorner\ ce1 \vdash ro\_eb_i\ \lrcorner$ $(1 \leq i \leq n)$

This provides a strategy for proving implementation. If the **no_hiding** and **no_scheme_defs** restrictions hold, we can expand an implementation relation into a finite collection of goals whose assertions are RSL logical value expressions. This is an important feature of RSL. In addition, as we will se in section B.8.5, the **no_hiding** restriction can be overcome.

B.8.4   Conservative extension

A class $ce1$ conservatively extends a class $ce0$ (in a given context) when the following conditions hold:

- $ce1 \preceq ce0$

- for any $ce2$ and ro_eb such that **no_new_capture**(ce1, ce0, ce2) and **no_new_capture**(ce1, ce0, ro_eb), if

    $ce1, ce2 \vdash ro\_eb$

    is provable by using inference rules and equivalence rules, then

    $ce0, ce2 \vdash ro\_eb$

    is provable by using inference rules and equivalence rules.

In fact, $ce1$ is a conservative extension of $ce0$ (in a given context) if

$ce1 \preceq ce0$

and

$ce0 \preceq$ **hide** names **in** ce1

where names comprises the names that occur in the signature of $ce1$ and not in the signature of $ce0$.

Proving that a class expression conservatively extends another class expression is not in general feasible, but there are rules for ensuring it by construction. See section 3.12.2.

B.8.5   Dealing with hiding

From *hide_elimination_inf* from section B.8.1.1, an assertion is justified in the context of **hide** names **in** ce if it is derivable in the context of ce and has no free occurrences of members of names. This gives us the meta-rule

[hide_implementation_inf]

$$\frac{ce1 \preceq ce0}{\textbf{hide } names \textbf{ in } ce1 \preceq ce0}$$

when no_capture(names, ce0)

hide_implementation_inf allows us to remove the hiding in the implementing class. (The applicability condition can always be satisfied by renaming the hidden names if necessary.)

If the class being implemented involves hiding there are two possibilities:

- All the hidden names in the class we want to implement are defined in the implementing class. In this case we have the following meta-rule:

[implementation_hide_inf]

$$\frac{ce1 \preceq ce0}{ce1 \preceq \textbf{hide } names \textbf{ in } ce0}$$

This allows us to remove the hiding in the class being implemented.

- Some hidden names are not defined in the implementing class. We now cannot use *implementation_hide_inf*, as the premise would be ill-formed. Instead, we extend the implementing class with declarations decls of these names; usually these declarations can be copied from the class being implemented. We check that this extension is conservative (usually, as noted earlier, by construction). We can then argue as follows:

  1. From the conservativeness of the extension

     $ce1 \preceq \textbf{hide } names \textbf{ in extend } ce1 \textbf{ with class } decls \textbf{ end}$

  2. Therefore, from the transitivity of implementation (easily proved from its definition), our goal

     $ce1 \preceq \textbf{hide } names \textbf{ in } ce0$

     holds if

     $\textbf{hide } names \textbf{ in extend } ce1 \textbf{ with class } decls \textbf{ end} \preceq \textbf{hide } names \textbf{ in } ce0$ (1)

  3. We can now apply *hide_implementation_inf*. Therefore (1) holds if

     $\textbf{extend } ce1 \textbf{ with class } decls \textbf{ end} \preceq \textbf{hide } names \textbf{ in } ce0$ (2)

Then we can use *implementation_hide_inf* to prove (2), since the implementing class now defines all the names hidden in the class being implemented.

B.8.6   Compositionality

When we do development in the large, we first create implementation relations between versions of component modules. Then we want to use the newer versions instead of the originals to create a new version of the system specification. We need to know if this new version of the system is an implementation of the old. This involves asking if the implementation relation is *compositional*. This section defines compositionality.

The implementation relation is regarded as compositional since it has the following two properties:

1. It is reflexive and transitive, i.e. we have the following meta-rules:

   [implementation_reflexivity_inf]

   $ce \preceq ce$

   [implementation_transitivity_inf]

   $$\frac{ce2 \preceq ce1, \quad ce1 \preceq ce0}{ce2 \preceq ce0}$$

2. We get the implementation relation between class expressions and declarations when the implementation relation holds between constituent class expressions, i.e. we have the following meta-rules:

[basic_implementation_inf]

class decl1 **end** $\preceq$ **class** decl0 **end**,
decl1 $\vdash$ **class** decls1 **end** $\preceq$ **class** decls0 **end**

class decl1 decls1 **end** $\preceq$ **class** decl0 decls0 **end**
when no_capture(decls1, decl1) $\wedge$ **no_capture**(decls0, decl0)

[extend_implementation_inf]

ce1 $\preceq$ ce0,
ce1$'$ $\preceq$ ce0$'$

extend ce1 **with** ce1$'$ $\preceq$ **extend** ce0 **with** ce0$'$
when no_new_capture(ce1, ce0, ce1$'$)

[hide_both_implementation_inf]

ce1 $\preceq$ ce0

hide names **in** ce1 $\preceq$ **hide** names **in** ce0

[rename_implementation_inf]

ce1 $\preceq$ ce0

use renamings **in** ce1 $\preceq$ **use** renamings **in** ce0

[scheme_implementation_inf1]

ce1 $\preceq$ ce0

class scheme S = ce1 **end** $\preceq$ **class scheme** S = ce0 **end**

[scheme_implementation_inf2]

extend class object X : cex **end with** ce1 $\preceq$
  extend class object X : cex **end with** ce0

class scheme S(X : cex) = ce1 **end** $\preceq$ **class scheme** S(X : cex) = ce0 **end**

[scheme_implementation_inf3]

extend class object X[b : T] : cex **end with** ce1 $\preceq$
  extend class object X[b : T] : cex **end with** ce0

class scheme S(X[b : T] : cex) = ce1 **end** $\preceq$
  class scheme S(X[b : T] : cex) = ce0 **end**

[object_implementation_inf1]

ce1 $\preceq$ ce0

class object O : ce1 **end** $\preceq$ **class object** O : ce0 **end**

[object_implementation_inf2]

extend class value b : T **end with** ce1 $\preceq$ **extend class value** b : T **end with** ce0

class object O[b : T] : ce1 **end** $\preceq$ **class object** O[b : T] : ce0 **end**

with the obvious extensions to several scheme and object parameters.

We see that all the constructions of declarations and class expressions from constituent class expressions give the same relation between the constructs as between the constituents.

The properties above of scheme declarations depend upon scheme declarations only extending their context conservatively, i.e. a scheme declaration has no effects on other entities until the scheme is instantiated

From these two compositional properties of implementation we can derive the following properties:

1. We have the following rules for scheme instantiations when the actual parameters are implemented:

   [instantiation_implementation_inf1]

   $$\frac{\text{ce0} \preceq \text{cex}, \quad \text{ce1} \preceq \text{ce0}}{\begin{array}{l} \textbf{scheme } S(X : \text{cex}) = \text{ce} \vdash \\ \quad \textbf{extend class object } O : \text{ce1 end with } S(O) \preceq \\ \quad \textbf{extend class object } O : \text{ce0 end with } S(O) \end{array}}$$

   [instantiation_implementation_inf2]

   $$\frac{\textbf{extend class value } b : T \textbf{ end with } \text{ce0} \preceq \textbf{extend class value } b : T \textbf{ end with } \text{cex}, \quad \textbf{extend class value } b : T \textbf{ end with } \text{ce1} \preceq \textbf{extend class value } b : T \textbf{ end with } \text{ce0}}{\begin{array}{l} \textbf{scheme } S(X[\,b : T\,] : \text{cex}) = \text{ce} \vdash \\ \quad \textbf{extend class object } O[\,b : T\,] : \text{ce1 end with } S(O) \preceq \\ \quad \textbf{extend class object } O[\,b : T\,] : \text{ce0 end with } S(O) \end{array}}$$

   with the obvious extensions to several scheme and object parameters.

   Loosely speaking: "instantiations of a scheme are implementations if the actual parameters are".

2. We have the following rules for scheme instantiations when their defining classes are implementations:

   [instantiation_implementation_inf3]

   $$\frac{\text{ces1} \preceq \text{ces0}}{\textbf{scheme } S0 = \text{ces0}, \textbf{scheme } S1 = \text{ces1} \vdash S1 \preceq S0}$$

   [instantiation_implementation_inf4]

   $$\frac{\begin{array}{l} \text{ceo} \preceq \text{cex}, \\ \textbf{extend class object } X : \text{cex end with } \text{ces1} \preceq \\ \quad \textbf{extend class object } X : \text{cex end with } \text{ces0} \end{array}}{\begin{array}{l} \textbf{scheme } S0(X : \text{cex}) = \text{ces0}, \textbf{scheme } S1(X : \text{cex}) = \text{ces1} \vdash \\ \quad \textbf{extend class object } O : \text{ceo end with } S1(O) \preceq \\ \quad \textbf{extend class object } O : \text{ceo end with } S0(O) \end{array}}$$

   [instantiation_implementation_inf5]

   $$\frac{\begin{array}{l} \textbf{extend class value } b : T \textbf{ end with } \text{ceo} \preceq \\ \quad \textbf{extend class value } b : T \textbf{ end with } \text{cex}, \\ \textbf{extend class object } X[\,b : T\,] : \text{cex end with } \text{ces1} \preceq \\ \quad \textbf{extend class object } X[\,b : T\,] : \text{cex end with } \text{ces0} \end{array}}{\begin{array}{l} \textbf{scheme } S0(X[\,b : T\,] : \text{cex}) = \text{ces0}, \textbf{scheme } S1(X[\,b : T\,] : \text{cex}) = \text{ces1} \vdash \\ \quad \textbf{extend class object } O[\,b : T\,] : \text{ceo end with } S1(O) \preceq \\ \quad \textbf{extend class object } O[\,b : T\,] : \text{ceo end with } S0(O) \end{array}}$$

   with the obvious extensions to several scheme and object parameters.

   Loosely speaking: "instantiations of schemes are implementations when their defining classes are".

From these compositional properties we see that developments consisting only of implementations of components will give implementation of the system.

B.9   Additional rules

There are a number of "rules" used for convenience in justifications that cannot be expressed in our syntax. These are in two groups:

- rules that affect what is displayed in goals
- tactics that involve a sequence of rules being applied

B.9.1   Rules affecting goals

The main rule here is *class_assumption_inf*, which can be visualized as

[class_assumption_inf]
$$\frac{\text{context, ce} \vdash {}_\llcorner \text{ro\_eb} {}_\lrcorner}{\text{context,} {}_\llcorner \text{ce} \vdash \text{ro\_eb} {}_\lrcorner}$$

This has the effect of moving the class expression forming part of the context out of the goal, so that it ceases to be displayed. There is also the converse

[class_extraction_inf]
$$\frac{\text{context,} {}_\llcorner \text{ce} \vdash \text{ro\_eb} {}_\lrcorner}{\text{context, ce} \vdash {}_\llcorner \text{ro\_eb} {}_\lrcorner}$$

B.9.2   Tactics

Tactics involve the application of a number of rules being applied in some sequence. When a tool is used, the tactics will typically be tool dependent. The tactics listed here are those used in the justifications in chapter 4.

The most common tactic is *simplify*, which transforms an expression to an equivalent one by applying a sequence of rules whose applicability conditions can be mechanically checked.

Another common tactic is to combine name change rules, such as *subtype_name_change*, with binding distribution rules, such as *all_subtype*.

Rules are only given for the single typing "b : T" where a typing list is possible. A common tactic, which is a generalization of *all_subsumption_inf* and is called *all_assumption_inf*, is used when there is a typing list following ∀. The tactic is to apply *typing_list_expansion* followed by *all_product2* and/or *all_product1* to distribute the ∀ through the typing list, followed by repeated applications of *all_subsumption_inf* and *class_assumption_inf* to put the resulting value declarations into the (non-displayed) context. For instance, if we have a goal

${}_\llcorner \forall \text{b1} : \text{T1, b2} : \text{T2} \bullet \text{ro\_eb} {}_\lrcorner$

we can apply *all_assumption_inf* to it to obtain

${}_\llcorner \text{ro\_eb} {}_\lrcorner$

provided **disjoint**(b1, b2). In the process, the value declarations

value b1 : T1, **value** b2 : T2

are added to the context, but not displayed.

The converse treatment, to combine *class_extraction_inf* and *all_deduction_inf* to extract a value declaration which is a typing from the (non-displayed) context and create a quantification of the condition in the goal, is *all_extraction_inf*.

Similar treatments can be given to typing lists in other constructs, and to multiple typings like "b1, b2 : T".

The rule *post_expansion* quoted in section 3.2.7 is a tactic based on the basic rule of the same name. The basic rule *post_expansion* can only be applied if there are no pre-names in the postcondition (or the result would be ill-formed). Hence the tactic is to apply *pre_name_absorption* to replace any pre-names and then apply the basic *post_expansion*. The same tactic is available for the derived rule *readonly_post_expansion*, but is generally unnecessary as there is no need to use pre-names when the value expression in the post expression is read-only.

assignment_sequence_propagation is a tactic which generalizes *assignment_unfold*. It may be applied to expressions of the form

v := e ; e1

provided **convergent**(v := e), **readonly**(e) and **assignment_disjoint**(v := e, e). It has the effect of replacing *e1* with an expression formed from *e1* by substituting *e* for any instance of *v* that may be evaluated before any possible further assignments to *v* or to any variables that may be read by *e*. Possible assignments to a variable are actual assignments and calls of functions with write access to the variable.

assignment_post_propagation is a similar tactic to *assignment_sequence_propagation*. It may be applied to expressions of the form

v := e **post** ro_eb′ **pre** ro_eb

provided **convergent**(v := e), **readonly**(e) and **assignment_disjoint**(v := e, e). It acts just like *assignment_sequence_propagation*, but on the expression *ro_eb′*.

Another tactic, *implementation_expansion_inf*, involves the meta-rule *implementation_intro-duction_inf* from section B.8.3:

[implementation_introduction_inf]

$$\frac{ce1 \vdash \textbf{properties}(ce0)}{ce1 \preceq ce0}$$

when no_new_capture(ce1, ce0, **properties**(ce0)) ∧
no_hiding(ce0) ∧ **no_scheme_defs**(ce0)

We know, when the applicability conditions hold, that **properties**(ce0) can be expanded into a conjunction of logical value expressions. *implementation_expansion_inf* is a tactic to apply *class_-assumption_inf* and then *multiple_and_split_inf* so that we get a collection of goals each of which is one logical value expression from **properties**(ce0) with a (non-displayed) addition of *ce1* to the context.

A number of other steps are also included in this tactic:

- If *ce1* is a hiding class expression then *hide_implementation_inf* is applied first to remove the hiding.

- If *ce0* is a hiding class expression, and all the hidden names are defined in the (possibly changed) *ce1*, *implementation_hide_inf* is applied to remove the hiding. (If this fails then the relation cannot be expanded further.)

- If any declarations in *ce0* are copied in *ce1* then the goals corresponding to the **properties** of these definitions are not generated; we know they can be proved.

- If the definition of a value, variable or channel has changed (so we cannot apply the previous step) but its type in *ce1* is a subtype of its type in *ce0* then the existential conjunct of the **properties** of the definition need not generate a goal; we know it can be proved. This includes in particular the common cases when the type in *ce0* is maximal and when the types in *ce1* and *ce0* are equal.

A further extension of this tactic can be used if there are object declarations in *ce0* whose class expressions involve hiding. We can use *basic_implementation_inf* to separate out the implementation relation for each object declaration, and then apply *object_implementation_inf1* (or *2*) to obtain an implementation relation between the object's class in *ce1* and its class in *ce0*. This allows us to deal with the hiding as we did above when *ce0* itself was a hiding class expression.

Or, of course, we may have already recorded the implementation relation between the object classes as a development relation and justified it separately.

This separation of the implementation relation for the objects depends on the objects' classes not mentioning any names defined in *ce0* and *ce1* respectively, which is one of our style guidelines: the only free names in class expressions should be the names of global modules or (for scheme bodies) the names of scheme parameters.

B.10   Deriving context rules

If an assertion *ro_eb* is provable only in a context, i.e.

context ⊢ ro_eb

holds, but *ro_eb* is not provable without the context, then the equivalence rule

ro_eb ≃ **true**   (1)

is a *context rule*. In practice, context rules arise from the **properties** function applied to the declarations in the context, and from theorems and development relations. Context rules typically include identifiers that are apparently free in the rule but are defined in the context, and hence are not interpreted as term variables.

The basic form (1) arising directly from a declaration is not always the most convenient form of a context rule and we can derive others from it using the proof rules. We list in tables B.2 and B.3 some of the most useful context rules derivable from various forms of type, variable and value declarations and from axiom declarations respectively.

The last rule in each of tables B.2 and B.3 requires **disjoint**(b, b1). This can be ensured by renaming *b1* if necessary.

In these tables, term variables that occur in the declarations are instantiated when the rule is derived, and so do not appear as term variables in the corresponding derived rules. The term variable *e* that occurs in some derived rules but not in the corresponding declarations must be chosen so as not to be bound in the context, so that it becomes a term variable. Since, as a consequence, the only term variable occurring in **subst_expr** when a rule is derived is its first argument, **subst_expr** is always expanded in the derived rules.

For example, the axiom

axiom [empty_def] empty = {}

gives the derived context rule

[empty_def] empty ≃ {}

in which there are no term variables. The axiom

axiom
  [is_in_empty] ∀ x : Elem • ~is_in(x, empty)

gives the derived context rule

[is_in_empty]
  is_in(e, empty) ≃ **false**
  when convergent(e) ∧ **pure**(e) ∧ **isin_subtype**(e, Elem)

since

subst_expr(e, x, is_in(x, empty)) = is_in(e, empty)

In the derived rule *is_in_empty* the only term variable is *e*, and the identifier "e" must be chosen so as not to be bound in the context; otherwise it would not be a term variable.

In addition, from any context rule derivable from the class expression of an object declaration in the context, a rule in which occurrences of names defined in the class expression are qualified can also be derived. For example, if the context contains

object O : **class value** x : **Int** • x > y **end**

Declaration	Context rule
type Tid = T	[Tid_def] Tid $\simeq$ T
type Tid = {| b : T • p_eb |}	[Tid_def] **subst_expr**(e, b, p_eb) $\simeq$ **true** **when convergent**(e) $\wedge$ **pure**(e) $\wedge$ **isin_subtype**(e, Tid)
variable v : T := p_e	[v_def] **initialise** ; v := p_e $\simeq$ **initialise**
value id : {| b : T • p_eb |}	[id_def] **subst_expr**(id, b, p_eb) $\simeq$ **true**
value id : T = p_e	[id_def] id $\simeq$ p_e
value id : T • p_eb	[id_def] p_eb $\simeq$ **true**
value id : T $\xrightarrow{\sim}$ a T1 id(b) $\equiv$ e1 **pre** ro_eb	[id_def] id(e) $\simeq$ **subst_expr**(e, b, e1) **when convergent**(e) $\wedge$ **pure**(e) $\wedge$ **isin_subtype**(e, T) $\wedge$ **subst_expr**(e, b, ro_eb)
value id : T $\xrightarrow{\sim}$ a T1 id(b) **as** b1 **post** ro_eb′ **pre** ro_eb	[id_def] id(e) **as** b1 **post subst_expr**(e, b, ro_eb′) $\simeq$ **true** **when convergent**(e) $\wedge$ **pure**(e) $\wedge$ **isin_subtype**(e, T) $\wedge$ **subst_expr**(e, b, ro_eb)

Table B.2: Some context rules derivable from declarations

where y is defined earlier in the context, then, provided neither O nor y is redefined later in the context, the derived context rule

O.x > y $\simeq$ **true**

will be available.

Use of these derived rules is somewhat like the use of rules involving tactics described in section B.9. In their usefulness, and in their tool dependence on precisely what is available, they are indeed similar. The difference lies in that a tactic starts with a given rule and may apply some others. Derived context rules, on the other hand, provide the user with a wider collection of rules to choose from. In this sense they are just like the derived proof rules for RSL in section B.7, but come from the context of the justification.

Axiom declaration	Context rule
axiom [id] ro_eb	[id] ro_eb $\simeq$ **true**
axiom [id] ~ro_eb	[id] ro_eb $\simeq$ **false**
axiom [id] ro_e = ro_e$'$	[id] ro_e $\simeq$ ro_e$'$
axiom [id] e $\equiv$ e$'$	[id] e $\simeq$ e$'$
axiom [id] $\forall$ b : T • ro_eb	[id] subst_expr(e, b, ro_eb) $\simeq$ **true** **when convergent**(e) $\wedge$ **pure**(e) $\wedge$ **isin_subtype**(e, T)
axiom [id] $\forall$ b : T • ~ro_eb	[id] subst_expr(e, b, ro_eb) $\simeq$ **false** **when convergent**(e) $\wedge$ **pure**(e) $\wedge$ **isin_subtype**(e, T)
axiom [id] $\forall$ b : T • ro_eb $\Rightarrow$ ro_eb$'$	[id] subst_expr(e, b, ro_eb$'$) $\simeq$ **true** **when convergent**(e) $\wedge$ **pure**(e) $\wedge$ **isin_subtype**(e, T) $\wedge$ **subst_expr**(e, b, ro_eb)
axiom [id] $\forall$ b : T • ro_eb $\Rightarrow$ e1 $\equiv$ e1$'$	[id] subst_expr(e, b, e1) $\simeq$ **subst_expr**(e, b, e1$'$) **when convergent**(e) $\wedge$ **pure**(e) $\wedge$ **isin_subtype**(e, T) $\wedge$ **subst_expr**(e, b, ro_eb)
axiom [id] $\forall$ b : T • e1 $\equiv$ e1$'$ **pre** ro_eb	[id] subst_expr(e, b, e1) $\simeq$ **subst_expr**(e, b, e1$'$) **when convergent**(e) $\wedge$ **pure**(e) $\wedge$ **isin_subtype**(e, T) $\wedge$ **subst_expr**(e, b, ro_eb)
axiom [id] $\forall$ b : T • e1 **as** b1 **post** ro_eb$'$ **pre** ro_eb	[id] subst_expr(e, b, e1) **as** b1 **post subst_expr**(e, b, ro_eb$'$) $\simeq$ **true** **when convergent**(e) $\wedge$ **pure**(e) $\wedge$ **isin_subtype**(e, T) $\wedge$ **subst_expr**(e, b, ro_eb)

Table B.3: Some context rules derivable from axiom declarations

Quality assurance checklists

This appendix provides some checklists intended to be useful in reviews and inspections of RSL modules and other entities.

We deal with modules, development relations and justifications. For each we give a checklist of issues to consider in reviews. This is intended to cover reviews by authors, individual reviews by others, or more formal reviews in meetings. Note that this does not imply that the checks must be carried out independently, or in the order in which they are presented. For example, it is generally sensible to do validation as soon as the checks that can be done automatically have been done — there is not much point checking further a specification that specifies the wrong thing!

C.1   Quality assurance for modules

Before writing any RSL module we should have a good (informal) idea of what it is to specify, and what its level of detail is to be. For an initial specification the notion of what it is to specify is most difficult, since there is no previous one to refer to. The need in such circumstances to merely sketch the modules and to be willing to redo the decomposition were discussed in the tutorial in chapter 2. For later development levels the important notion is to know what the appropriate degree of detail is. The new level should have a purpose, in that it makes a particular design decision — it describes a particular data structure, or a particular algorithm, or decomposes some task into smaller tasks.

At the start it is always useful to consider whether there is already something existing that will serve the purpose, possibly with some adaptation. The RAISE library of existing developments should be checked for possibilities of reuse. Correspondingly, we should check whether the module we are writing could be used elsewhere, or could be used elsewhere more easily if we generalized it, especially by parameterizing it. This not only makes it more re-usable, it also makes the system we are currently specifying easier to change during maintenance.

We are concerned with

- writing a specification in RSL, i.e. formulation

- checking a specification for conformance to requirements, i.e. validation

- checking a specification for conformance to a previous specification, i.e. verification

Note that only verification can be a formal activity. Validation is informal in that requirements are not written in RSL. Thus the initial specification can only be validated and not verified; later

479

specifications can be verified but will also be validated against non-functional requirements or detailed requirements not previously captured.

C.1.1   Formulation checks

We will assume a single module is being reviewed.

- Is it easy to read:
    - Are there enough comments for both the informed and the less informed reader? (These comments may be embedded in the specification or in supporting documentation.)
    - Are the names well chosen?
    - Is the layout clear?

- Is it clear what its functional and developmental purposes are?

- Are there cross references back to the requirements that it is supposed to meet?

- Are the design decisions that it encapsulates the appropriate ones?

- Can it use or be replaced by others that have been written previously?

- Can it be generalized, both with a view to use elsewhere and with a view to ease of maintenance and extension?

- Should it be decomposed into a main structure using others?

- Is the choice between scheme parameter and embedded object appropriate in each case?

- Is it as abstract as possible:
    - Are types abstract if possible?
    - Are constants and functions underdetermined if possible?

- Should anything that is currently visible in a module be hidden?

- If this module depends on others:
    - Are they all mentioned?
    - Have any changed since this module was formulated?

- Are all parameters to functions referred to in the definitions or axioms?

- Are all variables and channels referred to in access clauses referred to in the definitions or axioms?

- Are all variables referred to in access clauses with **write** access actually written to? In particular, when postconditions are used, are their values after execution sufficiently specified?

- What happens with typical and boundary conditions of parameters and variables?

- Do the comments match the specification?

- Can anything be simplified?

- Can any useful properties be added?

- Have any guidelines for style been followed?

- Are local standards adhered to?

- Have syntax, visibility and maximal type checking been carried out successfully?

- Have confidence conditions been generated and checked:

    - Are function and operator preconditions satisfied by all applications?
    - For explicit values and variable initialisations which are typed as subtypes, and for explicit function definitions with subtypes in their ranges, do the values given satisfy the subtype constraints?
    - For functions, operators, object arrays and maps with subtypes as domains, do all actual arguments satisfy the subtype constraints?
    - For variables and channels which are typed as subtypes, do all assignments and outputs respectively satisfy the subtype constraints?

- Are there possible implementations of all types?

- Are there possible implementations of all values that satisfy all the definitions and axioms?

- Do the calls of recursive functions and operations terminate? (This check will also apply to some but not all processes.)

- Can any process deadlock?

- Can any process livelock?

C.1.2 Validation checks

Validation is most important for the initial specification in each development, for which the requirements are the main input. Later development steps will be concerned with taking account of non-functional and detailed requirements. In each case the requirements should be recorded against the appropriate development, and cross referenced against the module first intended to capture them.

- Have all the appropriate requirements been met? (This is really two questions — has an attempt been made to meet them, and has this attempt been successful.)

- Have any inappropriate requirements been met? (This can be answered affirmatively if the requirement should be met at some other development level, when the module should be changed, or if the requirement is inappropriate at every level, when the requirement should be changed.)

- Have suitable comments been included in the module to show how requirements are being met?

- Have any suitable test cases been run, either by justification or by symbolic execution? If so, are the results in line with those predicted by the requirements?

C.1.3 Verification checks

The need for verification arises when a relation between two modules is created in the library.

The relation may be "implements", when the conditions to be justified may be provided by tools, or may consist of some properties which the user asserts.

Verification is covered by checking development relations, which is covered in section C.2.

C.2   Quality assurance for development relations

- If the relation stated is not "implements", is it sufficiently strong — could more properties be added?
- Could any change to the source and/or target allow a stronger relation to be stated? Would this be useful?
- Have syntax, visibility and maximal type checking of the properties been carried out successfully?
- Is the relation up to date, or have the relevant modules changed since it was formulated?
- Do you believe the stated relation holds?
- Are any justifications supplied?

C.3   Quality assurance for justifications

- Is the justification up to date, or have the relevant modules changed since it was formulated?
- Is the justification complete?
- Are there adequate comments to allow a reader to follow the strategy?
- Is the amount of displayed detail appropriate?
- If there are any informal steps, do you believe them to be correct, or should they be made more formal?
- Are all theorems and development relations in the context actually used?
- Is the justification circular? That is, do any of the theorems or development relations in the context have justifications dependent on this justification?

Bibliography

[1] American National Standards Institute. *Reference Manual for the Ada Programming Language*, February 1983.

[2] D.J. Andrews, J.F. Groote, and C.A. Middelburg, editors. *Semantics of Specification Languages*. Workshops in Computing. Springer-Verlag, 1993.

[3] P.M. Bruun et al. RAISE Tools Reference Manual. Technical Report LACOS/CRI/DOC/17, CRI: Computer Resources International, 1995.

[4] P.M. Bruun et al. RAISE Tools Tutorial. Technical Report LACOS/CRI/DOC/18, CRI: Computer Resources International, 1995.

[5] C.I.P. Language Group. *The Munich CIP Project, vol. II: The CIP Method*. Lecture Notes in Computer Science. Springer-Verlag, Heidelberg, Germany, 1988.

[6] B. Dandanell, J. Gørtz, J. Storbank Pedersen, and E. Zierau. Experiences from Applications of RAISE. In *[28]*, volume 670 of *Lecture Notes in Computer Science*, pages 52–63. Springer-Verlag, Heidelberg, Germany, 1993.

[7] B. Dandanell, J. Gørtz, J. Storbank Pedersen, and E. Zierau. Experiences from Applications of RAISE: Report 3. Technical Report LACOS/SYPRO/CONS/24, Cap Programator, Glostrup, Denmark, 1994.

[8] H. Ehrig and B. Mahr. *Fundamentals of Algebraic Specification 1, Equations and Initial Semantics*. EATCS Monographs on Theoretical Computer Science, vol. 6, Springer-Verlag, 1985.

[9] L.M.G. Feijs. An overview of the development of COLD. In *[2]*, 1993.

[10] C.W. George and S. Prehn. The RAISE Justification Handbook. Technical Report LACOS/CRI/DOC/7, CRI: Computer Resources International, 1994.

[11] J.A. Goguen and T. Winkler. Introducing OBJ3. Technical Report SRI-CSL-88-9, SRI International, 1988.

[12] J. Guttag. Abstract data types and the development of data structures. *Communications of the ACM*, 20(6), June 1977.

[13] J. Guttag, J.J. Horning, and J.M. Wing. Larch in five easy pieces. Technical Report 5, DEC SRC, Digital Equipment Corporation System Research Center, Palo Alto, California, USA, 1985.

[14] C.B. Jones. *Systematic Software Development — Using VDM, 2nd Edition*. Prentice-Hall International, 1989.

[15] H.B.M. Jonkers. Introduction to COLD-K. In *Algebraic Methods: Theory, Tools and Applications*, pages 139–205. Lecture Notes in Computer Science, Vol. 394, Springer-Verlag, Heidelberg, Germany, 1989.

[16] S. Kahrs, D. Sannella, and A. Tarlecki. Semantics of Extended ML: a gentle introduction. In *[2]*, 1993.

[17] K. Lano and H. Haughton. *Object-Oriented Specification Case Studies*. Prentice Hall, 1994.

[18] R.E. Milne. The proof theory for the RAISE specification language. Technical Report RAISE/STC/REM/12, STC/STL, Harlow, UK, 1990.

[19] R.E. Milne. The semantic foundations of the RAISE specification language. Technical Report RAISE/STC/REM/11, STC/STL, Harlow, UK, 1990.

[20] R.E. Milne. Transforming axioms for data types into sequential programs. In *[22]*, 1991.

[21] R.E. Milne. The formal basis for the RAISE specification language. In *[2]*, 1993.

[22] Joseph M. Morris and Roger C. Shaw, editors. *4th Refinement Workshop*. Workshops in Computing. Springer-Verlag, Heidelberg, Germany, 1991.

[23] The RAISE Language Group. *The RAISE Specification Language*. BCS Practitioner Series. Prentice Hall, 1992.

[24] J. Reher. A specification of the C++ integer types. Technical Report LACOS/SYPRO/-JR/3/V1, Cap Programator, Glostrup, Denmark, October 1993.

[25] J. Rumbaugh, M. Blaha, W. Premerlani, F. Eddy, and W. Lorensen, editors. *Object-Oriented Modeling and Design*. Prentice Hall, 1991.

[26] D. Sannella and A. Tarlecki. Extended ML: an institution-independent framework for formal program development. In *Category Theory and Computer Programming*, volume 240 of *Lecture Notes in Computer Science*, pages 364–389. Springer-Verlag, Heidelberg, Germany, 1986.

[27] M. Wirsing. *A Specification Language*. PhD thesis, Techn. Univ. of Munich, FRG, 1983.

[28] J.C.P. Woodcock and P.G. Larsen, editors. *FME'93: Industrial-Strength Formal Methods, First International Symposium of Formal Methods Europe*, volume 670 of *Lecture Notes in Computer Science*. Springer-Verlag, Heidelberg, Germany, 1993.

Index

The index is in two parts:

Terms References to the technical terms used in the book.

Rules RSL proof rules.

In each part page references in normal, roman type are to uses of the term or rule. Page references in bold type are to definitions.

E.1 Terms

E.2   Rules

abs_int_expansion, **456**

abs_real_expansion, **456**

all_always, **445**

all_annihilation, 280, **459**

all_application, **445**

all_assumption_inf, 273, 278, 280, 285, 286, 288, 297, 298, 302, 303, 306, 317, 318, 323, 325, 330, 332, **474**

all_commutativity, **445**

all_convergence, **445**

all_deduction_inf, **445**, 474

all_elimination_inf, **446**

all_evaluation, **445**

all_extraction_inf, **474**

all_implies, **445**

all_instantiation_inf, 310, **459**

all_list_left_induction, 169, 302, **445**

all_map_overide_induction, **445**

all_name_change, 293, **445**

all_nat_complete_induction, 303, **459**

all_nat_induction, 302, **444**

all_product1, **445**, 474

all_product2, **445**, 474

all_set_induction, **445**

all_subsumption_inf, 273, **445**, 474

all_subtype, 292, 297, **445**

always_absorption, 434, **446**

always_application1, 177, 317, **447**

always_application2, 317, 323, 325, **460**

always_application3, 317, **460**

always_convergence, **446**

always_elimination_inf, 317, 325, **447**

always_evaluation, **446**

always_idempotence, **447**

always_implies1, **447**

always_implies2, 325, **460**

always_post_application1, 317, **447**

always_post_application2, 317, **460**

and_annihilation, **462**

and_expansion, **458**

and_left_inf, 309, **442**

and_right_inf, **442**

and_split_inf, 271, 272, 309, **442**

and_true, **461**

application_evaluation, 312, 330, **444**

application_expansion1, **444**

application_expansion2, **444**

assignment_evaluation, 315, **448**

assignment_idempotence1, **448**

assignment_idempotence2, 320, **460**

assignment_post_propagation, 324, **475**

assignment_reduction, **448**

assignment_sequence, 316, **462**

assignment_sequence_propagation, 177, 316, 317, 319–321, 323, 325, 326, **475**

assignment_unfold, 314–316, **448**, 475

assumption_commutativity_inf, **463**

basic_implementation_inf, **472**, 475

bool_disjoint, **442**

bracket_expansion, **446**

card_empty, 306, **461**

card_expansion, **456**

card_singleton, 306, 428, 435, **461**

card_union, 306, **461**

case_analysis, 298, 304, **442**

case_expansion1, **453**

case_expansion2, **453**

case_expansion3, **453**

class_assumption_inf, 273, 278, 279, 288, 302, 303, 305, 323, 324, 330, 332, **474**

class_extraction_inf, **474**

composition_function_application, **455**

composition_map_application, **455**

concatenation_application1, **455**

concatenation_application2, **455**

contradiction_inf1, 310, **442**

contradiction_inf2, 310, 311, **459**

disambiguation_absorption, **446**

disambiguation_evaluation, **446**

divide_int_annihilation, 297, **461**

dom_composition, **455**

dom_comprehension, **444**

dom_convergence, **456**

dom_empty, 267, **444**

dom_override, **455**

dom_restriction_by, **454**

dom_restriction_to, **455**

dom_singleton, **444**

dom_union, **455**

elems_expansion, **456**

empty_concatenation, 269, 270, 277, **461**

empty_list_inequality, 278, 288, **461**

empty_set_equality, **456**

empty_text, **442**

equality_annihilation, 278, 288, **461**

exists_expansion, **445**

exists_implies, 285, 286, **459**